ECONOMY, CLASS AND SOCIAL REALITY

Issues in Contemporary Canadian Society

Edited by

John Allan Fry

Toronto
Butterworths

CANADA: BUTTERWORTH & CO. (CANADA) LTD.
TORONTO: 2265 Midland Avenue, Scarborough, M1P 4S1

UNITED KINGDOM: BUTTERWORTH & CO. (Publishers) LTD.
LONDON: 88 KINGSWAY, WC2B 6AB

AUSTRALIA: BUTTERWORTH PTY. LTD.
SYDNEY: 586 Pacific Highway, Chatswood, NSW 2067
MELBOURNE: 343 Little Collins Street, 3000
BRISBANE: 240 Queen Street, 4000

NEW ZEALAND: BUTTERWORTHS OF NEW ZEALAND LTD.
WELLINGTON: 77-85 Custom House Quay, 1

SOUTH AFRICA: BUTTERWORTH & CO. (SOUTH AFRICA) (PTY.) LTD.
DURBAN: 152/154 Gale Street

Canadian Cataloguing in Publication Data

Main entry under title:

Economy, class and social reality

Includes bibliographies.

ISBN 0-409-83100-X

1. Canada — Social conditions — 1965-   *
2. Canada — Economic conditions — 1971-   *
I. Fry, John Allan.

HN107.E36   309.1'71'064   C79-094559-2

For Britt

Acknowledgements

I would like to express my appreciation to the contributing authors for their participation. Each was more than occupied with other scholarly activities when I approached them, but all found time in their busy schedules to prepare a chapter for this book. I would also like to thank Butterworths and Mr. Peter Horowitz in particular for his encouragement and assistance. Professor B. Singh Bolaria has been more than generous with his time and comments at all stages of the work and the University of Saskatchewan generously extended indispensible financial assistance at various stages in the organization and preparation of the manuscript.

Finally I would like to thank my wife Britt and children Shaun, Somers and Stina for their patience while I worked on this project.

1979   John Allan Fry

Table of Contents

III   Class Consciousness

IV   Selected Social Issues

Introduction

The purpose of this book is to introduce sociology students to a number of important issues in Canadian society today. The breadth of the discipline is often limited only by the imagination and interests of its practitioners. Consequently, any such work must be selective in the choice of issues to be discussed. The parameters of *Economy, Class and Social Reality* have been in part determined by the general theoretical posture common to all contributors. Further than that, its scope reflects the particular interests of the editor.

The articles included seek to analyze various social issues in Canada from a critical perspective — that is, they attempt to reveal denied social possibilities and lay bare mute, even concealed, motives, relationships and problems. More generally the contributing authors have departed from the reifications, and apology of the sociological celebrationism which has characterized much work in the discipline. It is indeed distressing to see many students emerge from years of study with a wealth of social facts yet with scarce ability to conceptually organize this information for even a rudimentary holistic analysis of their society. Hopefully, the collective analysis presented here will offer students an alternative perspective on familiar social issues and suggest a more general approach to making sense of Canadian social reality.

J.A.F.

I

Economy and Class

The Deterioration of Economic Stability in North America

John Allan Fry

JOHN ALLAN FRY is an Assistant Professor of Sociology at the University of Saskatchewan. His current research interests include the Welfare State, Industrial Sociology and Classical Social Theory.

Sociology has always contributed to the reification of its object, however, the sociological celebrationism of North American society achieved its zenith in the first decades following World War II. This preoccupation with the achievements of the society was inspired by a confidence in the future of the economy expressed by the dominant economic analyses of the period.

For many, the postwar years marked the emergence of a qualitatively different economic structure and practice. The fear of communism appeared to necessitate national and international co-operation and planning, sustained arms spending and the containment and capitalist development of the Third World. Combined with revolutionary technological breakthroughs, these developments seemed to lay the basis for an unprecedented break with the past uneven and anarchical economic development under capitalism.

In retrospect, the late sixties were clearly the turning point in the relatively smooth-running North American economy. The discussions in this chapter will outline the foundations of that postwar stability and the forces which eventually undermined it.

The Re-Emergence of Inter-Imperialist Economic Competition

The inter-imperialist unity which emerged in the immediate aftermath of the Second World War may best be understood if one perceives its basis not in the widespread fear of communism, but rather as a result of the near complete crippling and destruction of all the major competitors of North American capitalism. Two world wars had lain Germany, Italy, France, Japan and Great Britain prostrate — stripped of practically all autonomous economic and military power.[1] In Britain there had been practically no net investment in industry during the war years, while on the continent the conflict had resulted in the near total devastation and exhaustion of the European nations' productive apparatuses.[2]

Largely through the instrumentality of the Marshall Plan, North America attempted to shore up the faltering Western European societies and thereby prevent their conversion to socialism as a result of indigenous socialist sympathies.[3] This system of grants totalled roughly thirteen billion dollars,[4] a relatively small price to pay for the revitalization of the capitalist system. Internationally, as Western Europe and other nations, confronted with independence movements in their colonial areas, were forced to grant independence, albeit reluctantly, to the majority of their colonies, these new nations were, to a great extent, simultaneously incorporated into a North American imperialist system.[5]

The end of the Second World War saw North America emerge as the undisputed leader of the capitalist world. Bolstered by the profits accumulated during the War[6] and the weakened military-economic position of her former rivals, she was able to dominate the capitalist system for the next 20 years. In the early postwar period North America overshadowed the international markets and investment fields while Western Europe and Japan were generally obliged to focus on their domestic markets. The combination of depleted capital resources and the need for vast domestic reconstruction in both Western Europe and Japan circumscribed the scope of their early postwar economic operations.

The need for global reconstruction, re-equipment and economic expansion in this period was complemented by a backlog of consumer demand, creating unprecedented economic growth potentialities for the entire system. A host of new productive techniques and products, deriving in large part from the technological breakthroughs achieved by the intense arms research of the wartime period, gave added scope to these economic opportunities. Thus, the postwar lull in inter-imperialist economic competition was largely the result of both the lack of necessity and the practical inability of the older imperialist powers to effectively compete with North America.

Particularly instructive on this point is the history of the Western economic embargo policy in the postwar years. With the decision to revitalize Western European and Japanese capitalism, the U.S. introduced the 'Foreign Assistance Act' of 1948. It was the first in a series of legislation culminating in the so-called 'Battle Act' of 1951, by means of which all aid recipients were obliged to impose U.S. formulated embargoes on trade with Soviet Bloc countries (and later China).[7] Violations of these lists were restrained not only by mutual agreement on the requirements of international security, but in many ways more decisively by the omnipresent fear of U.S. retaliatory aid restrictions aimed at the offending countries.[8]

Western European perspectives on this embargo policy were essentially less harsh. While Western Europe found little difficulty in accepting a policy aimed at what were traditionally considered strategic goods, the list imposed by the Americans went far beyond that conception. It was on the issue of trade in traditionally non-strategic commodities that there was reluctance to co-operate.[9] Inasmuch as North American trade with the restricted countries had always been minimal, the imposition of an extensive embargo policy required no serious alteration of its established trade and investment patterns. Western Europe on the other hand had always enjoyed substantial ties with Eastern Europe and the Soviet Union. Thus, this same embargo policy deprived Western Europe of vital markets and supplies[10] and obliged it to turn instead to North America. Though reluctant, the weakened economic condition of Western Europe, its financial indebtedness to America, as well as the more substantial income it accrued in these years from American aid than from possible East-West European trade,[11] weighed heavily in favor of the wisdom of adhering to the inflated embargo lists.

As Western European economies regained strength in the early and mid-fifties, the significance of American aid diminished. With the end of the postwar reconstruction boom, Western European economies began to attain capital resources and productive capacities surpassing domestic demand, and pressure mounted for the re-acquisition of a larger share of international trade and investment. Regarding Eastern Europe and the Soviet Union as traditional trading partners, these efforts were initially aimed at the re-establishment of broader trade ties in these areas. The death of Stalin, the slight easing of East-West tension, and the serious recession of 1953-54, complemented the increasing strength of Western European capitalism to mark 1953 as the beginning of the long period of European withdrawal from co-operation in the embargo policy.[12] The combination of these factors motivated, indeed necessitated, a gradual reconsideration of the wisdom of these trade restrictions. In 1954, against American wishes the Concom lists were revised. Simultaneously British and European pressure began to build for a parallel revision of the Chincom lists. The latter move was strongly opposed by the U.S. but finally effected unilaterally by the British, who were quickly followed by Western Europe.[13]

While the U.S. continued to unilaterally enforce a far more comprehensive embargo and attempted, usually unsuccessfully, to bring its Western European allies into line by exerting pressure through international organizations, after 1958 the entire policy began to rapidly disintegrate.[14]

The further aggravation of those economic factors (increasing productive capacity, raw material needs, and accumulating capital), which were critical in undermining the embargo policy, are also responsible for the broader deterioration of capitalist economic unity and co-operation.

While the Marshall Plan succeeded in re-establishing and revitalizing European capitalism,[15] this economic assistance also laid the basis for European economic independence and a subsequent re-emergence of economic competition between the capitalist nations.[16] In Japan the process of reconstruction began as early as 1946.[17]

With the saturation of the North American domestic market and the accumulation of surplus capital at the end of the first postwar economic cycle, American private capital began to flow into Western Europe.[18]

Indeed, some analysts such as Charles Kindleberger[19] have suggested that U.S. monopoly capitalists actively promoted the idea of a European Common Market on the assumption that they would capture the market before European firms had been able to build up adequate operations. In North America, industries were experiencing serious under-utilization of productive capacity and were ready made for such a market.[20]

This area offered investment opportunities, markets, skilled manpower, and political stability suitable to the requirements of North American productive capacities and capital surpluses. The massive infusion of state and private capital into both Western Europe and Japan was generally accompanied by the most advanced technology America had to offer. The technological lead gained by North American capitalism during the war was, thereby, substantially undermined. With their factories and capital goods either devastated or worn out, by the end of the war the older imperialist nations were obliged to rebuild from the bottom up. A situation which, while having obvious short-term disadvantages, entailed as well substantial long-term benefits. Either by purchase or imitation, the ensuing reconstruction utilized superior North American technology and capital goods[21] thus narrowing from the outset the technological lead enjoyed by North American capitalism.[22] These developments in turn hastened the attainment by Japan and Western Europe of capital strengths and degrees of technological sophistication enabling, indeed obliging, them to once again challenge their benefactor for larger shares of the available international markets, investment opportunities and raw material supplies.

While Western European and Japanese industries remained much smaller in scale than their North American counterparts and continued to trail technologically in most areas of production, by the mid-fifties the basis had been laid for the re-emergence of serious competition between North America and her, until recently, prostrate competitors. As a result, the early postwar competitive lull soon began to manifest the first signs of strain. The productive capacities and profits of the modernized industries of Western Europe and Japan began to outstrip domestic demand. The end of the first postwar expansion and reconstruction period led to growing capital surpluses, and investors in Western Europe and Japan once again turned to the international market. Thus by the mid- and late fifties the older imperialist centers, while still relatively much weaker than North America, were pressed by rising capital and productivity surpluses to rekindle inter-imperialist competition in an effort to maintain the high rates of investment necessary for continued and expanding prosperity. The technological boost offered them just a few years previously facilitated their resurgence as small but effective competitors on the international market.

While suffering the disadvantage of smaller scale, Japanese and Western European industries nevertheless enjoyed advantages in other areas. Although they had lost most of their colonial holdings during or immediately following the war, they were at the same time released from the taxing economic, political and military burdens of keeping these areas 'free' for foreign investment. The ready American acceptance of the role of world policeman enabled Western Europe and Japan to significantly share the benefits of a world kept 'free' largely by means of American dollars and efforts.[23] This was true not only of the Third World but of the defence of Western Europe and Japan themselves.

Obvious advantages accrue from enormous military expenditures. However, as costs continue to rise, as arms-spending-induced inflation persists in North America, as foreign military aid and involvement lead to worsening balance of payments situations, and as Japan and Western Europe compete more successfully on the world market, the disadvantages of vast military expenditures appear to be attaining more credence.

Further, North American superiority of scale and technological sophistication during the early postwar period compensated for the higher wages of its working class, but the erosion of these advantages in subsequent years has steadily pushed labour costs to the forefront in determining the competitive strengths of the various imperialist metropoles. First detectable in labour intensive industries,[25] the lower wage levels of the Japanese and Western European working classes[26] are frequently decisive factors in their competitive ability with the Northern American giant.

In the early sixties the approximate industrial wage ratio between Western Europe and North America was 1:2, while between Japan and North America it was 1:5.[27] While industrial wage costs between 1960 and 1968 rose in Japan and Western Europe at between four and five times the rate in North America,[28] this disproportional rate of increase has diminished substantially since 1967[29]. Thus the lower wages and salaries of the Western European and Japanese working classes remain a key factor in the competitive struggle. Further, it seems unlikely that in a tightening world market Japan and Western Europe will easily surrender one of the most significant competitive advantages they enjoy. Consequently, the coming decade will most certainly witness a tougher line being taken by capitalism in these areas in response to working class demands for wage and salary increases.

As for the wage struggle in North America, both the institutionally generated expectations and the precedent of relative working class affluence would appear to promise even more intense wage struggles, as rising expectations become less attainable.[30]

It is unlikely that American capitalism will be able to afford to continue to pay their working class the accustomed two to five times higher wages than that paid to their Japanese and European counterparts.[31] Thus it is probable that as North American capitalism's alternate competitive advantages are diminished,[32] their own working class, so long a relatively privileged sector of the global proletariat, will become the object of more severe exploitation.[33]

The above mentioned early postwar American advantage of scale, while generally still intact, is being undermined as a result of capital concentration in both Western Europe and Japan. In many areas such as the oil, steel, ship building, electrical appliance and chemical industries, this size differential has been practically eliminated.[34] While differences of scale still favour North American capitalism in the computer and car industries, here, too, the capital concentration in Western Europe and Japan is steadily eroding the American lead.[35]

Thus, in terms of favourable wage costs, comparable modernity of capital goods and technology, expanding scales of production and all round productive capacity and efficiency, Western European and Japanese capitalism are once again capable of effective competition with their North American counterpart. The growing capital and capacity surpluses arising from the disproportionally high industrial growth rates[36] of the older imperialist powers during the long postwar boom have not only made it possible for Western Europe and

Japan to challenge American economic hegemony, but more importantly these developments, coupled with the end of the postwar reconstruction boom, make it absolutely necessary that they do so. The high rates of investment underpinning the long postwar prosperity can no longer be realized by picking up left-overs from North American capitalism. The international market and investment field have become the only substantial alternative to counteract tendencial falling sales, investment rates and the concurrent general decline in economic prosperity. To the extent that American capitalism has attained a monopoly in the international market due to the inadequate early postwar industrial capacity of her rivals, moves by Europe and Japan to re-establish themselves in the area of international trade often lead to conflicting economic interests between these centres. The rising U.S. trade deficit, while deriving in large part from foreign military expenditures, stems also from this increased competition which has even moved into the previously U.S. dominated North American domestic market.

Disproportional growth rates favouring the older imperialist countries have characterized the last twenty years of western economic development.[37] It is perhaps most acute in the chemical industry where, between 1967 and 1970, Japanese and Western European firms experienced rates of growth ranging from two to eight times that of their rival companies in North America.[38] Nevertheless, while the postwar sprint of Japan and Western Europe has been impressive, the opportunities for further catching-up by means of rapid technological progress will probably diminish as they are obliged to rely more heavily on their own research rather than copying or purchasing American advances.[39] The narrower the technological gap the less there is to copy and innovate, and the stiffer the competition, the more covetous North American firms are likely to become of the technological advantages they retain. It appears, therefore, that not only the costs of policing world capitalism but also the research bill for its impressive scientific and technological advances, will fall more heavily upon the re-established rivals who for so long have been enjoying a relatively cheap ride at America's expense.

The advantages are clearly no longer all on one side and while North American capitalism is still relatively the strongest of the imperialist centres, it has been unable to prevent the erosion of the absolute economic superiority it enjoyed in the early postwar period.[40] The then axiomatic American economic dominance and consequent cohesion of the imperialist powers reflected in the economic constellation prevalent in the immediate aftermath of the Second World War, is once more problematic. Western Europe and Japan are feeling the necessity, as well as experiencing the ability, to compete with American capitalism on the international market.[41] The time is rapidly passing when one could simply consider all non-American capitalism as mere contented voluntary appendages of this industrial giant.

The heightening competition between the imperialist centres itself gives rise to a further intensification of this competition. The capital accumulation in the various metropoles find restricted investment opportunities in their domestic economies to the extent that the productive capacities of existing facilities are already more than adequate to meet aggregate demand in a largely monopoly market. In this way the surplus capital accumulated from domestic and foreign investments and sales pressures capitalists to extend the export of capital as well as commodities. This in turn demands and facilitates an enlarged scale of production both in the exporting and recipient countries.[42] Recent struggles between North America and Japan have revealed improved capital export opportunities to Japan to be a major concession sought (and won) by the Americans.[43] On this same line, the devaluation of the American and Canadian dollars, while contributing to an improved position for North American commodity exports on the world market, has also resulted in a worsening of the conditions for North American capital exports, as the costs in U.S. and Canadian dollars of establishing factories, etc. abroad has risen sharply.[44] Thus the increased competition for world markets and investment opportunities appears to be self-intensifying as profits realized through foreign investment eventually return to add to the pool of surplus investment capital, while the increasing productive capacity and efficiency of the productive apparatuses, spurred by the need to gain a competitive edge, results in a further hastening of the growth of surplus productive capacity. Taken together these developments seem to steadily renew and intensify pressure in the several capitalist metropoles towards rising capital and commodity exports as manifestations of their individual efforts to counteract tendencies toward economic stagnation. The development of the productive and investment capacities of the capitalist system are outstripping the requirements of available markets. Indeed, it seems reasonable to conclude that it is these surpluses which contribute most to the decreased fear of the enemy, as natural resources, markets, and capital investment opportunities in 'communist' countries become more attractive (and stable) outlets for the requirements of western economic expansion. When the chips are down, capitalism is far less biased about its customers than many politicians, economists and sociologists had supposed in the celebrationism of the fifties. The spate of political about-faces by leading Western nations in their posture toward numerous 'communist' countries should be seen as rooted less in a basic liberalization of

Western (and Eastern) political attitudes, and more in the chronic economic problems of capitalism (and socialism).

Increased competition between the major capitalist centres is by no means restricted to marketing and investment in the advanced industrial countries. Indeed, inasmuch as raw materials form the basis of industrial production and prosperity, (a point cogently demonstrated by the frequent price increases and delivery restrictions of oil from the Arab-world OPEC members), the Third World should be viewed as a major and inter-related arena for inter-imperialist competition.[45] The growing economic strength of Western Europe and Japan has been accompanied by a drive on their part to gain (or regain) either control, or at least a foothold, in the major resource areas of the Third World.[46] Along with the role of world policeman went definite advantages in the control and acquisition of Third World sources of raw materials. Indeed, the monopolization of the major sources of basic industrial raw materials is one of the most effective means of defeating competition.[47] It is this factor which must be appreciated in an understanding of North American efforts to gain monopoly control over even those resources for which they have an adequate and economical domestic supply[48].

Attempts to undermine the American advantage in this area may be witnessed not only in Western Europe,[49] but also in Japan (a country which at any given time has only enough industrial raw materials on hand for 20 days continued production as opposed to 45-60 days for its major rivals).[50] Japan, in particular, though in many respects also Western Europe, is faced with the prospect of either continuing its dependence on U.S.-controlled domestic and foreign supplies or developing alternate 'independent' sources. In a climate of increasing competition and in the wake of even the first manifestations of North American determination to undermine wherever possible the competitive advantages of its strengthening rivals,[51] Japan will most certainly continue its efforts to establish independent sources of raw materials. Only in this way can it deprive America of one of its major trump cards. Indeed, indications of the Japanese moves in this direction may be seen in its 1970 foreign investment guarantee plan. This programme was designed to guarantee up to 90 percent of investment losses incurred due to political or credit problems.[52] While the plan is applicable to investment in the advanced industrial countries as well as in the underdeveloped areas, it is clear that its primary intent is to secure investment against such problems in the more unstable Third World. Such guarantees, parallel in form and intent to guarantees sponsored by the U.S. government, are necessary in light of the rising investment uncertainty in major areas of the raw material rich Third World.

On this same issue, the seventies have seen moves by Japan to enter joint long-term raw material development projects with the Soviet Union in Siberia[53] and, in 1978, with China. It should be noted here that Japan is not alone in increasing trade and investment with the Soviet Union and China. Recent years have seen efforts by North America and Western Europe, as well as Scandinavia, to take advantage of the long latent economic opportunities in these areas. The vast resources of these parts of the world provide perhaps the most substantial single opportunity for Japanese capitalism to develop raw material supplies independent of American control. It should also be mentioned that these Japanese/Soviet and Japanese/Chinese resource development negotiations and projects are intrinsically tied to political agreements.[55]

Rooted in the growing capital and productivity surpluses, the rise in inter-imperialist competition[56] restricts even monopoly capitalism's ability to increase prices in response to rising costs *per se,* thus representing a major threat to the maintenance of the average rate of profit.[57] The narrowing technological gap between the imperialist metropoles and the increasing scale of production in Western Europe and Japan push the labour cost factor to a central position in the determination of national competitiveness.[58]

In the wake of growing inter-imperialist competition, structural unemployment in North America has reached serious proportions.[59] Further, international monetary crises, largely absent during the entire postwar period, have reappeared and intensified. Since 1969 their continual fluctuations have once again mirrored the existence of intense economic competition and raised the threat of international trade wars in the capitalist world[60] — a prospect which has loomed ever larger since the worsening of these crises in 1971.[61] Renewed international competition under the impact of growing capital and productive capacity surpluses and raw material needs, and the related shrinking of international markets, investment opportunities and inexpensive raw material supplies was, along with U.S. foreign military expenditures, the major factor contributing to the re-emergence of international monetary crises.[62] What is more, these monetary crises themselves threatened a further aggravation of this fundamental instability.[63]

While the monetary crises have continued to ebb and flow during the past ten years, the shattering of the 1944 Bretton Woods agreement by the dynamics of the very capitalist world it was designed to accommodate has yet to see the development of a lasting alternative. The unabated frequency of these crises since they first reappeared seems indicative of the fact that, while their effects are in many respects commonly disturbing to the affairs of all capitalist centres, the contradiction between immediate and long-term national interests on one hand, and systemic interests and priorities on the other, has placed a major obstacle in the way of a commonly acceptable solution. Unlike the situation which existed in 1944 at the adoption of the Bretton Woods agreement, the necessities and priorities of foreign trade and investment have reattained a position of more vital interest for all the capitalist nations. The loss by North America of absolute economic superiority[64] along with the re-establishment of the Western European and Japanese economies has altered the constellation of power in international capitalism — an alteration not reflected in, or able to be accommodated under, the terms of the Bretton Woods agreement. The growing capital and productive capacity surpluses in the older imperialist centres naturally create pressure for larger shares of the world market. Foreign trade and investment now assume positions of decisive importance for all major Western nations as each tries to achieve a favourable balance of payments, and as individual corporations seek new markets and investment opportunities to match their growing economic capabilities. As North American economic dominance is called more into question, so, too, is the leadership of the dollar among international currencies. Consequently the pivot of the Bretton Woods agreement has been undermined and America is now unable to unilaterally dictate the terms of a new agreement.

While there exists an over-riding interest on the part of the leading capitalist nations in achieving an acceptable solution, this requirement frequently conflicts with the often more immediate particular needs of the separate nations and economic blocs in their efforts to attain or maintain an adequate share of the international market. In short, the difficulty in curbing economically upsetting competition and monetary crises appears rooted in a general contradiction in the capitalist world between longer-range systemic interests and more immediate particular (national and/or regional) economic interests and necessities. The clear tendency for the growth of capitalism's productive capacities to outstrip (even to contribute to the decline of) demand in the world market is the central driving force behind this apparent dilemma. The obstacles facing a permanent solution to the monetary crises will be discussed further in a later section of this chapter.

Neither the existence of international competition nor the continued relative superiority of North American capitalism should be lost sight of. Further, it seems clear that the consequences for world capitalism of the economic collapse of one or another of its major partners/competitors would be catastrophic for the entire system. To reiterate, the major blocks of world capitalism appear caught in a dilemma. The more immediate prerequisites for national and/or bloc economic development and prosperity appear to increasingly necessitate effective and fierce competition for available world markets and investment opportunities. On the other hand, due to the complex and intrinsic trade and investment ties, the long-term economic disruption of one or more of the component nations as a result of sustained unsuccessful competition threatens disruption of the entire system and fosters or feeds forces working for socialist revolution. This contradiction between national and international, immediate and long-term interests, is reflected in the dual posture of co-operation and rivalry between the major capitalist powers. So long as productive capacity continues to expand faster than effective demand, an economically non-disruptive solution is difficult to envision. Therefore, as the scramble for markets, investment opportunities and control of the sources of industrial raw materials increases in intensity, it would be short-sighted to fail to take into account the emergence of significant economic pressures which threaten to undermine the stability of the entire system.

> During the entire postwar period, centripetal forces have been at work — those pulling the leading capitalist countries together under U.S. hegemony, and competitive strains working to break up the system. Hitherto, the centripetal forces have been the more powerful. From now on, the centrifugal forces may well assume the dominant position.[65]

The Limits of the Arms Spending Safety Valve

The notion that government spending on armaments provides North American economy with an unlimited and economically un-problematic safety valve for the traditional capitalist problems of uneven sectoral development and capital and productive capacity surpluses was a central premise in the analytic arsenal of the postwar economic celebrationists. Thus, fear of communism seemed to not only provide the motive for transcending inter-imperialist competition, but also the specific justification for the perpetuation of massive arms expenditures. Preparation for defense thereby provided international capitalism with a safety valve for its intrinsic expansionist pressures.

Clearly the medicative impact of American arms expenditures has been profound and should not be underestimated. Indeed, such spending is the only really novel feature of postwar state efforts in the U.S. at remedial economic intervention. Apart from defense, every other area of U.S. government expenditures is approximately the same percentage of the G.N.P. as in 1929.[66] After an initial postwar decline to 3.9 percent in 1947, it had climbed by 1953, under the impact of the Korean war, to a phenomenal 13.4 percent and has subsequently stabilized between 9 to 10 percent of the G.N.P. — a figure which represented approximately $78 billion in 1968.[67] In the U.S. these expenditures account for roughly 90 percent of the demand for aircraft and parts, 60 percent of the demand for non-ferrous metal, more than 50 percent of the demand for chemicals and electronic products, and over 34 percent of the demand for communication equipment and scientific instruments, etc.. Of the 18 major industries in the U.S., government arms spending represented 10 percent or more of their total market.[68]

Even with the enormous postwar reconstruction and expansion, and especially since 1957 when this boom petered out,[69] it has been the massive state defence expenditures which have largely kept the North American economy out of a postwar depression of the 1930's proportions.[70] With more than 9 percent of the labour force dependent on military budget supported jobs[71] added to the current 8 to 10 percent unemployment rate,[72] the nation would be suffering from an approximately 17 to 19 percent unemployment rate, a rate parallel to the depression years of the thirties.

Inasmuch as expenditures on armaments represent investments in a self-perpetuating market, they seem to be the ideal solution for the problems of overproduction and surplus capital accumulation.[73] The rapidity with which modern weapons become technologically obsolete guarantees a self-renewing market, while the frantic search for more technologically sophisticated weapons systems, sponsored and financed by the state, ensures expanding areas for capital investment.[74]

Quite apart from the more ideologically motivated objections to alternative forms of state stimulant spending, the self-renewing market of the arms sector seems to be the central reason for the support such expenditures receive from the business community. Not only do most alternate areas of state spending (public housing, medical research and care, education, etc.), conflict in large measure with the immediate interests of private capital, more importantly, they simply do not provide the scale nor the renewability of markets and investment opportunities adequate to meet the growing demands of North American capitalism.

Thus state arms expenditures have the multiple virtues of market renewability, arbitrary flexibility, non-competition with the interests of private capital, functional utility in the maintenance of foreign economic interests, and direct stimulation of the sensitive capital goods sector. These are the main factors influencing the disproportional state reliance on such an economic stimulation. This does not suggest that alternate measures have not been employed, but by comparison such measures have been minimal.

To emphasize a point made above, a major attraction of massive arms spending as an instrument of economic intervention is its superiority as a dampener of the impact of cyclical crises. The nature and dynamics of the capitalist economic cycle are such that the capital goods sector is most sensitive to, and is generally the starting (and ending) point of, economic downswings.[75] Thus, inasmuch as arms expenditures are primarily concentrated in this sector, they are more immediate in their effect at re-stimulating the economy by placing a floor under the downward swing of the economic cycle.[76]

These appear to be the general dimensions and rationale of American arms spending and, from the point of view of maintaining economic stability, they have until now achieved substantial successes. Such virtues aside, there exist certain current and potential obstacles and disadvantages to such an economic stimulant.

In a period of slow economic growth in world capitalism, investment in the defense sector becomes an important growth area.[77] Through foreign sales, the armament industry has long been a spearhead for international capitalist competition. The long postwar American superiority in this area has contributed immeasurably to the competitive edge it has enjoyed over its rivals in Japan and Western Europe. Once outfitted with American weapons systems, the purchasing countries have become greatly dependent upon the U.S. arms industry for further service, parts, resupply, etc., thus resulting in the effective consolidation of a long-term export market for the industry. Indeed, an indication of the priority given such sales may be seen in the U.S. pressure on Japan, in the wake of the unfavourable balance of payments and intensifying monetary crises of 1970, to double its purchases of American arms.[78] In the Third World, too, North American economic and military aid frequently entails the same long-range market-ensuring consequences[79] as has its postwar assistance to Western Europe and Japan.

The tightening world market obliges Western Europe and Japan to follow North America's example and consider the possibility of utilizing state arms expenditures to take up economic slack. Until quite recently neither Germany nor Japan, have, for political reasons, entered the arms market in a substantial way. However, even here the disintegration of allied imposed political restrictions have made possible the renewed utilization of this safety-valve. The re-emergence of inter-imperialist competition has already led to increased efforts by both Western Europe and Japan to undercut the North American monopoly even in this rather privileged market. Further, with American withdrawal from its peace keeping role in Western Europe, it is unlikely that European capitalism will long allow the continuance of the American domination of such a lucrative market.

The ability of arms spending to function as an economic stimulant in North America is further jeapordized as inter-imperialist competition grows in dimensions. It may then be expected that any move by one capitalist nation or bloc to expand arms spending and research for the purpose of domestic economic stabilization would be met, for both competitive (because of the export market) and strategic reasons, by retaliatory increases by other major capitalist centers. Thus, the virtue of arms spending and research as a domestic economic stimulant would seem to be gradually undermined as the struggle for strategic and economic advantage among the three main capitalist centers tends to perpetuate unabated growth in this sector.[80]

Another and perhaps more serious problem arising from sustained arms spending is the tendency towards permanent inflation. Especially for the aged, the non-unionized and the unemployed, inflation brings intensified social suffering in its wake. The consequent decrease in purchasing power may in turn lead to a further increase in unemployment as factories gear down. If there is a single outstanding characteristic of North American postwar capitalism, it is this sometimes slow, sometimes fast, but everpresent inflationary tendency.[82] In particular, the inflationary surges of the early fifties and the '56 to '58 period,[83] as well as those of '65, '67, '68 and '71, are each in their particular way reflections of sharp increases in military outlays.[84] Even apart from these spurts, inflation induced by massive state defence expenditures has been the hallmark of postwar North American capitalism.[85] These outlays have resulted in a steady rise in the amount of money in circulation without effecting a parallel increase in the amount of commodities on the market.[86] While increased purchasing power may bring about the immediate re-employment of workers and the re-utilization of idle productive capacity, in the long run when the wages of these workers and the profits of the companies concerned reappear on the market as demand for capital and consumer goods, without the production of these goods having been correspondingly increased, tendencial inflation is still the result.[87] It may well be that nothing short of a prolonged period of stagnation, with its ensuing chronic under-utilization of industrial capacity and with attendant unemployment reminiscent of the thirties, will bring this inflationary spiral to a halt.[88]

Along these same lines, were a situation to develop where restricted supplies of basic raw materials, productive capacity, and/or manpower did not permit the free and parallel expansion of both military and civilian production, it would entail the transfer to the military sector of raw materials, productive capacity and/or manpower necessary for the private sector. The ensuing process of protracted reproduction would lead to a shortage of private sector consumer and capital goods,[89] thus further aggravating the inflationary spiral.

The postwar years have not yet seen the emergence of this problem in North America in any serious dimension.[90] However, given the intensification of inter-imperialist competition for many relatively scarce and/or inexpensive raw materials, and the growing insecurity of numerous crucial Third World sources, it is not inconceivable that the future may witness problems of contracted reproduction due to restricted supplies of essential raw materials. It should also be noted that if and when such contracted reproduction does set in, it does not necessarily effect all economic sectors: rather it hits those in closest competition with each other for raw materials.[91] For the present and for the immediate future, however, it seems the most pressing problem arising from the inflationary tendency is the undercutting of bargaining-table wage gains made by the North American working class.[92]

On a different tack, it is significant that the ability of further arms expenditures to alleviate unemployment and stimulate safe investment oppportunities shows a tendencial decline. Technologically sophisticated weapons systems such as missiles, absorb a growing proportion of the total defense budget while at the same time requiring a declining proportion of the nation's manpower to construct and man them.[93] Clearly such developments should not be overshadowed, but it is nevertheless the case that as a proportion of the total defense budget, weapons, and weapons factories of high capital intensity are accounting for larger shares of the billions expended each year.[94] In terms of both the construction and the manning of the new weapons systems, growing technological sophistication implies a significant increase in the cost of creating employment through such spending.[95]

> Coupled with specialization, and partly as a consequence of it, go a rising capital and technological intensity in the arms industries. On both counts they become less able to underpin full employment even at the same level of relative expenditure. At a declining one, . . . their potency as an offset becomes increasingly questionable.[96]

The problem is, of course, not confined to the military sector. While up to 52 percent of all research conducted in the U.S. is done under the auspices of defense projects,[97] most of this is conducted either in public universities or contracted out to private firms. The consequent transfer to and use by the private sector of technological advances achieved by this state-sponsored research is further facilitated by the mobility of top personnel between the military, government, industrial and university sectors.[98] Such government financed research has led to enormous technological progress in nearly every field of production.[99]

The increase in the availability of new technology and scientific knowledge has lead not only to the development of new products, but also to the technological possibility for more rapid increases in the organic composition of capital. Under the press of intensified inter-imperialist competition and a related narrowing of the technological gap between the rival centres, this "technological possibility" is utilized to a greater degree.[100] Thus the relative (and real) decline in demand for labour in the field of military production and operation is accompanied by a subsequent and similar decline in demand within industry at large, as labour intensive industries are steadily eroded and new capital intensive ones are established and reinforced.[101]

One final point should be made in relation to these developments. Spurred by the inter-imperialist challenge and facilitated by technological advances, capital investments are more frequently replaced before they have been fully amortized. In those sectors defined by the state as 'strategic', the government guarantees the loss. However, in the non-military sector, this premature but competitively necessary industrial re-equipment causes an unutilizable increase in total productive capacity and a potential threat to the stability of the average rate of profit[102] as the average life-span of capital goods declines. Wherever possible the incomplete amortization is paid for either directly through the reduction of labour content, wage stagnation, or even outright wage cuts, or indirectly through increased taxes and inflation. In either event it is the working class (both domestic and, wherever possible, foreign) which pays these additional capital goods depreciation costs.

It should also be noted that North American military spending abroad in the form of military aid, base procurement payments, etc., has been a central factor contributing to the crisis in liquidity now confronting the American economy.[103]

Arms expenditures have clearly been a major mechanism for bottoming-out postwar economic downswings in North America. However, it should not be lost sight of that even this massive stimulant has been incapable of keeping the economy prospering and containing unemployment at acceptable levels.[104] Even considering these expenditures, the limited prosperity and economic stability achieved has hardly been possible without the considerable assistance of state deficit spending and a spiralling private debt.[105] Not only the national government but state, provincial, and local governments as well have become more reliant on borrowing in order to meet their governmental obligations.[106]

Taken together, the short and long-term limitations and adverse economic consequences of sustained arms spending on the scale pursued by the U.S. government during the postwar years suggest clear limitations on the efficacy of such an economic stimulant. In conclusion, although one must appreciate the fact that such expenditures have in the past — and indeed continue — to achieve an often extensive economic stability and prosperity in North America, nevertheless, limitations and problems do exist and their parameters and form are becoming increasingly manifest.[107]

The Third World and Capitalist Economic Stability

Many Western economists and sociologists have viewed Third World national liberation struggles as incapable of seriously disrupting North American economy.[108] Such a perspective appears to underestimate both the actual possibilities for successful national liberation in these areas and the vital role played by the Third World in world capitalism.

It is perhaps worth restating that the underdevelopment of the Third World areas is not the result of an historical accident causing a delayed economic 'take-off'. Rather it has been and still is the direct and necessary consequence of imperialist economic and political relationships.[109] While the major capitalist nations are characterized by extensive industrial development and the Third World areas generally reflect a gross lack of such development, it is important to appreciate that they do not exist in isolation from each other. Indeed, 'they are the top and bottom sides of one and the same world'.[110]

The uneven development between the advanced capitalist world and the Third World began, and is continually reinforced by, the unequal exchange which characterizes the economic relationships between these two areas of the capitalist world.[111] This unevenness continues to grow as the Third World steadily increases its share of the world population while receiving a diminishing share of the world's output.[112] Those Third World countries with the closest and greatest economic ties with the capitalist metropoles are generally the most acutely underdeveloped.

In the sixties, the dimensions of this discrepancy could be seen in a per capita income ratio between the advanced industrial countries and the Third World areas of 9/1.[113] Equally as telling were the ratios of 12/1 and 5/1 for per capita energy consumption and industrial steel consumption respectively.[114] In the wake of economic stagnation, these conditions have deteriorated more rapidly since the mid-sixties.

In a situation where already the 'topside' of imperialism — the advanced industrial countries — account for only 20 percent of the world population but 60 percent of world output, while the 'bottom side' — the Third World — accounts for 50 percent of world population and only 10 percent of the world production,[115] further deterioration in both relative and real human conditions become increasingly intolerable.

It is against this background that the potential success of Third World national liberation struggles and the importance of this part of the world for sustaining metropolitan affluence should be assessed. Inasmuch as imperialism is a two-headed coin of development and underdevelopment, it is reasonable to conclude that any effort by the 'losing partner' to end this relationship would entail the undermining of the affluence of the 'developed partner'. While the instruments for political and economic repression and containment in the underdeveloped areas are 'impressive', ". . . it does not necessarily follow that without and before the collapse of international capitalism nothing can be done about its liquidation."[116]

The Third World has long been a major source of super-profits for capitalism with investments in these areas realizing average profit rates from 50 to 400 percent greater than similar investments in the advanced industrialized areas.[117] The exploitation of relatively inexpensive sources of raw materials, land and labour has traditionally complemented the lower profit rates realized by international capitalism's larger investments in the metropole regions.[118] It is clearly the underdeveloped world's strengthened position as a supplier of numerous essential raw materials, however, which gives it most disruptive power over the advanced industrial nations. Since the early postwar years, the U.S. has experienced a larger and more diverse shortage of basic industrial and strategic raw materials. Indeed this domestic shortage is perhaps the most novel aspect of contemporary North American imperialism.[119]

The tendency towards increased import dependency seems unlikely to cease or decline as the gap between Third World and metropole production narrows.[120] It has been estimated that by the mid-eighties it will be necessary for the U.S. to import 54 percent of its annual oil consumption; overall it will be a net importer of raw materials.[121] It is sometimes argued that breakthroughs in recycling techniques and in the production of synthetic substitutes will more than counter this growing import dependency. Impressive though such achievements may be, however, they are seldom able to compensate with a supply which is large enough to meet the demands of the massive North American industrial apparatus and/or which can be produced at a cost comparable to the foreign supplies.[122] If there is one consistent characteristic of capitalist enterprise, whether monopolistic or not, it is that it seeks to maximize profits, in this case by exploiting the cheapest possible raw material sources.

The greater reliance of U.S. industry on Third World raw material supplies gives these latter areas substantial economic leverage. Should strategic areas of the underdeveloped world realign themselves politically and economically, raise their prices or utilize larger quantities of their raw materials domestically as a result of industrialization, it could have serious economic repercussions for North American capitalism. The result would be an undermining of both the super-profits earned in these areas as well as the productive potential of industry in the advanced industrial areas. Such developments would most certainly jeopardize North America's ability to buy-off its industrial working class to the extent to which they have been able in the past.[123]

Given the uncertain investment climate in numerous Third World areas, the U.S. would prefer to purchase raw materials in the more stable areas of Western Europe and Canada. Unfortunately, the geography of mineral deposits does not always coincide with the geography of political stability. Necessary sources are too often found in the required quantities only in the Third World.[124]

> . . . [It] should never be forgotten that however heavily imperialist exploitation weighs upon the Third World this exploitation needs the Third World and cannot do without it . . . the Third World is the sole or primary source of many products or raw materials without which many of the markets of imperialism would collapse and many of its most essential factories would come to a standstill.[125]

This increasing raw material dependence is further aggravated by increased competition between imperialist rivals. Western European aligned Third World areas which were opened to direct and indirect American exploitation through North American investment in Western Europe[126] will, in all probability, become less accessable as the strength of European capitalism increases and these states more effectively determine to protect their privileged sources. Considering, too, the rapid industrial growth rates of America's imperialist rivals, it is probable that the coming decades will witness a fierce struggle for access to and control of the raw materials, cheap labour and land, as well as the markets of those Third World areas which have for long been the more or less private domain of North American capitalism.[127] Indeed, as mentioned above, Japan has already moved towards establishing independent raw material sources. Any evaluation of the importance of trade between the U.S. and the Third World must be assessed in light of the adequacy of domestic supplies and the resurgence of inter-imperialist competition. Often, and perhaps this has been the source of many economists' apparent miscalculations, the growing overall proportion of world trade accounted for by inter-imperialist exchange, as opposed to trade between the advanced capitalist countries and the underdeveloped parts of the world,[129] has led to the conclusion that trade with the Third World is diminishing in importance. During the postwar years

Third World share of world trade fell from 31.3 percent in 1950 to 20.8 percent in 1963 and to 18.5 percent in 1967.[130] The point to be borne in mind, however, is that this trade is largely (90 percent)[131] an exchange of primary products for the manufactured goods of the advanced capitalist countries; whereas inter-imperialist trade is primarily an exchange of manufactured goods. There exists a qualitative difference between the two types of trade. Third World trade while less, is perhaps equal or more important to the stability of world capitalism inasmuch as it is largely concerned with raw materials and bulk foodstuffs.[132] Thus as Jallee points out:

> . . . [The] Third World has an ace up its sleeve; its hand is on the tap controlling the essential flow, and thus it enjoys a position of strength in one respect which must not be underestimated in a dynamic and changing world.[133]

Apart from its growing importance as a supplier of raw materials, there are still other, perhaps presently less important, but nevertheless latent sources of economic disruptive power enjoyed by the Third World. In an era of shrinking economic maneuverability, it is important not only to actively exploit these areas but also to hold open the investment door even though full advantage is not immediately taken of available opportunities. Along with the older imperialist nations the underdeveloped world has offered North American capitalism a convenient and often flexible safety-valve for problems of surplus capital and production.[134] Until recently this crisis exportation has helped cushion economic recessions and sustain upswings.

Particularly in the area of capital goods, North American exports to the Third World have performed this function of complementing the medicative effects of arms spending.[135]

Using steel as an example, the Third World accounts for 30 to 40 percent of U.S. exports[136] and as C.B. Baker, administrative vice-president of the United States Steel Corporation has stated:

> . . . [It] is largely due to the operation of our foreign aid program that the steel industry has managed to escape the full effects of the forces at work in the international market place.[137]

The role of the Third World as a recipient of commodity and capital exports has been somewhat limited by the comparatively smaller size of its domestic markets as well as by the fact that these markets are largely already under monopoly control.[138] It is likely that intensified inter-imperialist competition will accentuate the need to fully exploit these sources of cheap labour and land and take fuller advantage of the often closer proximity of raw materials. The metropole sponsored industrial development of the

Third World has almost exclusively focused on export sales and therefore, apart from wages, which necessarily remain low, was seldom, or only coincidentally, appropriate to the domestic needs of the host country, creating, in addition, a further drain on domestically generated capital. The drain on domestically generated capital and the undermining of domestic oriented industries and products are the direct consequence of foreign economic investment geared toward the more lucrative international market. The maintenance of low wages and capital drain, a condition of foreign investment in the first instance, ensure the weakness and unattractiveness of the domestic market.

The preceding discussion has given some indication of the international division of labour characterizing contemporary imperialism: The Third World supplying raw materials and the metropoles the manufactured good.[139]

The underdevelopment of the Third World is, for North America's part, sustained and expanded through a complex of aid programmes,[140] trade restrictions, selective investments, economic blackmail, and direct and indirect political and military intervention in the affairs of the underdeveloped countries in its orbit. Capital and productive capacity surpluses, diminishing domestic supplies of industrial raw materials, and the growth of inter-imperialist competition, all interact to make the development of underdevelopment and unequal exchange with the Third World a matter of unprecedented economic urgency.[141] If large parts of the Third World are underdeveloped it is not because they have yet to receive the midas touch of foreign capital, rather precisely the opposite is true — they have been 'touched' and the underdevelopment of their economies and misery of their peoples stand as testimony to that event. Advanced industrialization in these areas would threaten not only the export markets of U.S. monopolies[142], but, as mentioned above, would jeopardize necessary sources of inexpensive raw materials.[143] The obstacles confronting such industrialization are great, however, the stagnation of the Third World may turn out to be a major cause rather than a consequence of the weakening of the metropoles.

> The frightful differences in standard of living, the brutal subjection of one nation to another, prepare the way for colonial revolution which in turn pushes forward the industrialization of the underdeveloped countries and intensifies the international contradictions of capital.[144]

Parallel to the greater importance of the Third World to North American capitalism, is a growing hesitancy on the part of North American private capital to invest in face of a worsening investment climate through the underdeveloped areas. Unless initial investment can be amortized within approximately five years, fewer investors are prepared to take the risk.[145] Even with substantial U.S. government guarantees the unfavorable investment climate has already curbed substantial private investment in these areas.[146] Instability in the Third World does not negate the economic and strategic necessity of its material and human resources for North American capitalism. The devaluation of the dollar, while at least temporarily enhancing the competitive position of North America in the commodity export sector, also raises the cost of policing and keeping these areas free for further marketing and investment.[147] Thus the growing political and economic uncertainty in the Third World expressed through national liberation struggles, as well as the acquisition of power by nationalistic capitalist oriented governments, threaten to erode a cornerstore in North American postwar prosperity.

While the anti-development forces of North America should not be underestimated, neither should the possibilities for meaningful successes for the Third World. Political awareness is advancing inexorably[148] in the face of worsening poverty and repression. In Latin America per capita food consumption fell 7 percent between 1958 to 1959 and 1963 to 1964[149] and the per capita income inequality ratio between this part of the world and the advanced industrial areas has dropped from one-sixth in 1900 to one-twelfth in 1965.[150] It is improbable that North America's 6 percent of the world's population can indefinitely force 50 percent of the world's population to accept deprivation and humiliation as a permanent way of life. It is no exaggeration to say that: ". . . the tide or world revolution against exploitation . . . is flowing strong, much too strong to be turned back or halted."[151]

The postwar granting of political independence combined with a reinforced economic subservience in large areas of the underdeveloped world allowed North America to assume and tighten the imperialist grip[152] for a decade or so. It is difficult, however, to imagine what further peaceful concessions can be made in an era of renewed inter-imperialist competition and consequent shrinking economic elbow room, to placate a disillusioned and increasingly militantly politically-conscious people. The alternative is, of course, the repression of emerging national liberation sympathies and movements by coercion and force. The example of Indo-China, however, indicates the problematic ability of the U.S. to contain five to ten more Vietnams.[153]

It should be noted, too, that inasmuch as U.S. foreign defence spending is a major cause of its chronic balance of payments deficit over the past decade[154], and thus a central factor in the international monetary crises, the need for increased foreign military expenditures to curb the rising tide of national liberation struggles would most certainly aggravate this problem.

The growing importance of the Third World in the world capitalist economy implies a position of enhanced economic leverage and disruptive potential. The pitiful conditions of Third World inhabitants increase the likelihood that this leverage and disruptive potential will be utilized and reflected in a worsening economic situation within North America. The impact on the capitalist metropoles of the actions of the Third World OPEC countries scarcely requires comment. The tendency toward economic stagnation in America renders North American capitalism still more sensitive to both the further restrictions of its ability to utilize the wealth of the countries of the Third World[155], and the adverse economic effects of widespread and sustained policing.

Clearly it would be foolish to underestimate the ability of North America to continue to contain and exploit vast areas of the Third World. Through the use of its enormous economic, political and military resources it still holds the upper hand. Further, just as the export of military hardware tends to tie the recipient country to the supplying nation for replacements, repairs, parts, etc., on a broader scale, the export of North American civilian technology to the Third World creates a similar dependency, even when Third World areas achieve significant degrees of industrialization. Such technological imperialism is one more factor in the complex web of economic, political, military and cultural relationships which enforce the containment of the Third World within the world capitalist system. Limitations to containment and exploitation do exist, however, and the failure to consider them may lead to an underestimation of the real possibilities for successful national liberation struggles as well as the negative politico/economic effects such struggles may have on the North American economy:

> . . . [The] relations between the Third World and imperialism are dialectical and not all weapons are on one side.[156]
>
> . . . One can say that there is as yet no reason to abandon belief in a general crisis of capitalism — be it catastrophic or slow to develop. It is most likely to appear when the great revolution in the Third World passes from latency to reality.[157]

Apart from persistent anti-imperialist national liberation struggles, the capitalist Third World manifests a determination to compete with the capitalist metropoles in selected areas. The oil crisis, nationalizations, extensions of territorial boundaries at sea, etc., while not immediately removing the nations involved from the general framework of the world capitalist system, have nevertheless placed an added strain on the economic stability of the North American economy. Warren may be correct when he argues that Third World areas are tending to capitalist industrialization, nevertheless such industrialization, where realized, will most certainly lead to conflicts which, while not anti-capitalist, have substantial unstabilizing effects on the dominant position of North America in much the same manner as does inter-imperialist competition.

Economic Planning and Management

The relative calm and prosperity of the economy in the first postwar decade induced many analysts to anticipate an end to the cyclical crises which had plagued capitalist economic development since the inception of this order. The combined efforts of large corporations and nation states seemed to achieve unparalleled successes in corporate and national economic planning and management. Uneven and erratic growth appeared sure to fade into the past as a qualitatively new capitalism developed.

Persistent recessions do not imply immanent systemic collapse, however, their increasing frequency and severity in the nine slumps of '48, '53 to '54, '57 to '58, '61, '67, '70, '73, '74 to '75, and '77 to '78 suggests that the notion of a new capitalism free from traditional and fundamental contradictions was a trifle too optimistic.

Economic planning at the individual corporate level has necessarily become more sophisticated,[159] however, systemic management and planning even at a national level is far from realization.

While several large corporations may occasionally act in concert, it should be borne in mind that even the largest of corporations contributed individually only about 1 percent to the U.S. G.N.P. Admittedly large, but nevertheless a far cry from a planned national economy of the nature suggested by some. The market remains the central arena of the relationships not only between the large corporations, but also between each of them separately, and labour, suppliers, consumers, and smaller businesses.[160]

National economic planning is primarily a matter of attempting to co-ordinate the previously formulated investment plans of large firms and corporations while at the same time proposing certain government priorities.[161] Apart from the fact that the state generally has no means for enforcing such planning, these attempts at state economic intervention appear to be further restricted by the basic uncertainty of the investment and market calculations and projections collected from the various economic aggregates.[162] Much of this projected market and investment information is gathered by polling big business and thus suffers from the further defect that not all corporations are willing to co-operate. In the words of one state planner: "To a great extent we still rely today largely on hunches and the anticipation of other people's behavior."[163]

These estimates and 'enlightened guesses',[164] which form the basis of the state's efforts at economic management and planning, suffer from the additional uncertainties of the international market and labour unrest. While state economic intervention may decrease the severity of the downward phase and temporarily sustain the upswing, these achievements have frequently led to an overestimation of contemporary North American capitalism's ability to eliminate recessions (and depressions)[165] and the intensification of their more distant but also more adverse economic effects. Fierce competition in the international market, monetary crises, international trade uncertainties coupled with difficulties of controlling wage costs all serve to worsen existing problems involved in planning for sectoral equilibrium targets.[166]

The concerted efforts at economic planning in wartime Germany and Japan offer striking examples of the limitations of capitalist state planning in general.[167] More immediately instructive, however, has been the postwar attempts and failure at planning in Japan and especially in France. These have been among the most comprehensive and prolonged efforts to regulate the economies of advanced industrial capitalist societies. A model for other attempts at national planning,[168] the prolonged French effort under the direction of the 'Planning Board', has proven a consistent failure.[169] The scope and depth of the May '68 events in France should in themselves give some indication of its success in the eyes of the working class. It might also be noted that in Sweden, where state planning is more advanced than in the U.S., there is a persistent disjunction between planned, i.e., projected development of G.N.P. and its components, and actual developments.

Nevertheless, attempts in postwar North America have not been entirely without success at dampening the downward swings of economic cycles. While a variety of measures are available to the state, each with its own particular advantages and disadvantages,[170] the chosen option, as noted earlier, has been massive military expenditures resulting in turn in a swollen state debt, an unabated inflationary trend and the encouragement of an increased consumer and business debt. The previous discussion of this form of state stimulant has indicated both its short- and long-term disadvantages.[171]

Even this massive shot in the arm, however, complementing postwar reconstruction and expansion and the growth related to the automation revolution, was not adequate to maintain the boom of the fifties[172] — a 'boom' incidentally which has not witnessed a reasonable rate of full employment since 1953.[173] What has been achieved is that the North American economy, indeed the world capitalist economy, has avoided a depression of the dimensions of the thirties — a major achievement. Whether these successes can be maintained is another issue. In any event, the recessions and unemployment of the last three decades are a far cry from the well managed qualitatively new economic order portrayed by the celebrationism of the fifties and early sixties.

In an attempt to complement the defence expenditure effort to dampen recessions, the state has, on occasion, created new purchasing power (increased, in 1971, by 6 percent.[174]). While such measures may help solve the immediate problem, there are limits to the amount of extra purchasing power that may be introduced into the economy[175], and to the extent such 'money manufacturing' measures are chosen as the instrument of state economic intervention, it is the severity of the recession which determines the amount of new purchasing power to be created.[176] Such 'money creation' results almost immediately in an additional spurt to the already creeping (sometimes galloping) inflation. The dilemma confronting the state, therefore appears to be the unavoidable choice between crisis or inflation.[177]

Inflation can of course be tolerated within limits and until now at least that course has proven preferable. Limits there are, however, and when that point is reached the state must either find alternate anti-crisis measures (and they become increasingly difficult to find as the inflation spiral continues), or accept a severe economic crisis.

The fundamental contradiction which arises here is between the inflationary use of the dollar as an anti-crisis instrument in the North American economy on the one hand, and the dollar's use as a reserve currency in the international monetary system on the other.[178] Hence, in its role as an economic moderator in the state's efforts to dampen cyclical downswings and sustain upswings, it is important that there be as many dollars as necessary in circulation, which implies a flexible supply. These requirements, however, lay the basis for the general instability of the dollar's value due to the ensuing inflationary tendency. Yet, in its role as an international currency of account, it is important that the dollar's value be as stable as possible. Herein lies a fundamental contradiction between those capitalists engaged in trade with the U.S. (importers or those outside the U.S.) who want a flexible (and inflationary) supply of dollars, and others, such as central and private banks, holding large dollar reserves and credits, whose primary interest is in a stable dollar value.[179] This conflict of interest makes more difficult the achievement of a commonly acceptable long-term solution to the monetary crises which have emerged during the past half decade.

Spiralling corporate[180] and consumer debt in the postwar years has added to the illusion of perpetual boom and prosperity. In 1951 only 14 percent of consumer income went to debt servicing — by 1963 it had risen to 21 percent.[181] The trend did not end there, as the 1960s witnessed a growth of consumer debt at a rate of 50 percent faster than income growth[182]. The seventies have seen an even further aggravation of this trend.[183] To the short sighted this rapid increase in corporate and consumer debt seemed to go a long way in buoying up an economy with a steadily growing surplus productive capacity. So it did. However, while it may be difficult to delineate the precise limits of the percentage of income going to debt servicing, it is clear that there must a maximum percentage. Inasmuch as such a limit exists, it implies a final restraint on an economy which relies on debt to maintain stability.[184]

As for the corporate and business debt, its servicing necessitates an expanding gross profit and/or rate of profit. The dilemma creeping up on business is how to realize such profit increases at a time of declining markets and investment opportunities. Specifically, the problem is how to increase profits in a stagnant economy which boasts the lowest postwar industrial expansion rate in the advanced capitalist world.[185] Undoubtedly, a primary remedial measure will be a continued effort to reduce labour costs not only by further increases in the organic composition of capital, but by more direct and indirect forms of wage cuts to be levied at a working class that, at least since 1965, has had the lowest rate of wage increase in the advanced capitalist world.[186] Such measures, however, would seem indirectly to further exacerbate the already worsening economic situation inasmuch as workers, whose credit spending helps sustain the economy, require wages to service and extend this debt.[187] Indeed a central contradiction for contemporary capitalism is between the need on the one hand to drastically reduce labour costs by either increasing the organic composition of capital or by wage roll backs, while on the other hand, to sustain and extend aggregate demand by high levels of employment and real wages. This is a central contradiction in capitalism between labour's dual role as production cost factor and as consumer.

While helping curb recessions, the expansion of government, corporate and consumer debt has tended to steer the economy towards a far more serious dilemma. The problems solved in one area, only result in the emergence of economic difficulties in another, or in the prolongation and intensification of the original problem. The managers appear to have forgotten the necessary therapeutic effects of depressions. What used to bring the debt spiral to halt was the depression slump with its attendant price drop and the subsequent squeezing out of the financial superstructure.[188] In the present epoch, however, while the disproportional growth of debt and income is not a new phenomena to capitalism[189], the crucial difference lies in the fact that with the mitigation of the cyclical slump, no drop in prices occurs, nor is there a consequent squeezing out of the financial superstructure. As a result, state, corporate and consumer debt continues to swell, resulting in a situation where even mild economic setbacks shake the entire highly sensitized financial superstructure.[190] The dilemma facing economic planners is that the cost of avoiding a crisis now is a steady worsening of the debt/liquidity squeeze which becomes ever more explosive.[191]

In the short run, however, these efforts have been successful in converting what were (in their initial phases) depressions of the dimensions of that of the thirties to relatively mild and manageable recessions.[192] This was particularly true of the 1957-1958 recession. It should also be noted that in addition to any other adverse long range consequences of cyclical crisis management measures, the gains made in mitigating their severity appeared countered by their increased frequency and by the disappearance of any real boom phases.[193]

Generally, due to the postwar shortening of the business cycle, recessions increased from a prewar average of one every ten years or so to a postwar rate of roughly one every two, three or four years. The recession (or depression) phase of the cycle is characteristically a time for the renewal and expansion of fixed capital or productive machinery. In the postwar years several factors led to a shortening of the business cycle. First, as a result of the development of more rapid construction methods and techniques new and old factories were more quickly built and/or rebuilt and thus more rapidly returned to operation than previously.[194] Second, spurred on by the hastened rate of scientific and technological breakthroughs achieved through massive military and private research, the Third Industrial (or automation) revolution has resulted in a more frequent obsolescence of productive machinery.[195] Third, in the U.S. far-reaching government policy aimed at strategic industries allowed them to deduct from their profits depreciation sums which were often in excess of two or three times the actual wear. Consequently these industries were permitted to write-off the fixed capital of their plants in five years or less, at the expense of the taxpayer, and so further increase the frequency of the cycle.[196] Somewhat as a complement to this later point, it is worth mentioning that more than two-thirds of the new capital investments in the U.S. during the last decade went for the replacement and modernization of existing plants.[197]

Intensified international competition has served only to increase the tendency toward a shortening cycle. Thus, even with the underemployment of current productive capacities and substantial production surpluses, the hastened increase in the organic composition of capital under the press of competition and facilitated by massive defence research, reinforces the novel tendency toward a drastically shortened cycle. The rise in productive capacity which nearly always accompanies the reduction of labour costs through increases in the organic composition of capital deepens the existing problems of surplus production, under-utilized productive capacities, and declining aggregate demand.[198] Not only has the frequency of recessions in postwar North America increased, but it appears also that the upswing phase of the business cycle has been seriously reduced and even occasionally eliminated.[199] Even though more extensive state economic intervention has affected a dampening of the downward phase of the business cycle, it is reasonable to expect, indeed it is testified to by current trends, that subsequent economic crises will continue to deepen in comparison with those of the early postwar years.[200]

While state intervention efforts have achieved noteworthy successes, the problem of periodic cyclical crises is far from solved. Indeed the relative successes in this area appear slight as a long-range tendency towards more frequent and deepening crises sets in. Repeated attempts to counteract the pattern of uneven economic development have met either failure or only limited and short-term success.[201] If a major depression has been averted through extensive state economic 'management' (swelling state and private debt, sustained arms spending, inflationary monetary policies, etc.), it is not unreasonable to conclude that, "a capitalism which know 'only' recessions is certainly not a crisis free capitalism,"[202] and is, therefore, hardly of the qualitatively new order portrayed by the apologists of that system.

General Crisis of North American Capitalism

Inasmuch as capitalist prosperity depends upon the conjunction of expanding markets, investment opportunities and a high or stable rate of profit,[203] the continuance of the relative prosperity of the postwar years became more uncertain as events began to undermine the possibility for such conjunctions.[204] The rising surpluses of capital, production and productive capacity[205] are due to the non-realization of commodities in a more competitive and overcapitalized domestic and world market, to rising labour costs, and to the necessary replacement of unamortized fixed capital under the press of intensified competition. These problems are manifest in the growth of structural unemployment and the under-utilization of productive capacity.[206] Meanwhile, the increase in structural unemployment, itself a consequence of these problems, worsens the dilemma as the unemployed workers' effectiveness as consumers is drastically undercut.[207] Welfare and social assistance cheques in North America hardly compensate for the loss of purchasing power suffered by prolonged unemployment.

With growing Third World unrest and hostility towards foreign investment, even this traditional safety-valve of world trade for periodic overproduction is being undermined.[208] Inseparably related to problems of overproduction and surplus capacity is the problem of growing capital surpluses. The factors which lead to a squeeze on marketing possibilities also result in a relative and sometimes real decline in investment opportunities both at home and abroad. While North American capital export remains large, it tends to exacerbate the surplus capital problem inasmuch as these investments themselves pay dividends which are eventually transferred to the exporting country.[209]

As for domestic investment of this surplus capital, the already monopoly-dominated markets and surplus productive capacity in these areas restrict investment possibilities on a scale necessary to counteract the tendencial and disproportional rise in capacity, commodity and capital surpluses. Furthermore, in a domestic market which has come under intense competitive pressure from revitalized imperialist rivals, it is unlikely that large American corporations will see any advantage in building new plants to compete in a market which their present capacity already more than matches.

Coupled with this, the unabated and disproportional rise in government, corporate and consumer debt and military expenditures has spurred an inflationary spiral which has continued right through the recessions of the seventies.[210] Belatedly this problem is recognized by even those economists whose interest seems to lie primarily in propping up the system. In 1971 Samuelson stated:

> Creeping inflation is the malaria of the modern mixed economy. Like malaria it is uncomfortable to live with and just will not go away. But unlike malaria, there seems to be no known cure for creeping inflation that is better than the disease.[211]

'No known cure better than the disease' indeed; letting the crisis 'run its course' at this stage would, in all probability, mean running the risk (by government calculations) of from 20 to 25 million unemployed.[212] The likely political consequences of unemployment of these dimensions is more than North American capitalism cares to risk. The dilemma then is between solving the immediate problems of surplus capital, productive capacity and high structural unemployment on the one hand, and accepting a worsening of the overall economic situation as a consequence of measures taken to ensure short-term stability on the other.[213] Even this grim set of choices will not always be available as the economy slides closer to a general depression combining all negative options.

Creeping inflation coupled with a chronic balance of payments deficit over the last decade[214] has resulted in an undermining of the role of the dollar[215] as a currency of account on the international market.

State efforts to mitigate crises by the expansion of credit spending and inflationary monetary policies has led to an emergent contradiction between the dollar's use as an instrument in the struggle against cyclical crises, and its role as a reserve currency in the international monetary system.[216] The ensuing monetary crises of the late sixties and seventies shattered the 1944 Bretton Woods agreement[217] and shook the capitalist system to its roots.[218] The apparent uncorruptible stability of the postwar years was suddenly threatened with a degree of economic turmoil and uncertainty not witnessed since the depression of 1929.[219] The economist, Per Jacobsen, the director of the International Monetary Fund in 1963, addressing a group of economists at the time cautioned,

> . . . a new situation has arisen which shows certain similarities with what happened in the early 1930's . . . I do not intend to convey the idea that we must repeat the sad experiences of those years, but I do think we will have to take definite measures to see that they are not repeated.[220]

In the intervening 15 years not only have there been no successful measures to curb this situation, but on the contrary, there has occurred a steady worsening of the problems then present, plus the addition of several new ones. The long range prospects of expansion and prosperity seem far from promising.

The intensified inter-imperialist competition of our period continues to exacerbate contradictions between short- and long-range economic interests; national or bloc and systemic interests; labour as commodity and labour as consumer; and, nations as consumers and nations as competitors. The analogy of the parlour game 'Monopoly' seems appropriate here — when you win, you lose, simply because there is no one left to play the game. Indeed, capitalism remains the only economic system which experiences deepened economic, social and political crises precisely when and because it can produce *too much*.

The opening of the Soviet Union and China to Western economic penetration, however, may well prove to be one important stabilizing factor. The vast markets of these areas, if substantially opened to capitalist expansion as a result of the diplomatic scramble of the past half decade, may provide large secure areas for increased capital and commodity exports from the leading western nations. Both obstacles and opportunities exist. But to the extent that they do exist, the balance seems to have clearly shifted in favour of the former.

Advanced capitalism in general, and North American capitalism in particular, are clearly far from collapse and no doubt the future will hold further examples of its already well demonstrated tenacity and adaptability. It is also apparent, however, that the long period of postwar economic stability and prosperity in North America shows clear signs of strain. If the objective is to be a realistic evaluation of the conditions and tendencies of the North American economy, then those who are quick, not always without cause, to criticize the sometimes flippant 'doomsday' predictions aimed at that economic system, would do well to show equal critical scrutiny of their own often ill-formed and a historical evaluations of the elasticity and stability of the system. The task of assessing the direction of the North American economy is an extremely difficult one, and one which the foregoing discussions make no claim at realizing. What should be clear, however, is that the often conjunctural and undialectical economic analyses offered by many lingering celebrationists should be approached with caution. They can, and have, led to both premature and untimely social and political conclusions and to unnecessary revisions of theory and praxis.

NOTES

1. E. Mandel, *Europe vs. America*, p. 476.

2. M. Kidron, *Western Capitalism Since the War*, p. 1.

3. J. Phillips, "Economic Effects of the Cold War", p. 189.

4. G. Kolko, *The Roots of American Foreign Policy*, p. 40.

5. P. Sweezy, *Modern Capitalism and Other Essays*, p. 12.

6. E. Mandel, *The Decline of the Dollar*, p. 82.

7. G. Adler-Karlsson, *Western Economic Warfare 1947-1967*, p. 5.

8. *Ibid.*, p. 5.

9. *Ibid.*, p. 5.

10. *Ibid.*, p. 5.

11. *Ibid.*, p. 6.

12. *Ibid.*, p. 7.

13. *Ibid.*, p. 7.

14. *Ibid.*, p. 7.

15. *Ibid.*, p. 3.

16. Mandel, *Europe vs. America*, p. 11.

17. *Ibid.*, p. 11.

18. *Ibid.*, pp. 11-12.

19. See C. Kindleberger, *Europe's Postwar Growth.*

20. See Hearings Before the Subcommittee on Economic Statistics of the Joint Economic Committee of the U.S. 87th Congress, U.S. Govt. Printing Office, Washington, 1962, p. 13; See also H. Magdoff, and P. Sweezy *The Dynamics of U.S. Capitalism*, p. 49; See also, *The Economist*, Dec. 24, 1977, p. 35., See also OECD, *Economic Outlook*, July, 1977, p. 12.

21. Mandel, *Europe vs. America*, p. 13.

22. *Ibid.*, pp. 13-14.

23. Sweezy, *Modern Capitalism . . .*, pp. 12-13.

24. B. Rowthorn, "Imperialism in the Seventies — Unity or Rivalry?", p.33; see also Magdoff and Sweezy, *The Dynamics of U.S. Capitalism*, pp. 198-199 for a discussion of the recent U.S. shift to just such a policy.

25. H. Magdoff, *The Age of Imperialism*, pp. 41-42.

26. Rowthorn, "Imperialism in the Seventies — Unity or Rivalry?," p. 41; see also E. Mandel, "Where is American Going?", p. 13; and also G. Novack in E. Mandel and G. Novack, "On the Revolutionary Potential of the Working Class," p. 31.

27. Mandel, "Where is America Going?", p. 57, see also Mandel, *Marxist Economic Theory*, p. 146; and Mandel, "On the Revolutionary Potential of the Working Class, p. 31.

28. R. B. Sutcliffe and A. Glyn, *British Capitalism, Workers and the Profit Squeeze*, p. 57.

29. C. Levinson, *Capital, Inflation and the Multinationals*, p. 113; see also *The Globe and Mail*, June 3, 1978, "International Trade in Manufacturing"; see too *City Bank Money International*, Vol. 4, May, 1976.

30. See also J. Halliday and G. McCormack, "Japan and America: Antagonistic Allies", p. 70, regarding this possibility, and G. W. Domhoff, *Who Rules America?*, p. 201.

31. Mandel, "Where is America Going?", p. 12.

32. Mandel, *Europe vs. America*, p. 16; see also Y. Varga, *Politico-Economic Problems of Capitalism*, pp. 229-230.

33. Rowthorn, "Imperialism in the Seventies — Unity or Rivalry?", p. 35.

34. *Ibid.*, p. 35.

35. *Ibid.*, p. 35; see also Mandel, *Europe vs. America*, pp. 14-15.

36. Varga, *Politico-Economic Problems of Capitalism*, p. 229; see also Mandel, *Europe vs. America*, p. 9; see too *UN World Economic Survey, 1975*, pp. 63; and see OECD *Economic Outlook*, July, 1976, p. 40.

37. Sutcliffe and Glynn, *British Capitalism, Workers and the Profit Squeeze*, p. 95; see also *Fortune*, August, 1976, p. 126.

38. Levinson, *Capital, Inflation and the Multinationals* p. 171; and see Mandel, *Decline of the Dollar*, p. 83; and Halliday and McCormack, "Japan and America: Antagonistic Allies", p. 70.

39. Rowthorn, "Imperialism in the Seventies — Unity or Rivalry?", p. 70.

40. Mandel, *Decline of the Dollar*, p. 83; see also Mandel, *Europe vs. America*, pp. 9, 16; see too Varga, *Politico-Economic Problems of Capitalism*, p. 229.

41. Rowthorn, "Imperialism in the Seventies — Unity or Rivalry?", p. 45; see also Halliday and McCormack, "Japan and America: Antagonistic Allies", p. 70.

42. Mandel, *Europe vs. America*, p. 28.

43. Halliday and McCormack, "Japan and America: Antagonistic Allies", p. 66.

44. Mandel, *Decline of the Dollar*, p. 11.

45. H. Magdoff, "Is Imperialism Really Necessary?", p. 9.

46. T. Szentes, *The Political Economy of Underdevelopment*, pp. 168, 173; see also, Magdoff, "Is Imperialism Really Necessary?", p. 229.

47. Kolko, *The Roots of American Foreign Policy*, p. 86.

48. Magdoff, *The Age of Imperialism*, p. 166.

49. *Ibid.*, pp. 166, 173; see also Magdoff, "Is Imperialism Really Necessary?", p. 9.

50. Halliday and McCormack, "Japan and America: Antagonist Allies", pp. 68-69.

51. J. Halliday, "Washington vs. Tokyo: Wall Street vs. Maranouchi", p. 46.

52. Halliday and McCormack, "Japan and America: Antagonistic Allies", pp. 64-65.

53. Halliday and McCormack, *Japanese Imperialism Today*, pp. 232, 237.

54. Levinson, *Capital, Inflation and the Multinationals*, for a discussion of this point.

55. Halliday and McCormack, *Japanese Imperialism Today*, pp. 232 n. 1, 237.

56. Varga, *Politico-Economic Problems of Capitalism*, p. 230; see also Magdoff, "Is Imperialism Really Necessary?", p. 9.

57. Sutcliffe and Glyn, *British Capitalism, Workers and the Profit Squeeze*, p. 90.

58. Halliday, "Washington vs. Tokyo: Wall Street vs. Maranouchi", p. 46; Mandel, *Europe vs. America*, pp. 41-42.

59. B. Warren, "Capitalist Planning and the State", p. 19; see also OECD *Economic Surveys Japan*, July, 1977, p. 13. OECD *Economic Outlook*, July, 1976, p. 31.

60. Mandel, *Decline of the Dollar*, p. 11.

61. Magdoff and Sweezy, *The Dynamics of U.S. Capitalism*, p. 3; see also Sutcliffe and Glyn, *British Capitalism, Workers and the Profit Squeeze*, pp. 210-211.

62. *Ibid.*, p. 211.

63. *Ibid.*, p. 211.

64. Mandel, *Europe vs. America*, p. 5.

65. Magdoff and Sweezy, *The Dynamics of U.S. Capitalism*, p. 198, see also p. 12; and Halliday and McCormack, "Is Imperialism Really Necessary?", p. 9.

66. Sweezy, *Modern Capitalism . . .*, p. 77; see too P. Baran and P. Sweezy, *Monopoly Capital*, p. 153.

67. D. Horowitz (ed.), *Corporations and the Cold War*, p. 176.

68. Kidron, *Western Capitalism Since the War*, p. 27.

69. Magdoff and Sweezy, *The Dynamics of U.S. Capitalism*, p. 13.

70. Baran and Sweezy, *Monopoly Capital*, p. 153; see too, Sweezy, *Modern Capitalism . . .*, p. 27.

71. Baran and Sweezy, *Monopoly Capital*, p. 153.

72. OECD *Economic Outlook*, July, 1976, p. 31 and OECD *Economic Surveys Japan*, July, 1977, p. 13.

73. E. Mandel, *Marxist Economic Theory*, pp. 522-523.

74. Kidron, *Western Capitalism Since the War*, p. 39; see also Magdoff and Sweezy, *The Dynamics of U.S. Capitalism*, p. 13; and Baran and Sweezy, *Monopoly Capital*, p. 41.

75. Kidron, *Western Capitalism Since the War*, p. 41.

76. Magdoff and Sweezy, *The Dynamics of U.S. Capitalism*, pp. 9-10.

77. Y. Varga, *Twentieth Century Capitalism*, pp. 124-5.

78. Halliday and McCormack, "Japan and America: Antagonistic Allies", pp. 61-62.

79. Magdoff, *The Age of Imperialism*, pp. 132-33.

80. M. Kidron, *Western Capitalism Since the War*, p. 53.

81. Varga, *Politico-Economic Problems of Capitalism*, pp. 194-195; see also M. Kidron, *Western Capitalism Since the War*, p. 59.

82. Mandel, *Marxist Economic Theory*, pp. 526-527; see also *UN World Economic Survey, 1975*, p. 71; see too *Economic Council of Canada, 13th Annual Review, 1976*, c. 6-1; and *OECD Economic Outlook*, July, 1976, p. 43.

83. Magdoff and Sweezy, *The Dynamics of U.S. Capitalism*, p. 168.

84. Phillips, "Economic Effects of the Cold War", p. 175.

85. Magdoff and Sweezy, *The Dynamics of U.S. Capitalism*, pp. 167-8; see also Mandel, *Marxist Economic Theory*, pp. 526-7, and *An Introduction to Marxist Economic Theory*, p. 67.

86. Mandel, *Marxist Economic Theory*, p. 527; see also Mandel, *An Introduction to Marxist Economic Theory*, pp. 67-68.

87. Mandel, *Marxist Economic Theory*, p. 527.

88. Magdoff and Sweezy, *The Dynamics of U.S. Capitalism*, p. 168.

89. Mandel, *Marxist Economic Theory*, pp. 524-25; see also Varga, *Politico-Economic Problems of Capitalism*, p. 218.

90. Mandel, *Marxist Economic Theory*, p. 524.

91. *Ibid.*, p. 525.

92. P. Baran, *The Political Economy of Growth*, p. 129.

93. Baran and Sweezy, *Monopoly Capital*, pp. 213-214.

94. *Ibid.*, p. 214.

95. *Ibid.*, pp. 213-214.

96. Kidron, *Western Capitalism Since the War*, p. 55.

97. *Ibid.*, p. 41.

98. See the work of G. W. Domhoff and C. W. Mills.

99. M. Kidron, *Western Capitalism Since the War*, pp. 41-42; see also Mandel, *An Introduction to Marxist Economic Theory*, p. 57; J. Phillips, "Economics Effects of the Cold War", pp. 185-186; and Mandel, *Europe vs. America*, pp. 33-35.

100. M. Kidron, *Western Capitalism Since the War*, p. 55.

101. Baran and Sweezy, *Monopoly Capital*, p. 215; see too B. Seligman, *Most Notorious Victory*, for a more comprehensive discussion of these consequences.

102. Depending on whether or not this 'cost-burden' is shifted onto workers and consumers.

103. J. D. Phillips, "Economic Effects of the Cold War", pp. 200; see also OECD *Economic Outlook*, July, 1976, p. 31.

104. Warren, "Capitalist Planning and the State", p. 19; see also Phillips, "Economic Effects of the Cold War", p. 176.

105. Mandel, *Decline of the Dollar*, p. 29; see also *Business Week*, Nov. 7, 1977, p. 22; see too *Canadian Statistical Review*, Nov. '77, p. 112.

106. Magdoff and Sweezy, *The Dynamics of U.S. Capitalism*, p. 14.

107. Kidron, *Western Capitalism Since the War*, p. 56; see also Baran, *The Political Economy of Growth*, p. 121.

108. H. Marcuse, *Five Lectures*, p. 95.

109. For the statistical basis of this conclusion see data in D. Cooper (ed.), *The Dialectics of Liberation*, pp. 102-103; Szentes, *The Political Economy of Underdevelopment*, p. 50; A. Emmanuel, *Unequal Exchange*, p. 265; Baran, *The Political Economy of Growth*, p. 196; P. Jallée, *The Pillage of the Third World*, p. 49.

110. D. Cooper (ed.), *The Dialectics of Liberation*, pp. 102-103.

111. Emmanuel, *Unequal Exchange*, p. 265.

112. Sweezy, *Modern Capitalism . . .*, p. 16.

113. Jallée, *The Pillage of the Third World*, p. 9, for a more detailed breakdown.

114. *Ibid.*, p. 9.

115. Sweezy, *Modern Capitalism . . .*, p. 16.

116. Szentes, *The Political Economy of Underdevelopment*, pp. 291-2.

117. See Mandel, *Marxist Economic Theory*, pp. 454-5 for examples of this discrepancy.

118. Magdoff, *The Age of Imperialism*, p. 45; and Mandel, *Marxist Economic Theory*, pp. 454-5.

119. Magdoff, *The Age of Imperialism*, pp. 45 and 48.

120. Jallée, *The Pillage of the Third World*, p. 27.

121. Halliday and McCormack, *Japanese Imperialism Today*, p. 237.

122. Magdoff, *The Age of Imperialism*, pp. 45-46; see also Magdoff, "Is Imperialism Really Necessary?", p. 8.

123. Kolko, *The Roots of American Foreign Policy*, p. 55.

124. Jallée, *The Pillage of the Third World*, pp. 99-100.

125. *Ibid.*, p. 110.

126. Magdoff, *The Age of Imperialism*, p. 16.

127. Magdoff, "Is Imperialism Really Necessary?", p. 9.

128. Halliday and McCormack, "Japan and America: Antagonistic Allies", pp. 64-65.

129. Mandel, *Europe vs. America*, p. 81; Mandel, *Marxist Economic Theory*, p. 524.

130. Mandel, *Europe vs. America*, p. 81.

131. Jallée, *The Pillage of the Third World*, p. 53.

132. *Ibid.*, p. 111.

133. T. Kemp, *Theories of Imperialism*, p. 19.

134. Magdoff, *The Age of Imperialism*, p. 21.

135. Mandel, *Marxist Economic Theory*, p. 480.

136. Magdoff, *The Age of Imperialism*, p. 121.

137. Quoted in *Ibid.*, p. 129.

138. *Ibid.*, p. 38.

139. *Ibid.*, p. 20.

140. *Ibid.*, pp. 132-134.

141. J. O'Connor, "The Meaning of Economic Imperialism", p. 142.

142. Mandel, *Marxist Economic Theory*, p. 491.

143. Kolko, *The Roots of American Foreign Policy*, p. 60; Mandel, *Marxist Economic Theory*, p. 479.

144. Mandel, *Marxist Economic Theory*, p. 465.

145. Baran, *The Political Economy of Growth*, p. 200.

146. D. Horowitz, *Imperialism and Revolution*, p. 155; see also C. Levinson, *Capital, Inflation and the Multinationals*, p. 110.

147. Kolko, *The Roots of American Foreign Policy*, p. xviii.

148. Emmanuel, *Unequal Exchange*, p. 264; Sweezy, *Modern Capitalism . . .*, p. 14; see also Jallée, *The Pillage of the Third World*, p. 110.

149. Kolko, *The Roots of American Foreign Policy*, p. 61.

150. *Ibid.*, p. 62.

151. Baran and Sweezy, *Monopoly Capital*, p. 280; see also Sweezy, *Modern Capitalism*, p. 14.

152. Mandel, *Marxist Economic Theory*, p. 480.

153. Horowitz, *Imperialism and Revolution*, pp. 258-261.

154. See *U.S. News and World Report*, June 14, 1971, pp. 52-53.

155. Magdoff, "Is Imperialism Really Necessary?", p. 4; Kolko, *The Roots of American Foreign Policy*, p. 52; P. Jallée, *The Third World in World Economy*, p. 139.

156. Jallée, *The Pillage of the Third World*, p. 112.

157. *Ibid.*, p. 103.

158. See H. Magdoff and P. Sweezy, "Economic Stagnation and the Stagnation of Economics, p. 7; and Varga, *Politico-Economic Problems of Capitalism*, p. 211; see, too, *OECD Economic Outlook*, July, 1976, p. 73, 74 (U.S.A.); see also *OECD Economic Surveys*, July, 1977, p. 27; see also *OECD Economic Outlook*, July, 1977, p. 12; finally see *The Economist*, Dec. 24, 1977, p. 35.

159. Baran and Sweezy, *Monopoly Capital*, p. 53.

160. *Ibid.*, pp. 53, 55.

161. Mandel, *An Introduction to Marxist Economic Theory*, p. 71.

162. P. Baran, *The Longer View*, p. 121.

163. Quoted in *Ibid.*, p. 121.

164. *Ibid.*, p. 121.

165. Varga, *Politico-Economic Problems of Capitalism*, p. 238.

166. Goldfinger, "Capitalist Planning and the State", p. 23.

167. Mandel, *Marxist Economic Theory*, p. 367.

168. E. Mandel, "Workers and Permanent Revolution", p. 185.

169. Goldfinger, "Capitalist Planning and the State", p. 22.

170. Baran, *The Longer View*, pp. 119-130.

171. Magdoff and Sweezy, *The Dynamics of U.S. Capitalism*, pp. 9-10.

172. *Ibid.*, pp. 8, 14.

173. *Ibid.*, p. 8.

174. Mandel, *Decline of the Dollar*, p. 81.

175. Mandel, *Marxist Economic Theory*, p. 532.

176. *Ibid.*, p. 532.

177. *Ibid.*, p. 532.

178. *Ibid.*, p. 532.

179. Mandel, *Decline of the Dollar*, pp. 105-106.

180. See figures in Magdoff and Sweezy, *The Dynamics of U.S. Capitalism*, p. 15; see also *Statistical Abstracts of the U.S.*, 1976, p. 490; *The Economist*, Nov. 19, 1977, pp. 30, 103; *Business Week*, Nov. 7, 1977, p. 22; *Canadian Statistics Review*, Nov., '77, p. 112.

181. See figures in Magdoff and Sweezy, *The Dynamics of U.S. Capitalism*, p. 14.

182. See figures in *Ibid.*, pp. 17-18.

183. Information on consumer debt and servicing in 1970s.

184. See figures in Magdoff and Sweezy, *The Dynamics of U.S. Capitalism*, p. 14.

185. See comparative data in Varga, *Politico-Economic Problems of Capitalism*, p. 211; see also *Business Week*, Nov. 21, 1977, p. 138; *UN World Economic Survey*, 1975, p. 63; *Monthly Review*, January, 1977, p. 8; *Economic Council of Canada*, 13th Annual Review, 1976, p. 81.

186. See the results of a 1974 study done by the Swedish Employers Association and reported in 'Dagens Nyheter', Feb. 15, 1974; see also, Varga, *Politico-Economic Problems of Capitalism*, p. 211; see also *City Bank Money International*, Vol. 4, No. 4,

May '76; OECD *Economic Outlook,* July, 1976, p. 40; UN *World Economic Survey,* 1975, p. 62; UN *Bulletin of Statistics,* Sept. 1977, pp. xx and 146.

187. Varga, *The Dynamics of U.S. Capitalism,* p. 15; see also Mandel, *Decline of the Dollar,* p. 40.

188. H. Magdoff and P. Sweezy, "The Long-Run Decline in Liquidity", p. 13; see also Mandel, *Europe vs. America,* pp. 90-91.

189. Magdoff and Sweezy, "The Long-Run Decline in Liquidity", p. 12.

190. Varga, *The Dynamics of U.S. Capitalism,* p. 192.

191. Magdoff and Sweezy, "The Long-Run Decline in Liquidity", p. 192.

192. Mandel, *Marxist Economic Theory,* p. 531; see also Sweezy, *Modern Capitalism . . .,* p. 76.

193. Varga, *Politico-Economic Problems of Capitalism,* p. 236; Sweezy, *Modern Capitalism . . .,* p. 76.

194. Varga, *Politico-Economic Problems of Capitalism,* p. 234.

195. M. Dobb, *Capitalism Yesterday and Today,* pp. 58-59; Jallée, *The Pillage of the Third World,* p. 102; Varga, *Politico-Economic Problems of Capitalism,* p. 234.

196. *Ibid.,* p. 235.

197. *Ibid.,* p. 235; see also *Business Week,* Nov. 21, 1977, p. 138; UN *World Economic Survey,* 1975, p. 63.

198. See Sweezy, *Modern Capitalism . . .,* p. 199, for figures from 1970; see also J. Bright, *Automation and Management,* pp. 80-81; and Magdoff and Sweezy, "Economic Stagnation and the Stagnation of Economics", p. 7.

199. Varga, *Politico-Economic Problems of Capitalism,* p. 236; see also *New Left Review,* Feb/April 1977, pp. 101-102; see also *Monthly Review,* January, 1977, p. 8; see too *Business Week,* Nov. 21, 1977, p. 138; finally see UN *World Economic Survey,* 1975, p. 63.

200. Varga, *Politico-Economic Problems of Capitalism,* p. 236.

201. Goldfinger, "Capitalist Planning and the State", p. 17; see also Varga, *Twentieth Century Capitalism,* p. 85.

202. Mandel, *Marxist Economic Theory,* p. 534.

203. Mandel, *Decline of the Dollar,* p. 90.

204. *Ibid.,* p. 90.

205. Baran and Sweezy, *Monopoly Capital,* p. 218; see also Magdoff and Sweezy, "Economic Stagnation and the Stagnation of Economics", p. 7, for figures on capacity

utilization in manufacturing 1960-1970; see too, *The Economist*, Dec. 24, 1977, p. 35; see too OECD *Economic Council Outlook*, July '76, pp. 73, 74; and see OECD *Economic Outlook*, July, 1977, p. 12.

206. Jallée, *The Third World in World Economy*, p. 139; see also Sutcliffe and Glyn, *British Capitalism, Workers and the Profit Squeeze*, pp. 73-74.

207. P. Sweezy, *The Theory of Capitalist Development*, p. 177.

208. Mandel, *Marxist Economic Theory*, pp. 488-489.

209. Baran and Sweezy, *Monopoly Capital*, pp. 107-108.

210. Magdoff and Sweezy, *The Dynamics of U.S. Capitalism*, p. 2; see also OECD *Economic Outlook*, July, 1976, p. 43; *UN World Economic Survey*, 1975, p. 71.

211. Quoted in Levinson, *Capital, Inflation and the Multinationals*, p. 11; see also U.S. Secretary of Economic Affairs, quoted on p. 22.

212. Mandel, *Decline of the Dollar*, p. 26.

213. Magdoff and Sweezy, *The Dynamics of U.S. Capitalism*, pp. 178-9.

214. Mandel, *Decline of the Dollar*, p. 45; see also Magdoff, "Is Imperialism Really Necessary?", p. 9; and Horowitz (ed.), *Corporations and the Cold War*, p. 200.

215. Mandel, *Decline of the Dollar*, p. 7.

216. Magdoff and Sweezy, "The Long-Run Decline in Liquidity", p. 12.

217. Magdoff and Sweezy, *The Dynamics of U.S. Capitalism*, p. 2.

218. Mandel, *The Decline of the Dollar*, p. 10.

219. Magdoff and Sweezy, *The Dynamics of U.S. Capitalism*, p. 2.

220. Quoted in Varga, *Politico-Economic Problems of Capitalism*, pp. 238-9.

Readings

Adler-Karlsson, Gunnar, *Western Economic Warfare 1947-1967*, Uppsala: Almqvist & Wiksell A.B., 1968.

Albinowski, Stanislow, *Commercial Policy of the E. E. C.*, Warsaw: Western Press Agency, 1965.

Arrighi, Giovanni, "International Corporations, Labor Aristocracies, and Economic Development in Tropical Africa", in R. I. Rhodes (ed.), *Imperialism and Under-development*, New York: Monthly Review Press, 1970.

Baran, Paul A., *The Longer View*, New York: Monthly Review Press, 1970.

Baran, Paul, A., *The Political Economy of Growth*, New York: Monthly Review Press, 1957.

Baran, Paul A. and Paul M. Sweezy, *Monopoly Capital,* New York: Monthly Review Press, 1966.

Berle, A. A. and G. C. Means, *The Modern Corporation and Private Property,* New York: Harcourt Brace Jovanovich, 1932, 1968.

Bluestone, Barry, "Capitalism and Poverty in America: A Discussion", *Monthly Review,* Vol. 24 (1972), pp. 65-71.

Bright, James A., *Automation and Management,* New York, Plimten Press, 1958.

Bright, James A., "Does Automation Raise Skill Requirements?", *Harvard Business Review,* July-August, 1958.

Bright, James A., *Research, Development and Technological Innovation,* Homewood (Illinois): R. D. Irwin Inc., 1964.

Bright, James A., "Skill Requirements and Wage Aspects of Automation", paper delivered at the U.S. Labor Relations Council Conference, Washington, D.C., November 8, 1960.

Cooper, David (ed.), *The Dialectics of Liberation,* Harmondsworth: Penguin Books, 1968.

Dobb, Maurice, *Capitalism Yesterday and Today,* London: Lawrence & Wishart, 1958.

Dobb, Maurice, *Economic Growth and Underdeveloped Countries,* London: Lawrence & Wishart, 1963.

Domhoff, G. William, *Who Rules America?,* Englewood Cliffs (N.J.): Prentice-Hall, 1967.

Duboff, Richard, "Trade War Exercises", *Canadian Dimension,* Vol. 9, No. 6, (July, 1973), pp. 37-44.

Eakins, David W., "Business Planners and America's Postwar Expansion", in David Horowitz (ed.), *Corporations and the Cold War,* New York: Monthly Review Press, 1969.

Emmanuel, Arghiri, *Unequal Exchange,* New York, Monthly Review Press: 1972.

Fischer, George (ed.), *The Revival of American Socialism,* New York: Oxford University Press, 1971.

Foster, W. T. and W. Catchings, *Money,* Boston: Houghton & Mifflin, 1925.

Frank, Andre Gunder, *Latin America: Underdevelopment or Revolution,* New York: Monthly Review Press, 1969.

Geltmann, Emanuel and Stanley Plastrik, "Labor's Decade — Maybe", *Dissent,* (August, 1971), pp. 365-375.

Gerassi, John, "Imperialism and Revolution in America", in David Cooper (ed.), *The Dialectics of Liberation,* Harmondsworth: Penguin Books, 1968.

Goldfinger, M., "Capitalist Planning and the State", *Dissent,* April, 1971.

Gordon, David M., "American Poverty: Functions, Mechanisms, and Contradictions", *Monthly Review,* Vol. 24 (1972), pp. 72-79.

Gorz, Andre, *Strategy for Labor,* Boston: Beacon Press, 1964.

Halliday, Jon, "Washington v. Tokyo: Wall Street v. Maranouchi", *New Left Review,* (May-June, 1971), pp. 39-46.

Halliday, Jon and Gavan McCormack, "Japan and America: Antagonistic Allies", *New Left Review,* (January-February, 1973), pp. 59-76.

Halliday, Jon and Gavan McCormack, *Japanese Imperialism Today,* New York: Monthly Review Press, 1973.

Hamilton, Richard F., *Class and Politics in the United States,* New York: John Wiley & Sons, 1972.

Horowitz, David (ed.), *Containment and Revolution,* Boston: Beacon Press, 1967.

Horowitz, David (ed.), *Corporations and the Cold War,* New York: Monthly Review Press, 1969.

Horowitz, David, *Imperialism and Revolution,* London: Allen Lane, 1969.

Horowitz, David (ed.), *Marx and Modern Economics,* New York: Monthly Review Press, 1968.

Jallée, Pierre, *The Pillage of the Third World,* New York: Monthly Review Press, 1968.

Jallée, Pierre, *The Third World in World Economy,* New York: Monthly Review Press, 1969.

Kaysen, Carl, "The Social Significance of the Modern Corporation", *American Economic Review,* (April 6, 1960).

Kemp, Tom, *Theories of Imperialism*, London: Dobson Books, 1967.

Kidron, Michael, *Western Capitalism Since the War*, London: Weidenfeld & Nicolson, 1967.

Kindleberger, Charles, *Europe's Postwar Growth*, Cambridge: Harvard University Press, 1967.

Kolko, Gabriel, *The Roots of American Foreign Policy*, Boston: Beacon Press, 1970.

Lange, Oscar, "Marxian Economics and Modern Economic Theory", in David Horowitz (ed.), *Marx and Modern Economics*, New York: Monthly Review Press, 1968.

Lefebvre, Henri, *The Explosion*, New York: Monthly Review Press, 1969.

Lefebvre, Henri, *The Sociology of Marx*, New York: Vintage, 1969.

Levinson, Charles, *Capital, Inflation and the Multinationals*: London: George Allen & Unwin, 1971.

Magdoff, H., *The Age of Imperialism*, New York: Monthly Review Press, 1969.

Magdoff, H., "The American Empire and the U.S. Economy", in Robert I. Rhodes (ed.), *Imperialism and Underdevelopment*, New York: Monthly Review Press, 1970.

Magdoff, H., "The Economic Aspects of Imperialism", in George Fischer (ed.), *The Revival of American Socialism*, New York: Oxford University Press, 1971.

Magdoff, H., "Is Imperialism Really Necessary?", *Monthly Review*, Vol. 22, No. 5, (1970), pp. 1-14; Vol. 22, No. 6, (1970), pp. 1-13.

Magdoff, H. and Paul M. Sweezy, *The Dynamics of U.S. Capitalism*, New York: Monthly Review Press, 1972.

Magdoff, H. and Paul M. Sweezy, "Economic Stagnation and the Stagnation of Economics", *Monthly Review*, Vol. 22, No. 11, (1971), pp. 1-11.

Magdoff, H. and Paul M. Sweezy, "The Long-Run Decline in Liquidity", *Monthly Review*, Vol. 22, No. 4, (1970), pp. 1-17.

Magdoff, H. and Paul M. Sweezy, "The Mind of the Ruling Class", *Monthly Review*, Vol. 24, No. 2, (1972), pp. 1-15.

Magdoff, H. and Paul M. Sweezy, "War and Crisis", *Monthly Review*, Vol. 22, No. 2, (1970), pp. 1-12.

Mandel, Ernest, *Decline of the Dollar*, New York: Monad Press, 1972.

Mandel, Ernest, *Decline of the Dollar*, New York: Monthly Review Press, 1970.

Mandel, Ernest, *Europe vs. America: Contradictions of Imperialism*, New York: Monthly Review Press, 1970.

Mandel, Ernest, *An Introduction to Marxist Economic Theory*, New York: Young Socialist Alliance, 1967.

Mandel, Ernest, *Late Capitalism*, New York: Schocken, 1978.

Mandel, Ernest, *Marxist Economic Theory*, Vols. 1 & 11, London: Merlin Press, 1968.

Mandel, Ernest, "Where is America Going?", *New Left Review*, No. 54, (March-April, 1969).

Mandel, Ernest, "Workers and Permanent Revolution", in George Fischer (ed.), *The Revival of American Socialism*, New York: Oxford University Press, 1971.

Mandel, Ernest and George Novack, *On the Revolutionary Potential of the Working Class*, New York: Merit Publishers, 1969.

Marcuse, Herbert, *Five Lectures*, Boston: Beacon Press, 1970.

Mills, C. Wright, *Power, Politics and People*, New York: Oxford University Press, 1963.

Morril, Richard C. and Ernst H. Wohlenberg, *The Geography of Poverty in the United States*, New York: McGraw-Hill, 1971.

Nathanson, Charles F., "The Militarization of the American Economy" in David Horowitz (ed.), *Corporations and the Cold War*, New York: Monthly Review Press, 1969.

Nicolaus, Martin, "The Crisis of Late Capitalism", in George Fischer (ed.), *The Revival of American Socialism*, New York: Oxford University Press, 1971.

O'Connor, James R., "The Meaning of Economic Imperialism", in Robert I. Rhodes (ed.), *Imperialism and Underdevelopment*, New York: Monthly Review Press, 1970.

Phillips, Joseph D., "Economic Effects of the Cold War", in David Horowitz (ed.), *Corporations and the Cold War*, New York: Monthly Review Press, 1969.

Rhodes, Robert I. (ed.), *Imperialism and Underdevelopment*, New York: Monthly Review Press, 1970.

Rowthorn, Bob, "Imperialism in the Seventies — Unity or Rivalry?", *New Left Review*, No. 69 (September-October, 1971), pp. 31-54.

Schon, D. A., *Beyond the Stable State*, New York: Random House, 1971.

Seligman, Ben B., *Economics of Dissent*, Chicago: Quadrangle, 1968.

Sutcliffe, R. B. *Industry and Underdevelopment*, London: Addison-Wesley, 1971.

Sutcliffe, R. B. and Andrew Glyn, *British Capitalism, Workers and the Profit Squeeze*, Harmondsworth: Penguin Books, 1972.

Sweezy, Paul M., "The Future of Capitalism", in David Cooper (ed.), *The Dialectics of Liberation*, Harmondworth: Penguin Books, 1968.

Sweezy, Paul M., *Modern Capitalism and Other Essays*, New York: Monthly Review Press, 1972.

Sweezy, Paul M., *The Theory of Capitalist Development*, New York: Monthly Review Press, 1968.

Sweezy, Paul M., "Workers and the Third World", in George Fischer (ed.), *The Revival of American Socialism*, New York: Oxford University Press, 1971.

Szentes, Tamas, *The Political Economy of Underdevelopment*, Budapest: 1970.

U.S. Government Printing Office, *Measures of Productive Capacity*, "Hearings before the Subcommittee on Economic Statistics of the Joint Economic Committee", Washington, D. C., 1962.

Varga, Y., *Politico-Economic Problems of Capitalism*, Moscow: Progress Publishers, 1968.

Varga, Y., *Twentieth Century Capitalism*, London: Lawrence & Wishart, 1963.

Wachtel, Howard M., "Capitalism and Poverty in America: Paradox or Contradiction?", *Monthly Review*, Vol. 24, No. 2 (1972), pp. 55-61.

Warren, Bill, "Capitalist Planning and the State", *New Left Review*, No. 72 (March-April, 1972), pp. 3-30.

Warren, Bill, "Imperialism and Capitalist Industrialization", *New Left Review*, No. 81 (September-October, 1973).

Williams, William Appleman, "The Large Corporation and American Foreign Policy", in David Horowitz (ed.), *Corporations and the Cold War*, New York: Monthly Review Press, 1969.

Canada: Economy, Opportunity and Class

Roy T. Bowles and Prudence Craib

ROY T. BOWLES is a Professor of Sociology at Trent University. His current research interests include Canadian Class Structure and Political Economy.

PRUDENCE CRAIB is an Associate Dean of Arts and Science at Trent University. Her current research interests include Canadian Class Structure and Political Economy.

Introduction

This essay is intended as a basic introduction to a perspective upon a set of concepts which can be used in the analysis of Canadian society. These ideas will, we think, make it easier for the reader to understand the connections between a number of specific social issues and problems which Canada faces and the basic structural features of the society as a whole. Our central themes can be summarized here: modern Canada is faced with major dilemmas. These dilemmas arise out of the institutional characteristics of the economy and the relationship between the economy and the structure of social class in Canadian society. Many of the issues faced by millions of individual Canadians are aspects of the dilemmas facing the society as a whole, and can be better comprehended in the context of an understanding of the economy and the class structure.

Dilemmas Facing Canada

The Canada of today is perceived both by Canadians and by outsiders as a society which, while it enjoys considerable advantages

51

in comparative international terms, is nevertheless facing a series of deep and perplexing dilemmas. An examination of the positive aspects of Canadian society reveals many indications of relative well-being. There are high levels of economic activity in many parts of the country and in some sectors of the economy. Sophisticated technologies are present and used in many industries. There is a relatively high standard of living, at least for a large and visible segment of the population living in major centres. This standard of living has not lagged noticeably behind that of similar segments in the United States and Europe. There is a continuity in political institutions which appears, on the surface, to be coping with issues which are subject to policy control. These are the characteristics often described as the advantages present in advanced industrial societies.

On closer examination, however, there are major weaknesses in Canadian society. There are persistent instabilities in major segments of the Canadian economy which affect the Canadian labour market in such a way that many individuals experience economic insecurity. In comparison to other countries, significantly larger numbers of workers are concentrated either in the relatively unstable resource sectors or in the disadvantaged working conditions charac- teristic of non-unionized service industries. The Canadian state apparatus is severely limited in its ability to act autonomously. Foreign ownership of significant sectors of the internal economy confront it with limitations on its power to act effectively in the national interest. In summary, many Canadians do not share the advantages which are widely assumed to be available to almost all individuals in advanced industrial societies, and Canadian society as a whole is able to function with less autonomy in economic processes and policy making than would be expected.

We suggest that there are three major features of the Canadian economy which account for many of these dilemmas. Firstly, throughout Canadian history there has been, and there continues to be, a heavy reliance of the whole economy on the export of staples. Secondly, the manufacturing sector is relatively poorly developed and is possibly declining. This means that Canada has always been dependent upon the importation of manufactured goods. Thirdly, there is an exceptionally high level of direct foreign investment in, and therefore control of, the Canadian economy. As a consequence, a relatively small number of major multi-national corporations exercise control of this direct foreign investment in Canada.

The central focus of our analysis is on certain basic features of the Canadian economy which contribute to the character and persistence of the dilemmas cited above. This is because many current social issues or dilemmas are directly affected by the nature of the economy. For example, unemployment results from the inability of the economy to provide jobs for all who are willing and able to work. The underemployment of university graduates, that is, their inability to find jobs appropriate to their training, results from the limited demand in the economy for highly educated manpower. The increasing difficulties encountered by federal and provincial governments in sustaining the levels of social services which are deemed necessary to well-being and equity among the Canadian people is also rooted in economic factors. The nature and productivity of the economy as a whole affects the income available to governments. Canadian governments at all levels spend money to provide services and subsidies which give both direct and indirect support to business enterprises. During most parts of the last few decades there has been sufficient surplus to provide high levels of support for medical care, education, and social services. But these surpluses are declining and such services, as a consequence, are increasingly curtailed. Without understanding the basic features of the economy we cannot identify the roots of the social concerns which these changes generate.

Here we must make a more general point. The Canadian economy is a capitalist economy. As such it manifests in some form all of the problems associated with capitalist economies. The Canadian economy is also profoundly integrated into the North American economic system. As a consequence, it will manifest many of the problems which are apparent in the economy of the United States. There are, however, special characteristics of the Canadian economy which make it more vulnerable than the economies of most other advanced industrial nations to shifts in the structure of international capitalism and also the national capitalism of the United States. Therefore, we are focusing our primary attention on these special characteristics of the Canadian economy.

The Economic Base: Concepts For Analysis

We will organize our analysis around three conceptual issues: (1) the particular ways in which the Canadian economy is divided into primary, secondary and tertiary sectors, and the relative importance of each sector; (2) the dominance in the economy of the production of primary staple goods for export and the consequences of this dominance, and (3) the nature and quality of metropolitan-hinterland relations between Canada and other nation-states as well as within Canada.

1. The Division of the Economy Into Sectors

It is useful to divide economic activities of all types into three categories: (1) primary extractive industries which gather or produce some basic raw material such as furs, timber, wheat, metal ores, or petroleum; (2) secondary industries which convert raw materials into products ready for comsumption; and (3) service or tertiary industries whose activities do not as a rule produce tangible commodities but rather provide service for people or other industries. This distinction is important because each type of industry employs people with certain types of occupational skills. Also, these three sectors of the economy experience different types of modification as a consequence of changes in technology, market conditions, and both national and international politics.

The most important primary extractive industries in Canada are fishing, timber production, mining, farming, and petroleum production. In these industries, the materials may be subjected to some elementary processing to facilitate easier transportation. Grain is threshed, trees are sawn into boards, ores are concentrated and fossil fuels are converted into basic components. In secondary manufacturing or processing the materials are converted, often as a result of elaborate technological and industrial processes, into a form usable by the consumer. For example, lumber is converted into furniture or houses and metals are transformed into such products as factory tools, automobiles, or computers. Examples of tertiary or service industries include wholesale and retail trade, entertainment, transportation, banking and finance, and finally the administration of all types of government services. Some tertiary industries, for example, transportation and trade, involve the distribution of manufactured products. Others provide services. For example, the entertainment industry provides places and organizes events for the enjoyment of customers; governments organize and manage education, social welfare, and health care programs for the benefit of of citizens.

Compared to other advanced capitalist countries, Canada has a very well-developed primary extractive sector and a well-developed service sector. The secondary manufacturing sector, however, is relatively under-developed. This pattern has important consequences for the stability of the Canadian economy. Primary industries are subject to fluctuating supplies (for example, crop yield and fishing catches are highly variable from year to year), to intense competition from alternative suppliers all over the world, and to both rapidly fluctuating demands and few alternatives markets. Hence, economic instability — periods of boom and bust — characterize many primary industries. Service industries are also very responsive to economic fluctuations. Any decline in consumer income means fewer people can purchase the commodities or services offered. For example, if incomes decline people spend less on entertainment and holidays so recreational and tourist enterprises experience declines in business. Reduced production of ore in mines means a reduction in the demand for explosives and equipment so the companies who have been supplying these commodities experience decline. By contrast, secondary industries seem, in general, to be more constant or stable. They can seek raw materials from a variety of sources. They can develop alternative markets if necessary and many industries are able to convert to new product lines with relatively moderate new investment.

As a consequence of Canada's weakness in secondary manufacturing industries her economy is subject to more dramatic and controllable swings than the economy of the United States and most other advanced industrial countries. There is also mounting evidence that because of the patterns of development of the international economy Canada, like Britain, is becoming involved in a process of "de-industrialization". That is, the amount of secondary manufacturing in Canada is actually declining because the large multinational corporations which are so dominant in the secondary sector are shifting some of their manufacturing capacity to the Third World, where labour costs are lower and government regulations are fewer. If this is the case, Canada's whole economy is likely to become even more vulnerable to the fluctuations which affect the primary and tertiary sectors.

2. The Importance of Primary, Extractive or Staple Production

Export staples are raw materials which are gathered or produced in one country or region for shipment to and marketing in another country or region. Some parts of the world acquire most of their income by extracting or producing raw materials and exporting them to other areas for use. For example, the economies of many Caribbean countries have relied heavily on the production of cane sugar and related products. Canada has produced and exported cod fish, furs, forest products and wheat for long historical periods. Currently, she is producing and selling oil and gas as well as hydroelectric power. The Canadian economy has been, to a greater degree than that of most developed economies, dominated by the production of such export staples. In terms of the categories already outlined this means that primary industries have always been more important in Canada than in other countries.

In fact, the production of staples for export has been so important to Canadian development that a significant school of Canadian historians have taken the growth and consequences of staple trades as their major focus of study. A few of the major conclusions reached by authors working within the staples approach to Canadian history will be summarized here.

Growth in the staple industries has been the most important factor in growth in the Canadian economy as a whole. Conversely, shifts in the staple industries have had great impact on the Canadian economy, often precipitating serious regional declines. The activities involved in the production of raw materials for export, together with the development of transportation and other aspects of the economic structure for this, have provided both incomes and opportunities for domestic investment in Canada. Each period of major economic growth in the history of Canada has been a period in which some new staple was developed or in which significant expansion in some staples occurred. For example, the introduction of the timber trade to Canada in the early nineteenth century and the expansion of wheat production on the Prairies in the early twentieth century both produced major booms. The severity of the Great Depression in Canada is understandable in terms of the enormous fluctuations in the world wheat market. Much of the growth in the economy since World War II has resulted from the production and export of energy sources, namely oil, hydro-electric power, and uranium.

The overall growth produced by expansion in a staple occurs because this expansion stimulates activities in other areas. Each staple export industry has "spread effects," that is, the growth in the export staple itself spreads out to produce consequences in other parts of the economy. Watkins has used the concept of "linkages" to show more specifically how general growth is stimulated by staple production. "Backward linkage is a measure of inducement to invest in the home-production of inputs, including capital goods, for the expanding export sector". Every staple requires certain types of equipment and supplies for its production. For example, the production and export of wheat required the manufacture of farm machinery and the construction of railroads. Growth in the Canadian economy during the wheat boom was, in part, growth in the manufacture of farm machinery and railroad equipment. "Forward linkage is a measure of inducement to invest in domestic industries using the output of the export industry as an input". Secondary processing of any raw material is an example of forward linkage. "Final demand linkage is a measure of the inducement to invest in domestic industries producing consumer goods for the export sector". For example, when a new resource-based town is established there is a need for the construction and staffing of schools, for medical services, for recreational facilities, and many other services. (Watkins, 1971: 54-55). To summarize, the growth of each Canadian staple industry has been linked to economic demands or growth in other areas of the economy.

Historically, as well as today, the social structure of Canadian society has been shaped by the staples which have been produced and the technologies used to produce them. The exploitation of a given staple in a particular environment — whether it be wheat on the Prairies or timber in the Ottawa Valley — is possible only if a suitable technology can be developed and applied. Once a particular technology (including tools, machines, and knowledge) is applied some clear consequences follow. Typical forms of economic organization develop to co-ordinate the activities within the trade. Particular occupations are created, indeed each staple trade creates a particular occupational structure. As the technology for exploiting a staple changes, the tasks to be performed change and the occupational structure and co-ordinating organizations must also change.

If one views the Canadian economy only in terms of expanding staple industries and the way in which they stimulate growth, then tremendous optimism seems justified. But part of the dilemma facing Canada results from the fact that staple industries, and particularly those based on non-renewable resources, also decline in due course. When declines occur in a staple producing industry they are followed by reductions in demand through all of the linkages or related industries.

3. Metropolitan—Hinterland Relationships

The concept of metropolitan-hinterland relationships, as we shall use it here, focuses attention on the characteristic economic relations between countries or between major economic regions which differ in their make-up and also in their relative economic and political power. Attention is drawn to the nature of the world trading system and the role which different countries play within it, rather than simply to the internal analysis of each country. A metropolitan country (such as the United States) is at the "centre" of a large-scale or world trading system and has a more developed or sophisticated economy. It draws basic resources for its own economy from the less developed or hinterland areas or the "peripheral" areas of the world trading systems. In terms sometimes used, the metropolitan country has an economic empire and the hinterland countries are its economic colonies. Trading patterns between a metropolis and a hinterland tend to be unequal and in general more benefits accrue to the former than to the latter. In particular, a metropolitan centre has the greater bargaining power when negotiating trading relationships with more peripheral areas.

The British Empire was based on metropolitan-hinterland trade, and Canada was an economic colony (as well as a political colony) within it. In recent years, Canada has been called an economic colony of the United States.

Forces that have major effects on economic and social developments in the hinterland often have their origin in the metropolis. For example, the Canadian timber trade with Britain began because Napoleon blockaded the Baltic ports in order to cut the British off from a critical source of timber supplies. The pulp and paper industry grew in Canada as a consequence of the increasing size and distribution of American newspapers.

It is important to note that only under certain conditions does metropolitan exploitation of resources in a hinterland lead to the establishment of stable and self-sustaining economic patterns in the hinterland. If the staple trade is conducted in such a way that local entrepreneurs can accumulate capital and if there are local resources and access to markets which make possible the development of other industries, there is the potential for economic growth which is not dependent on the staple as such. In the absence of these conditions, a hinterland is likely to flourish during a period of staple exploitation but to stagnate or decline afterward.

Metropolis-hinterland relations have developed between regions in Canada. Groups of Canadian capitalists developed during the nineteenth century in Montreal and Toronto by playing an intermediate role within the British trade system. These interest groups had the organizational capacity and access to capital which were necessary to extract, transport and trade in primary products located in other widely dispersed regions. Historically, as these groups pursued their interests, central Canada developed metropolitan influences over some other areas in the Dominion. Regional disparities in Canada are, in large part, understandable as products of metropolitan-hinterland relations. Through most of Canadian history, interest groups in Southern Ontario have been able to affect, and in some cases determine, the economic developments of other regions or provinces.

To summarize concretely, Canada was a fur trading hinterland for France during the French Regime. After the conquest, Canada was a hinterland for Great Britain supplying furs, timber and wheat. Since early in this century, but particularly since World War II, Canada has become a hinterland of the United States, producing minerals, pulp and paper, and energy resources for the economy of that country. Canadian raw materials are also supplying the manufacturing economy of Japan. In each period of Canadian history the capacity for internal economic development has been shaped by Canada's essentially subordinate economic relationship to some strong metropolitan economy.

Because historically Canada has always been a hinterland economy many internal policies or decisions have been responses to events in, or policies of, other countries. Many Canadian social issues and problems can be seen as having their roots in Canada's hinterland position in the world economy, and her consequent inability to control significant aspects of her own internal economic and political processes.

The Economic Opportunity Structure

In an earlier section we discussed the general way in which the staple trades affect growth or decline in the Canadian economy and the way in which they have shaped the patterns of social organization in the society. We now wish to explore more specifically the impact of such changes in the economy on the class structure of society. Before we do this it will be helpful to introduce the concept of the economic opportunity structure.

Most people in Canada are aware that there are only certain things that one can do to gain an income. There are certain types of businesses that one might establish or certain types of occupations in which one might seek employment. Most people are also aware that a certain number of each possibility exists in any one geographical area or historical era.

It will be helpful to re-phrase this more technically. An economic opportunity is a chance to gain income. An entrepreneurial opportunity exists when it is possible to bring together capital equipment, resources, and labour to produce some product which can be sold at a profit. Such opportunities may be large in scale, for example, those available to the major contractors in the construction of a railway or pipeline. Or they may be relatively small in scale, for example, when a local contractor can buy equipment and materials and hire craftsmen to build houses for sale in a single community. The businesses that can reasonably be operated and their numbers make up the set of entrepreneurial opportunities available at any one time. An employment opportunity is a chance to sell one's labour power — that is, one's time and capacity to do work — for a wage or salary. The types and amounts of labour which entrepreneurs (the private sector) and governments (the public sector) are willing to purchase make up the set of employment opportunities available at a given time. In conventional economic terms this is the demand side of the labour market. Thus, the economic opportunity structure of a society is the total of all the different ways of gaining an income which exist at any one time. It consists of all of the businesses which might be operated together with all of the kinds of employment available.

The opportunity structure is not identical to the occupational distribution of people into jobs in a society. This is because during a period of rapid economic expansion there may be more opportunities than can actually be filled by the people in the society. For example, during the early twentieth century there were many more opportunities to establish prairie farms than there were people to occupy them. When a new technology, for example, the computer, is introduced there may be more employment opportunities in related fields than there are qualified people. Conversely, during periods of economic decline or the general introduction of labour-saving machinery, there may be more people who are prepared to do a certain type of work than there are jobs available in that field. For example, because of the introduction of large mechanical tree harvesters in British Columbia there are many more "loggers" than there are employment opportunities for loggers.

The structure of economic opportunity is very directly a product of the economic structure of the society. When the economy expands the number of economic opportunities increases, when it declines the number of economic opportunities decreases. When the basic type of economic activity changes, or the technologies in use are modified, some kinds of opportunities are eliminated and others are brought into being.

The importance of export staples in the development of the class structure of Canadian society and hence for Canadians as individuals can be demonstrated by showing how shifts in the staple trades have affected the opportunity structure. Each staple trade has opened a set of entrepreneurial opportunities (both large-scale and small-scale) and a set of employment opportunities. The expansion of the timber trade in the St. Lawrence drainage basin in the early nineteenth century can be used as an example. The British demand for Canadian timber created an opportunity for large-scale timber merchants to hire crews for the cutting and rafting of logs, to arrange for the shipment of timber from Quebec to Britain, and to sell it for a profit. Employment opportunities were created for woodsmen and raftsmen. Backward linkages to transportation provided opportunities for entrepreneurs to establish shipbuilding yards and for craftsmen to be employed in shipbuilding. In time, forward linkages were expressed in the opportunity for entrepreneurs, often operating on a small scale, to establish saw-mills. Final demand linkage was expressed in the opportunities for farmers near the lumber camps to produce foodstuffs for workers in the timber trade and each associated activity.

The fundamental point is this: each staple trade creates a particular opportunity structure. The opportunity structure of a staple trade consists of all of those entrepreneurial opportunities and all of those employment opportunities created in the production of the staple and in the activities linked to or stimulated by the production of the staple.

A discussion of certain features of the opportunity structure of the staple trades yields important insights into the ways in which the Canadian economy and Canadians are made vulnerable by Canada's heavy reliance on the export of resources. Many discussions of economic growth in Canada have assumed that any one activity would stimulate other economic activity and hence continuing growth and expansion of opportunities. Thus it has often been assumed that any development of Canadian natural resources would contribute to self-sustaining economic activity in Canada. The kind of examination we have undertaken of the links between the staple industry and other economic and social sectors reveals that this is not necessarily the case. Certain opportunities are dependent on a given staple trade and disappear once the trade declines. Some significant part of the instability in the Canadian economy and of the insecurity faced by Canadians arises from the fact that many of the economic opportunities in Canada are to be found in staple trades which experience wide fluctuations or are dependent on non-renewable resources.

The Canadian Class Structure

In the preceding sections we have discussed the basic features of the Canadian economy and the way in which the operation of the economy produces a particular economic and hence occupational opportunity structure. In this section, we will discuss the concept of social class as a means of understanding other, but related, developments and issues in a society. When the economy at a particular time is viewed concretely rather than abstractly, the opportunities which it creates can be seen as socially fixed positions which depend on the character of the economic processes present. When the opportunity structure is filled with people, its shape and form are perceived and experienced as the class structure of the society. An analysis of the class structure of Canadian society is fundamental to an understanding of Canadian social issues or social problems for one very fundamental reason: events and developments in a society have different consequences for those in different social classes.

Our basic approach to the analysis of class positions in any society focuses on an examination of the relationship of individuals to the economic processes of the society. The two most fundamental aspects of this are their relationship to property and their relationship to work. In regard to the relationship to property the basic question we ask is: Does the individual own productive property? Productive property consists of such things as land, factories, machines, raw materials and other things used in the production and distribution of commodities. (Consumer property, such as television sets, pleasure cars, and homes, is not included). When considering the relationship to work we ask: Does the individual sell his labour power to others? Does the individual buy the labour power of others for use in the productive process? If a society had a simple class system consisting of capitalists and proletariat, we could identify only two groups of people:

Capitalists	**Proletariat**
Own productive property	Do not own productive property
Employ the labour power of others	Sell their labour power in the market place

Clearly, there has never been a time when the class structure of Canada (or any other nation) was this simple. Nevertheless, by using the two criteria of ownership versus non-ownership of productive property and purchasing versus selling of labour power, we can identify one of the most fundamental divisions between the classes which make up Canadian society.

Three general comments will help students apply this discussion of class. First, the discussion itself is applicable to any capitalist society. But, a class analysis of Canada must take into account the distinctive characteristics of Canadian society. The distinctive characteristics of Canadian society result from the fact that Canada has a particular set of economic processes rooted in a specific pattern of staple production and export. Second, all members of a particular class are not identical. Hired farmhands are different from railway workers and both are different from school teachers, although all these groups sell their labour. Some authors use the phrase *class fragment* to refer to some part of a class whose members share distinctive characteristics in their relationship to the economy. While Canada has the same broad classes as other capitalist societies, the class fragments which make up these classes will differ from those which are present in other societies. Third, a variety of consequences arise out of class position. Those in different class positions differ from each other in their ability to control people and resources, the amount and form of income they receive, their chances to accumulate capital, the amount of security or insecurity they have in their positions, the chances they have of transferring their skills and resources to other activities, and the kinds of activities required of them as a consequence of their relationship to the work process.

In each period of Canadian history one can identify capitalists and members of the proletariat. The analysis of the Canadian class structure will be more adequate, however, if we identify fragments of each class and in addition, identify an underclass. Within the capitalist class we will discuss the following fragments: large-scale capitalists based in foreign metropolitan centres whose actions have major consequences in Canada; small-scale capitalists; and independent commodity producers. Among the proletariat, we will make a distinction between those who sell manual labour and those who sell mental labour as well as a distinction between unionized and non-unionized workers. The underclass is characterized by the fact that its members do not have a continuous involvement in the operating economy.

1. The Capitalist Class

(i) Metropolitan or Foreign Large-Scale Capitalists

In every period in Canadian history there has been a group of large-scale capitalists *located outside of Canada* who have played a very important role in Canadian society. Capitalists located in metropolitan France and especially in Britain wished to accumulate profit by trading in some raw material found in Canada. Capitalists located in the United States have and do directly own many Canadian enterprises. Members of this foreign metropolitan capitalist class have controlled Canadian resources, have made decisions which had major consequences in Canadian society, and through their influence on governments have had a major role in shaping the international and national policies which affect Canada. The statement that Canada is an economic hinterland or an economic colony is, in part, understandable when the power and interests of this metropolitan capitalist class are examined and are seen to have shaped Canadian society in fundamental ways. Hence, one cannot analyze the class system of Canadian society by looking at Canadian society alone. It is necessary to understand that the class system of Canadian society includes a group of powerful capitalists located outside of Canada.

(ii) Major Canadian Based Capitalists

There is also a significant category of major Canadian based capitalists who own or control very large concentrations of productive property and set the general tone and standards of both economic and social life. They are frequently either dominated by, or work in collaboration with, the foreign metropolitan capitalist group. They employ the labour power of large sectors of the proleteriat to perform the actual tasks of production. Their property and the labour they hire is managed through large-scale organizations employing many specialists. Their own work activity is organizational, it consists of directing the organization as a whole rather than performing the productive work itself. Because of their control of property and organizations, large-scale capitalists are able to make decisions which have far-reaching consequences at many levels of society. These decisions may change the lives of individual workers or affect the careers of politicians. They have also shaped the institutions within which people live. Members of this group receive significant proportions of their income through returns on investments made by themselves and by their ancestors as well as from current business revenues and salaries. When shifts in the economy make certain activities less profitable, large-scale capitalists are frequently able to transfer their capital and organizational capacity to other activities.

(iii) Small-Scale Capitalists

A third group which has been represented in most Canadian periods consists of small-scale capitalists. Members of this group own or control small businesses which they operate themselves. Typical examples are local merchants who own or operate independent stores, craftsmen operating their own businesses (for example, small-scale building contractors), and owners of small, independent service establishments such as restaurants and motels. Small-scale capitalists participate in these businesses through direct personal interventions rather than through elaborate organizations. They are often engaged in the physical activity of production or service themselves. Compared to large capitalists, they employ relatively little hired labour. Indeed, in many enterprises, the only workers involved are the owner and members of his family. The principal source of income for this group is current business revenues. Small-scale capitalists experience significant insecurities because even short run shifts in the economy may reduce current revenues and threaten their income as well as their investment.

(iv) Independent Commodity Producers

Independent commodity producers are small-scale capitalists, but their importance in the case of Canada is such that they deserve special discussion. The typical case of the independent commodity producer is the family farmer. He owns his own land, machinery, and livestock. He combines this property with his own labour and that of members of his family to produce commodities. A major proportion of these commodities are sold in a cash market. Another example of an independent commodity producer might be an inshore fisherman who owns his own boat and equipment and catches fish for sale on the market. It should be noted that agriculture, fishing, and similar activities can be organized on principles other than those of independent commodity production, for example, the activities may be conducted by large corporations.

Independent commodity producers have typically been subject to tremendous fluctuations of, and insecurities in, income. These insecurities result firstly from the vagaries of environmental factors over which the producers have little or no control, and which cause production to vary greatly from year to year. Secondly, the value of the commodities produced varies widely, and is often affected by fluctuations in demand at the level of international markets. Thus, the prices received for their commodities, and even their ability to sell them varies from year to year. Thirdly, the capital required to establish a farm or similar business is often obtained through loans which must be repaid even during years of poor harvest or depressed prices.

2. The Proletariat and Fragments Within It

We define the proletariat as those people who sell their labour power and as a consequence are dependent on being offered employment or being kept in employment by others. While there are exceptions, most members of this group have not owned significant productive property nor have they derived significant income from sources other than employment. The basic relationship between a member of the proletariat and his employer is the cash nexus. That is, the employer agrees to pay for work, and the employee agrees to work for a wage or salary. When the employer no longer has need of the employee's services, he terminates the relationship and stops paying him. Reliance on the sale of labour power obviously creates insecurities for members of the proletariat; when the capitalists (or the state as an employer) no longer needs labour the proletariat either have no income or must adjust to living on the drastically reduced income which is available through unemployment insurance or the social welfare system.

(i) Mental and Manual Labour

Some of the conventional terminology surrounding social class creates confusions which need to be eliminated before we proceed. The term "proletariat" is associated often with the term "the working class" and many associate both of these terms with blue-collar or manual workers. White-collar workers or clerical and sales workers are often thought of as "middle-class" and assumed to have positions in the class system which are fundamentally different from those of blue-collar workers. This view rests on observations about differences in working environments and prestige, but ignores basic patterns which arise from being an employee. We use the term proletariat to refer to all of those workers who sell their labour, regardless of the kind of labour they sell. On closer examination and within our frame of reference, many of those who are conventionally regarded as middle-class turn out to be proletariat. The typist in an office, the teller in a bank, and the clerk in a store are all selling their time and ability to do work in the same way as the assembly line worker in a factory or the mechanic in a garage. The same is true of many people who regard themselves as professionals, for example, school teachers, nurses, and many engineers. These different occupational groups may be selling different types of labour, but they are all alike in that they sell their labour to an employer, they own no productive property, they do not control the conditions under which they work, and their security in their jobs depends on the willingness or ability of the employer to keep purchasing their labour power. With the rapidly expanding opportunity structure of the 1950s and 1960s, some groups, for example, school teachers and professors, misunderstood the true nature of their relationship to work and to employers and thought themselves permanently secure in their positions. The constricting opportunity structure of the 1970s and the discussions of redundancy and layoffs have reminded many in these groups that they do not own their jobs, but rather sell their labour.

There are different fragments within the proletariat. In spite of the fundamental similarity shared by all those who sell their labour, not all members of the proletariat can be viewed as identical. When workers sell their labour power, they place their time and ability to do work at the disposal of an employer. The most important criteria in terms of which fragments of the proletariat can be distinguished from one another is the *type of work* (or type of ability to do work) which is sold to the employer. In this paper, we will consider only the division between those who sell manual labour and those who sell mental labour, though more refined distinctions are possible and some workers might be hard to classify neatly into one category.

Let us develop this basic division by focusing on the example of a single manufacturing firm, using illustrative material provided by Miller and Form (1964: 111-113). Those who sell manual labour to the firm are engaged directly in the physical process of producing the material commodities made by the firm. These include foundry workers, milling machine operators, drill press operators, lathe operators, and similar categories of workers. Those workers who sell mental labour to the firm are not engaged directly in production, rather, they are engaged in the planning, co-ordination and supervision of production and in the sale of the resulting commodities. Their work might be understood as the communication that is necessary to keep the production process flowing. This group commonly called white-collar workers includes managers, secretaries, inspectors, accountants, engineers, draftsmen, salesmen, advertising personnel, and so on. The importance of their work to the on-going production process is caught by Miller and Form:

> The office, it seems, is closely related to activities in the shop. Some of the workers order materials for the shop; others sell the products made. Some of the men are constantly planning to improve the machines in the shop. Others are concerned with coordinating the work of the departments. Then there are "specialists" who keep track of green pieces of paper and put them into envelopes. Everything must be recorded, and this is the job of the younger women in the office (Miller & Form, 1964: 113).

As the societies become more complex, and particularly in the twentieth century when more economic activity comes to be concentrated in larger organizations, the proportion of the proletariat who sell their capacity to do mental work compared to those selling the capacity to do physical work increases dramatically.

(ii) Unionized and Non-Unionized Workers

We also regard unionized and non-unionized workers as separate fragments of the proletariat. In recent decades, one of the most important distinctions within the proletariat has been between those workers who have been able to gain unionized protection and those who have not. (In 1975 only 37 percent of the paid labour force in non-agricultural industries were members of unions (Canada Year Book, 1976-77: 386)). Some union contracts provide moderate protection of job security in that they specify that workers shall be given a certain amount of notice and employers must follow specific procedures before layoffs take place. Most unions protect individual workers from arbitrary dismissal or changes in the condition of employment by an employer. For example, the conditions under which an individual may be ordered to either work short hours, work overtime, or move to a lower job classification are likely to be specified in the union contract. By contrast, non-unionized workers are much more likely to be forced either to comply with the dictates of their employer or to lose their jobs. In periods of rapid inflation, such as the past decade, if wages do not increase commensurately, the real purchasing power of workers declines. Workers in strong unions are more likely to be effective in bargaining for increases in wages and benefits which maintain pace with the cost of living than are workers who are unprotected by unions. There are major differences in the strength of unions and often differences in the efforts which unions make to defend or advance the interests of different categories of workers. Nevertheless, workers organized into unions are, by virtue of the mechanisms that they have for protecting themselves from certain insecurities produced by economic forces, best regarded as a fragment separate from non-unionized members of the proletariat.

A summary statement is required at this point. The proletariat have been defined as those who sell their labour power. The proletariat can, for various analytical purposes, be divided into fragments. Two initial criteria can be used to identify fragments: firstly, the distinction between manual and mental labour and secondly, the separation of workers into unionized or non-unionized workers. These distinctions provide the reader with a focused perspective in terms of which various concrete problems can be approached and do not pretend to constitute an exhaustive analysis of the Canadian proletariat. These criteria may, however, be used more specifically to identify further class fragments. For example, one can distinguish between members of the proletariat employed in the private sector and those employed by various branches of the state. The first question in studying a group of workers is what characteristics arise from the fact that they sell their labour, that is, from the fact that they are proletariat? The second question is what characteristics arise from the specific conditions under which they sell their labour, that is, from the fact that they belong to a particular fragment of the proletariat?

3. The Underclass

The groups discussed above are characterized by the nature of the positions they occupy in the operation of the economy. There are yet others in the society who seem so marginal or insecure in their connection to the economy that it is necessary to refer to them in different language. We will use the term *underclass* to refer to these individuals and groups. We have in mind many people who are often regarded as the "underprivileged" of the society, but we wish to focus attention on why they are underprivileged. In terms of our earlier discussion, the underclass consist of those who cannot locate and take up economic opportunities of a permanent character, either because such opportunities do not exist or because they lack the qualifications to move into those opportunities which do exist. The term *underclass* is perhaps best considered as a concept that sensitizes the reader to an extensive range of demeaning and frustrating processes and phenomena which are experienced by a number of people in Canadian society.

A wide variety of people may be included in the underclass. In many depressed areas, the number of economic opportunities is so much smaller than the number of people seeking them that some people are excluded more or less permanently from participation in the labour force. Many native Indians, because of their geographic isolation on reserves and the cultural isolation and discrimination which they experience, are effectively excluded from access to opportunities. Some people, because of their age and/or sex, experience great difficulty in locating and retaining access to economic opportunities. In the current situation of high unemployment, for example, many of those between the ages of 15 and 24 experience the reality of a marginal and unreliable connection to the economy. The same is true of women and the elderly.

The boundary between the underclass and the proletariat as a whole cannot be drawn with rigor. There are many unskilled and non-unionized workers in marginal enterprises who may work only seasonally, or for irregular and unpredictable hours, and receive very low wages. In the main, it is useful to think of those whose relationship to the labour market is characteristically erratic and poorly rewarded as members of the underclass. In addition, downswings in the economy of the nation or of a region may sever the connection which many people have had with the economy through employment, and, if the downswing is of long duration, leave them permanently without alternative opportunities.

From the perspective of the operation of the economy as a whole, many segments of the underclass serve as an industrial reserve army. That is, if there is a high labour demand they are called up to serve, but when demand for labour declines they can be laid off. Women, youth and the elderly and members of some minority groups certainly experience this pattern of being the last hired and the first fired, particularly in those large segments of the labour market which are not unionized. The practice of paying women less than men for the same work and of setting minimum wages for students which are lower than those for non-students indicates that women and students are not considered full "citizens" of the economy and hence can be treated differently from others.

4. The Historical Development Of The Canadian Class System

Some necessarily brief historical material will illustrate how the class categories we have presented can be used in the analysis of Canadian society during different periods. By 1850, the economy of central Canada (Ontario and Quebec) had been relatively well developed on the basis of the timber trade and the wheat trade with Great Britain. (There was also some trade with the U.S.) The exporting of wheat and timber and the importing and forwarding of manufactured goods were all highly concentrated in the hands of a relatively few companies, each of which controlled large quantities of capital and large organizations. Many of these organizations operating in Canada were subsidiaries of British firms or had British partners. Thus, there existed in Britain a segment of a metropolitan capitalist class whose actions affected Canada. The owners of Canadian companies and the Canadian based partners in British firms made up a class of major Canadian capitalists. The farmers growing agricultural products for export were independent commodity producers. Small merchants linked the farmers to the large traders and, together with local craft enterprises, serviced the consumer needs of the population. These were the small-scale capitalists. There was also a significant proletariat. The workers who physically cut and rafted timber, those who constructed the transportation system, and those who loaded, unloaded and manned the boats and ships were selling their physical labour power. Clerks in trading companies and in government were selling their mental labour power. The situation of the Indians in much of central Canada during this period shows how shifts in the economy can produce an underclass. During the fur trade, the Indians had been the basic producers and were firmly integrated into the general economic processes of the society. With the decline of the fur trade the Indians were no longer a necessary labour force. They lost their integration with the economy and gradually became confined to reserves where they were unable to develop other forms of economic integration. They had become part of the underclass.

Many major changes occurred in the Canadian economy and Canadian society between 1850 and 1930. The prairies were settled, new mineral resources were developed, and significant industrialization occurred. Canada became less closely tied to the British economy and more closely integrated into the economy of the United States. These changes had important consequences for the class structure.

The members of the metropolitan-based capitalist class who had the most influence in Canadian affairs were no longer British merchants. They were now the American owners of Canadian enterprises. Many of the members of the class of large-scale capitalists in Canada, as had most Canadian capitalists in the past, concentrated their efforts on the organization of commerce and transportation. The discovery of new resources and the development of new industries had, however, permitted an increase in the number of Canadian capitalists who were involved in manufacturing and processing. Most of the people engaged in agriculture were, as they had been in the past, independent commodity producers. Only one in four of the non-agricultural workers was self employed. The other three-fourths were paid workers, that is, they were selling their labour power. The sale of mental labour power was becoming more important. Almost one-fifth of the employees in manufacturing were classified as supervisory and office workers.

With the depression of the 1930s, significant sections of the economic opportunity structure collapsed. Many who had been selling their labour power could no longer find employment. Many small-scale capitalists, whether farmers or businessmen, went broke. Large numbers of people became unemployed and were, for the decade, members of the underclass because they had no meaningful tie to an operating economy. Here we emphasize the point that many people became members of the underclass not because of their own inadequacies, but because there was no place for them in the economic opportunity structure.

With World War II, the depression ended and the economy expanded enormously and very rapidly. Unemployment virtually disappeared. Many members of the industrial reserve army, particularly women and youth, were called into the active labour force. Then, as now, when the economy demands labour many segments of the underclass become active members of the proletariat. However, at the end of the War women were induced by economic forces and propaganda to return to their roles as full-time wives and mothers.

Since World War II there has been an increasing concentration of control in the economy. Large-scale enterprises have expanded in number and power and have expropriated many of the opportunities previously available to small capitalists. Also, agribusiness and changing farming technology have reduced the number of farms. This, together with changes in such industries as fishing, has reduced the proportion of Canadians operating as independent commodity producers. Thus, today a much smaller and diminishing proportion of the population are small-scale capitalists.

There continue to be large-scale Canadian capitalists, but control of the Canadian economy is now concentrated in fewer hands than ever. In addition, because of the growth in American ownership of Canadian enterprises, it is probably true that the impact of the foreign metropolitan-based capitalist class on Canadian affairs is now greater than it has been at any period since early in the nineteenth century.

Another consequence of the increasing concentration of economic control in the private sector and the growth of bureaucracy in the public sector has been an acceleration of the proletarianization of the Canadian labour force. More Canadians are connected to their employer fundamentally through the fact that they are paid a price for their labour power. There continue to be differences in working environments, but blue collar manual production workers, white collar clerical staff, technicians in laboratories, and professionals such as engineers are often basically alike in that the employer (often a large corporation) employs them because of their capacity to do specialized work and lays them off when there is no longer a need for that kind of work.

For most of the first 25 years following World War II, there was a rapidly expanding opportunity structure in Canada. There was a general labour shortage, particularly in the semi-skilled category, which was filled to a significant extent by relatively heavy immigration. The expanding economy also created opportunities for labour requiring specialized levels of education or technical training. To fill these openings highly trained manpower was recruited through immigration and a larger educational system was put in place to train Canadians.

The 1970s have seen a general constriction in the economy and hence in the opportunity structure. This process has been exacerbated by the fact that the products of the "baby boom" have also come onto the job market in large numbers during this period. Many of the troublesome social issues or social problems we are beginning to identify as particularly intractable can be understood if they are seen to be, in part, a consequence of this change. This constriction is the result of many factors. More sophisticated and capital intensive technologies have reduced the demand for labour. Computers, for example, have modified the demand for specialized manpower in a number of lower managerial and white collar occupations. Educational establishments expanded in the 1960s, but because of falling birth rates there are now fewer children and young people who need education. This has resulted in a decline in the demand for teachers at all levels. The increasing American ownership of Canadian industry has meant that local opportunities in research and development have not expanded as rapidly in Canada as it was originally assumed they would. The development of new mining resources in other parts of the world has reduced the demand for some Canadian minerals. Thus, unemployment continues to rise.

Because of this constriction in the opportunity structure many people are underemployed, that is, they have advanced training or education which they are unable to use in their work. In addition, large numbers of people have been pushed into the underclass. For example, many young people are unemployed or find employment in only temporary and marginal jobs. In some depressed areas of the country, a large proportion of the labour force can find no employment at all. A relatively large number of people find their only employment in the non-unionized and often most insecure parts of the tertiary service sector.

Economy, Opportunity, and Class: Interconnections and Consequences

The Canadian economy has a well-developed set of primary industries. That is to say, the resource extractive sector of the Canadian economy is relatively sophisticated and, by standards applied in western industrial countries, is well run. Canada has a large land mass and a very diversified set of raw materials. There are systems for developing agricultural products, ocean products, forest products, minerals, and several types of energy resources for economic gain.

The secondary sector of the Canadian economy is relatively underdeveloped. Many Canadian raw materials are shipped out of the country in an unprocessed or partially processed state. If the forward linkages of Canadian industry were developed to their full potential there would be much more secondary manufacturing in Canada. One of the reasons for the limited secondary processing is that the large multinational corporations which own Canadian resources find it to their advantage to do the processing outside of the country. In addition, a relatively large proportion of the manufactured goods used by Canadians are imported, hence the final demand linkage to manufacturing of consumer products is sometimes to activities outside of Canada.

The tertiary or service sector of the Canadian economy is well developed. Those parts of the economy which are oriented to the delivery of services and the distribution of consumer goods to the Canadian population are complete and effective by the standards of capitalist societies. In addition, finance, communication and transportation are all well-developed and integrated.

The dominance of foreign multinational ownership of Canadian industry and resources is having an increasingly adverse effect on the Canadian opportunity structure. The export of raw materials for secondary processing means that forward linked economic opportunities in the chain of activity associated with the exploitation of a staple are located outside of Canada rather than in Canada. If the research and development work necessary to the utilization of a staple product is conducted in the headquarters of an American-based multinational corporation, then the opportunities for this kind of work are available to people outside of Canada rather than to Canadians. When Canadian raw materials are extracted and exported, economic opportunities are created for Canadians to work in the extractive activities themselves, for example, to be hewers of wood and drawers of oil. Opportunities are also created in the service industries such as transportation, communications, retail trade, and community services. To phrase the point in general terms, the exploitation of Canadian resources for export by foreign-based multinational corporations creates a broad range of economic opportunities, but a significant portion of these opportunities are located outside of Canada and are generally not available to Canadians.

We stated earlier that the shape of the Canadian class structure, as reflected in the character of the fragments which make up the capitalist class and the proletariat, could be understood in terms of the structure of the Canadian economy and technology. The relative size of different class fragments in Canada is a result of the particular metropolitan-hinterland relationships which have been developed in the Canadian economy. As many have noted, the industrial fragment of the Canadian capitalist class is not as well-developed as the commercial fragment (Naylor, 1975.). Historically, this can be explained by the fact that Canadian development up to the beginning of the twentieth century provided relatively few opportunities for manufacturing entrepreneurship, compared to the opportunities available in Britain and the United States. Major opportunities were available in commerce, finance and transportation. At present, the weakness of the manufacturing fragment of the Canadian capitalist class results from the fact that the dominant U.S. capitalists operating in Canada retain most opportunities in manufacturing for plants in their home country.

The relative importance of different fragments of the proletariat in Canada is also a consequence of metropolitan-hinterland relations and staple trade. The concentration of research and development in the head offices of U.S. multinationals means that the fragments of the Canadian proletariat which exist by selling very sophisticated technical and scientific capabilities, for example, engineers, research scientists, and technicians, is relatively small. The export of Canadian materials for processing and manufacturing reduces the size of that group of Canadians sometimes thought of as the aristocracy of blue-collar workers, that is, those members of the proletariat who work in sophisticated manufacturing plants and are protected by relatively strong unions. Because Canadian corporations provide services such as transportation, communication and finance for both foreign and domestic companies extracting Canadian staples, the mental and manual fragments of the proletariat working in these sectors will be quite large. The Canadian state at both the federal and provincial levels has undertaken to provide the infrastructure of facilities and services which would facilitate the development of Canadian resources. As a consequence, state employees are an important part of the Canadian proletariat.

The underclass of Canadian society at any given time may make up a larger proportion of the Canadian population than is characteristic of other industrialized societies. Because the staple industries in the primary sector experience pronounced fluctuations in particular products at various times there are almost always large numbers of people in some regions of Canada who cannot find economic opportunities. The proletariat in many parts of the service sector have virtually no union protection and certain parts of the service sector (for example, tourism) fluctuate widely. As a result, many people are pushed for varying periods of time into the underclass. Because the Canadian state is so limited in its capacity to effectively control major economic units it does not have the capacity to manage the economy in order to prevent the production of more members of the underclass.

The Ultimate Dilemma

We began this paper with a discussion of the dilemmas facing Canada. We shall end by stating clearly the dilemma which makes it difficult to solve all other dilemmas.

The economic activities conducted in Canada, or conducted

elsewhere but based on Canadian resources, produce economic surpluses. We pose the question: "In whose hands does economic surplus accumulate?" This question raises more implications than can be pursued here, but a few points can be made. Some capital is accumulated in the hands of strong Canadian capitalists and is not necessarily available for the betterment of Canadians generally or Canada as a nation. Economic surpluses which result from the processing of Canadian staples outside of Canada are not available to Canada because they are beyond the reach of Canadian governments. Economic surplus accumulated in Canada but under the control of foreign corporations can be directed toward the achievement of ends chosen by Canadians only with tremendous difficulty. Foreign owners can withdraw their funds. Major multinational corporations are particularly immune to pressure because they can switch activities and assets to areas other than Canada without suffering harm to the total corporate income. The ultimate dilemma is that the economic surpluses which are generated by economic activity in Canada or based on Canadian resources cannot be easily directed toward ends chosen by Canadians.

In this paper we have presented a framework for the analysis of Canadian society together with some historical illustrations of how this framework can be applied. We have emphasized the importance of the economic base, the opportunity structure, and the class structure. In particular, we have emphasized the connections between these three dimensions of society. The current Canadian condition is a result of persistently reinforced patterns of historical development which continue to shape our present economic and social structure.

NOTES

References noted here are suggestive rather than exhaustive. An extensive and current bibliography providing material relevant to the themes discussed in this paper is A User's Guide to Canadian Political Economy edited by Clement and Drache (1978). The most direct introductions to the staples school of Canadian economic history are Easterbrook and Aitken (1975) and Easterbrook and Watkins (1970), the later of which includes a bibliographic essay. The concept of the opportunity structure draws on Lockhart's "Future Failure" (1975) and Pentland's "The Development of a Capitalist Labour Market in Canada" (1959), as well as general treatment of the labour market. Anderson (1974) provides a useful introduction to class analysis. The general idea of class fragments are from Poulantzas (1975). Johnson (1972) discusses proletarianization of the Canadian labour force. Macpherson (1962) discusses independent commodity production. Discussions of the Canadian capitalist class rely heavily on Clement (1975), Porter (1965) and Creighton (1970). The general perspective applied to power is developed in Bowles (1979). The concept of metropolis-hinterland relations is clearly developed and applied to Canada by Lower (1971; 1973) and the idea of central and peripheral economies is expressed in the literature of economic dependency, examples of which appear in Cockcroft, Frank, and Johnson (1972). Specific discussions of U.S. metropolitan domination over Canada and of multinational corporations are Levitt (1970), Clement (1977), and Hutchison (1978). Marxist writings generally are important in emphasizing the primary importance of economic factors but the works of Mills (1961) and Steward (1955) are also useful. A recent collection of essays presenting excellent and pertinent analyses of Canada is Panitch (1977).

Readings

Anderson, Charles H, The Political Economy of Social Class, New York: Prentice Hall, 1974.

Bowles, Roy T., "Societal Economic Power in Canada: A Framework for Analysis", Journal of Canadian Studies. (Forthcoming).

Cockcroft, James D., Andre Gunder Frank and Dale L. Johnson, Dependence and Underdevelopment: Latin America's Political Economy, New York: Doubleday, 1972.

Clement, Wallace, The Canadian Corporate Elite: An Analysis of Economic Power, Toronto: McClelland and Stewart, 1975.

Clement, Wallace, Continental Corporate Power: Economic Linkages Between Canada and the United States, Toronto: McClelland and Stewart, 1977.

Clement, Wallace and Daniel Drache, A User's Guide to Canadian Political Economy, Toronto: James Lorimer, 1978.

Creighton, Donald, The Empire of the St. Lawrence: A Study in Commerce and Politics, Toronto: Macmillan Company of Canada, 1970.

Easterbrook, W.T. and Hugh G.J. Aitken, Canadian Economic History, Toronto: Macmillan Company of Canada, 1975.

Easterbrook, W.T. and M.H. Watkins, Approaches to Canadian Economic History, Toronto: McClelland and Stewart, 1971.

Hutcheson, John, Dominance and Dependency: Liberalism and National Policies in the North Atlantic Triangle, Toronto: McClelland and Stewart, 1978.

Johnson, Leo A., "The Development of Class in Canada in the Twentieth Century", in Gary Teeple (ed.), Capitalism and the National Question in Canada, Toronto: University of Toronto Press, 1972.

Levitt, Kari. Silent Surrender: The Multinational Corporation in Canada, Toronto: Macmillan Company of Canada, 1970.

Lockhart, Alexander, "Future Failure: The Unanticipated Consequences of Educational Planning", in Robert M. Pike and Elia Zureik (eds.), Socialization and Values in Canadian Society, Volume II, Toronto: McClelland and Stewart, 1975.

Lower, Arthur, R.M., "Metropolis and Hinterland." South Atlantic Quarterly Vol. 70, (1971).

Lower, Arthur R.M., Great Britain's Woodyard: British America and the Timber Trade, 1763-1867. Toronto: McGill-Queen's University Press, 1973.

Macpherson, C.B., Democracy in Alberta: Social Credit and the Party System. 2nd edition. Toronto: University of Toronto Press, 1962.

Miller, Delbert C. and William H. Form, Industrial Sociology: The Sociology of Work Organizations, New York: Harper & Row, 1964.

Mills, C. Wright, White Collar: The American Middle Class, New York: Oxford University Press, 1961.

Naylor, Tom, The History of Canadian Business, 1867-1914. Vols. 1 and 2. Toronto: James Lorimer, 1975.

Panitch, Leo, The Canadian State, Toronto: University of Toronto Press, 1977.

Pentland, H.C., "The Development of a Capitalistic Labour Market in Canada", The Canadian Journal of Economic and Political Science Vol. 25, (1959).

Porter, John The Vertical Mosaic: An Analysis of Social Class and Power in Canada, Toronto: University of Toronto Press, 1965.

Poulantzas, Nicos, Classes in Contemporary Capitalism, London: NLB, 1975.

Steward, Julian H., Theory of Culture Change: The Methodology of Multilinear Evolution, Urbana: University of Illinois Press, 1975.

Watkins, M.H., "A Staple Theory of Economic Growth", in W.T. Easterbrook and M.H. Watkins (eds.), Approaches to Canadian Economic History, Toronto: McClelland and Stewart, 1971.

Uneven Development: Some Implications of Continental Capitalism for Canada*

Wallace Clement

WALLACE CLEMENT is an Associate Professor of Sociology at McMaster University. His current research interests include Canadian Class and Economic Structure and the Canadian State.

Anyone interested in discovering Canada's place within the world system will soon find it necessary to turn to its roots in Canadian history. The present uneven development of the society is founded on Canada's external dependence and the way this dependence has been mediated by dominant Canadian capitalists. There has long existed an unequal alliance between the dominant fraction of the Canadian capitalist class and foreign capitalists located earlier in the United Kingdom and now in the United States. A full understanding of the current structure of power in the Canadian economy demands an examination of *both* external pressures and demands on Canadian resources and markets and the classes and fractions of classes that have encouraged and benefited by this foreign penetration in Canada, as well as those classes that have suffered.

It will be argued here that an unequal alliance has been struck between the dominant fraction of the Canadian capitalist class and foreign capitalists and that this alliance has benefited each to the overall distortion of the Canadian economy, resulting in a pattern of uneven development and a focus on resource exploitation. It will also be argued that the Canadian state has been distorted as well and that the outcome has meant the relative dependency of the Canadian state within the continental context. Finally, some

An earlier version of this paper was presented at the Western Sociology Association meeting, Calgary, Alberta in December 1977.

ways this structure of power and uneven development have influenced Canada's class formation will be examined. This essay may be regarded as a preliminary statement on development following *Continental Corporate Power* (Clement, 1977a), especially my attempt to specify some of the implications of the power structure it uncovered.

First, however, it is necessary to provide a summary statement on Canada's pattern of uneven development.

Uneven Development of the Canadian Economy

Uneven development has two main expressions in Canada. These are in its regional inequalities and in the sector specific activities of fractions of the capitalist class. By the latter it is meant that foreign and Canadian capitalists have their respective strengths in specific sectors of the economy. Foreign capitalists, through branch plants and markets, dominate the sphere of circulation and service: finance, transportation, utilities, and the media. This division of activity has facilitated a complementary relationship between *dominant* Canadian and foreign capitalists; it has also been the reason for the unequal character of their alliance. Since the sphere of circulation is predicated on the activity generated by the sphere of production, Canadian capitalists have entered into an unequal alliance whereby their own growth and well-being is based on the lead of foreign capitalists.

Regional uneven development is related to the fact that the centre of Canadian manufacturing and finance is located in the 'golden triangle' between Windsor, Toronto, and Montreal. The rest of the country relies on key resources. For the North, it is mining and minerals, following traditional furs; in British Columbia, it is wood, pulp and paper, fish, agriculture, and some hydro; it is gas, petroleum, and potash along with grain on the Prairies; mining and pulp and paper in northern Manitoba, Ontario, and Quebec, along with hydro; in Atlantic Canada, it is pulp and paper, agriculture, fish, some coal, and hydro. These regions feed the 'golden triangle' and U.S. markets with their resources and, in turn, consume the finished products from these centres. The economies of these different parts of the country, in turn, produce different types of class structures in these regions (see Clement, 1978).

Both forms of uneven development result from the effects of foreign pressures which have penetrated and shaped Canada. Initially France and then the United Kingdom colonized what is now Canada in search of its staple commodities and as an outlet for their surplus capital, used to create the nation's infrastructure — its roads, canals, ports, railways, and financial institutions. These colonial powers provided a ready outlet for Canada's commercial staples — fish, fur, timber, and wheat — while the colonies were a ready market for the converted raw materials.

William Lyon Mackenzie characterized the dependent condition of British North America well when he said in 1824:

> Our foreign commerce, confined and shackled as it is, and it has been, is entirely in the hands of the British manufacturers...Our farmers are indebted to our country merchants, our country merchants are deeply bound down in the same manner, and by the same causes, to the Montreal wholesale dealers. Few of these Montreal commission merchants are men of capital; they are generally merely the factors or agents of British houses, and thus a chain of debt, dependence and degradation is begun and kept up (quoted in Ryerson, 1968:106-107).

Because the primary form of capital used by the United Kingdom in Canada was portfolio or loan capital, this necessitated the development within Canada of an indigenous capitalist class and a stable state structure which could guarantee these loans and oversee their investment. This arrangement continued until, in 1846, with the abolition of the Corn Laws in Britain, there was a movement to free trade and the end to Canada's privileged position within the Empire. Canadian capitalists then floundered in search of another imperial centre with which the country could become attached. Many signed the Annexation Manifesto of 1849 calling for commercial union with the United States; they settled for the Reciprocity Treaty of 1854. Soon followed Confederation whereby central Canadian capitalists would become their own colonizers, turning east and west. The foundation of their economy remained that of mediators between Canada's resources and foreign markets, but alongside this there was beginning to be developed small scale manufacturing interests that had grown to serve the Canadian market. These were basically local in nature and tied to the local populations in Ontario, Quebec, and the Atlantic Provinces.

The position of the small scale manufacturers was, however, a precarious one. Dominant capitalists controlled the transportation networks essential for getting goods to market and the pools of capital essential for expansion. In addition, the United States by this time had become an important industrial nation, itself searching for outlets for its products and sources of raw material. These two forces combined represented the demise of indigenous Canadian industrialization, particularly in Atlantic Canada.

Uneven Development and Regionalism

T.W. Acheson has summarized the position of Atlantic Canada within Confederation in the following way:

> [A] crisis occurred in the depression of 1874-79, when the British and American markets for Canadian wood products and grains experienced a sharp downturn. To further aggravate the situation many American businessmen, faced with contracting domestic markets, began dumping large quantities of manufactured products on the Canadian market at substantially reduced prices. The combination of failing markets and foreign competition drove hundreds of manufacturers into bankruptcy and seemed to threaten the very survival of the small and comparatively inefficient Canadian manufacturing sector (Acheson, 1977: 91).

In light of a declining demand for Canadian staples and the dumping of surplus production by U.S. capitalists on the Canadian market, Sir John A. Macdonald devised the now famous National Policy of 1879. This policy was based on a program of tariffs to bring industry into Canada, railways to produce a national economy, immigration to fill the West, and production of wheat destined for the world commodity markets. It served to stimulate manufacturing within Canada but, as will be seen, did little to sustain it. As Acheson has illustrated:

> The National Policy increasingly fulfilled its promise of making the entire domestic market available to Canadian producers. Thus, in reaction to the problems of an international economy which was unable to consume Canadian staples, and in response to the demands of a variety of concerned business interests, the Canadian government moved to restore the traditional metropolis-hinterland economic relationships....The effect of the reorganization was to create a new economic metropolis, centered on Montreal, replacing the traditional British and American centres (Acheson, 1977:93).

All did not fare equally well under this new structure; ". . . the Canadian metropolis was unable to perform most of the functions usually associated with a dominant centre...The most critical metropolitan failure was the inability of the central Canadian market to consume the output of these new regional industries" (Acheson, 1977:95). The result was the destruction of Atlantic industry, its takeover by central Canadian capitalists by the First World War and its replacement by branch plant industries and central Canadian banking consortia. From that point on, the Atlantic region became a "client economy."

John Baker has shown the scale of this demise. In Atlantic Canada "there was a decline in the number of persons employed in manufacturing, from 69,529 in 1890 to 43,719 in 1920 (reaching a low of 24,538 in 1933)" (Baker, 1977:201). The root of this demise was in the overproduction of manufacturing output in central Canada and the control by financial capitalists of central Canada. Following Confederation, the new federal state implemented policies resulting in "the effective prohibition of independent community banking (as had existed in Atlantic Canada) and the establishment of a branch banking system, controlled from Montreal and Toronto" (Baker, 1977:298). These centrally controlled banks caused a shortage of loan capital and higher interest rates, thus undercutting the ability of Atlantic manufacturers to compete.

For Atlantic Canada, what was once a thriving manufacturing centre now reverted to staples production and dependency. Whereas staples had accounted for 32 percent of the Atlantic output in 1911, this grew to 38 percent by 1951 (see Acheson, 1977:98). Not only did the region return to staples production, it also turned to the U.S. market as its primary outlet. By 1966 two-thirds of Atlantic exports were sent to the United States and forest, mines, and fish products accounted for 85 percent of their exports, (see Acheson, 1977:113n). The decline in manufacturing coincided as well with the growth of the state and service sectors, so that more than anywhere else in Canada, Maritime workers were employed in these sectors.

The weight of the National Policy shifted the benefits to central Canada. By the time its effects were fully felt, central Canada housed the major financial centre of the nation and extended its power to the east through branch plant operations. It also established a monopoly over manufacturing. By 1910, four-fifths of Canada's manufacturing capacity was located in Ontario and Quebec. But increasingly this capacity was no longer controlled by small scale Canadian capitalists. Some had shifted into the hands of Canadian financial capitalists in the steel, pulp and paper, and food and beverages industries as they expanded into corporate ventures by buying out many small operators and creating monopolies. Outside these areas of industry, U.S. capitalists led the way, particularly in the technology intensive secondary manufacturing and resource sectors. This only served to reinforce and aggravate the problems of regionalism in Canada. By 1931, two-thirds of U.S. controlled manufacturing plants were located in Ontario, with Quebec accounting for another 16 percent. Today Ontario receives 62 percent of the taxable income from U.S. controlled manufacturing companies even though it has only 36 percent of the population (see Clement, 1978). All other regions are significantly under-represented. Thus the penetration of the Canadian market by U.S. branch plants to avoid the tariff 'barriers' served to draw even more economic power into the centre, further distorting the economy and failing to really build a national economy since it was immediately drawn into a continental one where the United States dominated.

Besides the Atlantic region, central Canadian capitalists also extended their dominance to the West. Following a path blazed by the Hudson's Bay Company, the Canadian Pacific Railway (CPR) was given control over most of the West's productive land. In the vision of central Canada dominance, the West was turned into a resource hinterland so central Canadian capitalists could continue their historic role as mediators of Canadian resources for the markets of the world. This left the producers of the West vulnerable. As Paul Phillips has shown:

> The farmer had to sell his output, mainly grain, on an unprotected (European) international market, but had to buy his finished goods on a highly protected domestic market increasingly dominated by American manufacturers. What is significant, of course, is that the western producer had no control over either his market or his supplier...caught between the fluctuating world grain prices and more stable finished-goods prices, the western producer suffered wide variation in real income (Phillips 1977:21).

Added to their burden was the discriminatory freight rates imposed by the CPR whereby the wheat rate "was almost three times that for comparable distances in competitive eastern areas" and consumed "half of the farmer's gross income from his grain crop" (Regehr, 1977:118-119). At least until the Second World War, the agrarian *petit-bourgeoisie* as expressed in the Social Credit and Co-operative Commonwealth Federation parties dominated the politics of the West in reaction to the domination of their markets, transportation systems, financial sources, and implement supplies. While unable to defend themselves against the exploitation of this system, they did manage to develop important institutions to moderate its impact with, for example, the introduction of the Wheat Board and the co-operative movement.

Today freight rates continue as a major obstacle to development in the West. As fewer and fewer farmers are needed to work the more mechanized farms, people are forced off the land and into the urban areas but find little employment in manufacturing industries. It has been difficult to attract manufacturers to the region because the freight rates make it more profitable to remain in central Canada and ship to regional markets. For example, the rate per hundredweight to ship iron and steel products by rail from Toronto to Vancouver is 168¢ but from Toronto to Saskatoon it is 247¢. Ensuring that a minimum of processing will occur with the grains, it costs 92¢ per hundredweight to ship from Saskatoon to Moncton while the rate for mill feed is 162¢ (see Regehr, 1977:132-133).

Unlike the Atlantic region, however, the West, since 1947, has had petroleum as an important lever in its dealings with central Canada. This entire industry, as one of the key industrial staples, is dominated by foreign, largely United States controlled, oil companies. When western oil came on stream, the world oil monopoly had already been established and it simply became one more domain for the Seven Sisters that controlled the markets and technology necessary to develop these resources. While petroleum gave the West an important counterpoint against central Canada, it in fact drew the West into a greater structure of dominance. As Larry Pratt has convincingly argued, "Canadians are not receiving fair value for the exploitation of their resources; that it is the handful of multinational companies, holding almost exclusive leasing privileges in the tar sands, that are dictating the conditions for their development" (Pratt, 1976:17). The costs of such dependence are enormous as the provincial governments became completely dependent upon a single resource for their survival. The multinational companies shift the risk and costs to the state while at the same time ensuring their own profitability. "Thus government must shoulder the enormous financial burden of building the massive infrastructure required to service and supply these remote projects, providing equity and debt financing, royalty holidays, guaranteed returns and prices, ensure labour stability, train a work force, underwrite environmental studies and costs — all of which carries a price tag in the billions" (Pratt, 1977:95).

A repeat of Canada's history of uneven development is again taking place, now in the North. Bearing the stamp of the staple, the Berger Report calls the North "an area of production remote from the main markets of Canada and from the homes of those who own and invest in its resources...The first great staple industries in the North were the fur trade and whaling; then followed by mining; now there is gas and oil" (Berger Report, 1977:117). Each of these staples has left its mark on the North, but the most recent developments in mining and minerals are the most disruptive, serving exclusively outside interests. As Mel Watkins has shown, the fur trade involved the native people as gatherers of fur. They acted as independent commodity producers selling their products to the fur trading companies, thus giving them a measure of autonomy and control over their homeland. With mineral production, however, capitalists demand "both rights to the use of land and people who will work for a wage" (Watkins, 1977:88). The linkages generated by this search for industrial staples benefit industrialized parts of the country but have only disruptive effects on the traditional economy of the native people. Moreover, the benefits of this development accrue primarily to the United States and not even to industrialized Canada. As Edgar Dosman has shown: "In most well-established countries, the development of a peripheral region would be largely a domestic issue. In Canada, however, the development of the North was inextricably linked to the issue of the Canadian relationship with a foreign power, the United States" (Dosman, 1975:xiv). This is because the United States is the major recipient of Canadian gas and oil exports and because the companies controlling these resources are U.S. controlled companies. As has been characteristic of the entire Canadian economy, the exploitation of natural resources for foreign markets has placed Canada in a vulnerable position in the world system. In the North this means the destruction of the native people's final homeland, their last refuge from a mode of production which destroys their traditional culture and livelihood.

Uneven Development and the Capitalist Class

It has been demonstrated that uneven development has an important expression in the distortion it has caused in the regional nature of the Canadian economy, creating an unequal alliance between fractions of the capitalist class. While the indigenous fractions of Canada's capitalist class were nurtured on British portfolio investment and found their niche in finance, transportation and utilities, U.S. investment had a very different impact. Direct investment, as expressed in the branch plants of multinational corporations, involves an entire 'package' consisting of technology, access to markets, access to capital and management. Unlike portfolio investment, over time direct investment expands and widens the scope of control for its owners. In time it eventually expands at a rate faster than new investment, using both internally generated capital and capital borrowed within the investing country, and actually drains off more capital than is invested from without. This point was reached in Canada during the early 1960s. Branch plants do not require the development of an indigenous capitalist class for their operation since they remain externally controlled. They serve, rather, to displace existing capitalists in the activities they engage in or prevent them from emerging. In Canada these firms found a welcome ally in the dominant indigenous capitalist class, anxious to invest in their secure operations and to benefit from the activity they generated.

In response to demands for natural resources to feed industrialization at home and in search of expanded markets for their own products, U.S. corporations began to penetrate the Canadian economy with great force after the Second World War. In 1946, 35 percent of Canada's manufacturing was foreign controlled but this rose to 50 percent by 1953, and 56 percent by 1957; in mining and smelting the increases during the same years were from 38 percent to 57 percent to 70 percent. Thus, in the course of a decade, the productive cornerstones of Canada's economy ceased to be Canadian owned and became foreign owned. Much of the impetus for the United States penetration of Canadian resources came as a result of an inventory conducted after the wartime experience of resource shortages in the United States. A Presidential Commission was struck and issued The Paley Report, entitled *Resources for Freedom*, in 1952. In this report 22 key resources were identified as central to the United States maintaining its dominant position in the capitalist world. Canada was listed as the primary source for 12 of these (nickel, copper, lead, zinc, asbestos, iron ore, sulphur, titanium, cobalt, petroleum, natural gas and newsprint).

These developments were welcomed by many Canadian capitalists. They particiapted in foreign ownership in a variety of ways. For example, by 1970, Canadian capitalists had committed some $5.8 billion directly to U.S. controlled companies in Canada through investments, representing 21 percent of the value of U.S. direct investment. They also benefited from the secure loans they made, guaranteed by the foreign parents, the transportation and utilities they used and the access to technology and foreign markets they provided. These Canadian capitalists were also given positions on the branch plants of these companies in Canada. In fact, of the indigenous fraction of the dominant capitalist class in Canada, 31 percent sit on the boards of U.S. branch plants. In addition, 7 percent of the members of the Canadian economic elite hold positions directly on the boards of companies in the United States. Of the 113 dominant Canadian companies, 63 (or 56 percent) are interlocked with U.S. dominants; of the 194 dominant U.S. companies, 73 (or 38 percent) have interlocks with dominant Canadian companies (see Clement, 1977a:172-180). The direction of these ties is from U.S. manufacturing to Canadian finance and back again, suggesting that at least a part of Canada's capitalist class is able to operate comfortably within the continental economy.

An additional expression of Canada's uneven development is evident in Canada's relationship with the rest of the world. Investment from Canada falls into two types, closely corresponding to the relative strengths of Canadian and foreign capitalists within the Canadian economy. The first is real Canadian investment abroad, located primarily in finance, transportation, and utilities. At the pinnacle of this are the five dominant Canadian banks. As the people at the Development Education Centre have argued:

> The Canadian banking trusts chose very early an international strategy, rather than bearing the risks of boom and bust in the Canadian 'staples' economy or in underwriting a potential national manufacturing strategy. Profits were more stable and insured in cooperation with Wall Street or London, no matter whether the action was at home or abroad (Development Education Centre, 1977:50).

The fortunes of Canada's banks abroad followed those of first the British and then the U.S. empires. For example, "branches and sub-branches of Canadian banks in the Caribbean and Latin America peaked at 140 in 1926; that figure was not reached again until 1958" (Chodos, 1977:11). Today, riding on the crest of U.S. hegemony, Canadian banks have grown to be the third largest in international financial circles. The five dominant banks earn a fifth or more of their total revenues from foreign operations and this share has been increasing. The international operations expanded at a rate of 667 percent between 1966 and 1976, considerably faster than the 394 percent growth in domestic operations for the same period.

Besides the indigenous Canadian investment abroad, there is a second rather unusual form of 'Canadian' investment abroad. This is go-between investment whereby branches, typically of U.S. companies, are used to control other branches in the rest of the world. As early as 1929, companies like Union Carbide, Ford Motor Company, Standard Oil of New Jersey, and Aluminum Company of America used Canadian subsidiaries as a means to avoid U.S. laws and take advantage of preferential Canadian tariffs. Today this pattern remains and a good deal of 'Canadian' foreign investment in the manufacturing and resource sectors is actually controlled outside of Canada, with the Canadian branch acting as a go-between (see Clement, 1977a:115-117). Thus foreign investment distorts not only Canada's national economy but its international relations as well. In the economic as well as the political and military domains, Canadians have a role as mediator, acting as a kind of 'bumper' between U.S. imperialism and the rest of the world.

The strategy of Canadian capitalists and the Canadian state is to attempt to expand even further the multinational operations of Canadian corporations. Acknowledging that this will lead to even greater concentration within Canada, they argue that Canada must develop these giant companies if it wants to compete internationally. This would certainly benefit Canada's largest capitalists but at the same time will undercut smaller capitalists in Canada and make the working class even more vulnerable to the whims of both Canadian and foreign multinationals and those who control them.

The Relative Dependency of the Canadian State

It has been argued to this point that the Canadian economy is characterized by uneven development and this has been illustrated in terms of the regional nature of the economy, various fractions of the capitalist class, and as it affects 'Canadian' investment abroad. One important area where this unevenness expresses itself is in the Canadian state. The contradictory forces within the society become manifest in the state. The most fundamental of these are:

(1) Two, or three if you include the native people, nations within a single state;

(2) A state that has at least 12 governments with many of the critical functions of the state falling outside the federal domain; and

(3) A state which, in light of the previous fragmentation, attempts to reconcile the demands of various fractions of the capitalist class, each with some degree of power and political importance.

A vast territory, constant encroachment on its powers by the United States, two or more nations, uneven development, ill-defined northern frontiers with conflicting ownership claims, ethnic diversity, a persistent petty bourgeoisie with demands differing from the working and capitalist classes, tremendous foreign ownership — these are all features of Canadian society having a bearing on the nature of the state.

The problem is not simply to provide an analysis of the state but one of creating an analysis of society. It is an illusion to think the state operates independent of society. It is both generated by society and influences that society; in other words, the state is wedded to the socio-economic make-up of society.

Questions concerning the relative autonomy of the state have become important points of debate with the resurgence of Marxist theories of the state. This position acknowledges that the state in a capitalist society is used to further the general interests of the most powerful sectors of a society and in order to do so 'stands back' from the particular interests of some dominant sectors or fractions. In Canada this autonomy has not been evident. Instead, there has been contradiction, confusion, and conflict *within* the state itself. The fundamental role of the state in any capitalist society is not only to regulate or mediate relations between classes but it is also critical for regulating intra-class relations. In Canada this task is pushed to the extreme because of the fractions of the capitalist class already outlined. In Canada it is also important to note fractions of the state itself, especially differences between federal and provincial levels and between government and other parts of the state apparatus, such as regulatory boards and agencies and the public bureaucracy.

The major division within Canada is between big and medium sized capitalists rather than between Canadian and foreign capitalists, and the overall weight of the Canadian state is such that it reinforces these dominant capitalists. Canadian capitalists, especially those in the giant banks, life insurance, trust and holding companies, back winners, whatever their nationality, since their interests are inextricably tied into the international system of capital.

Basic to the Canadian state and its various branches is the need to balance contradictory requirements on the part of U.S. and Canadian capital. The outcome has been that some Canadian capitalists who 'fit' the demands of U.S. capitalists have benefited by Canada's distorted development and struck an unequal alliance while others have been left by the wayside. While it is important for the state's legitimacy to project an appearance that this does not occur or that they are acting to prevent it, in the end state policies have followed the demands of the most powerful sectors of the society. This is not simply because they are ideologically predisposed to do so but because the most powerful are those that can make things happen, get things done. They are the backbone of all economic activity and thus crucial to the viability of any capitalist state.

One outcome of such practice is a highly concentrated economy but this does not bother the state (except that it has to legitimate it — such as was done recently in the Royal Commission on Corporate Concentration). Part of the concentration in Canada is internally induced and some of it is imported but as far as the state is concerned, it is in the concentrated areas that 'planning' can take place, both articulating demands of capital on the state and for the state to have an input into the economy (e.g., Bank of Canada). But in large part this is an illusion. The state under these conditions has its input under terms dictated by private capital; that is, ventures it advocates must be made profitable. Consequently capitalists must be induced or subsidized in their activities or have conditions provided that artificially make them competitive internationally (e.g., the uranium cartel).

Underlying many of the contradictions of Canadian society is the uneven development discussed earlier. It is quite apparent why this would lead to confusion on the part .of the Canadian state in its performance of its accumulation function. Canada is an advanced industrial society whose mainstay is resources rather than manufactured products, whose industrial capacity is mainly foreign owned, and a trading nation that sends over two-thirds of its exports to one country (the United States) and receives over two-thirds of its imports from that same country.

Moreover, as both a recipient of, and base for, foreign investment, the Canadian state is forced to 'play both sides of the fence'. It must maintain the legitimacy of foreign investment since it sanctions a good deal of it in the rest of the world under the guise of Canadian investment abroad, while at the same time it must contend at home with the massive problems it causes.

As a result, there is no clear focus for the Canadian state. It is a state of confusion since it contains within it contradictory interests and forces. Consequently, it is weak in its ability to deal with basic economic problems: trade, inflation, unemployment, development strategies, etc.

A recent example illustrates the point. The Canadian state was aware that Inco Ltd. was about to expand its operations into Guatemala, regardless of what the Canadian state did. In response it performed an illusion. It turned Inco into a Canadian company simply by changing its official classification. Suddenly there exists a 'Canadian' company that can operate in the world system and give Canada a place in that system. As a further indication of the rationality of the irrationality of the system is the fact that it has exempted the company from normal taxation so Inco can 'modernize' its Canadian operations, which means mechanization and automation that eat up jobs. In addition, they provided a $78 million loan through the Export Development Corporation to Inco for its Guatemala operations. The net impact in Canada is the loss of about 4,000 jobs.

Another example of state policy wrought with contradictions is the Foreign Investment Review Agency (FIRA). It was established as an instrument of legitimation, in response to nationalist pressures, both broadly based and from small Canadian business. It was, however, soon turned on its head by the powerful forces that support dominant capital. Provinces cried out that they cannot be cut off from foreign investment. Politicians ran around the world saying it did not really make any difference and the agency itself became a conduit for foreign investment by providing services for foreign capital and giving their actions legitimacy. For example, Claude Bennett, the Ontario Minister of Industry said: "We'll try to clear up the misunderstanding that the FIRA rules are rigorous. We'll show them [foreign investors] that it's not difficult to get through it, and we'll simplify the processing of their applications."

(*Macleans*, 1 Nov., 1976:40). Since October, 1975, FIRA has approved over 80 percent of the takeover bids, certainly not a record that would suggest any attempt to reduce foreign control. Indeed, the government has been bending over backwards to attract even more. In 1978 the federal and Ontario provincial governments offered Ford Motor Company a subsidy of $75 million to build an engine plant in Ontario rather than Ohio.

In its rush to meet the increasing demands on its resources, the various branches of the Canadian state have found themselves running to the New York money markets. The costs of building a resource infrastructure are enormous. In 1976, government borrowing was $8 billion, of which $3.5 billion was raised outside Canada. Compare this with the $7.6 billion borrowed by private business, only $400 million of which was raised outside (see *Weekend Magazine*, 18 Dec., 1976:4). Canada is being made capital poor because of the costs of foreign ownership and because of the demands being placed on its revenues. The Canadian state is now in a position where it must borrow to repay interest on its loans. According to Garth Stevenson: "By 1973 interest charges on all provincial debts amounted to nearly $1.2 billion, substantially more than the total of *all* provincial expenditures in 1950"(Stevenson, 1977:84-5). By 1977 all levels of government were making interest payments of $8.94 billion annually. Ottawa alone paid over $225 million in interest in 1977 on *foreign* loans (see *Globe and Mail*, 7 April, 1978:B1; 3 May, 1978:1-2). It is not possible for the state to continue indefinitely in its give-aways and concessions.

The closeness of the capitalist class in Canada to the state makes it all the more difficult for the state to be autonomous. This is especially so when fractions of the capitalist class, at times in concert and at times in conflict, have very close relations with different branches and levels of the state (see Clement, 1977b). Since corporate power is political power, these interests become translated directly into contradictory state policies and behaviour. As the scope of these demands enlarge and call for increasing state action, the contradictions must become manifest.

Canada's Class Formation

In previous sections the focus was on the capitalist class and its various fractions with only a few oblique references to the effects of uneven development on other classes. As with the state sector, it will only be possible here to suggest some ways uneven development has affected the class structure of Canada. This is an area of continuing research so the following must be regarded as a very preliminary outline.

It was illustrated earlier that there is an unequal distribution of manufacturing capacity in Canada with the industrial heartland residing in the 'golden triangle'. Outside this area most productive workers are part of a 'resource proletariat' whose jobs are in activities like mining, minerals, pulp and paper, lumber, fishing, or hydro. They tend to live in single industry towns far from major urban centres and their costs of living are high. Most important, they tend to work in non-renewable resources and their livelihood is constantly threatened by exhaustion of these resources or fluctuations in world markets. The boom-bust cycles in Canada's resource proletariats are legion; there are constant fluctuations between labour shortages and labour surpluses in these industries because their fate depends on external demands.

Traditionally, many of the people working in staple industries were independent commodity producers. In fact, up to the Second World War, the petty bourgeoisie was the most powerful class outside the capitalist class and accounted for much of the political resistance to the dominant class. Increasingly they have been drawn into wage labour. In 1957, 79 percent of the labour force were paid workers. By 1976 this increased to 89 percent, while the proportion working for themselves decreased from 12 percent to 5 percent. In numerical terms, this means an increase over the past ten years from 4,540,000 paid workers to 8,272,000 and a decrease of the self-employed with no employees from 667,000 to 512,000. It is important to note, however, that the decline of the traditional petty bourgeoisie of fishermen, farmers and small shopkeepers has not meant a proportionate increase in the traditional working class. What has occurred instead is a dramatic rise in the number of state workers, thus resulting in a situation where a major part of the working class is directly in the employ of the various branches of the state. It is from this new set of state workers that much of the militancy in the post-Second World War era has emanated and where much of the growth in unionization (particularly national or Canadian unions) has taken place. The militancy is particularly evident here because it is these employees' wage demands that the state can best control and under periods of restraint attempts to hold back their wages.

Hugh Armstrong has shown that the state sector has grown more rapidly than any other, accounting for more than a third of all new jobs since the Second World War. It has increased from 8.9 percent in 1946 to at least 21.2 percent of the labour force in 1974, with provincial employees increasing at a much faster rate than federal ones (see Armstrong, 1977:296). Because of the increasing pressure for legitimation on the state with the myriad of contradictions it must face, the state has grown to meet these demands. In addition, the increasing foreign investment since the Second

World War has been highly capital intensive and concentrated, about four and a half times the size of Canadian non-financial corporations in terms of assets and over six times as large by equity and profits, thus requiring much less labour. Moreover, much of the value added in these industries occurs outside Canada thus employing fewer people than would be the case if the manufacturing were done here. Thus the Canadian state is forced into a position of employing a larger share of the labour force and dealing with inordinately high unemployment.

Along side this is the general growth of clerical workers. This is the result of two types of changes, those within factory offices and a growth of 'clerical industries'. The first process is reflected in the following figures for Canada: the proportion of administrative and office workers in Canadian manufacturing increased from 11 percent in 1917 to 19 percent in 1939 to 22 percent in 1954, and 28 percent in 1971. The second is the rise of 'paper empires' such as companies in the commercial sector (banks, trust companies, life insurance, real estate, etc.) which are primarily clerical, and to some extent, sales oriented. Their main activity is record-keeping which involves accounts, stocks, payrolls, etc.

Related to changes in the clerical stratum of the working class are those in service occupations and retail trade. The trend in Canada since the Second World War is toward a rapid increase in the proportion of occupations located in 'service-producing' as opposed to 'goods-producing' sectors. Between 1946 and 1973, the former increased by 199 percent while the latter expanded by only 14 percent. Particularly rapid is the expansion in services such as community, business and personal services, and public adminis-tration, which increased by 266 percent, while finance, insurance, and real estate increased by 239 percent and trade by 161 percent. Looked at differently, in 1946 the 'goods-producing' sectors accounted for 60 percent of employment while in 1973 this had fallen to 37 percent while 'service-producing' sectors accounted for 63 percent. Within the 'goods-producing' sector only construction, which ex-panded by 145 percent, is higher than the average expansion of 88 percent. These figures, of course, do not take into account the expanding proportion of administrative jobs within the 'goods-producing' sector, accounting for, as was mentioned, 28 percent of the jobs in manufacturing in 1971. This means there are many more people in the labour force being supported by ever fewer people producing surplus value. An economy cannot be maintained merely by 'pushing paper.' It must be based on the actual creation of value.

The decline of the primary sector is not an uncommon phenomenon in industrialized nations. Typically, however, it results in a rise in the secondary sector and only much later in an expansion of the tertiary sector. In Canada the decline in the primary sector is matched by a rise in the tertiary sector, and remains unchanged in the secondary sector. Most of the change in the primary sector involves agricultural jobs. These persisted in importance up to the Second World War, as late as the early 1940s accounting for one-quarter of the labour force (declining from two-fifths at the turn of the century), while today they are only one-twentieth of the labour force. This is a result of the increasing mechanization and capitalization of farms. A large part of the demise of farmers is also accounted for by state policies regarding tariffs and the fact that processors of agricultural products have become highly concentrated and fallen into the hands of U.S. capitalists who command the world markets (see Clement and Janzen, 1978). Almost the entire shift, in aggregate terms, has gone to 'white-collar' jobs, especially clerical, sales, and lower-level technical and professional occupations.

Another factor of importance is the weakness of Canada in terms of research and development, with much of this taking place under the command of parent corporations outside of Canada. Of related concern is the exporting of resources and the importing of processed goods which means that labour and skill intensive jobs are also exported. As the studies by Pierre Bourgault have shown, ". . . when we examine the nature of our imports and exports, we find that we export mainly raw materials and resource-based products while importing most manufactured goods, particularly those which have a high knowledge content," that is, those jobs involving advanced technology and skilled labour (Bourgault, 1972:82). Little wonder Canada's unemployment rate runs at nearly 10 percent *officially* and about a million people. Canada's uneven development affects not only the distribution of the labour force but also the number of jobs in the labour force itself. Even the rapid increase in state employment has not been able to meet the demand for jobs caused by the capital intensive foreign control of Canada's productive sectors and the decline of the traditional petty bourgeoisie.

The ability of Canadian labour to exercise its power is also strongly affected by the uneven development of the economy and the development of multinational corporations. The Canadian labour movement is highly fragmented with divisions between national and international unions, between trade, industrial, and public unions, between French and English speaking unions, and between organized and unorganized workers. Added to this is the flexibility capitalists have in dealing with labour as they become multinational in their operations. The recent lay-offs by Inco and Falconbridge reflect their ability to shift production outside the country and weaken the power of labour. An illustration that this is not unique to foreign controlled multinationals is provided by Massey-Ferguson, a part of the Argus holdings. In 1968, Canadian workers at Massey-Ferguson were demanding wage parity with their U.S. counterparts in the same company. Massey-Ferguson threatened to withdraw its operations from Canada. Their threat was successful, resulting in a strike settlement without parity. Massey-Ferguson applied the same threat to the Canadian government over recommendations from the Carter Commission on Tax Reform and was successful in having the recommendations rejected.

The vulnerability of Canadian labour to the flexibility of multinational corporations and to the vagaries of a resource-based economy means that the working class must be constantly on guard for its jobs and standard of living. It is no longer possible, on a large scale, to escape wage labour by 'striking out on your own'. The traditional areas of small business such as shopkeepers and farmers have been thoroughly penetrated by capitalism. The capital requirements to enter either now pose an insurmountable barrier for virtually all workers to accumulate from deferred consumption (that is, out of personal savings). Those who escape wage labour do so mainly by entering into contractual relations with large corporations to manage concessions or chains in the fast-food business or corner stores. There they have little more control over their lives than they did as wage labour because the corporation sets the rules and regulations by which they must abide and shifts much of the risk onto the individual running the branch operation.

It is not possible in the space of this paper to develop a detailed analysis of transformations in Canada's class structure as affected by uneven development. The purpose has rather been to suggest that there are important implications of uneven development not only for the capitalist class and the Canadian state but also for the kind of work people do in this country. The experiences of inflation, lay-offs, unemployment and rising state expenditures are related directly to the kind of economy Canada has and to its relationship with broader continental and world forces. Obviously, much remains to be done.

Readings

Acheson, T.W. "The Maritimes and 'Empire Canada'", in David Jay Bercuson (ed.), Canada and the Burden of Unity, Toronto: Macmillan, 1977.

Armstrong, Hugh, "The Labour Force and State Workers in Canada", in Leo Panitch (ed.), The Canadian State: Political Economy and Political Power, Toronto: University of Toronto Press, 1977.

Baker, John, "The Underdevelopment of Atlantic Canada, 1867-1920", Unpublished Master's thesis, McMaster University, Hamilton, 1977.

Berger Report, *Northern Frontier, Northern Homeland*, Vol. 1, Ottawa: Minister of Supply and Services Canada, 1977.

Bourgault, Pierre, *Innovation and the Structure of Canadian Industry*, Ottawa: Science Council of Canada, 1972.

Chodos, Robert, *The Caribbean Connection*, Toronto: James Lorimer and Co., 1977.

Clement, Wallace, *Continental Corporate Power: Economic Elite Linkages Between Canada and the United States*, Toronto: McClelland and Stewart, 1977(a).

Clement, Wallace, "The Corporate Elite, the Capitalist Class and the Canadian State", in Leo Panitch (ed.), *The Canadian State: Political Economy and Political Power*, Toronto: University of Toronto Press, 1977(b).

Clement, Wallace, "A Political Economy of Regionalism in Canada", in D. Glenday, H. Guidon and A. Turowetz (eds.), *Modernization and the Canadian State*, Toronto: Macmillan, 1978.

Clement, Wallace, and Janzen, Anna, "Just Peachy: The Demise of Tender Fruit Farmers", *This Magazine*, Vol. 12, 2, (1978).

Development Education Centre, "Corporate Power, the Canadian State, and Imperialism", in John Saul and Craig Heron (eds.), *Imperialism, Nationalism and Canada*, Toronto: New Hogtown Press, 1977.

Dosman, Edgar, *The National Interest: The Politics of Northern Development 1968-75*, Toronto: McClelland and Stewart, 1975.

Phillips, Paul, "National Policy, Continental Economics, and National Disintegration", in David Jay Bercuson (ed.), *Canada and the Burden of Unity*, Toronto: Macmillan, 1977.

Pratt, Larry, *The Tar Sands: Syncrude and the Politics of Oil*, Edmonton: Hurtig, 1976.

Regehr, T.D., "Western Canada and the Burden of National Transportation Policies", in David Jay Bercuson (ed.), *Canada and the Burden of Unity*, Toronto: Macmillan, 1977.

Ryerson, Stanley B., *Unequal Union: Confederation and the Roots of Conflict in the Canadas, 1815-1873*, Toronto: Progress Books, 1968.

Stevenson, Garth "Federalism and the Political Economy of the Canadian State," in Leo Panitch (ed.), *The Canadian State: Political Economy and Political Power*, Toronto: University of Toronto Press, 1977.

Watkins, Mel, "From Underdevelopment to Development", in Mel Watkins (ed.), *Dene Nation: The Colony Within*, Toronto: University of Toronto Press, 1977.

Canadian Foreign Aid

Harley D. Dickinson

HARLEY D. DICKINSON is a Canada Council
Doctoral Fellowship holder and a graduate student
at the University of Lancaster. His current research
interests include Canadian Foreign Aid and the
Definition and Care of Mental Illness.

An understanding of the phenomena commonly referred to as underdevelopment can only be based upon an historical-structural analysis of the socio-economic political system which has given rise to that underdevelopment. In recent years it has become more and more widely accepted that the existing international economic system is at the root of underdevelopment. This conception that the dynamics and processes of *capitalist* development have led to the overdevelopment of other areas finds expression in the 1975-1976 Annual Report of the Canadian International Development Agency (CIDA), where it is stated that;

> At the time of the Bandung Conference the industrialized nations were forced to realize, with feelings of mingled fear and guilt, that the prevailing international order left two-thirds of humanity, in a manifestly disadvantaged position (CIDA, 1977: 9).

The Bandung conference was held in 1958 and since that time the proportion of people who have been left in a manifestly disadvantaged position has increased. In further regard to this phenomena it has been noted that the Aid programs in existence have only been able to raise *per capita* income in the underdeveloped countries by about 2 or 3 percent in the last 25 years. Given the prevailing rate of inflation, this, in fact, represents a substantial decline in terms of real income.

This article will be a brief attempt at showing how over $118 billion of foreign aid have actually resulted in a decline in the living standards of the vast majority of the earth's population. Although the $118 billion represents the total amount of aid "donated" to the underdeveloped countries by *all* of the developed capitalist countries, attention for the present purposes will be focused on Canadian aid.

This in and of itself represents a substantial amount, for CIDA had a budget for 1977-1978 of $1.1 billion; up from $973 million in 1975-1976. As a result, Canada is in the position of being about the fifth or sixth largest contributor of foreign aid from among the world capitalist countries. This leads one to ask the question, why does Canada continue to administer foreign aid funds to the under-developed world, when it has been almost universally accepted that the existing plans, both bilateral and multilateral, have been abject failures in terms of promoting development? To adequately answer this question one must first answer the question, why have the existing foreign aid plans failed? Once one has the answer to this question it becomes clear why foreign aid programs as they are presently structured still persist.

In order to answer these questions it is necessary to clarify the dynamics of the "prevailing international order", which is the world capitalist system. Capitalism has one fundamental motive, the need for profits. It was this need for profits, coupled with the uneven development of the world capitalist system which, to a large degree, gave rise to the age of colonialism. The countries in which capitalism first developed had gained an advantage over the rest of the world due to the pillage and exploitation of the newly discovered areas. This pillage of the world resulted in vast quantities of capital being accumulated in Europe, and most especially Britain. With this initial accumulation of capital came the need to profitably invest it. As this investment was made in Europe it resulted in the development of capitalistic relations of production (which include an increasing efficiency in the productivity of labour).

With an increase in the productivity of labour there develops a need to secure a market for the vast quantities of manufactured goods produced. This requirement, coupled with the fact that as the productivity of labour increases the relative cost of the labour decreases in comparison to the cost of the raw materials, resulted in an attempt on the part of capital to lower the proportion of total costs of production accounted for by the cost of raw materials. With the objective of increasing profits by securing sources of cheap raw materials (as well as markets for the manufactured goods of the industrialized metropoles) the gaze of capital eventually came to focus on the so-called backward areas of the world. This was the beginning of the age of colonialism. Labour in these underdeveloped areas of the world was very cheap in comparison to the industrialized countries. This advantage was further accentuated by the destruction of the indigenous social, economic and political structures of these underdeveloped areas and the imposition of colonial organizational structures whose primary purpose was to facilitate the exploitation of the colonies for the sake of profits. This exploitation of the cheapness of raw materials due to the low level of wages in the colonies was made more acute by the creation of a slave economy — where, in fact, the cost of labour amounted to nothing more than the minimum required to ensure the physical existence of the slaves.

With the colonial system and slavery it would appear that the problems faced by capitalism with regards to ensuring profits would have been solved. This was not the case, however, because, like any social system, capitalism is a dynamic process which constantly changes. Once it had ensured itself a source of cheap raw materials, and cheap labour power, it was the industrialized areas themselves that were the source of falling rates of profit. The wages of the industrial workers in the metropoles were now relatively more than the raw materials from the colonies. To overcome this obstacle it was necessary to lower the costs of production in the metropoles themselves. There were several ways in which this could be done. The amount paid out for labour could be reduced in absolute terms, i.e., wages could be lowered in real terms, or wages could be reduced in a relative way, i.e., by increasing the productivity of labour. Since the lowering of wages in an absolute sense is very difficult, not to mention the threat of such action to the stability of the social order, the usual way of circumventing this problem of decreasing profits was to increase the productivity of labour. Simply put, this means that for the same wages the workers produce more goods. This could be achieved by increasing the length of the working day, a move that does, however, have an absolute upper limit of 24 hours. As a result, lowering the cost of production is usually done by mechanizing and/or automating the production process. This lowers the cost of production because once the machine and equipment have been paid for, it is cheaper to maintain them in operation than it is to pay the wages of people to do the same job. Thus with the labour power in the metropoles again relatively less expensive than the raw materials that were being imported from the colonies, the eyes of the capitalist class again turned to the colonies to look for ways to lower the costs of raw materials.

Here a problem arose: you cannot get labour any cheaper than that of slaves. So how do you lower the cost of the raw materials? The answer lies in making the labour of the underdeveloped world more productive. The way in which this was done was already known, namely, to import capital and industrialize the labour process that was used in the creation of the necessary raw materials. The capitalist relation of production was instituted in the colonies. As Ernest Mandel states:

> With the massive export of capital to the underdeveloped countries for the organization of the capitalist production of raw materials there,

the quantitative difference in the accumulation of capital and the level of productivity between the metropolitan countries and the economically backward ones was suddenly transformed into a qualitative difference. These countries now became dependent as well as backward (Mandel, 1975: 60).

At this point in the development of capitalism it became a source of decreasing profits to maintain the vast colonial structure, and there ensued a wholesale granting of "independence" to the former colonies. Independence, however, was more an illusion than a reality because of the position of economic dependency in which these former colonies found themselves. Finally, after the Second World War, as was pointed out in the quotation from the CIDA Report, there suddenly developed a concerted attempt, motivated by both guilt and fear, to help those "less fortunate" countries. This help took the form of foreign aid. The task to which attention will now be turned is that of outlining, and supplementing this outline with empirical data, the part that foreign aid in general, and Canadian foreign aid in particular, plays in the world capitalist system. In particular, the focus of attention is the area known as the Commonweath Caribbean, as this area receives the greatest amount of Canadian aid on a *per capita* basis.

In his book entitled the *Age of Imperialism*, Harry Magdoff develops five points which he maintains are the purposes or consequences of foreign aid. These propositions were developed with U.S. foreign aid as the focus of analysis, and therefore must be modified somewhat for application to the Canadian situation.

The first of these propositions is the least applicable to the Canadian situation and therefore will be largely ignored. In it Magdoff states that U.S. foreign aid is an attempt to help implement the worldwide political and military policy of the United States. Canada is not a major world military power, and therefore an adaptation of this proposition is not very appropriate. This is not to imply that the Canadian government has no international military commitments. Canada is party to several joint military ventures such as the North Atlantic Treaty Organization (NATO), the North American Air Defence Command (NORAD), and the United Nations Peace Keeping Forces. However, within all these organizations Canada plays the role of a very junior partner. Also Canada does not include military expenditures under the heading of aid.

The remaining four propositions, in a reworked form, are much more applicable to the Canadian situation. These propositions state that the purpose or consequence of Canadian Foreign aid is;

(1) to enforce the open door policy; for freedom of access to raw materials, trade, and investment opportunities for Canadian-based business,

(2) to ensure that such economic development as does take place in the underdeveloped countries is firmly rooted in capitalist ways and practices,

(3) to obtain immediate economic gains for Canadian-based businessmen seeking trade and investment opportunities, and

(4) to make the aid recipients increasingly dependent on Canadian and other capital markets.

All of these propositions are very closely interrelated, and thus a degree of overlap will exist in regards to the evidence presented to substantiate them. For this reason the propositions are, in a couple of instances, discussed in pairs. This helps facilitate the presentation and examination of evidence.

The first and second propositions are very closely related, and therefore will be discussed together. Canada is a member, and active participant, in several multinational agencies and institutions, which ostensibly have as their objectives the distribution of funds and the implementation of strategies and policies directed toward the development of certain underdeveloped countries. These institutions include the International Bank of Reconstruction and Development (IBRD), or as it more commonly known, the World Bank, the International Development Association (IDA), the International Finance Corporation (IFC), both of which are affiliates of the World Bank. Canada, as well as being a founding member and architect of the World Bank, was also integrally involved with the creation and development of the International Monetary Fund (IMF). Canada is also involved with the United Nations, and the several committees and/or agencies of the United Nations that are concerned with the problems of underdevelopment, such as UNESCO and UNDP.

Teressa Hayter, in her book entitled *Aid as Imperialism*, goes into great detail in discussing the structure and policies of the World Bank and the closely affiliated IMF. In this work, which will not be summarized here, Hayter concludes that the World Bank has as its major concern the repayment of debt of the underdeveloped countries, and the maintenance of the existing capitalist economic order (Hayter, 1971: 32).

The IMF, the World Bank and the associated organizations of IDA and the IFC are very closely related in terms of co-ordination of activities and long and short-term goals, although they are formally separate institutions. The degree of interrelatedness extends from close physical proximity of head offices in Washington, D.C., to the existence of interlocking directorships [see H.D. Dickinson, *Canadian Foreign Aid and the Developmental Process of The Commonwealth Caribbean*, unpublished M.A. thesis, Department of Sociology, University of Saskatchewan, 1978, for a more detailed discussion of the interrelationship]. Of the directors who represent the major capitalist nations in these organizations, the five who represent the United States, the United Kingdom, the Federal Republic of Germany, France and Japan are appointed, and control a total of 42.97 percent of the voting power in the IMF. If one adds the voting power of Canada to that of the previously mentioned five directors from the IMF, who also hold appointments at the World Bank, this accounts for a majority of the voting power of the World Bank.

As of 1975 the appointed members of the Boards of Directors of the World Bank and the IMF have two overlapping directors, William S. Byrie of the United Kingdom, and Jacques Henri Wahl of France. It should also be noted that Jacques de Groote, the elected director from Belgium, also sits on the Board of Directors of both institutions.

If this inspection of the key decison makers of these international organizations is continued it will be found that the representatives from Canada on the Boards of Governors of IDA and the IFC are the same men. Canada's representative in both cases is Donald S. Macdonald (former Liberal Cabinet Minister), and a recently admitted member to David Rockefeller's Trilateral Commission, (an organization whose express goal is the representation of the economic interests of the multinational corporations). The alternate to Donald Macdonald in the IDA and IFC is Paul Gerin-Lajoie, the president of the Canadian International Development Agency (CIDA).

Another feature of these multinational agencies is that they have been structured in such a way that one member country does not simply get one vote. Rather the decision making structure is such that there are now 20 directors, most of them representing a variety of countries, and some of them representing up to 20 countries, with voting rights based on the proportion of capital subscribed by the country of origin of the directors. Thus the original architects of the so-called Bretton Woods institutions of which Canada was a founding member, were able to create a form of world government which does not have an equitable representation structure.

Canada is also a member of the Organization for Economic Co-operation and Development which was established in 1960. Other members of OECD are Australia, Austria, Belgium, Denmark, Finland, France, the Federal Republic of Germany, Greece, Iceland, Ireland, Italy, Japan, Luxembourg, The Netherlands, New Zealand, Norway, Portugal, Spain, Sweden, Switzerland, Turkey, the United Kingdom and the United States. The OECD has as its objectives the promotion of policies designed

> . . . — to achieve the highest sustainable economic growth and employ-
> ment and a rising standard of living in member countries, while
> maintaining financial stability, and thus to contribute to the develop-
> ment of the world economy;

— to contribute to sound economic expansion in member as well as non-member countries in the process of economic development;

— to contribute to the expansion of world trade on a multilateral, non-discriminatory basis in accordance with international obligations (OECD, 1976: preface).

In an attempt to help achieve these objectives the OECD has set up specialized committees. One of these committees is the Development Assistance Committee (DAC). This committee consists of representatives from all of the member countries except Greece, Iceland, Ireland, Luxembourg, Portugal, Spain and Turkey. In addition, the Commission of the European Economic Communities is represented.

The membership of OECD and especially DAC leads to the conclusion that the goals and policies of this organization, like those of the World Bank Group and the IMF, are firmly rooted in the capitalist system. Although capitalism is portrayed by many theorists as being the embodiment of "free" trade, which, according to these same theorists, is the "natural" process that is guided and controlled by Adam Smith's invisible hand of the market, it is becoming ever more difficult for these intellectual workers to adhere to this explanatory system in the face of logical and empirical evidence, although some are very tenacious in their adherence to this doctrine. Hence one finds such contradictory and nonsensical statements as the following, which appeared in the 1976 Annual Report of the Development Assistance Committee:

> There is a growing realization that international economic relations cannot be entirely governed by mechanisms which operate on principles of complete automaticity. The 'hidden hand' of price adjustments operating in free and open markets is the most efficient mechanism known to man for the allocation of resources. But in selective areas, where intervention is of crucial importance to world economic health and stability, governments acting in concert must be prepared to assure that markets are structured to meet their common objectives. (DAC Annual Report, 1976: preface).

Statements such as this point out very clearly the dilemma faced by those in capitalist organizations who are trying to cope with problems of underdevelopment and yet still maintain the prevailing socio-economico-politico order, or, to put it in the words of the DAC Report, to maintain "world economic health and stability". It is clear that the "most efficient mechanism known to man for the allocation of resources", i.e., the "hidden hand of the free and open market", which should bring about the development of the underdeveloped world, is not the most efficient mechanism for the allocation of resources from the point of view of the DAC members. Rather, these representatives of the most powerful capitalist countries are concerned with insuring "that markets are structured to meet their

common objectives", which do not embrace the most efficient allocation of resources.

The dilemma is now clear. The world capitalist powers, in order to
achieve their common objectives, must interfere with the workings
of that mysterious "hidden hand" which they claim would most
efficiently take care of the allocation of resources, and hence they
are interfering with the development of the now underdeveloped
countries. If "governments, acting in concert must be prepared to
assure that markets are structured to meet their common objectives"
in an attempt to maintain world economic order, then it must be
concluded that the common objectives of certain world governments
(DAC members) are based on an inefficient allocation of resources,
and surely it is clear that this inefficient allocation of resources
is at the root of underdevelopment.

The maintenance of the prevailing economic order is achieved in
part through the aid-administering operation of these multilateral
agencies. Control and domination is also achieved through the extension of bilateral aid, which is aid administered on a direct govern-
ment-to-government basis. Education is a field which figures
predominately in Canadian bilateral and multilateral aid, and it is to
this area that attention will now be turned.

One way of looking at the role that education plays in the maintenance and perpetuation of the capitalist system is evidenced by
the following simplified conception of ideology. Richard Lichtman
points out that

> ... [p]ower over material production confers power over the production
> of consciousness. The ruling class exercises its power to distort
> consciousness through its control over the means of intellectual
> production — schools, churches, the daily press, etc. (Lichtman, 1975:
> 54).

Although such a conspiracy type explanation may have some
validity, it is not an adequate explanation by itself. Recourse must
be had to a theoretical explanation of the relationship which exists
between the day to day lives of people, (i.e., their existential conditions), and the conceptions of reality and expectations for social
interaction that arise from their incorporation within a given social
structure (i.e., expected patterns of social interaction). If consciousness is simply a reflection of the objective existential conditions
which confront people, then it becomes impossible to explain the
existence of false consciousness, or mistakes in people's perceptions
of that social reality. However, Lichtman has pointed out that the
social relations of capitalist commodity production themselves are
inherently mystifying. To put it in his own words he states that
". . . the mystification of consciousness is viewed as ingredient in

and constitutive of economic exploitation through whose agency it influences the remainder of conscious life" (Lichtman, 1975: 56).

The education system is a major mechanism by which people are trained and prepared for the occupation of a position in the economic sphere of life. Thus there exists a close relationship between the education process and the mystification of consciousness that is 'ingredient in and constitutive of' economic exploitation. In this regard Lichtman has further pointed out that

> . . . productive forces cannot be isolated from social relations of production for the compelling reason that productive forces are not "things", but human beings, men and women *trained in the technical and social division of labor,* in the rules that inculcate deference to authority and subservience to class domination, as well as in the use of mechanical apparatus (Lichtman, 1975: 57).

From this perspective it can be seen that any attempt to separate the education process from the social relations of production is in fact reifying interrelated social processes. To put it another way, the intimately interrelated social processes of education and economic production are artificially separated from each other in an attempt to facilitate social analysis, and then these analytical, arbitrary categories are perceived to be a concrete representation of the social reality in the static form created for the purposes of analysis.

This reification of social processes is part and parcel of the creation of ideology which is the mystification of consciousness ingredient in and constitutive of economic exploitation. Having outlined the relationship between education, ideology and the social relations of production, the discussion will now be directed towards an outline of the role that Canadian Foreign Aid plays in the Commonwealth Caribbean. The 1975-1976 Annual Report of CIDA states that;

> Over the years hundreds of Canadian advisers and educators have served in the Caribbean on CIDA assignments and thousands of students and trainees from the West Indies have studied in Canada or in third world countries under CIDA auspices. On January 1, 1976 there were 40 advisers and educators in the region while 219 students and trainees were in Canada and 272 CIDA sponsored Caribbean students followed courses at the University of the West Indies and other institutions in the region.' (CIDA, 1977: 51)

The extent of CIDA's involvement in the education process of the Commonwealth Caribbean is further indicated by the following list of education and/or education-related projects that receive CIDA funds. In 1958, the beginning of Canada-West Indies Aid relations, a committment of $10 million was made, a large proportion of which was directed to education programs. Even after the collapse of the Federation in 1962, the date that it was supposed to achieve independence, Canada continued to support education programs on the individual islands. By 1966 CIDA had made a separate $5 million committment to the University of the West Indies. In 1977 the committments were as follows:

Jamaica
— In 1977 the final year of a four-year program to develop a technical teacher training department at the College of Arts, Science and Technology was begun. Funded with a $0.92 million grant and a $0.30 million loan, it involves provision of equipment, staffing assistance, and counterpart training. There are three advisers in Jamaica and five Jamaicans studying in Canada under this project.

— Four Canadian advisers are assisting Jamaica's Ministry of Education in the development of a technical vocational planning unit. This project is funded with a $350,000 grant.

— Construction of 42 schools has just been completed under a $2 million loan which was used to purchase structural steel. CIDA previously built 128 prefabricated primary schools with $1.5 million in grants.

Guyana
— The Guyana Electricity Corporation (GEC) was provided with $5.5 million worth of Canadian equipment to help expand its distribution network. Computed in the last year, this project is part of a multi-donor project costing $25 million. Canadian advisers have set up a training program for the GEC and training awards have been provided for GEC employees.

— Agreements have been signed for providing the country with a veterinary diagnostic laboratory; technical assistance and some equipment for an applied science institute which will be concerned with the national development of resources and in fisheries development study.

Belize
— A grant of $2.8 million to cover the cost of a Canadian project team leader, two engineers and an administrator and training of Belizeans. (The project is a water and sewer system for Belize City).

— A grant of $462,000 for road-building equipment, workshop tools and equipment and training related to the production of bananas.

— $1.193 million for various types of training in Canada.

Windward and Leeward Islands

— (Antigua, Dominica, Grenada, Montserrat, St. Kitts-Nevis, St. Lucia, St. Vincent.) These islands in the eastern Caribbean are considered LDC (least developed countries) under CIDA's Aid program.

— Construction of 20 primary and junior secondary schools and additions are being made possible by a grant of $10 million.

— Training of technical and vocational teachers is under way with a grant of $1 million. CIDA grants are also financing the training of animal health assistants ($275,000), public works technicians ($360,000), hotel staff ($115,000), and agricultural experts ($480,000).

— Construction of a large junior secondary school in St. Lucia was completed with a grant of $3.9 million and Canadian staff is being provided while local counterparts are being trained.

— $180,000 grant for curriculum and materials development in St. Lucia. The grant offers salaries of two specialists and cost of some equipment.

University of the West Indies

The regional institution is supported by 14 Caribbean governments and has campuses in Jamaica (Mona), Trinidad (St. Augustine), and Barbados (Cave Hill) and extension facilities in Dominica, Grenada, Montserrat, Antigua, St. Kitts, St. Lucia and St. Vincent.

Canada has assisted the university since the early sixties with grants, personnel and scholarships and has funded construction of student residences in Trinidad and Barbados and two faculty buildings in Trinidad and Jamaica. A CIDA-financed extension centre in Belize was completed recently.

A management studies program under a twinning arrangement with the University of Western Ontario and financed with a CIDA grant of $1 million was completed recently. The program is West Indian in content and environment. Another $0.6 million has been used to errect new buildings on the Jamaica and Trinidad campuses complete with classroom and office facilities; special course material have been developed and UWO professors are acting as consultants and teachers. Some 28 West Indian students have entered Western's Business School over a four-year period and are to return to the Caribbean as teachers.

The UWI also processed the 1970 census returns of various

Caribbean countries, using a computer supplied by Canada in 1971.Statistics Canada provided training and advisory assistance.

CIDA also financed construction of residences for the Marine Biology Laboratory at Discovery Bay, Jamaica ($320,000) and supports the examinations research unit to develop standards for school exams throughout the Caribbean ($237,000) (CIDA Background paper 1977: 2-12).

Viewed from the perspective of the theory of ideology it can be seen that education, technical assistance and training serve to perpetuate and reinforce the integration of underdeveloped countries into capitalist ways and practices. Long after the original aid commitments to these types of programs have been expended the effects of educational and training programs continue to exist. Once teachers and experts are trained into capitalist relations and methods the concomitant ideology of capitalist existence will be passed on from instructor to student, and the structure is maintained.

The third proposition that was taken from Magdoff states that foreign aid has the purpose and/or effect of obtaining immediate economic gains for Canadian-based businessmen seeking trade and investment opportunities. This is clearly related to the first proposition, i.e., the enforcement of the open-door policy, which has already been discussed. Thus any information used to support proposition three can also be used to support proposition one.

The preceding discussion of ideology, although useful and essential for an understanding of the problems of underdevelopment, is often quite abstract. Therefore attention will now be turned to an analysis of trade and investment patterns which exist between Canada and the countries of the Commonwealth Caribbean. In proportional terms Canada's trade with the countries of the Commonwealth Caribbean is quite insignificant, amounting to about 2 percent of Canada's total trade. However, one must not be lulled into the use of a simplistic quantitative explanation or interpretation of the importance of the amount of trade. Most of the trade of the underdeveloped countries with the developed capitalist metropoles, according to the theory of imperialism, should be in the area of raw materials from the underdeveloped regions in exchange for manufactured goods and food stuffs from the developed metropoles. The 1975-1976 Annual Report of CIDA describes Canadian Caribbean trade and investment relations in the following way:

> . . . [In] addition to strong trading ties and agreements, private Canadian investment holdings in the Caribbean exceed half a billion

dollars. Banking, insurance, bauxite extraction and processing, travel and tourism are among Canadian interests (CIDA, 1977:51).

Although the amount of trade as measured in dollars is small, this does not give a true representation of the importance of the trade. Aluminum, for example, which is produced from bauxite, is essential for the maintenance of the contemporary economic and political systems, for it is used as a conductor of electricity and it is presently essential for the production of both commercial and military aircraft.

The following table shows the exports of Canada to the Commonwealth Caribbean, and in accord with the theory of imperialism it is found that the content of this trade falls into three major categories: (1) Food, Feed, Beverages and Tobacco, (2) Fabricated Materials, Inedible, and (3) End Products, Inedible.

Table 1 presents the goods that are imported by Canada from the countries of the Commonwealth Caribbean. A look at this table indicates that most of the goods fall into the categories of: (1) Food, Feed, Beverages and Tobacco, and (2) Crude Materials, Inedible.

The theory of imperialism accurately predicts this content of the trade between a developed metropole like Canada and a more underdeveloped hinterland like the area that constitutes the Commonwealth Caribbean. The only possible exceptions to this generalization is the trade which exists between Canada and the Bahamas and Bermuda. However, this apparent discrepancy can be explained by making reference to the content of the trade flows of these two areas, and other parts of the developed capitalist world.

For example, Bermuda in 1974 imported about 78 percent of its import commodities from the USA, Puerto Rico, the Netherland Antilles. A full 84 percent of all imports came from 'developed market economies' or capitalist countries. This is down from about 95 percent in 1971. Bermuda in 1974 also exported 58 percent of its export commodities to developed market economies, which was down from 89 percent in 1971. This seems to indicate a move towards decreasing dependence on the developed capitalist economies.

The same general trend is evident in the statistics relating to the Bahamas. We see that in 1970 about 85 percent of the Bahamas imports came from developed market economies, particularly the United States, Puerto Rico and the United Kingdom, and about 15 percent came from developing market economies. In 1974 these figures have been reversed, with 82 percent of imports coming from developing market economies, especially Nigeria, Saudi Arabia and Iran, while about 18 percent come from developed market economies, especially the United States — Puerto Rico which account for 12 percent of that total. A look at the export figures show that the Bahamas exports about 96 percent of all its commodities to the developed market

TABLE 1
IMPORTS BY COUNTRY AND SECTION
January to September

COUNTRY	YEAR	Live Animals	Food, Feed, Beverages and Tobacco	Crude Materials, Inedible	Fabricated Materials, Inedible	End Products, Inedible	Special Transactions, Trade	All Sections	Year-to-Year Percentage Change	Proportion of Imports in Categories 2 and 3
Bahamas	1975	1	614	10,240	8,538	2,054	474	21,920		
	1976	4	1,276	240	5,188	1,658	95	8,462	-61.4	.24
	1977		1,235	40	1,493	2,347	125	5,240	-38.1	
Bermuda	1975	1	6	2	66	226	129	430		
	1976		6		127	364	138	636	47.8	.01
	1977		9	1	579	100	679	1,368	115.1	
Belize	1975		1,115	4	1	1	157	1,277		
	1976		1,149		1		4	1,155	-9.6	.99
	1977		562		3		3	567	-50.9	
Barbados	1975		4,387	3		595	376	5,361		
	1976		3,049	4	29	1,064	109	2,254	-20.7	.56
	1977		2,731	4	109	1,875	129	4,848	14.0	
Guyana	1975	58	1,490	7,317	5	243	48	9,162		
	1976	17	1,017	1,936	121	144	158	3,393	-63.0	.99
	1977		5,504	4,115	8	33	49	9,708	186.9	.99
Jamaica	1975		4,797	7,532	72	388	234	13,022		
	1976		4,811	4,780	62	1,612	595	11,860	-8.9	.97
	1977		20,460	19,183	72	1,000	347	41,061	246.2	
Leew.-Wind. Is.	1975		587			22	48	657		
	1976		439		3	19	7	469	-28.7	.80
	1977		325		7	44	29	405	-13.6	
Trinidad-Tobago	1975	13	3,974	1,917	10,422	160	77	16,562		
	1976	18	5,274	8,899	3,058	100	158	17,507	5.7	.76
	1977	19	5,012	29,388	10,555	56	155	45,186	158.1	

Source: *Trade of Canada: Imports by Countries Jan. - Sept. 1977.* (Ottawa: Statistics Canada, Dec. 1977). Vol. 34 - No. 3. Catalogue 65-006

TABLE 2
DOMESTIC EXPORTS BY COUNTRY AND CATEGORY
January to September

COUNTRY	YEAR	Live Animals	Food, Feed, Beverages and Tobacco	Crude Materials, Inedible	Fabricated Materials, Inedible	End Products, Inedible	Special Transactions, Trade	All Sections	Year-to-Year Percentage Change	Proportion of Exports in Categories 2, 4, and 5
Bahamas	1975		5,550	178	532	3,553	241	10,055		
	1976		4,754	3,418	423	3,237	387	12,218	21.5	.99
	1977		3,966	3	314	3,653	43	7,979	-34.7	
Bermuda	1975	35	3,781	8	1,330	3,284	116	8,554		
	1976	22	3,207	7	1,021	10,269	657	15,184	77.5	.99
	1977	5	2,774	9	1,008	3,569	65	7,431	-51.1	
Belize	1975	4	384		470	1,054	50	1,962		
	1976		241	4	195	776	128	1,343	-31.6	.99
	1977		106	8	224	823	1	1,162	-13.5	
Barbados	1975	15	3,676	34	2,396	3,650	110	9,881		
	1976	20	3,942	45	3,519	3,529	388	11,444	15.8	.99
	1977	9	3,289	69	3,772	4,984	22	12,146	6.1	
Guyana	1975		811	24	4,221	4,844	577	10,477		
	1976	—	909	45	4,258	3,730	273	9,216	-12.0	.97
	1977		282	181	1,492	4,833	2	6,789	-26.3	
Jamaica	1975	18	11,758	425	11,915	14,383	163	38,663		
	1976	65	8,706	17	10,968	11,199	430	31,384	-18.8	1.0
	1977	9	11,285	29	6,513	7,616	38	25,489	-18.8	
Leew.-Wind. Is.	1975		6,746	10	3,078	1,910	81	11,826		
	1976		4,541	17	1,951	1,908	956	9,372	-20.8	.91
	1977		4,920	52	4,468	4,602	1,318	15,359	63.9	
Trini-dad-Tobago	1975	15	6,638	105	10,026	6,071	181	23,021		
	1976		11,225	28	9,236	5,823	384	26,710	16.0	1.0
	1977	21	17,544	34	13,616	8,012	36	39,262	47.0	

Source: Trade of Canada: Exports by Countries, January-September 1977. (Ottawa: Statistics Canada, December, 1977). Vol. 34 - No. 3 Catalogue 65-003 Quarterly.

economies, with the United States — Puerto Rico accounting for 90 per cent of this total. This is about the same as it was in 1970.

Table 3 of the Bahamas and Bermuda illustrates that the theoretically expected content of trade flows does in fact hold in general, even though it does not hold as far as the specific case of Canada is concerned.

It was seen (Table 1) that virtually all of the countries of the Commonwealth Caribbean import a substantial proportion of their total imports from the Food, Feed, Beverages and Tobacco Category. A partial explanation of this fact lies in the control and utilization of agricultural land which characterizes most of the world's underdeveloped colonial and ex-colonial countries. The exports of these areas are often concentrated in one or two commodities, and quite often the commodities are agricultural goods. This is the case in most of the countries of the Commonwealth Caribbean. During colonial times all of the prime agricultural land was organized into plantations for the growing of export crops, especially sugar and tropical fruits. These agricultural commodities have remained an integral part of the islands' economies and hence the best agricultural land is not available for growing food for domestic use, with the result that food must be imported while at the same time agricultural products for foreign markets dominate the area's exports.

This general condition of most underdeveloped countries is further aggravated in the Caribbean due to the fact that the islands also support a large tourist industry. Robert Chodos in his book *The Caribbean Connection* points out that:

> The tourist industry is notoriously dependent on imports — especially the kind of tourist industry prevalent in the Caribbean. Tourists are served steaks flown in from Miami, Idaho potatoes, French wine and Scotch whisky. Before it has had a chance to multiply most of the tourist revenue has left the country. Some of it, such as money siphoned off by a foreign hotel owner from his share of a package tour price paid in North America, never even enters the country (Chodos, 1977: 174).

This problem, of tourism not bringing much money into the host country's economy on which the multiplier effect can operate, is further magnified by the expatriation of profits by the foreign owned tourist hotels. The tourist industry, although it is supposed to bring money into the host economy, also serves to increase and perpetuate the problems of dependency and subservience to the developed metropoles. This is so because the tourist industry requires, especially in relatively inaccessible places like the Caribbean Islands, great expenditures on infrastructure projects. For example, Chodos states that:

TABLE 3
TRADE OF THE BAHAMAS AND BERMUDA FOR 1974
(thousands of $US)

Imports

Commodity, Category and Country	Quantity	Percentage of Total Imports
Bahamas		
Food and Live Animals	65,618	.034
Beverages and Tobacco	13,476	.007
Minerals Fuels etc.	1,594,409	.84
Chemicals	37,582	.019
Basic Manufacturers	72,428	.037
Machines, Transportation Equip.	68,770	.036
Misc. Manufactured Goods	44,388	.023
Total		.99
Bermuda		
Food and Live Animals	35,000	.23
Mineral Fuels Etc.	20,291	.13
Basic Manufacturers	21,813	.14
Machines, Transportation Equip.	25,583	.165
Misc. Manufactured Goods	30,238	.195
Total		.86

Exports

Commodity, Category and Country	Quantity	Percentage of Total Exports
Bahamas		
Beverages and Tobacco	13,853	.009
Crude Materials excluding Fuels	10,610	.007
Mineral Fuels etc.	1,320,791	.91
Chemicals	51,648	.035
Total		.96
Bermuda		
Mineral Fuels etc.	9,493	.276
Chemicals	16,307	.475
Total		.75

Source: Yearbook of International Trade Statistics 1975 Vol. I, Trade by Country (New York: United Nations, 1975).

Antigua is arguably, the country most seriously ravaged by tourism. The tourist industry developed less because of any inherent advantages of the island than because the big jets from North America could land at the airstrip the Americans had built to serve their military needs during World War II (Chodos, 1977: 174-175).

This brings us back to the role of Canadian foreign aid to these islands. With regards to this Baum states that:

> Foreign aid has often funded the infrastructure — the airports, the roads, the water, the electricity services — needed for tourism. Without the initial heavy capital expenditures needed for an infrastructure, tourism could only be a marginal industry on any island, for the means would not be there to serve and attract great numbers of people. And the basic fact of a lack of capital to provide such finding is true of all the islands, especially the smaller islands that do not have any but a single-line economy, namely agriculture. Without foreign aid funding the necessary infrastructure, tourism could not exist as an industry (Baum, 1974: 98).

The following quotation from Allan J. MacEachen, who was Secretary of State for External Affairs and Minister responsible for International Development, brings to light the government's perception of the role of foreign aid. He states that "the development projects we help to launch . . . are typically those that are uneconomical for private investors — and yet must be undertaken to make other projects possible or profitable" (MacEachen, 1975).

Looking to the historical data that is presented in the works of Dobbs and Mandel, it is found that capital originating in the second half of the nineteenth century from the developed countries of Europe, such as Britain, France, Belgium and Holland, was concentrated in railway construction. Mandel explains this by pointing out that

> . . . the extension of this world-wide communications network was a precondition for the gradual extension of their domination over the internal markets of the less developed countries which had been drafted into the malestrom of the capitalist world economy (Mandel, 1975: 51).

Technology has advanced greatly since the second half of the nineteenth century, and the forms of communications systems that are now necessary to control a market or source of raw materials has expanded. Hence, infrastructure investments are no longer concentrated in railway construction. Capital is now invested in airports, electricity generation, port facilities, telecommunications, roads etc. Though the content of capital investment may have changed, the reasons and effects of this investment have remained the same within the capitalist system.

The infrastructure projects that Baum points out as being necessary for tourism as an industry to develop are precisely the same forms of capital intensive projects that are necessary, and always have been necessary, for successful capitalist enterprise.

The following list of CIDA sponsored projects in the Caribbean gives an idea of the extent to which infrastructure projects take up Canadian foreign aid, and the extent to which these programs provide 'trade and investment opportunities for Canadian based business'.

Jamaica
— Phase four of the bridge rebuilding program got underway early in 1976 with a loan of $1.6 million for the supply of Canadian steel and related equipment. The earlier phases resulted in construction of 26 bridges and involved loans of $18 million.

— The Sugar Industry Research Institute was provided with a $125,000 grant for an operations research study to improve the transport of sugar cane from field to factory.

— A $425,000 project involving improvements to the engineering workshop of the Jamaica Railway Corporation has just been completed. The project was carried out by CANAC Consultants Ltd. of Montreal.

— Jamaica's Ministry of Communications has been provided with seven engineers to assist in the implementation of their road and bridge building program. The project was financed by a $750,000 grant.

— Advisers are also participating in assistance to the operations management of the Jamaica Airport Authority at a cost of ($80,000).

— A loan of $2.5 million has been made available to the Jamaican Development Bank for lending to entrepreneurs who wish to purchase goods and services in Canada.

— A $10 million development line credit has been made to the Ministry of Finance to purchase Canadian goods and services for specific development projects in the agriculture and manufacturing sectors.

— Assistance to the Ministry of Communications and works and the Central Data Processing Unit (CDPN) in the development of: —
(1) Management information systems (MCU) and (2) electronic data processing policy and the operation of a government unit. P.S. Ross is the consultant involved and currently has four advisers in Jamaica ($980,000 grant).

Guyana

— Under an agreement signed in May, 1977, Canada is providing the country with a $7 million loan at 0/10/50 and a grant of $1.25 million to help develop its forest industry. The Guyana Agricultural Co-operative Development Bank administers the fund and provides loans to Guyanese forestry producers to purchase Canadian logging, sawmilling and road building equipment. Proceeds of loan repayments by Guyana producers will be reinvested in the forestry sector for 15 years. The goal is to double the production of the forestry sector within five years. The grant covers the cost of technical assistance to the Guyana Forest Department. Eight Canadian advisers in forestry related subjects will help the department develop a long-term system for managing the countries forest which covers more that 80 percent of the land area. Technical assistance is also being provided to Guyana Timbers Ltd., the largest sawmilling firm in the country. This program is the largest commitment by Canada to Guyana in 13 years of development co-operation.

— The Guyana Electricity Corporation (GEC) was provided with $5.5 million worth of Canadian equipment to help expand its distribution network.

— Four navigation beacons were installed at Timehri International Airport and additional landing aids were being provided. The Guyana Air Corporation received $145,000 worth of freight handling equipment.

— Two water drilling rigs and ancillary equipment worth $1 million have been provided.

Belize

— Canada's major contribution to the country in the past year was provision of a loan of $7.9 million for construction of a water and sewer system for Belize City to meet demands for at least a decade beyond its completion date around 1980. A grant of $2.8 million covers the cost of a Canadian project team leader, two engineers and an administrator and training of Belizeans, while another for $679,000 was for engineering services.

— $2 million loan to the Belize Development Finance Corporation (DFC) to be loaned to private borrowers in agricultural, industrial or tourist development; a grant of $200,000 was made to the DFC for technical assistance;

— A $300,000 line of credit was opened to enable the Belize Government to purchase material and equipment in Canada;

— A grant of $462,000 for road-building equipment, work shop tools and equipment and training related to production of bananas;

— $197,800 for purchase and equipment for an airport.

Barbados
— The largest Canadian development project in Barbados is the modernization and expansion of the Granteley Adams International Airport under a $10 million CIDA loan. Construction was begun in January, 1977 supervised by International Airport Consultants of Montreal and completion was scheduled for the end of 1978.

— Expansion of the Island's water system is being carried out under a $3.5 million loan, largely used for purchase of pipes and equipment in Canada.

Windward and Leeward Islands — (Antigua, Dominica, Grenada, Montserrat, St. Kitts-Nevis, St. Lucia and St. Vincent)
— These islands in the Eastern Caribbean are considered as LDCs (least developed countries) under CIDA's development assistance program. Aid to the islands is concentrated in agriculture, transport, water development and education. The major input to date has been in the development of the airport facilities of the islands. Airports are vital to one of the major growth industries — tourism. A $12 million grant was allotted in 1975-76 for an airport expansion program to meet current and projected demand until 1983. The funds will be spent on improving airport facilities in most of the islands with the largest share, $6.9 million, going to Coolidge International Airport in Antigua.

— The airport program includes architectural, engineering, construction, supervision and administration costs. Canadian contractors undertake the designing.
Sharing the funds are: St. Vincent, $665,000 for a new air terminal building and runway resurfacing; Montserrat, $131,000 for an extension to the air terminal building and related improvements; St. Lucia, a $3,350,000 air terminal building was completed in 1975 and a further $1 million spent in 1977 to resurface the runway; St. Kitts-Nevis, $2.5 million to expand the air terminal building at Golden Rock Airport and $250,000 to resurface the runway at Newcastle Airport.

— Various phases of water development programs were carried

on in all of the islands under grants and loans totalling about $12 million.

Trinidad and Tobago
— Canada's major recent contribution to the development of Trinidad and Tobago has been the supply of $2.3 million worth of equipment under a development loan for the country's rural electrification program.

— $220,000 worth of equipment for the Trinidad and Tobago Metal Industries Company;

— $500,000 feasibility study for the Port of Spain arterial highway.

Among other contributions provided through development loans are:
— $500,000 worth of hospital equipment (CIDA, *Background Paper*, 1977: 2-11).

This information shows how much Canadian aid goes into infrastructure projects, which makes it possible for Canadian based businessmen to realize a greater return on their investments. This data can also be shown to be a source of immediate economic return to Canadian based businessmen. This point will be returned to later.

The following quotation by A.H. Zimmerman, Vice-President and comptroller of Noranda Mines and the President of Northwood Pulp and Timber Ltd., gives a clear insight into the perception that is held of Canadian foreign aid, as administered under by the present structure, by multinational corporations:

> Concerning Foreign Aid, I have good reason to feel that the new management of this important federal department has recognized the need for closer relations with industry and that the machinery will be put together to eventually give the Canadian small and medium sized exporter the same advantages as enjoyed by his U.S. counterpart (Zimmerman, 1973: 71).

The business community should well be pleased with the assistance that is offered them by the present CIDA structure. It is stated in the 1975-76 Annual Review of CIDA that:

> An important feature of Canada's continuing efforts to broaden its relations with developing nations is the action taken to encourage private industry to play a greater role in international cooperation (CIDA, 1977: 80).

The document goes on to say that:

The more advanced developing countries, those with annual *per capita* incomes of $350 or more, are likely to offer the best returns on Canadian investment because most have acquired the minimum of infrastructure, such as roads and energy sources, required for industrial growth (CIDA, 1977: 80).

This applies to most countries in the Commonwealth Caribbean, with the exception of some of the very small islands of the Leeward and Windward group. It is especially likely that private investment will yield 'the best returns' when the necessary infrastructure is developed and paid for through Canadian foreign aid, which comes from public funds.

Canadian Foreign Investment in the Commonwealth Caribbean

Although one constantly hears of the problems created by foreign investment in Canada, the Canadian based business community itself has prodigious investments abroad. According to the latest figures available from Statistics Canada we see that the book value of Canada's direct investment abroad at the end of 1975 amounted to $10,674 million, an increase of $1,367 million or about 15 percent over that recorded a year earlier (Statistics Canada, Dec. 12, 1977: 12). By far the greatest proportion of that investment is in the United States, with a total of $5.680 million or 53 percent of the total of Canadian direct investment abroad being invested there. An increase of $40 million brought direct investment in all other North American countries, including those in the Caribbean, to $929 million, of this $854 million was invested in the countries of the Caribbean. This represents 8 percent of the total. Table 4 shows Canadian direct investment abroad by location of investment.

Table 5 gives a breakdown of Canadian direct investment in the Western Hemisphere (excluding the U.S.A.) by industry between 1973 and 1975 inclusive.

One of the advantages of direct foreign investment is that control lies in the hands of the investor, in this case the Canadian based business community. This means that the profits, interest, dividend payments etc. resulting from the investment can be realised in the home country. One of the disadvantages is that if the economic and/or political climate of the foreign country is not suitable (stable) the whole of the investment can be lost along with all of the profits and benefits such as sale of parts and servicing, extra business generated, etc., which accrue to the country of origin of the original investment.

TABLE 4
CANADIAN DIRECT INVESTMENT IN THE CARIBBEAN
AND WESTERN ATLANTIC ISLANDS* YEAR ENDS 1971-1975
(millions of dollars)

Location	1971	1972	1973	1974	1975
Commonwealth:					
Bahamas	143	160	178	181	142
Bermuda	190	258	351	424	462
Jamaica	113	110	114	105	118
Trinidad & Tobago	4	3	16	18	24
Barbados	4	6	5	8	6
Other	12	8	7	7	9
Sub-total	466	545	671	743	761
Non-Commonwealth:	45	58	74	84	93
Total, Caribbean & Western Atlantic Islands	511	603	745	827	854

*North America and Caribbean excluding U.S.A. and Mexico
Source: *Balance of Payments Division* (Ottawa: Statistics Canada, February 23, 1978).

TABLE 5
CANADIAN DIRECT INVESTMENT IN THE WESTERN HEMISPHERE
(EXCLUDING U.S.A.)
BY INDUSTRY, 1973-75
(millions of dollars)

Industry group	Commonwealth Developing			Non-Commonwealth Developing			Total		
	1973	1974	1975	1973	1974	1975	1973	1974	1975
Manufacturing	44	42	29	225	277	356	269	319	385
Merchandising	38	42	46	1	3	1	39	45	47
Petroleum	38	36	70	6	6	12	44	42	82
Mining	89	108	83	96	113	148	185	221	231
Other*	466	519	539	713	818	879	1,179	1,337	1,418
Total	675	747	767	1,041	1,217	1,396	1,716	1,964	2,163

*Includes utilities, financial and "other" industries.
Source: *Balance of Payments Division* (Ottawa: Statistics Canada, Feb. 23, 1978).

The EDC

The Canadian government is cognizant of the above problem, and has taken actions to assuage any fears that might lead to a reduction of foreign investment by the Canadian based business community. The steps taken by the Canadian government have resulted in the formation of the Export Development Corporation (EDC). The predecessor of the EDC, the Export Credits Insurance Corporation was established in 1945, the same year that many other international agencies that were previously discussed were established.

The EDC is a financially self-sustaining Canadian Crown Corporation established to facilitate and develop export trade by the provision of insurances, guarantees, loans and other financial facilities. The EDC offers:

— Export Credits Insurance, to insure Canadian firms against non-payment when Canadian goods and services are sold abroad;

— Long-term Loans to foreign buyers of Canadian capital equipment and technical services;

— Guarantees to financial institutions against losses incurred in financing either the Canadian supplier or the foreign buyer in an export transaction;

— Foreign Investment Guarantees to insure Canadians against loss of their investment abroad by reason of political action (EDC, 1976: Introduction).

All persons carrying on business in Canada are eligible to benefit from the services offered by the Export Development Corporation. Export loans are made under the authority of the Corporation's Board of Directors, and at the risk of the Corporation, which is a Crown Corporation. In special circumstances deemed to be in the "national interest" loans of up to $850 million may be made under the authority of and at the risk of the Canadian Government. Once made these loans are administered for the government by the EDC. The Export Development Act which was amended in 1974, provides up to $4.25 billion for loans and guarantees authorized by the Export Development Corporation's Board of Directors (EDC, 1976: 7).

The EDC has been expanding its support for Canadian based exports and investment abroad dramatically over the years. For example, in 1975 financial support of exports from Canada, in the form of loans, insurance and guarantees totalled $2.046 billion. This constituted a 20 percent increase over the $1.701 billion of the preceding year, 1974 (EDC, 1976: 4).

The Annual Report goes on to point out that during its 30 years of existence the corporation has supported more than $10 billion worth of export business — half of this within the last five years. In 1975 the EDC was serving 'this crucial area of national interest' by providing insurance, guarantees, loans and other financial facilities for more than 10 percent of all Canada's overseas exports.

There are several major spheres of interest of the EDC. The first of these is to help make Canadian-produced goods competitive on the world market. This is done through the activities of the Export

Loans Division. EDC makes long-term loans usually in some relationship with Canadian banks or other financial institutions. These loans, although they are made to a foreign buyer, are never actually in the recipient's control. The funds are dispersed directly to the Canadian exporter.

In order to receive such a loan the export transaction must involve the export of capital goods and related services which justify a repayment term normally in excess of five years. The project must be commercially viable and achieve maximum Canadian content in terms of labour and materials as determined by the EDC. The EDC also stipulates that there should be economic or other benefits to the buyer or buyer country.

The total amount loaned by the EDC since its inception is $2,933 million, and the amount of signed agreements outstanding net of repayments was $2,529 million. $344.9 million was dispersed to Canadian based exporters during 1975, and $81.1 million was received in principal payments from borrowers. The Canadian banking industry is also beginning to take a more active role in the activities of the EDC. In 1975 the Canadian banking industry extended $200 million in loans to foreign borrowers who wished to purchase goods from the Canadian based capital goods industries (EDC, 1976: 8).

Since 1961 the Export Development Corporation has made the following loans to countries of the Commonwealth Caribbean (See also Table 6):

Bahamas	$19.067 million
Barbados	$ 9.527 million
Bermuda	$73.075 million
Guyana	$ 5.200 million
Jamaica	$29.604 million

Source: *Export Development Corporation 1975 Annual Report*

Another major aspect of the EDC's activities is carried out by the Export Credits Insurance Division. This branch of EDC insures Canadian exporters against non-payment when they grant credit to foreign buyers under contracts involving the following classes of export transactions:

— Consumer goods sold on short-term credit usual for the particular trade, and which normally ranges from documentary sight draft to a maximum of 180 days;

— Capital goods such as heavy machinery sold on medium-term credit which may extend to a maximum of five years;

TABLE 6

CANADIAN EXPORT FINANCING TO THE CARIBBEAN ARRANGED
FROM JANUARY 1, 1975 TO DECEMBER 31, 1975
Under the Authority of the Board of Directors of the EDC

Country	Borrower	Products Financed	Principal Exporter	Repayment Terms	Amount of Financing (Millions of Dollars)
Bahamas	The Incorporated Trustees of the Church of England in the Bahamas	Modular components and Services for construction of a college	EBS Systems Ltd.	20 s.a. 6 months after completion but not later than June 30, 1977	2.0
Barbados	The Barbados Telephone Company Ltd.	Telephone Equipment and Services	Northern Electric Company Ltd.	20 s.a. 6 months after delivery but not later than March 15, 1976	1.2
Bermuda	Shell Bermuda (overseas) Ltd.	Six 31,250 metric ton oil tankers	Saint John Shipbuilding and Drydock Co. Ltd.	14 s.a. 6 months after delivery	110.9

Source: *Export Development Corporation 1975 Annual Report* (Ottawa: EDC, 1975).

— Services such as the supply of design, engineering, construction, technological, and marketing services to a foreign customer; photogrammetric and geophysical surveys, etc.;

— "Invisible" exports such as the sale or licensing to a foreign customer of any rights in a patent, trademark or copyright advertising fees, fees to auditors, architectural consultants etc.;

The main risks that are covered by an EDC insurance policy are:

— Insolvency of the foreign buyer;

— Failure of the buyer to pay the exporter within six months after due date the gross invoice value of the goods which he has duly accepted;

— Repudiation by the buyer which does not result from a breach of contract by the exporter and where proceedings against the buyer would serve no useful purpose;

— Blockage of funds or transfer difficulties which prevent the Canadian exporter from receiving payment;

— War or revolution in the buyer's country;

— Cancellation or non-renewal of an export permit and the imposition of restrictions on the export of goods not previously subject to restriction;

— Any other cause outside the control of both the exporter and the buyer which arises from events occurring outside Canada and the continental United States of America (EDC, 1976: 15).

More Canadian exports were insured under this program in 1975 than in any previous year. The volume of business insured by EDC on its own account in 1975 was $878,902,000 exceeding by more than $100 million the previous high set in 1974. The Government of Canada also underwrote a total of $31,797,000 which was administered by EDC. This figure shows a marked drop from the previous year's total of $160,590,000, largely the result of improved wheat markets. Of the total amount insured by EDC, $726,457,000 pertained to exports of consumer goods and services, and the balance, $152,445,000, pertained to capital goods and related services. Fully 10 percent of the actual credit insurance risks underwritten during 1975 were for the Central American/Caribbean area. The following table gives the breakdown for the Caribbean area.

TABLE 7
ACTUAL CREDITS INSURANCE RISKS UNDERWRITTEN
DURING 1975 BY COUNTRY
(thousands of dollars)

Country	Amount
Antigua	$ 300
Bahamas	1,351
Barbados	3,081
Belize	221
Bermuda	2,588
Guyana	3,862
Jamaica	12,619
St. Kitts	192
St. Lucia	340
St. Vincent	395
Trinidad-Tobago	9,504
Other	160
Total	$ 34,613

Source: *Export Development Corporation 1975 Annual Report* (Ottawa: EDC, 1975).

The following breakdown of the insured exports shows that about 88 percent of the commodities insured fall into the two categories Fabricated Materials, Inedible, and End Products, Inedible. This is precisely what one would expect based upon the theory of capitalist development which was briefly presented earlier.

Another aspect of EDC operations is meant to "insure Canadians against loss by reason of political actions. EDC insurance can cover expropriation, war or insurrection, or inconvertability, that is the inability to repatriate earnings or capital" (EDC, 1976: 21). These insurance policies can have a term of up to 15 years, and can only be cancelled by the investor, not EDC, as long as the contract conditions are maintained. The cost of this insurance to the investor is about two-thirds of one percent of the investment per annum.

The purpose of this insurance is to make Canadian based investors competitive with the nationals of other countries that have similar schemes. The following quotation taken from the 1975 Annual Report of EDC, indicates that even if the activities of the EDC are not able to make Canadian-based investors competitive on the world market in terms of prices charged, they must surely be in the forefront in terms of returns on investment.

With an aggregate maximum coverge of $70 million, 39 contracts of insurance have been signed up to December 31, 1975. These are in support of investment ranging from $45,000 to $14 million . . . Under the EDC program, all forms of investment and all industrial sectors are eligible for insurance cover. The major criteria determining support is that the investor maximize the benefits to Canada and the host country. Benefits to Canada from foreign investments insured under this program have proved to be substantial. For the $70 million of risks underwritten, there have been corresponding sales of $80 million in capital equipment and $140 million in technical services. On-going sales of components and raw materials will be $120 million, and dividends and interest to be repatriated to Canada are anticipated to be $110 million, for a total return to this country in excess of $450 million (EDC, 1976: 22).

A flow of funds in and out of underdeveloped countries such as depicted in the above quotation, i.e., $70 million in, $450 million out, seems to mitigate against economic, and social development— (see also Table 8).

The Caribbean region receives 23 percent of the investments insured under this program. This is the second largest proportion for a region, and is surpassed only by the 36 percent which goes to Asia. On a per capita basis EDC seems to insure a disproportionate amount of investment in the Caribbean region. If all the investments reap a 640 percent return to Canada, it is no surprise that the Caribbean with a population of about 4.5 million is underdeveloped. However, in terms of fulfilling its objectives the EDC is obviously an unqualified success.

The EDC makes this fact very clear in its own succinct analysis of the Foreign Investment Guarantees Insurance:

> Since the program started in 1971, the number of contracts in force has risen from four to 35 and the aggregate maximum coverage stands at $68.4 million, up from $43.5 million last year (1974). The immediate calculable return to Canada in sales of capital equipment, technical services, spare parts, raw materials and dividends and interest is expected to be more than $450 million. Put another way, each dollar of risk assumed will produce at least seven dollars worth of benefits to Canada, a major contribution to the nations balance of payments (EDC, 1976: 5).

Given that this is a benefit to Canada and a major contribution to the balance of payments, the recipient countries must be losing out, for if every Canadian dollar invested in some other country brings seven dollars back into Canada, every Canadian dollar invested also deprives the "recipient" country of at least seven dollars worth of benefit. As was previously pointed out, 23 percent of that insured investment is in the Commonwealth Caribbean totalling approximately $16 million worth of insured investment. This in turn generates about $112.7 million "worth" of benefits to Canada, which hardly seems conducive to the development of the Caribbean.

Thus it appears that the EDC has as its major goal the perpetuation, for the benefit (profit) of Canadian based business, the existing world economic order, i.e., the economic system which makes it profitable to the extreme to invest in "developing" countries. This is in opposition to the professed goals of CIDA which, in its public

TABLE 8
1975 EXPORTS INSURED BY COMMODITY
(thousands of dollars)

Commodity	Amount	Commodity	Amount
Live Animals		*Fabricated Materials, Inedible*	
Livestock	$ 5,836	Leather	$ 609
Other animals	94	Steel products	70,968
		Wood pulp	179,522
	$ 5,930	Wood and wood products	55,267
		Newsprint, paper &	
Food, Feed, Beverages, Tobacco		paper products	122,454
Wheat	$31,797	Chemicals	1,449
Flour, malt, cereals	9,758	Chemical products	20,934
Fruit & Vegetables	14,119	Aluminum products	280
Meat	4,091	Copper & products	2,727
Vegetable oils & Seeds	3,716	Other non-ferrous metals	23,675
Milk products	2,646	Refractory products	56
Fish	6,234	Fabrics, woven & other	18,109
Other food &		Asbestos products	171
agricultural products	5,459	Other fabricated materials	10,288
	$77,820		$506,509
Crude Materials, Inedible		*End Products, Inedible*	
Furs, dressed &		Autos, trucks & parts	$ 38,379
undressed	$ 711	Farm machinery	20,407
Hides & skins	1,132	Industrial machinery	66,779
Other crude animal		Locomotives	17,397
products	485	Measuring equipment	5,764
Iron ore & steel scrap	4,844	Marine equipment	1,557
Asbestos fibres	3,957	Communications &	
Other crude materials	8,651	related equipment	11,344
		Other electrical equipment	8,173
	$19,780	Personal & household goods	10,639
		Pharmaceuticals	2,554
		Aircraft & components	7,086
		Other end products	47,151
		Services	63,430
			$300,660
		Total	$910,699

Source: *Export Development Corporation 1975 Annual Report* (Ottawa: EDC, 1976).

statements, claims that it is precisely this economic system which
has brought about the crisis of underdevelopment that is the plight
of most of the earth's population. In a section of CIDA's Annual
Review entitled the *Origins of the International Imbalance* the
following is found:

> At the time of the Bandung Conference the industrialized nations
> were forced to realize, . . . with feelings of mingled fear and guilt,
> that the prevailing international order left two-thirds of humanity
> in a manifestly disadvantaged position . . .
>
> . . . The years to follow and further research into the matter would

lead to the even more dramatic findings: the underdevelopment of a large portion of humanity was directly related to the over-development of a minority of well-endowed nations. The analyses were categorical; the international economic order then prevailing caused injustice to the poorest countries (CIDA, 1977: 9).

This economic order, *i.e.*, the world capitalist system, still exists and as CIDA points out, after almost two UN Development Decades,

> . . . underdevelopment is now more pronounced than ever; it points up the major contradiction in international economic relations: accumulation of wealth by some, impoverishment or stagnation among the rest (CIDA, 1977: 13).

The activities of EDC, and the private business that EDC supports, perpetuate and extend the process of development-underdevelopment that is a result of the existing economic system. There are very powerful elements or interest groups in society that have representatives in government and other agencies that are very concerned with maintaining the existing structure intact. R. Harmston, Director of the Canada Council for International Cooperation, speaking before the House of Commons Subcommittee on International Development of the Standing Committee on External Affairs and National Defence on June 8, 1976 stated that:

> The very change of policies, particularly fundamental policies that we are talking about here, is going to take years. We of course are impatient for an accelerated progress. There are major forces in society that want either status quo or want a different sort of process and the large economic interests, I think, are very clearly among those. Certainly Industry, Trade and Commerce (IT and C) and Finance reflect those interests very clearly . . . (House of Commons, Issue No. 21 Doc. 16, sem #21, June 8, 1976).

EDC is a very successful enterprise in and of itself, and it too is one of those "major forces" and "large economic interests" that wish to maintain the *status quo*. Evidence as to the size of EDC's economic interests can be seen when it is known that in the 1975 fiscal year total gross revenues from loans, export credits insurance, foreign investment guarantees and interest on investments amounted to $87.389 million. This represents an annual record for EDC's operations, and is up 35 percent from the 1974 total of $64.659 million. Net earnings for this Crown Corporation also increased to $12.838 million, up from $11.585 million in the preceding year. This represents an 11 percent gain in corporate profitability. The Canadian government received $1.474 million as its share of earnings for programs undertaken by the corporation at the risk of the Government (EDC, 1976: 4-5).

The EDC also helps make investment more profitable for private enterprise, witness for example the return per dollar of capital investment abroad, *i.e.*, seven dollars of benefit for every dollar invested. Given that Harmston's analysis of the Ministries of IT & C and Finance is correct this should come as no surprise, for direction of EDC is vested in a twelve-member Board which is chaired by;

(1) the Deputy Minister of Industry, Trade and Commerce, and includes,

(2) the President of EDC,

(3) the Undersecretary of State for External Affairs,

(4) the Governor of the Bank of Canada,

(5) the Deputy Minister of Finance,

(6) the Senior Assistant Deputy Minister of Industry, Trade and Commerce.

(7) the President of the Canadian International Development Agency, all of Ottawa.

(8-12) the other five Directors are appointed from private industry (EDC: Introduction: 12).

Thus it seems reasonable to assume, given the evidence of EDC activities, and the composition of the Board of Directors, that EDC is among those that "want either a status quo or want a different sort of process. . .". The most interesting fact to come to light, however, is that the President of CIDA is one of the Directors.

CIDA and EDC ostensibly have contradictory mandates. As opposed to promoting and supporting private industry at home and abroad, CIDA's "primary role is to promote economic and social development, particularly among poorer developing countries. The EDC's mandate is to promote export of Canadian goods and services (CIDA, 1977: 99).

The activities of EDC are primarily concerned with maximizing the benefits to Canadian based industry, while CIDA is supposedly more concerned with maximizing the benefits, in terms of economic and social development, to the poorest of the underdeveloped countries. It is stated in the 1975-1976 Annual Review of CIDA that because both organizations are involved in the international transfer of resources, their objectives are complementary in many cases. Although it would seem that given the *stated* objectives of both organizations that their objectives could not be complementary, it is true that there is an overlap in some projects and a definite meshing in terms of others. This complementarity seems to favour the interests and goals of EDC and private enterprise.

CIDA and the Business Community

The 1977 CIDA Background Paper on the Commonwealth Caribbean lists several projects where CIDA funds are loaned or granted to a receiving nation or organization for the purchase of goods and services in Canada, from private Canadian based concerns. For example:

— A loan of $2.5 million has been made available to the Jamaican Development Bank for lending to entrepreneurs who wish to purchase goods and services in Canada.

— A $10 million development line credit has been made to the Ministry of Finance to purchase Canadian goods and services for specific development projects in the agriculture and manufacturing sectors.

— Under an agreement signed in May, 1977, Canada is providing the country with a $7 million loan at 0/10/50 and a grant of $1.25 million to help develop its forest industry. The Guyana Agricultural Cooperative Development Bank administers the fund and provides loans to Guyanese Forestry producers to purchase Canadian logging, sawmilling and road building equipment (CIDA, Background paper, 1977: 56).

The list of examples goes on and on, and has been previously outlined in the list of infrastructure projects that are funded by CIDA.

Many of the projects that CIDA finances intermesh with the interests of EDC and private investors insofar as the funds and expertise go into infrastructure projects, which by themselves are not profitable, but which are necessary to make other business and investment operations profitable. To requote Allan MacEachen, former Secretary of State for External Affairs and Minister responsible for International Development, regarding CIDA's activities in Asia and Africa, and equally applicable to the Caribbean, it can be seen that the developing projects that are launched by CIDA "are typically those that are uneconomical for private investors — and yet must be undertaken to make other projects possible or profitable" (MacEachen, 1975).

CIDA takes great pains to render assistance to the business community in terms of investment incentives and feasibility studies. In 1970 the Secretary of State for External Affairs announced a program "to provide incentives to Canadian businessmen seeking to invest in Third World countries. At that time CIDA's Business and Industry Division was created to administer the program. . ." (CIDA, 1977: 109). The purpose of this Division is to bring together investors from Canada and countries of the underdeveloped world. CIDA keeps a roster of Canadian firms interested in investing in underdeveloped countries and tries to match these firms with investment opportunities in particular countries. This is done in two major ways, as outlined by CIDA. The first way is to maintain contacts with the Trade Commissioners through the Canadian embassies in the underdeveloped countries, to maintain contact with foreign government representatives in Canada, and with local industrial development banks and businessmen. People in these offices are all in a position to understand the various investment climates and to be on top of commerical developments.

The other major method used by CIDA to help Canadian based investors get into the underdeveloped world is a more recent development and it consists of pilot projects by which consultants are sent to selected countries to identify possible industrial projects in which Canadian resources could be used (CIDA, 1977: 109).

Once a company or Canadian investor has expressed an interest in investing in an underdeveloped country the Business and Industry Division collects all the relevant data about the firm, such as, size, location, annual sales, line of production, total equity, capabilities and interests, and matches companies to potential investment opportunities.

The company is then eligible for financial assistance. CIDA states that:

> To be eligible for starter and feasibility study assistance, businesses must be at least 51 percent Canadian-owned. If a Canadian firm wishes to arrange a visit to a developing country, it can apply to the division for starter study assistance. Under this program a Canadian company is eligible for a grant of up to $2,500 to examine the investment opportunity on site by sending one or more representatives to the developing country. If the results of this preliminary study are positive, the firm may apply to undertake a feasibility study, which is more detailed investigation. Subject to guidelines established by the Treasury Board, the division can pay the lesser of $25,000 or 50 percent of the allowable costs of the study. After the feasibility study the firm should have enough information to decide whether or not it wishes to proceed with the investment. Apart from providing financial assistance, the division will also be able to provide assistance if the firm should encounter any difficulties in carrying out its feasibility study (CIDA, 1977: 109).

It is apparent from this that CIDA perceives at least part of its role to be the encouragement of private investment in underdeveloped countries. It is this investment, and the concomitant flow of resources out of the underdeveloped countries that have been identified, almost universally, as the major causal factor of underdevelopment. CIDA acknowledges the fact that it is the prevailing economic relationships between developed and underdeveloped countries that is the major cause of underdevelopment, as has been pointed out in previous quotations where it is identified that the existing economic order left two-thirds of humanity in a manifestly disadvantaged position, and also that the underdevelopment of some countries results directly from the overdevelopment of others (CIDA, 1977: 9).

Within this context it appears as though CIDA is trying to play two contradictory roles; (1) that of trying to provide "development assistance" that is going to result in independent economic development of the recipient countries (especially through the funding of infrastructure projects), and (2) that of providing information, financial and technical support and expertise for Canadian based businessmen who wish to profitably invest in Third World countries.

As has been argued throughout this study, it is precisely this type of investment relationship that has historically resulted in the underdevelopment of the "recipient" countries.

The efficacy of CIDA in achieving the first goal may be questioned if we note that:

> CIDA relies on private enterprise to implement most of the projects the agency plans, contracts for, and administers. Apart from its contributions to multilateral aid programs, *most of its budget goes to private contractors, consultants, suppliers and manufacturers in Canada,* (author's italics) (CIDA, 1977: 107).

From this quote alone it becomes evident that the Canadian foreign aid policy has the undeniable and clearly intended effect of providing "immediate economic gains for Canadian based businessmen seeking trade and investment opportunities" (proposition 3). Thus if we take CIDA at its word it ends up sounding more like it is fulfilling the mandate of the Export Development Corporation (EDC) than its own stated objective, which is:

> To support the efforts of developing countries in fostering their economic growth and the evolution of their social systems in a way that will produce a wide distribution of the benefits of development among the populations of these countries, enhance the quality of life and improve the capacity of all sectors of their population to participate in national development efforts (CIDA, 1977: 104).

The convergence or complementarity of CIDA's and EDC's actions and programs is not surprising if one looks at the decision-making structure of both organizations, and the composition of the Boards of Directors. The orientation of CIDA sponsored aid programs is decided by Cabinet based on the advice of the Secretary of State for External Affairs. The recommendations of the Secretary to Cabinet come from the President of CIDA who is assisted by a high-ranking interdepartmental committee, called the Canadian International Development Board, which he chairs (CIDA, 1977: 104-105).

The structure of this decision-making board, and the Board of Directors for the Export Development Corporation is as follows:

Canadian International Development Board; CIDA	Board of Directors; EDC
(1) The President of CIDA	(1) The President of CIDA
(2) The Under-Secretary of State for External Affairs	(2) The Under-Secretary of State for External Affairs
(3) The Deputy Minister of Finance	(3) The Deputy Minister of Finance
(4) The Deputy Minister of Industry, Trade and Commerce	(4) The Deputy Minister of Industry, Trade and Commerce (Chairperson)
(5) The Governor of the Bank of Canada	(5) The Governor of the Bank of Canada
(6) The Secretary of Treasury Board, and	(6) Senior Assistant Deputy Minister of Industry, Trade and Commerce
(7) The President of the International Development Research Centre.	(7) The President of EDC
	(8) Five Directors are appointed from Private industry.

It can be seen from looking at the composition of these two powerful organizations that both are dominated by what R. Harmston, the Director of the Canadian Council for International Co-operation, has called the representatives of major economic interests that want either a *status quo* or a different sort of (development) process, namely the Ministries of Industry, Trade and Commerce and Finance. One feels safe in stating that the Bank of Canada represents a bastion of conservatism in international relations.

This decision-making structure explains why Canadian foreign aid, in spite of all the public statements regarding its objectives and intentions, is firmly rooted in the traditional capitalist patterns of investment, and hence serves to perpetuate the conditions that it is ostensibly trying to eliminate. Thus it comes as no surprise that in the 1976 Annual Review CIDA is forced to conclude that "all in all, underdevelopment is now more pronounced than ever. . ." (CIDA, 1977: 13).

Proposition Four — Dependency of Underdeveloped Countries

Proposition number four, states that one of the effects of foreign aid is to make the receivers of aid "increasingly dependent on Canadian and other capital markets".

In the 1975-1976 fiscal year Canada's aid programme was split in the following manner:

TABLE 9

	Amount ($) (in millions)	Percentage of total
Bilateral (excluding bilateral) Food Aid)	406.39	45.0
Bilateral Food Aid	119.32	13.2
Multilateral Food Aid	103.32	11.4
Multilateral (excluding multilateral Food Aid)	215.34	23.9
Non-governmental Organizations	31.86	3.5
Other	.38	- -
International Development Research Centre	27.00	3.0
Total	903.51	100.0

Source: *Canada and Development Co-operation CIDA Annual Review, 1975-1976.*

Bilateral aid (including bilateral food aid) totalled $525.71 million dollars, or 58.2 percent of the total budget for 1975-1976. Although bilateral aid has fallen into disfavour Canada has a good reputation for the terms on which its grants aid. That is, in 1975 the terms of Canadian official development assistance (ODA) continued to be highly concessional, with grants constituting 96 percent of the overall commitments. Although most bilateral aid was tied to procurement in Canada, CIDA claims that a liberalization of these procurement conditions is now in sight, with the advantage shifting to the underdeveloped countries.

Although this may seem to belie the validity of the statement that foreign aid increases the dependence of the recipient countries, this perception is misleading. Even though Canadian "development assistance" is 'given' on easy terms, the principal itself is repayable, and in any event, as was shown earlier, this money never gets into the hands of the recipients for ". . . most of its (CIDA's) budget goes to private contractors, consultants, suppliers and manufactures in Canada".

The proportion of grants to loans that were distributed by CIDA in the 1975-1976 fiscal year was 63 percent to 37 percent. CIDA also provided over 90 percent of the loans according to the 0/10/50 formula.

This refers to a 0 percent interest charge, 10 years grace for repayment of the principal and 50 years to maturity. The remaining proportion of the loans were provided according to the 3/7/30 formula which indicates a 3 percent interest rate, 7 years grace for repayment of the principal, and 30 years to maturity (CIDA, 1977: 19).

These conditions and terms do in fact appear to be very concessional, but, as was explained above, the principal must be repaid, and thus adds to the overall debt burden of the underdeveloped countries. Even grants, although not so obviously creating dependence of the underdeveloped countries on the metropolitan capital markets, do create a dependency in terms of the knowledge, expertise, technology and need for replacement parts for machinery on the developed capitalist metropoles.

Even with this being the case, it is clear that Canadian aid is administered according to some of the most concessional terms of any DAC member country. However, even concessional terms are not enough to really help the poorest of the underdeveloped countries. In 1969, the Pearson Commission reported that the total debt of the underdeveloped countries, referred to euphemistically as "developing" countries, including both commerical and concessional flows, was in excess of $110 billion dollars. This report also goes on to point out that these countries are paying more than $11 billion a year to service that debt. This sum is more than all the new official development assistance of all industrialized countries combined.

The five years since 1969 have seen the situation worsen. The total reported outstanding debt of underdeveloped (developing) countries in 1974 was $118.321 billion. The servicing of that debt in 1974 totalled $15.623 billion. Tables 10 and 11 break this down by category of lender, and by income group of the "developing" countries.

It is quite clear from this that no matter how concessional CIDA's terms are, they will not solve the problems of indebtedness and underdevelopment of the underdeveloped countries. Simply to be able to service the existing debt the underdeveloped countries of the world must have recourse to the commercial lending institutions, which will further increase indebtedness. This process, if uninterrupted, perpetuates itself, and no matter how concessional the terms of a loan the principal must be repaid which strengthens dependence on the world's capital markets.

Shifting attention from the general to the specific, and concentrating for a moment on the Commonwealth Caribbean, it can be seen that since 1965-1966 Canadian Bilateral disbursements in the region have amounted to $175 million, including disbursements in the 1976-1977 fiscal year of $21.834 million (CIDA, Background Paper, 1977: 2). As a proportion of total Canadian aid this amounts to only about 4

TABLE 10
TOTAL REPORTED DEBT OF DEVELOPING COUNTRIES (DISBURSED) AT END 1974 AND THEIR DEBT SERVICE IN 1974, BY CATEGORY OF LENDERS

Creditor	Debt outstanding		Debt Service					
	$ million	% of total	Total		Interest payments		Amortization payments	
	$ million	% of total	$ million	% of total	$ million	% of debt[c]	$ million	% of debt[c]
	1	2	3	4	5	6	7	8
1. DAC countries	82,079	69	10,659	68	3,740	5.2	6,918	9.6
—ODA	32,142	27	1,550	10	697	2.4	853	2.9
—Other official (OOF)	8,042	7	1,234	8	420	6.0	814	12.2
—Private export credits	34,328	29	6,034	38	1,996	6.6	4,038	13.6
—Other bilateral private debts[a]	7,567	6	1,841	12	627	9.0	1,213	18.0
2. Multilateral organisations	15,110	13	1,334	9	670	5.2	664	5.2
—of which IDA	4,519	4	80	..	30	0.8	50	1.3
3. Centrally-planned economies	7,334	6	728	5	124	1.9	604	9.4
4. Oil producers	1,454	1	103	1	33	6.9	70	15.0
5. Other developing countries	2,595	2	648	4	220	9.4	428	19.0
6. Other[b]	9,749	8	2,151	13	978	12.9	1,174	18.5
Total	118,321	100	15,623	100	5,765	5.8	9,858	9.9

a. Principally guaranteed bank credits and bonds.
b. Principally euro-currency debt, guaranteed.
c. Debt at the end of 1973.

Source: IBRD and OECD/IBRD reporting systems.
Source: 1976 Review Development Co-operation: Efforts and Policies of the Members of the Development Assistance Committee.

TABLE 11
TOTAL REPORTED DEBT (DISBURSED) AT END 1974 AND DEBT SERVICE IN 1974 OF DEVELOPING COUNTRIES, BY INCOME GROUP

Income group	Debt Outstanding $ million	%	Debt Service $ million	%	Population 1973 million	%	GNP 1973 $ billion	%
	1	2	3	4	5	6	7	8
Least-developed countries	4,967	4	339	2	270	13	26	3
Under $200 per capita[a]	23,653	20	1,604	10	1,030	52	133	16
$200-$374 per capita[b]	8,114	7	1,012	7	170	8	52	6
$375-$699 per capita	17,333	15	2,049	13	206	10	110	13
$700-$999 per capita	17,611	15	2,379	16	149	7	126	15
$1,000 per capita and more	30,137	26	4,709	30	182	9	274	32
Total non-oil developing countries	96,848	82	11,752	76	1,737	86	695	82
Oil producers	20,517	18	3,733	24	279	14	151	18
Total developing countries (excluding unallocated)[c]	117,365	100	15,485	100	2,016	100	846	100

a. Excluding Indonesia (oil producer).
b. Excluding Nigeria (oil producer).
c. Excluding unallocated amounts $956 million.

Source: *IBRD and OECD/IBRD reporting systems.*

percent, but it must be remembered that measured on a *per capita* basis the Caribbean region receives more Canadian aid than any other area of the world.

Canadian Food Aid

Canada is one of the largest contributors of food aid to the under-developed countries of the world. One would assume, especially based on the information that is made *easily* accessible to the public, that food aid is the one form of foreign aid that may in fact be beyond reproach or question.

The Canadian government had made a public commitment, presented as point eight in *Canada: Strategy for International Development Co-operation 1975-1980,* to give priority to the poorest developing countries. Here it is stated that "the development assistance program will direct the bulk of its resources and expertise to the poorest countries of the world" (CIDA, 1975; 26). This document goes on to state that:

> Because their fragile economies are least able to withstand serious shortages, Canada recognizes that special consideration must be given to these countries. In addition to receiving a large share of Canada's bilateral funds, countries in this category would, in the normal course of operation of the aid program, have greater access to grants rather than loans, technical assistance, local cost financing and food aid, in order to take into account their special situation and to improve the effectiveness of the assistance they receive (CIDA, 1975; 26).

It would appear from this that a substantial proportion of Canadian aid is directed towards the structurally induced suffering that is the plight of the inhabitants of the LLDC's (i.e., the least less developed countries). This perception seems to be substantiated if we look at the figures that represent the type and channels of Canadian aid for the decade from 1966 to 1976.

TABLE 12
PROGRAM EXPENDITURES DISTRIBUTION BY PROGRAM
COMPONENTS, DECADE TO DATE
($ millions)

Bilateral	$1,669.61	47.6%	Total Bilateral	$2,289.57	65.3%
Bilateral Food Aid	619.96	17.7%	Total Food Aid	809.39	23.1%
Multilateral Food Aid	189.43	5.4%	Total		
Multilateral	839.92	23.9%	Multilateral	1,029.35	29.3%

Source: *Canada and Development Cooperation* CIDA *Annual Review 1975-1976* (Ottawa: CIDA, 1976).

Canada made strong commitments to give food aid at the World Food Conference in Rome. In reference to this, the Annual Report of CIDA states that:

> Particular attention was also paid to the food aid program through which the Canadian government has undertaken in particular to provide one million tons of cereals per year for the next three years. For the year 1975-1976, the second year of the program, $225.5 million were devoted to food aid. This amount is to increase to $250 million in the next fiscal year (CIDA, 1977: 20).

One gathers the impression from this that Canada has pledged to give food aid and other forms of bilateral aid to the poorest of the underdeveloped countries. Things however are not always what they seem. Mr. Roche, in a preamble to a question put to Paul Gerin-Lajoie, the President of CIDA, before the Canada Commons Standing Committee on External Affairs brings to light the fact that:

> ... 80 percent of Canadian food aid and virtually 100 percent of bilateral aid, is sold by the local authorities. I suggest that CIDA has mis-represented this situation to the Canadian people. Certainly there is no doubt that the average Canadian believes that our food is given to the people in need. Even the Prime Minister has no idea that the exact opposite is the case (Standing Committee on External Affairs Proceeding, No. 22, 16-5-1975: 20).

Of the one million tons of food that the Canadian government pledged at the Rome Food Conference, Mr. Roche points out that 59.2 percent will be sold to the local people. The selling of this food is not the focus of this objection, although it is reprehensible. What is being objected to is the fact that CIDA is presenting a false impression regarding the administration of its aid programs. The strategy position very clearly implies that Canadian aid and especially Canadian food aid and other forms of bilateral aid are aimed at alleviating the suffering of the most destitute peoples of the world. However, when food aid is sold by the local authorities it is precisely those people who are the poorest who cannot be relieved by the "aid". In fact, this being the case Canadian aid does not "help" these people at all — not even as a stop-gap measure.

An example of the deliberately constructed misrepresentation of CIDA's aid programs and the rift that exists between stated policy and practical tactics can quite clearly be seen in terms of Canada's "aid" programs to Bangladesh and Pakistan. Included as part of CIDA's aid to these countries is an arrangement that is being made to write off their debts to the Export Development Corporation. This form of aid in no way affects the lives of the poorest of the poor, and hence stands in contradiction to public policy statements, and strategy statements of CIDA.

If CIDA wants to achieve its stated strategy goals it must be willing to ensure that Canadian "aid" in fact reaches the people that the Canadian public are led to believe it is helping. Even the President of CIDA states that the food rationing system by which the local authorities in Bangladesh sell Canadian food aid "has a large bias towards serving the urban areas, which by Bangladesh standards are basically middle class. Its effectiveness in terms of feeding the poor could be improved substantially" (Standing Committee on External Affairs Proceedings No. 22, 16-5-1975: 21).

The conclusion that is reached from this analysis is that there is not even a substantial relief of suffering and death as a result of Canadian aid, let alone a basic redistribution of wealth, which is universally acknowledged as the *only* way in which underdevelopment can be eliminated. Not only is Canadian aid ineffective at altering the world economic order in the direction of more equality, due to the structure and form of its administration, it is perpetuating the very conditions it is ostensibly trying to alter.

Before drawing this discussion to a close it will prove to be fruitful to outline the relationships that exist between Canadian banking interests in the Commonwealth Caribbean, and the developmental process.

Canadian Banking Interests in the Commonwealth Caribbean

It must be remembered that Canadian commercial banking interests are dominant in this area. The Bank of Nova Scotia, the Royal Bank of Canada and the Bank of Montreal are all especially prominent in the Caribbean area. In 1963 an unpublished report by the Bank of Nova Scotia states that it (the Bank of Nova Scotia) "opened, in Kingston in the summer of 1889. In 1906 it became the Jamaican government's banker for the island, and in the same year it opened two more branches in Port Antonio and Montego Bay" (Baum, 1974: 21).

It is pointed out by Baum that it is not unusual for Canadian Banks in the Caribbean to loan up to 120 or 130 percent of the funds on deposit at any given time. It is from the profit made on these loans, investment and/or deposit funds that the salaries of the islands' bank employees are paid. It is also these profits which in turn give rise to a multiplier effect; which is used to hire and train local talent and to import needed expertise. These things are not paid for by imported capital, as is often claimed by vested interest groups, but rather through profits made on the deposits of the island people. This situation can exist because the Canadian banks are multinational corporations which, as was discussed previously, are a direct result of the actions and laws of the Canadian government directed at creating a monopoly situation. Baum, drawing on the analysis of E.P. Neufeld, recognized authority on Canadian Banking, points out that Neufeld has

> ... placed considerable emphasis on the freedom of the closed circle of banks to shape their own legislative rules. Over the years banks have not labored under restrictive legislation with respect to their borrowing and lending activities. Changes in lending regulations came soon after they were sought by the industry. Laws touching on bank liabilities were not restrictive, with the possible exception of cash reserve requirements. Incidentally it might be noted that reserves may bear more of a relationship to short-term funding of government debt than to the safety of bank deposits. Thus, to the extent that cash reserve requirements constrain banks, they do so to further the interests of government rather than the saving public (Baum, 1974: 18).

The Canadian government and its associated institutions have a vested interest in maintaining a *status quo* in terms of economic and financial arrangements in the Commonwealth Caribbean.

The Canadian government is also deeply involved with the Caribbean Development Bank, (CDB), and has contributed 20 percent of the Bank's authorized capital. Britain controls another 20 percent, and the remaining 60 percent is controlled by thirteen of the regions' governments. Relative to the size of the population of the area, some 4 million people, the resources of the Bank are quite large. Under the leadership of its first president, Sir Arthur Lewis, the Bank is developing 'its own thrust' which has, and will continue to have, an effect on the direction of development in the Caribbean area. Baum presents this idea in the following way:

> The Caribbean Development Bank is apt to shape its own direction and build upon its rather strong financial base. That direction may not always comport with what some of the Bank members may think best in the pursuit of their own national goals. Yet what Canada has done is not subject to retraction. Canada has played a large part in building a financial institution which, in time, can have an important role to play in the kind of economic and social structure that will evolve in the Caribbean. There are some kinds of aid programs that can be stopped without their function coming to an end (Baum, 1974: 109).

Canada has played a large part in shaping the future of the Caribbean area through its involvement with the Caribbean Development Bank. Baum summarizes the role of the Bank, which came into existence in 1969, as follows:

> In many respects the Bank can be viewed as a special lender of last resort. It is a merchant bank that will make loans on potentially profitable undertakings, but only if the funds are not otherwise available from private enterprises. Moreover the Bank will not make a

loan to member governments if the purpose is merely to help those governments fund a debt. Nor will it loan to private entities if the purpose is to provide working capital. Primarily the Bank is concerned with the potential multiplier effect of the business venture on the economy (Baum, 1974: 108).

Canadian involvement with the organization and structure of the Caribbean Development Bank is a good example of how Canadian foreign aid (even that distributed through multilateral channels) perpetuates and increases dependence on Canadian and other capital markets. Since funds will not be loaned to member governments to enable them to service debt, the more "aid" Canada gives to this area the greater becomes it debt burden. This increased dependency as a deliberate policy of the Canadian International Development Agency is outlined in Baum's book, *The Banks of Canada in the Commonwealth Caribbean,* in the section relating to the Caribbean Development Bank being the alternative to sugar rebates. Based on this, one is forced to conclude that as the professed goal of decreasing the amount of aid distributed via bilateral channels is achieved, the effect is to increase rather than decrease dependence of the underdeveloped hinterlands on the developed metropoles, and the overall socio-economic structures remain unchanged.

The foregoing discussion of the activities of the Canadian International Development Agency and related institutions has been an outline of Canadian state support, at the economic and financial level, for international capitalist enterprise. One clear conclusion that can be drawn from the available data is that Canadian foreign aid does not promote development *of* the recipient nations' economies, but it does promote development *in* these economies. The key distinction to be made between development of an economy and development in an economy is one of *control*. Foreign aid in general, and, for the purposes of this study, Canadian foreign aid in particular, supports foreign control rather than indigenous control over the recipient nation's economy. This results in a situation in which independent development of the host nation's economy is stifled. For example, if a subsidiary of a foreign (Canadian) country's corporation, or even a foreign owned company operating in a host nation's economy, is encouraged not to expand its operations, it will return a substantial rate of surplus to the "home base" or parent because retained earnings are not reinvested but expatriated. On the other hand if the subsidiary or foreign owned enterprise is encouraged to reinvest its earned surplus abroad, the amount of surplus earned abroad will grow. This generates a greater surplus which results in the return of a lower proportion but a higher absolute amount to the home base, while at the same time expanding the parent's control abroad. No matter what the policy of the foreign owned and/or controlled enterprise, surplus will flow back to the investing metropole, resulting in the development of the investing area, and the underdevelopment of the receiving area. In the age of monopoly capitalism, which is dominated by the multinational corporation, this process of underdevelopment is further aggravated due to the fact that these economic giants very seldom invest their own capital abroad, but in collaboration with the huge multinational financial and banking interests, as well as the native elites of the receiving nations, raise most of the capital on the domestic market, or generate it from retained earnings as mentioned above.

Canada, due to the nature of its historical development, is characterized by three distinct segments (or fractions as they are referred to by Clement) of the Canadian capitalist class. One fraction or segment is the dominant indigenous elite which is "very active in finance, transportation and utilities, to a lesser extent in trade, and much less in manufacturing and resources" (Clement, 1977: 25). These are the people who hold the uppermost positions in Canadian controlled dominant corporations. There is also that fraction of the capitalist class that is referred to by Clement as the middle-range indigenous fraction. This element is active mainly in small-scale manufacturing, and is not international in scope, as is the dominant indigenous fraction. The middle-range indigenous fraction tends to act in a service capacity to the dominant foreign corporations in the sphere of production, or else to serve regional markets in Canada (Clement, 1977: 25). The third fraction or segment is the dominant comprador fraction which is active in manufacturing and resources. Most of the foreign corporations that this segment of the capitalist class works for are owned and controlled in the United States. The fact that this fraction of the capitalist class is also engaged in activities at the international level points out the go-between nature of its role. With regard to this fraction of the Canadian capitalist class Clement states that "it also acts as an intermediary for a significant amount of foreign direct investment flowing out of Canada" (Clement, 1977: 25). As an example of this aspect of the comprador elite's activities Clement points out that:

> Ford Motor Company of the United States holds 85 percent of the stock in Ford Motor Co. of Canada, thus making the Canadian operation a branch plant. This Canadian-based company in turn holds 100 percent of Ford Motor Co. of Australia, New Zealand, South Africa and Singapore and operates plants in Malaysia (Clement, 1977: 25 footnote).

It can be quite clearly seen that the fraction of the capitalist class that occupies executive positions in this type of branch plant operation are in fact comprador elites. The distinctive characteristic of comprador elites is that they function as directors and advisers but must follow directives and policies set by the foreign (U.S.) based parent corporation. (Clement points out that at the end of 1973 the United States accounted for 79 percent of all foreign direct investment in Canada (Clement, 1977: 94)). Most of the U.S. direct investment in Canada is concentrated in manufacturing (44 percent) and resources (39 percent) with very little in other sectors. For example, finance accounted for 8 percent, the trading sector for 5 percent and utilities for only 2 percent (Clement, 1977: 95, figures for 1967). Thus one must conclude that in the sectors of manufacturing and resources, or the industrial sector of the economy, Canada is a dominated, dependent satellite of United States based multinationals.

The "dominant indigenous elite", to use Clement's phrase, who operate in the complementary areas of finance, transportation and utilities have entered into an alliance with the dominant comprador elite, and hence with the foreign elite which controls the parent companies. Clement provides more figures pointing out the net change in book value of investments in Canada over the 13 years ending in 1967. In railways there was no U.S. investment, while Canadians added $1.4 billion; in utilities the figures are U.S. controlled $0.3 billion, Canadian controlled $10.6 billion; in merchandising and construction, U.S. $0.6 billion, Canada $7.2 billion. This compares to investment in both manufacturing and resources which show that United States controlled branches added $5.9 billion in manufacturing, while Canadian controlled companies added $4.7 billion.[1] In the area of resources the figures are U.S. controlled $6.2 billion, Canadian controlled $2.6 billion (Clement, 1977: 95).

The specific historical conditions which led to this situation are detailed by Clement, and therefore it will not be necessary to outline these developments at this point. However, to state this process succinctly, it is found that the situation arose partly because when Canada was a part of the British Empire, most of the British based investment in Canada was portfolio investment. This investment, directed to the utilities, finance and transportation sectors of Canada's resource base, was intended to service the British industrial sector abroad. With the repayment of this debt these sectors of the Canadian economy came to be under the control of an indigenous Canadian elite who ended up servicing the U.S. development and takeover of the manufacturing and resource sectors of the economy by the more highly developed U.S. businesses.

The Canadian elites have not been able to regain control of the manufacturing and resource sectors of the economy which are owned and controlled by U.S. businessmen because of the nature of their investments. A large proportion of the U.S. investment in Canada is direct investment and therefore it cannot be repaid as can portfolio investment. *The Financial Times of Canada,* June 26, 1978, reports that about $40 billion of a total of $68.6 billion long-term foreign investment in Canada in 1975 was direct investment, with the remainder being of the portfolio type. It is to a large degree because of this that the resource and manufacturing sectors of the economy have not, and cannot, within the present political and military structure, pass into the hands of the indigenous Canadian capitalist elite.[2]

This does not mean that Canadian indigenous industrial capitalism is non-existent; although it is not strong internationally, as Clement says, ". . . it does have an international presence" (Clement, 1977: 124). This is especially true in the area of South and Central America, and especially in the Caribbean. However, due to its underdevelopment in the industrial sector which is a direct result of the domination and control in this area by United States based multinationals ". . . the overall standing of Canada within the hemisphere is still a paradoxical one displaying simultaneous dependence and dominance" (Clement, 1977: 125). In the age of monopoly capitalism and imperialism the development or underdevelopmental of a nation (or region) depends upon whether the economic activities of that area are integrated as a satellite into the economic activities of other nations or regions. A relationship between equals may be considered symbiotic, but the relationships between powerful and weak areas are parasitic. To use Clement's example, if one looks at the relationship between Canada and Britain or Europe at the present time one has a rough approximation of symbiosis. The relationship between Canada and the United States is parasitic (with the United States being the parasite). The relationship between Canada and Latin America or the Caribbean is also parasitic, however, in this case Canada is the parasite.

One must conclude from this that there are degrees of development, overdevelopment and underdevelopment that characterize the economic relationships that exist between Canada, the United States and the Caribbean. Due to uneven development, even within an area such as Canada, various sectors of the economy can experience differing degrees of development or dependence. In Canada the development of the manufacturing and resource sectors of the economy have been induced and predominantly controlled by external forces, primarily subsidiaries of U.S. multinationals. The circulation, transportation and utilities sectors of the Canadian economy have conversely been controlled by a highly developed sector of the indigenous Canadian capitalist class. This fraction of the Canadian capitalist class has extended it operations and interests into other underdeveloped areas of the world (for the purposes of this study attention was focused on the area of the Caribbean) rather than trying to compete with the dominant U.S. corporations for control of the Canadian economy. Within this set of economic relationships the

U.S. benefits doubly, whereas in the Caribbean (or Latin America generally) the non-capitalist classes especially bear the burden of both sets of relationships: that is, U.S. multinationals pursuing resources, markets and extension of their control of the Caribbean economies, and Canadian extensions of the financial and utilities sectors. The United States based multinationals benefit whether the extension into the underdeveloped country's economy is the result of direct investment, of if it is 'go-between' investment by a Canadian based subsidiary or branch plant of the United States based mother company. First the U.S. capitalist class who control the multinational corporations benefit from the control that direct investment gives them of both the Canadian and the Caribbean economies, and, second, this same class also benefits from the financial activities and the extension of transportation and utilities services by the indigenous Canadian capitalists in the underdeveloped areas (Clement, 1977).

This type of discussion gives rise to the question of Canada being an exploited satellite, or an exploiter of less developed areas in its own right. This question, however, is off the mark, for as has been shown in a brief outline given above,[3] depending on which sector of the economy one looks at, and which fraction of the Canadian capitalist class one analyzes, the answer one is forced to put forth is that Canada is both. That is, Canada is an exploited satellite of the U.S. multinationals in the sphere of manufacturing and resource exploitation and is an exploiter of other areas in the spheres of finance, utilities and transportation. This is not meant to imply that these various sectors of economic activity are independent of each other. The financial, transportation and utilities sectors of the economy are often referred to as circulation industries, and as such they are dependent for their very existence on the productive sectors of the economy, and vice versa. However, within the relationship of mutual dependence that exists between production and distribution (circulation) one is able to speak of the independence of the owning and controlling elites to make specific investment decisions. For example it is possible to speak of CPR deciding to invest in one project or another, but it is not possible to speak of its independence to invest or not to invest in absolute terms. Thus the systemic demands of capitalism are such that if a capitalist or a capitalist enterprise is to remain in existence, profitable investments must be made, but independence to decide on individual project exists. If the Canadian controlled CPR decided to invest some of its capital in the construction of a railroad in some underdeveloped country it would have to make this decision in terms of potential profitability. In order for an industry in the circulation sector of the economy to be profitable it has to have something to circulate. This means that there has to exist resource-exploiting industry or manufacturing industry to service. Given the structure of the Canadian economy in particular, but even the world capitalist economy in general, the chances are that the resource or manufacturing industries that the Canadian-controlled circulation industries are able to service are going to be foreign owned and controlled (most probably U.S. owned and controlled). Thus even though it is possible to speak of some Canadian capitalists as having independence to make this or that investment decision, it must be kept in mind that there is a high degree of dependence on foreign industrial capitalists to provide profitable outlets for Canadian circulation capital. The relationship of dependence on the U.S. industrial capitalist class is even more pronounced in the case of Canada due to the intricate web of interlocking directorships which characterize the continental corporations. Although these interlocking directorships help eliminate uncertainty with regard to investments, this confidence is bought at the expense of independence on the part of the Canadian capitalist elite.

The internationalization of capitalist activity which is inevitable given the dynamics of monopoly capitalism, and which leads to the exploitative relationships discussed above, raises another question: that is, is Canada an imperialist power? This question can be reformulated in the following way — although the economic exploitation of underdeveloped areas by advanced monopoly capitalism is a *necessary* condition for imperialism, is it also a *sufficient* condition? In order to answer this question it is necessary to have a precise definition of imperialism. Such a definition has been developed by Sweezy. This definition states that there are five basic characteristics of imperialism:

> (a) several advanced capitalist countries stand on a competitive footing with respect to the world market for industrial products; (b) monopoly capital is the dominant form of capital; and (c) the contradictions of the accumulation process have reached such maturity that capital export is an outstanding feature of world economic relations. As a consequence of these basic economic conditions, we have two further characteristics; (d) severe rivalry in the world market leading alternately to cutthroat competition and international monopoly combines: and (e) the territorial division of the "unoccupied" parts of the world among the major capitalist powers (and their satellites) (Sweezy, 1968; 307).

It can be seen from this definition of imperialism that "the territorial division of the whole world by the biggest capitalist powers" is a necessary condition of imperialism. This territorial division of the world requires a strong military presence to maintain these divisions. As was pointed out earlier in the study, Canada does not have the military resources or strength to enforce the interests of the Canadian capitalist class through the exercise of military power. This observation has led Clement to conclude that:

> While Canadian multinationals cannot be said to have dominated any of these areas [Central and South American countries] in the way that U.S. multinationals have, they were helped into the region first as protégés of the British Empire (particularly in the Caribbean) and now in the wake of the United States. They depend to a large extent on the climate created and maintained by the United States in its sphere of influence (reinforced by political and military control) for their continued operation. Thus some Canadian capitalists have enjoyed great privileges within that sphere of influence (Clement, 1977: 122).

One is inclined to conclude from this that Canada, or more precisely the Canadian capitalist class, does not and, given the existing world power distribution, cannot occupy the position of an independent imperialist power because of the lack of independent military might.

This does not mean that the operations of the Canadian state through such affiliated agencies and corporations as CIDA and EDC do not support the extension of indigenous Canadian capitalists into the underdeveloped countries of the world and aid and facilitate their exploitative activities there. Nor does it mean that the activities of CIDA and EDC do not facilitate U.S. imperialism through assistance given to Canadian based subsidiaries of U.S. multinational corporations. Clement cites a very good example of how the operations of the Export Development Corporation support the international activities of Canadian based foreign owned business:

> One EDC loan of note (over $26 million) was made to Brazil and in 1971 was guaranteed by the Brazillian government. It stipulated that $23 million of the $26.5 million must be used to buy equipment from seven "Canadian" companies, all foreign-owned (six in the United States and one in Britain) (Clement, 1977: 123).

Given the evidence that is available one is further drawn to conclude that the Canadian state through its various agencies and crown corporations does aid U.S. imperialism and also facilitates the indigenous Canadian capitalist elite's monopolistic expansion into the underdeveloped countries, especially in the sectors of finance, transportation and utilities.

However the extension and support of the international operations of monopoly capital, although a necessary condition of imperialism, is not a sufficient condition of imperialism, and therefore one is inclined to conclude that the activities of the Canadian capitalist class do not constitute imperialism.

NOTES

1. Clement points out that Canadian-controlled capital that goes into manufacturing is in sectors relatively distinct from U.S. dominated sectors, such as the food and beverages, steel, and pulp and paper industries (Clement, 1977: 94).

2. The *Financial Times of Canada*, June 26, 1978 reports as of 1974 that if Canadians set out to buy back the assets of foreign direct investment, they would have to find about $2.5 billion a year just to keep the total from rising, even if not a cent of new investment money was flowing north over the border.

3. The structure of the Canadian capitalist class, and its interlocks and relationships with the U.S. capitalist class is extensively discussed and articled by Wallace Clement in his books *The Canadian Corporate Elite* and *Continental Corporate Power*.

Readings

Baum, Daniel Jay, *The Banks of Canada in the Commonwealth Caribbean*, New York: Praeger Publishers, 1974.

Canada: Strategy for International Development Cooperation 1975-1980, Ottawa: CIDA, 1975.

Canada and Development Cooperation, Annual Report 1975-1976, Ottawa: CIDA, 1977

CIDA Background Paper, *Canadian Development Assistance to the Commonwealth Caribbean*, Ottawa: CIDA, 1977.

Canadian Direct Investment Abroad, Ottawa: Statistics Canada Daily, December 12, 1977.

Chodos, Robert, *The Caribbean Connection*, Toronto: James A. Lorimer and Co., 1977.

Clement, Wallace, *Continental Corporate Power*, Toronto: McClelland & Stewart, 1977.

Development Cooperation: Efforts and Policies of the Members of the Developmental Assistance Committee, 1976 Review, Paris: OECD, 1976.

Export Development Corporation: Introduction, Ottawa: EDC, [197?].

Export Development Corporation, 1975 Annual Review, Ottawa: EDC, March 31, 1976.

Hayter, Teressa, *Aid as Imperialism*, London: Penguin Books, 1971.

Lichtman, Richard, "Marx's Theory of Ideology", *Socialist Revolution*, Vol. 5, No. 23 (April, 1974).

MacEachen, Hon. Allan J., Secretary of State for External Affairs and Minister Responsible for International Development, *International Development Cooperation*, Ottawa: CIDA, 1975.

Magdoff, Harry, *The Age of Imperialism: The Economies of U.S. Foreign Policy*, New York: Modern Reader Paperbacks, 1969.

Mandel, Ernest, *Late Capitalism*, London: HLD Atlantic Highlands, Humanities Press, 1975.

Minutes of Proceedings and Evidence of the Sub-Committee on International Development of the Standing Committing on External Affairs and National Defence (House of Commons, Issue No. 21, Tuesday, June 8, 1976, First Session, Thirtieth Parliament, 1974-15-1975 Doc. 16, S9M #21).

Standing Committee on External Affairs and National Defence Proceedings No. 22, 16-5-1975.

Sweezy, Paul M., *The Theory of Capitalist Development*, New York: Modern Reader Paperbacks, 1968.

World Bank Annual Report 1976, Washington: International Bank for Reconstruction and Development, 1976.

Work Bank and IDA: Questions and Answers, Washington: International Bank for Reconstruction and Development, September, 1971.

Zimmerman, A.H., *Canada's Options and Objectives*, Note: from a syposium presented by the Canadian Export Association. Toronto: Canadian Export Association, 1973.

II

Unemployment and Underemployment

The Capitalist Labour Market and Income Inequality in Canada

Leo A. Johnson

LEO A. JOHNSON is a Professor of Sociology and History at the University of Waterloo. His current research interests include the Canadian Labour Market, Canadian Class Structure and Political Economy.

Since World War II innumerable government studies, reports and pieces of legislation have concerned themselves with the problem of poverty and income inequality in Canada. In these studies the location, social characteristics and personal attributes of the poor have been enumerated, analysed and commented upon, apparently to little avail. As one recent investigation has shown:

> Over the entire 1951-1973 period there is a slight tendency towards increasing inequality. This is generally true regardless of the inequality measure or unit of analysis examined. . . .

> It seems an inescapable conclusion that income inequality has not diminished over the period under observation. This is certainly surprising in the light of the great expansion of social security programs over the period most of which are supposed to be redistributive in nature (Love and Wolfson, 1976:74).

Thus, in spite of all the public outcry that Canada has become a "welfare state", the income gap between rich and poor has not diminished in almost three decades.

In all these studies of poverty and inequality there is, however, a curious omission. Although the vast majority of Canadians depend upon wages and salaries for their incomes, aside from a few superficial references to the "working poor", no real study has been made of the way that the existence of capitalism, and, in particular, of the way that the capitalist labour market has affected the distribution and levels of personal income in Canada.

Although this study cannot do more than raise some general questions and suggest some hypotheses concerning the effects of the capitalist labour market on income distribution, it is hoped that it will provide a basis for further exploration.

In the first place, it is important to recognize that the labour market in a capitalist economy is just that, a market, and as such is governed by the typical market forces of supply and demand. This is not to say that supply and demand are the only forces at work. After all, even market forces are affected in their operation by the particular social customs, biases, legalities and pressures of society at large. These factors, however, do not replace supply and demand, but rather shape the manner in which supply and demand are expressed in social terms. Thus when Hugh and Pat Armstrong point out that in the capitalist labour market men and women are effectively segregated in their participation, they are not demonstrating that the market forces of supply and demand are absent, but rather that they have been channelled to maximize economic return to employers by the exploitation of sexism (Armstrong and Armstrong, 1975).

In analyzing the operations of the capitalist labour market, four kinds of competition must be considered: competition between the system of the capitalist production of goods and services and the sector of production remaining in the hands of individual producers and distributors; competition among employees and potential employees for available jobs; competition among employers and potential employers for the cheapest and most productive employees, and competition between employers and employees in negotiating the actual terms of employment. It is the outcome of these competitions which determines who receives an earned income and what amount of income they receive.

Although certain occupations such as doctors, dentists, retail merchants and farmers continue to operate outside of the wage labor market, as Table 1 shows, such self-employed occupations make up only a very small part of income opportunities in Canada. Since 1951 the self-employed sector has been reduced from 12.2 percent of all gainfully employed persons to only 8.1 percent in 1975. In contrast, the proportion of persons dependent upon wages and salaries has remained relatively steady, increasing from 85.5 percent in 1951 to 86.5 in 1975. The increase of persons living off investment income has made up the difference. Although some of these self-employed individuals earn high incomes (the self-governing professions such as medicine, law and dentistry are particularly well paid) most individuals in the private sector earn low incomes. In

TABLE 1
DISTRIBUTION BY SECTOR OF PERSONS GAINFULLY EMPLOYED, CANADA: 1951, 1971, 1975

	Persons Gainfully Employed					
	Number			Percent		
	1951	1971	1975	1951	1971	1975
Wages and Salaries — Business & Private	2,938,570	5,566,905	6,442,314	73.1	62.1	61.6
— Gov't. & Institutions	498,640	2,177,287	2,600,843	12.4	24.3	24.9
— Total	3,437,210	7,744,192	9,043,157	85.5	86.4	86.5
Self-employed—Commodity Producers-Primary	199,470	298,470	305,133	5.0	3.3	2.9
—Commodity Producers-Secondary		71,833	83,786		.8	.8
—Commodity Distributors	255,050	211,289	227,513	6.3	2.4	2.2
—Service Operators		107,689	131,679		1.2	1.3
—Professionals	35,270	72,911	94,578	.9	.8	.9
Total	489,790	762,192	842,689	12.2	8.5	8.1
Investors	94,230	453,631	577,446	2.3	5.1	5.5
Total Gainfully Employed	4,021,230	8,860,015	10,463,292	100.0	100.0	100.1

Source: Taxation Statistics, 1953, 1973, 1977.

particular, in those sectors such as farming, fishing and retail sales, which have relatively open entry, competition is fierce, with many individuals existing on the edge of bankruptcy — practitioners of the "peasant art" of self-exploitation. In spite of competition from their compatriots and the gradual erosion of these sectors by competition from capitalist big business, these independent operators fiercely resist absorption into the even greater alienation of the wage labour market.

Since the 1950s some significant changes have occurred in the capitalist labour market. First, there have been some fundamental changes in the composition of the labour force. As Table 2 shows, participation rates among males under 25 and over 65 declined sharply between 1955 and 1970. In contrast, participation rates among prime-aged males (25 to 64) remained generally unchanged. Female participation rates for those under 24 and over 65 remained stable, while participation rates for prime-aged females (25 to 64) rose sharply.

Over all, these changes generally cancelled each other out, and total participation rates rose only marginally from 51.6 percent in 1955 to 53.8 percent in 1970. Since 1970 the patterns have changed somewhat. Male participation rates for those under 25 reversed the previous pattern, rising sharply from 51.7 percent to 57.7 percent. Among males 25 to 44 participation rates were stable, while for the group 45 and over there was a general decline. For all groups of females under 65 there was a sharp increase participation in rate. Participation rates for females over 65 remained unchanged. The net result was an increase in total participation rate from 53.8 percent to 56.8 percent in just four years.

There were also equally important changes in the pattern of employment. As Table 1 shows, although there was little change in the over all proportion of the labour force who worked for wages and salaries, there was a large change in the location of that employment. In 1951 only about 14.5 percent of persons who worked for wages and salaries were employed by governments and institutions (schools, hospitals, jails, etc.). In 1975 this proportion had doubled to 28.8 percent. In other words, of the 5,605,947 new jobs created, 3,503,744 were created in the private sector and 2,102,203 (37.5 percent) were created by government and institutional expansion. Thus while job opportunities in the private sector were increased by 119.2 percent, those in the public sector increased by a remarkable 421.6 percent.

There has, however, been some drastic changes in the pattern of job creation in the past few years. In the private sector, from 1951 to 1971, the rate of job creation was approximately 3.3 percent per

TABLE 2
PARTICIPATION RATES BY AGE AND SEX,
CANADA, 1955-1974, JANUARY AVERAGES

	14-24			25-44			45-64			65+		
	M	F	T	M	F	T	M	F	T	M	F	T
1955	64.4	37.5	50.7	96.4	23.2	59.3	89.9	17.9	54.8	31.1	3.8	17.5
1960	58.9	38.5	48.6	97.3	27.2	61.8	91.5	24.9	58.8	28.7	5.5	16.9
1965	52.4	36.2	44.3	97.0	31.5	63.8	90.8	32.5	61.7	25.9	6.2	15.9
1970	51.7	38.9	45.1	96.0	38.8	67.3	89.5	35.2	62.0	20.9	4.7	12.0
1974	57.7	45.2	51.6	96.3	45.4	70.8	87.9	37.6	62.3	18.8	4.7	11.0

Source: *Historical Labour Force Statistics, 1944*

year compounded. From 1971 to 1975 this rate increased somewhat to 3.7 percent annually compounded. In contrast, in the public sector the rate of new job creation, between 1951 and 1971, was approximately 7.6 percent per year compounded. Between 1971 and 1975 this rate dropped sharply to 4.5 percent per annum compounded. If the pattern of job creation had continued at pre-1971 levels, some 214,000 additional jobs would have been created.

When a potential employer, whether business, government or an institution, comtemplates hiring an employee, they do so within the context of definite economic incentives and constraints: the businessman by the need to make a profit, and government or an institution by the need to retain public support within the constraint of the taxpayer's willingness to pay. Thus before a job can be offered to anyone, important calculations have to be made. In these calculations a potential employer must consider competition by other employers to secure the opportunity, competition among employers to acquire the most suitable employees, availability and cost of skills amongst employees, degree of competition among suitable employees for jobs, etc.

Thus, before a job opportunity is created, employers must have a relatively clear picture of what kind of employee they want and what wages or salaries and conditions of labour they can offer and still remain within the constraints imposed by their self-interest. Of course, because profits and the viability of the opportunity are enhanced by reducing wages, salaries and conditions of labor to minimum levels, there is a constant incentive for employers to do so. As Joe Davidson, the militant former president of the Canadian Union of Postal Workers discovered, under capitalism governments as well private employers share this characteristic:

> As long as there have been employers, they have tried to buy the services of labour as cheaply and sell the products as dearly as possible. I assume they will keep on doing it, and also that workers will always try to band together to avoid being the victims of abuses of power by their employers (Davidson and Deverell, 1978: 186).

Thus in any analysis of the capitalist labour market it must be kept in mind that before any job is created under capitalism, it must benefit some employer first. As Pierre Elliot Trudeau has so nicely phrased the matter, under capitalism, no one has a right to a job.

From the point of view of the employee or potential employee, a similar calculation takes place. There are, however, some fundamental differences in the circumstances surrounding the calculations made by potential employees. In order to earn a living under capitalism, an individual must either possess skills that are marketable directly to the public (such as those possessed by a doctor or dentist), possess the assets necessary to create or trade commodities or perform a service (such as a farmer, shopkeeper, electrician or barber), possess or control assets which other people require in order to make a living (such as a rentier or capitalist), or to acquire access to such assets by hiring oneself to someone who possesses them. Thus anyone who lacks either directly marketable skills or the ownership or control of marketable assets becomes dependent for his or her livelihood on someone who does. This dependency may be direct, as in the case of children in a family, or an employee hired to a capitalist, or indirect, as in the case of charity received from institutions, or state welfare.

For the approximately ten million Canadians who are directly dependent upon the capitalist labour market (that is, the nine million persons working for wages and salaries plus the one million or more who are unemployed and want work), when they compete for a job, for an opportunity to earn a living, they compete for jobs whose regularity, duration, conditions of work and remuneration are already generally determined. Thus if the only job opportunity that is available is one whose remuneration is substandard or inadequate for the person's needs and responsibilities, or whose conditions are brutal, dangerous or inhumane (for example, such as those traditionally experienced by asbestos miners) then that is the job that must be competed for — the alternative is the even less satisfactory dependency of welfare.

In the current situation when ten million adults are dependent upon the capitalist labour market, but employers (business and government) require only nine million employees, then one million people will be unemployed and remain dependent directly or indirectly upon the charity of others. Individually the one million surplus employees are incapable of changing the general situation. If John or Mary quit or are fired from their jobs and Joe or Jane are hired to replace them, we may condemn John and Mary for being lazy or for being malcontents and praise Joe and Jane for their responsibility and initiative, but in the larger picture nothing has changed — only the faces are different.

Over the long run, important changes in the capitalist labour market do occur, but these changes are slow. When an employer invests money in fixed assets, he does so only where there is a reasonable expectation of long-term profitability or benefit. Moreover, when such investments are made, the employer will use every strategy available to ensure the investment's continued profitability and utility. Such investor "conservatism", therefore, tends to inhibit rapid structural change in the labour market. Thus the employer's relationship to job creation includes strategies of structural change, but only at a measured and "responsible" pace. In contrast, when the individual employee enters the job market, because of that person's lack of resources and state of dependency, the entry is made under considerable time pressure. To the employee, therefore, the job market is a given, and fixed condition, to which the individual must relate in immediate terms.

Competition among employees for the available job opportunities comes from three sources: from persons with jobs attempting to better themselves, from persons without jobs atempting to get jobs, and from foreign workers who hope to better themselves by immigrating to Canada. In the latter case the Canadian government takes a particularly active role. Every month the Department of Employment and Immigration takes a survey of employer needs and adjusts the immigration point system to allow entry to immigrants possessing skills or characteristics that employers claim are in short supply. The purpose of such labour supply management is to increase competition among employees and to keep worker incomes down to customary levels or, as the managers of the program put it, to prevent "wage distortions". Such a reduction of competition among employers and the enhanced competition among employees has the result of improving the employer's bargaining position when engaged in the hiring or negotiating process, and, of course, aids the employers in their attempts to acquire employees at profitable rates. On the other hand, government interventions to increase competition among workers prevents workers from benefitting from market forces when their particular skills and attributes are in demand and in short supply. The frequently-made complaint that Canadians refuse to work at certain dirty, difficult or dangerous jobs merely indicates that wage levels in those areas are not allowed to rise to competitive levels. Rather than allow the normal market forces to operate in these areas, employers put pressure on the government to bring in immigrants from low wage economies who will work for wages below the Canadian norm; that is, below the level of wages and salaries established by domestic competition and Canadian circumstances.

In assessing the net impact of the capitalist labour market upon income distribution, certain general characteristics stand out: first, there are only nine million income opportunities, but ten million persons competing for them; second, the self-employed sector of the economy has shrunk steadily in proportional terms as its growth rate lagged far behind the wage labour sector; third, the nine million income opportunities provided in the wage labour sector differ drastically in both the quality of employment and level of income offered. Thus opportunities in the wage and salary sector range from the few dollars a week earned by paper boys and girls to the $300,000 per annum received by the president of Canadian Pacific Railways.

In all cases these opportunities have to be competed for, and the losing competitors end up competing for less desirable opportunities. The weakest one million competitors, of course, end up with no job at all.

In the following tables which illustrate various distributions of earned income, several preliminary factors must be kept in mind: first, not all the tables are drawn from the same source, so comparisons between tables must be made with caution; second, these tables include all types of earners, private and public, self-employed and wage and salary earners; third, in the tables drawn from taxation data, changes in taxation law, especially between 1971 and 1975 have made direct comparisons with earlier data more difficult.

Table 3 illustrates in general terms the drastic impact that part-time and seasonal jobs have on annual average incomes. Of the 9,272,760 Canadians who received earned income in 1970, 1,798,170 (19.4 percent) worked on a full-time basis but found less than 40 weeks work; 1,059,215 (11.4 percent) worked full time from 40 to 48 weeks; 1,597,750 (17.2 percent) worked part-time while only 4,817,630 (52.0 percent) found full-time work on a year round basis. In 1970, on average, there were 476,000 persons without jobs actively seeking work. In such a situation, there can be little doubt that many persons who wanted and needed full-time year round jobs were forced to accept part-time or seasonal work. The alternative for them was no job at all.

As Table 3 shows, there is a significant relationship between the level of income earned and the duration of employment, and whether the individual worked on a full- or part-time basis. Thus, in 1970 the 3,661,420 men who were gainfully employed on a full-time, year round basis received an average income of $8,076 per annum. In contrast, the 409,350 men who were employed full-time but worked for only 14 to 27 weeks earned an average of only $2,650. Similar comparisons can be made for women and part-time workers.

These average income figures, however, tell only a very small part of the story. What is hidden behind the averages is a pattern of income distribution in which a small minority of Canadians enjoy high incomes while many persons earn incomes which would not, by themselves, maintain a typical family above the poverty line. Tables 4 to 6 give the distribution of earned incomes as reported by the federal *Taxation Statistics*. In examining these tables several factors stand out. First, even when one allows for the effects of inflation, there has been an enormous increase in personal reported earnings since 1951. Between 1951 and 1975 earning power increased by 381 percent over all, and by 64 percent on a per earner basis. Thus it is clear that the money was there for all earners to enjoy a much higher

TABLE 3
PERSONS 15 YEARS OF AGE AND OVER, WHO WORKED FULL-TIME AND PART-TIME IN 1970, BY WEEKS WORKED, SHOWING AVERAGE EMPLOYMENT INCOME, 1971

Weeks Worked		Worked			Worked full-time			Worked part-time		
		Total	Male	Female	Total	Male	Female	Total	Male	Female
Total	No.	9,586,280	6,093,085	3,493,190	7,870,030	5,388,080	2,481,950	1,716,250	705,005	1,011,240
With income	:	9,272,760	6,023,320	3,249,440	7,675,010	5,346,325	2,328,685	1,597,750	676,995	920,755
Average employment income	$	5,392	6,574	3,199	6,125	7,111	3,864	1,867	2,341	1,518
1-13 weeks	No.	1,036,620	492,740	543,880	529,015	282,645	246,375	507,600	210,100	297,505
With income	:	987,195	474,280	512,910	508,460	274,465	234,000	478,730	199,820	278,915
Average employment income	$	998	1,328	692	1,248	1,591	845	732	967	565
14-26 weeks	No.	993,325	519,485	473,835	629,050	357,645	271,400	364,275	161,840	202,435
With income	:	956,780	509,350	447,435	611,010	352,280	258,735	345,770	157,070	188,700
Average employment income	$	2,155	2,650	1,592	2,514	2,973	1,889	1,520	1,925	1,184
27-39 weeks	No.	971,820	572,635	399,185	694,065	446,070	247,995	277,755	126,565	151,190
With income	:	943,055	566,465	376,590	678,695	442,425	236,265	264,360	124,040	140,325
Average employment income	$	3,646	4,395	2,521	4,174	4,788	3,026	2,291	2,992	1,672
1-39 weeks	No.	3,001,765	1,584,860	1,416,900	1,852,130	1,086,360	765,770	1,149,630	498,505	651,130
With income	:	2,887,025	1,550,095	1,336,935	1,798,170	1,069,175	728,995	1,088,860	480,920	607,935
Average employment income	$	2,246	2,883	1,508	2,783	3,369	1,922	1,361	1,802	1,013
40-48 weeks	No.	1,300,650	818,640	482,015	1,084,575	740,560	344,015	216,080	78,075	138,000
With income	:	1,259,985	811,810	448,175	1,059,215	736,045	323,165	200,765	75,765	125,010
Average employment income	$	5,700	6,849	3,619	6,205	7,162	4,026	3,037	3,810	2,568
49-52 weeks	No.	5,283,865	3,689,585	1,594,285	4,933,330	3,561,155	1,372,175	350,540	128,430	222,110
With income	:	5,125,755	3,661,420	1,464,330	4,817,630	3,541,100	1,276,525	308,125	120,315	187,810
Average employment income	$	7,087	8,076	4,614	7,356	8,230	4,932	2,892	3,571	2,458
40-52 weeks	No.	6,584,515	4,508,225	2,076,300	6,017,905	4,301,715	1,716,190	566,620	206,505	360,110
With income	:	6,385,740	4,473,225	1,912,505	5,876,845	4,277,155	1,599,690	508,895	196,080	312,820
Average employment income	$	6,813	7,853	4,381	7,149	8,046	4,749	2,949	3,663	2,502

Source: *Canada Year Book*, 1975: 324.

standard of living. Second, in 1951, there was a great deal of disparity between high and low income earners. In that year the top quintile of earners received about 7.5 times as much income as that received by the lowest quintile of earners. Third, as Tables 5 and 6 make clear, the new income received during the 1951-1975 period was even more severely skewed in distribution than were the incomes in 1951. Whereas in 1951, the top quintile of earners received 41.8 percent of all earned income, between 1951 and 1975 they received in addition 55.4 percent of all new income. Thus by 1975 the top quintile was receiving some 47.1 percent of all earned income. Similarly, the fourth quintile of earners increased their share of total income from 22.9 percent to 24.8 percent. The share of all other quintiles of income earners declined. By 1975 the top quintile of income earners received 15.2 times as much income as did the bottom quintile. Thus between 1951 and 1975 the rate of disparity between the top and bottom quintile of earners had more than doubled. In the competition for incomes the strongest competitors had gained virtually all the new wealth while the weakest competitors had actually lost purchasing power. It is this general pattern of earnings which lies behind the problem of poverty in Canada.

At the very top of the income ladder is a small elite of 398,320 individuals, (or 3.3 percent of the total persons filing taxation returns), who received more than $25,000 per year. This group received a total of 16.1 billion dollars, or 14.6 percent of all income reported by Canadians in 1975. Put another way, the top 3.3 percent

TABLE 4
INCOMES OF CANADIANS BY QUINTILES, CURRENT DOLLARS,
1951-1975

	1951	1961	1971	1975*
Total Reported Income — (millions of dollars)	$10,469	$21,480	$56,016	$105,609
Total Earners — (thousands)	4,102	5,964	9,533	12,002
Average Reported Income	$ 2,552	$ 3,601	$ 5,876	$ 8,799
Average Reported Income				
— Lowest Quintile	$ 710	787	897	1,349
— Second ..	1,572	2,021	2,766	3,924
— Third ..	2,222	3,082	4,827	7,053
— Fourth ..	2,917	4,272	7,327	10,928
— Fifth ..	5,339	7,845	13,562	20,733

*In order to make the data more equivalent, items 7, 8 and 25 (Family Allowances, Unemployment Insurance Benefits and Capital Gains Tax) have been subtracted from the 1975 totals.
Source: *Taxation Statistics*, 1953, 1963, 1973, 1977.

TABLE 5
INCOMES OF CANADIANS BY QUINTILES, 1971 CONSTANT DOLLARS,
1951-1975

	1951	1961	1971	1975*
Total Reported Income (millions of dollars)	$15,862	$28,640	$56,016	$76,252
Total Earners (thousands)	4,102	5,964	9,533	12,002
Average Reported Income	$ 3,867	$ 4,802	$ 5,876	$ 6,353
Average Reported Income				
— Lowest Quintile	$ 1,076	$ 1,049	$ 897	$ 974
— Second ..	2,381	2,694	2,766	2,833
— Third ..	3,366	4,109	4,827	5,092
— Fourth ..	4,420	5,696	7,327	7,890
— Fifth ..	8,090	10,460	13,562	14,970
Percentage of Reported Income Received				
— Lowest Quintile	5.6	4.4	3.1	3.1
— Second ..	12.3	11.2	9.4	8.9
— Third ..	17.4	17.1	16.4	16.0
— Fourth ..	22.9	23.7	24.9	24.8
— Fifth ..	41.8	43.6	46.2	47.1
	100.0	100.0	100.0	100.0

*See note, Table 3
Source: *Taxation Statistics*, 1953, 1963, 1973, 1977.

TABLE 6
PROPORTION OF NEW INCOME RECEIVED BY AVERAGE MEMBERS
OF EACH QUINTILE OF INCOME EARNERS IN 1971 CONSTANT
DOLLARS AND BY PERCENT, 1951-1975

	1951-61	1961-71	1971-75*	1951-75*
Bottom Quintile	-$ 27	-$ 152	+$ 77	-$ 102
Second ..	+ 313	+ 72	+ 67	+ 452
Third ..	+ 743	+ 718	+ 265	+ 1,726
Fourth ..	+ 1,276	+ 1,631	+ 1,563	+ 3,470
Fifth ..	+ 2,370	+ 3,102	+ 1,408	+ 6,880
Average Change	+ 935	+ 1,074	+ 476	+ 2,485
Bottom Quintile	− .6	− 2.8	+ 3.2	− .8
Second ..	6.7	+ 1.3	+ 2.8	+ 3.6
Third ..	15.9	+ 13.4	+ 11.1	+ 13.9
Fourth ..	27.3	+ 30.4	+ 23.7	+ 27.9
Fifth ..	50.7	+ 57.8	+ 59.1	+ 55.4
	100.0	100.1	99.9	100.0

*See note, Table 3
Source: *Taxation Statistics*, 1953, 1963, 1973, 1977.

of earners received as much income as did the bottom 42.4 percent of earners. Indeed, that small elite group received as much income as did the total of all earners (1,912,543) living in Newfoundland, Nova Scotia, New Brunswick, Manitoba and Saskatchewan combined (Income Statistics, 1975, tables 1 (first series) and 13.

Although this small elite of earners received a very disproportionate amount of income, that figure again tells only a very small part of the story. They also control a large proportion of the accumulated wealth of the country. In addition to whatever privately held property they own (farms, business, etc.), they receive 22.9 percent of all bond interest, 21.6 percent of all bank interest and 60.0 percent of all taxable dividends (Taxation Statistics, 1977, table 15). The latter figure is particularly important because its represents virtually total control of all Canadian-owned corporations.

But, within this small elite of 398,332 persons earning $25,000 or more in 1975, there is a "super-elite" whose earnings were greater than $100,000 per year. Members of this group of earners, numbering only 11,134 (less than one-one thousandth of all earners) in 1975, are the greatest beneficiaries of the capitalist system in Canada. Tables 7 and 8 make it clear the degree of benefit capitalism confers on this super-elite, as compared to the income and wealth possessed by the

TABLE 7
CANADIAN NON-ELITE EARNERS; INCOMES AND
LIQUID WEALTH, 1975

	Under $3,000	$3,000-13,000	$13,000-25,000
Total number in group	2,428,087	6,856,594	2,319,387
Percent of all persons reporting incomes	20.23	57.13	19.32
Percent of income received	3.40	52.00	29.98
Average annual income, 1975	$1,550	$8,396	$14,311
Index of earnings: average = 100	17	91	155
Average income from dividends & bond and bond interest	$190	497	868
Index: average = 100	29	76	132
Estimated average value of investments in stocks, bonds and interest-bearing bank depositsı	$3,810	$9,930	$17,359

I. Asset value is estimated at twenty times dividends, interest and dividend and interest exemptions.
Source: Taxation Statistics, 1977, table 2

TABLE 8
THE CANADIAN ECONOMIC ELITE: INCOME & LIQUID
WEALTH, 1975

	Average: All Earners	$25,000 - 100,000	$100,000 and up
Total number in group	12,002,400	387,198	11,134
Percent of all persons reporting incomes	100.00	3.23	.09
Percent of income received	100.00	12.95	1.67
Average annual income, 1975	$9,223	$37,017	$165,889
Index of earnings: average = 100	100	401	1,799
Average income from dividends & bank and bond interest	$658	$4,208	$34,721
Index: average = 100	100	640	5,277
Estimated average value of investments in stocks, bonds and interest-paying bank depositsı	$13,157	$84,167	$694,421

I. Asset value is estimated at twenty times dividends, interest, and dividend and
   interest exemption.
Source: *Taxation Statistics, 1975*, Table 2

vast majority of Canadians. Not only do the super elite receive
eighteen times the annual income of the average Canadian, but they
own an average of almost $700,000 each in liquid assets (stocks,
bonds and interest-bearing bank deposits). This is 182 times the
average owned by the lowest 20 percent of income earners, and
seventy times that owned by the average income earner in the $3,000
to $13,000 range.

It should not be assumed, however, that the lavish incomes and
great personal wealth of the super-elite arise primarily from their
personal excellence as competitors. As Wallace Clement pointed out,
the chief determinant of individual economic success in Canada is
inherited class position (Clement, 1975: 172-269). For the super-elite
of earners, the advantages gained by inherited wealth, attendance at
the right schools, membership in the best clubs, and relationships
with and marriage into other wealthy and powerful families, all
determine that they will be the real winners in any competition for
income. In this way the elite reproduces itself with but few additions
from the lower classes. Thus the real competition in the capitalist
labour market is amongst those born into non-elite families, all of
whom are competing for the opportunity to earn the modest incomes
and marginal security of those jobs paying less than $25,000 dollars
per year. Only 1 or 2 percent can ever rise above that level.

Over the last two decades politicians and the media have fostered
the belief among Canadians that government policies have had the
result of increasingly redistributing wealth from the rich to the poor.
As W. Irwin Gillespie has pointed out:

A myth is in the process of becoming entrenched in the Canadian body politic. . . . We refer to the myth that Canadian society has become increasingly more redistributive away from the rich to the poor during the postwar period. The claim that Canadian governments have been successful in increasing the degree of redistribution such that the share of command over resources of the poor has increased considerably at the expense of the rich has moved off the popular podium into popular literature. The claim may also lie behind recent provincial and federal moves to 'tighten up on welfare clients', restrain spending on unemployment insurance payments and expand tax loopholes for the rich (Gillespie, 1976: 419-20).

Gillespie's study of the total impact of government taxation and expenditure policies on family incomes is particularly useful. His approach, using orthodox neo-classical economic concepts, is to examine the net transfers of wealth in both money and services (e.g. roads, military and education) at given levels of family incomes. His results (to non-Marxists) are surprising:

In short, *the increasing contributions of the middle — and upper-middle — income Canadians to the redistributive mechanism of the public sector during the 1960s generated the major gains to rich Canadians: each rich Canadian family gained three times more than each poor Canadian family and six times more than each Canadian family in the lower - middle-income class* (Gillespie, 1976; 432-3, Gillespie's italics).

The pattern of government intervention in order to increase aid to the rich at the expense of middle-income families, Gillespie found, continued into the 1970s:

The evidence does not support the belief that over time governments have been successful in increasing the degree of redistribution from the rich to the poor such that the "share" of command over resources of the poor has increased significantly. Quite the contrary: the small relative gain of the poor during the 1960s has been eroded during the early 1970s leaving the poor with no improvement in their "share" over the longer period. On the other hand, the considerable gain of the rich during the 1960s has persisted during the 1970s, thus giving the rich an improvement in their "share" over time. For the most part, the relative improvement of the rich has been at the expense of the median and upper-middle-income families (Gillespie, 1976: 435).

Such is the justice of the "Just Society": the increasing power of the rich to command greater and greater proportions of wealth through earnings is parallelled by their ability to influence government to bias taxation and expenditure policies to their benefit.

Given the growing disparity between rich and poor earners and the tendency of government to bias taxation and spending towards the benefit of the rich, neither the capitalist labour market nor "liberal" welfare policies appear to offer hope to either the non-working poor or the vast majority of the income-earning population. With the standard of living of the poor worker already below the poverty line, the middle and upper-middle income earners are being squeezed to further enrich the income elite. Little wonder, therefore, that welfare policies have failed to redistribute incomes while the middle classes are in revolt against the burdens of increased taxation. Unfortunately, because of the myth of the increased redistribution of wealth to the poor, this middle class anger is aimed in the wrong direction. It is the rich and powerful who are the main beneficiaries of the capitalist labour market and government policies in Canada, and the government continues to guarantee that such will remain the case.

Readings

Armstrong, Pat and Armstrong, Hugh, The Double Ghetto: the Segregation of Woman's Work in Canada, Toronto: McClelland & Stewart, 1978.

Adams, Ian, et. al., The Real Poverty Report, Edmonton: Hurtig, 1971.

Canada, Senate, Poverty in Canada (Report of the Special Senate Committee on Poverty), Ottawa: 1971.

Canada, Taxation Department, Taxation Statistics, Ottawa: 1953, 1963, 1973 and 1977.

Clement, Wallace, The Canadian Corporate Elite, Macmillan, Toronto: 1975.

Clement, Wallace. Continental Corporate Power, Toronto: McClelland & Stewart, 1977.

Davidson, Joe and Deverell, John. The Autobiography of Joe Davidson, Toronto: James Lorimer and Company, 1978.

Economic Council of Canada, The Challenge of Growth and Change (Fifth Annual Report), Ottawa: 1968.

Gillespie, W. Irwin, "On the Redistribution of Income in Canada", Canadian Tax Journal, Vol. XXIV, No. 4, (July-August, 1976).

Gonick, C.W. (Cy), Inflation and Wage Controls, Winnipeg: Canadian Dimension, 1976.

Gonick, C.W. (Cy), "Poverty and Capitalism", Canadian Dimension, Vol. 6, No. 5, (October-November, 1979).

Hamilton, Richard and Pinard, Maurice. "Poverty in Canada: Illusion and Reality", Canadian Review of Sociology and Anthropology, Vol. 14, No. 2, (May, 1977).

Harp, John and Hofley, John R. eds., Poverty in Canada, Scarborough, [?], 1971.

Johson, Leo A., "The Development of Class in Canada in the Twentieth Century", in Gary Teeple (ed.), "Capitalism and the National Question in Canada, Toronto: University of Toronto Press, 1973.

Johnson, Leo A., "Illusions or Realities: Hamilton and Pinard's Approach to Poverty", Canadian Review of Sociology and Anthropology, Vol. 14, No. 3, (August, 1977).

Johnson, Leo A., Poverty in Wealth, The Capitalist Labour Market and Income Distribution in Canada, Toronto: New Hogtown Press, 1974.

Levant, Victor., Capital and Labour: Partners: Two Classes — Two Views, Toronto: Steel Rail, 1977.

Love, Roger and Wolfson, Michael C., Income Inequality: Statistical Methodology and Canadian Illustrations, Ottawa, Statistics Canada, 1976.

Marx, Karl, Wage-Labour and Capital, New York: C.H. Kerr, 1933, 1948.

Oja, G. and Love, R., "Canadian Low Income Statistics", Canadian Statistical Review, (January, 1976).

Statistics Canada, Historical Labour Force Statistics, Ottawa, 1974 and 1976.

Statistics Canada, Income Distributions by Size in Canada, Ottawa, 1971, 1974, 1975 and 1976.

Unemployment Indexes — The Canadian Context*

Robert Stirling and Denise Kouri

ROBERT STIRLING is a Professor of Sociology at the University of Regina and Acting Head of the Sample Survey Data Bank Unit. His current research interests include the Political Economy of Agriculture and Unemployment Studies.

DENISE KOURI is a graduate student in the Department of Sociology and Social Studies at Regina University and a Laboratory Instructor and Computer Analyst with the Sample Survey Data Bank Unit at that University. Her current research interests include Womens Studies, Unemployment and Poverty.

Introduction

A fundamental aspect of a materialist approach to social theory is the recognition that specific theories, and their accompanying methodologies, do not arise in a social vacuum, but rather are rooted in material relations of production and therefore serve specific economic and political interests. Accordingly, conventional, or orthodox, economic theory (from classical to Keynesian) generally serves the interests of the ruling class. For this reason, it has often been referred to as bourgeois economic theory. The key aspect of bourgeois economic theory, in this context, lies in serving to disguise the fundamental characteristic of capitalist production namely, the exploitation of workers by capitalists in the generation of surplus value and wealth. Fundamental concepts of conventional economics such as the concepts of equilibrium, supply and demand (or market

*We wish to express our appreciation for helpful comments and criticisms from Paul Gingrich, Bill Livant, Pam Smith and Don Kossick.

forces), and the thesis that such mechanisms achieve optimum resource allocation and general socio-economic well-being, can seriously mislead the student of capitalist society into not observing its fundamental qualities — exploitation, unequal distribution of wealth, class oppositions and dialectical change. Marxist theorists, such as Cornforth (1977), have pointed out that conventional economic theory has been, and continues to be developed by the ruling class for this very purpose — that is, in order to obscure the exploitative purposes of its economic activities.[1]

If the working class is to acquire a theory and methodology which objectively describes capitalist society, it must develop one itself. This process will require the development of concepts and propositions which arise from practical efforts to apply knowledge in order to change capitalist society. The struggle to produce change will in turn result in a new set of concepts and propositions, that is, in a theory which is empirically more accurate than the first. Only through this continuous cycle — a dialectical process of mental and practical activity — can empirically true theory emerge (Mao, 1967). Whether or not concepts and propositions from existing bourgeois theory can be usefully retained in this context becomes a problem to be solved through practical and empirical observation. The issue of unemployment is an example of this kind of problem.

There are many arguments about what the "unemployment rate" measures and how it should be interpreted. All but the most conservative, however, believe that the level of unemployment in Canada is high. Even the existing definitions, for example, reveal two important characteristics about unemployment in Canada. First, Canada's unemployment rate is one of the highest of any of the major industrialized capitalist countries (Figure 1). Only the United States has rivalled Canada for the honour of having the highest unemployment rate since 1960 (except for a brief period after 1965 when unemployment in the United States dropped and British unemployment rose). Second, while there has been considerable variation in the annual unemployment rates, since the Great Depression of the 1930s the unemployment rate in Canada has been gradually rising. A careful examination of Figure 2 shows that, in the period since the Depression, the unemployment rate experienced several cycles, with lows in 1944, 1947, 1951, 1956, 1966 and 1974. Notice that each of these lows is higher than the previous low, thus producing the steady upward trend illustrated in Figure 2. Similarly, if we draw a trend line through the high points in the cycles, a less regular but still upward trend is also indicated.

While labour force surveys were not regularly conducted in Canada during the 1930's Depression, the official estimates indicates that from 9.1 percent to 19.3 percent of the labour force were unemployed

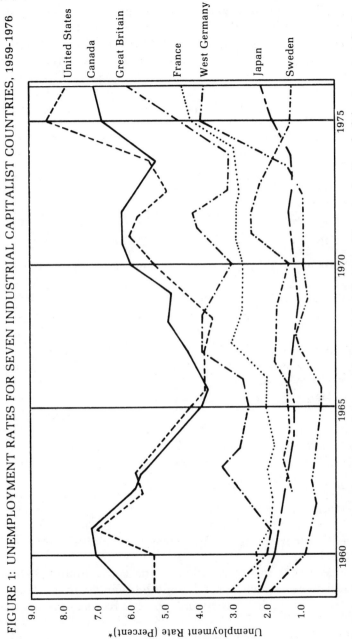

FIGURE 1: UNEMPLOYMENT RATES FOR SEVEN INDUSTRIAL CAPITALIST COUNTRIES, 1959-1976

*The unemployment rates have been adjusted to coincide with U.S. definitions. The rates for Canada did not require adjustment.
Source: Sorrentino, 1970, 1972; and Moy and Sorrentino, 1977.

Data For:

FIGURE 1: UNEMPLOYMENT RATES FOR SEVEN INDUSTRIAL
CAPITALIST COUNTRIES, 1959-1976

	U.S.	Canada	Great Britain	France	West Germany	Japan	Sweden
1959	5.5	6.0	3.1	2.4	1.8	2.3	N.A.
1960	5.5	7.0	2.0	2.5	0.8	1.7	N.A.
1961	6.7	7.1	1.9	1.9	0.5	1.5	1.5
1962	5.5	5.9	2.8	1.8	0.4	1.3	1.5
1963	5.7	5.5	3.5	2.1	0.5	1.3	1.7
1964	5.2	4.7	2.5	1.6	0.3	1.2	1.5
1965	4.5	3.9	2.2	2.0	0.3	1.2	1.2
1966	3.8	3.6	2.4	2.1	0.3	1.4	1.6
1967	3.8	4.1	3.8	2.7	1.0	1.3	2.1
1968	3.6	4.8	3.7	3.2	1.2	1.2	2.2
1969	3.5	4.7	3.7	2.8	0.7	1.1	1.9
1970	4.9	5.7	3.1	2.8	0.8	1.2	1.5
1971	5.9	6.2	3.9	3.0	0.8	1.3	2.6
1972	5.6	6.2	4.2	3.0	0.8	1.4	2.7
1973	4.9	5.6	3.2	2.9	0.8	1.3	2.5
1974	5.6	5.4	3.2	3.1	1.7	1.4	2.0
1975	8.5	6.9	4.7	4.3	3.8	1.9	1.6
1976	7.7	7.1	6.4	4.6	3.8	2.1	1.6

during those years. The question has been raised, however, as to whether this was an adequate measure of the actual level of unemployment at the time.

In the United States, for example, other estimates, from non-government sources, suggest an unemployment rate of 20 to 35 percent (Woytinski, 1940). These estimates, based upon partial survey data and a variety of assumptions and statistical techniques not used in the official calculation of the unemployment rate, raise the hypothesis that there were many more people looking for jobs than the unemployment rate measured. Could this also be true for Canada?

The debate over the appropriateness of the conventional definition of the unemployment rate in measuring the true level of unemployment is therefore not a new one. However, with unemployment rising, as it has in recent years, the question is taking on a more urgent, and public, focus.

While many economists working in the conventional theoretical frameworks have been concerned about the unemployment "measurement problem," they have commonly settled for the existing definitions. As one example of this, note a comment by the U.S. Presidential Committee to Appraise Employment and Unemployment Statistics: "The concept of unemployment now in official use is a reasonable one. It represents a conscientious and well designed effort over a long period of time to resolve a wide range of difficult issues" (1962:14).

The purpose of this article is to illustrate the relationship between

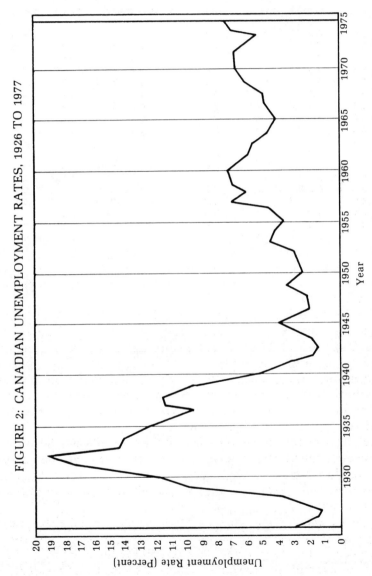

FIGURE 2: CANADIAN UNEMPLOYMENT RATES, 1926 TO 1977

Source: *Statistics Canada, 71-201 Annual,* Dominion Bureau of Statistics, National Income and Expenditure Accounts, 1926-1977.

Data For:
FIGURE 2: CANADIAN UNEMPLOYMENT RATES, 1926 TO 1977

Year	Rate	Year	Rate
1926	3.0	1953	3.0
1927	1.8	1954	4.6
1928	1.7	1955	4.4
1929	2.9	1956	3.4
1930	9.1	1957	4.6
1931	11.6	1958	7.0
1932	17.6	1959	6.0
1933	19.3	1960	7.0
1934	14.5	1961	7.1
1935	14.2	1962	5.9
1936	12.8	1963	5.5
1937	9.1	1964	4.7
1938	11.4	1965	3.9
1939	11.4	1966	3.6
1940	9.2	1967	4.1
1941	4.4	1968	4.8
1942	3.0	1969	4.7
1943	1.7	1970	5.9
1944	1.4	1971	6.4
1945	1.6	1972	6.3
1946	3.4	1973	5.6
1947	2.2	1974	5.4
1948	2.3	1975	6.9
1949	2.9	1976	7.1
1950	3.6	1977	8.1
1951	2.4		
1952	2.9		

the conventional theoretical perspectives and their attendant techniques for measuring unemployment. Alternate theoretical perspectives and measures are also examined with a view to unmasking a few of the important characteristics of unemployment in Canada.

Conventional Labour Force Theories

Certain theories about the labour force can be labelled "conventional" because they are the most common or popular among academics, the media and particularly state bureaucracies. The function of the state in capitalist societies has been to serve the interests of the ruling class in two important ways (O'Conner, 1973). First, it enhances the accumulation of capital by members of the capitalist class through its various programs and policies enshrined in and protected by its legal system. Examples of these programs and policies are incentive grants and bonuses extended to manufacturers, depletion and exploration allowances for oil and mining companies, trade policy, regulation of the nation's currency, incomes policy or "wage and price" controls, labour legislation, and so forth. Second, it must legitimate exploitation; the production process whereby labour generates surplus value which becomes the property of capitalists. A sufficient number of people, including workers, must at least acquiesce in this process of exploitation or else the state and the capitalist system of production will be threatened. Once again, the systems of "welfare" and of "justice" — the law, courts and police — play an important legitimate function. Also important is the ideology, and the theory on which it is based, which the state presents as justification for the acceptance of capitalist production. Conventional theories have a history of use by representatives of the ruling class, including the state, in order to legitimate the economic order, to rationalize its periodic changes, and to organize and enhance the accumulation of capital.

Classical and Neoclassical Theories

Conventional explanations of the labour force are commonly traced to the classical economic theory of Adam Smith and David Ricardo. Classical theory claims that general unemployment is impossible. An important assumption of classical (and neoclassical) theory is known as "Say's Law" which argues that demand adjusts to supply, that the sale of output produces an equal amount of income, and hence that there can be no imbalance in the circulation of commodities into money and subsequently into commodities again, since income will buy an equivalent amount of output (Sweezy, 1970:136ff). The lack of such an imbalance in the economy therefore, implies continuous full employment. Of course, workers might voluntarily decide not to sell their labour power and hence be unemployed although they obviously could not persist with this decision for very long. And in the short run, while the economy may be adjusting to various internal fluctuations (for example, in the demand and supply of commodities from different sectors), and external disturbances (for example competition from foreign economies or wars), some involuntary unemployment could result from the fact that changes cannot be made instantaneously. This temporary, involuntary unemployment became known as "frictional" unemployment emphasizing its marginal character (Peitchinis, 1965:199ff). Workers who are "between jobs" make up most of the frictional unemployment category. Hence for classical (and neoclassical) theory, an economy can be at full employment even though there is a certain amount of frictional unemployment.

Neoclassical economists, such as Leon Walras and Alfred Marshall, accepted these basic assumptions but added an important refinement to classical theory, the concept of marginal utility. In their view consumers would spend their money (income) on an additional unit of a product depending upon the additional (marginal) satisfaction (utility) they receive from it. The price of a product would usually depend upon its marginal utility. Of course firms that produce products are also consumers.

The concept of "marginal productivity" is used to explain the production decisions of firms. Given a certain level of production, the next addition unit of an input will cause a definite change in a firm's output, that is, a marginal product. Therefore, there is a sense in which the ability to produce a marginal product is contained in each input.

Labourers, like other factors of production, are thought to have marginal productivities. What determines a worker's marginal productivity? By definition, it is his/her capacity to generate an additional amount of output if he/she is added to the configuration of inputs at a given level of production. This in turn depends upon his/her level of skill, submission to the regimen of the work place, stamina or perseverance, and so forth. Hence, conventional theories define marginal productivity as a characteristic of the individual worker (or class of workers), with the production system as a "given". In other words, a worker's level of productivity is "up to him/her". Similarly, the average productivity of a class of workers — women, Blacks, Indians, youth — depends upon the aggregate of all of the free individual decisions of the members of that class.[2]

While the concept of marginal productivity is usually used to explain the variation of workers' wages it is also claimed that, given a "minimum wage" regulation, workers (or classes of workers) with very low marginal productivities may not be in demand at all by producing firms since there may be no way that any firm can profitably put them to work. They will be unemployed and, given the existing level and methods of production, they will stay unemployed unless they personally change their productivity (by acquiring more education, being more diligent, etc.). As well, the unscientific prejudices of employers about the marginal productivities of certain workers are thought to result in racist and sexist hiring practices and therefore in wide differences in the labour force participation of Indians, Blacks, women and youth, compared to white, middle-aged males (Gordon, 1972).

One should notice that the state has a very limited role with respect to unemployment within the neoclassical or classical perspectives. Peitchinis argues:

> A major factor contributing to the absence of positive government action against unemployment [at the time of the Great Depression] was the absence of a respectable economic theory justifying government intervention. The existing theories postulated that equilibrium will

be re-established in the economy by the market mechanism (Smith);
and that goods buy goods and, therefore, excess production cannot last
(Say's Law of Demand). There were, of course, advocates of government intervention, but their ideas were considered to be political
rather than economic. In view of this, government measures were
designed to relieve suffering rather than to stimulate economic activity
— they were relief measures rather than unemployment remedies.
(Peitchinis, 1965:224)

Since only "frictional" unemployment is thought to be possible in the
neoclassical system, state intervention is limited to welfare
programs, and efforts to retrain workers, help them to find jobs,
and to relocate. Particular emphasis is placed upon ways to improve
workers' marginal productivities such as through more education and
migration to places where the demand for workers is greatest.

The classical and neoclassical theories do not deny that unemployment can be produced by forces that are "external" to an economic
system. Indeed, this is the only source of fundamental economic
change according to these views. One example is *seasonal unemployment* caused by regular annual changes in production by certain
industries. In Canada, several industries such as construction,
agriculture, forestry, fishing and trapping, are seriously affected
by the winter climate. Extremes of high summer employment and
high winter unemployment have been typical of the Canadian
economy. "Perhaps 20 percent to 25 percent of total official unemployment in Canada in recent years can be labelled seasonal unemployment" (Economic Council of Canada, 1976:193).

Classical and neoclassical theories guided the initial attempts in the
early 1900s to gather information about the Canadian labour force.
Since unemployment was thought to be largely impossible in the
Canadian economic system, no systematic attempt was made to
measure it. A regular labour force survey was not conducted. Only
during Census enumerations were labour force statistics collected.
Farrall reports that:

> ... the Census concepts such as the 'gainfully occupied' were developed
> primarily to measure secular changes in the occupation and industrial
> composition of the work force. The 'gainfully occupied' concept did not
> distinguish unemployment (Farrall, 1973:21).

Workers who had an "occupation" were considered to be in the
labour force regardless of whether they were working (employed) or
looking for work (unemployed). "Any actual unemployment that
occurred in the real world could be explained away as a voluntary
and temporary phenomenon, a residual that fluctuated with the
volume of employment" (Farrall, 1973:21).

This approach prevailed in Canada until the 1930s. But the Great
Depression provided a serious and fundamental challenge to the

validity of the classical and neoclassical theories. Unemployment rose to 9 percent in 1930 and remained at or well above this level for the next ten years. The concepts of frictional and seasonal unemployment could scarcely explain this event. Unemployment during the Depression was not often voluntary! How could this be explained?

Keynesian Theory

Into this crisis of bourgeois ideology came John Maynard Keynes (1936).[3] He found most serious fault with the classical doctrine expressed in "Say's Law" (a critical observation whose accuracy was surely enhanced by the conditions of the Depression). According to classical theory the economy would tend to remain at equilibrium of supply and demand, with full employment. But Keynes was able to show that the equilibrium point for an economy might also be at high levels of unemployment or alternatively at high levels of price inflation.

Say's Law rested upon the argument that all income is spent either in the consumption of consumer goods or, through savings, in investment in capital goods and labour. A problematic aspect of this argument is that it implicity assumes that exactly that part of income which is devoted to savings will determine the extent of entrepreneurial investment in capital goods and labour. Keynes denied this assumed relationship in which the level of savings had a causal influence upon the level of investment. A major determinant of the level of savings, he claimed, is the level of income. That is, people will tend to save a certain proportion of their income, spending the rest upon consumption, and as income rises, the proportion saved also tends to rise. The level of income, in turn, is determined by the level of investment. But if savings do not determine the level of investment, then what does? To answer this question Keynes turned to a number of "psychological" explanations. Entrepreneurs would estimate the profits from given investments based upon "expectations" and "business mood" in addition to the cost of borrowing as expressed in the interest rate. But the investment decisions were assumed to take place within a given level of consumption, that is, within a given aggregate demand for goods and services. If there were little demand, then businessmen would not likely engage in production that could not be sold.

Hence it is the level of aggregate demand that determines how much the economy will produce. This level of output, in turn, determines how many people will be employed. As long as aggregate demand, and the levels of output and employment are suitably matched, the economy will remain at equilibrium regardless of how many are unemployed. For example, during the Depression low wages and prices meant that demand was low and because of this, the levels of output and of employment were also low. The system was relatively stable even though unemployment was very high.

What is the solution to a situation of high unemployment? From the classical perspective, no solution is necessary since the condition is only temporary and adjustment to equilibrium is immanent. From the Keynesian perspective, however, the condition arises as a result of a low level of demand, a cautious business mood and pessimistic expectations of businessmen. Furthermore, it is the responsibility of the state to correct this situation and to return the economy to full employment. One important corrective measure available to the state involves deficit financing. By creating demand for the goods and services of the private sector, the state can introduce conditions that are conducive to increased investment which will create new employment. As well, the state can increase the money supply, and in so doing reduce interest rates and increase the level of investment. Economic and fiscal policy thus became very important state functions as Keynesian theory replaced classical and neoclassical theories as the dominant bourgeois description of capitalism (O'Conner, 1969:392ff).

Two definitions of unemployment flow from macro-economic theory such as that of Keynes. Macro theory leads to the conclusion that an economy may never rest at equilibrium but rather continuously fluctuates between recession (low investment, high unemployment) and inflation (high investment, low unemployment). Unemployment caused by reduced consumer and investment demand corresponding to a movement from inflation to recession is called *cyclical unemployment* (Peitchinis, 1965:195ff). Figure 2, (page 173), illustrates several periods of cyclical unemployment in recent history: 1953-1954; 1956-1958; 1959-1961; 1966-1968; 1969-1971; 1974-1975; and 1976-1977.

Some unemployment is thought to be like frictional unemployment in that it results from a "mismatch" of workers and jobs, however, it is of longer duration and is "caused by an imbalance between changes in the structure of the economy and changes in the occupational structure of the labour force. A maldistribution in the occupational composition of the labour force relative to the skills demanded by the economy is the result" (Peitchinis, 1965:200). This is called *structural unemployment*. For macro theory, it follows from the principle that income, and hence demand, ultimately produce employment. But over time, these causes themselves will vary, for example, as the population moves, as consumer tastes shift, as government policies change, and so forth. Hence, there will likely be a fairly continuous mismatch of the occupational skills of the work force and the skills required by entrepreneurs to meet this changing demand. In 1964 the Economic Council of Canada thought that 3 percent unemployment would be required for structural reasons in the Canadian economy by 1970 (1964:38). However, 12 years later the work of the Council seemed to indicate that structural unemployment in the Canadian economy had been increasing from something less than 3 percent in 1953 to perhaps between 4 to 5 percent in 1975 (1976: 194-5).

The Labour Force Survey

Keynesian theory was first applied to the measurement of unemployment in the late 1930s in the United States and in the labour force surveys that began in both the U.S. and Canada in the early 1940s. Two main principles redirected the new measurement away from previous neoclassical practice, namely, that (1) unemployment is the result of a lack of aggregate demand and hence (2) it is not entirely a voluntary act on the part of workers. Farrall points out that the application of Keynesian theory led to the conclusion that "[all] persons who offered their labour at the current market price but who were unable to find a buyer were involuntarily unemployed". Keynesian theory directed ". . . attention at the stock of unemployment occurring in a deficient demand economy . . . . In practical terms the concept of activity rather than the concept of status by occupation became the key element in policy-makers' data demands" (Farrall, 1973:21). This led to some measurement problems. For example, using a survey technique and an interview with a specific respondent, how does one determine if the person is employed, unemployed or not in the labour force? What specific, standard questions should be asked? The answers to these questions became central to the measurement practice. "The pragmatic 'seeking-work' criterion which demonstrates willingness and availability of the unemployed was taken from the eligibility rules of the United States Unemployment Insurance Act" (Farrall, 1973:22). Specifically, the criteria used by the Canadian Labour Force Survey (before its revision in 1976) to identify these labour force categories were as follows:

> The employed includes all persons who, during the reference week:
>
> a) did any work for pay or profit;
> b) did any work which contributed to the running of a farm or business operated by a related member of the household;
> c) had a job, but were not at work, because of bad weather, illness, industrial dispute, or vacation, or because they were taking time off for other reasons. Persons who had jobs but did not work during the reference week and who also looked for work are included in the unemployed as persons without work and seeking work.

The *unemployed* includes all persons who, during the reference week:

a) were without work and seeking work, *i.e.*, did not work during the reference week and were looking for work; or would have been looking for work except that they were temporarily ill, were on indefinite or prolonged layoff, or believed no suitable work was available in the community; or

b) were temporarily laid off for the full week, *i.e.*, were waiting to be called back to a job from which they had been laid off for less than 30 days.

Those *not in the labour force* include all civilians 14 years of age and over (exclusive of institutional population) who are not classified as employed or unemployed. This category includes those: going to school; keeping house; too old or otherwise unable to work; and voluntarily idle or retired. (Statistics Canada, 71-001, Dec. 1974. 99-100. Italics added.)

One should notice that the *labour force* is defined as the civilian non-institutional population 14 years of age and over who were either employed or unemployed during the reference week.

These definitions were made operational in the labour force survey by a carefully worked out sequence of questions. However, the questions which were most important for categorizing respondents into each of the three labour force categories were "indirect" or general. For example, two of the questions which the interviewer would ask the respondent about the person in question were: "What did . . . do mostly last week?" and "Did . . . do anything else last week?" "Such indirect questions generally required further explanation on the part of the survey interviewer, who, on the basis of the response to these questions, was required to mark the questionnaire according to one of several general categories — 'worked', 'looked for work', 'went to school', 'kept house', etc." (Statistics Canada, Labour Force Survey Division, 1976a:3). Consequently, a respondent who was not working but didn't bother to mention that he/she looked for work during the reference week, or who did not look for work because he/she believed no suitable work was available in the community but failed to explain this to the interviewer, would be classified as "not in the labour force" rather than "unemployed". Such persons, who want to work but are not working and have not looked for work recently for various reasons, are called *discouraged unemployed* or *hidden unemployed*, since in most official labour force surveys they appear as persons who are "not in the labour force" and hence are not included as part of the unemployment rate (although some information about this group has usually been made available in the official publications based upon the Canadian Labour Force Survey).[4]

The unemployment rate is calculated as follows:

$$\text{unemployment rate} = \frac{\text{number unemployed}}{\text{number unemployed} + \text{number employed}} \times 100$$

An analysis of the way in which concepts are measured in the Labour
Force Survey reveals that current methods have, on the whole, the
An analysis of the way in which concepts are measured in the Labour
Force Survey reveals that current methods have, on the whole, the
effect of decreasing the numerator and increasing the denominator
of the expression on the right hand side of this equation and hence
of decreasing the unemployment rate. For example, the phrase "did
any work" in the definition of the employed inflates the denominator
since it means that some members of this category will be under-
employed, such as involuntary part-time workers. Since these
persons want full-time work, they should also be represented in some
way in the numerator of the expression. One can conceive of other
ways in which the demoninator will be exaggerated as a result of the
phrase "had a job, but were not at work, because of bad weather [or]
illness. . . ". This definition obscures such conditions as a lack of
industrial diversity or occupational flexibility in the economy and
hence a high degree of susceptibility to seasonal unemployment, and
a poor record of occupational health or the "rehabilitation" of injured
workers. Similarly, the numerator is made smaller by requiring that
to be unemployed one must not only have a job but also to have looked
for work during the reference week rather than to simply "want a job"
or "have looked for work in the recent past". The requirement that
the respondent must "speak up" and tell the government interviewer
his/her "excuses" for not looking for work no doubt exacerbates this
undercounting problem.

Counter arguments to this analysis claim that the measurement
techniques overestimate the numerator by not requiring the respondent to "prove" that he/she looked for work (and therefore was
available for work), by allowing "excuses" for not looking for work
(being temporarily ill or not believing suitable work was available)
or by allowing persons who were waiting to be called back to work to
be counted as unemployed. While the respondents' truthfulness
affects many forms of data collection, surveys may be affected
somewhat less since the respondent has nothing to gain from a false
reply. What about the "excuses" for not looking for work? The case of
illness seems straightforward — we would not want a definition of
unemployment based upon temporary sickness since it would be quite
variable over time nor would it provide a reliable measure of the stock
of unemployed persons who could be put to work. But if a person
believes that no suitable work is available, is he/she clearly
unemployed or are his/her expectations "unreasonable"? The question
of "reasonableness" identifies one of the practical differences between
classical and Keynesian theory. The classical perspective assumed
full employment, therefore suitable employment would be available,
and the respondent's claim is therefore unacceptable. But for Keynes,

the level of employment was the result of aggregate demand in a specific economy. Hence, for some proportion of the labour force suitable work (in the right location, or offering the "going wage") might not be available and, until this condition could be corrected, these persons should be counted as unemployed. Finally it is obvious that those who are "waiting recall" are unemployed in the Keynesian perspective even though they "have an occupation" in the classical mode of measurement. Once again, the Keynesian perspective justifies this specific inclusion.

The Revised Labour Force Survey

The period following World War II marked the strengthening of forces in the economies of the capitalist world, such as increasing concentration of productive resources and the creation of oligopolies, and the domination of world markets by the U.S. and its efforts to defend against encroachments on the capitalist world, which led to increases in *both* unemployment and inflation (Gonick, 1976). The simultaneous increase of inflation and unemployment was not easily reconciled with Keynesian theory and, as the phenomenon became ever more obvious in the late 1960s and 1970s, Keynesian doctrine lost its hegemony among bourgeois ideologists. The debate over how to properly measure unemployment (and inflation) increased as state supported committees and commissions were struck to study the problem.[5] Important changes were made to the U.S. Current Population Survey in 1967, while a Revised Labour Force Survey was instituted in Canada in January, 1976.

Since no economic doctrine had hegemony by the mid-1960s, one may ask what theory guided these revisions to the official North American labour force surveys. Perhaps the most important change was a return to neoclassical theory. For example, Farrall comment on the 1967 U.S. revisions that ". . . their objective was to obtain a more restrictive definition of unemployment by removing the category of 'inactive seeker' from the unemployed" (Farrall, 1973:23). Further,

> . . . neoclassical theory appears to advocate the exclusion of some active seekers from unemployment status if they (a) represent speculative, precautionary (wait) or search unemployed; (b) have unreasonable reservation-wage demands, i.e., failure to search in all avenues of job mobility; and (c) lack of the necessary qualifications for the jobs they are seeking (Farrall, 1973:25)[6]

But Farrall concludes that ". . . many of the categories of unemployment suggested above are essentially untestable" (Farrall, 1973:25). In other words, to measure these new exclusions would require something like a massive form of surveillance of workers and potential workers by the state, an enterprise which would be too costly and, perhaps, too oppressive for the current ideology of the Canadian state. Certainly the measurement could not be adequately accomplished by modifications to the more modest Canadian Labour Force Survey.

However, the 1976 revisions to the Canadian Labour Force Survey did try to take some of these concerns into account. The changes in measurement attempted to provide data which would permit an analysis of the flows of persons between the labour force categories, rather than simply the stock of, say, unemployed each month. Of course to measure flows, one must also have a measure of stock and for this purpose the Survey retained the concept of labour force activity (i.e., working, or not working but looking for work) during a reference period, which had been developed while the Keynesian perspective was dominant. The revisions produced the following changes in the definitions of the three labour force categories:

(1) The minimum age for members of the labour force was raised to 15 from 14 years.

(2) The unemployed were defined as those who
(a) were without work, had actively looked for work in the *past four weeks* (ending with the reference week), and were available for work (i.e., they were full-time students seeking part-time but not full-time work, or they reported that there was no reason why they could not take a job in the reference week with these two exceptions: 'own illness or disability' or 'personal or family responsibilities')

(b) had not actively looked for work in the past four weeks but had been on layoff for 26 weeks or less and were available for work;

(c) had not actively looked for work in the past four weeks but had a new job to start in four weeks or less from reference week, and were available for work.
(Statistics Canada, 71-001, Dec. 1976: 81-2)

In other respects the definitions remained either exactly or approximately the same. However, the revisions introduced another important change which did not involve the definitions directly but rather the construction of the questionnaire. Instead of the "indirect" technique used in the previous Labour Force Survey, the Revised Survey used direct questions such as "What has . . . done in the past four weeks to find work?" or "Was there any reason why . . . did not look for work last week?" and "In the past [6] month(s) has . . . looked for work?" This allowed more precise classification of respondents into each of the three labour force categories. Other revisions included a substantial increase in the sample size for the survey to about 55,000 households by 1977 (residents of the Yukon and Northwest Territories, persons living on Indian reserves, inmates of institutions and full-time members of the Armed Forces continued to be excluded).[7]

Conceptually, the revisions may be summarized as follows:

One, the definition of the unemployed has been narrowed to something more in line with neoclassical theory by eliminating many of the "excuses" for not looking (such as believing that no suitable work was available in the community).

Two, the amount and accuracy of data has been increased through direct questioning and increasing the sample size. This allows users of the data a certain range of alternatives in calculating their own labour force categories, unemployment rates, etc.

These conceptual changes are reflected in the empirical counts of the unemployed categories. The two surveys were run concurrently during 1975. This data revealed that more employed persons were counted by the Revised Survey than by the previous survey (about 2.1 percent more for the Canadian annual average). "The use of direct questions results in more complete reporting of part-time and short hours employment and identifies more persons who had a job but were not at work during the survey reference week" (Statistics Canada, Labour Force Survey Division, 1976a:3). For these reasons women (all ages) and men aged 15 to 24 showed the greatest increase. Also, in the prairie region, female employment increased since more farm wives were able to report unpaid farm work as a result of the new questions. The revised survey also found more persons unemployed than the previous survey (about 1.3 percent for the 1975 Canadian annual average). "In particular, the revised survey shows substantially higher unemployment levels for women, and a decrease in the level of unemployment for men" (Statistics Canada, Labour Force Survey Division, 1976a:4). Here we find that the direct questioning concerning methods of searching for work resulted in more housewives reporting that they did in fact look for work as well as doing housework (and hence they were really unemployed rather than not in the labour force) and at the same time, men who were out of work, especially during seasons of unemployment, were found by the revised survey to have not looked for work without an acceptable "excuse". Hence they were classified as not in the labour force rather than unemployed. One might think of a seasonally employed Newfoundland fisherman as an example of the effect of this revision — during the nonfishing season, if he didn't look for work, he would have been unemployed according to the previous survey but not in the labour force according to the revised survey. The revised survey decreased the 1975 annual average unemployment rate for Newfoundland by 3.3 percent. As a result of these revisions, the revised survey produced an unemployment rate for the country that was actually slightly lower than the previous survey (0.1 percent lower for the 1975 Canadian annual average).

The Revised Labour Force Survey has produced more complete data since January 1976 which permits one to devise alternate unemployment rates by varying certain assumptions. We turn now to some examples of alternate definitions and measures.

Alternate Definitions and Measures of Unemployment

A considerable range of alternative measures of unemployment can be calculated using official Labour Force Survey data. Four such measures have been calculated below to illustrate their monthly (and seasonal) variations for 1977 (Figure 3). Rate 1 which represents the conventional unemployment rate varied from a high of 9.2 percent in March to a low of 7.3 percent in October. We have already noted that the conventional rate does not take account of underemployment. That is, it counts as employed those part-time workers who want full-time work but cannot find it. As well, it counts as unemployed, those who are looking only for part-time work. To take account of these two corrections we have converted the measures of both unemployment and employment to "full time equivalents" by adjusting for the ratio of the number of usual hours worked per week by part-time workers in comparison to full-time workers. (This adjustment varied between 35.1 percent and 38.5 percent for 1977. It had to be estimated at 35.3% for the months January to April where no data was available.) Unemployment Rate 2 illustrates a measure of unemployment which takes into account the effect of (1) counting part time labour force participation in full-time equivalents and (2) counting the time "unemployed" (in full-time equivalents) of part-time workers who want full-time employment. The effect was to increase the unemployment rate by about 1 percent except during July and August when the increase was about 1.2 percent (probably due to more students who could only find part-time work), and September and October when the increase was slightly less than 1 percent. For the next correction we focus on those who are officially counted as "not in the labour force". A number of these "non labour force participants" have looked for work in the past six months but not in the past four weeks because they "believed no work was available", or were "awaiting recall" (i.e., supplementary teachers), or for "personal reasons" (i.e., "gave up" and turned to some non-labour force activity such as being a housewife, volunteer work, etc.). In our third measure of unemployment , we have included all of the first two categories and one-half of those with personal reasons for not looking on the assumption that they want work (since they looked in the past six months) and are available for work.[8] Rate 3 illustrates that the effect of these corrections is a further increase of about 1 percent (or 2 percent over the conventional rate). The seasonal variation is similar to Rate 2. Finally, there may be other persons who are counted as being not in the labour force but who want work and are available even though they have not been searching for work. To make a liberal correction for this possibility we have counted as unemployed all those "not in the labour force" who reported that they left their last job because of "lost job or laid off" as well as one-half of those who left for "personal responsibilities" or who "retired" and one-quarter of those who went to "school".[9] Of course, the standard labour force survey categories are not well suited for measuring these "potential workers" who are currently not in the labour force. No doubt some of those persons who left their last job because of "own illness", or "other reasons" or who have "not worked in the last five years" or have "never worked" (to exhaust the list of possible categories), want to work and are available, but there is currently no way of knowing how many. Hence we have restricted ourselves to selecting all or portions of the four categories from which potential workers would seem, at face value, most likely to be drawn. Rate 4 illustrates that these corrections had the effect of increasing the unemployment rate to between 15.6 percent and 18.6 percent. This represents an increase over the conventional rate of between 8.1 percent and 9.8 percent with the greatest difference occurring in the winter season, particularly January, and the least difference in the summer months, particularly June. However the seasonal variation of Rate 4 is somewhat different than the conventional rate, declining more sharply during the spring (when firings and layoffs as well as the school population declines) and failing to decline in the autumn (as the school population, and to a lesser extent, the layoffs and firings increase).

During the periods of peak unemployment, how many persons are unemployed? Using the conventional definition there were about 944,000 unemployed persons in March. (About 9,350,000 persons were employed while the total population age 15 years or older was about 17,138,000.) However, if we use Rate 3 as our measure, the equivalent of about 1,086,000 full time workers were unemployed (in July) and by using Rate 4 we discover that the equivalent of about 1,959,000 full time workers (or almost 2 million) were unemployed (in February). Each of these measures suggests that there was a substantial reserve of unemployed workers in Canada during 1977. But is it likely that the size of that reserve was at times more than double the estimates provided by the conventional measure of

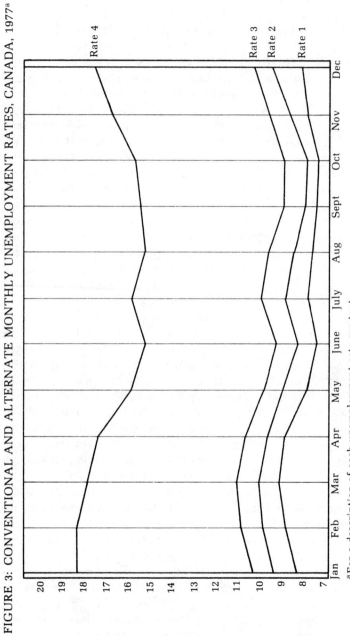

FIGURE 3: CONVENTIONAL AND ALTERNATE MONTHLY UNEMPLOYMENT RATES, CANADA, 1977[a]

[a]For a description of each unemployment rate see text.
Source: *Statistics Canada*, Cat. 71-001, Monthly.

Data For
FIGURE 3: CONVENTIONAL AND ALTERNATE MONTHLY UNEMPLOYMENT RATES, CANADA, 1977

	Jan.	Feb.	Mar.	Apr.	May	June	July	Aug.	Sept.	Oct.	Nov.	Dec.
Rate 1	8.8	9.1	9.2	8.8	7.7	7.5	7.9	7.5	7.5	7.3	7.9	8.3
Rate 2	9.6	10.1	10.1	9.7	8.8	8.6	9.2	8.7	8.1	8.1	8.7	9.4
Rate 3	10.6	11.1	11.2	10.8	9.8	9.6	10.1	9.7	8.9	8.9	9.7	10.5
Rate 4	18.6	18.6	18.2	17.8	16.1	15.6	16.1	15.7	15.8	15.9	16.8	17.7

unemployment, as suggested by Rate 4? There are several sources of partial evidence that we can examine to help us form a preliminary opinion about this rather important question.

Data collected by the Revised Labour Force Survey (post-1975) indicates that a large proportion of the non-labour force (about 40 percent — 3 million on an average monthly basis for 1977) have worked during the past five years (Statistics Canada, Cat. 71-001). Allowing for monthly variation, another 30 to 35 percent, or about 2 million, have had work experience, but not within the past five years, and only some 25 to 30 percent have "never worked". Hence there is a large pool of working experience and skills (some more current than others) among Canadians who are not in the labour force. Excluding those who have "never worked", this inventory of potential workers could have been as large as 5 million in 1977. Of course, this figure in no way indicates how many potential workers would actually be supplied to the Canadian labour force since most of these people, at a specific time, were not available for work, being retired or ill, having personal responsibilities (such as child raising), or attending school, and so forth.

The Revised Labour Force Survey provides data on flows between the three labour force categories although so far only flows into unemployment are available (Statistics Canada, Labour Force Survey Division: 1978). Hence we can only make weak inferences about the size of the reserve labour pool in terms of how many workers it tends to actually supply to the Canadian labour force. In any given month, the ranks of the official "unemployed" are increased from two sources: (1) those who were previously "employed", and have either lost their jobs or quit, and (2) those who were previously "not in the labour force".[10]

During 1977 the latter category composed 23.3 percent, on an average monthly basis, of all new "unemployed", or about 244,000 persons. However, not all persons flowing from "out of the labour force" into "the labour force" go into the "unemployed" category. Most probably go directly into the "employed" category. As there is no direct measure of the size of this latter group, we must estimate it from our knowledge of the number of new "unemployeds". If we estimate that these new "unemployeds" composed 25 percent of all labour force entrants, in any given month (a conservatively high estimate since the conventional rate would suggest 8 percent), then the total flow into the labour force, into both "employed" and "unemployed" becomes 244,000 + 732,000, or 976,000. These persons can be considered to have been the previous month's "potential workers", and this calculation suggests that the size of the reserve labour pool in Canada in any one month, in 1977, should be increased by about 1 million workers. If we add these potential workers to our calculation of the unemployment rate, we discover that they have the effect of increasing the conventional rate by about 9 percent, that is, to between 16 to 18 percent. Of course the conventional rate did not rise to this high level since an approximately equal number of workers in the labour force — both employed and unemployed — simultaneously moved out of the labour force (one of the flows on which we have no data). And so long as the Labour Force Survey requires a person without work to actively search for work in order to be counted as unemployed, then we cannot know what proportion, if any, of these labour force "leavers" remained available to supply labour. However, we can infer, from consideration of our two separately defined estimates, namely (1) the substantial number with work experience who are nevertheless not in the labour force and (2) the rather high monthly flows from "out of the labour force" into "the labour force", that Canada had a large labour reserve of unemployed workers during 1977, the size of this reserve being likely no less than 1 million and perhaps as many as 2 million persons.

The fact that a reserve labour pool exists and the inadequacy of surveys to measure it is often best revealed in depressed and underdeveloped regions in Canada. It is well known, for example, that Newfoundland has a persistent unemployment problem. The People's Commission on Unemployment used another approach to estimate "real unemployment" in that province (Newfoundland and Labrador Federation of Labour, 1978: ch. 3). Starting with the observation that if more jobs were available many more people would readily take them, the Commission reasoned that the *participation rate* in Newfoundland, that is, the percentage of the working age population (15 years and over) who are in the labour force (either employed or unemployed) would be about the same as the participation rate in Ontario. Since Ontario has a history of relative regional development and industrialization in Canada, its participation rate tends to be much higher than most of the other regions with the recent exception of Alberta. Hence the difference between the actual number of employed in Newfoundland, and the number who would be in the Newfoundland labour force if that province enjoyed the same participation rate as Ontario, provides an estimate of the number who were actually unemployed. The Commission estimated that the true unemployment rate for Newfoundland in 1977 should have been 34 percent, an increase of 18.1 percent over the conventional rate of 15.9 percent.

Table 1 presents the results of applying this estimating technique to Canada and the ten provinces for 1977. In this case, we have used Alberta, the province with the highest participation rate, as the standard since even in Alberta in 1977, 4.4 percent of the labour force were unemployed (by the conventional definition). The assumptions

TABLE 1

ESTIMATES OF THE RESERVE OF UNEMPLOYED BASED ON PARTICIPATION RATES
AND EMPLOYMENT/POPULATION RATES, CANADA AND THE PROVINCES, 1977[a]

	Conventional Unemployment Rate (%)	Participation Rate (%)	Employment/Population Rate (%)	Unemployment/Population Rate (%)	Reserve of Unemployed Number ('000)	Real Unemployment Rate (%)
Canada	8.1	61.5	56.5	10.0	1725[b]	15.0
Newfoundland	15.9	50.6	42.6	23.9	90	35.9
P.E.I.	10.0	57.3	31.1	15.4	14	23.2
Nova Scotia	10.7	55.3	49.4	17.1	103	25.7
New Brunswick	13.4	53.8	46.6	19.9	99	29.9
Quebec	10.3	58.8	52.7	13.8	655	20.8
Ontario	7.0	64.4	59.9	6.6	414	9.9
Manitoba	5.9	61.6	58.0	8.5	63	12.8
Saskatchewan	4.5	61.4	58.6	7.9	54	11.9
Alberta	4.4	66.5	63.6	2.9	39	4.4
B.C.	8.5	61.8	56.6	9.9	186	14.9

Participation Rate = $\dfrac{\text{No. in labour force}}{\text{No. of working age}} \times 100$

Employment/Population Rate = $\dfrac{\text{No. employed}}{\text{No. of working age}} \times 100$

Unemployment/Population Rate = $\dfrac{\text{No. Unemployed}}{\text{No. of working age}} \times 100$

Note that: Participation rate = Employment/Population Rate + Unemployment/Population Rate.

[a]The estimates adjust the participation rates for each province, and for Canada to that of Alberta (66.5%).

[b]The discrepancy between this estimate and the sum of the provincial estimates is due to a rounding error in the calculations.

raise the Canadian unemployment rate from 8.1 percent to 15.0 percent, an increase of 6.9 percent. The Maritimes are subject to the greatest increases although even Saskatchewan, with a relatively low conventional unemployment rate of 4.5 percent would increase by 7.4 percent. Table 1 also indicates that Quebec makes up almost 40 percent of the total Canadian unemployment reserve. The assumptions on which this technique is based lead to several inaccuracies in its estimates. For example, the technique does not take account of the amount of hidden unemployment that existed in Alberta in 1977. To do so would drive the real unemployment rate up even further.[11] Nevertheless, it does illustrate the ideological component of measurements of unemployment. There are important historic reasons in the development of Canadian capitalism which have ensured that the level of employment in Newfoundland cannot be equal to the levels of employment in Ontario or Alberta. To make Newfoundland equal to Alberta in calculations of unemployment is to create a mental fiction, something that has never been accomplished in Canadian economic history. But the technique demands that we recognize that very fact when we measure the number who are prepared to work.

A Saskatchewan Labour Force Survey done in 1973, (before the Statistics Canada Labour Force Survey was revised), provided data for a preliminary indication of the size of that province's reserve of unemployed, as well as some of their characteristics.[12] The survey was modelled on the Federal Labour Force Survey, having a similar sample design, (although the sample size was 6,000 households as compared to 1,800 in the Federal survey at that time), a similar interview format and many similar questions in the interview schedule. Many other questions, however, were added in an attempt to more precisely describe the members of the three labour force categories. The reference week for the Saskatchewan survey was the week ending July 14, 1973 while for the Federal survey it was the week ending July 21, 1973 (not a major difference). The results of the Saskatchewan survey produced two interesting differences from the Federal survey results.

The official unemployment rate for Saskatchewan in July, 1973 was 1.9 percent. However, using the same definitions as the Federal survey, the Saskatchewan survey found an unemployment rate of 4.9 percent (a statistically significant difference, that is, it was not likely a chance result). This puzzling result seems hard to explain since it should not result from sampling error. Why would the Saskatchewan survey interviewers find more persons unemployed than the Federal survey interviewers? Perhaps they were more exhaustively trained or more closely supervised. Perhaps, since they represented the University and not the Federal government, they got different information from respondents. None of these reasons seem very compelling. A more likely reason is based upon the fact that the determination of conventional unemployment in 1973 used indirect questioning, *i.e.*, "What did . . . do during (the reference week)?" Often this question had to be followed up with further exploratory questions (called probes) by the interviewer. If the probing revealed that a respondent who was not working did not look for work because she believed no work was available, an unemployed person would thus be "found". In other words, part of the discrepancy may have been due simply to the different ways that the interviewers asked the questions. (If true, the advantages of direct questioning are obvious.)

The Saskatchewan survey also looked for hidden unemployment. It asked those who were not in the labour force, "Did you want a job during the week of July 8-14?" The weighted results indicate that about 9,666 persons in the province did want a job. Adding in these hidden unemployed, the unemployment rate increased to 7.2 percent, a 5.3 percent jump from the official rate of 1.9 percent. When asked, "What is the main reason you are not looking for work?" these hidden unemployed identified such reasons as being unable to arrange daycare or family responsibilities, believing no work was available, health "problems" or a disability, in school, awaiting recall, age or appearance, and a host of more specific, personal reasons. The survey next asked those remaining in the non-labour force category, "Would you be interested in working (either full-time or part-time) if there were changes in the job market or in your household or personal situation?" The weighted results indicate that about 62,715 persons in the province would have replied "yes" to this question. If we include these as unemployed, the Saskatchewan rate for July increases by 18.1 percent over the official rate to 20.0 percent. When asked "What are these changes?" the respondents indicated such things as better health, child care or housework, completion of school, approval of spouse, satisfactory pay, working conditions or meaningful work, and many very specific, personal answers.

Who were those potential workers who either "wanted work" or "were interested in working", if conditions changed? Eighty-seven percent were women and 51 percent lived in the four largest cities. One-quarter of them were in their twenties, 29 percent had work experience during 1972 and they had spent an average of 4.9 weeks looking for work during 1972 (compared to 5.75 weeks for the conventional unemployed and 4.6 weeks for those remaining out of the labour force).

Various efforts, similar to the ones above, have been made to estimate the size of the unemployment pool in the United States. DuBoff (1977) drew on several sources to develop a time series of annual unemployment rates concluding that ". . . the official rate tends to be *at least* one-third too low." He notes also that unemployment has affected a very large number of Americans for relatively long periods of time. Leggett *et al.* (1977) completed a labour force survey in New Brunswick, New Jersey, and concluded that the unemployment rate for that city for 1975 was 43 percent, a count which included ". . . jobless persons who failed to seek a job in the last twenty-eight days; . . . unemployed single women with children . . . [and] unemployed fourteen and fifteen years old who were not in school, a category dropped from the labour force by the B.L.S. [Bureau of Labour Statistics] in 1967," and excluded ". . . the retired, the married housewives, the permanently disabled, the high school and college students and the strikers as unemployed *even when they sought work*" (Leggett *et al.*, 1977: p. 5, italics in original). A "winter seasonal" unemployment rate was also calculated at 23 percent, a figure which was reduced to 15 percent if the conventional B.L.S. definition was used, and compared to the official B.L.S. rate of 9 percent. Once again this 14 percent discrepancy appears to have two causes, namely (1) a change in the definition of who is "not in the labour force" rather than being unemployed (the difference between 23 percent and 15 percent), and (2) non-sampling error related to the diligence with which interviewers pursued their tasks, especially among the more suspicious, poverty-ridden, slum dwellers in the city (the difference between 15 percent and 9 percent).[13]

Even the limited evidence that we have summarized above leads to the conclusion that a large pool of unemployed workers exists in the Canadian and the U.S. economies. However, the evidence is not at all clear on the exact size and the characteristics of this unemployed reserve.[14] For Canada, the number may be somewhere between 1 to 2 million, suggesting unemployment rates between 10 to 20 percent, although some studies have suggested even higher unemployment rates particularly in underdeveloped regions and cities.

The existence of such a large unemployment pool, especially in conjunction with the experience of high levels of inflation, seriously questions the validity of current conventional economic theories, both Keynesian and neoclassical. In the face of the resulting ideological crisis, attempts have been made to shore up the faltering theories by involving exceptionalist explanations (*i.e.,* that unemployment insurance and welfare programmes cause unemployment) and by blaming "lazy" workers and labour unions for having unreasonable demands for wages and working conditions. However, none of these *ad hoc* explanations can explain the size of the unemployment pool. Accordingly, we must adopt a theoretical perspective which incorporates a large unemployment pool into its general (or unexceptional) explanation of capitalist production. We turn now to a brief examination of such an alternate theory.

An Alternate Labour Force Theory

Confronted with persistent and relatively large numbers of jobless people we turn to an explanation of capitalist production which sees unemployment as one of its fundamental or necessary features. Marx provided such an explanation in his discussion of "the general law of capitalist accumulation" (Marx, 1967: ch. 25). The explanation has a number of propositions which can be reviewed briefly. As the historical successor to feudalism, the capitalist mode of production ushered in "free" or unindentured labour. Peasants and serfs were no longer in bondage to a master but were "free" to sell their labour power to any entrepreneur who would combine it with the means of production (raw materials, machinery, etc.) so as to produce commodities. From the entrepreneur's point of view the object of this exercise was not only to recover the cost of capital and of labour, but also to retain a quantity of surplus value accomplished by being able to pay less for the labour than the value it contributed to the commodities produced. Hence the value of the final commodities produced "F" can be thought of as having three general cost components namely, the value of the constant capital "C" (the land, factories, machinery, etc.), the value of the variable capital "V" (primarily wages for labour), and the surplus value "S" retained from unremunerated labour by the capitalist. Thus, $C + V + S = F$. Some might think that the capitalists would spend all of their surplus value on typical consumer items such as food, houses, cars, holidays and so forth. But Marx observed that any capitalist who behaved this way would not continue to be a capitalist for very long! Indeed, to keep from being driven out of business by other competitive capitalists, it was necessary for the wise entrepreneur to (1) appropriate as much surplus value as possible and (2) quickly reinvest it in more capital. This is not only a subjective or personal goal of each capitalist. It is also an essential or objective aspect of the system of production itself. For example, to successfully compete against other capitalists an entrepreneur must produce commodities as cheaply and efficiently as possible. At a given wage level, efficiency can primarily be increased by adopting new technology. This will have the effect of either increasing the amount of output, making each unit less expensive to produce and hence increasing the margin of profit, or it can mean that less variable capital (in particular labour) will be used in the production process. Once a new technology has been adopted in an industry, it usually makes the existing technology obsolete, hence all of the entrepreneurs in that industry will either have to make the added investment in new capital or else go out of business. We can notice some important characteristics of capitalism from this example. Capitalist production, at least in its early stages, encourages a very high rate of accumulation and capital formation. It also leads to concentration of the ownership of capital since some entrepreneurs are continuously going out of business as the "victims" of competition among capitalists. These "fallen" entrepreneurs, who are usually smaller scale capitalists such as "small" businesspersons and farmers, "drop" into the ranks of the working class and increase the supply of "free" labour. The supply of labour is also increased relative to the economy's level of output by virtue of the drive by capitalists to adopt new technology and hence substitute capital for labour. However this characteristic of capitalist production needs some closer examination.

Efforts to increase the amount of capital accumulation initially lead to an increased demand for labour since it is only through increasing the amount produced that more surplus value can be appropriated (at a given wage). This tendency would sooner or later use up the supply of labour and the competition between capitalists for workers would surely drive up wages which, in turn, would decrease or even eliminate the amount of surplus value that could be appropriated. This contradiction is resolved and wages are kept down by introducing a counter trend which has the effect of increasing the supply of labour. That trend is the drive by capitalists to substitute capital (and "labour saving" technology) for labour. It has the effect of producing a "reserve army of labour" which ". . . consists of unemployed workers who, through their active competition in the labour market, exercise a continuous downward pressure on the wage level" (Sweezy, 1970:87). The reserve army can be made up of workers who are unemployed either because they have been displaced by capital (new technology), or because the substitution of capital for labour has meant that they were never hired. Hence we have identified two opposing tendencies: the drive to accumulate capital forces wages up while the reserve army of labour forces wages down. "It follows that the stronger the tendency of wages to rise, the stronger also will be the counteracting pressure of the reserve army, and *vice versa*" (Sweezy, 1970:88). For example, Marx observed that ". . . it is capitalistic accumulation itself that constantly produces, and produces in the direct ratio of its own energy and extent, a relatively redundant population of labourers . . ." (Marx 1967:630). In other words, the drive to accumulate *forces* entrepreneurs to substitute capital for labour and hence produce the reserve army of labour. The tendency to concentration of ownership of capital only serves to accelerate this trend. The combination of these two tendencies ". . . may mean an absolute decline in the demand for labour, or it may mean simply that the demand for labour lags behind the growth of total capital" (Sweezy, 1970:88-9).

> But if a surplus labouring population is a necessary product of accumulation or of the development of wealth on a capitalist basis, the surplus-population becomes, conversely, the lever of capitalistic accumulation, nay, a condition of existence of the capitalist mode of production. It forms a disposable industrial reserve army, that belongs to capital quite as absolutely as if the latter had bred it of its own cost. Independently of the limits of the actual increase of population, it creates, for the changing needs of the self-expansion of capital, a mass of human material always ready for exploitation (Marx, 1967: 632).

As the economy moves through its chaotic but necessary cycles of expansion and recession, the reserve army of labour is alternately diminished and replenished. Similarly the magnitude of the effect of the reserve army on wages will vary (less effect when the reserve army is diminished and more effect when it is replenished). However, the direction of the effect is always the same, *i.e.,* to hold wages down.

Workers who work part-time or are wholly unemployed make up the reserve army (as opposed to the active army of labour whose members are fully employed). Marx identified three forms of the reserve army. The *floating* form consisted of workers who were sometimes displaced from employment and at other times rehired, in other words, they cycled in and out of employment and were located at the "centres of modern industry". The *latent* form refers to potential workers, currently underemployed or unemployed in industries such as agriculture, but who are not actually drawn into other employment until a demand for them arises. The constant depopulation of rural areas in Canada illustrates the magnitude of this potential or latent form. Finally, the *stagnant* form refers to workers who have very irregular employment, are subject to the highest levels of exploitation (long hours and low wages), are recruited primarily from the "decaying branches of industry" (*i.e.,* the technologically least advanced) and who sink below the working class average in terms of proverty. In summary,

> . . . the greater this reserve army in proportion to the active labour-army, the greater is the mass of a consolidated surplus-population, whose misery is in inverse ration to its torment of labour. The most extensive, finally, the lazarus-layers of the working class, and the industrial reserve army, the greater is official pauperism (Marx, 1967:644).

With the advent of imperialism and the increasing domination of production by monopolies in the later stages of capitalism, the fundamental need for a reserve of unemployed workers was not reduced. A number of observations about the Canadian economy that are consistent with Marx's original explanation can be presented. For example, one important fact is that the concentration of ownership in many Canadian industries (such as the resources, food processing and retailing, and many manufacturing sectors) has progressed to the point where there are only a few firms (a condition called "oligopoly"). Then, the competition between firms changes. No longer do they engage in price competition, rather, the firms hold or even advance their prices in the face of declining demand and to compensate for lower sales they reduce the supply of their commodity by cutting back production (Gonick, 1976:ch. 2). In this way, they generate unemployment and add to the reserve army of labour. This source of unemployment is additional to the traditional forms identified by Marx (described above).[15] Imperialism is characterized by the fusion of bank capital with industrial capital into major corporate multinational conglomerates which partition the world in order to dominate the supplies of raw materials and the demand for commodities. Usually a state, such as the United States, plays a major role in securing world markets for these multinational firms. One of the effects has been to concentrate manufacturing in certain "developed" centres while other regions become important as sources of supply for raw materials, with manufacturing taking on a secondary importance.[16] In these latter regions, of which Canada is one, the potential for employment is dependent upon the "primary" or resource based industries. But the employment potential of these industries has been reduced by a high rate of adoption of technology (substitution of capital for labour) in the resource sector. One can conclude, therefore, that the employment potential of the Canadian economy has definite constraints.

A brief examination of some Canadian data substantiates these explanations. One of the historic roles of Canadian agriculture has been to give up labour to the industrial and commercial sectors of the economy. The number of persons employed in agriculture has been continuously declining since World War II. Some of these persons who migrate from farms to the industrial and commercial centres of Canada have been farm workers, but most have been farm entrepreneurs and their family members who have been squeezed out of business as a result of the competition between farmers themselves and between farmers as one sub-class of capital and other forms of capital, such as agri-business firms (for example, those which supply farmers with inputs — machinery, fuel, fertilizer, feed — and those which wholesale and process farm products — grain traders, packers). While this depopulation of rural areas and supply of labour cannot go on indefinitely, it is still continuing at a reduced rate in the 1970s. For example, between 1971 and 1976, Canadian agriculture lost another 36,000 employed persons, a drop from 6.3 percent of the Canadian employed labour force to less than 5 percent. Nevertheless, farm products still make a major contribution to the Canadian economy in both domestic and export markets. This is also true for other primary industries, especially those involved with mineral and forest resources. However, the proportion of the labour force involved in the entire Canadian primary industry sector is below 10 percent. Indeed, it dropped from 9.1 percent of the Canadian employed labour force in 1971 to 7.4 percent in 1976. All of these Canadian primary industries have experienced heavy substitutions of capital for labour thus replenishing the supply of labour. The manufacturing and construction sectors have taken up some of the extra supply of labour but the percentage increase has been marginal, with the total proportion of labour in these sectors remaining below 30 percent of the Canadian employed labour force from 1971 to 1976. Instead, the main increase in Canadian employment has come from the service producing sector which includes transportation, trade and finance, personal services and of course the services of the state. Together, the service sector accounts for almost two-thirds of Canadian employment, increasing from 62.6 percent in 1971 to 65.5 percent in 1976. But many jobs in this sector, as well, are being lost to machine technology. And the potential is very great for an ever more rapid substitution of capital for labour given the current state of computer technology and its wide range of service applications. We can see, therefore, that Canadian capitalist production has produced and continues to produce a reserve army of labour in various ways.

To summarize the alternative explanation, we have observed that a capitalist system of production tends to produce a surplus or reserve army of labour by substituting capital for labour. Far from being incidental to the capitalist economy, it is an essential aspect of the generation and accumulation of wealth by entrepreneurs. From this perspective the matter of whether unemployment is voluntary or involuntary is not an important distinction. The level of unemployment is determined by the structure of capitalist production; the subjective whims of individual workers — whether they look or don't look for work during a specific reference week — are minor variations within this structural source of unemployment. The important point is that members of this reserve can be recruited into the active labour force, a fact which our earlier presentation of data confirmed in the case of Canada. Finally, the importance of this reserve is that it effectively places limits on the rise of wages and generally serves to keep the level of surplus value and capital accumulation high.

Conclusion

Conventional theories about the labour force do not visualize high levels of unemployment as an integral part of a capitalist economy at or approaching equilibrium. Classical and neoclassical theories deny structural unemployment allowing only short-term frictional unemployment, a temporary condition that exists while the economy readjusts to an external influence. In this view, if a person is without work, it is because of his/her own personal voluntary decision — he/she quits, or is poorly trained, lazy and so forth. While higher levels of structural unemployment are theoretically possible in the Keynesian theory, in practice Keynesians expect that the state will undertake any incomes and fiscal policy specially designed to keep unemployment levels acceptably low. In doing so, the state must trade off higher inflation for lower unemployment and *vice versa*. They argue that a certain amount of unemployment is necessary in a growing and regionally extended economy such as Canada's. Hence the state's goal of "full employment" actually includes a few percentage points of unemployment and this figure has been creeping upward from 3 percent to 5 percent or more during the past two decades (Gingrich, 1978).

But the level of unemployment in Canada is far above 5 percent. The official measurement of Canadian unemployment has been derived from the propositions of the conventional theories. Consequently, these measurement criteria have excluded many potential workers who are unemployed or partly employed. Even the official counts reveal unemployment rates reaching 8 percent. But if we include all those who don't have work, want to work and would be employed if suitable work were available, then the unemployment rate appears to jump to 10 to 20 percent leaving a reserve of unemployed or under-employed persons of between 1 to 2 million. An alternate theory is required to explain this reserve of unemployed.

Marx explained that a reserve army of labour consisting of various forms of unemployed and underemployed workers is systematically generated by the capitalist system of production. Such a reserve serves to hold wages down and thus enhance the creation of surplus value and capital accumulation. The reserve is produced by entre-preneurs being forced to substitute capital for labour in order to increase efficiency and remain competitive. The gradual development of monopoly capitalism and world imperialism increased the likeli-hood that the reserve army will be large, especially in certain underdeveloped regions. These explanations appear to be appropriate for the history and current condition of the Canadian economy. For example, capital substitution for labour in agriculture has provided a continuous supply of labour in Canadian history. Since Canada is heavily dependent on resources and primary industries such as agriculture the demand for industrial labour is very limited. Instead, most employed Canadians work in the service sector. The potential for the replenishment of the reserve army from this sector is very great given the current technologies which can rapidly replace workers with machines.

Finally, it is clear that the conventional theories about unemployment are not only wrong, they also serve to rationalize, mystify, and legitimate the currently rising levels of unemployment. To the extent that they are used to justify state expenditures and regulations, they serve the interests of the ruling class or that portion of it which benefits. O'Connor has pointed out ". . . that macro-theory is at one and the same time the science and ideology of the ruling class — or, more precisely, the dominant stratum of the ruling class, the corporate oligarchy" (O'Connor, 1969:394). Therefore, it is important to realize that the difference between the official unemployment rate and the real unemployment rate cannot be compromised by "splitting the difference". Such an average would obscure the fact that there is not only a quantitative difference between the two rates but a qualitative difference as well. Each rate has its own movements and forms its own contradictions. It takes two very different methodologies to arrive at each rate. Conventional theories cannot embrace the real unemployment rate nor is the official rate of much use to a Marxist explanation of Canada's economy. Hence, it is doubtful that a working class which seeks to develop a critical view of Canadian capitalism will be able to usefully retain much from the conventional explanations of the labour force.

NOTES

1. It is important to note two factors which, although not taken into account here, are fundamental to a full analysis of ideology in relation to class interests. First, the development of ideology supportive of the ruling class does not necessarily have to be a conscious, direct effort on the part of representatives of that class. Second, and relatedly, theories which serve a ruling class by disguising the process of exploitation may be generated by other classes as well, for example the petty bourgeoisie and representatives of co-operative capital. Therborn (1976) provides an informative discussion of these issues.

2. We do not take up the erroneous, reductionist hypothesis that there is systematic variation in the biological make-up or "native ability" of various classes of workers which produces important differences in their levels of productivity. For a critical review of one form of this hypothesis see Armstrong and Armstrong, 1978.

3. Many of Keynes' "discoveries" had been anticipated by the Polish economist Michael Kalecki. But it was left for Keynes, responding to the challenge that the Depression posed for conventional theory, to make the ideas well known and dominant among academics and state bureaucracies (see Kalecki, 1966).

4. Some estimates of the number of hidden unemployed in Canada in 1977 are presented on page 185.

5. Canadian examples were the "Committee on Unemployment Statistics" which reported in 1960, and the background papers and discussion surrounding the "Statistics Canada Labour Force Survey Data Users Conference" held in Ottawa in 1973. In the U.S. a major study was that of the "President's Committee to Appraise

Employment and Unemployment Statistics" (or the "Gordon Committee") which reported in 1962 and more recently the "President's Commission on Federal Statistics". For a discussion of some of the debates see Gordon, 1968 and Wood, 1972.

6. The "speculative" and "precautionary" unemployed, called the "search" unemployed, are thought of as elements of frictional unemployment except that their decisions to stop working in anticipation of finding a better job (speculative) or not to start working so as to remain available for a more desirable job (precautionary) are viewed as voluntary decisions and hence their unemployment is not attributable to the economy and should not be counted.

7. The sampling frame is relatively complicated, employing a multi-stage stratified cluster design in which the strata are thought to be relatively homogeneous units, based on certain socio-economic criteria, and the clusters are relatively heterogeneous units within the strata. The design involves randomly selecting clusters within the strata, and at a subsequent stage randomly selecting households within the clusters. Since the survey is conducted monthly, a household will remain in the sample for about six months using a system of rotation. A local, trained interviewer, supervised by Statistics Canada personnel, initially visits the household, collecting information from a responsible person about each household member 15 years or older, using the standard questionnaire. When the interviewers send in their completed questionnaires, they are carefully checked (for example for obvious errors, such as being incomplete, etc.) and ultimately a computer based system checks the responses for "validity" using as criteria, internal consistency and consistency with previous monthly data for the same respondent. Computer based systems subsequently produce the aggregated totals that appear in published form and on tape. Clearly the Labour Force Survey is a very large undertaking which requires careful planning and strenuous attention to accuracy in order to produce acceptable results. But costs must also be minimized, which means a trade off with completeness of the data as well as precision (Statistics Canada, Cat. 71-526, 1976).

8. The numbers added have been adjusted to reflect the proportion of full-time and part-time participants (expressed as full-time equivalents) in the labour force.

9. Adjusted as described in Note 8.

10. This latter category includes a small number who became 15 year olds during the month and therefore spent no time designated as "not in the labour force".

11. As well, our calculations have ignored the existing capacity of each province's population to supply labour. A correction could be made by applying age specific participation rates for Alberta to the appropriate age categories in each province. The aggregate effect would not be great. Further, the choice of Alberta as the standard is arbitrary. If countries with even higher participation rates were chosen as the standard (the United States, Sweden or the Soviet Union) then the estimate of the Canadian labour reserve would be increased.

12. The survey was comissioned jointly by the Province and the Federal Department of Manpower, and was conducted by the Sample Survey and Data Bank Unit, University of Regina. Generous assistance from Statistics Canada is also acknowledged.

13. Some of this latter difference is also due to sampling error since the B.L.S. survey has the effect of averaging unemployment over several other urban areas in the vicinity of New Brunswick and not only the city itself.

14. There is another source of error in the conventional measurements which would lead to a discussion beyond the scope of this paper. We have mentioned that the fundamental concepts in the conventional framework, "employed," "unemployed,"

"labour force," and "not in the labour force," tend to obscure the class contradictions in Canadian society by focussing our attention on people — all people — who work or don't work, as if this were their individual choice. Why is it that the comparable terms which describe the other side of the "labour market" — "employers," and especially "unemployers," — are much less commonly used? To use these terms, a theoretical framework would have to recognize that the labour force status of a person is not her own choice. However, notice as well that the measurement of these concepts lumps "the many" with "the few". They make what are objective opposites look statistically alike — an employed labourer with a bank president; a welfare mother with a woman of wealthy class both "not in the labour force"; an unemployed university graduate with a "housewife" holding a degree but having become resigned to the conclusion that no work is available; and so on. Finally, the use of common statistics such as means and standard deviations, and the statistics based upon the assumptions surrounding the normal curve, themselves entail this "many/few" error since they summarize objective opposites into what appears to be a unified whole. For example, the 1977 annual average number of unemployed in Canada was 862,000. But in March, 1977, 1,944,000 were unemployed whereas in October 1977, only 787,000 were unemployed. In this case, seasonal variation is obscured by quoting an annual average. While the unemployment rate in 1976 was 7.4 percent for all of Canada, six of the ten provinces had rates above this average — indeed the median unemployment rate for the ten provinces was 8.5 percent. What has been obscured in this case is regional variation. But it is objective differences or contradictions such as these which need to be studied and demystified, not obscured. To what extent this will require a "new statistics" is an important methodological question.

15. Another tendency that has become very pronounced during advanced capitalist production parallels Marx's explanation of the reserve army of labour. Much of the new technology that has been adopted by capitalist firms (especially large scale firms) has not only had the effect of replacing labour but also of reducing the skills necessary to perform the remaining jobs. This generalized "deskilling" of jobs and workers is, of course, accompanied by a reduction in wages. And it increases the size of the reserve army by automatically making a block of unskilled persons now suitable candidates for the deskilled jobs. (See Braverman, 1974, and Lockhart, for an analysis and description of this trend.)

16. The recent tendency to deindustrialize the developed centre by moving factories to underdeveloped countries to take advantage of their lower wage costs has not fundamentally changed this global organization of capital.

Readings

Armstrong, Pat and Hugh Armstrong, *The Double Ghetto: Canadian Women and Their Segregated Work,* Toronto: McClelland & Stewart, 1978.

Braverman, Harry, *Labour and Monopoly Capital: The Degredation of Work in the Twentieth Century,* New York: Monthly Review Press, 1974.

Canada, Economic Council of Canada, *Economic Goals for Canada to 1970,* Ottawa: Queen's Printer, 1964.

Canada Economic Council of Canada, *People and Jobs: A Study of the Canadian Labour Market,* Ottawa: Information Canada, 1976.

Canada, Dominion Bureau of Statistics, *National Income and Expenditure Accounts 1926 - 1968,* Ottawa: Queen's Printer.

Canada, Statistics Canada, *Historical Labour Force Statistics,* (Cat. 71-201 Annual), Ottawa: Information Canada, 1977.

Canada, Statistics Canada, *The Labour Force,* (Cat. 71-001 Monthly), Ottawa: Information Canada, 1974-1977.

Canada, Statistics Canada, *Methodology of the Canadian Labour Force Survey,* (Cat. 71-526), Ottawa: Information Canada, 1976.

Canada, Statistics Canada, *Notes on Labour Statistics*, (Cat. 72-207 Annual), Ottawa: Information Canada, 1973.

Canada, Statistics Canada, Labour Force Survey Division, "Revision of the Labour Force Survey", Ottawa: Statistics Canada, 1976 [a].

Canada, Statistics Canada, Labour Force Survey Division, "Comparison of the 1975 Labour Force Survey Estimates Derived from the Former and Revised Surveys", (Research Paper No. 1), Ottawa: Statistics Canada, 1976 [b].

Canada, Statistics Canada, Labour Force Survey Division, "Flows in Unemployment", (Research Paper No. 17), Ottawa: Statistics Canada, 1978.

Cornforth, Maurice, *Materialism and the Dialectical Method*, New York: International Publishers, 1968.

DuBoff, Richard, "Unemployment in the United States: An Historical Summary", *Monthly Review*, Vol. 29 (November, 1977).

Farrall, Kim, "Theories, Concepts and the Art of Measurement: Economic Theories' Relationship to the Labour Force Survey Concepts" in Statistics Canada, *Notes on Labour Statistics* (Cat. 72-207), Ottawa: Information Canada, 1973.

Gingrich, Paul, "Unemployment: A Radical Analysis of Myth and Fact", *Our Generation*, Vol. 12 No. 3, (1978).

Gonick, Cy, *Inflation and Wage Control*, Winnipeg: Canadian Dimension, 1976.

Gordon, David M., *Theories of Poverty and Unemployment*, Lexington, Mass.: Lexington Books, 1972.

Gordon, R.A. "Employment and Unemployment", in *International Encyclopedia of the Social Sciences*, David L. Sills. (ed.), New York: Crowell Collier and MacMillan, Inc., 1968.

Kalecki, Michal, *Studies in the Theory of Business Cycles*, Warszawa: Polish Scientific Publishers, 1966.

Keynes, John M., *The General Theory of Employment, Interest and Money*, London: MacMillan & Co, 1936.

Leggett, John C., Jerry Gioglio, Mari Scanlon and Paula Toth, *Break Out the Double-Digit: Mass Unemployment in the City of New Brunswick*, New Brunswick, N.J.: John C. Leggett, 1977.

Mao, Tse-Tung, "On Practice", in *Selected Works of Mao Tse-Tung*, Peking: Foreign Languages Press, 1967.

Marx, Karl, *Capital*, (Vol. 1), New York: International Publishers Co., Inc., 1967.

Moy, J. and C. Sorrentino, "An Analysis of Unemployment in Nine Industrial Countries", *Monthly Labour Review*, Vol. 100 No. 4, (1977).

O'Connor, James, "Scientific and Ideological Elements in the Economic Theory of Government Policy", *Science and Society*. Vol. 33 No. 4, (1969).

O'Connor, James, *The Fiscal Crisis of the State*, New York: St. Martin's Press, Inc., 1973.

Peitchinis, Stephen G, *The Economics of Labour: Employment and Wages in Canada*, Toronto: McGraw-Hill Company of Canada Limited, 1965.

People's Commission on Unemployment, *Now That We've Burned Our Boats*, St. John's: Newfoundland and Labrador Federation of Labour, 1978.

Sorrentino, C., "Unemployment in the United States and Seven Countries", *Monthly Labour Review*, Vol. 93 No. 4, (1970).

Sweezy, Paul M., *The Theory of Capitalist Development*, New York: Monthly Review Press, 1970.

Therborn, Goran, *Science, Class and Society*, London: New Left Books, 1976.

United States, President's Committee to Appraise Employment and Unemployment Statistics, *Measuring Employment and Unemployment*, Washington, D.C.: United States Government Printing Office, 1962.

Wood, J., *How Much Unemployment: The Methods and Measures Dissected*, (Research Monograph No. 28), London: Institute of Economic Affairs, 1972.

Woytinsky, W. S., *Additional Workers and the Volume of Unemployment in the Depression*, Washington: Committee on Social Security of the Social Science Research Council, 1940.

The Economic Context of Women's Labour Force Participation in Canada*

M. Patricia Connelly

M. PATRICIA CONNELLY is an Associate Professor of Sociology at St. Mary's University. Her current research interests include Women in the Canadian Economy and Sociology of Labour.

Recently in Canada, as well as elsewhere, more and more married women are entering the labour force. Most attempts to explain this increasing participation have been done within a framework of traditional economics using a consumer choice perspective. The major assumption underlying the consumer choice model is the existence of an opportunity structure. Based on this assumption the question of women's labour force participation becomes a matter of personal choice. The explanation that follows concerns the factors affecting that personal decision to work or not to work.

However, data collected on the basis of the consumer choice model suggest that the decision of women to work is not so much determined by a capacity to take advantage of existing opportunities as it is structured by class conditions. By 1971 the majority of working women were married and the married women most likely to work were those with husbands who have low incomes. Such data clearly points to a class structure rather than an opportunity structure. These women do not freely choose to work but are economically compelled to do so.

With the major assumption of the consumer choice model in question it appeared necessary to pose the whole problem in a different way and to develop a more appropriate framework for analysis. This paper outlines a tentative step in this direction. An

I would like to thank Lorna Marsden, Herb Gamberg, and Henry Veltmeyer for their helpful comments and suggestions. I would also thank Olive Ross for her editorial assistance.

expanded concept of a reserve army, based on Marx's theory of capitalist development, is used as the framework of analysis. On this basis the problem in question is re-posed by shifting the focus from the factors influencing women's subjective decision to enter the labour force to the objective conditions under which they participate.

Specifically, this is done by examining the conditions under which women work in Canada in a way that parallels Marx's analysis of the conditions under which the capitalist system was formed. As capitalism developed it contracted the basis for agricultural labour, 'freeing' a significant proportion of the labouring population in the primary sector. At the same time a need was created for this surplus labour in the secondary sector of the economy. Similarly, as capitalism matures in Canada it contracts to some extent the basis for domestic labour, 'freeing' married women while at the same time creating a need for female labour in the tertiary sector of the economy. Under these conditions women are economically compelled to enter the labour force and constitute in effect a reserve army for the capitalist labour market.[1]

Elsewhere it has been shown that the expansion of the Canadian industrial and occupational structure has created a demand for female labour (Connelly, 1978). In this paper it is argued that married women are both freed (within limits) and economically compelled to enter the labour force. Which is to say, that Canadian women are used as a reserve army of labour.

The Entrance of Married Women into the Labour Force

In the average family in Canada the family's existence has been maintained by the husband's wage. His wage was expected to buy the necessary amount of commodities converted by the housewife into the family's subsistence. If the husband's wage is insufficient to buy the commodities necessary to meet a reasonable standard of living, then the housewife has two alternatives to prevent the family's standard of living from declining. She can intensify her labour in the home by cooking more, that is, using fewer of the more costly prepared foods; mending rather than buying new things; shopping more carefully; and generally trying to stretch her husband's wage. Secondly, she can seek employment outside the home, if jobs are available.

Recently more and more married women are working outside the home rather than intensifying their labour in the home because, under present conditions in Canada, they can accomplish more in economic terms by doing so. The data clearly show that married women in Canada have been entering the labour force in increasingly larger proportions. In 1931 the participation rate of married women was only

3.5 percent. The 1941 census showed only a slight increase to 4.5 percent. The percentage more than doubled in 1951 to 11.2 percent and doubled again in 1961 to 22 percent. By 1971 the percentage of all married women participating in the labour force had risen to 37 percent, (see Table 1).

TABLE 1

FEMALE LABOUR FORCE PARTICIPATION, CENSUS YEARS 1931-1971 [a]

Year	Participation rate				Married women as a percent[b] of total women in labour force
	Married %	Single %	Other %	Total %	
1931	3.5	43.8	21.3	19.3	10.0
1941	4.5	47.2	17.3	20.3	12.7
1951	11.2	58.3	19.3	24.1	30.0
1961	22.0	54.1	22.9	29.5	49.8
1971	37.0	53.5	26.5	39.9	59.1

[a.] Statistics from the 1931 Census are for the age group 10 and over. Statistics from the 1931-51 Censuses are for the age group 14 and over. Statistics from the 1961 and 1971 Census are for the age group 15 and over. Figures exclude those on active military service; Newfoundland is included from 1951 on; the Yukon and Northwest Territories are not included.

[b.] Including permanently separated.

Sources: DBS, 1961 Census, Advance Report N. AL-1 (Catalogue No. 94-500).
Table from: Spencer and Featherstone, 1970, p. 12, and Statistics Canada, 1971
Census, Vol. III, Catalogue 94-706, Table 14, Catalogue 94-774, Table 8.

This increase of married women in the labour force meant that by 1961 married women made up a larger proportion of the female labour force (49.8 percent) than single women (those never married, 42.3 percent) although they comprised a lesser proportion than single, divorced, and widowed women combined (single and other categories, 50.2 percent). However, by 1971 the percentage of married women (59.1 percent) had increased to the point where it was greater than the combined percentage of single, divorced, and widowed women in the labour force (see Table 2, Chart 1).

It should be noted that the 'married' category in Table 2 includes both married women who were living with their husbands as well as those who were separated. Since our interest is in married women living with husbands it is important to deduct those women who are separated from their husbands and need to work by virtue of being the only breadwinner. The Census does provide a count of married women living with their husbands who were in the labour force and these figures for 1961 and 1971 are included in a footnote to Table 2. In 1961, 42.3 percent of the labour force was composed of women who had never married, 44.9 percent of married women living with their husbands, and 12.8 percent of widowed, divorced, and separated

TABLE 2
MARITAL STATUS OF WOMEN IN THE LABOUR FORCE, CANADA[d] 1931-1971 [a]

Marital Status	1931 No.	(10+) %	1941[b] No.	(14+) %	1951 No.	(14+) %	1961 No.	(15+) %	1971 No.	(15+) %
Single	537,657	80.7	665,623	79.9	723,433	62.1	746,310	42.3	1,018,815	33.4
Married[c]	66,798	10.0	105,942	12.7	348,961	30.0	877,794	49.8[e]	1,803,870	59.1
Other	61,335	9.2	61,237	7.4	91,927	7.9	139,758	7.9	230,478	7.5
Not stated	69	-	38		-		-		-	
Total[d]	665,859	99.9	832,840	100.0	1,164,321	100.0	1,763,862	100.0	3,053,100	100.0

a. Statistics from 1931 Census are for age group 10 and over. Statistics from 1931-1951 Census are for age group 14 and over. Statistics from 1961 Census are for age group 15 and over.
b. Not including persons on active service.
c. Including permanently separated.
d. Including Newfoundland (1951 on) but not Yukon and Northwest Territories.
e. Married women who were living with their husbands and working numbered 791,685 or 44.9 percent of the female labour force in 1961; and 1,669,580 or 54.7 percent of the female labour force in 1971.

Sources: *Occupation and Industry Trends in Canada, 1901-1951*, DBS, Table 9
DBS, 1961 Census, *Advance Report No. AL-1* (Catalogue No. 94-500), Table 2.
DBS, 1931 Census, Vol. VII, Table 55; Table 26.
Table from: Canada Dept. of Labour, 1965, p. 21; and Statistics Canada, *1971 Census*, Catalogue 94-706, Vol. III, Part 1, Table 14.

210

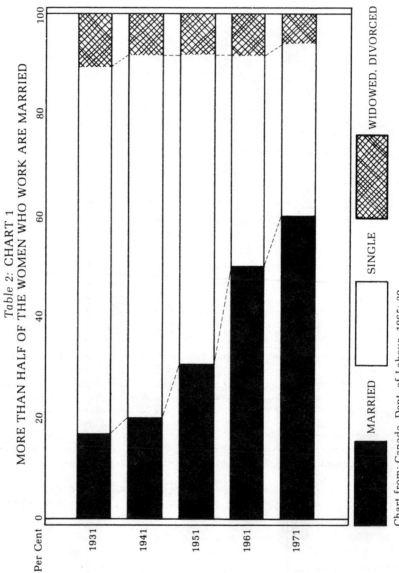

Table 2: CHART 1

MORE THAN HALF OF THE WOMEN WHO WORK ARE MARRIED

MARRIED   SINGLE   WIDOWED, DIVORCED

Chart from: Canada, Dept. of Labour, 1965: 20.

women. In 1971, 33.4 percent of the female labour force was composed of women who had never married, 54.7 percent of married women living with their husbands, and 11.9 percent of widowed, divorced, and separated women. Therefore, today more than half of the Canadian women working are married and living with their husbands.

Of course, it is true that when the housewife takes a job outside the home it means an increase in the cost of maintaining the family. Now, the cost of daycare or babysitters, prepared foods, laundry, more clothes and labour-saving devices must be included in the family's subsistence. These added costs must be met by the house-wife's wage. There is a trade-off of the increased cost of the family's subsistence resulting from the housewife working outside the home for the additional income her employment brings in (Seccombe, 1975). However, it would not make economic sense for her to work if only an equal exchange between lost domestic labour and the housewife's wage took place. What does occur is that once the extra cost of maintaining the family, which results from the housewife's working outside the home, is met there is still a small amount of her wage left.

That housewives have a small portion of their wage left after costs are deducted is certainly not because women's wages have risen. On the contrary, women's wages in Canada have declined relative to men's wages over the years. MacLeod did a trend analysis for the period 1946 to 1968 comparing male and female earnings in manufacturing industries. He concluded that:

> On the whole no improvement has been made over the 22-year period examined. Although pay ratios have risen in certain industries in certain time periods, there have been very few industries which showed significant improvement. The situation is as stagnant as a polluted river. The consistency of the pay differentials is particularly interesting in view of the large increases in the number of women working and the technological advances which have opened up new kinds of jobs and produced major changes in the nature of work performed in most, if not virtually all industries (MacLeod, 1972: 41).

Between 1967 and 1972 the dollar difference between female and male full-time workers' salaries increased in every occupation (Table 3). For example, in 1967 the difference between women's and men's salaries in clerical occupations was $1,925 and in 1972 it was $2,807. The average annual earnings of men employees in clerical occupations increased by $2,221 from 1967 to 1972 compared with $1,339 for women (Table 3). MacDonald (1975: 4) says that "women who work full-time in Canada earn on the average about 60 percent as much as male full-time workers". Moreover, she states that "the gap in wages and salaries between women and men is *increasing* — in all the provinces, and anyway you look at it" (also *cf* Gelber, 1975).

TABLE 3
AVERAGE EARNINGS[a] OF WOMEN AND MEN FULL-YEAR WORKERS[b]
BY OCCUPATION[c] IN 1967 AND 1972, SHOWING DOLLAR DIFFERENCES
BETWEEN THE YEARS, CANADA

Occupation	Salary Increases 1967 to 1972		Differences between increases in men's and women's salaries
	Women	Men	
Managerial	$3176	$4600	$1424
Professional and Technical	2292	3183	891
Clerical	1339	2221	882
Sales	1479	3471	1992
Service	779	2766	1987
Transportation and Communication	1167	3120	1953

Occupation	Difference Between Men's and Women's Salaries	
	1967	1972
Managerial	$5052	$6476
Professional and Technical	4294	5185
Clerical	1925	2807
Sales	3804	5796
Service	2594	4581
Transportation and Communication	2080	4033

a. Earnings include wages and salaries and net income from self-employment.
b. These are workers who reported having worked 50-52 weeks.
c. Individuals were classified according to their job at the time of the survey; individuals who were not in the labour force at the time of the survey are excluded. Some occupations that were incomplete for one sex, or that were not comparable between 1967 and 1972 are not shown in the table.

Source: Canada, Dept. of Labour, Women's Bureau, 1975b, Table 6.

When the earnings of female and male full-time, full-year workers are compared for 1971 we do indeed find that women earn only 59 percent of what men earn (Table 4). This is the same ratio that existed in 1961 showing that the gap has not narrowed. When all female (including part-time) and male wage earners in 1971 are compared the gap increases. In 1961 women earned 54 percent of what men earned but by 1971 this had declined to 50 percent.

The gap between female and male wages is sometimes explained as resulting from the occupational segregation of women. Gunderson (1976) examined what the overall ratio of female to male earnings would look like if females had the same occupational distribution as that of males while retaining their own earnings within an occupation. On this basis, he found that "the ratio of female to male earnings would be approximately .54 which is less than the actual ratio of .59 for full-year, full-time workers". Adjusting for differences in occupational distribution by sex does not by itself raise the ratio of female to male earnings. For the broader occupational groupings (i.e., those of Table 4), occupational desegregation would not reduce the wage

TABLE 4
RATIO OF FEMALE EARNINGS TO MALE EARNINGS,[a] ALL AND
FULL-TIME WAGE EARNERS, BY OCCUPATION, CANADA,
1961 AND 1971

Occupation	1961 Census[b]		1971 Census	
	All Wage Earners	Full-year[c] Full-time	All Wage Earners	Full-year[c] Full-time
Manager/Professional [d]	.46	.56	.49	.56
Clerical	.61	.74	.59	.67
Sales	.35	.45	.34	.49
Service	.47	.47	.37	.50
Primary	.43	.60	.38	.47
Blue collar[e]	.53	.59	.47	.53
Other	-	-	.47	.55
All occupations	.54	.59	.50	.59

a. Earnings figures are for wage and salary earners and exclude those self-employed in unincorporated business. 1961 and 1971 ratios are not strictly comparable. In 1961, wage and salary data were collected, with fine breakdowns to the income level of $12,000, with an openend class of $15,000 or more. For calculating averages, all incomes of $15,000 or more were given the value of $15,000. This means that, for occupations that had any incomes of $15,000 or more, the averages are too low. The groups most likely to be affected are the managerial and professional; in 1971 actual earnings were collected, so that the same bias does not exist in 1971 data.
b. 1961 occupational groupings are based on the 1951 Census categories and are not directly comparable with the 1971 figures, which are based on the CCDO groupings (see notes to Table 4.8 in Gunderson).
c. Worked 49-52 weeks for 35 or more hours per week.
d. 1961 figures are an unweighted average of the ratios for managers and professional and technical, used because the two groups had approximately equal numbers in 1961.
e. 1961 ratios are a weighted average of the ratios for transportation and communication with craft, production, and related workers. The latter ratio was weighted by 3 to reflect the fact that there were approximately 3 times as many craft, production, and related workers as transportation and communication workers. 1971 figures consist of CCDO occupations 81-95, which include crafts, production, transportation, communication, and construction workers.

Sources: 1961 data are derived from Sylvia Ostry, *The Female Worker in Canada*, (Ottawa: Queen's Printer, 1968), Table 16. 1971 data are from special 1971 Census tabulations from Statistics Canada.
Table from: Gunderson, 1976: 121.

gap unless accompanied by more equal wages within each occupation (Gunderson, 1976, p. 122). Gunderson also estimated what female earnings would be if women were paid according to the pay structure for males. He found that, "paying both sexes according to the male pay structure would raise female earnings from 60 percent of male earnings to 93 percent. The remaining 7 percent is due to differences in age, marital status, education, and residence between males and females" (Gunderson, 1976: 126).

Since the overall price of female labour has declined relative to the overall price of male labour, higher wages cannot be the reason that part of the housewife's wage remains after deducting the cost to the family incurred by the loss of her domestic labour. The reason has to do with the productivity of labour in the industrial sector which has risen significantly relative to the productivity of domestic labour. As capitalism develops the housewife has to work more hours in the home to make up for one hour spent in producing wage goods.

The following section draws on Seccombe's (1975: 92-94) argument regarding the productivity of domestic and industrial labour, which is part of an ongoing debate in the *New Left Review*.

Productivity of Industrial Versus Domestic Labour

Although the productivity of domestic labour has increased in absolute terms it has fallen behind the productivity of industrial labour. The Canadian Royal Commission on the Status of Women reports:

> Comparison with much earlier studies suggests that hours spent on housework have not decreased as much as one would expect in a technological age. The question therefore arises whether or not housework has been influenced by the same forces of technological change that have transformed and continue to alter the rest of the economy (The Canadian Royal Commission on the Status of Women, *Report,* 1970: 34).

The answer to that question is that housework has not been influenced by the same forces of technological change that have altered the rest of the economy. This is because domestic labour has no direct relation with capital. Domestic labour is not paid a wage, is not part of variable capital, and does not create surplus value: therefore, the capitalist has no interest in increasing its productivity. Within industrial production, on the other hand, any increase in the productivity of labour increases surplus value, raises profits, and gives one capitalist a competitive advantage over another.

The result has been that new technology and new ways of organizing and dividing labour have been introduced into industrial production to increase productivity while the domestic labour process has advanced only to the extent that new technology is introduced into the household via commodity consumption. Also women can accomplish their household work in less time, given that many of the services once performed by domestic labour are being displaced or altered by the State and by the production and service sector of the capitalist economy. The Royal Commission on the Status of Women describes this phenomenon as follows:

> Mechanization of the old processes of spinning, weaving, cutting and sewing has transferred the manufacture of clothing from the home to

the factory. Commercial laundries have taken over much of the cleaning. Truck-gardening, canning, freezing and pre-cooking have lessened the importance of the home in the production, preservation, and preparation of food.

Other functions, which had stayed in the home, have been greatly altered. Meal preparation has been changed by the introduction of a wide variety of appliances. New quick-freezing techniques for fresh food, along with improvements in canning and pre-cooking techniques and the addition of chemical fortification to foods, make it possible for the family to eat varied and nutritious meals with much less preparation in the home (The Royal Commission on the Status of Women, Report, 1970: 34-35).

The advance of technology and the rising productivity of labour in the industrial sector has lowered the cost of many consumer goods. The lower cost has put them almost within reach of the majority of people. At one time only the wealthy could afford these products and they were considered by most people to be a luxury. However, as more goods are produced in a shorter time mass consumption of these goods becomes an imperative for the ongoing capitalist system. New needs are created among the population so that the greater amount of goods produced have a ready market. These needs are created partly through psychological means by way of advertising but mainly through not developing alternatives or through encouraging the erosion of existing alternative ways of doing things. For example, the automobile is a necessity and not a luxury if an adequate public transportation system does not exist. In the household, refrigerators and stoves are no longer luxuries. Most households in Canada today find it necessary to have a stove and refrigerator (see Table 5).

According to the 1941 Census at that time half of Canadian households had no installed baths or showers and 45 percent of households had no inside toilets (Popoluk, 1968). Few people would question the necessity of these facilities today. Podoluk states:

> Other examples of items that might be considered necessities of the 1960s are consumer durables such as television sets or automobiles. When television sets first became available in the early 1950s only the middle and upper income classes could afford them; currently, families who do not own television sets appear to be those residing in parts of the country still not reached by television stations, or families who can afford television but consider it a status symbol not to own one (Podoluk, 1968: 184).

By the late 1960s even welfare budgets recognized that expenditures on television ownership should not disqualify recipients from receiving assistance.

As capitalism develops, then, what was once a luxury for a few becomes a necessity for the majority. Women are not working for labour-saving devices which are luxuries or 'extras'. They are working for necessities (which must be constantly replaced as a result

TABLE 5
PERCENTAGES OF CANADIAN HOUSEHOLDS SURVEYED THAT HAD
CERTAIN HOUSEHOLD EQUIPMENT, 1948-1968*

Item	1948	1953	1958	1963	1968
Hot and cold running water	-	62.57	73.50	84.86	90.97
Gas or electric stove**	48.49	62.73	76.66	87.24	94.03
Mechanical refrigerator	29.26***	66.33***	86.24***	94.20	97.44
Home freezer	-	2.22	8.17	17.66	29.16
Electric washing machine	59.21	76.38	84.28	86.81	83.57
Vacuum cleaner	32.02	48.01	60.94	72.45	-
Electric sewing machine	-	23.43	36.30	49.03	-
Gas or electric clothes dryer	-	-	-	21.60	36.79
Automatic dishwasher	-	-	-	2.08	5.08
Floor polisher	-	-	-	-	55.01

*   Does not include households in the Yukon, Northwest Territories or on Indian reservations.
**   Includes piped and bottled gas and oil or kerosene.
*** Includes both gas and electric refrigerators. The number of gas refrigerators, however, dwindled rapidly, so that their exclusion from the statistics after 1958 probably makes little difference.
- No statistics available.

Source: Dominion Bureau of Statistics, *Household Facilities and Equipment*, Ottawa, Queen's Printer: 1948, 1953, 1958, 1963, 1968, Cat. no. 64-202.
Table from: Royal Commission on the Status of Women in Canada, 1970: 34.

of planned obsolescence) that cannot be purchased by one wage and in most cases are just beyond the second wage (note the rise in the use of credit).[2]

The Economic Necessity for Married Women to Work Outside the Home

Evidence that married women *need* to work outside the home can be found by examining several Canadian studies dealing with women in the labour force. In 1955-56, for example, the Canadian Department of Labour conducted a survey of married women working outside their homes in eight Canadian cities.[3] One of the aims of this survey was to discover why these married women were working. Why they were working became apparent when they considered the husband's income alone and then his income combined with that of his wife (Table 6). When considering the husband's income alone only 14 percent of the families would have had at least $4,000 to live on. However, when the wife's income was also considered half of the families (51 percent) had incomes of $4,000 or more.

It is interesting to note that in 1954, according to the Dominion Bureau of Statistics, 43 percent of all non-farm families, whether there was one income or more, were in the "$4,000 and over" group (Canada,

Dept. of Labour, (1958).[4] With the husband's income alone the families in this survey would have been well below a cross section of Canadian urban families in income; but with the addition of the wife's income these families compared favourably with others. According to the authors of this study: "The extreme importance of the economic motive in keeping these married women at work outside the home is one of the most outstanding findings of this survey" (Canada, Dept. of Labour, 1958: 48).

TABLE 6
MARRIED WOMEN WORKING: PERCENTAGE DISTRIBUTION
BY HUSBAND'S INCOME AND BY COMBINED INCOMES

Amount of Income $	Husband %	Combined %
Under 2000	24.9	8.0
2000-2999	21.8	12.3
3000-3999	29.6	17.0
4000-4999	10.5	20.2
5000 plus	3.5	31.0
Unknown or not applicable	9.7	11.4
Total	100.0	99.9

Table from: Canada, Department of Labour, 42.

In 1961, data on husband and wife family income distribution again confirmed the importance of the wives' earnings. Table 7 shows that half of all husband-and-wife families (including those with wives that work outside the home and those with wives that don't) had incomes of $5,000 or more. In families where the wives do not work outside the home 45 percent had incomes of $5,000 or more. In families where the wives do work outside the home almost two-thirds (64.8 percent) had incomes (including the wives' earnings) over $5,000. However, when the earnings of the wives are excluded only slightly more than one-third (36.1 percent) of those families with working wives have incomes over $5,000 (see Chart 2). Removing the wives' earnings results in an income distribution which is lower than that of families with non-working wives. It would appear, then, that husbands in families with non-working wives have higher incomes than husbands in families with working wives (Podoluk, 1968: 133). Married women whose husbands have low incomes are clearly compelled to find employment outside the home.

Again in 1971 data show that the lower the family's income (excluding the wives' earnings) the greater the likelihood that a married woman will work outside the home. Table 8 shows that almost half (47 percent) of the women whose family income is less than $3,000 (excluding her own earnings) participate in the labour

TABLE 7
PERCENTAGE DISTRIBUTION OF HUSBAND-AND-WIFE FAMILIES
BY SIZE OF FAMILY INCOME,
INCLUDING AND EXCLUDING EARNINGS OF WIVES

Income Group	All Families With & Without Wives Working	Families Without Wives Working	Families With Wives Working Including Their Income	Families With Wives Working Excluding Their Income
Under 3000	19.1	22.0	10.4	22.6
2000-4999	30.9	33.1	24.9	41.3
5000-6999	24.7	22.5	31.3	14.4
7000-9999	15.8	13.0	24.0	17.7
10,000+	9.4	9.4	9.5	4.0
Totals	100.0	100.0	100.0	100.0
Average income	$5839	$5652	$6387	$4739
Median income	5000	4677	5894	4308
Families (number)	3,357,386	2,427,062	830,324	

Source: Unpublished data, 1961 Census of Canada.
Table from: Podoluk, 1968, Table 6.6.

TABLE 8
LABOUR FORCE PARTICIPATION RATES OF MARRIED WOMEN,
HUSBANDS PRESENT BY FAMILY INCOME EXCLUDING
WIVES' EARNINGS

Family Income Excluding Wives' Earnings	Participation Rate of Wives
3000 or less	47
3000-5999	44
6000-8999	44
9000-11,999	38
12,000-14,999	33
15,000 or over	27

Source: Special 1971 Census tabulations from Statistics Canada.
Table from: Gunderson, 1976, Table 4.3.

force. As the family income (excluding wives' earnings) rises, the economic need for married women to work outside the home decreases and so does their participation in the labour force.

What we have seen, then, is that between 1951 and 1971 the participation rate of married women in the labour force more than tripled (see Table 1). It is the married women whose husbands earn the least that are most likely to be working outside the home. The question is do these women work to get the 'extras' that their husband's income won't buy? or are they working because their husband's wage can no longer buy what is *necessary* to maintain their family at a reasonable standard of living? The evidence points strongly to the latter explanation: married women work in order to maintain their family's economic position.

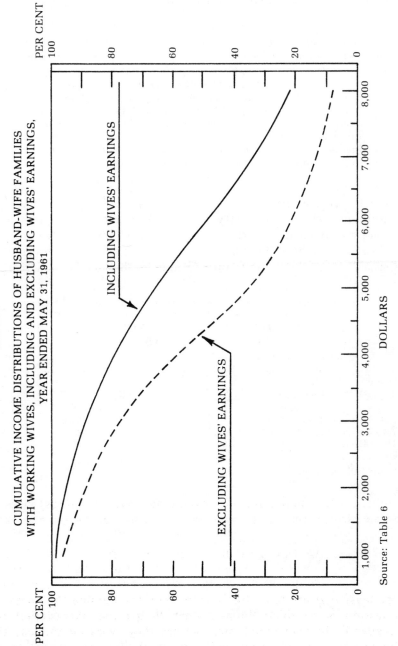

CHART 2

CUMULATIVE INCOME DISTRIBUTIONS OF HUSBAND-WIFE FAMILIES
WITH WORKING WIVES, INCLUDING AND EXCLUDING WIVES' EARNINGS,
YEAR ENDED MAY 31, 1961

PER CENT

INCLUDING WIVES' EARNINGS

EXCLUDING WIVES' EARNINGS

DOLLARS

Source: Table 6

The Department of Labour's publication *Women at Work in Canada: 1964* indicated that many women were working out of need.

> Since the thirties the level of living of the population, including the "real" incomes that sustain it, has risen remarkably. The standard of living — that level at which people feel they are comfortably off and not deprived of anything important — has increased also; the availability of a wide range of consumer goods has assisted in the latter process. Yet a considerable proportion of male wage-earners, in fact the majority, do not earn the $6,000 or so per year that is necessary to move consumption much beyond food, clothing, and shelter. For many Canadian families, however, the earnings of the wife added to those of the husband just succeed in bringing total income up to a fairly comfortable level (*Women at Work in Canada: 1964*, 1965: 6).

According to Johnson (1974) there has been a growing disparity between rich and poor workers since 1951 despite the rise in *per capita* income. This disparity has contributed toward the restructuring of family earning patterns. Multi-earner families have increased enormously since 1951 until, by 1971, almost two-thirds (64.9) percent) of all Canadian families had more than one income recipient (see Table 9).

TABLE 9

PERCENTAGE DISTRIBUTION OF FAMILIES BY NUMBER OF INCOME RECIPIENTS, 1951-1971

Number of Income Recipients in Family*	1951**	1961**	1971
None	0.4	0.5	0.3
One Recipient	57.0	53.2	34.7
Two Recipients	29.7	34.7	47.6
Three Recipients	8.7	8.6	11.6
Four Recipients	3.0	2.4	4.3
Five or More Recipients	1.1	0.6	1.4

*   Excludes unattached individuals.
** Excludes families with one or more farmers.

Sources: Canada, Dominion Bureau of Statistics, *Income Distributions* (Cat. 13-529), Table 14; Canada, Statistics Canada, *Income Distributions by Size in Canada 1971* (Cat. 13-207), Table 25.
Table from: Armstrong and Armstrong, 1975.

The Armstrongs[5] have convincingly argued that married women's "earnings supplement the family's income, thus helping the family maintain its financial status in spite of the increasing disparity for individuals in general" (Armstrong and Armstrong, 1975: 22). Using quintiles they illustrated the growing inequality in individual income distribution between 1951 and 1971. Over this twenty-year period it was found that all individuals with income, all wage earners, and all unattached individuals with income in the lowest three quintiles (lowest three-fifths of the population) received a decreasing share of the total income. At the same time the top two quintiles received an increasing share. Table 10 shows that the top two-fifths of wage earners increased their share of the total income from 65.3 percent in 1951 to 69.8 percent in 1971. A corresponding decline was experienced by the other three-fifths of the population so that by 1971 two-fifths of all wage earners earned 70 percent of the total income, while the remaining three-fifths earned 30 percent.

TABLE 10
PERCENTAGE DISTRIBUTION OF TOTAL INCOME BY QUINTILES,
1951-1971

Year	Lowest Quintile	Second Quintile	Third Quintile	Fourth Quintile	Highest Quintile
All Individuals					
1951*	3.2	9.2	17.4	25.2	45.0
1961*	3.1	8.9	17.2	26.0	44.8
1971	2.0	7.2	15.5	26.0	49.2
1971**	2.3	9.2	15.8	25.8	45.8
Wage Earners					
1951*	4.2	12.0	18.6	25.0	40.3
1961*	3.7	11.7	18.7	25.6	40.3
1971	2.3	10.1	17.8	25.8	44.0
Unattached Individuals					
1951*	2.7	8.9	16.1	25.8	46.6
1961*	3.1	7.8	14.8	26.6	47.7
1971	2.9	8.0	14.9	25.8	48.5
1971**	3.3	9.2	15.8	25.8	45.8
Families					
1951*	6.1	12.9	17.4	22.4	41.1
1961*	6.6	13.5	18.3	23.4	38.4
1971	5.6	12.6	18.0	23.7	40.0
1971**	6.4	13.5	18.5	23.8	37.8

*   Excludes farm income.
** Represents income after income taxes, but no other taxes have been removed.

Sources: Canada, Dominion Bureau of Statistics, *Income Distributions*, (Cat. 13-529), Tables 9 and 12; Canada, Statistics Canada, *Income After Tax, Distributions by Size in Canada, 1971*, (Cat. 13-210), p. 16.
Table from: Armstrong and Armstrong, 1975.

In comparing the distribution of incomes among Canadian families, however, the pattern which exists for individuals does not repeat itself. Rather, the families in the two lowest quintiles experienced only a slight decline in proportion of the total income and the families in the middle group increased their share. The top group, on the other hand, had a reduction in their proportion of the total income (Armstrong and Armstrong, 1975: 21).

It is married women's earnings which prevent the family income distribution from matching that of the individual income groups. As our earlier discussion illustrated, women with husbands who have low incomes are most likely to work. Therefore, the fact that these women are working explains why the bottom two quintiles did not decline significantly and why the middle quintile improved their positions slightly. It also follows that women in the highest income groups are least likely to work outside the home and therefore the decline in the share of the total income experienced by the highest quintile can be explained by this fact.

In summary, it would appear that as the standard of living in Canada rises, married women whose husbands earn low incomes must work outside the home to maintain their relative standard of living. Married women do not work in order to close the gap between rich and poor families; rather they work to prevent the difference from increasing. To stay at home and try to stretch their husband's wage is no longer a viable alternative. To maintain what is now considered a reasonable standard of living, families must purchase a growing number of goods and services which are rapidly becoming indispensable. In order to be financially able to purchase these goods and services many wives must work outside the home. The existence of these goods and services is a prerequisite for women taking outside employment. At the same time it is the production of these goods and services that women themselves once produced in the home which has led to the expansion of 'female' occupations. In other words, married women are 'free'[6] to work because of the creation of necessities which, in fact, determine their need to work. It is the accumulation process itself by expanding the occupational structure and creating 'female jobs' which determines women's participation in the contemporary labour force. The form of this participation is that of a relatively permanent reserve army which is the ultimate cause of women's oppressive labour conditions.

NOTES

1. For a detailed explanation of women in Canada as a reserve army as well as the specific form of reserve army that married women constitute, namely, the institutionalized inactive reserve, see M.P. Connelly, *Last Hired, First Fired: Women and the Canadian Work Force,* Toronto: The Women's Press, 1978.

2. Baran and Sweezey (1966) explain how and why the capitalist system creates new needs; builds in obsolescence; and increases consumer debt.

3. While the sample did not represent a cross section of working women in the categories of divorced, widowed, and separated, for married women living with their husbands "the sample is fairly representative, and they make up 88% of the total" (Canadian Dept. of Labour, 1958, p. 11).

4. As the authors point out the combined incomes of husbands and wives in the sample cannot be precisely compared with total incomes for Canadian families (Canada, Dept. of Labour, 1958, p. 42).

5. This part of the discussion is based on Armstrong and Armstrong's (1975) important article on female segregation in the Canadian labour force.

6. The family as a private unit of consumption is required in a capitalist society. Consequently "a residual portion of the (domestic) work that accomplishes this consumption is structurally necessary regardless of advances in household technology, child care services etc." (Seccombe, 1975, p. 92).

Readings

Armstrong, H. and Armstrong, P., "The Segregated Participation of Women in the Canadian Labour Force, 1941-1971", *Canadian Review of Sociology and Anthropology*, Vol. 12, No. 4, (November 1975).

Baran, P.A. and Sweezy, P.M., *Monopoly Capital*, New York: Monthly Review Press, 1966.

Canada, Department of Labour, *Married Women Working for Pay*, Ottawa: Queen's Printer, 1958.

Canada, Department of Labour, *Women at Work in Canada: 1964*, Ottawa: Queen's Printer, 1965.

Canada, Department of Labour, Women's Bureau, *Women in the Labour Force: Facts and Figures*, Ottawa: Information Canada, 1975.

Canada, Statistics Canada, *1971 Census*, Ottawa: Information Canada.

Connelly, M.P., "Canadian women as a reserve army of labour"; Unpublished doctoral dissertation, Ontario Institute for Studies in Education, University of Toronto, 1978.

Gelber, S., "The Compensation of Women", in Canada, Dept. of Labour, *Women's Bureau '74*, Ottawa: Information Canada, 1975.

Gunderson, M., "Work Patterns", in G. Cook (ed.), *Opportunity for Choice*, Ottawa: Information Canada, 1976.

Johnson, L.A., *Power and Wealth*, (Rev. ed.), Toronto: New Hogtown Press, 1974.

McDonald, L., "Wages of Work: A Widening Gap Between Men and Women; *Canadian Forum*, (Apr.-May, 1975), pp. 4-7.

MacLeod, N., "Female Earnings in Manufacturing: A Comparison with Male Earnings", in *Notes on Labour Statistics, 1971*, Ottawa: Information Canada, March 1972 (Catalogue No. 72-207 Annual).

Podoluk, J.R., *Incomes of Canadians*, Ottawa: Queen's Printer, 1968.

Royal Commission on the Status of Women in Canada, *Report*, Ottawa: Information Canada, 1970.

Seccombe, W., "Domestic Labour — Reply to Critics", *New Left Review*, No. 94, (1975).

Spencer, B.G. and D.C. Featherstone, *Married Female Labour Force Participation: A Microstudy*, Ottawa: Queen's Printer, 1970.

Educational Opportunities and Economic Opportunities — The "New" Liberal Equality Syndrome

Alexander Lockhart

ALEXANDER LOCKHART is an Associate Professor of Sociology at Trent University. His current research interests include Canadian Post Secondary Education.

Compared to the previous two decades, the 1970s saw a massive about-face in popular attitudes toward, and public support of, higher education in Canada. While these changes have been argued in terms of abstract philosophical principles, a sociological understanding is most cogently pursued in the context of some wider understandings of how Canada's educational institutions have developed historically in relationship to the changing structure of economic opportunity.

We may usefully begin in the late 1840s when Egerton Ryerson challenged the traditionalist educational policies of the Upper Canada establishment. In essence, Ryerson's reforms followed closely the strategy of the American progressivist movement, i.e., the institutionalization of universal, free, compulsory and comprehensive public schooling as the means of promoting economic modernization and social justice.[1]

Yet despite the widespread adoption in Canada (excluding Quebec) of Ryerson's liberal educational model, the century that followed his famous 1849 Report was one in which Canada, by comparative Western world standards, remained industrially underdeveloped and socially conservative. Indeed, as Johnson (1972) has documented, the late nineteenth and early twentieth century period was one in which Canadian economic and social policy served to reduce those classically liberal economic opportunities which elsewhere (especially in the United States) were at this time expanding very rapidly. This failure on the part of Canada to realize reasonably the economic and social goals of liberalism, in liberalism's golden age, has been explained by some (e.g., Clark, 1968; Lipset, 1963; Porter, 1965) in terms of the particular normative legacy of British colonialism, and by others (e.g., Innis, 1956; Myers, 1972) in terms of the more general (and hence continuing) imperatives of imperialism. Either way, it is clear that despite the school reforms Canada retained a comparatively traditional economy[2] and a conservative socio-political institutional pattern until at least the mid-point of the current century.

What ultimately did facilitate some modicum of progress toward economic modernization (in central Canada) came not from early educational reform but from Canada's involvement in the two great wars. However, by the end of the Second World War, the classical liberal model of free market determined opportunities had itself been outflanked by the consolidation dynamics of large scale capital. As the functions, and hence opportunities, that had once been open to small entrepreneurs became increasingly absorbed into the corporate monoliths, the "old" liberal ideology that emphasized social independence and economic competition began to be displaced by a "new" liberal doctrine.

These ideological revisions began in the United States, where a major "culture lag" (Ogburn, 1966) crisis was occurring as a result of the irreversible growth of corporate-statism in a nation whose origins were so clearly committed to the practice of *laissez-faire*. The "new" liberal doctrine began with the proclamation of the "post-industrial" society (Drucker, 1957). The essential difference between this kind of society and its "industrial" antecedent was that the free market rationality had been superseded by an organizationally sponsored technological rationality.[3] Thanks to the combining of science with the large-scale organization, scarcity was alleged to have been vanquished. Thus the "hidden hand" of the autonomous market mechanism was no longer required as the ultimate allocator of harsh necessity. On the contrary, it was argued that both economic growth and the social good now required expert planning and the fulfillment of "discretionary" needs through administered marketing. This, in turn, required the intervention of the corporate-state at all levels (Galbraith, 1967). As a consequence, the Adam Smith ideal of the independent, inner-directed entrepreneur, seeking to fulfill real consumer needs by competitively offering judicious buyers the most product for the least cost, had become a dangerous anachronism. The business leadership model now advocated was that of the other-directed organization man working co-operatively within the authority structure of the modern corporation seeking to create unthought-of "wants" amongst an increasingly captive mass consumer market (Riesman, *et al*, 1953; Whyte, 1956; Leiss, 1976).

Such an ideological revision was, of course, nothing more than an *ex post* attempt to legitimize the encroachment of monopoly capital upon the once dominant (in the United States) "old" middle class entrepreneurial sector and to redefine the locus of "new" middle class opportunity away from anticipating independent business careers and toward an acceptance of entering white collar employment (C. Wright Mills, 1956).

However, given the popular commitment to the old liberal rhetoric of free men and free markets (even in Canada), such an attempt would not have likely gained much support had it not been for the parallel development of a major new economic theory which provided some essential identity transformations. This theory was widely labelled the theory of "human capital". Its primary postulate was that as the scale and complexity of production increased, "knowledge" had replaced ordinary capital as the critical input factor through which the liberal goals of national economic growth and individual success could be achieved.[4] Thus by the simple act of defining knowledge as the newly functional equivalent of capital, it was *theoretically* possible to claim that those who "possessed" organizationally relevant knowledge were in the same relative social position as those who had fomerly owned the means of production. The fact that these "techno-structural" experts and managers were employees of organizations, and as such might well suffer the same sorts of "de-skilling" and redundancy disadvantages that employed workers have traditionally experienced under the regime of capital (Braverman, 1974) was neatly sidestepped by the invocation of a second assumption, *i.e.,* that the imperatives of the "post-industrial" society were such as to render the demand for the techno-structural experts always in excess of the potential supply. Under this totally unproven assumption, it could be logically argued that those individuals who attained the necessary higher educational certifications would hold the same power over their employers as these owners of the physical means of production had formerly held over their less knowledgeable labourforce, *i.e.,* the prerogatives that attend control over the most scarce production factor (Burnham, 1962; Galbraith, 1967).

The popular acceptance of these human capital postulates, coupled with the (then) cold war fear of Russia's emerging technological sophistication, caused a major and rapid shift in public educational philosophy. Gone was the "old" liberal "pragmatic" concern for a "common core" curriculum that would hopefully provide everyone with the "basic" competence through which an equity start in life's competitive race might be assured (Dewey, 1959). In its place was a highly technical concern for testing, measuring and sorting students into differential learning "streams", each of which was linked to socially stratified occupational levels (Conant, 1959).

The essential individual opportunity mechanism of the "new"

liberalism was thus rooted in the notion of early meritocratic educational selection for later occupational rewards (or punishments) as the necessary replacement for the "old" liberal notion of comprehensive schooling as the common preparation for the real world of free market place competition. However, given the elite traditions of higher education (even in America), this shifting of the field of life-success competition from the market place to the learning place required not only curricular changes in the schools, but accessibility changes in higher education, if the liberal goal of "equal opportunity" were to be upheld. While any attempt to render the traditionally exclusive universities "open" to the masses would require very heavy public financing, the human capital theory justified such an "investment" in terms of the widespread public returns that would allegedly flow automatically from an increase in the availability to the private sector of such a vital new production factor.

Thus, under the American-born theory of human capital, the State was to play a central and active role in creating the scientific and educational infrastructures as the primary instruments of national economic policy. In so doing the State could also claim to be promoting a new and more active form of social justice through the sponsorship of a meritocratic form of equal opportunity provision. And, like other "metropolitan" concepts of the day, the "post-industrialization" ideology and human capital theory became popular in "hinterland" nations seeking a place within a rapidly changing international economic order.[5]

In Canada, where the old mercantile form of monopolistic privileges had inhibited the full development of industrial capitalism, the theory of "post-industrialism" suggested the possibility of a leapfrog jump from a moribund primary to an expansionary tertiary sectoral predominance without passing through the slow-growth secondary stage. Indeed, it could even be argued that Canada's earlier failure to commit itself to the classical forms of social liberalism left it in an advantageous position to "engineer" the necessary state interventionist policies through which a rapid human capital formation could proceed. And, to be sure, this seemed to be the case. Utilizing the extraordinary wartime powers which C.D. Howe had established in the realm of state sponsorship of scientific and technological development, the federal government moved swiftly after the secession of hostilities to create a major "in house" (direct government) research and development establishment under the aegis of the Science Council of Canada.[6] The intended purpose of these lavishly funded state sponsored laboratories was to pioneer break-throughs in the most advanced areas of potentially profitable technology and then to make these discoveries freely available to Canadian based private industry.

However, as Porter (1965) pointed out, it is one thing to sponsor the high technology research facilities deemed necessary for attaining the threshhold from which the leap into "post-industrialism" could occur, but it is quite another to staff such institutions from domestic sources in a nation that had steadfastly maintained an elitist and classically oriented higher educational system. But by the time Porter published his liberal critique of Canadian society, the Canadian government had already moved to transform and harness higher education to the human capital master plan. However, because education falls under provincial government jurisdiction, this had to be approached indirectly through ideological and financial manipulation.

The ideological instrument was created in the form of the Economic Council of Canada which was given broad terms of reference. In the words of Lester B. Pearson, the Council was "expected to create an economic consensus, the kind of economic understanding we need if we are to make the most of our resources, achieve and maintain a high level of employment, and compete successfully in the new trading world" (quoted in *Leader Post*, February 21, 1978: 6). The ECC responded with much publicized reports[7] which reiterated almost verbatum the arguments of the American "post-industrial" prophets in general and the human capital economic theorists in particular. In so doing they created a vision of Canada emerging in the 1980s as a super-modern world economic power — provided the nation's current economic resources were focused almost exclusively upon the building up of the necessary higher educational infrastructures through which the critical human capital formation could proceed.

Given the ubiquity of the human capital onslaught, and its major premise which held educational reforms to be central to the realization of the "new" liberal economic and social success goals, it is hardly surprising that public support was high for radical changes in educational philosophy and financing. Provincial government after provincial government sponsored Royal Commissions into public school reform, all of which mimicked J.B. Conant's (1959) call to the American public to harness high school education to "the national purpose" in preparing the masses for further human capital processing at either the direct vocational or further higher educational levels.[8]

Having achieved the necessary "economic consensus", the federal government found few objections to moving into the provincial jurisdiction at the level of financing higher educational expansion. Indeed, the 1960s was a decade in which Canada led the world in expanding higher educational facilities — especially in the scientific disciplines and at the post-graduate levels.

Over this critical decade, the federal share of university funding grew from 21 to 52 percent. In terms of overall fiscal commitments, the Canadian higher education expenditures grew from $273 million in fiscal 1960-61 to $1,767 million in fiscal 1970-71, or nearly three times the growth in GNP over the same period. Expressed as a proportion of total educational spending, the universities' share rose from 16 to 24 percent.

As a measure of the relative importance given to human capital expansion, Canada's public support for education rose from 14 percent of all government spending in 1960 to 21.6 percent in 1970. Expressed as a proportion of the GNP, educational spending increased from 4.6 percent to over 9 percent in the ten-year period.

A cross-cultural comparison of proportional spending on education reveals that Canada closed the decade of the 1960s with the highest proportion of its GNP devoted to education of any of the major industrial nations in the world, including both the United States and Russia.

This focusing of national economic resources on higher education met the ECC's stated goal of achieving something close to parity with the United States in terms of the university-going participation rate. Between 1960 and 1970, university enrolments grew by 310 percent in comparison to an increase in the university aged population of only 60 percent. Thus the stable, prewar university participation rate of 4 percent increased by a factor of over six times to 30 percent by 1971. Although this growth rate still trailed behind the United States (at 40 percent) overall, Canada had managed to reach or surpass proportionate equity with the U.S. in the critical human capital formation areas of science, engineering and post-graduate studies. For example, the growth in Canadian doctoral degrees over the 1961-71 period was nearly twice the increase in all degrees granted, and 83 percent of these Ph.D.s were in the fields of science and engineering.

Thus, if the human capital theory were correct, Canada should have entered the 1970s as a leading member of the exclusive "post-industrial" club. Specifically, its rate of economic growth should not only be high, but it should surpass that of conventional industrial economies. This growth should have occurred primarily as a result of high technological innovations in electronics, nuclear and related "software" fields. Further, with over a third of its new-entrant labour force now in possession of higher educational degrees, the rate of net upward mobility as measured by the early acquisition of highly rewarding employment, should be similarly high.

Unfortunately, the decade of the 1970s was ushered in not with the statistics of economic growth and the widespread realization of individual occupational success, but rather with economic recession and unmet occupational expectations. A review of the thin evidence used to support the "post-industrial" and human capital theories provides some useful insights as to why the 1970s have not measured up to expectation. To begin, as numerous recent documentaries on the Canadian economy testify, the high technology industries in Canada are to an extraordinary degree foreign-owned subsidiaries. As Levitt (1970) points out, these Trojan horse industries not only fail to transfer higher research and managerial functions to their hinterland operations but have also siphoned off the rather considerable innovations which Canada's government-sponsored laboratories have made available to them. Thus the anticipated growth in scientific and managerial employment within Canada's private sector did not materialize. For a time this was thinly disguised by the educational expansion itself which *briefly* absorbed virtually all its own human capital output. But by the mid-70s the teaching and professorial reservoir was full to overflowing.

However, Canada's hinterland status cannot fully explain the current debacle, for a major surplus of highly educated manpower has emerged in virtually all industrial nations, including the American metropolis itself. Clearly, the postulates of the human capital theory itself have failed to demonstrate real world validity. The notion that "knowledge" could remain in short supply and hence offer the possessor market advantage was naive in the extreme. Not only was the publicly sponsored higher educational expansion designed to increase the available supply of knowledge workers to the private sector, but the very computer-based innovations which the human capital theorists saw as increasing the demand actually had the opposite effect. For as the research of Bright (1958) and Whisler (1970) reveals, after a brief period during which the introduction of computer technology increases the technical and managerial load, its ultimate effect is to reduce significantly the number of higher level knowledge workers required and to fragment and reduce the knowledge required of those who remain.

In Canada, official recognition of the early indicators of this failure of the human capital inspired public policy to achieve the desired social and economic goals was slow in coming, despite the emergence in the early 1970s of signficant counterevidence from within the governmental research establishment itself. For example, a review of the scientific employment trends published by the Science Council of Canada (Kelly, 1971) revealed the extent of the failure of Canadian industry to follow the government's lead in promoting R and D activities. According to the data presented, the private sector had managed to account for only five percent of the new scientific employment that had resulted from the massive expansion of scientific education during the 1960s, and even this small proportion was on the decline. By 1970, Canada's private sector was only

providing "about 300 employment opportunities for [science] graduates. . . annually through retirement and other forms of attrition — a
negligible proportion of the 14,000 science and engineering graduates
now produced each year by Canadian universities" (Kelly, 1971:21).

The report goes on to point out that throughout the university
expansionary period, the absorption of the exponentially increasing
number of new scientists had been almost wholly within government
created "in house" research establishments and university faculties.
Thus the earlier "evidence" of insatiable demand for scientists was
revealed to be nothing more than a self-fulfilling prophecy that could
only continue so long as those institutions that were to prime the
pump could absorb virtually all of the resulting flow.

The implication that such a situation must at some critical point
reverse itself into a self-defeating prophecy was further reinforced
by von Zur-Muehlen's (1972) projective analysis of future Ph.D.
employment prospects — a study that was ironically sponsored by the
ECC. Using demographic data, von Zur-Muehlen showed that the
university expansion period was rapidly ending, that precisely
because of the earlier rapid expansion the professorial workforce
currently in place was extraordinarily young, and that as a result,
replacement rates over the next 20 years or more would be in the order
of one percent, or 250 positions annually. This employment potential
compares with a national Ph.D. output which by the early 1970s
reached 13,800 annually and continued to grow.[9]

Although both of these studies focus exclusively upon the market
situation of those with the highest level degrees, a Statistics Canada
survey (Zsigmond, Picot, Devereaux and Clark, 1976) of the job-
getting patterns of all the 1974 graduates of Ontario's post-secondary
institutions provides a broader picture. According to this study, the
unemployment rate of the university graduates four months after
labourforce entry was 11.9 percent (unadjusted). The comparable
community college graduate unemployment rate was 9 percent, with
the overall Ontario unemployment at 3.7 percent (unadjusted). Under
these circumstances it is quite obviously absurd to assume that the
wide distribution of higher educational opportunities is equivalent
to the extension of life-chance opportunities. It is equally obvious
that the emergence of surplus human capital must undercut the
legitimacy of treating educational spending as a retrievable investment in future economic growth.

The slowness of government to recognize and react to the accumulating evidence that the human capital forecasts were delusionary
no doubt reflected the massive consensus which the earlier commitment to these policies had engendered. However, the early 1970s saw
the beginning of a tactical retreat from official sponsorship of the
"post-industrialization" formulae. As before, the early warning

signals of incipient policy change appeared in the form of special committees and Royal Commissions charged with the task of "fundamental re-examination" of existing science and education policies.

The retreat from Canada's "hot house" science policy was initiated by a cabinet directive instructing the Senate Standing Committee on Science Policy to evaluate the effectiveness of government "in house" research in promoting the expansion of private sector R and D activities. After conducting extensive and highly visible public hearings, the Committee recommended that the government abandon its direct scientific leadership policy by curtailing "in house" R and D activities (and hence employment of scientists and engineers) in favour of a limited programme of subsidies for scientific research within the private sector itself. Given the record of Canada's by now predominantly foreign-owned industrial sector with respect to domestic R and D activities, this amounted to a near total abandonment of the notion that a new economy could be created around high technology production and service activities.

As for educational policy, the Province of Ontario heralded the retreat from its former leadership in human capital production with two commissioned reports on the future directions of that Province's school and university support provisions. The so-called "Hall-Dennis Report" (1968) gained instant international notoriety as the most "radical" set of curricular and pedagogical change proposals to have appeared anywhere under official government sponsorship, an observation that took on added significance when the government implemented the main recommendations.

The Hall-Dennis educational model was clearly, indeed proudly, borrowed from A.S. Neill's *Summerhill* (1960). Its condemnation of "instrumentalism" in public education was total, and its euphoric celebration of the "expressive" was underscored by the Report's presentation in unorthodox format — multi-colour typography and finger-painting illustrations.

The principal recommendation was something close to the total destructuring of elementary and secondary school curricula such that teachers could choose their subjects and presentation methods as freely as students could choose to engage in all, any, or none of these offerings without fear of "failure".

While this unheralded and, for many, "shocking" advocacy of a Rousseauian student-centred approach as the replacement for the now well established subject-centred school philosophy was presented for the most part in terms of psychological development needs, its somewhat more circumspect extension in the form of the Wright Commission's Report (1972) on future directions in post-secondary education was, in our view, more to the real point.

The Wright Report noted at the outset that the existing post-secondary educational structures had been almost forcibly erected upon a foundation that reflected "often contradictory" assumptions about the ability of higher education to facilitate economic modernization, social mobility aspirations and high rates of future economic returns on current investments. The Commissioners then question, with admirable hindsight, the ability of the educational institution *alone* to perform this "panacea" function with respect to facilitating broader social and economic transformation goals.

The Commission further rejects the notion that higher educational provisions should in any significant way reflect national *economic* policy planning. Rather, education should be returned to its proper location as a broadly *cultural* institution. To the extent that higher educational services must be economically accounted, the Commission is explicit in its view that education must be entered as a "consumer good" and not as an "investment" in future production assets. Their reasoning here is brief, but insightful; for the majority, higher education will become a form of leisure time activity "in a society destined to require shorter work hours" (Wright Commission Report, 1972: 33). To the extent that higher education will remain costly, though not as expensive as in the past (because of the proportional decline in scientific and professional preparatory programmes), the division of costs between the individual "consumer" and the society should be properly negotiated as part of the wider "political process", *i.e.*, subject to popular rather than expert evaluation of social benefit.

As with the Hall-Dennis Report, the Wright Commission recommended a destructuring of destination oriented higher educational programmes and encouraged a "flexible" approach to free course selection and institutional transfers which would ideally continue on and off over a lifespan of pursuing knowledge "for its own sake".

Thus by linking apparently "radical" notions of educational practice with some very traditional *laissez-faire* concepts of individual rights and responsibilities, the social contract implications of the human capital education model were tacitly broken. Indeed, the Wright Report makes it quite clear that the student who accepts a place in such an educational model also accepts a personal responsibility for any "future failure" (Lockhart, 1975) that may derive from his current curricular choices. But as with other examples of *laissez-faire* advocacy, there are likely to be latent structural forces already in place which ensure that individual "free choice" will result in quite predictable social outcomes. Or as a recent OECD re-examination of Canada's educational policies notes:

> The practice of [curricular] "flexibility" . . . may easily prove to be a form of selection built into even the primary school at the early stages,

with mostly irreversible effects on [later opportunity] development of individual pupils. In many instances in Canada the form of [individual programme] adaptation looks suspiciously like traditional streaming... (OECD, 1975: 7)

Most certainly, if an infinitely variable and individualized set of curricular options has any sociological implications, it is that only those individuals who make the appropriate choices, at the right time and in the proper sequence, from primary school through to the completion of their secondary educations, would be in a position to "qualify" for entry into those now much more limited professional or quasi-professional post-secondary programmes. And given what educational sociology has documented with respect to which social groups most, and least, monitor the educational choices of their children, and which are most, and least, effective in making decisive interventions amongst the school personnel on behalf of their children (Halsey, et al, 1961), we cannot help but conclude that these educational policies heralded a tactical retreat not only from the human capital notion of mass education as an economically regenerative force, but also from the "new" liberal notion of education as the great equalizer of life chance opportunities.

But, as we have argued elsewhere (Lockhart, 1977), this hasty sponsorship of such apparently radical educational policy by one of Canada's most traditional provincial governments may well have been as much motivated by the desire to goad the public into a reaction, to which the government could "democratically" respond, as it reflected the need to retreat quickly from the prior policy. If so, then the strategy was successful. Educational traditionalists, who had for years been silent in the face of the popular "equal opportunity" policies, were quick to organize a highly vocal "back to basics" movement. The ensuing public education debate was thus between those who would celebrate the "noble savagery" of youth and those who had no doubt as to the moral purification powers of highly structured mental exercise.

In the course of this debate, the plight of the un- and under-employed university graduates reached the level of a public scandal. The effect was to swing public opinion to the side of "tradition" since, as the back-to-basics advocates argued, in the days when "rigour" apparently prevailed, graduates got jobs. Thus the brief experiment in consumer oriented education served to disguise the failure of education as capital investment policies to achieve their goal of equalizing life-chance opportunities. The official response to the back-to-basics lobby was to reverse their still-born free choice curricular policy in favour of a return to central control over curriculum and didactic formalism in teaching methods — a formula which has long been recognized as functional in the early separation of the privileged few from the under-privileged many.

The potentially restrictive effect of these lower school policies upon future university participation rates in combination with the certain decline in the university-aged population that will occur after 1980 (Zsigmond, 1975) brought an abrupt end to the free spending post-secondary expansionary programmes. While "cutbacks" in government support for universities occurred everywhere, it was in the over-expanded Ontario system that the restrictive formula was most clearly articulated. The vehicle was the Report of the Special Program Review which the Provincial government established in 1975 to review a wide range of spending priorities. The recommendations relating to post-secondary education stood the prior human capital "investment" and "equal opportunity" policies on their head:

> . . . [No] further public support should be directed toward increasing student participation rates.
>
> The Province's percentage share of total operating costs should be reduced and tuition fees correspondingly increased. . . .
>
> The attitudes of employers and society as a whole should be adjusted to discourage reliance on paper credentials in determining eligibility for employment. . . . (Government of Ontario, 1975: 127).

There can be little doubt that these recommendations reflected a rather generous share of public opinion. The reasons why should now be apparent. If public "investment" in higher educational expansion was sold to the public explicitly in terms of general economic benefits and particular occupational mobility opportunities, then the failure of this investment to yield the anticipated returns was bound to result in widespread disenchantment.

If there is a lesson to be learned from all of this, it is that educational reform, whether it be motivated by "old" or "new" liberal notions of equality, cannot hope to overcome the more fundamental sources of inequality in a society that bases its core social relationships upon differential access to the basic economic resources that must ultimately determine the real life-chance opportunities not only of individuals but more importantly of whole social classes.

NOTES

1. See Wexler (1976) for a comprehensive review of the progressivist education movement and its relationship to wider socio-economic forces.

2. Easterbrook and Watkins (1967) provide a useful selection of readings in Canadian economic history.

3. See McDermott (1969) for a detailed exposition.

4. The human capital literature is extensive, but the following are representative: Becker, 1964; Denison, 1962; Schultz, 1961: 1-7.

5. The diffusion of these concepts throughout the Western Bloc nations was strongly promoted by the Organization for Economic Co-Operation and Development (OECD).

6. The linkage between these wartime developments and Canada's post-war science policy was clearly made by an OECD examining team which noted "that during the Second World War, Canada by a concentrated national effort was able to marshal its substantial scientific capabilities and weld them into an effective force directed toward achieving the national goal of victory". They go on to note that the Canadian government believes that its post-war economic success is largely dependent on a similar "broad national plan of action that will fully utilize the creative abilities of scientists and engineers" (Gunning, 1969: 3).

7. See in particular the First and Second *Annual Reviews* (1964: 1965) of the Economic Council of Canada.

8. A relevant and succinct review of these Reports is provided in Johnson (1968).

9. See also Auerbach, et al, (1976).

Readings

Adelman, Howard, The Holiversity: A Perspective on the Wright Report, Toronto: New Press, 1973.

Auerbach, Lewis and Andrea Gerber, Perceptions 2: Implications of the Changing Age Structure on the Canadian Population, Ottawa: Science Council of Canada, 1976.

Baran, Paul A. and Paul M. Sweezy, Monopoly Capital, New York: Monthly Review Press, 1966.

Becker, Gary S., Human Capital: A Theoretical and Empirical Analysis, New York: Columbia University Press, 1964.

Berg, Ivan, Education and Jobs: The Great Training Robbery, New York: Praeger, 1970.

Braverman, Harry, Labor and Monopoly Capital, New York: Monthly Review Press, 1974.

Bright, James R., Automation and Management, Cambridge: Division of Research, Graduate School of Business Administration, Harvard University, 1958.

Burnham, James, The Managerial Revolution, Harmondsworth: Penguin Books, 1962.

Clark, S.D., The Developing Canadian Community, (2nd ed.), Toronto: University of Toronto Press, 1968.

Conant, James B., The American High School Today, New York: McGraw Hill, 1959.

Denison, Edward F., Sources of Economic Growth in the United States, New York: Council of Economic Development, 1962.

Dewey, John, Democracy and Education, New York: Macmillan, 1959.

Drucker, Peter F., Landmarks of Tomorrow, New York: Harper and Row, 1957.

Easterbrook, W. and M. Watkins, Approaches to Canadian Economic History, Toronto: McClelland and Stewart, 1967.

Economic Council of Canada, First Annual Review, Ottawa: Queen's Printer, 1964.

Economic Council of Canada: Second Annual Review, Ottawa: Queen's Printer, 1965.

Galbraith, John K., The New Industrial State, Boston: Houghton Mifflin, 1967.

Government of Ontario, The Report of the Special Programme Review, Toronto: Executive Council of the Province of Ontario, 1975.

Gunning, Harry E., "Canadian Science Policy and the OECD Report: A Critical Analysis", Science Forum Vol. 12, (1969).

Hall-Dennis Report, Living and Learning: The Report of the Provincial Committee on the Aims and Objectives of Education in the Schools of Ontario, Toronto: Ontario Department of Education, 1968.

Harvey, Edward, Educational Systems and the Labour Market, Don Mills: Longman Canada, 1974.

Horowitz, Gad, "Conservatism, Liberalism and Socialism in Canada", *The Canadian Journal of Economics and Political Science*, Vol. 32, (1966).

Innis, H.A., *Essays in Canadian Economic History*, Toronto: University of Toronto Press, 1956.

Johnson, F. Henry, *A Brief History of Canadian Education*, Toronto: McGraw-Hill, 1968.

Johnson, Leo A., "The Development of Class in Canada in the Twentieth Century", in Gary Teeple (ed)., *Capitalism and the National Question in Canada*, Toronto: University of Toronto Press, 1972.

Kelly, Frank, *Prospects for Scientists and Engineers in Canada*, Ottawa: Information Canada, 1971.

Kerr, Clark, *The Uses of the University*, Cambridge: Harvard University Press, 1964.

Leiss, William, *The Limits of Satisfaction*, Toronto: University of Toronto Press, 1976.

Levitt, Kari, *Silent Surrender: The Multinational Corporations in Canada*, Toronto: Macmillan, 1970.

Lipset, S.M., *The First New Nation*, New York: Basic Books, 1963.

Lockhart, Alexander, "Future Failure: The Unanticipated Consequences of Educational Planning", in Robert Pike and Elia Zureik (eds.), *Socialization and Values in Canadian Society*, Toronto: McClelland and Stewart, 1975.

Lockhart, Alexander, "Education Policy Development in Canada: A Critique of the Past and a Case for the Future", in R.A. Carleton, D. Colley, and A. MacKinnon (eds.), *Education, Change, and Society: A Sociology of Canadian Education*, Toronto: Gage, 1977.

McDermott, John, "Technology: The Opiate of the Intellectuals", *New York Review of Books*, (July 31, 1969).

Mills, C. Wright, *White Collar*, New York: Oxford University Press, 1956.

Myers, Gustavus, *A History of Canadian Wealth*, Toronto: James Lewis and Samuel, 1972.

Neill, A.S., *Summerhill: A Radical Approach to Child Rearing*, New York: Hart, 1960.

OECD, *External Examiners' Report on Educational Policy in Canada*, Paris: November 18, 1975.

Ogburn, William F., *Social Change with Respect to Cultural and Original Nature*, New York: Dell, 1966.

Ostry, Sylvia, *Canadian Higher Education in the Seventies*, Ottawa: Information Canada, 1972.

Porter, John, *The Vertical Mosaic*, Toronto: University of Toronto Press, 1965.

Repo, Marjaleena, *I'm a Ph.D. Who Needs a Ph.D?* Toronto: Graduate Students' Union, University of Toronto, 1970.

Reisman, David et al, *The Lonely Crowd*, Princeton: Yale University Press, 1950.

Rowntree, John and Margaret Rowntree, "The Political Economy of Youth", *Our Generation*, Vol. 6, (1968).

Schultz, T.W., "Education and Economic Growth", in *Sixtieth Yearbook of the National Society for the Study of Education*, 1961.

Wexler, Philip, *The Sociology of Education: Beyond Equality*, Indianapolis: Bobbs-Merrill, 1976.

Whisler, Thomas L., *The Impact of Computers on Organizations*, New York: Praeger, 1970.

Whyte, William H. Jr., *The Organization Man*, Garden City: Doubleday, 1956.

Wright Report, *The Learning Society: Report of the Commission on Post-Secondary Education in Ontario*, Toronto: Ministry of Government Services, 1972.

Zsigmond, Zoltan, *Patterns of Demographic Change Affecting Education*, Quebec City: The Canadian Teachers' Federation Conference on Financing Education, 1975.

Zsigmond, Z., G. Picot, M.S. Devereaux, and W. Clark, *Future Trends in Enrolment and Manpower Supply in Ontario*, Ottawa: Statistics Canada, 1976.

Von Zur-Muehlen, M., "The Ph.D. Dilemma in Canada: A Case Study", in S. Ostry, *Canadian Higher Education in the Seventies*, Ottawa: Economic Council of Canada, 1972.

III

Class Consciousness

The Persistence of Working-Class Consciousness in Vancouver

John C. Leggett

JOHN C. LEGGETT is a Professor of Sociology at Rutgers University and Co-Director of the Institute for Labour Studies. His current research interests include Class Consciousness, the State, and the U.S. Labour Market.

The Focus

What are the sources and political consequences of working-class consciousness in a seaport community characterized by a long tradition of class struggle at the workplace and by class voting in provincial and national electoral politics? This kind of question cannot help but fascinate students of working-class politics of such seaport communities as Marseilles, Glasgow, Liverpool, Yokohoma, Shanghai, Oslo, Stockholm, Helsinki, Genoa, and, of course, Vancouver, B.C. Vancouver strikes us as being in many ways ideal for the study of class politics and class consciousness not only because of its seaport tradition and associated class politics but also because a study of consciousness allows us to test a key hypothesis advanced by Clark Kerr and Abraham Siegel some time ago, namely, that class consciousness should be both extensively prevalent in communities dependent upon maritime, longshore and forestry industries and sharply related to how the communities' workers relate to the political realm.

Of course, there are those who contend that class considerations should be of incidental significance in determining how working-class people think and act politically, especially under conditions sometimes described as streamlined industrial capitalism, a society bereft of any form of contradictions which might urge workers to acquire a class frame of reference. Presumably status considerations, political imagery, job consciousness, and leadership charisma should sway political decisions made by working class people. Working *class* politics become confined, from this point of view, to the early periods of industrial capitalism.

Another perspective would hold that while revolutionary class consciousness may well be more frequently the case during the period of primitive capital accumulation, economic and organizational conditions can still foster a sense of working-class identity, create a widespread rejection of capitalist myths on the distribution of wealth within the context of *current* industrial capitalism, engender working-class solidarity, and even go so far as to militate in favour of a deep sense of economic equality. From this point of view, one which the author entertains, class consciousness will evolve unevenly, with certain clusters of workers proving to be more class conscious when their objective positions create economic insecurity and when they belong to organizations such as militant unions. These unions can help to create an experience of economic deprivation, work-site action, and political mobilization. Furthermore, once workers have achieved a medium or high degree of class consiousness, irrespective of its sources, they will vote for a pro-labour candidate, especially when they belong to union organizations that favour such candidates.

The Expectation

This argument would hold that certain objective positions help to foster class consciousness: (1) membership in a proletarianized ethnic group; (2) belonging to the category of uprooted workers; (3) involvement in economically insecure positions such as the lesser skilled and unemployed; and (4) membership in unions located in a community where unions have taken the lead in confronting both the employers and the state.

By contrast, workers should be the least class conscious and hence the least likely to vote labour when they belong to non-proletarianized ethnic groups; have grown up in industrial regions, fill skilled positions, and fail to belong to unions in the community under consideration. Thus, in Vancouver, some of the most class conscious workers might well consist of Italian workers who had emigrated from Southern Italy, became unskilled or semi-skilled workers employed in work sites located in the longshore, maritime, logging, pulp, paper and sulphide, woodwork, and construction industries, in turn functioning in a community context of extensive union organization with a long history of class struggle. Further, Vancouver's class conscious workers, irrespective of the origin of their awareness and commitment, should most likely cast a class conscious vote for a New

Democratic Party candidate when the candidate is strikingly pro-labour and the economic conditions are those of incipient recession.

The Research Setting

The author was involved in studies of 810 Vancouver blue collar workers made just after the summer federal election of 1968, in which it was found that many of these economic and organizational conditions were *absent*.

The economy had not yet fallen into recession, although by 1968 many people could observe that the boom of the mid-1960s had clearly run its course. Also working against a class conscious vote was the behaviour of the NDP candidates at that time. Neither of the NDP choices (one each for Burnaby-Seymour and Vancouver-East) had campaigned in the ridings so as to stress class issues such as unemployment. Rather the campaign was dominated by NDP efforts to answer the sometime campy performances of Pierre Elliot Trudeau, the spring-board master of the pool-side bourgeoisie. Furthermore, although groups like the Vancouver-Italian working class might qualify as a subpopulation simultaneously subjected to (a) economic exploitation and hence loss of surplus value which they created, and (b) ethnic discrimination and associated occupational insecurity within an ethnic group overwhelmingly working class in composition — in other words an Italian blue collar population subject to double exploitation — the Vancouver-Italian working class has held few if any leading positions either inside organized labour or within the NDP. Without such leadership, Italian workers are not that visible either in the union or in the NDP setting. Without this visibility, their collective identity as a militant force may develop, but only with the greatest difficulty. In this sense, they have certainly been different from the unionized, blue collar blacks studied 18 years ago in Detroit, many of whose members had occupied significant and visible positions within organized labour and the Wayne Country Democratic Party. Both the C. I. O. and the Democratic Party and its front groups had always worked to press blacks forward in union and non-union situations — both on and off the picket lines. In these group contexts, the blacks experienced and hence stressed to an unusual degree — precisely because of the utterances of black leadership — the class and class-racial quality of problems facing Detroit's black working class population. As a result, blacks scored exceedingly high on matters of class consciousness.

One more consideration worked against the importance of consciousness, among both Italians and other groups, in the 1968 federal election. The British Columbia unions and the NDP organizations *did* not stress class issues and thereby attempt to attach these topics to NDP candidates despite increased unemployment among blue collar workers. There was none of David Lewis' 1972 "throw out the corporate bums" oratory, a formula which, by the way, may well have helped the NDP to sweep working class areas in the lower mainland, Vancouver Island, the Upper Coastal areas, and the Interior.

So it was with some trepidation that we did our 1968 survey study of workers living in Burnaby-Seymour and Vancouver East. We conducted the study just after the Federal election had been held. We randomly selected and interviewed approximately four hundred male workers from each of these ridings. We did not randomly select adults at the door, and hence include women in the study, since to do so would have more than doubled the costs of our effort. And our funds were exceedingly limited. Any future study of the working class, however, must include women since they quite obviously play a very important role in the labour force. In the future, funds will simply have to be obtained or such studies should not be conducted.

In our limited 1968 study, we used a modified measure of working-class consciousness based upon an earlier study (1960 Detroit), and we classified workers as either low, medium or high in terms of consciousness.

FIGURE 1
GENERAL CLASSIFICATION OF WORKMEN ON FOUR ASPECTS OF
CLASS CONSCIOUSNESS

WORKERS TYPED ACCORDING TO CLASS PERSPECTIVE	EGALITARIANISM	MILITANCY	SKEPTICISM	CLASS VERBALIZATION
Militant Egalitarians	$+^1$	+	+	+
Militant Radicals	$-^2$	+	+	+
Skeptics	-	-	+	+
Class Verbalizers	-	-	-	+
Class Indifferents	-	-	-	-

The idea of the development (acquisition) of class-consciousness can be expressed most simply as a movement from a low level of class consciousness (cognitive) to a high level of class-consciousness valuative — (see Figures 2 and 3).

The actual *process* of the development of working-class conscious-

FIGURE 2
WORKMEN AND FOUR ASPECTS OF CLASS CONSCIOUSNESS
Vancouver

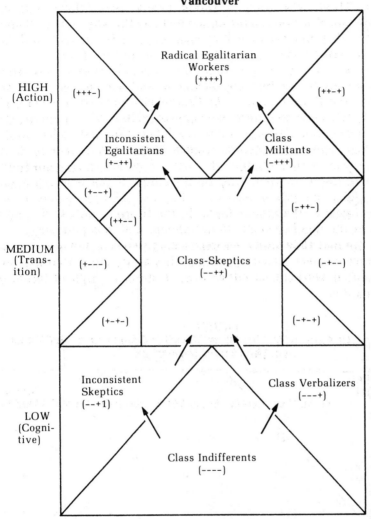

ness (in terms of the categories we have used) is indicated by the arrows. One of the central theoretical points to be made is that while the *idea* of the *development* of class-consciousness remains the same (as in the Detroit Study, even though the Vancouver conditions are considerably different), the process of acquisition varies with community conditions — (see Figures 2 and 3).

At the same time, we are not saying that simply because workmen fall into one of these two "path flows" that they must of necessity acquire consciousness in the sequential manner indicated by the diagram. Acquisition of consciousness may be uneven, much as revolution may skip stages and later reverse to include them.

FIGURE 3
WORKMEN AND FOUR ASPECTS OF CLASS CONSCIOUSNESS
Vancouver
With Frequency Counts

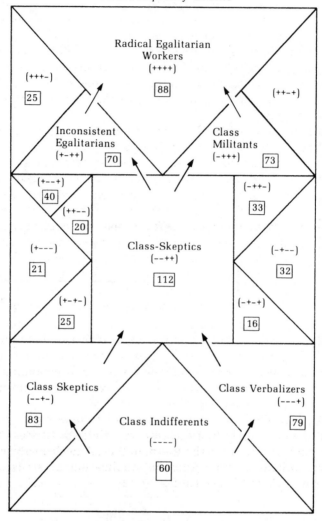

The Results: A Preliminary Analysis

For a number of reasons, we have only begun to analyze the data. Nonetheless, for what they are worth, here are the data so far analyzed:

(1) The Italian workers proved to be only slightly more class conscious than the other workers, although clearly they were up-front (see Table 1).

(2) The highly uprooted were somewhat more class conscious than those less uprooted (see Table 2).

(3) The unskilled were slightly more class conscious than the semi-skilled and skilled (see Table 3).

(4) The unionized were to a similar degree more class conscious than their non-unionized counterparts (see Table 4).

(5) The unionized Italian workers were slightly *less* class conscious than the non-unionized — in part because there were proportionately fewer uprooted among the unionized (see Table 5).

(6) The unionized, highly uprooted proved to be strikingly class conscious (see Table 6).

(7) When one takes into account union membership, uprootedness and ethnicity, the unionized and non-unionized Italian workmen demonstrated the same level of consciousness (see Table 7). Why there should be a condition of no difference is hard to explain, unless a disproportionately large number of these non-unionized workmen turn out to be unskilled construction workers — a group highly exploited in the city of Vancouver. Of interest also is the emergence of a particular category of unionized, class conscious workers. On matters of uprootedness, they score low; on the question of ethnicity, they constitute part of the "other" category — but on the question of class consciousness, 68 percent scored high, 23 percent as medium, and 9 percent as low. Further data analysis will indicate the make-up of members of this "other" category.

(8) Irrespective of the sources of consciousness and of the small statistical differences among the various segments of labour on consciousness, we can observe that they voted overwhelmingly for the NDP, and hence against Trudeaumania, when they were highly class conscious (see Tables 8 and 9).

One more point. We found class consciousness to be highly related to political ideology, including the anti-imperialist attitudes of B.C. workers on such questions as the Vietnam War, American ownership of Canadian industry, and futher nationalization of areas of the economy here in Canada (see Tables 10-12).

TABLE 1
ETHNICITY AND DEGREE OF WORKING-CLASS CONSCIOUSNESS

Ethnicity[a]	Working Class Consciousness			
	High	Medium	Low	Total
Italian	47%	41%	12%	100% (93)
Canadian	33%	34%	33%	100% (217)
British	37%	36%	28%	100% (211)
Other	31%	42%	27%	100% (224)

[a] Based upon place of birth — not nationality descent lines. The latter is now being tabulated.

TABLE 2
UPROOTEDNESS AND WORKING-CLASS CONSCIOUSNESS

Uprootedness[a]

Uprootedness[a]	Working Class Consciousness			
	High	Medium	Low	Total
High	41%	40%	19%	100% (238)
Medium	34%	37%	29%	100% (306)
Low	32%	35%	33%	100% (249)

[a] Uprootedness is based upon degree of occupational-cultural distance of worker, at time of birth, from urban-industrial-commercial setting.

TABLE 3
SKILL LEVEL AND WORKING-CLASS CONSCIOUSNESS

Skill Level	Working Class Consciousness			
	High	Medium	Low	Total
Unskilled (laborers)	41%	35%	24%	100% (167)
Semi-skilled (industrial)	35%	41%	25%	100% (150)
Skilled (craft)	35%	36%	29%	100% (314)
Service (mixed)	34%	35%	31%	100% (102)

TABLE 4
UNION MEMBERSHIP AND WORKING-CLASS CONSCIOUSNESS

Union Membership	Working Class Consciousness			
	High	Medium	Low	Total
Union	40%	35%	25%	100% (535)
Non-union	27%	42%	31%	100% (260)

TABLE 5
ETHNICITY, UNION MEMBERSHIP AND WORKING-CLASS CONSCIOUSNESS

Ethnicity	Union Class Consciousness				Non-Union Class Consciousness			
	High	Medium	Low	Total	High	Medium	Low	Total
Italian	46%	46%	8%	100% (59)	51%	37%	12%	100% (34)
Canadian	37%	32%	31%	100% (156)	22%	39%	39%	100% (59)
British	40%	34%	26%	100% (144)	31%	39%	30%	100% (67)
Other	39%	36%	25%	100% (177)	19%	48%	33%	100% (100)

TABLE 6
UPROOTEDNESS, UNION MEMBERSHIP AND WORKING-CLASS CONSCIOUSNESS

Uprootedness	Union Class Consciousness				Non-Union Class Consciousness			
	High	Medium	Low	Total	High	Medium	Low	Total
High	46%	36%	18%	100% (149)	31%	45%	24%	100% (88)
Medium	40%	29%	31%	100% (210)	22%	45%	33%	100% (92)
Low	33%	37%	30%	100% (168)	29%	34%	37%	100% (78)

TABLE 7
UNION MEMBERSHIP, UPROOTEDNESS, ETHNICITY, AND WORKING-CLASS CONSCIOUSNESS

Uprootedness	Ethnicity	Union Class Consciousness				Non-Union Class Consciousness			
		High	Medium	Low	Total	High	Medium	Low	Total
High	Italian	55%	35%	10%	100% (51)	55%	35%	10%	100% (29)
	Canadian	(1)	(1)	(1)	— (3)	(0)	(0)	(0)	— (0)
	British	54%	23%	23%	100% (35)	24%	43%	33%	100% (24)
	Other	48%	28%	24%	100% (60)	16%	55%	29%	100% (38)
Medium	Italian	(1)	(0)	(0)	— (1)	(0)	(0)	(0)	— (0)
	Canadian	54%	15%	31%	100% (80)	25%	41%	34%	100% (32)
	British	55%	21%	24%	100% (62)	29%	46%	25%	100% (24)
	Other	54%	19%	27%	100% (67)	14%	51%	35%	100% (35)
Low	Italian	(2)	(3)	(2)	— (7)	(1)	(2)	(1)	— (4)
	Canadian	47%	18%	35%	100% (93)	26%	36%	38%	100% (39)
	British	50%	17%	33%	100% (46)	38%	29%	33%	100% (21)
	Other	68%	23%	9%	100% (22)	29%	29%	42%	100% (14)

aBased upon place of birth — not nationality descent line. The latter is now being tabulated.

TABLE 8
DEGREE OF WORKING-CLASS CONSCIOUSNESS AND VOTE IN THE 1968 FEDERAL ELECTION (BY RIDING) — VOTERS AND NON-VOTERS

Burnaby-Seymour

Class Consciousness	Candidates				Non-Voters	Total
	Douglas (NDP)	Perrault (Liberal)	McLean (Conservative)	Price (Socred)		
High	56%	17%	1%	—	26%	100% (133)
Medium	38%	25%	3%	2%	32%	100% (140)
Low	35%	24%	3%	1%	37%	100% (116)

Vancouver-East

	Winch (NDP)	Kennedy Liberal	Manuel (Conservative)	Meyer (Socred)	Non-Voters	Total
High	37%	11%	—	2%	50%	100% (151)
Medium	28%	15%	1%	1%	56%	100% (160)
Low	25%	10%	3%	—	62%	100% (106)

TABLE 9
DEGREE OF WORKING-CLASS CONSCIOUSNESS AND VOTE IN THE 1968 FEDERAL ELECTION (BY RIDING) — VOTERS ONLY

Burnaby-Seymour

Class Consciousness	Candidates				
	Douglas (NDP)	Perrault (Liberal)	McLean (Conservative)	Price (Socred)	Total
High	77%	22%	1%	—	100% (98)
Medium	56%	37%	4%	3%	100% (95)
Low	56%	37%	5%	2%	100% (73)

Vancouver-East

	Winch (NDP)	Kennedy (Liberal)	Manuel (Conservative)	Meyer (Socred)	Total
High	74%	22%	—	4%	100% (76)
Medium	63%	33%	2%	2%	100% (71)
Low	68%	25%	7%	—	100% (40)

TABLE 10
WORKING-CLASS CONSCIOUSNESS AND AMERICAN ACTION
IN VIETNAM[a]

Level of
Class
Consciousness — American Action in Vietnam

	Correct	Wrong	Don't Know	Not Ascertained	Total
High	16%	64%	13%	7%	100% (284)
Medium	19%	52%	18%	11%	100% (300)
Low	20%	41%	26%	13%	100% (222)

[a]We used the following question: "Do you think American action in Vietnam has been .. correct.. wrong.. do not know?" The question was asked just after the completion of the TET Offensive of Spring, 1968.

TABLE 11
WORKING-CLASS CONSCIOUSNESS AND AMERICAN OWNERSHIP
OF CANADIAN INDUSTRY [a]

Level of
Class
Consciousness — American Ownership of Canadian Industry

	Bad	Doesn't Matter	Good	Not Ascertained	Total
High	55%	8%	32%	5%	100% (284)
Medium	45%	12%	38%	5%	100% (300)
Low	33%	11%	49%	7%	100% (222)

[a]We used the following question: "Do you think that American owernship of Canadian industry is. . . good for Canada. . . bad for Canada. . . does not matter?"

TABLE 12
WORKING-CLASS CONSCIOUSNESS AND PUBLIC OWNERSHIP
OF INDUSTRIES [a]

Level of
Class — Favours Public Ownership of Industries Besides Those Presently
Consciousness — Owned by the State

	Yes	No	Undecided	Total
High	65%	30%	5%	100% (284)
Medium	56%	37%	7%	(100%) (300)
Low	46%	45%	9%	100% (222)

[a]The question used was: "Do you feel that any industries, other than those which are now publicly owned (C.N.R., Air Canada, and B.C. Hydro, for example) should be publicly owned?" — followed by: "If yes, which ones?"

Five Case Studies

But perhaps of more interest than tabular data would be how the workers themselves spoke out on matters of power, class, and privilege. Maybe the best way to portray these expressions would be to discuss how the first five workmen interviewed reacted to questions pertinent to class consciousness.

The first blue collar worker, a machinist of Scotch-Irish descent, and we might add, an occasional church-goer (Anglican), gave replies which epitomize the absence of a fully crystallized, class conscious point of view. What emerged from the interview was a grab bag of cognitive categories and attitudes nonetheless replete with class references.

We asked this Canadian-born workman the following question: "Do you think city officials show favoritism to any groups of the population?" He replied in the affirmative, and then said that: "Big Business has too much say. Big community firms downtown . . . . Blocks 42-52" [Blocks 42-52 have reference to a special downtown construction project being conducted by private enterprise and favoured by Vancouver City Hall]. Yet the respondent didn't think any person or groups of people have enjoyed special powers or privileges. Still there was an egalitarian strain in the mind of this unionist who earned a respectable eight to nine thousand dollars in 1967. This propensity surfaced in his *positive* response to the following question: "Do you think that the wealth of the country should be divided up equally so that people will have an equal chance to get ahead?" Not unexpectedly, this worker did waffle on the "harder" question dealing with equality. He was asked: "In your view, would it be a good thing if Canadian society were changed so that all persons received an equal share of the wealth and lived in equal conditions". He couldn't decide between a "yes" and "no" reply, but rather set up the following contingency: "If everybody does their job. Otherwise there'll be a lot of free-loaders. You could have a welfare state which is no good for a country".

It is conceivable, then, for a worker to look positively, albeit with hesitation, towards equality and still to have real doubts about at least one form of the welfare state. No centre-to-right continuum is apparently involved.

This worker's concern with free loaders proved consistent with his Social Credit provincial voting preference. We found that like many blue collar Socred provincial supporters during the 1960s, he identified himself with the working class and voted NDP federally. A native of British Columbia, he had voted federally for Harold Winch.

This worker was then told the following story concerning the 1966 Vancouver Lenkurt Strike.

I'm going to read you a story on an accident which occurred in Vancouver a few years ago. I'd like to get your opinion on this matter. In 1966, a union was negotiating with a company in Vancouver. The company agreed that while negotiations were going on, there would be no overtime required of the plant employees. However, the company then ruled that the workers had to work overtime or be fired. Some of the workers followed local leaders in the plant in a walk-out to protest this ruling. This was done without the support of many of the official union leaders. The company fired the 257 men and women who walked off their jobs. These workers then set up a picket line around the plant. The company reacted by going to a judge and getting a court order, called an *exparte injunction* to stop the picketing. Although some of the leaders of the pickets and some of the pickets obeyed the injunction order, most continued to picket the plant. The company sent in private police who joined the RCMP to enforce the injunction. Police and pickets clashed. Nine of the pickets were arrested. A trial was held several months later and the accused were fined and jailed for alleged violence and refusing to obey the injunction. The union was able to eventually get most of the strikers rehired. But it refused to pay these men strike-pay and most of these men lost their seniority when they were rehired.

When told the story, this member of the International Union of Machinists spontaneously recognized the strike in question by refering to the Lenkurt Electric dispute. What is of perhaps more interest, is the fact that he approved of the action taken by the Lenkurt strikers. Subsequently, he answered affirmatively to the following questions:

"If a similar conflict were to happen today, at the same plant, would you support this group?"

"If such an incident occurred at your plant today, would you support this group or would you figure that it is none of your business?"

"Would you walk out with the others?"

"Later on in this conflict, would you join the picket line set up before the injunction was issued?"

Interestingly, and perhaps revealing a Socred bias in favour of "law and order", the respondent answered negatively to the following and final question:

"In this same situation, would you stay on the picket line after the injunction was issued?"

This same worker, by the way, believed that the American military action in Vietnam had been wrong.

Our second workman, a retired tool and die maker born and raised in the Western Ukraine, where his father had worked as a mill-wright, was a once-a-week, church-going Greek Orthodox whose views were, nonetheless, anything but reactionary. When asked whether city officials showed favouritism to any groups of the Vancouver population, he replied by saying, "The property owners — especially the real estate dealers". Again, when asked whether any persons or groups of people enjoyed special powers or privileges, he replied: "Block Brothers . . . They are either German or German descent". Yet when asked his reaction to the soft question on equality ("Should the wealth of the country be divided up equally so that people will have an equal chance to get ahead?"), he replied negatively and added: "That is a fool's paradise . . . It's all abstract". In his reply to our "harder" question on equality ("In your view, would it be a good thing if Canadian society were changed so that all persons received an equal share of the wealth and lived in equal conditions?") this workman (who had moved from the Ukraine to Canada in 1921) gave a flat "no" for an answer and added: "Impossible. You could do it. But it wouldn't last. Every fast buck artist on the road would make a killing. We would need social legislation in the form of a dictatorship so that the fast buck artist can't overcome the people". Then, referring to the present, he added: "It must become a crime to profiteer — to exploit one must become a criminal". His "world hypotheses" were clear: he did not believe that equality was possible; nor did he believe that exploitation should be tolerated — a fascinating mixture of pessimism and sense of justice.

This thoroughgoing NDP supporter did make an interesting reply to the following question: "When business booms in Vancouver, who gets the profits?" His answer was: "The profiteers, the business people. The middleman never loses anything. The middleman is a useless parasite: unproductive, profiteer, exploiter. He never suffers a loss . . . Always gains to improve his standard of living. I mean the businessman guys who buy islands by evading income tax. The businessmen maintain standards of profits at the working man's expense". Yet when we asked: "Which class do you belong to?", he did give a reply by no means indicative of full class consciousness: "There is no class. It depends on the circumstances. Every man is a working man". Apparently, from this man's point of view, exploiters are workers.

More important than matters of consistency-inconsistency was his focus on employment justice. He believed that the provincial government had not been trying to do enough on unemployment, education, and health. Furthermore, he held that the influence of Big Business on Canadian government had been too much.

On the Lenkurt Strike-arrest-imprisonment question, he did not spontaneously recognize the dispute as the 1966 Lenkurt hassle, but he did "approve with qualifications" the action of the workers in this case and added: "When the police were sent in, it shows how corrupt the government is. The unions should start a political party to protect themselves". When asked if a similar conflict were to happen today, at the same plant, would he support this group, he replied affirmatively. Finally, he answered positively to the hard-line question: "In this same situation, would you stay on the picket line after the injunction was issued?", and added: "The injunction is an illegal instrument. They are not just. So I would break them".

The third worker, a longshoreman in his early fifties, was of German-Russian descent, Lutheran, and Alberta born and raised. He was a member of the longshoreman's union (ILWU). He did not know whether city officials showed favoritism to any groups of the population but he did believe that city officials don't pay attention to the needs of some kinds of people: "Welfare people do pretty good, but some get the run-around". This consistent NDP voter did not know whether any persons or groups of people enjoyed special powers or privileges. Nor did he believe in either form of egalitarian sharing of wealth. He did not know who gets the profits when business booms in Vancouver, but he did view himself as working class and had a high regard for Harold Winch (former NDP MP from Vancouver East). He also took a down-the-line militant position on the Lenkurt Strike questions. He also viewed American military action in Vietnam as wrong.

Our fourth worker was a thirty-five year old Italian working class bricklayer who emigrated to Vancouver in 1957. He proved to be quite militant. Born and raised in Odine, a city in the Po River Valley of Northern Italy, an area well-known for its "red" sympathies, he came from a working class family in which the father was a bricklayer with less than a high school education. Not too surprisingly, the son took his first job as a bricklayer. Upon emigrating to Canada, he retained this occupation and became a member of the International Bricklayer and Teraso Workers Union. In Vancouver he laboured as a terrazzo layer; he was working full-time when interviewed. He gave Roman Catholicism as his religious preference but seldom attended church.

In the first part of the interview, he offered few indications of class consciousness. He did not know whether city officials showed favoritism to any groups of the population, and on matters of welfare, he seemed reactionary. Like many first impressions, our initial assessment proved wrong, and he turned out to be anything but right-wing on these matters.

In the interview, conducted in Italian by one of our staff people, he was asked whether or not city officials pay attention to the needs of some kinds of people. He ducked a "yes" "no" response and went on to say that: "City officials give away too much money to people who don't work. Everyone should do something. Otherwise people become ill if provided with welfare. City officials should provide them with work instead".

As the interview progressed, the respondent began to open up. When asked the question: "Which class do you belong to?" he replied: "The working people". When questioned: "When business booms in Vancouver, who gets the profits?", he gave a class conscious reply. Unlike many Vancouver workers who said "everyone" or "everybody", he replied: "Big shots . . . Anyways, of course, the big profits go to the big shots". His non-use of the functional categorization and preference for class categories was very similar to the preference of many Detroit workers studied eight years earlier. Not too surprisingly, this unionized Italian worker took the hard line on the hard question of equality (". . . all persons should receive an equal share of the wealth and live in equal conditions") and added: "Everyone should have the same opportunity. We're all human beings". Yet when reacting earlier in the interview to the "softer" question on equality, ("The wealth of the country should be divided up equally so that people can have an equal chance to get ahead"), he ducked the question and criticized the union and the government and their particular relationships to equality: "The problem here is with the unions. You get two to five dollars per hour. A union man can get more if he goes on strike. This is bad for the country. The government should look after it and give everyone — all people — a good wage. Look at me. I earn $3.95 per hour, and we are going to go on strike for a seventy-five cent increase. The government should make us remain at work. I've nothing against unions. They're good. But the government should say when enough is enough. I've been in the Union as a member for eight years. I've got lots (later in the interview he said that in 1967, by working six and seven days a week, he earned between eight and nine thousand dollars) . . . some poor guy has nothing. That's not fair. Everybody should be the same. The poor guy should have his share too. Why should he be made to starve? That's not fair".

During the Lenkurt question, the interviewer discovered that this worker was a straw-boss, a low level foreman in charge of a small group of six to eight bricklayers who worked along with him. Despite this grey zone status between worker and management, he went down the line on the Lenkurt militancy question, including recognition of the need to stay on the picket line even after an injunction had been issued. He observed: "Each worker has different opinions. I can't force anyone to work if he doesn't want to. I remember the top brass saying that when some workers refused to work overtime, they're the first to go".

In another question on militancy, this one concerned with the neighbourhood, we told this worker the following story (in Italian):

Public opinion people like myself often ask the people we talk with to use their imagination in answering questions. Now imagine the following situation. All of the people in your neighbourhood are working people, and all rent their homes and apartments. People in your neighbourhood have been complaining about the high rent and poor housing in your neighbourhood and the landlords refuse to do anything about it. If these working-class people in your neighbourhood were to get together and form an organization to try to do something about these problems, that is, to try to force the landlords to change things for the better, would you support this group or figure it was none of your business?

| Support | Figure it's none of your business | Unsure |

If support this group:

	Yes	No	Unsure
a. Would you join it?			
b. Would you go to the group's meetings?			
c. Would you contribute money to it?			
d. Would you take part in a neighbourhood demonstration such as picketing the landlord to do something about it?			

We then asked whether he should "support this group or consider it none of his business". He said he would support it. Next we asked whether he would join the group ("yes") . . . would he go to group meetings ("yes") . . . would he contribute money to it? ("I can always spare at least two dollars for the people"), and, finally, he indicated that he would "take part in a neighbourhood demonstration such as picketing the landlord to do something about it".

Although this worker couldn't vote, because he lacked Canadian citizenship, he favoured Tommy Douglas and the NDP, and he believed that unions should contribute money to political parties. He then added: "But here, too, our unions are run by the States. We should have Canadian unions. I pay seven dollars a month — three dollars stay in Canada, four dollars go to the States. It should all stay in Canada". He definitely believed that unions should affiliate with a political party — he had in fact given four dollars to fight B.C. Bill 42, the notorious anti-Labour bill passed by the Socred government and geared to limit union funds spent for political purposes.

The class consciousness of this worker, then, proved to be considerable. Further, it was related to his political ideology. He believed that American military action in Vietnam had been wrong: "They should look after the Negroes, not the Communists in Vietnam. I don't care if they're Communists. If they want to be Communist, that's alright. Let them be Communists. It's stupid, killing people for nothing. But the killing makes them — the Americans — feel bigger". Further, he held that: "All big corporations should be publicly owned. It would be much better for us if the government makes money. They would spend it for us. But if the individual makes it, he keeps it. That's not good". Not too surprisingly, he held that American ownership of Canadian industry is bad for Canada.

Of course this class-nationalistic attitude toward American ownership does not indicate his acceptance of the nationality pecking order within Canada. His critical opinions on this matter came forth after we told him the following story:

> Now, imagine a situation where a rich country club in Shaughnessy is selecting a few members. It is hard to get into this club because it is *exclusive* and there are lots of people applying to get in. Now, in this one situation it just happens that every individual who wants to join the club has almost the same amount of education, income and occupational skill. These people who want to join are similar in many other ways as well. However, they differ in one and only one important way: there are five different nationality groups among the applicants. There are roughly the same number of people of Indian, Italian, English, German and French descent. My question is, of these five groups, which nationality group members have:

a. The *least* chance of getting into the country club?

_____

b. Why do you think so? _____

_____

_____

c. The *best* chance of getting into the country club?
   (REPEAT THE NAMES OF THE FOUR REMAINING GROUPS)

_____

d. Why do you think so? _____

_____

_____

e. The *second best* chance of getting into the country club?
   (REPEAT THE NAMES OF THE THREE REMAINING GROUPS)

_____

f. Why do you think so? _____

_____

_____

g. The *third best* chance of getting into the country club?
   (REPEAT THE NAMES OF THE REMAINING TWO GROUPS)

_____

h. Why do you think so? _____

_____

_____

i. The *fourth best* chance of getting into the country club?
   (REPEAT THE NAME OF THE REMAINING GROUP)

_____

j. Why do you think so? _____

_____

_____

We asked who would have "the *least* chance of getting into the country club?" He replied: "To get in you have to be a big shot. Everyone's supposed to be the same but they discriminate. I'm sure they wouldn't pick Italians or any other group before the English". Subsequently our interviewer asked: "Who would have the best chance of getting into the country club?" He said: "I really don't know how they pick. Maybe they're prejudiced against Italians. I tried to get into a gun club nearby — I like to hunt — but they told me that the membership was filled".

The fifth worker among the 810 was of Ukrainian-Danish background and around 50 years of age. Born and raised on a farm in Denmark, his father was a carpenter and a farmer until the respondent moved to the city at age ten. His first full-paying job was that of a salesworker. During the late 1950s he emigrated to Vancouver where he became a unionized sheet-metal worker. By 1967 he was earning between nine and ten thousand dollars. Because he never became a citizen, he could not vote in the federal election although he did favour Harold Winch. He viewed himself as working class and believed that businessmen get the profits when business booms in Vancouver. A militant when it came to action, he gave an organizational answer on the matter of continuing to picket, after an injunction had been issued, by saying, "That depends on what the union official says". On the soft measure of equality, he said "yes", but added, "but it can't be". On the harder measure he said "no": "It would be a good thing if people could handle it, but no matter how much you give them, they wouldn't be any good anyways".

On political ideology he proved to be relatively conservative as well. While he viewed American action in Vietnam as wrong, he also believed that American ownership of Canadian industry was good for Canada: "We can't do without it because there isn't enough people and money here; but American ownership is also bad..."[sic]. He also felt that public ownership of industry had gone far enough.

These case histories plus the tabular data indicate that it doesn't take a very high degree of class consciousness for a worker to vote for, or in other ways favour, both the NDP and left-liberal positions on politics. Not unexpectedly, it would also seem that whenever workmen are extremely class conscious, almost all favour the New Democratic Party.

Concluding Comments

We have skipped lightly over certain areas which demand additional concern in order to get to the basic results of the study. In another essay we would like to dwell at length on (1) how we conceptualized and operationalized working-class consciousness; (2) how our findings compared with those of an earlier Detroit study — with an analytic emphasis on racial bipolarization and one big union in Detroit; (3) the problems and limitations of using survey analysis in studying working-class consciousness; (4) how workers feel about the connection between class questions and voting after experiencing three years of a B.C. provincial government led by the NDP (1972-75).

Certainly it is clear that a high degree of working-class class consciousness and social democracy are not necessarily compatible. In fact, historically, militant workers have clashed with social democratic regimes intent on imposing state arbitration, in favour of employers locked into conflicts with militant employees. Such a triangular fight did develop during the Barrett-NDP period, as the government moved successfully to pass anti-labour legislation of a sort one would ordinarily expect from a Social Credit government committed to sever links with working people. Because of the near-Draconian anti-labour legislation passed by the NDP government, many B.C. workers have learned to look to their unions as the first line of defense and to define social democracy in power as less than adequate to meet their day-to-day work-site problems of pay and working conditions.

Finally, with the 1972-75 learning experience of Vancouver workers as an example, we can by no means say that the NDP cultivates the class conscious vote. On the contrary, the policy of the NDP in power was to press ahead with a populist-technocratic appeal — one replete with self-evident contradictions — to deny most explicitly the importance of any form of class analysis. That being the case, the NDP has more than amply demonstrated two things:

(1) The NDP most emphatically is not the party of class conscious labour;

(2) Class conscious workers might well consider another political alternative — the creation of a Marxist Canadian Commonwealth Federation.

Readings

Kerr, Clark and Abraham Siegel, "The Inter-Industry Propensity to Strike: An International Comparison", in A. Kornhauser, R. Dubins and A.M. Rose (eds.), *Industrial Conflict*, New York: Arno Press, 1954, 1977.
Leggett, John C., *Class, Race and Labor*, Toronto: Oxford University Press, 1969.
Lukacs, George, *History and Class Consciousness*, Cambridge, Mass.: MIT Press, 1971.
Mannheim, Karl, *Ideology and Utopia*, New York: Harcourt, Brace Jovanovich, 1955.
Marx, Karl, *The German Ideology*, Moscow: Progress Publishers, 1976.
Porter, John, *The Vertical Mosaic*, Toronto: University of Toronto Press, 1965.

Quebec Labour and the Rise of Working-Class Consciousness

Paul Willox

PAUL WILLOX is a Lecturer in Sociology at the University of British Columbia. His current research interests include Quebec Society, Political Economy and Working-Class Consciousness.

The 15 November 1976 election of an *indépendantiste* government in Quebec has diverted attention from a mass movement which, though more erratic than the separatist movement in its development, is emerging as a vital — ultimately, perhaps even determining — factor in the Quebec political equation: namely, a radicalized labour movement which identifies itself as the vanguard of a working class with interests fundamentally opposed to those of the capitalist economic and political system. In addition to clarifying the political drama unfolding in Quebec, an understanding of the origins and evolution of this movement is of importance in illuminating the particular socio-economic tensions characteristic of a satellized economy and certain critical stresses in the fabric of advanced capitalism as a whole.

The essential historical context of the Quebec labour movement's development is found in the legacy of Quebec's eighteenth century conquest and the subsequent alliance of convenience which evolved between the Anglo-Canadian polity and the Quebec wing of the Roman Catholic Church whereby the latter, in its initially-unchallenged role as institutional guarantor of *la survivance* of French Canada, conceded effective control of the Quebec economy to the English in exchange for a relatively free hand in shaping the educational and cultural formation of the Québécois. That the ensuing correspondence of ethnic and economic divisions could have the effect of stimulating popular critical awareness of class cleavages was foreseen as early as 1838 when Britain's Lord Durham warned in a report on the Quebec colony:

> If they prefer remaining stationary, the greater part of [French
> Canadians] must be labourers in the employ of English capitalists.
> In either case it would appear that the great mass of French Canadians
> are doomed, in some measure, to occupy an inferior position, and
> to be dependent on the English for employment. The evils of poverty
> and dependence would merely be aggravated in a ten-fold degree,
> by a spirit of jealous and resentful nationality which should separate
> the working class of the community from the possessors of wealth
> and employers of labour . . . . (quoted in Milner, 1973:ix).

The radicalization of workers was in fact forestalled by the
Catholic Church's comprehensive control of the French Canadian
schools, political organizations, and press. Systematically opposing
the "alien values" of urbanization and industrialization while
permitting the substance of these processes to develop unhindered,
Quebec's ecclesiastical regime generated a steadily widening tension
between culture and economy. As Anglo-American investment was
increasingly attracted by Quebec's combination of abundant natural
resources, cheap labour, and proximity to large markets, the vision
of a rural conservative Catholic *patrie* so assiduously propagated
by the Church became progressively anachronistic and hence
problematic as an effective tool of socialization. A measure of the
Church's difficulty can be seen in the fact that by 1901 40 percent
of the Quebec population were already living in cities, and that
by 1941 this figure had risen to 63 percent, the highest level of
urbanization in Canada (Trudeau:4). Fear of the inevitable social
tensions inherent in their parishioners' proletarianization elicited
increasingly shrill exhortations from the Catholic hierarchy. Typical
of these was Monseigneur Bruchési's 1903 appeal to Quebec workers
concerning social inequalities:

> To claim to ban from the world this inequality or to revolt against
> it would be a chimera . . . . What God has decreed, what Christ
> has maintained, men will not change one iota. His creatures until the
> end of time will be divided into two great classes, the class of the
> rich and the class of the poor . . . . We counsel workers to submit to
> their condition patiently, their eyes turned toward heaven (quoted in
> Trudeau:63).

Realizing that such an approach would not be sufficient to stem the
inroads of international unions (active in Quebec even before the
turn of the century), the Church sponsored the establishment in
1921 of the Confédération des Travailleurs Catholiques du Canada
(CTCC), a "righteous" alternative for Québécois workers unable to
resist the temptations of unionization. With a priest at the head of
each local, the CTCC enjoyed an official approval which enabled it to
quickly garner the major share of Quebec's slow but steady union
growth after World War I. By 1932, of the 11 percent of industrial

workers in Quebec belonging to unions, 59 percent — or 25,000 members — were affiliated to the CTCC (Milner, 1973:118). However, though the CTCC initially achieved the Church's goal of preventing the emergence of a secular, class-conscious, "anit-national" labour movement, the basic crisis engendered by the Church's continuing attempt to propagate an outmoded culture and political ideology continued to emerge inexorably, a fact reflected in the eventual recovery of international union recruiting — by 1951 the CTCC's membership of 88,000 constituted only 34 percent of Quebec unionists (Milner, 1973:118) — and in the gradual disaffection of the CTCC itself. In an effort to refurbish nationalism as a device of effective mass-mobilization against this erosion of its power, the Catholic hierarchy in the late 1920s and 1930s tacitly approved sympathetic Quebec politicians' flirtations with the rising fascist ideologies of Europe. During this period a veritable panoply of quasi-fascist movements arose in Quebec espousing authoritarian "corporatist" solutions to the Quebec malaise. Some, like the secretive Ordre Jacques Cartier, sought to infiltrate the leadership of designated "key" institutions, while others, most notably Adrien Arcand's Parti National Social Chrétien, openly expressed agreement with Germany's Nazi movement. But the quintessential practitioner of the new authoritarianism was Maurice Duplessis, who became Premier of Quebec in 1936 at the head of a newly-formed Conservative/ breakaway-Liberal coalition called the Union Nationale. Taking his cue from the preceding corrupt Liberal administration of Louis Taschereau, Duplessis added ample use of porkbarrel patronage tactics to his party's platform of authoritarian Catholic corporatism, and in the process fashioned a formidable political combination which — with the exception of 1940-44 — kept his party in power until 1960 (with Duplessis remaining Le Chef until his death in 1959). That the Union Nationale's open-door, union-busting, minimum-royalties policies toward multinational corporations contradicted the party's vote-getting warnings against big capitalism on the hustings reflected both the political skill of Duplessis and the enduring nature of the post-1760 compact between conqueror and conquered which conceded the economy to the former in exchange for the socio-cultural autonomy of the latter.

But blatant recourse to ballot-box manipulation and heavy-handed repression of dissidents (through means such as the 1937 Padlock Law which empowered the provincial government to close down any premises used for undefined "communist" purposes) failed to obscure the gradual spread of Québécois' discontent with the Salazarist-backwater fate consigned to them by Duplessis and the Catholic Church. Helping crystallize and articulate this discontent was a small group of critically-minded social scientists at Laval University headed by Dominican priest Georges-Henri Lévesque. By the end of World War II Laval graduates such as Jean Marchand were attaining leadership in the CTCC and other unions and reorienting them toward greater assertiveness of labour's interests. Thus by 1943 the CTCC began edging away from its Catholic affilition, deconfessionalizing the leadership of locals. Sensing that the Church's own interests would one day be comprised by an overly-close association with the Union Nationale and that the doctrine of Christianity was not credibly served through such an alliance, some priests pressed for a more sympathetic Catholic attitude toward the nascent labour movement, but most of the hierarchy continued to take a hard-line attitude. The shifts occurring within Quebec's political constellation were highlighted in 1949 when Duplessis attempted to curb union growth through particularly severe labour-code restrictions — a move which brought about a common front between the CTCC and the international unions, and provoked misgivings from the Church leadership, in turn forcing Duplessis to withdraw the measure. Later in the same year, under the activist leadership of the CTCC's new president, Gérard Picard, asbestos workers struck the American-owned Johns-Manville Company in what quickly became an epic test of strength between Quebec's old-style corporatist regime and a labour movement seeking collective bargaining already secured elsewhere in North America. Brutal intervention by the Duplessis government against the workers prompted a total disavowal by the Catholic Archbishop of Montreal and compelled unprecedented coverage by the previously intimidated French-language media. Though Duplessis eventually won the asbestos struggle, his victory was a pyrrhic one, for the confrontation further politicized the unions and created division within Quebec's ruling alliance. The 1950s saw a series of additional confrontations, each one heightening the politicization of labour and the disaffection of both church and business with Duplessis' authoritarianism. By decade's end, the unions' cries for unfettered collective bargaining rights and the extension of basic social services were finding an increasingly sympathetic hearing from a church concerned about its weakening influence on workers and from a business community seeking to integrate Quebec more harmoniously into the general North American framework of advanced capitalism. The commonality of these perspectives — a desire for *rattrapage*, i.e., a rapid "catch-up" modernization of Quebec — provided the basis for the provincial Liberals under Jean Lesage to build a reformist coalition (including Radio-Canada journalist René Lévesque, himself politicized by involvement in a 1959 broadcasters' strike) which swept to power in the 1960 election.

The ensuing transformation of the Quebec economic and social infrastructure, known universally in Quebec as the Quiet Revolution, (early and mid-1960s), included a curtailment of the official harassment of unions and a complete severing of church ties by the CTCC, which renamed itself the Confédération des Syndicats Nationaux (CSN) in 1961. The two other principal union centrals to emerge during this period were the internationally-affiliated Fédération des Travailleurs du Québec (FTQ) — formed in 1956 in the wake of the AFL-CIO merger in the United States and the parallel establishment of the Canadian Labour Congress — and Quebec francophone teachers' central, the Corporation des Enseignants Catholiques, which deconfessionalized itself in the 1960s under the name Corporation des Enseignants du Québec (CEQ), later the Centrale des Enseignants du Québec. All three centrals enjoyed rapid growth during the Quiet Revolution, with membership between 1960 and 1968 rising from 95,000 to 215,000 in the case of the CSN, 100,000 to 215,000 with the FTQ, and 12,000 to 68,000 in the CEQ (Milner, 1978:177). Overall, union membership in the period increased 7 percent more quickly than the province's quickly-growing labour force; by 1968 39.1 percent of Quebec's workers were organized (Ethier:20.22). The most spectacular growth occurred in the CSN and CEQ (much of the FTQ's expansion merely consolidated already-organized workers); this in turn was a result of the Lesage government's extension of collective bargaining rights to workers in the rapidly expanding public sector. A prohibition of public sector union affiliation with political parties militated against public sector recruitment by the FTQ, as the latter was linked through the Canadian Labour Congress to the New Democratic Party. The CSN and CEQ accordingly gained the upper hand, with the result that 106,000 of the 120,000 members recruited by the CSN between 1960 and 1968 came from Quebec's swelling public service ranks (Milner, 1978:177).

At the outset of the Quiet Revolution, Quebec's unions exhibited a fervent optimism that Lesage's modernization policies would reduce the province's high unemployment levels and widen economic opportunities for the francophone majority who, according to a 1961 survey of male salary and wage earners in Quebec based on an average labour income indexed at 100, earned only 91.8 as opposed to the 142.4 earnings of workers of British origin (Canada 3:23). Fuelling this optimism was the amalgam of reform and nationalism articulated by the Liberals — "Masters in our own house" was the Party's 1962 re-election slogan — which seemed to imply an activist intervention in the economy by the Quebec state to redress the full spectrum of economic, social, and cultural grievances of francophone workers (e.g., the language-of-work issue with its attendant implications of social-mobility). However, by the mid-1960s it was becoming clear that Lesage's modernization program, while including such popular measures as the introduction of various long-overdue social services (previously opposed by the Catholic Church as an intrusion in the parochial domain), was facilitating rather than stemming external control of the Quebec economy, and that this satellization was in turn resulting in declining growth in Quebec's labour-intensive manufacturing sector and accelerating growth in the capital-intensive, minimum job-return resource-extraction sector — a tendency which continued during the ensuing Union Nationale regimes of Daniel Johnson (1966-68) and Jean-Jacques Bertrand (1968-70). One measure of this shift and Quebec's consequent failure to generate a sufficient number of new jobs to keep pace with its expanding labour force can be seen in a comparison with the neighboring province of Ontario: during the years 1961-65 the rate of growth of Quebec's manufacturing industry was only 9.3 percent as opposed to 21.0 percent for Ontario. Had Quebec's growth rate equalled its neighbor's throughout the 1960s, the province would have gained 100,000 new jobs in the manufacturing sector alone (CSN, 1972:135). In the context of Quebec's rapidly growing labour force — which by the end of the 1960s was adding 75,000 new workers a year in one of the world's highest *per capita* growth rates — this failure to produce new jobs in such a key sector had a major detrimental impact on Quebec's already high unemployment. In conjunction with the continuing migration of rural and small-town job-seekers to metropolitan areas, such unemployment increases had the further effect of exacerbating urban poverty: by 1966 the Montreal Labour Council estimated that 58.4 percent of that city's population lived in poverty — the poverty line being defined as 1966 earnings of less than $5,000 for a family of four or $2,500 for singles (Jauvin:35). In 1967 the Health Service of the City of Montreal estimated that 44 percent of the city's families had a deficient diet, with 20 percent of the children not learning to speak until after the age of three years, and 20 percent being below normal size and weight (Jauvin:41). The housing situation became correspondingly grave: the 1961 census indicated that 86,000 dwellings in Montreal were overpopulated. By 1970, despite a large population increase, only 2,238 low-rent dwellings had been constructed by the city — as opposed to the estimated 70,000 needed during that period (*Canadian Dimension*, Vol.7, No.5:49).

    In addition, the rapid expansion of public services during the Quiet Revolution and the concomitant acceleration of state expenditures placed growing tax burdens on Quebec workers. Between 1961 and 1970, for example, Quebec government expenditures as a percentage of Quebec's gross national product rose from 17.99 percent to 31.84 percent (Lemoine:65). As the aim of this state expansion had been to strengthen the Quebec economy through increasing direct and indirect support for the private sector, the burden of financing this support fell increasingly on the only other shoulders remaining: those of the individual taxpayer. Thus, between 1961 and 1970 corporation taxes increased by 47 percent while those paid by individuals increased by 905 percent (Lemoine:69). Including revenue from sales taxes (the bulk of which are paid directly or indirectly by individuals as consumers), the net result was that between 1961 and 1970 the corporate share of Quebec's total tax revenues declined from 23 to 10.8 percent while the share paid by individual citizens rose from 68 to 86 percent (Lemoine).

With Quebec's economic satellization having rendered the growth of manufacturing industries problematic, the Liberal regime of Robert Bourassa (1970-76) opted for a strategy of subsidizing large-scale extraction of natural resources for export as a means of generating increased profits, consumption of goods and services, and employment, the characteristic capital-intensity of such primary-sector development notwithstanding. The most spectacular manifestation of this accelerated-extraction approach was the mammoth James Bay project, wherein over $10 billion were raised to divert the flow of certain northern rivers in order to produce hydro-electric power for export. The steady rise in the government's fiscal outlays on such projects in turn had the effect of forcing the government to re-allocate its revenue and expenditure patterns so as to simultaneously raise individual taxation and enforce severe restraints on public sector salaries and individual transfers (the provincial government's second and third biggest spending items respectively at the beginning of the 1970s), thereby freeing more capital for resource-extraction support.

Given this nexus of satellization, chronic unemployment, and escalating tax burdens on the work force, one might logically expect an increasing politicization of Quebec's workers in both the province's fiscally-pressed public sector and economically-vulnerable private sector. Such in fact was the case by the early 1970s — i.e., in response to the forementioned pressures, a significant and growing minority of Quebec workers came to explicitly identify themselves as an exploited class whose interests are separate from and opposed to the interests of industrial owners and their government supporters.

One level of data indicating the growth of labour militancy in Quebec during this period is found in the incidence of strikes and expressions of labour sympathy for political violence. With reference to strikes, the number of work-days lost in Quebec through strikes and lock-outs increased from 207,240 days in 1960 to an annual average of 1,473,000 days in the years 1966-70 (Ethier:26). Especially volatile in this regard was the public sector, which accounted for over 60 percent of the workers involved in Quebec strikes and lock-outs between 1965 and 1971 and over 40 percent of lost work-days during that period (Ethier:25). With reference to political violence, the data is less direct but no less revealing: between 1962 and 1972 there were, for example, eighty-five separate bombing incidents in the province, of which eighteen involved factories and corporate offices, several of the latter coming during strikes and other labour disputes (Laurendeau:213-221). There is no evidence to suggest that any labour unions were involved in the perpetration of this violence, nor is any such link being suggested here. What can be documented, however, are expressions of growing union sympathy with the motivations of those expressing violent dissent with Quebec's politic-economic status quo. Thus, for example, the October 1970 kidnappings of British Trade Commissioner James Cross and Quebec Minister of Labour Pierre Laporte by the Front de Libération du Québec (FLQ) and the subsequent television broadcast of the FLQ's manifesto (which denounced "the corporations which exploit the working people" and "the aggression organized by high finance through the marionettes of the federal and provincial governments") evoked sympathetic responses from two regional Central Councils of the CSN. Michel Chartrand, president of the CSN's Montreal council, articulated this response by asking: ". . . Who's scared of the FLQ? Are the workers terrorized by the FLQ? Are the students terrorized by the FLQ? The only people afraid of the FLQ are those who should be scared — the power elite" (quoted in Milner, 1973:205). While disavowing terrorist tactics, both the Montreal and Laurentian Central Councils endorsed the FLQ manifesto, as did Montreal's union-backed municipal opposition party, the Front d'Action Politique. When the federal government subsequently suspended Canadian civil liberties for six months under the terms of the War Measures Act and rushed over 7,500 soldiers into Quebec (a move which was followed by the FLQ assassination of Labour Minister Laporte), the leaders of Quebec's three largest union centrals, the CSN, FTQ, and CEQ, joined the leaders of the farmers' Union des Cultivateurs Catholiques and the Parti Québécois to denounce "the almost rigid military atmosphere that we can discern in Ottawa" (quoted in *Canadian Dimension*, Vol. 7, No. 5:6). In similar fashion, when a prolonged strike against the Montreal daily newspaper *La Presse* erupted into street violence in October 1971 involving ten thousand demonstrators battling with police and resulting in the death of a demonstrator, leaders of the CSN, FTQ, and CEQ voiced their support for further confrontations if these proved to be necessary. Typical was the comment of FTQ president Louis Laberge, who declared before a rally of 14,000: "We give serious warning to the wealthy and to the established powers that this first victim might be followed by others, but in future the victims won't only be on our side" (quoted in Chodos:100).

A second level of data indicating the growing radicalization of the Quebec labour movement during this period is to be found in the shifting political patterns within the union centrals. The ideological evolution in this connection was unmistakably in the direction of a militant working-class consciousness. In the case of the FTQ, the transformation was especially rapid. As late as 1969 federation president Laberge had warned that political involvement by organized labour would "pervert unionism and provoke its destruction" (quoted in Tremblay:150); similarly, in early 1971 Laberge declared: "I'm a practical guy, not a dreamer. I believe in evolution not revolution . . . and while I don't agree with the present system, I don't want to destroy it" (quoted in Chodos:101). By November 1971, however, Laberge's tone had completely changed:

> Whatever model of society we're looking for, we now know that the one we have in Quebec, generally in North America, is not made for us. We have examined the political and economic machine which is trying to demolish us, and we have come to the conclusion that there is nothing we can expect from its good will. We now have to fight with the ardour of the original trade-union militants. . .the origins of our roots, when trade unionism's liberating goal was global.
> The worker is not composed of detached pieces. If he is a slum dweller, an exploited consumer, a citizen faced with anti-democratic powers or a tool of production exhausted by an employer and thrown out onto the pavement, he's still the same man, and it's he as a whole that must be liberated. . . .
> The definition of all the particulars of the society we want to build is less urgent than the development of a strategy for smashing the present system, a system which does not permit and never will permit all the reforms needed to build a veritable 'just society' (quoted in Chodos:101-2).

Also by the end of 1971, the Twelfth Congress of the FTQ had endorsed the manifesto, *L'Etat, rouage de notre exploitation*, in which implications of class conflict were clearly drawn:

> Unemployment presents itself as one of the most visible and cruel forms of the exploitation by imperialism and external domination in Quebec . . . Only control of [the] surplus would permit the Quebec economy to be oriented in terms of Quebec's needs . . . Capitalism can never re-establish any sort of equilibrium. And we who suffer the consequences . . . must correct the situation FTQ:128).

In a similar vein, a 1972 FTQ manifesto declared that "all the means of production are in the hands of a few owners who use them only for their own priority, maximum profit" and that workers "must take control of the means of production . . . to liberate us from this prison that work now constitutes" (quoted in Milner, 1973:208-9).

During the same period and in parallel fashion, the CEQ, the union central representing most of Quebec's francophone school teachers, moved from white collar-professional assumptions to an explicit class-analysis of Quebec's malaise and the role of teachers therein. In October 1971 the CEQ's new self-definition as proletarian was outlined in a "white paper":

> The teacher is proletarianized. He is a wage-earner from whom one purchases his capacity to produce at the ideological level, telling him what to say and how to say it, what to do and how to do it . . .This process of debasement. . .is not. . .a voluntary plan by identified persons, but rather the implacable logic of a system which concentrates all the means of decision and action in the hands of a small group of private owners of the means of production. . .(CEQ, 1971:15).

In the summer of 1972 an additional CEQ manifesto entitled *The School in Service to the Dominant Class* called for a "fight for radical change in social relations and against the enemy of the workers, the capitalist system". Similarly, in December 1973 CEQ president Yvon Charbonneau, dismissing Quebec's parliament as "a caricature" and declaring that Québécois "are bludgeoned, as workers and as consumers, by foreign and other capitalists," called for the "liberation of Quebec workers" (CEQ 1973:1-3).

But perhaps the most significant manifestation of the radicalization of the Quebec labour movement was evidenced by the CSN. By the mid-1960s the CSN's positive attitude toward the provincial government was changing in response to a hardening economic climate, a slowdown of government ardour for social reforms, and the reintroduction of certain restrictions on the right to strike in the form of *lois d'exception* aimed particularly at public sector employees (Le Borgne:23-25). The resultant process of self-reevaluation was epitomized by CSN president Marcel Pepin's candid acknowledgment in 1968 of organized labour's need to widen its critique of the state and economic structure:

> . . .Everywhere in the world, unionism is considered to have aged and become bourgeois. What is sure is that it is no longer in the avant-garde of movements of social transformation. . .I am strongly of the opinion that all working people expect from the union movement defense and protection against all those who exploit them in favour of a social and economic regime which permits and even encourages this (CSN, 1970:151-152).

The role of the state as an enforcer of corporate interests was a theme pursued with increasing vigour by the CSN in the following four years — a period marked by growing conflict between the CSN and the Quebec government over the wage-levels and unionization rights of public sector workers. Out of this conflict emerged a deepened CSN critique of the state rooted in a class-analysis of Quebec society exemplified by the CSN manifestos of September and October 1971, *There is No Future for Us in the Present Economic System* and *Let Us Rely Solely on Our Own Means:*

> American imperialism has confined Quebec capitalists to the least lucrative sectors. . .To compensate for their weakness in the face of the American giant, Quebec capitalists called the State to their aid. This was the origin of 'maîtres chez nous'. . .and the Quiet Revolution. . .But. . .'maîtres chez nous' will be realized only when it is true for everybody, instead of a slogan to hide the leftover privileges for the owning class of Quebec. . .From now on Québécois workers know they cannot count on national capitalists nor on a government at the service of the capitalists or the imperialists. Québécois workers also know that their labour is the real backbone of Quebec's wealth: a mine shaft is worth nothing without the miners' work. But it is the workers who pay for all the defects of capitalism: unemployment, inflation, work insecurity, lack of housing, of hospitals, of schools, of old people's homes, gaps in the distribution of food, clothing, leisure services, etc., etc. The fundamental cause of this state of things is simple: the workers do not own the factories in which they work (CSN, 1972:123, 159, 161).

This explicitly class-conscious analysis of Quebec society, which concluded with a call for "the replacement of the present system, which is dominated by the bourgeoisie, by a classless society, that is, an economic system controlled by the workers of this society" (CSN, 1972:173), was formally endorsed by delegates at the June 1972 CSN Congress. What makes such endorsation particularly revealing from a sociological viewpoint is not only the fact that of the three major union centrals in Quebec the CSN was the most occupationally-diversified, but also that the CSN's decision-making structure is the most open and democratic, *i.e.*, the structure least amenable to dictation from the central's leadership (Milner, 1973:186-7).

That an emergent class consciousness was reflected in a significant number of Quebec workers by the early 1970s is dramatically demonstrated by a third level of evidence: the "Common Front" strike of May 1972. The basic background to this strike was that, following a stalemate in negotiations between the provincial government and the CSN-FTQ-CEQ "Common Front" representing 210,000 unionized public sector workers, the Common Front unions voted overwhelmingly in favour of strike action. Fearing that union demands for $100 per week minimum wages (the poverty level for a family of four according to the Canadian Senate's Poverty Report) and strengthened job-security guarantees would create a dangerous precedent for the private sector (a point made by Quebec's finance minister), the Liberal regime of Premier Robert Bourassa attempted to force the strike to an end by the imposition of a dictated wage "settlement" and substantial fines against union locals and individual workers that did not immediately return to work. In addition, Marcel Pepin, Louis Laberge, and Yvon Charbonneau, the presidents of the CSN, FTQ, and CEQ, were sentenced to one year in prison. Despite a majority vote by the centrals' members to defy the government, the three presidents counselled workers to return to work in the face of the state's determination to utilize heavy legal sanctions. Notwithstanding this counsel, workers reacted massively and angrily to the actual jailing of Pepin, Laberge, and Charbonneau. A spontaneous general strike erupted, involving not only the two hundred thousand public sector workers but also several hundred thousand other workers including, significantly, unorganized workers as well as union members. A wide spectrum of institutions was involved, ranging from automobile factories to schools. The strike lasted from 10 to 17 May 1972, gathering momentum to the point that several towns were physically taken over by workers. Typical of these was the mining town of Sept Îles (population 27,000) on the north shore of the St. Lawrence River, where workers (having, incidentally, the highest wage-level in Canada at the time) closed the town's port on 10 May, barricaded all highways, seized the airport, closed down all "non-essential" businesses, and took over the local radio station. A Canadian Armed Forces airlift of police the following day lifted the road barricades and reoccupied the radio station, though the mayor ordered the police out of the station at the day's end in response to a union — in this case the FTQ affiliate of the United Steelworkers of America — request "that the workers may continue to use it to inform the population" (quoted in *The Last Post*, (July, 1972:26). Despite the military-police intervention, the town remained closed down and under worker control until 17 May, when the CSN-FTQ-CEQ Common Front called a province-wide truce in order to facilitate the reopening of negotiations with the government (which by this point was backing down from its hard-line position). In all, nine towns were taken over by Quebec workers in this manner: Saint Jérôme, Sainte Hyacinthe, Joliette, Murdochville, Sept. Îles, Hauterive, Thetford Mines, Lévis, and Baie Comeau (Solidaire:103). Virtually every sector of the society was touched by the May upheaval: newspapers and television stations were struck, 23 radio stations were seized by workers, hospitals were taken over (and in the case of the Albert Prévost Psychiatric Hospital in Montreal a worker council involving non-medical and nursing staff as well as doctors assumed formal administrative control, proclaiming "North America's first liberated hospital"), the entire construction industry of the province shut down, multinational corporations' factories (e.g., General Motors in Sainte Thérèse and Uniroyal in Saint Jérôme) were closed by worker walkouts, as were many other institutions ranging from large "chain" food stores to universities to lumber mills (Chodos: passim). Indeed, in terms of numbers and sectors affected, Quebec's May 1972 Common Front strike, in many ways reminiscent of the May-June 1968 upheaval in France, ranks as the most effective general strike in North America in this century.

The significance of the strike as a barometer of working-class consciousness is indicated by several facts: (a) it occurred virtually spontaneously and was occasioned by frequent articulations of class consciousness — epitomized by the "worker bulletins" and "music of the resistance" aired on the occupied radio stations; (b) white-collar as well as blue-collar workers, and private sector as well as public, sector workers, participated; (c) workers in prosperous regions, e.g., Sept Îles, as well as economically depressed regions, e.g., Saint Jérôme, took part in the strike action; (d) despite major attempts by government, business, and the mass media to encourage workers to quit the Common Front in favour of a newly formed, less militant breakaway central called the Confédération des Syndicats Démocratiques (CSD), Common Front solidarity remained largely intact for the conflict's duration, with only 19,000 workers in the entire province leaving the Front to join the CSD (Chodos:140).

In addition to the general economic factors which constituted the basis for the increase in Quebec workers' militancy in the early 1970s, several non-economic factors were important contributory elements. The first of these was government repression (e.g., the Common Front jailings in 1972). In this connection, a relationship between the utilization of strict legal sanctions for social control and the creation of foreign-investor confidence in Quebec was suggested by the findings of a survey of American and Canadian investor attitudes to Quebec conducted by Fantus, a Chicago consultant subsidiary of the New York brokerage firm Dun and Bradstreet. The survey, commissioned by the Bourassa administration in 1970, reported that Quebec's jobless rate is actually an attraction to investors: ". . .The unemployment rate in Quebec is probably the highest of any province in Canada. This tends to keep wages low" (quoted in Isacsson:14). On the other hand, Fantus reported there was growing investor distress at the increased militancy of Quebec's labour unions — the latter being variously described by the investors interviewed as "very militant", "too active politically", "very dangerous", and "very socialistic" (quoted in Isacsson:15). To remedy this situation and retain Quebec's investment inflow, the interviewees called for stricter labour regulations, "elimination of the radical nationalist groups", "better control on extremist movements", and "stricter law enforcement to ensure respect for authority" (quoted in Isacsson). While the hypothesis that the mounting repressive sanctions against labour during this period reflected a specific effort to implement the Fantus report's findings cannot be documented, the systematic nature of the repression and its politicizing effects were noted succinctly in a statement issued by the CSN, FTQ, and CEQ presidents from their prison cells at the height of the Common Front strike:

> Within the current union conflict, there is an over-riding social struggle. The Liberal establishment. . .has chosen the clubbing of the workers as its trademark. . .This government, as an employer, cowers before its real 'boss', the private sector. . .Repression turns a simple panic into a battle, a participant into a combattant, a diverse group of individuals into a force of solidarity. . .and finally, it obliges everyone to choose sides (quoted in Chodos: 133-4).

Four year later (1976) CEQ president Yvon Charbonneau stated his belief that the prospects of future economic uncertainty would generate further repression:

> What has happened at the negotiation tables of the public sector is happening in other domains also. I think there is a rise of authoritarianism. . .which is the corollary of a great loss of credibility. When they are no longer able to impose themselves morally, all they can do is pound their fists on the table and provoke crises. . .This government that we have does not really govern; it is manipulated, it is the marionette of the economic conjuncture, of inflation, or of financial constraints. . .All this means that in order to seem to govern, the government must make noise to try to impress people. . .This manifests itself in negotiations, in certain laws, in a general stragegy. There is definitely a rise of authoritarianism (quoted in Dupont:135).

A second significant non-economic factor stimulating the rise of working-class consciousness was the organized political-education campaigns undertaken by the union centrals. In the case of the FTQ and CEQ, wide distribution was given to their various critiques of the Quebec economic and social structure, e.g., the FTQ's *L'Etat, rouage de notre exploitation* and assorted special publications of the CEQ, and a series of local and regional public assemblies were organized to discuss these critiques. In the case of the CSN, these techniques were augmented by comprehensive political education courses offered by local union committees and circulation of detailed critiques of the mass media's discussion of labour affairs, e.g., *La Grande Tricherie* (1973).

A third contextual factor promoting labour radicalization was the rise of a Quebec nationalism focused critically on those institutions perceived to be instrumentalities of Quebec's colonization, for, as noted earlier, the paralleling of ethnic and economic divisions has increasingly had the effect of stimulating popular critical awareness of class cleavages in Quebec. Paradoxically, this rise of a socially-critical nationalism was aided by the very longevity of corporatist and conservative Catholic ideological dominance in Quebec, i.e., this conservative dominance until the Quiet Revolution limited the impact of North American liberalism on the political consciousness of Québécois. The abrupt collapse of corporatism in the early 1960s in turn had the effect of leaving a relative ideological vacuum in Quebec — a vacuum quickly filled in part by various anti-capitalist and national-liberation perspectives emergent in the West in the mid- and late-1960s. (The rapidity of Quebec's ideological transformation in the 1960s was epitomized by the precipitous decline in the influence of the Catholic Church: in the Diocese of Montreal, for example, the percentage of the population actively practising Catholicism declined from 65 percent in 1961 to 50 percent in 1967 to 30 percent in 1971. Among the younger population, i.e., the 15 to 35 age group, this figure declined to 12 percent— see *Québec-Presse*, 3 Nov. 1974).

Finally, the rivalry between Quebec's labour centrals, particularly between the CSN and the FTQ, injected a degree of inter-union competition which, in the socio-economic context of Quebec, obliged union to outbid union in relevant analyses of, and political responses to, worker grievances. Considerations of recruitment in effect served as a propellent for ideological radicalization. This was especially evident in the FTQ's concern not to be outflanked by the more radical CSN.

The rise of *indépendantiste* nationalism and the Parti Québécois in the late 1960s and early 1970s evoked increasing attention and sympathy from the Quebec labour movement. The historic issues of language-of-work and ultimate assimilation by non-francophone immigrants were asserted with more urgency than ever, labour's concern being rooted in both Québécois nationalist sentiment and workers' fear of job-competition in the context of Quebec's chronic unemployment. In addition, labour's desire for major economic and social reforms logically implied support for a left-reformist party at the very least, and in the absence of a labour party, the Parti Québécois became the political beneficiary of this support. Moreover, as the bitterness and acrimony between labour and the Bourassa regime deepened in the period 1972 to 1976, union support for René Lévesque and the PQ became firmer. (Hostility to Bourassa also had the effect of healing much of the strident inter-union conflict which resurfaced after the 1972 Common Front settlement). On the fundamental question of Quebec independence, however, organized labour remained ambivalent, with the only central to formally endorse the PQ in the November 1976 election — the

FTQ — studiously avoiding pronouncement on the independence issue. Despite such ambivalence, massive electoral support was given to the PQ by all three major centrals in the 1976 campaign — providing the PQ with its margin of victory in the opinion of some observers — and the PQ's victory was enthusiastically welcomed by the labour movement as a whole. Largely in repayment for this support, the Lévesque regime granted a series of union demands (including a ban on the use of strike-breakers) in amendments to the province's labour code in December 1977.

While bringing an immediate improvement in the general climate of labour relations, the accession to power by the Parti Québécois has also produced new challenges to the labour movement. First, the mobilization of public debate over the forthcoming independence referendum has effectively pre-empted public interest in labour issues. In the second place, the new government's relatively sympathetic attitude to labour has removed the focus of hostility which provided much of the basis of both Common Front co-operation between the CSN, FTQ, and CEQ and rank-and-file support of union militancy. In general, the FTQ — now the largest of the centrals (with 280,000 members as opposed to the CSN's 160,000) — has emerged as a firm supporter of the government. The more radical leadership of the CSN and CEQ has faced challenges from pro-PQ elements, and while the ideological lines of these two centrals retain formal majority support, a noticeable political quiescence had fallen over union memberships by 1978.

There is, however, reason to believe that this quiescence will prove to be temporary. It seems likely new worker discontent will be spawned by the economic destabilization which has occurred in Quebec since the PQ's election, exemplified by a 1977 growth rate half of the all-Canada rate, a December 1977 unemployment rate of 11.4 percent, a declining job-creation rate (24,000 new jobs in 1977 as opposed to 38,000 in 1975 and 130,000 in 1973), and a hemorrhage of hundreds of millions of dollars of private Quebec investment funds into the eastern United States. Moreover, the advent to power by the PQ portends further fiscal pressures on the public sector, given the PQ's ideological predilection for use of the state apparatus as a means of redressing the historical imbalance between Anglo-Canadian and American entrepreneurs on the one hand and Québécois entrepreneurs on the other. Some measure of the Québécois bourgeoisie's propensity to seek countervailing state aid can be gauged by the fact that in early 1978 francophones constituted a majority in only 14 of the province's 105 largest private companies and only 9 percent of the remaining 91 companies' directors. As Quebec Finance Minister Jacques Parizeau has noted, state aid to the francophone business community is a cornerstone of PQ economic strategy:

> In Quebec, the state must intervene. It is inevitable. It is what gives the people the impression that we are more to the left. If we had, in Quebec, 25 companies like Bombadier, and if we had important banks, the situation might be different. We have no large institutions, so we must create them (quoted in Gonick:35).

The fiscal implications of such an interventionist approach are enormous, and will place the party in diametrical conflict with its electoral committment to expand social service programs. The inevitable deterioration of the already severe fiscal crisis of the Quebec state is already forcing a tougher government line with public sector unions, and in the long run will compell the PQ regime to cut back social services, thereby further alienating the labour movement. That the PQ's bourgeois nationalism will ultimately prove to be an inadequate vehicle for labour interests was stressed by CSN president Norbert Rodrigue in 1976:

> The necessity of a workers' party is no longer disputable. . .for the Parti Québécois, even though it represents a hope for a certain number of union militants. . .is a traditional, fundamentally non-labour party. It has not pronounced itself against capitalism; it has supported illusions, it has aroused deception (quoted in Dupont:102).

Clashes between the CSN and the Lévesque regime erupted as early as February 1977 when the government rejected a CSN request to nationalize Aluminum Company of Canada hydroelectric facilities in the Saguenay region with a brusqueness which led the CSN vice-president to denounce "this so-called government of the workers" (*Le Devoir*: 17 Feb. 1977). Similarly, the CSN and CEQ vehemently opposed the government's last-minute removal of certain anti-"scab" provisions in its December 1977 labour code amendments — unlike the FTQ, which remained supportive of the government. This division within union ranks may in fact foreshadow a temporary polarization of Quebec labour into pro-PQ and anti-PQ wings, with the former gravitating to the FTQ and the latter to the more radical CSN and CEQ — which, in November 1977, issued a joint declaration of intent to eventually merge. The latter group's misgivings about Quebec independence PQ-style were indicated in late 1977 by CSN ex-president Marcel Pepin:

> I would easily become an *indépendantiste* for cultural reasons, but the economic aspect makes me say that to separate from Canada would be adventurism for Quebec workers.
> If there is a big price to be paid (for separation), it won't be the national bourgeoisie who will have to pay it, it will be the mass of workers (quoted in Gordon:2).

As the economic situation continues to deteriorate, it would seem likely that the FTQ will be obliged to follow the CSN and CEQ into opposition to the PQ, thus restoring the Common Front solidarity of the Bourassa years. On the other hand, two additional factors will continue to pose obstacles to the further development of working-class consciousness. First, the labour struggles of the early 1970s and their critical portrayal by the mass media have contributed to a considerable anti-union backlash in public opinion: a 1977 poll by the Centre de Recherche sur l'Opinion Publique indicated that 54 percent of the Quebec public believe that unions have too much power, and that 84 percent desire restrictions on public sector workers' right to strike (*Financial Post*: 29 Oct. 1977). Second, the pressure for new jobs will be diminished by demographic trends: the Economic Council of Canada predicts that Quebec's 1975 to 1985 working-age population growth rate will be only half the 1965 to 1975 growth rate, and that by the mid-1980s the growth will have ceased altogether (*Financial Post*: 19 Nov. 1977).

Despite these factors, the consolidation and expansion of the radical, highly politicized, class-conscious elements within Quebec's labour movement is a distinct possibility in the long-term in light of Quebec's economic deterioration. Insofar as public opinion is concerned, the public's negative image of unions appears to be fully matched by its hostility to large corporations: a 1973 Canadian Institute of Public Opinion poll showed that 55 percent of Québécois blamed management for strikes while only 15 percent blamed labour — in contrast to Ontario, where 18 percent blamed management and 41 percent blamed labour (Bennett:56). Moreover, even with declining working-age population growth rates, job pressures will remain as increasing numbers of women are obliged to enter into the labour force to bolster family earnings in the face of chronic stag-flation and growing tax burdens. In addition, international indicators suggest that the province's economy will be damaged in the 1980s by a gradual deindustrialization of the American-dominated secondary sector as American owners cut back the operations of their less profitable branch-plants in response to European and Japanese competitive pressures and as Canada's foreign trading partners (as well as domestic constituents outside Quebec) force the federal government to lift the specific tariffs currently protecting Quebec's inefficient textile industries. Also, as the separatist debate rages, the debilitating effects on Quebec's economy engendered by the province's uncertain political future will multiply. (Nor will this process necessarily be ended by the electoral defeat of the PQ; the record of similarly frustrated nationalist movements elsewhere in the world demonstrates that blockage of the parlimentary route to independence might well drive a minority of separatists to FLQ-style violence, in turn provoking a Belfast-like crisis). Such economic stagnation will unleash further cross-pressures on the Quebec government for both investment-aid to the private sector and social-services aid for the

Quebec population at large. Irreconcilable in the context of Quebec's deteriorating economic circumstances, these cross-pressures will ultimately render social-democratic brokerage politics impossible and force a polarization of the forces advocating such conflicting expenditure priorities. It is in the resultant sequence of fiscal squeezes, rising taxes, cutbacks in social services, narrowing employment and "quality of life" opportunities, labour-protest mobilizations, government repression, and labour politicization that one can discern the potentiality of an increasingly class-conscious labour movement in Quebec.

Signficantly, the Trilateral Commission established by David Rockefeller warned in its 1975 report, *The Crisis of Democracy*, that a similar sequence faces the advanced capitalist world as a whole, and that the very survival of democratic institutions will hang in the balance as governments committed to present economic priorities seek to sustain industrial expansion:

> What are in doubt today are . . . the political institutions inherited from the past. Is political democracy . . . a viable form of government for the industrialized countries of Europe, North America, and Asia? Can these countries continue to function during the final quarter of the twentieth century with the forms of political democracy which they evolved during the third quarter of that century? . . . The demands on government and the needs for government have been increasing steadily. . . . The cause of the current malaise is the decline in the material resources and political authority available to government to meet these demands and needs (Crozier: 2, 169).

Claiming that "governability and democracy are warring concepts", the Commission report warned that "the balance has shifted too far against governments" (Crozier: 173) and that, in the specific case of Canada, the maintenance of an expanding economy within a capitalist framework will require drastic curbs on the demands of labour:

> Labour groups are not impeded . . . from making outrageous demands due to the absence of a strong public philosophy and to prevalent doubt as to whether fairness underlies the general allocation of influence and resources. . . . In the absence of a strong national ethos, governments are hamstrung in their efforts to cope with such prevalent difficulties as inflation and labour/management difficulties (Crozier: 208).

It is precisely this escalating clash of values over what should be the priorities governing disposition of society's increasingly pressured fiscal and other resources that will generate and condition future labour conflict in Quebec — and throughout the Western world.

Readings

Bennett, Arnold, "Labour and the Quebec Election", *Our Generation*, Vol. 9, (1973).

Canada, *Report of the Royal Commission on Bilingualism and Biculturalism*, Vol. 3. Ottawa: Information Canada, 1970.

Canadian Dimension, Vol. 7, No. 5. (December, 1970).

Chodos, Robert and Nick Auf Der Mer (eds.), *Quebec: A Chronicle 1968-1972*, Toronto: James Lewis & Samuel, 1972.

Confédération des Syndicats Nationaux, *Le deuxième front: rapport moral du président de la CSN au congrès 1968*, second edition. Montreal: 1970.

Confédération des Syndicats Nationaux, "We Can Rely Only on Our Own Means", in *Quebec Labour*. Montreal: Black Rose Books, 1972.

Corporation des Enseignants du Québec, *Premier Plan: livre blanc sur l'action politique*, Quebec: 1971.

Corporation des Enseignants du Québec, "Les syndicats et l'opposition extra-parlementaire: notes pour l'allocution du président devant le syndicat des professeurs de Québec métropolitain", Quebec: 1973.

Crozier, Michel and Samuel P. Huntingdon, Joji Watanuki, *The Crisis of Democracy: Report on the Governability of Democracies to the Trilateral Commission*, New York: New York University Press, 1975.

Dupont, Pierre and Gisèle Tremblay, *Les Syndicats en Crise*, Montreal: Les éditions Quinze, 1976.

Ethier, Diane and Jean-Marc Piotte, Jean Reynolds, *Les Travailleurs contre l'Etat bourgeois: avril et mai 1972*, Montreal: Les éditions de l'Aurore, 1975.

Fédération des Travailleurs du Québec, *L'Etat, rouage de notre exploitation*, Montreal: 1971.

Financial Post, The, 29 October and 19 November, 1977.

Gonick, Cy, 1977 "The New Patriotes" in *Canadian Dimension*, Vol. 12, (April, 1977).

Gordon, Sheldon E., "Merger before Referendum" in *The Financial Post*, 26 November, 1977.

Isacsson, Magnus, "Quebec: Nothing Satisfies the Investors" *The Last Post*, Vol. 2, (July, 1973).

Jauvin, Pierre, *Sous-développement au Québec et dans le monde*, Montreal: Centre d'animation de culture ouvrière: 1971.

Last Post, The, "Sept Îles revolts", Vol. 2, (1972).

Laurendeau, Marc, *Les Québécois violents: un ouvrage sur les causes et la rentabilité de la violence d'inspiration politique au Québec*, Quebec: Les éditions du Boréal Express, 1974.

Le Borgne, Louis, *La CSN et la Question nationale depuis 1960*, Montreal: Les éditions Albert St-Martin, 1976.

Le Devoir, 17 February, 1977.

Lemoine, B. Roy, "The Growth of the State in Quebec", in D. Roussopoulos (ed.), *The Political Economy of the State*, Montreal: Black Rose Books, 1973.

Milner, Henry, *Politics in the New Quebec*, Toronto: McClelland and Stewart, 1978.

Milner, Henry and Sheilagh Hodgins, *The Decolonization of Quebec: An Analysis of Left-Wing Nationalism*, Toronto: McClelland and Stewart, 1973.

Québec-Presse, 3 November, 1974.

Solidaire, "Chronology of the May General Strike" in *Radical America*, Vol. 6, (September-October, 1972).

Tremblay, Louis-Marie, *Le Syndicalisme québécois: idéologies de la CSN et de la FTQ, 1940-1970*, Montreal: Les Presses de l'Université de Montréal, 1972.

Trudeau, Pierre Elliott (ed.), *La Grève de l'amiante: une étape de la révolution industrielle au Québec*, Montreal: Les éditions Cité libre, 1956.

IV

Selected Social Issues

A Tale of Two Medians

Bill Livant

BILL LIVANT is an Associate Professor of Psychology at the University of Regina. His current research interests include Marxist Social Psychology and the Political Economy of Communications.

_____

Part I

The tale told here is short. Not because it is a short tale, but because I know only the beginning. Still, there are interesting things even there.

The tale has a background; a few informal observations which I must describe first. When the weather comes on the radio in the morning, they always report the expected *high* and the expected *low*. They *never* report the expected *average*; any kind of average.[1] Why not? When I asked people about this they gave two kinds of answers. A few . . . statistically minded psychologists . . . told me that they ought to give an average too. It would be "fairer"? But most people said that the highs and the lows told them something that *made a difference*. Here in Saskatchewan, for example, to be told on a January day that it will go down to -35C. that night tells something important: if you visit a friend, and leave your car unplugged for a few hours, your engine block will freeze and you'll have a fine bill on your hands. There will be *qualitative change* in your engine. That's important quantitative information. On the other hand, for me to hear now in March that, . . . finally! . . . the expected high will go above zero C. tells me I can get the ice off my walk.

The highs and lows are the way *we need* quantitative information on the weather. We don't need the average; it doesn't tell us about a change of quantitative variation into quality. Neither does the weather bureau need it. It keeps the average for its records. But it thinks so little of it that, even though it takes hourly readings, it computes the average by summing only the high and the low and dividing by two.[2]

This was an odd experience. Every statistics book I had read had told *first* about the "average", the "middle", the "central tendency"; and only *afterwards* about the "range", the "dispersion", the "variance". As one colleague put it to me: "How can there be a variance unless there's a center for it to vary *around*?"[3] Indeed, I felt the weatherman had cheated me of a missing middle.

But the more situations I examined, the more I found people act like the weatherman. Students talk of whether they will be able to make enough money this summer. But how much is "enough"? "Enough" turns out to be enough to go back to school next year; "not enough" is to have to drop out. I found this question of "enough" in a much more agonizing form in studying the peasants in pre-liberation China. "Enough" grain left over after you pay the landlord means living through the winter or starving in the snow. It seems people have good reason to be interested in quantitative changes *mainly* in terms of qualitative changes; they are interested in a difference *that makes a difference.*

This makes clearer why the fastest selling book in modern times is the *Guinness Book of World Records.* First published in October 1955, by May 1978 global sales in 19 languages had reached 34,000,000 copies.[4] What accounts for the enormous popularity of Guinness? Probably several reasons; but one stands out. To pick up Guinness is to enter a world where quantity changes into quality on every page. Or does it? Often we are not sure whether we would dare to take a bite of the largest tomato; for it seems a different vegetable, one too royal to be bitten. And the smallest watch, could we still manage to wear it? And since Guinness records both the largest clock and the smallest watch, when does one become the other?

Guinness is a book of *limits*, of points of movements of quantity where one thing *changes* into another. Some limits are only one-sided; there is a *Most* but not a *Least*. Others are two-sided; there is both a *Most* and a *Least*. But even the two-sided limits, those with a maximum and minimum, don't work the same way. The limits are asymmetric.[5] This is especially apparent in records of speed, as we can confirm with a variable speed tape recorder. To slow down a voice to the limit where its human quality begins to give way to something else is very different from speeding it up to a limit. The "something else" is very different in the two cases.

Guinness is a book of changes. The same practical interest that we have in the weather report is magnified in Guinness almost into magic.

Guinness is hardly a Marxist book. Yet there is something useful to be learned from it. There is often a curious discrepancy between the way Marxists view society *politically* and the way they view the *data* they draw from it.[6] What would Marxists think of a Marxist class analysis that *starts* with the petty bourgeoisie, that starts by trying to find the "middle" of a society?

Not much. We know that the middle cannot be found in itself. We know that the middle is a contradiction; if we start with the middle as the basis of our description we won't be able to see it. In short, we won't have any idea what "the middle" is in the middle *of*. A *Communist Manifesto* written around "the middle" would have been a muddle. For Marx and Engels knew that a description that begins with the middle has a *symmetry*, a *pre-established harmony* built into it from the beginning.

Rather, Marxists begin with the *asymmetric* nature of classes. This is reflected in the *quantitative* division of society into *Many* and *Few*. These categories have *objective* reality. They are what psychologists would call the basic "figure-ground" of quantity. Unlike any number of qualities we could mention . . . height, weight, colour, etc. . . . . they are *inherently quantitative*. For Marxists, the problem of class analysis and class practice always requires a correct determination, a correct division of the whole society into the Many and the Few. this problem occurs again and again in every new situation.

There is no reason to abandon this outlook when we deal with *data*. And since "the middle", the "central tendency" is given such importance in the present approach to how to deal with data, it is a good first step to take a careful look *inside* "the middle". It may hold some surprises.

Part II

We can begin looking at the center of a distribution by looking *for* it; by actually trying to find it. I pass out to the students a collection of unordered scores and ask them the following question: "Let us find the Mean and the Median of this distribution. Which do you think you can find more quickly?" The overwhelming majority of students say the Median.

This expectation is an echo of the texts they read. "It can be seen that calculating the Median value of a set of scores is even simpler than finding the Mean. All we have to do is rank the scores in order from lowest to highest, and then read off . . ."[7].

"All we have to do . . . ." But when we actually *do* it, what do we find? When the sample is small . . . when there are just "a few" elements in the collection . . . indeed you can find the Mean faster than the Median. But as the number of elements increases . . . as "a few" becomes "many" . . . this *reverses*. The point of reversal need not require a great number of scores; in the informal experiments I have tried, a dozen or so is enough. And as the collection increases, as the sample approaches a census, the difference increases dramatically. It takes longer and longer to find the Median compared with the Mean.

The difference is even more dramatic when there is a calculator handy. With a calculator the Mean can be found in a wink. But it is no help at all with the Median; one might as well not have it.

Of course, when we think about it we see why the Median is harder to find. To find the Median, I must display the dispersion in order to find its "center". For the Median, the dispersion of scores and their center are not independent.

Their interdependence is shown by another fact. To find the Median, the "center", and to find its dispersion — its quartiles — we must do exactly the same thing: divide the ordered array in two. The Median divides the whole array in two: the Quartiles divide the parts produced by the Median in two.

Again, this is not what we are usually taught, when those pictures are put up on the blackboard with the same "center" and different dispersions; and conversely, distributions with the same dispersion and different centers. We are taught, rather, that they are conceptually separate. "The difference in dispersion is quite independent of any differences that may exist in central tendency".[8]

Now, the Median is said to contain *less* information from the distribution than the Mean:

> . . . the mean responds to every change whereas the median and the mode respond only to *some* changes. For this reason, the mean is often described as 'sensitive' and as 'reflecting' the entire distribution.[9]

If this is so, why should the measure of the center that contains *less* information be *harder* to find?

Silly? Perhaps. It was such silly questions that led me to look at the kinds of changes to which the Median is "sensitive" and "insensitive". For example, in an income distribution, the Median is sensitive to the movement of *people*, but insensitive to the movement of *income*. (In fact, for this reason, it is the most commonly cited example of a "skew" distribution where the Median is to be preferred as a center). The Median distinguishes between *many* people and *few* people. And it distinguishes between a person and a dollar. For the Mean, a person and a dollar are equivalent. But not for the Median; for each element, a person is the *main* feature, a dollar is the secondary one.

Perhaps this "insensitivity" of the Median had another side? Perhaps it masked a sensitivity which was not immediately obvious? Such silly questions lead us back to the simplest distributions, to facts which everyone knows.

Part III

We will confine ourselves to simple "univariate" data, where a number of cases, N, is measured on some magnitude. It may be the weight of birds, the test scores of students, the income of households. Below is some simple data on the money a pickpocket found in the pockets of 36 people:

Dollars:	$0	$1	$2	$3	$4	$5	$6	$7	$8	$9	$10
People:	1	2	3	4	5	6	5	4	3	2	1
Sum Dollars:	$180										
Sum People:	36										

The frequency distribution practically plots itself. This data is beautifully symmetric; the Mean, Median and Mode all coincide at $5 (see Figure 1).

It is often important to *cumulate* frequencies; this gives us the familiar *ogive*. The frequencies must be ranked, and since we can cumulate from high to low or low to high, ogives come in pairs. From the intersection of the ogives, we can read the Median directly (see Figure 2).

From the ogives we can also read off how many . . . (or what percentage) . . . of the people had more . . . (or less) . . . than x, y, or z dollars in their pockets. But we cannot read how much of all the *dollars* were found in x, y, z number . . . (or percentage) . . . of the *people*.

We can answer questions like this:

(a) What is the income of the person who gets *less* than half the people, and *more* than half the people?

But not questions like this:

(b) What is the income of the person so that half *of all the income* is made by the people who make *more* than he does, and half *of all the income* is made by the people who make *less*?

Why not? Because the ogives cumulate only *one* aspect of the data, but there are *two*. However, there is nothing that forbids us from doing it. On the horizontal axis, we simply rank the people, from the lowest to the highest amount of money in their pockets.

FIGURE 1
FREQUENCY DISTRIBUTION

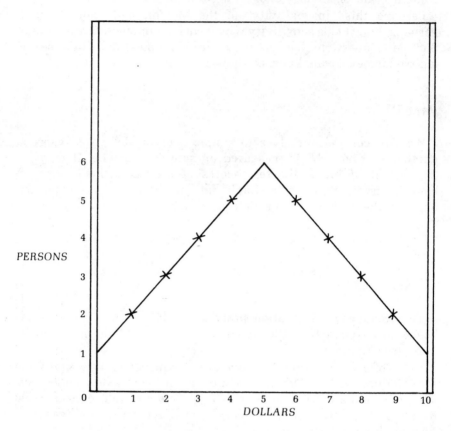

PERSONS

DOLLARS

On the vertical axis, we cumulate their total dollars. Again, we can accumulate from lowest to highest, or highest to lowest; and we get a pair of curves, plotted from the pickpocket data (see Figure 3).

The lowest-to-highest curve is the Lorenz curve. Though I have not seen it used in psychology and it is not mentioned in statistics texts for psychologists, it has a long history in the study of income distribution.[10]

These two curves intersect at the point we are looking for. Half of all the money the pickpocket found ($180) was in the pockets of the 12 people to the right of it; half was in the pockets of the 24 people to the left.

This is not exact. The point of division in half may, and often does, fall between people. But there is a particular point of division at which *someone's* money is being added in. This point has a particular value. It is the amount of money in the pocket *of the*

FIGURE 2
OGIVES

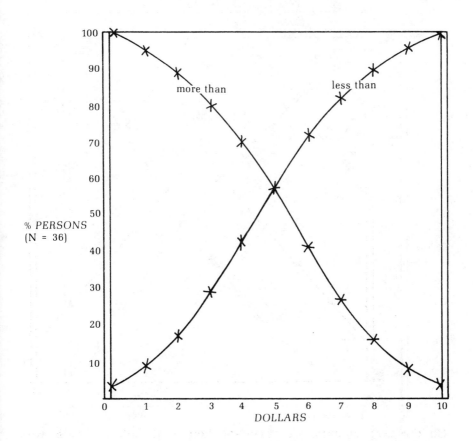

person being added in which cumulates the money to half the total. That is, $90.

To find this value, we need only go back to the ogive (Figure 2) and read it off. From the pickpocket data, this value is $6.17. This is the answer to question (b) above. *This is a second Median* in the *same* data. It divides the mass of accumulated money in half. Half the money was found in the pockets of people with more than $6.17; half with less. The familiar Median we found to be $5.00; we shall call it M_1. This second Median we shall call M_2.

We cannot easily grasp M_2 from the frequency distribution, nor from the ogives alone. We must go to the Lorenz curve before it appears to the eye.

Notice that M_2 and M_1 are not equal, even though the frequency distribution is perfectly *symmetric*. We have all learned from our texts that when a frequency distribution is symmetric, the measures

292

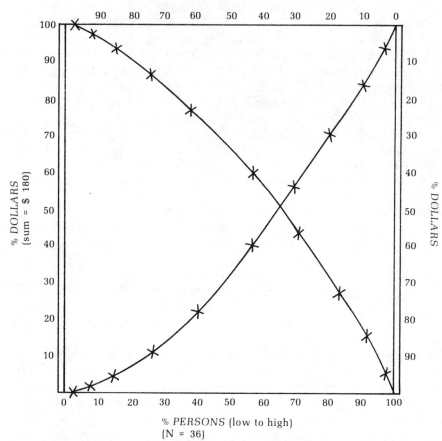

FIGURE 3
LORENZ CURVES
% PERSONS (high to low)

% DOLLARS (sum = $ 180)

% DOLLARS

% PERSONS (low to high)
(N = 36)

of central tendency — Mean, Median, Mode — all coincide. Only when the distribution is "skew" do they separate. But not M_1 and M_2. M_1 and M_2 will differ not only when the frequency distribution is skew but also when it is symmetric. The pickpocket data is not an exception. The only case where M_1 and M_2 will be equal is where every person has the same number of dollars. That is, where there is no dispersion at all.

In any distribution, if we find the value of the "center" that divides the people equally in two, that value will divide the dollars in two unequally. If we find the value of the "center" that divides the dollars equally in two, that value will divide the people unequally in two. Both these values exist; in the simplest "univariate" data, they are both definite magnitudes of variable. But they cannot be the same value.[11]

So the same data has, in fact, *two different "centers"*, Medians 1 and 2.

It is worth considering the implications of two different centers in the same simple data. Aren't the familiar Mean, Median — (our M_1) — and Mode also different centers in the same data? Yes they are. But *only of one side* of the data. That is why we could read them all from the frequency distribution (see Figure 1). The same is true of the various kinds of Means. In addition to the familiar Arithmetic Mean, we could calculate the Geometric Mean, the Harmonic Mean, the Quadratic ("root square") Mean. The familiar Standard Deviation itself is a Difference Mean.

All these are simply *different mathematical* operations on one side of the data. But the two Medians are the *same mathematical* operation on the *two different qualities* of the data. Unlike the other statistics, they measure an *inherent difference within the center of the data*. This is why they *never* coincide.

If there is a difference within the center, its behaviour as the frequency distribution changes should be very interesting. I said earlier that I know only the beginning of this tale. Nevertheless, we can see a few simple facts already. If the frequency distribution remains symmetric, but its dispersion increases, M_1 stays the same, M_2 *increases*. The Mean increases also, but not nearly as much as M_2. If the frequency distribution skews to the right, M_1 increases slightly, M_2 increases dramatically, and the Mean increases slightly more than M_1 but much less than M_2. If the frequency distribution skews to the left, the movement is reversed. M_1 decreases slightly, M_2 decreases dramatically; the Mean decreases slightly more than M_1 but much less than M_2.

These results on the behaviour of the two Medians and the Mean are very elementary; they hardly begin to scratch the surface. Yet simple as they are, they allow us to look at the Mean from another angle. As everyone knows, to find the Mean in our pickpocket example, we divide the mass of dollars by the mass of people, N. We must accumulate the total of both, but we need not *cumulate by rank*. That's why we can sum up scores in any order we please.

In the pickpocket data, we need to know that N=36. To find M_1, we must also find N. But we must *cumulate persons by their dollar-ranks*. So, whereas the Mean is sensitive only to the *mass* of persons, N, M_1 is sensitive to *both* their mass *and* their cumulated dollar-ranks. But we need not know the total mass of *dollars*.

Thus the denominator of the Mean contains only *part* of the information about persons which we find embodied in M_1.

To find M_2, we can compare it with the numerator of the Mean. This numerator is sensitive only to the mass of dollars. M_2 is also sensitive to the mass of dollars. In the pickpocket data, we need to know that his total loot is $180. But to find M_2, we must also *cumulate dollars by their person-ranks*. So, whereas the Mean is sensitive only to the mass of dollars, M_2 is sensitive to *both* their mass *and* their cumulated person-ranks. But we need not know the total mass of *persons*.

Thus the numerator of the Mean contains only *part* of the information about dollars which we find embodied in M_2.

$Median_1$ is sensitive to both the mass and dollar-rank of persons. $Median_2$ is sensitive to both the mass and person-rank of dollars. The Mean is sensitive to the mass of both and the rank of neither.

Now let us place the Mean in its most "comfortable" symmetric setting, the normal distribution. In any actual distribution, it has a particular value. Why does it have *this* value rather than another? We can divide this question in two.

Why is it as *high* as it is; why isn't it lower? It is as high as it is *mainly* because of the mass of *dollars above* it, *not below* it. The mass of dollars above it contribute *many* dollars to its numerator, the dollars below it contribute *few*.

And why is it as *low* as it is; why isn't it higher? It is as low as it is *mainly* because of the mass of persons *below* it, *not above* it. The mass of people below it contribute *many* persons to its denominator, the mass of people above it contribute *few*.

So the Mean is sensitive *mainly* to the *dollars above* it and the *people below* it. The parameter that shows us the first aspect of the Mean is $Median_2$. The parameter that shows us the second is $Median_1$.

Even in a perfectly symmetric distribution, the Mean is not the center of stability. It is better seen as a *limit*, a temporary limit of the *opposing* tendencies of people and dollars. In a symmetric distribution, this opposition is still "manageable"; the Mean still serves as a measure of its "center". But as many people with little income accumulate, and few people with much, the symmetry begins to skew, and the Mean, the "center" breaks down.

But our two Medians do not. They were different from the beginning.

Part IV   ,

All our texts discuss the Median. But we have found that what is called *the* Median is really only M_1; it is really only *one side* of the Median which has *two*.

If this view is correct, why has it been overlooked? Why have the two sides been invisibly collapsed into one?[12]

Recall that earlier (in Part II) we found that the Median is regarded as a *weaker* measure of central tendency than the Mean. The

Mean is the preferred measure. Only when the distribution skews and the Mean becomes questionable do we need to resort to the Median.

It is important to ask just what "weakness" means. It is *insensitivity* to *some* changes in the data. The weaker measure appears to "throw away" information which the stronger does not. But there are two ways of looking at this "insensitivity". We can look at it *passively*, as simply a "lack" or "deficit", as a kind of "inability" to respond. Or we can detect in that insensitivity an *active resistance* to certain kinds of movement in the data. The insensitivity is not a feebleness but a stubbornness.

This is not just a metaphor. For when we take the first view, we are not able to see the question which the second view forces on us. Is there a *hidden* aspect of "*The*" Median which we do not yet see; an aspect which *is* sensitive to just those changes to which the former aspect *is not*?[13]

To ask such a question is to search for the strong side of the weak thing; and to see the weakness in strength. The Median$_1$, in its stubbornness, refused to erase the distinction as the Mean did, between a person and a dollar. Just because it was so stubborn, it led us to Median$_2$; and through this to the asymmetric division of the simplest symmetric distribution.

Guinness should record the humble Median$_1$ under: Most Stubborn Statistic.

NOTES

1. It is a pity . . . though not an accident . . . that the morning news doesn't report the Index of Unemployment the way it reports the weather. "Expected high today, 10 degrees Celsius, expected low, minus 3 . . . And now, today's unemployment. Statistics Canada's expected low: 7% . . . Stirling-Kouri's expected high: 20% . . ."

   The reader of the Stirling-Kouri paper in this volume may want to consider whether "splitting the difference", taking an average of the high and low would clarify or muddle the real state of unemployment, and for whom.

   The answer stands out in relief when we look at the *name* which the number counts. E.P. Thompson tells us how the word, "Unemployed" came into the English language:

   > There is a legend abroad that 'unemployment' was outside the semantic frame of the 1820s. Perhaps it stems from an unwise statement in G.M. Young, *Victorian England* (Oxford 1936), p. 27, that 'unemployment was beyond the scope of any idea which Early Victorian reformers had at their command, largely because they had no word for it': to which is added the authority of a footnote: 'I have not observed it earlier than the sixties'. In fact (as is often the case with these semantic 'datings') the statement is wrong. (Cuckoos generally arrive in these islands some weeks before they are announced in The Times). 'Unemployed', 'the unemployed', and (less frequently) 'unemployment' are all to be found in trade union and Radical or Owenite writing

of the 1820s and 1830s: the inhibitions of 'Early Victorian Reformers' must be explained in some other way.

E.P. Thompson, *The Making of the English Working Class*, (Pelican 1963) p. 853 fn. 3.

Obviously, the English bourgeoisie of the day did "a deed without a name" (*Macbeth* IV:1). They needed none. But the actual unemployed *did* need a name. It is not possible to "split the difference", and take the average of these two "estimates".

Today, beneath billions of numbers still lie the names. "Unemployed" was a semantic Black Hole in the 1820s. Today the Black Hole is . . . "Not in the Labour Force". See the Stirling-Kouri paper. My paper, in a sense, takes off from Note 14 in theirs.

I want to thank Bob Stirling for critical support. But he is not to be blamed in any way for the present Tale.

2. "The mean temperature for any one day is one-half the total of the maximum and minimum temperatures for that day" (*World Almanac and Book of Facts*, Newspaper Publishers Enterprise Association, Inc., 1977, p. 796).

3. This comment only echoes what the texts tell us. For example, one author, after discussing the central tendency takes up dispersion, "which is *quite independent* of any differences that may exist in central tendency . . . The second important feature of a set of scores is the extent to which they are spread out *on either side of the central value*". (S. Miller, *Experimental Design and Statistics*, Methuen 1975, p. 40. Authors emphases).

4. Guinness book of records holds this record itself — see *Guinness Book of World Records* (ed: N. McWhirter, Bantam, 1979, p. 214). Another recent bestseller which extends the "Guinness principle" is *The Book of Lists* (eds: Wallechinsky, D. Wallace, and I. Wallace, Bantam 1978). The editors report that "readers and media alike found these lists and responded with overwhelming affirmation . . . we were inundated with call-ins . . . readers' letters poured in from every corner of the continent" (p. xviii).

5. A lovely example of this asymmetry are the lists of "The 9 Breeds of Dogs that Bite the Most", and "The 9 Breeds of Dogs that Bite the Least" (*The Book of Lists*, p. 125).

6. The masters of Marxism — Marx, Lenin, Mao — always appreciated quantitative data. And why not? We would expect this from a world view that understands the transformation of quantity into quality, that understands the quantitative preparation of qualitative leaps.

Marx and Lenin's appreciation of quantitative data is too well known to have to document. Mao, also, did not regard the problem of quantity and quality in production as beneath him:

> Fifth, several things were swept away last year. One was the principle of doing things with greater, faster, better and more economical results. The demand for greater and faster results was dropped, and with it the demand for better and more economical results was swept away, too. No one, I think, objects to doing things better and more economically; it is just doing things with greater and faster results that people don't like and some comrades label "rash". As a matter of fact "better" and "more economical" are meant to restrict "greater" and "faster". "Better" means better in quality, "more econo-mical" means spending less money, "greater" means doing more things, and "faster" also means doing more things. This slogan is self-restricting, since it calls for better and more economical results, that is, for better quality and

lower cost, which precludes greater and faster results that are unrealistic. I am glad that a couple of comrades have spoken on this question at the present session. Besides, I've read an article on it in the newspaper. Our demand for greater, faster, better and more economical results is realistic, in conformity with the actual conditions and not subjectivist. We must always do our utmost to achieve greater and faster results; what we oppose is only the subjectivist demand for greater and faster results. In the second half of last year, a gust of wind swept away this slogan, which I want to restore. Is this possible? Please consider the matter.

"Be Activists in Promoting the Revolution", in *Selected Works* V, 1957, p. 491.

Politically, his basic formulation of the problem of *unity* and *struggle* contains a quantitative aspect. Here he explains the meaning of "both unity and struggle".

You have not yet won state power but are preparing to seize it. Towards the national bourgeoisie a policy of "both unity and struggle" should be adopted. Unite with them in the common fight against imperialism and support all their anti-imperialist words and deeds, while waging an appropriate struggle against their reactionary, anti-working class and anti-Communist words and deeds. It is wrong to be one-sided; struggle without unity is a "Left" deviationist mistake and unity without struggle is a Right deviationist mistake. Both mistakes occurred in our Party and we learned bitter lessons from them. Later, we summed up the two kinds of experience and have since adopted a policy of "both unity and struggle", that is, to struggle whenever necessary and unite whenever possible. The aim of struggle is to unite with the national bourgeoisie and win victory in the struggle against imperialism.

"Some Experiences in Our Party's History", in *Selected Works* V, 1956, p. 329.

Unite *whenever possible*. Struggle *whenever necessary*. These ideas contain the notions of *maximum* and *minimum*. It is too bad this is not in *Guinness Book of World Records* as a guide.

In my final example, Mao wrote in 1941 how class power in society is reflected in the power even to gather data.

Speaking generally, the infant bourgeoisie of China has not been able, and never will be able, to provide relatively comprehensive or even rudimentary material on social conditions, as the bourgeoisie in Europe, America and Japan has done; we have therefore no alternative but to collect it ourselves.

"Preface to Rural Surveys", in *Selected Works III*, 1941, p. 13.

7. Miller, *Experimental Design and Statistics*, p. 37.

8. *Ibid.*, p. 37 — (see Note 3)

9. Weinberg, G.H. and J.A. Schumaker, *Statistics: An Intuitive Approach*, Belmont, Cal.: Brooks/Cole, 1969, p. 13. Authors' emphasis.

10. See R. Love, and M.C. Wolfson, *Income Inequality: Statistical Methodology and Canadian Illustrations*, Ottawa: Statistics Canada, 1976.

I believe there is a reason psychologists don't know it. They are accustomed to dealing with the qualitative aspects of data indifferently simply as "scores". Hence they do not see, for example, the number of items remembered by the whole population in a memory test as a *real material* magnitude; as something that exists in the world, capable of expansion, contraction and redistribution in the real population.

We cannot get away with this when we deal with the material magnitudes of production and distribution. Then we are forced to see that *both* quantities in the "univariate" distribution are real; they are not just "scores" to which we can take any attitude we please. They are real relations of possession, accumulation, etc.

Love and Wolfson recognize this, but tend to fall into a more sophisticated form of the error when they make the measure of income inequality purely relative (see pp. 22-3). The reason given is that the measure should be unaffected by changes in the unit of measurement. Well and good. But there remains the *real growth* of productive forces, population, etc; these changes are not due to changes in the unit of measure. And they lead to qualitative changes. The growth of a baby is not because the ruler shrinks; the baby really grows. To think otherwise is to turn the real relation between measurement and reality inside out.

11. There is a point worth noting here. Sometimes, the frequency distribution of data is Bi-Modal. It is often said that the reason it is Bi-Modal is that there are two different populations being measured as if they were one. For example, a distribution of heights of college students often has one Mode for the men, another for the women. Separate the scores of men from women and the bi-modality would disappear.

This views bi-modality as a kind of "imperfection" in the data, which "ought not" to be there. The idea of *inherent* bi-modality is seen as something to be avoided, a last resort. Medians 1 and 2 cast a different light on this question. They show us that while *some* distributions may be bi-modal *some* of the time, *all* distributions are *Bi-Medial* all of the time. From this point of view, the idea of inherent bi-modality as a wide-spread property of the data becomes much more plausible.

12. This question reaches beyond the Medians alone. Consider our simple pickpocket data. Is it univariate or bivariate? All the texts would say it's univariate. We are only measuring one variable on people, the amount of money in their pockets. But it has *two different centers*; as soon as we cumulate persons by their dollar-ranks, and cumulate dollars by their person-ranks, we see that each is secondarily involved in the determination of the other. So it is *not* univariate.

But is is not bivariate either, in the way we usually think of it. Again, the reason is the same. The two aspects of the data are inherently non-independent. Their interdependence is not an empirical result. The Lorenz curve shows us that the *very classification* of either aspect of the variate, without the other, *disappears*. Therefore:

(a) it is not bivariate because the two aspects of the data are *interdependent, but*
(b) *it is not univariate because the two* aspects of the data are interdependent.

It is the *collapse* of these two aspects into one which opens the door for the "Jacob's Ladder" of statistics: "multivariate" data as a *combination* of "univariates". When we see the inherently bi-variate character of univariate data, we can't proceed this way. This theoretical collapse has another side, too: the theoretical *total separation* of the *mass* from the *rank* of data. This is the base for the separation of parametric from non-parametric statistics. Thus, variables are piled on top of each other *because* the rank and the mass aspects of even the simplest variable are separated from each other.

It may be objected that in treating univariate data as if it were "bivariate", we have erased the difference between the object and the quality (or attribute) we are measuring. We have erased the difference between a person and a dollar, between a whole and a part.

This, of course, is just what the Mean does as a measure of "the center". In this paper we have done something else. We have *translated* the *qualitative difference* between a person and a dollar *into a quantitative asymmetry in the measure of the "center"* of the data. This is the meaning of the division of the Median in two.

13. *Seeing* the data is much more important in statistical analysis than we often allow. It is unfortunate how quickly we often race through the descriptive

aspect of statistics to get on with the "serious" business of "crunching the data". This practice is based on a view that quantitative qualities like *Many* and *Few* are really only *pre*-quantitative; a kind of quantitative baby-talk which we can cast off as soon as we get to the "real thing". They are seen as qualities we can leave behind us when we begin a mature scientific elaboration of quantitative movement.

Hand-in-hand with this view goes another: the downgrading of the powers of *practical perception* in the realm of quantity. These powers are discounted as very primitive. The perception that sees in the data that *only* a few cases are different from the rest, or that *even* a few cases are different from the rest, is thrown away. This is an important reason why present conceptions of *statistical significance* and *actual significance* described in the same data are worlds apart. This gap over "significance" is a source of demoralization to students.

But a different view is possible; one which sees practical perception as potentially very powerful, capable of being educated. Quantities like Many and Few exist in the data objectively. They are capable of statistical elaboration. We need to spend much more time *describing what's there* in the data before going on to "crunch" it.

For interesting remarks on this question, see J. Cohen, *Chance, Skill and Luck*, (Penguin, 1960, ch. 9).

Readings

Bakan, David, "The Significance of Psychological Research", in David Bakan, *On Method: Toward a Reconstruction of Psychological Investigation*, San Francisco: Jossey-Bass, 1967.

Cohen, John, *Chance, Skill and Luck: The Psychology of Guessing, Gambling, and Luck*, Baltimore: Penguin, 1960.

Engels, Fredrich, *Anti-Dühring*, Part 1, Section XII, "Dialectics: Quantity and Quality," San Francisco: China Books, 1976.

McWhirter, N. (ed.), *Guiness Book of World Records*, N.Y.: Bantam Books, 1979.

Miller, Steve, *Experimental Design and Statistics*, London: Methuen, 1975.

Moroney, M.J., *Facts from Figures*, Harmondsworth: Penguin, 1952.

Wallechinsky, David and Irving Wallace, *The Book of Lists*, N.Y.: Morrow, 1977.

The Welfare State and Its Ideology

Angela Wei Djao

ANGELA WEI DJAO is an Assistant Professor of Sociology at the University of Saskatchewan. Her current research interests include Industrial Sociology and the Ideology of the Welfare State.

Ideology of the Welfare State

The term "welfare state" usually prompts the layman and the social policy professional alike to enumerate the various welfare programs in Canada and compare them with those in the "socialist" countries of northwestern Europe. This preoccupation with the quantity of welfare measures invariably leads to a concern with the cost and abuse of welfare. Fears of socialism notwithstanding, what is overlooked is the fact that the welfare state is based on and committed to a structure of social inequality produced by the capitalist process of industrialization. The express goal of the welfare state is indeed the redistribution of income so that every citizen is ensured a minimum acceptable standard of living (Schottland, 1967). Some welfare measures, controversial and slow in coming in Canada, do provide the destitute with basic means of subsistence. But the total welfare system accomplishes little in the redistribution of income. On the contrary, it tends to perpetuate the gap between the rich and the poor. Thus in Canada as in the social democratic states of Europe, the assertion that the welfare state is "creeping socialism" is only partially correct: it is not socialist but it creeps (Offe, 1972).

The discrepancy between the express goal and the real workings of the welfare state is masked by the ideology of the welfare state.[1] Historically, the laissez-faire theories in the liberal tradition formed the essential ideology of industrial capitalism. It was argued, in theory at least, that individuals on their own could and should achieve their well-being, with little or no state intervention. Only widows and orphans could have some legitimate claim on the charity of the community (Wallace, 1950). During the Great Depression, the action of the federal and provincial governments ushered in a de facto welfare state in Canada (see Armitage, 1975; Finkel, 1977). By its unemployment relief measures, the Canadian state recognized and implemented the principle of public responsibility for individual welfare.

Since the economic crisis of the 1930s, a modified ideology emerged in Canada as in all advanced capitalist societies. It would account for the realities of state intervention in social welfare without altering the basic socio-economic structures of capitalism. In this updated ideology, the welfare state

> . . . is considered a natural and inevitable response to various societal changes that contain the potential to disrupt social stability and impair individual well-being. These underlying pressures are frequently thought of as industrialization and urbanization. The welfare state in its broadest dimensions (as opposed to specific policy and program alternatives) . . . is considered to reflect a continuous unfolding of logical and necessary responses to social developments, predetermined by society's major values and institutions . . . (Galper, 1975:13).

This concept of the welfare state is essentially a liberal view for there is no opposition to capitalism or individualism (Galper, 1975: 33-44); in fact, the welfare state is seen as a natural outcome of capitalist development. The most important assumptions of this view are still that there is widespread opportunity in the capitalist system for individualistic competitive achievement; that the individual knows what is in his/her best interest; and that the well-being of the community is the sum of individual well-beings. What is new is that the welfare state programs are seen as means enabling the individual to pursue his/her best interest.

All the same this view of the welfare state represents a significant departure from the pre-welfare state ideology which maintained that the individual alone was responsible for his well-being or impoverishment. It will be shown in this paper that some pre-welfare state notions of individualism persist; they are voiced in connection with the people on public assistance. But by and large there is acceptance of the welfare state itself. The crucial question is what does the welfare state do? Officially the welfare state is said to intervene on behalf of the less privileged, the poor, the dispossessed, etc. But as we shall see, the welfare state in Canada operates on two levels, with one system for the poor and another for the non-poor. The ideology of the welfare state is, therefore, made up of some factual statements about the welfare system for the poor, some misconceptions about those dependent on the welfare system for the poor, and general concealment of the welfare system for the non-poor.

The ideology has at least three consequences. First of all, in highlighting the subsistence given to the poor, it persuades the public to accept humanized capitalism. Secondly, in retaining some pre-welfare state notions of individualism, it moves people to be indignant about real or assumed welfare abuse by the poor. In blaming the victims of poverty, the ideology at the same time glosses over the real causes of social inequality and poverty. And, thirdly, in concealing the welfare system for the non-poor, especially the wealthy, the ideology prevents people from criticizing the virtual absence of income redistribution in Canada.

The Welfare State Programs

Programs of the welfare state are usually classified into cash transfers for income security and in-kind transfer programs. A classification scheme of the important programs is presented in Figure 1.

FIGURE 1
SELECTED PROGRAMS OF THE WELFARE STATE

A Social Services: In-kind Transfers[a]	B Income Security: Cash Transfers
1. Universal services:	1. Transfer to the poor:

- Health services
  - Primary education
  - Secondary education
	- Social assistance
	  - Guaranteed income supplement
	  - Spouse allowance

2. Personal and community services:	2. Transfer to the non-poor:

- Information and referral
  - Counselling
  - Family planning
  - Crisis intervention
  - Child welfare
  - Day care
  - Services for the disabled
  - Home support services
  - Social integration centres
  - Social adaptation services
  - Employment-related services
  - Community development
	- The Income Tax Act
	  - "Occupational" welfare
	
	3. Universal programs:
	
	  - Family allowance
	  - Youth allowance
	  - Old age security
	
	4. Social insurance programs:
	
	  - Canada/Quebec pension plan
	  - Unemployment insurance

[a]The distinction between universal services and some personal/community services is largely administrative. Those listed under personal/community services are shareable services between the federal and provincial governments under the present arrangements.

There is little income redistribution in Canada because the poor and the non-poor have their separate welfare systems. This will be shown in this section with reference to only two cash transfer programs: social assistance for the poor and tax expenditures in the Income Tax Act for the non-poor, listed under B 1. and B 2. in Figure 1 respectively. There is no significant decrease in income inequality effected through the other cash or in-kind transfers. If anything, the non-poor derive proportionally greater benefits from some of the social services and social insurance programs (see Armitage, 1975; Canada National Health and Welfare; 1977; National Council of Welfare, 1978).

Welfare for the Poor

For most Canadians, welfare is social assistance, the program for the poor. Relief for the poor is traditionally considered a local matter, a legacy of the Elizabethan poor laws. The underlying belief was that only the local authorities could separate the undeserving poor from the truly needy (Adams et al, 1971). This legacy was implicitly inherited by Canada insofar as the British North America Act did not impose any obligation on the Dominion or the provinces to provide welfare services. The Act merely designated public charities along with education and hospitals as within the provincial sphere of jurisdiction, "any subsequent action being permissive, not mandatory" (Wallace, 1950:384). As things went, charity to the indigent was handed by the parish or the local community well into the twentieth century.

Although federal funds were used for relief since the Great Depression, it was not until after the Second World War that the involvement of the national government in general welfare was gradually written into law. The Canada Assistance Plan (1966) consolidated previous federal-provincial cost-sharing programs including unemployment assistance, old age assistance, blind and disabled persons assistance, child welfare and administrative costs. By the Plan the federal government entered into agreements with the provinces to reimburse 50 percent of the costs incurred in provincial or municipal assistance to the needy. However, the pattern of decentralization of control is essentially unchanged. The administration of social assistance is left to the provinces. In seven provinces, some allowances are administered by the municipalities (Statistics Canada, 1977a:283). The rates of assistance and conditions of eligibility are set by each province. The differences among the provinces are not so much determined by differential living costs as differential provincial ability or willingness to spend on the poor (Armitage, 1975:133). Thus the definition of a recipient's needs and the way these needs are met are both somewhat arbitrary. The rates established by all the provinces are below the poverty line, whether one uses the poverty line provided by the Economic Council of Canada, Statistics Canada or Canadian Council on Social Development.

On the other hand, the provinces must meet three conditions for federal reimbursement of costs. First, provinces or municipalities cannot establish any residence requirements as criteria for assistance eligibility. Second, assistance must be based on need, regardless of causes. In other words, there must be a needs test, usually in the form of an interview by the intake officer. And, third, there must be some procedure for appeal.

These three conditions are symbolic of the national scope of the welfare state. They do not detract the expediency of having the lower levels of government in control of social assistance. That the coverage of social assistance is broad but discretionary is left intact. As Armitage has noted:

> It is broad in that there are no exclusions from coverage in the way that social insurance programmes exclude persons who do not satisfy defined criteria. This leads to social assistance programmes supporting all those persons whose need is not met by other income security programmes (persons unemployed for more than one year, persons disabled but not severely disabled, elderly persons who are not yet sixty-five, etc.). Coverage is discretionary because no person is assured a right to benefit. Instead, his or her circumstances are examined and assessed by the administering agency which then makes a judgement as to whether "need" exists. Subject to limited rights of appeal, the agency's judgement is final (Armitage, 1975:134).

The way social assistance is administered has exacted "a high price in civil liberties for the provision of subsistence income," a conclusion reached by the Canadian Civil Liberties Education Trust (1975:107) after it conducted a survey of welfare practices across the nation. The survey researchers were dismayed at the departure from common law requirements of "due process" in welfare administration and the substantial unawareness of any appeal machinery on the part of recipients. The state, through the welfare program, seems to intrude on the most intimate situations in the lives of recipients. It encroaches on the privacy of marriage, of cohabitation, of unwed mothers and of the home.

The state is also intruding on freedom of choice: whether and/or where to work, where to live, and what to consume. There is no legal definition of "employability;" nor are there precise and consistent guidelines for the administrators (Buttrum, 1976). Yet applicants and recipients are constantly classified or declassified as employables. As a condition of receiving assistance, they are sometimes required to comply with a variety of employer demands (Canadian Civil Liberties, 1975).

The periodic use of vouchers is probably the most stigmatizing aspect of the welfare system for the poor. Not only is the voucher a symbol of poverty and dependency, but it also intrudes upon the recipient's freedom of choice as it restricts what to buy and, sometimes, where to buy.

> The decision to grant vouchers, instead of cash, is frequently made by welfare administrators on the basis of their personal impressions of the recipients' competence at handling money . . . . Many recipients have alleged that they are not even told why they are given vouchers instead of cash (Canadian Civil Liberties, 1975:108).

The litany of flagrant violations of civil liberties in the administration of social assistance goes on. The recent story of a "welfare bum" (Mott, 1977) unfortunately suggests that the program has improved but little. What is clear is that various encroachments on personal privacy and freedom of choice are allowed and carried out all "[in] the interests of safeguarding public funds" (Canadian Civil Liberties, 1975:107). The state's concern for welfare expenditures tends to modify its ethical priorities, the civil libertarians observed. But there is a further consequence: it shapes the public's ideological thinking. The welfare state in providing subsistence to the poorest members of the society holds them in deep distrust while in effect exercising comprehensive control over their lives. Welfare practices which embody such orientations of the state naturally support and encourage the welfare bum stereotypes among the non-poor members of the society. In other words, the perpetuation of certain myths about the welfare poor must be attributed in part to the way social assistance is administered.

The dehumanization, the public humiliation, the disregard for civil liberties and personal freedoms of recipients and applicants, and, above all, careful accounting of where the tax money goes, have all become ingrained features of the welfare system for the poor. They keep it highly visible for the rest of the society. The welfare system for the non-poor in contrast has none of these things. It is so well hidden that even some of its beneficiaries are not aware of it.

Welfare for the Non-Poor

The most important welfare program for the non-poor in Canada is the Income Tax Act (National Council of Welfare, 1976). The income tax system is a source of revenue for the government. It can be used to bring about a more equitable distribution of income in society. On the one hand, tax money is transferred, through income security programs such as social assistance and old age security, to those who have little or no earning capacity. On the other hand, revenue collection is based on the ability-to-pay principle so that people with higher incomes are taxed at higher rates.[2]

The ideal of income redistribution through the Income Tax Act to reduce the disparity between the rich and the poor is an official policy of the Canadian government (see Gillespie, 1976). Yet if the ability-to-pay principle were really operational, how could the changes in the income shares of the various groups resulting from the income tax system be so modest (see Table 1)? The answer lies in other provisions in the Income Tax Act which negate the intent of progressive taxation. These provisions ensure a tax break to certain groups and individuals who can then save substantial amounts of money which progressive taxation would have otherwise required them to pay (National Council of Welfare, 1976).

The savings are in the form of deductions and exemptions from income, tax deferrals, tax reductions, credits against tax and preferential tax rates. They are collectively called tax incentives or loopholes. But these savings for some individuals are in fact revenue lost (*i.e.* spent) by the government. So the more accurate terminology would be tax subsidies (to some individuals) or tax expenditures (by the government) (National Council of Welfare, 1976:6).

How these tax expenditures are government subsidies to the non-poor is demonstrated by an example given by the National Council of Welfare. A person "makes" $20,000 in a year, $19,000 in wages and $1,000 in interest from a savings account. The tax on $20,000 is $5,020.[3] Provisions in the Income Tax Act, however, allow this income tax payer to deduct up to $1,000 in interest before he arrives at his taxable income. In other words, his $1,000 of interest income is tax free. So he only pays on $19,000. It amounts to $4,640, which is $380 less than the tax on $20,000.

> The entirety of this $380 tax savings is due to the special deduction for interest income. In a very real sense, then, the government has spent — by not collecting the tax — the amount of $380. From the point of view of the taxpayer, he has received a subsidy of $380 — a reward, as it were, for having saved enough money in the bank to have gained $1,000 in interest.
>
> The government could have chosen to collect the full tax on $20,000 and then paid this person, through a direct transfer, a grant of $380 as the means for giving him this "reward". The government would have ended up with the same net revenue and the taxpayer with the same net income. Furthermore the government accounts would have shown that it had spent $380. However because the

subsidy is accomplished through an exemption from taxes, it never appears as a government expenditure (National Council of Welfare, 1976:13).

TABLE 1

DISTRIBUTION OF INCOME BEFORE AND AFTER INCOME TAX
1974 AND 1975

	1974			1975		
	Share of Total Income			Share of Total Income		
Income Group a	Before Income Tax %	After Income Tax %	Change %	Before Income Tax %	After Income Tax %	Change %
Bottom 20%	4.0	4.6	+ .6	4.0	4.6	+ .6
Second 20%	10.9	11.7	+ .8	10.6	11.5	+ .9
Third 20%	17.7	18.2	+ .5	17.6	18.2	+ .6
Fourth 20%	24.9	24.9	0	25.1	25.1	0
Top 20%	42.5	40.6	-1.9	42.6	40.6	-2.0

aThe unit in each group is a family or an unattached individual.

Sources: Statistics Canada, Income After Tax, Distribution by Size in Canada 1974 and Income After Tax, Distribution by Size in Canada 1975, Ottawa: Supply and Services Canada, 1977.

The concealment of subsidy in a tax exemption does not make it any less a form of governmnt expenditure. It has been estimated that in 1974, 17 out of approximately 60 tax subsidies in the personal income tax system cost Canadians $6.4 billion.[4] This sum was "equal to well over one-fifth of the entire federal budget in 1974 . . . (and) four and a half times the cost of the Olympic games" (National Council of Welfare, 1976:16). The sum was also 12 times the total amount of funds transferred from the federal government to the ten provinces and the territories for all the social welfare expenses incurred in 1974 (Statistics Canada, 1977a:977).

Tax subsidies benefit Canadians differentially, the higher their income, the greater their benefit (see Table 2). The poorest income earners, whose incomes fall below the taxpaying threshold, receive no benefit at all.[5] Deductions and exemptions always give greater benefit to those with higher incomes because they take money out of the income bracket which is taxed at the highest rate applicable to that income. Thus although income tax rates are progressive, its intended purpose of distributing the tax burden according to the ability to pay is defeated by allowing incomes to be taxed at lower rates, or, more simply put, by granting subsidies to higher income earners.

Of the estimated $6.4 billion the government spent on 17 tax subsidies in 1974, the average benefit to a person with income

TABLE 2
ESTIMATED % DISTRIBUTION OF TOTAL BENEFITS FROM THE 17 TAX
SUBSIDIES AND AVERAGE BENEFIT PER TAXPAYER, 1974

Income Group	% of All Tax Filers	% of Total Benefits from the 17 Tax Subsidies	Average Benefit Per Taxpayer
Under $5,000	38.4	12.5	$ 243.75
$ 5,000 - 9,999	31.5	27.9	484.65
$10,000 - 14,999	18.7	26.5	788.06
$15,000 - 19,999	6.8	14.3	1,177.46
$20,000 - 24,999			1,786.93
$25,000 - 49,999	} 4.6	} 18.8	2,426.73
$50,000 +			3,989.78
	100.0	100.0	

Source: National Council of Welfare, *The Hidden Welfare System*, Ottawa: National
Council of Welfare, 1976.

over $25,000 was ten times that to an individual with income under
$5,000 (see Table 2). Moreover, all those with income under $10,000,
i.e., 70 percent of all tax filers, received altogether 40 percent of
the benefits, whereas the top 11 percent of tax filers received 33
percent.

The best known deductions are contributions to the registered
retirement savings plans, registered home ownership savings plan
and registered pension plans, interest income deduction and child
care deduction. Even if these tax subsidies were intended as
incentives to foster national savings among the "ordinary" Canadians,
the way they are implemented makes them both arbitrary and unjust
because they accrue the greatest benefits to the wealthy but only
modest benefits to the low and middle income tax payers.

It may be argued that the purpose of most exemptions, *e.g.*, those
for wholly dependent children, for blind and disabled persons, for
students, etc., is to lessen the financial burden of specific categories
of people with special needs. Such an aim is of course reasonable
and socially justifiable. It will be more equitably met by means of
tax credits. But the tax exemption mechanisms now in use always
guarantee the greatest benefit to those who already have the most
income (National Council of Welfare, 1976).

While these deductions and exemptions undermine the progressive
tax structure, "the income tax system remains the only part of
Canada's tax structure that is at all redistributive from the rich
to the poor" (National Council of Welfare, 1978:6). The rest of the
Canadian tax system does not even begin with any idea of pro-
gressivity. In fact some of the non-income taxes used to fund social
insurance programs (*i.e.* contributions to Canada Pension Plan/

Quebec Pension Plan, and premiums on unemployment insurance and provincial health services) are regressive because they place the heaviest burden on the low income earners. Yet pension and unemployment insurance benefit payments to higher income tax payers are greater (see National Council of Welfare, 1978).

In addition, publicly provided services such as primary and secondary education and health care are in-kind government transfers. In theory, as these services are universal, the poor and the rich could derive the same kinds and amounts of benefits from them. There is even an assumption that benefits of universal health care to low income families are above average because of the correlations among low income, poor health and age. But again the higher income groups seem to get greater benefits from the publicly provided services. Available information on utilization of health services in Ontario suggests that in 1974-75 "average medical benefits for families with income above $14,000 was 60 percent higher than the average for families with incomes less than $8,000" (Canada National Health and Welfare, 1977:46).

Taken together, tax subsidies through the income tax system, regressive features of the non-income taxes, and greater benefits from the social insurance programs and universal social services make up the hidden welfare system for the non-poor, and especially the wealthy in Canada. The poorest Canadians who are stigmatized and scapegoated because of their dependence on social assistance are not likely to find out about it. The lower and middle income citizens, who are indignant about the real or imagined abuse of social assistance, are largely unaware of the fact that they bear the greatest burden of the cost of the hidden welfare sytem. There is no needs test for the recipients of this welfare system; the only criterion for eligibility is high income. No accounts of this welfare system are kept. There is no public debate. "The government already has all of the information to make known the extent, the costs and the beneficiaries of the hidden welfare system. It has simply chosen not to make these known" (National Council of Welfare, 1976:34).

Ideological Beliefs about Welfare

Given the structure of the welfare state described above, certain public perceptions and beliefs about social welfare are likely to develop. There is limited information on ideological beliefs about welfare in Canada. A province-wide survey conducted in Alberta in 1972 revealed that although most respondents approved of government involvement in welfare programs, they thought that many "undeserving poor" were abusing the system. They felt that only the sick, the aged and the single-parents should get public assistance (Alberta Health and Social Development, 1973).

The same pattern of perceptions was found in a survey conducted in one Alberta city in 1977. In the second study, the 'welfare bum' stereotypes were examined in greater detail. Table 3 shows that respondents on the whole tend to believe that personal short-comings and faults are important causes of poverty. Furthermore, most respondents hold some perjorative views about the welfare recipients.

TABLE 3
BELIEFS ABOUT CAUSES OF POVERTY AND
SOCIAL ASSISTANCE RECIPIENTS[a]

	Agree %	Disagree %	
1. The following are important reasons for some people being poor:			
a. they do not manage money well	97	3	(100%)
b. they do not try hard enough	90	10	(100%)
c. they have loose morals	38	62	(100%)
d. they spend all their money on liquor	85	15	(100%)
2. Women on welfare have illegitimate babies to increase the money they get.	26	74	(100%)
3. Recipients who can work do not try to find jobs to support themselves	55	45	(100%)
4. Most recipients do not tell their social workers the truth about their financial matters.	53	47	(100%)
5. A lot of people are moving to Alberta to get better welfare benefits.	47	53	(100%)
6. What percentage of the people who are getting welfare do you think *do not deserve* it, and are abusing the system?			
less than 3% of the recipients	4		
about 5 %	6		
about 10%	12		
about 30%	30		(100%)
about 50%	34		
more than 75%	14		

N = 585
[a]All items in this table, with the exception of #6, are virtually the same as those used by Feagin (1975). #2 to #5 incl. were also used by Kallen and Miller (1972). Some items have been slightly reworded for presentation here.

Available information on social assistance recipients contradicts the three perjorative views held by the majority of the respondents (*i.e.* reponses to #3, #4 and #6 in Table 3). In 1977, 319 social assistance cases, that is 0.88 of one percent of an approximate total of 36,320 cases in Alberta, were investigated for possible welfare abuse. The investigations resulted in only five convictions for fraud with another 15 cases still under examination. In 120 of the cases investigated, people who received welfare overpayments agreed to pay the money back. In the rest of the cases, no criminal activity was found or overpayment was due to some administrative error.[6] Moreover, approximately 6,000 cases, 17 percent of a total of 35,602 cases on social assistance in mid-1977, were classified as employables. But 87 percent of these were already fully or partially participating in the labour force, and another 12 percent were preparing for employment (Alberta Department of Social Services, 1977).

With regard to #2 and #5 in Table 3, American studies show that 31 percent of the children in welfare families were born out of wedlock (Williamson, 1974) and that people move to cities or regions which are perceived as employment opportunity havens with no conscious consideration for levels of welfare benefits (De Jong and Donnelly, 1973). Information on illegitimacy in welfare families and migration in search of better benefits in Canada is unavailable; therefore, one cannot say whether respondents' views on these issues are erroneous. It should be pointed out, however, that responses of the majority to #2 and #5 are not in the anti-recipient direction. But it would appear that some perjorative views about the recipients are myths and misconceptions.

Respondents' tendency to believe in individualistic causes of poverty and negative stereotypes about the social assistance recipients indicate the persistence of some pre-welfare state notions of individualism. The logic runs something like this. Some people are poor because they do not try hard enough or because they waste their money on liquor. If poverty is caused by individuals' own failings, then giving assistance to the same indolent, irresponsible and dishonest people would only confirm them in their bad habits. Hence there is a great deal of suspicion and even hostility towards the recipients.[7] Welfare practices, as we have seen, reflect the same kind of feelings from the officials of the state.

Yet the same survey respondents more or less support the idea of the welfare state: 63 percent agree that the government has the responsibility to ensure that all citizens have the necessities of life regardless of circumstances, and 83 percent think that welfare programs would be better provided by the government than by private charity organizations.

Support for the welfare state and the popularity of the 'welfare bum' stereotypes may appear to be contradictory; such a pattern of beliefs point to the inherent contradictions in capitalist ideological systems. However, one explanation can be suggested. As has been mentioned at the beginning of the paper, the ideology of the welfare state is essentially one of liberalism. It still retains a commitment to individualistic competitive achievement in the capitalist system and a faith in an opportunity structure for social mobility. Because of the "side-effects" of industrialism and urbanism, state intervention in promoting citizens' well-being is conceded to be necessary. Although its higher ideal is the redistribution of income in society, the ideology has emphasized the provision of welfare programs — for the poor — as the principal form of state intervention. Welfare programs, providing income security and adaptation/rehabilitation services, are meant to help the unfortunate to regain that competitive edge in the educational system, the labour market, the mobility structure, etc., so that they can become independent and pursue their self-interests. Insofar as welfare cases do not diminish and welfare costs keep on rising, it is then argued that the social assistance recipients choose to be a burden on society for hasn't the state done enough for them already? The recipients are seen as failures in a double sense: once for being unable to provide for themselves and again for not being rehabilitated. Putting the blame on the poor themselves and uncritically accepting the principle of government responsibility are, therefore, complementary components of the ideology of the welfare state. Without the ideological filter, however, the contradictions between these two sets of beliefs and tendencies would probably show up, for a critical examination of what the welfare state is doing and what it claims to be doing will force some rethinking about the stereotypical welfare bum.

As has also been demonstrated above, there is insignificant income redistribution in Canada. Whatever income redistribution effected by progressive taxation and the provision of assistance to the poor is thwarted by the welfare system for the non-poor. The extent to which the welfare system for the non-poor is hidden can be seen from the results in Table 4. In the 1977 survey, there is almost unanimous agreement that social assistance (known as social allowance in Alberta) is welfare. There is less public perception of universal cash transfers, social insurance plans and in-kind transfers as social welfare. Least of all are the tax subsidies for the non-poor seen as social welfare.

In view of the above, it is interesting to note that the majority of respondents (54 percent) say that they know a few things about the welfare system. Another 22 percent claim that they know a fair amount or quite a lot about social welfare. It could be reasonably assumed that most respondents in assessing their knowledge about the welfare system did not have the welfare programs for the rich in mind. It would seem that except for the 8 percent or 10 percent of the respondents who regard tax subsidies as welfare, most of them are quite unaware of their ignorance. The exclusion of these welfare

TABLE 4
PUBLIC PERCEPTION OF WHAT IS WELFARE

Question: Would you say whether the items listed below are part of the welfare system?

Item[a]	Yes %	No %	Uncertain %	
(Cash transfer to the poor)				
Social assistance	98	-	2	(100%)
(Universal cash transfers)				
Family allowance	57	37	6	(100%)
Old age security	42	50	8	(100%)
(Social insurance programs)				
Unemployment insurance	34	61	5	(100%)
Canada pension plan	21	73	6	(100%)
(Universal social services)				
Alberta health plan	32	62	6	(100%)
Education	21	70	9	(100%)
("Cash transfers" to the non-poor)				
Registered home ownership savings exemption	10	77	13	(100%)
Registered retirement savings exemption	8	79	13	(100%)

N = 585
[a]Sub-headings in parentheses ( ) were not in the questionnaire.

programs for the non-poor from the range of public perceptions and hence from public scrutiny shows one facet of the ideology of the welfare state. The ideology of the welfare state prevails among the public to the extent that there is such ignorance along with support for government involvement in welfare programs for the poor and negative stereotypes of poor welfare recipients.

Conclusion

Although government responsibility for citizens' well-being is accepted in principle, some perjorative views about poor Canadians receiving public aid are common. The welfare programs for the non-poor are not perceived as such. Thus public reaction to the two welfare systems has been different: sense of outrage is rampant in the case of one, and conspicuous by its absence in the other.

Ideological beliefs about social welfare which have been discussed here point to an important condition in the development of ideologies, namely, ignorance. There are two types of ignorance with regard to social welfare: inaccurate knowledge about the poor on public assistance, and lack of knowledge about the rich and their welfare programs.

In summary, the ideology of the welfare state is based on individualism in the liberal tradition. Its key components are desirability of state intervention in promoting social welfare and suspicion towards the poor. State intervention should, however, be interpreted with caution. The official goal of state intervention is to reduce income inequality in society; in practice, state intervention amounts to a few programs providing subsistence income to the poor. The ideology masks the real workings of the welfare state, so that the structure of social inequalities in society is left intact.

NOTES

1. Ideology, as the term is used in this paper, is defined as: "A pattern of beliefs and concepts (both factual and normative) which purport to explain complex social phenomena with a view to directing and simplifying socio-political choices facing individuals and groups" (Gould & Kolb, 1964:315, parentheses in the original).

2. An example of progressive taxation would be as follows. The tax rate for taxable income of $760 or less is 9 percent in Ontario in 1978, whereas taxable income over $91,000 is taxed at a rate of 62 percent (National Council of Welfare, 1978:2). The National Council of Welfare, not to be confused with the federal government department of National Health and Welfare, is a citizen advisory body. Its mandate is to advise the Minister of National Health and Welfare on welfare matters. The 21 members, including low income citizens as well as professionals, are appointed by the Governor-in-Council but serve on the Council in their personal capacities rather than as representatives of organizations.

3. This amount of tax is calculated using 1976 tax and exemption rates applicable to an Ontario resident.

4. The 17 tax subsidies on which the National Council of Welfare estimate is based are those on which there is sufficient information. They do not include (1) personal exemption and the deductions for expenses directly related to earning an income; (2) tax reductions through "dummy" companies set up by high income earners such as managers and professionals, or tax reductions through other exotic loopholes; (3) revenue lost because some individuals with very, very high incomes paid no income tax at all (National Council of Welfare, 1976:18); and (4) revenue lost because some people filed fraudulent tax returns.

5. The poor whose income is too low to be taxed are also taxpayers. They pay sales taxes, federal and provincial; property tax through their rent; and part of corporation income tax which is passed on to the consumers.

6. Information on welfare investigations is taken from The Lethbridge Herald, July 13, 1978. Letter to the Alberta Department of Social Services and Community Health requesting a copy of the investigations report has not been answered at the time of writing three months later.

7. In 1973, Canada Assistance Plan had a total caseload of 522,547. Altogether 1,218,560 Canadians (recipients and their dependants) were given assistance under the Plan (Statistics Canada, 1976:260).

Readings

Adams, Ian, William Cameron, Brian Hill & Peter Penz, *The Real Poverty Reporty,* Edmonton: M.G. Hurtig Ltd., 1971.

Alberta, Department of Health and Social Development, *Public Attitudes Towards Public Assistance in Alberta,* Edmonton: Queen's Printer, 1973.

Alberta, Department of Social Services and Community Health, *Quarterly Statistical Review April-June 1977,* Edmonton: Department of Social Services and Community Health, 1977.

Armitage, Andrew, *Social Welfare in Canada: Ideals and Realities,* Toronto: McClelland and Stewart Ltd, 1975.

Bailey, Roy and Michael Brake, (ed.), *Radical Social Work,* New York: Pantheon Books, 1975.

Buttrum, Jon, "What is Employable?", *Canadian Welfare* Vol. 52(3), (1976).

Canada, National Health and Welfare, *The Distribution of Income in Canada: Concepts, Measures and Issues,* Ottawa: Health and Welfare Canada, Long Range Welfare Planning Directorate, 1977.

Canadian Civil Liberties Education Trust, *Welfare Practices and Civil Liberties — A Canadian Survey,* Toronto: Canadian Civil Liberties Education Trust, 1975.

De Jong, Gordon F. and William L. Donnelly "Public Welfare and Migration", *Social Science Quarterly,* Vol. 54 (1973).

Feagin Joe, *Subordinating the Poor: Welfare and American Beliefs,* Englewood Cliffs: Prentice-Hall, 1975.

Finkel, Alvin, "Origins of the Welfare State in Canada", in Leo Panitch (ed.), *The Canadian State,* Toronto: University of Toronto Press, 1977.

Galper, Jeffry, *The Politics of Social Services,* Englewood Cliffs: Prentice-Hall Inc., 1975.

Gillespie, W. Irwin, "On the Redistribution of Income In Canada", *Canadian Tax Journal,* Vol. 24(4), (1976).

Gould, Julius and William L. Kolb, (eds.), *A Dictionary of the Social Sciences,* Complied under the auspices of the United Nations Educational, Scientific and Cultural Organization. London: Tavistock, 1964.

Kallen, David and Dorothy Miller, "Public Attitudes Toward Welfare", *Social Work,* Vol. 16, (1971).

Lethbridge Herald, The, 'The welfare myth', July 13, 1978.

Mandell, Betty Reid, (ed.), *Welfare in America: Controlling the "Dangerous Classes",* Englewood Cliffs: Prentice-Hall Inc., 1975.

Mott, Margaret E., "A 'Welfare Bum's' Story", *Canadian Welfare,* Vol. 53(2), (1977).

National Council of Welfare, *The Hidden Welfare System,* Ottawa: National Council of Welfare, 1976.

National Council of Welfare, *Bearing the Burden, Sharing the Benefits,* Ottawa: National Council of Welfare, 1978.

Offe, Claus, "Advanced Capitalism and the Welfare State", *Politics and Society,* Vol. 2 (1972).

Ross, David, *Canadian Fact Book on Poverty,* Ottawa: The Canadian Council on Social Development, 1975.

Schottland, Charles I., ed., *The Welfare State,* New York: Harper and Row, 1967.

Statistics Canada, *Canada Year Book 1975,* Ottawa: Supply and Services Canada, 1976.

Statistics Canada, *Canada Year Book 1976-77,* Ottawa: Supply and Services Canada, 1977[a].

Statistics Canada, *Income After Tax, Distributions by Size in Canada 1975,* Ottawa: Supply and Services Canada, 1977[c].

Wallace, Elizabeth, "The Origin of the Social Welfare State in Canada", *Canadian Journal of Economics and Political Science,* Vol. 16, (1950).

Waxman, Chaim I., *The Stigma of Poverty,* N.Y.: Pergamon Press, 1977.

Williamson, John B., "Beliefs about the Welfare Poor", *Sociology and Social Research,* Vol. 58, (1974).

Confessions of a T.V. Addict

Gerald B. Sperling

GERALD B. SPERLING is an Associate Professor
of Political Science at the University of Regina. He
is also a programme producer at CBC Regina. His
current research interests include the Canadian
Media and the Canadian State.

Why do we — who know the "Beverely Hillbillies" is bullshit — sit
and watch such banality? What does the acceptance of death but
not sex on network T.V. tell us about ourselves and the broadcaster's
image of us? How accurate is T.V. news reportage? Why is there
so much bad T.V. and who is responsible for it? Make no mistake
I am not *really* talking about T.V. here. I am talking about dissi-
dence, repression, censorship, the brutality and stupidity of much
of our culture, the dangers of being passive in a time when the
individual is merely cannon-fodder, the lying and cheating and
killing our 'patriots do in the sweet name of the American way'
(Harlan Ellison, 1969).

An analysis of the effect of the media in capitalist society must
take into account two dialectically related phenomena: (1) the
media as an enterprise and (2) the media as a legitimating instrument
for the preservation of the existing social order.

While much effort has been spent pointing out the methods by
which the media[2] act to maintain the existing system of social
relations in any historical epoch, it should not be forgotten that
the media in Canada is a business, as indeed it is in all capitalist
countries. For the owners and managers of the enterprises that
purvey the cultural commodities that characterize the media, the
profits that their enterprises generate are paramount.[3]

This is not to morally condemn these men and women; rather
it is to recognize that this commitment to making their enterprises
profitable goes far to explain the generally poor quality of much
that is exhibited on television and also, paradoxically, to justify

those few nuggets of genuinely high quality production that occasionally make their way into Canadian living rooms.

Even more paradoxically, it appears that, proportionately, the greatest production values, the greatest creative energy, and the greatest innovations go into the production of commercials. Apparently, commercials are more appealing, and more professional, than the material between them. As Michele Landsberg has observed:

> Television isn't programmes. Programmes, are the rickety props for the real stuff of TV: the commercials. And *whatever one says about programmes, the commercials have all the lavish production values that our TV-smart kids* have been trained to recognize and appreciate (Emphasis mine).[4]

On this point, the commercials (especially those produced for national network consumption) seem particularly to convey in no uncertain terms the ideological values that most accurately portray the existing social order. For example, during 1977 Canadian viewers were treated to a series of 'institutional ads' paid for by the major insurance companies which in graphic terms (a dove struggling to be released etc.) gave us the clear ideological message: "Let's free enterprise". Whether the insurance companies of Canada in fact represent the interests of "free" enterprise is the subject for another essay.

While it may be difficult to measure precisely the effects of television on the belief systems of the mass of the population, we can observe what the message of television is. By and large, most television programmes tend to idealize life under our social system, while at the same time emphasizing the merits of extreme individualism.

> . . . The important point is that there is immeasurably more about television, public and commercial, to confirm conservative-minded viewers in *their* attitudes than is the case for 'radical' ones; as far as the latter are concerned, television, in any serious meaning of the word is a permanent exercise in dissuasion.
>
> The mass media cannot ensure complete conservative attunement; nothing can. But they can and do contribute to the fostering of a climate of conformity, not by the total suppression of dissent, but by the presentation of views which fall outside the concensus as curious heresies, or, even more effectively treating them as irrelevant eccentricites, which serious and reasonable people may dismiss as of no consequence. This is very 'functional'.[5]

This essay and the attached review materials will deal primarily with the question of ideology and content. However, it should be noted that there is renewed discussion amongst some academics on the political economy of the consciousness industry. Specifically,

Dallas Smythe in his seminal article, "Communications: Blindspot of Western Marxism",[6] postulates in essence that time spent watching television by the working class in capitalist society is work in the Marxist sense, that is, it is an activity that creates value from which surplus is extracted. As Smythe puts it:

> . . . The materialist answer to the question — What is the commodity form of mass produced advertiser supported communications under monopoly capitalism? — is audiences. The material reality under monopoly capitalism is that all non-sleeping time of most of the population is work time. This work time is devoted to the production of commodities in general (both where people get paid for their work and as members of audiences) and in the production and reproduction of labour power (the pay for which is subsumed in their income). Of the off-the-job work time, the largest single block is time of the audiences which is sold to advertisers. It is not sold by workers but by the mass media of communications. Who produces this commodity? The mass media of communications do by the mix of explicit and hidden advertising and 'programme' material. . .

> In their time which is sold to advertisers, workers (a) perform essential marketing functions for the producers of consumers goods, and (b) work at the production and reproduction of labour power.[7]

These fundamental questions posed by Smythe and supported by Livant[8] have been neglected by many left-wing and liberal scholars. Certainly, the struggle for audiences by T.V. executives trying to beat their opponents in the ratings game, so as to maximize advertising rates, is as least as important as the ideological message that these same executives put in their programmes, as well as what they put in the commercials that pay for these programmes. Furthermore, I suspect that network executives themselves spend more time worrrying about the effects on corporate income of a fall in the ratings than they do on whether "All in the Family" is delivering precisely the correct ideological mix of racism, liberalism, patriotism, and respect for motherhood.[9]

However, in the present historical context, when there is a struggle for the "minds of men", when it is increasingly important to those who control the existing social order that all of us, regardless of class, has a monolithic view of how our own local communities operate, and have also reached a basic agreement on the "state of the world", it may be more important to see specifically just how concretely this monolithic view is conveyed.

Television is not the only medium through which the dominant ideas of modern capitalism are conveyed. Note here, that by 'dominant ideology' I mean that system of beliefs about the nature of life, death, work, leisure, power, etc., that primarily serves the interests of the ruling class in any epoch. This ideology may at any one point actually be reality, may reflect it, or may, as is usual, paint a picture of reality that is functional to the interest of the ruling class but that may only coincidentally indicate the truth.[10]

Robert Cosbey has done original research on the messages contained in modern mass media. He deals with the ideological signals and systems that are delivered in comics, Harlequin romantic fiction, as well as in popular television stories. In "Mass Media Stories — What are they doing to our Heads?"[11] he deals with media treatment of workers and unions:

> In our real world it is the many productive workers who keep society going, but you wouldn't know that from watching T.V. stories or reading comics. There, you will find workers in offices, like Dagwood (but very seldom see them actually working), and you'll find people doing vague work in advertising agencies, like 'Mary Tyler Moore', and some working entertainers, like the 'Partridge Family'. But where among all these people, are *real* workers, the kind that keep the world going with their work?
>
> You'll find doctors in Real Workers' stories, doing their professional jobs. You'll find detectives, and policemen — lots and lots of policemen — going about their duties. But where are the workers? And where are the unions? . . .
>
> The workers in mass media stories are there to be put down and laughed at, not to be admired like the doctors and policemen. The workers are always lazy or helpless. In fact a lot of mass media stories carry . . . the propaganda message of the helpless worker taken care of by the generous boss.[12]

Over the past seven years, I have been involved in a mixed media exercise, the reviewing of television on radio. The idea for this exercise came out of the fertile imagination of Sheila Moore, the original producer of CBC Saskatchewan's morning radio show.

What follows is an annotated and edited selection of these reviews. The reader will note that the majority of these reviews have a positive 'flavour' about them. Partly, this is a reflection of the fact that I chose 'good' programmes (the minority) to show up the 'bad' (the vast majority). Furthermore, how many times can one person attack "All in the Family", "Phyllis", "Fantasy Island" or "Chico and the Man"?

These reviews deal with some of the main ideological questions which television in Canada has confronted and embraced in the decade of the seventies.

Finally, I must confess that as a member of the first generation of television children I, too, have been a boob tube junkie for too many years.

April 29, 1974

MAUD AND ARCHIE BUNKER

"Maud" is a sort of upper middle class offspring of the notorious Archie Bunker. Norman Lear is executive producer of both programmes, and both have the stage-like quality of having the action, such as it is, take place basically in the living room of the main protagonists. In fact, both of these shows have the positive attraction of concentrating on the spoken word to get their message across, a fact which makes them superior to most situation comedies. Again, both concentrate on contemporary social and political themes, and both have appeal because they are more or less blunt in their treatment of those themes. However, this bluntness should not be confused with that real biting satire often evident in American perspectives of their society.

While Bunker, played by Carrol O'Connor, has become a hero to many because of his outspoken bigotry, Maud, acted by Beatrice Arthur, is a heroine because of her persistant struggle for liberal causes. There is something insidiously wrong in all of this and I think that we are being taken for a ride in both cases. With "All in the Family", the voice of liberalism is represented by Bunker's son-in-law Meathead, who comes off as a twit and yes, a meathead! Surely Bunker would have to be a fool not to be able to show up his son-in-law as a weak defender of liberalism. On the other hand, Maud, who inevitably wins all the struggles for progress, be they racial tolerance or women's liberation, fights against the overwhelming forces of reaction represented by a narrow-minded, lascivious, neighbour-doctor and a timid, ambiguous, businessman husband. Yes, Maud gets her husband to give a $1,000 to support a type of Black Panther movement, but she keeps her black maid, whose name, incredibly enough, is Florida.

And yes, Maud wins her right to hold a job against her husband's wishes and forces him to adjust to being waited on only by Florida and not by his wife *and* the black maid. But what is this job that she fights to keep? Selling real estate in wealthy Westchester County. In this particular case, as in most others, the very serious question of discrimination against women in the job market is not even approached, let alone dealt with seriously.

In a word, if "All in the Family" is modishly reactionary, "Maud" is radical chic. Both programmes appear to be presenting serious themes critically through the use of satire. But both make such a sad joke of their themes, that bigotry becomes acceptable in the one case, and liberal causes become farcical playthings for the rich in the other.

•   •   •   •

September 9, 1974

IMPERIAL OIL AND LABOUR DAY

Recent commentators in the U.S. have noted that it is impossible under the United States system of enterprise for good television to survive for very long. In the opinion of American critic Andrew Kopkind, every generation gets the soap operas it deserves. I think that it is more complicated than that.

About ten days ago there was a backgrounder after the CTV national news which implied that the Arabs were taking unfair advantage of the energy crisis by charging very high prices for their oil and investing their super-profits in the United States and Europe. Now who sponsored this insight; this behind the news scoop? Why, none other than Imperial Oil! A few days later I read in the *Globe and Mail Report on Business* that higher prices and lower demand are forcing cutbacks in oil production in Alberta and Saskatchewan. I do not pretend to understand all of this, but I doubt very much if Imperial Oil is going to go to any great lengths to clarify the issues. And why should they? They are in business to make money, not to go to heaven. And so I concluded that as long as such insights are sponsored by self-interested parties it is totally unfair to say that we deserve the television that we get.

Which brings me to my point for today. For Labour Day news coverage CBC television had Sheldon Turcotte of CBC Vancouver, talking about transit workers in Toronto and Montreal, and interviewing Joe Morris of the CLC. Turcotte said, in effect, that workers, management and governments had better settle these issues because the public was getting very impatient. My own feeling is that Turcotte's report was at best anti-union. While I question the propriety of using the one day in the year officially put aside for the working people of Canada as time to attack labour, if that is what CBC and Turcotte wants to do, that's fine. What I am really offended about is Turcotte's claiming to speak on behalf of the public. Just what public is he talking about? Trade unionists, farmers, Indians, big businessmen, small businessmen or himself? It is bad enough when *politicians* claim to be representing the views of the public, but it is very dangerous for members of the working press to elect themselves as tribunes speaking for the people, especially over the public air waves. Actually, I suspect that, given the rate of inflation today, the vast majority of working people have sympathy for those fighting rising prices with their only effective weapon, the strike.

● ● ● ●

September 30, 1974

PAYDAY

This week I made a point of watching CBC's new show about workers entitled "Payday". And you know, it's not bad. This week the programme looked at the situation of oil workers in Alberta.

The documentary was concise, comprehensive, and informative and simply appeared to want to inform us about work in the oil industry. To achieve that end the producers showed us both happy workers and unhappy workers, male workers and female workers, white workers and native workers, professionals and tradesmen. The material covered was presented not from the academic point of view of the outside observer, but from the point of view of the workers themselves. We learned from a skilled mechanic that his biggest beef about working in the remote oil sands was the living conditions; the company had not made it clear that he would be living in a summer camp while working. We learned from the wife of the worker how many young wives are going stir-crazy with nothing to do but wait for their husbands to return from their jobs. A young woman operator of heavy earth machinery told of how the men were adjusting to her presence and yet how the work place was *still* theirs, implying that this will not always be the case. A Native worker compared being on welfare with his present apprentice mechanic job and told us that now he was feeling productive, that he was now his own man with control over his own labour power. The programme was tied together by host Bob Oxley and the United Steelworkers' Marc Zwelling, who pointed out that there is a definite shortage of skilled and unskilled labour for such massive projects; that oil workers will have to be certificated like other trades; that workers on these projects because they are in such high demand, will be able to make advances not only in the area of wages but in the fields long considered to be exclusive management rights — pensions, housing and so on. Indeed, Zwelling made it abundantly clear that real communities will have to be built in these remote areas, communities with good schools, technical institutions, and recreation facilities. The frontier slums which we call company towns will no longer be adequate if the oil companies want the oil wells drilled, and the oil processed by Canadian workers.

In sum, a good programme.

•   •   •   •

November 4, 1974

CRTC VS. CBC[13]

What made an impression on me this week is the struggle between the CRTC and the CBC which surfaced in a syndicated article by the Toronto Star's Richard Gwyn. Basically, what is involved is the CRTC's demand that the CBC move towards the elimination of all commercials of foreign programming over prime time television. On the advertising question, the only difference appears to be over timing, with the CRTC's Pierre Juneau being in a big hurry to implement such changes and the CBC's Picard having a more 'go-slow' attitude.

I have never been able to understand the contradiction between asking the CBC to play a nation-building role while at the same time demanding that it, in part, at least, finance this role through the sale of commercial time. The companies who pay for advertising do not have as their primary purpose the building of the Canadian nation. Therefore, they will choose to finance programmes that sell their products, such as "Maude", "All in the Family", and "The Carol Burnett Show." These are not programmes that have anything to do with Canadian culture.

As for the prime time argument, Picard's position is that we cannot fully replace the American shows with Canadian shows because the Canadian talent to produce these programmes is not currently available. I do not believe that there is insufficient Canadian talent to produce the necessary programming.

We certainly have done well in the export of actors, writers, producers to the U.S. More importantly, what does worry me is that if we wait too long, the Canadian programming we ultimately get in prime time may be nothing more than carbon copies of U.S. shows.

•   •   •   •

February 17, 1975

MACLEAR

This was the last in a series of half hour programmes hosted by CTV's Michael Maclear and, as he suggests, it may have been the best. This week Maclear took us to Elliott Lake, urainium capital of the world.

In 30 minutes Maclear informed us that there are one million Canadian workers suffering from silicosis, and that one in five Canadian workers have been injured on the job. He showed us men with 10 percent silicosis, men with 15 percent silicosis, and the horrendous sight of one totally helpless man with 100 percent silicosis. He talked with men dying from cancer, and with their wives, and with the widows of miners who have died from silicosis.

And why are these deaths allowed to happen? Maclear makes it abundantly clear. He pulls no punches. A silent conspiracy of profit hungry corporations (the mine officials at Elliott Lake would not be interviewed by Maclear), government bureaucracies, and medical men, together with the absolute need, nay the desire, of these workers to earn a living for themselves and their families, results in the maiming of men, and in their slow, painful destruction by such diseases as silicosis and lung cancer.

As Maclear puts it, we live in a system where only the fittest survive. Companies like Dennison Mines, Rio Algom, Rio Tinto take healthy young men who want to work, then they work them for five, ten, fifteen years until, finally, with their health undermined, they cast them aside to struggle with the slow bureaucracies of compensation boards.

Did you know that there are 202 game wardens in Ontario and only 27 mine inspectors?

Three times as many man-days of work are lost through industrial disease and accidents as through strikes, yet strikes get the headlines. The profits of the corporations grow while the bodies of the workers die.

Maclear is to be congratulated for speaking out and for allowing the men and women who create the wealth in this country to speak out. It would have been interesting to hear from the mine owners, who get a good portion of that wealth, but, as I said, they refused to be interviewed.

•   •   •   •

February 20, 1975

NOTES ON THE SOAP OPERA SYNDROME FOR "THIS COUNTRY IN THE MORNING"*

The first question is why people watch these things? Let's take a typical day in the life of "Another World", the only hour-long soap opera.

Mack Cory, wealthy publisher from Bay City, is planning a secret marriage to Rachael Frames, with the ceremony to take place in

Mack's New York townhouse. Mack is a man in his late fifties. He is terribly well preserved. Rachael must be in her early thirties. She is even more terribly well preserved, given that this is to be her third or fourth marriage. Carol Lamont is making all the arrangements for the wedding, while Iris Kerrigan, Mack's daughter, who looks older than her father, is plotting with Phillip (who always wears riding britches) and with Louise, Mack's maid to break up the wedding. Carol loves Robert who is married to Lenore, who is loved by Vic who is loved by Barbara.

It is important to pause at this point. You see, Lenore used to work in Robert's firm, but he wants her to stay at home and look after their lovely family. Barbara is envious of Lenore, possibly because Vic loves Lenore, but probably because Barbara, who now works in the office, would like to have a home and family while Lenore is envious of Barbara because *she* would like to work in the office. As Lenore says to Barbara: "Women have to make certain choices that men never have to face up to."

Incidentally, Steve Frames, who works in the same office, is Rachael's second husband, having made her pregnant with Jamie while she was still married to Russ, a doctor who works in the same office as Dave Gilchrist who was intended to be the best man at Mack's hurried wedding. You remember Mack?

Russ, upon hearing from Dave that Mack is marrying Rachael, rushes over to Iris's place to tell her. Here he meets with his Aunt Liz who really wants to marry Mack. She, of course, is more Mack's age. She becomes distraught upon hearing the bad or good news (it all depends on your point of view) and falls into an emotional embrace with Russ. This embrace is seen by Dennis, Iris's eleven-year old son and by the way he looked at Russ and Liz, I suspect that he suspects that Dr. Russ may be carrying on with *his* Aunt Liz, which shouldn't surprise him given the other goings on in "Another World".

Why do people watch these things? They're all the same — everybody is rich, lives in marvellous houses and are very thin. In fact that's the one thing they all have in common; they are thin. Except for Rachael's mother who is terribly decent, is fat, sixtyish and has just had a baby by her new fat cop husband Gil.

It's a fantasy world in which all problems are soluble with love, where the basic institutions of marriage and fidelity are not challenged, and most important every problem has an individual solution. There are no unions or collective action.

---

*This item is drawn from notes prepared by the author for an interview by the host of the now-defunct radio show "This Country in the Morning".

· · · ·

March 3, 1975

VIOLENCE AND T.V. WATCHING AS WORK

Dr. Bernard Brown, Director of the U.S. Institute of Mental Health, has said: "Repeated exposure to violent T.V. programmes can produce insensitivity to cruelty and violence because it gradually extinguishes the viewer's emotional response and builds the feeling that violent behaviour is appropriate under some circumstances . . .". I might add that those circumstances may not be those which are acceptable in society today.

Now, from what I read in the papers there is an increasing recognition in Canada of the seriousness of this situation. For one thing [former] Solicitor-General Almand announced consideration of curbs on violence shows in Canada. For another, the CRTC is going to make its own study of the impact of such shows on Canadian children.

A recent survey in the U.S. revealed that there are over seven instances of brutality per hour on American television. What was interesting about this survey was that of the ten most brutal TV programmes as rated by the critics, none were amongst the most widely watched programmes by the population at large. In other words, in spite of their relative lack of popularity, the most brutal shows were still being aired, many of them in prime time. Some of these violent, not so popular programmes were "Kung Fu", "Kojak", the "Rookies", and "Hawaii 5-0".

So it seems that the old argument that the public gets what it wants does not hold as much as in the past.

I was in Vancouver over the weekend and had a long talk with my old friend, communications expert Dallas Smythe. Apparently, another recent survey indicated that an aggregate of time during which the tube is on in families with at least two adults is over 80 hours per week. Now this does not mean that both adults watched the T.V. for this long period; it just means that they were home and around while the set was on. Even so, this could be a lot of viewing time. From these figures, Dr. Smythe suggested that we now must consider T.V. watching not as leisure, but as unpaid labour. Work that is necessary in order to ensure that high consumption patterns of goods and services we may not need are maintained. An intriguing idea, for if you consider T.V. viewing as work, and especially work for which you receive no wages, then you may begin to understand why so many people emerge from their T.V. rooms tired, listless, and bored. They've just spent several hours on the job.

•   •   •   •

April 1, 1975

THE SPANISH CIVIL WAR

What I want to talk about today is the CBC Wednesday night special which treated us to a very intelligent analysis of Spain and the Spanish Civil War.

"To Die in Madrid" was a truly remarkable documentary based upon film shot by war correspondents and film makers, many of whom died during the fighting. The film made no bones about the fact that it stood *for* the Spanish Republican government made up, as it was, of communists, socialists, and anarchists; *for* the Spanish people who died in the hundreds of thousands during the Civil War; and *against* the obscurantist Spanish church; the ruthless Spanish officers who led the revolt against democracy; and most of all *against* the fascism which put out the flickering light of a better life for millions of Spaniards for some 40 years. The film documents the valiant stand made by the international brigades in the defense of Madrid. Few Canadians are aware that, proportionately, Canada sent more men to fight in the Spanish Civil War than any other country. Of the 1,200 Canadians that did go to Spain in 1936-37 only some 600 returned, the others having fallen on the battle fields.

And another thing about these international brigades and the men that filled their ranks, is that while some went for adventure and others went because of the depression, many of these courageous men went to fight in Spain, not in spite of their beliefs, but precisely because they were communists who had the quaint idea that the duty of a good communist was to fight for the rights of workers and poor farmers no matter where they lived nor what language they spoke. I stress this because sometimes this simple truth is too easily forgotten even by some of those veterans of the Spanish Civil War.

The other major portion of the CBC's programme on the War was a recent documentary entitled "Will the Past Win?" which attempts to take a long look at the War and at modern day Spain. On the whole this film was quite informative. But, in my view the underlying theme of the film was wrong. According to this film, the whole problem of Spain is Spain and the Spanish people, their peculiar history, their long association with something called sensuous Islam, their love of blood sports like bull fighting, (I couldn't help thinking of our love of blood sports like hockey, boxing and football), and the traditional harshness and narrowness of the Spanish church (again the Basque exception is not fully explained). All of this is presented by way of an explanation of the complications of the Spanish Civil War. The war of the Spanish people against fascism was only the beginning of the whole world's struggle against that scourge. One need not look into the idiosyncracies of the Spanish character, as fascinating as these may be, to explain the horrors of the Spanish Civil War.

My point is that western scholars have this habit of attempting to make each and every historical occasion completely separate from all that has preceded it. In this view the modern history of Spain is perceived as a discrete set of events that has nothing to do with the rest of the world.

In dealing with events such as the Spanish Civil War there is also a tendency to become morbid and to mourn the defeat of the Spanish people. And yet on the same evening of the special I noticed in the news that the peoples of Viet Nam and Cambodia seemed very firmly on course in their struggle to gain national independence and the chance to make their society a better place in which to live.* A lot of these people have died in this struggle and their deaths should not be taken lightly. But, to bring us back to Spain, the peoples of Indo China have suffered in the name of the same ideals that motivated the Spanish people in their battle against Franco. And so I do not feel sad at viewing once again the defeat of democracy in Spain; rather I feel exhilarated knowing that their fight is not over. In fact their brothers and sisters in Indo-China are today demonstrating once again that the power of a people aroused, will, in the end, overcome the armies of reaction, whether these armies are supplied by Hitlers and Mussolinis or by Nixons and Fords . . ..

---

*Events in Indo-China in 1978-79 raise some doubts about the accuracy of this statement. (Author's note)

•   •   •   •

May 5, 1975

THE OCTOBER CRISIS I

Recently the CBC aired Robin Spry's documentary on the October 1970 crisis in Quebec. Spry very wisely resisted the temptation to dwell upon the kidnappings and the execution which precipitated the crisis. Instead he concentrated on presenting a rather complete social history of Quebec since World War II. We learned that the rapid industrialization of Quebec during the 1940s created a militant working class, a class which had been torn from the backward narrow nationalism of Duplessis and the Quebec Catholic Church. We find that during the 1940s and 1950s intellectuals and journalists like Trudeau and Pelletier had thrown their lot in with this working class and had marched on their picket lines under the guns of the Quebec Provincial Police. We also see how Trudeau and others from the Cité Libre group were persuaded by Mike Pearson to transfer their zeal and skills to the federal sphere. With hindsight we can see that old Mike Pearson was not so dumb, after all. Just think of the difficulties in Quebec if the Prime Minister in October 1970 had been an English-Canadian like John Turner or Robert Stanfield.

One very effective moment in the documentary is the videotape of a Montreal broadcaster reading the F.L.Q. manifesto. We must remember that when the War Measures Act was in force the act of reading or discussing the manifesto could be a cause for immediate arrest. I hope that viewers read the translation of the manifesto that Spry provided, for it shows that the F.L.Q., for all their drastic tactics, had a very clear understanding of the class basis of the tensions prevailing then and now in Quebec. And Spry makes it very clear that the ideas in the manifesto were received sympathetically by the Quebec populace. Indeed, it may be that this sympathy for the ends, and not the means, of the F.L.Q. by the people of Quebec was the real cause for the calling out of the army. Finally, the famous confrontation between CBC reporter Tim Raffe and Trudeau reveals, at least for me, the Prime Minister's view that in order to preserve his notion of democracy it may be necessary to remove all ordinary civil rights and put troops in the streets. And if you don't like that idea then you're a bleeding heart.

All in all an excellent film, which tells us a great deal about Canada and Quebec. What is also clear is that the question of independence for Quebec was not killed by the War Measures Act in 1970. On the contrary, politics in Quebec has moved substantially to the left since that time.

•   •   •   •

October 27, 1975

OCTOBER CRISIS II

Five years after the historic crisis that shook the Canadian body politic the CBC has finally pulled itself together enought to present a reasonably comprehensive and accurate picture of just what happened during those trying times. Furthermore, and to its credit, the corporation has not refrained from giving us some sort of interpretation of those events.

For one thing, there is some new information presented: first, it was the Mafia who first located Laporte's body; second, federal authorities, provincial authorities, and the Montreal city police were prepared for an occurances such as the October 1970 kidnappings. It was also useful to learn, in detail, of the differing rationales for the imposition of the War Measures Act. For Trudeau this was one of those occasions when the extreme authoritarianism of the War Measures Act was necessary in order to preserve the existing social order in Quebec, so as to counteract the large public sympathy that existed for the socialist and separatist aims of the F.L.Q., if not for their methods. It was to this end that the list of people arrested during that fateful morning of October 15 included so many left leaning personnages from the P.Q., from trade unions, from radical pressure groups. For Mr. Bourassa the purpose was not to apprehend an insurrection but to find the kidnappers.

The programme also reveals the existence of a small team of strategic planners reporting directly to the Prime Minister. These planners calculated options for the P.M., basically in terms of the most effective way of manipulating public opinion (in passing I wonder whether a similar team of manipulators is working for the P.M. during his current attempts to deal with the present economic crisis).

Statements by such eminences as Eric Kierans and Bob Stanfield that they privately opposed the War Measures Act but publicly supported it (Kierans for reasons he could not explain and Stanfield for fear of splitting his party and alienating an electorate whipped up to a frenzy by the Trudeau propaganda machine) lead one to be skeptical of well-meaning public figures in times of crisis.

The description of the attitudes and practices of the police during the crisis are both hilarious and frightening. On the one hand we have the police using the mythical visions of a Jesuit priest as a means of finding the hideouts. We also see the police poring over copies of *Winnie the Pooh* for some locational clues because Jasper Cross was an avid fan of A.A. Milne.

On the other hand, the documentary demonstrates quite clearly the drift towards fascism amongst certain segments of the Montreal police. In 1969, for example, it appears that the riot squad of that police force seemed willing to seize power in the city in order to win their demands for more money and for better equipment.

Finally, the film was effective because of its neat interplay of actual documentary footage with dramatization of the events by actors.

•   •   •   •

March 16, 1976

CBC-T.V. AND ADVERTISING

This past week, I have spent less time watching T.V. than reading about it and I must say that the printed word does have its attractions. The most recent issue of that little journal, *This Magazine*, published in Toronto, presented some interesting figures on T.V. expenditures. Did you know that it costs $30,000 to tape a half-hour weekly segment of "King of Kensington", $65,000 to film a half-hour episode of "Sidestreet" or the "National Dream"? And herein lies the reason why so much prime time on both major networks is taken up with American imports. Because, while the American shows apparently cost almost double those of Canadian shows to produce, they can be purchased from the American production houses very cheaply. For example, the CBC could purchase a full hour of "Police Story" from the U.S. for only $4,000, while it would cost $130,000 to produce a Canadian one-hour cop show. In other words, it is not simply the preferences of Canadian audiences that explain why the large amount of prime time on both networks is taken up with American shows. It is simple economics. It is much cheaper to purchase imported programmes than it is to produce Canadian programmes.

If one takes into account the fact that advertising revenue makes up about one-sixth of the CBC's annual income — the other $300 million comes from the annual grant from Parliament — one can see why the American imports are so important to CBC brass, and why they are essential to CTV executives who receive no subsidy from the federal government. Therefore, on CBC in prime time, that is from 7:00 to 11:00 every evening, about one-third of the programming is American. On CTV two-thirds of prime time programming are U.S. imports.

One way out of this mess might be to cancel all advertising on CBC and increase the CBC's budget by about $100 million, a mere 25 percent. In return for this investment we would be guaranteed a 100 percent Canadian television network which would certainly be a boon to Canadian producers, technicians, and artists, to say nothing of the viewers. Of course, there is no guarantee that the Canadian "Police Story" might not turn out to be as mindless and violent as the American. But it may be worth the gamble. If you think that it is too expensive, just think about the $1½ billion that we may be paying that pillar of the corporate community, Lockheed, for the Orion aircraft. A crazy idea? Maybe. But certainly one to think about while we wait for the arrival of cable and the three U.S. channels.

•   •   •   •

September 21, 1976

LLOYD ROBERTSON AND MARY HARTMAN

Regarding the departure of Lloyd Robertson from CBC to CTV, for reasons that apparently have something to do with Lloyd's desire to do something other than read the news, I can only comment that on those few occasions when Robertson did attempt to play the role of intelligent anchorman — for example, for the special following Chou En Lai's death; or the American Republican convention; or, most notoriously, during the Olympics — Lloyd Robertson did not reveal himself to be curious or knowledgeable. Bland and inoffensive, yes, but a committed journalist? Perhaps the commercial atmosphere of the private network will bring out facets of Robertson's character that he has successfully hidden from his huge audience for the past six years.

Speaking of CTV, more than one ardent hockey fan who in the past had denounced the nervous squeaks of Howie Meeker's hockey coverage, felt that CTV's between period shows during the recent Canada Cup Tournament were dull, slow paced, and seemed, ineptly, to be tied to the endless commercial breaks. The secret of the hard sell on television is, of course, to make sure that the viewer does not run to the bathroom before the commercial comes on.

"Mary Hartman, Mary Hartman", the anti-soap opera, deserves a review in depth. However, today, I simply want to point out that this programme, perhaps the first truly innovative show on television in the past 20 years, is outrageously satirical, confusing, irreverent, and at first sight, even a little crazy. If you want to know what I mean just imagine a programme that deals quite explicitly with the love, no, sex life of a typical white working class family in the United States, where the housewife states clearly that her lifestyle is determined by the magazine *Family Circle* and the commercials for laundry products that she sees on T.V., where her grandfather exposes himself in an elementary school yard and where her sister seems to be a nyphomaniac, and so on. Remember that you can see this show five times a week. I'll be saying more about "Mary Hartman, Mary Hartman" in weeks to come.

• • • •

November 30, 1976

TELEVISION AND THE KID*VID GHETTO

Did you know that the average American youngster watches the tube for close to four hours a day? Or that by the time he or she enters kindergarten, the American child has already spent more time watching television than he would to earn a college degree? More specifically, the American high school graduate will have attended school for more than 11,000 hours, but will have viewed T.V. for more than 22,000 hours. During this time he will have received 350,000 commercials and have witnessed 18,000 murders.

I don't have figures yet for Canadian viewers, but I would be surprised if a similar horror story does not prevail here. But what of the effect of all this upon children, and, of course, ultimately upon the future of the nation? For one thing, many American observers point to television as one of the main causes of declining math and reading scores amongst American children. If the kids are watching the tube, then they aren't reading. As far as violence is concerned, over 50 studies in the United States conclude that televised violence tends to stimulate aggressive behaviour in children and foster their tolerance of violence as the sole way to solve problems. Kids who become accustomed to violence on T.V. may also tend to be apathetic about real life violent situations that they come up against.

As for stereotypes, most shows in the American 'Kid*Vid Ghetto', that Saturday morning children's show time slot, depict heroes as white men and women as simpering idiots, while minorities as either absent or stupid. All of this may result in children acquiring racist and sexist attitudes. The commercials aimed at children during prime time Kid*Vid viewing concentrate on selling the kids junk food: pre-sweetened cereals, sugared tarts, gum, cookies, and so on: which does wonders for their teeth and good looks.

•   •   •   •

December, 1976

ONE CANADIAN AND THE KING

Actually, I am finding CBC's "One Canadian", the recreation on television of John Diefenbaker's memoirs, a most fascinating series. Whatever opinions one may have about Diefenbaker and his government, this in-depth recounting of Diefenbaker's life in politics — shamelessly written from the Chief's point of view — does demonstrate the good uses to which the technique of television may be put. For here we have on film the man himself, celebrating his victories, pillorying his foes, and all in that ponderous grandiloquence which would be buffoonery from anybody else but Diefenbaker. The series is well researched and the researchers, as well as Diefenbaker, I assume, have taken great care in juxtaposing Diefenbaker's claims with film clips, interviews, and stills which buttress Diefenbaker's interpretation of the historical events of which he was a part.

Let me take last week's programme, which dealt with American imperialism, as an example. On the programme, Diefenbaker claims that he lost the 1963 election because of American intervention. He has the American Ambassador of the period, Thomas Merchant, giving a seminar to the Canadian press corps on how to attack Diefenbaker. He has American magazines such as *Newsweek* showing unflattering photos of the Chief on the front cover. Most seriously, he has Mike Pearson taking his marching orders from the United States, completely reversing his stand on nuclear weapons on Canadian soil so as to demonstrate the folly of Diefenbaker's defense policy.

I have two comments here: for one thing we have to ask why the United States found Diefenbaker so unacceptable. He certainly was not unfriendly to U.S. business interests. U.S. investment in Canada grew continuously during the Diefenbaker years. I suspect that Diefenbaker was viewed by the U.S. Defence and State departments as an annoyance because he did have the nasty habit of making mildly nationalistic statements. And given the paranoia prevalent in the U.S. in that period, (I am thinking primarily of the American failure to topple the Cuban Revolution), Pearson and Liberal continentalism must have seemed preferable to Diefenbaker's Red Toryism. My second comment is that we all know for certain what only people on the Left believed in the 1960s, and that is, that successive U.S. governments have had no compunction whatsoever in destablizing duly elected governments of foreign countries, if those governments engaged in policies which in any way threatened U.S. business or state interests, which usually are the same thing. Who would have believed that John Diefenbaker was an anti-imperialist?

One other short comment, I am disappointed that "King of Kensington" has not lived up to its promise of having topical comments written into the programmes. The producers claim that these have been eliminated because the audience does not recognize the characters to whom reference is being made. I find this explanation unacceptable as I suspect that the citizens of Davidson, Saskatchewan know who John Turner is. However, the citizens of Cincinatti, Ohio do not. And if you are trying to sell a series to the States you don't want to clutter up the programme with too many exotic Canadian references. There's that nasty American Imperialism again.

● ● ● ●

January 11, 1977

MARIA

Allan King, Canada's premier director, who last summer was directing *Who Has Seen the Wind* down in Arcola, has produced in "Maria" a small masterpiece of didactic theatre. "Maria" tells the story of the daughter of a Toronto Italian immigrant couple who decides, partially out of her own suffering in a sweat shop, and partially because of her commitment to her fellow workers, to organize a union in the garment plant where she works.

Why call this little story about definitely unglamorous people a masterpiece? Why indeed! Because it does what I think all great art should do — portray through one medium or another the essentials of reality and distill the facts of life in such a way as to highlight what is truly important in complex real life situations.

Once Maria decides to help organize the union she and her fellow workers are confronted with all of the classic union busting tactics. The special blandisments; the boss buys Maria a birthday cake, and paints the ladies' washroom. The harassments; the boss lays off one employee who has signed a union card. The threats; a foreman puts a knife to the throat of one of the workers. The attempts to divide the employees on racial lines, with Greeks being lined up against Italians, and Italians against West Indians and so on. The lies; another foreman tells Chinese workers that signing a union card is against the law in Canada. And finally, the tearful ideological pleas from the employer that both workers and management are one happy family and that the union will only divide the family.

All of this is portrayed as taking place in and about a plant which is clearly located in Toronto. "Maria" is not a play set in the 1930s. This could have happened yesterday. It certainly does happen here and now in Saskatchewan. One need only look at the docket of unfair labour practices before the Saskatchewan Labour Relations Board to see that these backward anti-union attitudes and tactics are still with us. And this, of course is what makes "Maria" such a poignant piece.

King uses black and white film, probably to point out that the real world of class struggle is stark and gray. Furthermore, the play does not romanticize the employees in the plant. They *do* divide on ethnic lines. Maria's own fiancé rejects her union activity. To her credit Maria, when asked by her boyfriend to choose between him and a life of security as the wife of a small businessman and the union, does not hesitate: "That's easy", she says, "the union".

For once I can unequivocally say "Bravo" to the CBC for this drama. I hope that it is rerun soon.

    •   •   •   •

January 25, 1977

MARY HARTMAN, MARY HARTMAN

For the most part television programmes are packages that are repeated, hour after hour, season after season. Everything is predictable. There is the game show package, the cop show package, the sit-com package, the variety package, the soap opera package and so on. But "Mary Hartman" does not fit into any pattern. And perhaps that is why the programme is so popular in the States and seems to be becoming all the rage here. It certainly is different, or as a student at the university put it to me the other day, "That show is weird". Just listen to the current problem occupying the life of our heroine — she has just made love with the fiancé of her younger sister. This incident has taken place in the hospital bed of the fiancé, where he is recuperating from a heart attack brought on by his last effort to seduce Mary Hartman. Oh yes, he is a policeman, whose role in life, as he puts it, is to fulfill the differing needs of each and every woman he comes into contact with. The thing is that he fulfills all their needs in the same way.

Certainly, this is not your normal television fare. However, let me take a shot at the other reasons for this show's popularity. For one thing, it relentlessly satirizes the consumerism of North American society. No product from Hamburger Helper to T.V. dinners is safe. For another, it presents an almost vicious critique of psychology, social work and psychiatry. It presents the practitioners of these disciplines as at best fools, at worst unthinking charlatans. I think that people enjoy this attack because in their hearts they know that these professionals do little to alter the fundamental hopelessness of the lives of many people who live in North America. Work in "Mary Hartman" is portrayed as being alienated, meaningless, and unchangeable. Mary's husband Tom, when he is not having incoherent arguments with his wife, is beating his head against the powers that be in the auto plant where he works. He is trying against all odds, and significantly by himself, to change the system of work that is driving him and his fellow workers crazy.

As you can see, this programme is complex and I shall return to it again. But let me conclude by stating that I think basically the show is different, and therefore successful, because it attempts to confront the reality of our lifestyles in a satirical, and a tragic way. You can't say that about "Mary Tyler Moore", or the "Fonz", or the "Waltons".

● ● ● ● ●

February 22, 1977

"WHAT BREADBASKET?"

Let me say *a very few* kind words about this special, which purported to give us the real story behind the troubles besetting Canada's grain trade. The photography was beautiful. Great wide expanses of wheat fields, blue skies, lumbering combines. The cameramen were clearly seduced by the golden flesh of the Saskatchewan prairie.

But what about the substance of this programme? It was biased, distorted, and full of half truths to the point that if one did not know better, one might have concluded that this was an hour long paid commerical for the inland terminal, free market, multi-national grain trade lobby. A few examples should suffice. The programme took its direction mainly from interviews with two Saskatchewan farmers, Al Coulter and Darryl Rumble. Typical farmers these — one with an airplane and another with an indoor, kidney-shaped swimming pool complete with a whirlpool bath! Are these farmers representative of producers in the West? I doubt it. Are there any farmers who support the Canadian Wheat Board or the Wheat Pools or orderly marketing? Apparently the producers of "What Breadbasket?" could not find them.

Many farmers are against free competition, against the market place, against the Winnipeg Commodities Exchange. Did anyone producing this programme ask why? For all of the program's implicit and explicit attacks upon the Wheat Board, did it occur to Bill Smith, the producer, director and writer of this show, to point out that the Canadian Wheat Board was set up because the free enterprise system of grain marketing had failed in the post World War One period, and that the Winnipeg Grain Exchange was about to go broke?

Mr. Coulter told us that his grandfather was one of the founders of the Wheat Pool. He then went on to inform the viewer that by 1970, "something" had to be done." But why were the pools organized in the first place? "What Breadbasket?" omitted to point out that wheat pools were organized as self defense organizations of farmers against the depredations of the private elevator companies.

Indeed we are left with the impression that "Operation Lift", the programme which paid farmers a pittance not to grow wheat, was a plot of the Wheat Pool. Nowhere are we informed that this hated programme was the brainchild of Otto Lang.

Cargill Grain (Canada) emerged unscathed from Sunday night's programme. Indeed, their image was one of a struggling corporation attempting to achieve efficiency through competition in the market place. "What Breadbasket?" did not mention that Cargill has been charged and convicted of selling below-grade grain; that the Government of India is suing Cargill and other large grain companies for millions of dollars because of failure to fulfill delivery requirements to that country; that the U.S. Government has accused both Cargill (Canada) and Cargill Company of the U.S. of issuing false invoices and declarations regarding rapeseed screenings; and that Cargill in Red Deer recently pleaded guilty to 11 charges of violating the Canadian Wheat Board Act by making false entries on elevator records and by accepting deliveries in excess of quotas.

But enough of Cargill. Their public record is available to all who would care to spend a couple of hours in the Library.

One more distortion should be enough to clinch it. The programme told us that grain loading on the west coast poses a great problem. Somehow, according to "What Breadbasket?", Seattle has the answer. Of course, the authority for this is a man who conducts tours of the terminals in Vancouver. Don't talk to terminal management. Don't talk to the unions concerned. If you did, you would learn that over the past five years, 40 million bushels of grain a year, on average, were loaded on ships in Seattle, while in Vancouver an average of 248 million bushels a year were loaded. Six times as much! But let's not allow facts to clutter up this documentary film.

It is indeed unfortunate that such an unbalanced, prejudiced view of Canada's grain trade has been aired.[14]

•   •   •   •

March 22, 1977

THE WOODSWORTH PHENOMENON

What I have to say about this programme will probably not amuse the producer, Jeanine Locke, the NDP, or most probably J.S. Woodsworth. I looked at this film twice last week, once in the privacy of a room at the CBC-T.V. studio alone with my thoughts and my cigar and once down at the Centre of the Arts, together with an imposing list of New Democratic Party luminaries. Each time I came away feeling that I had spent an hour with a man — nay, a God-like creature — who had been given a mission to preach to the masses and, like all real prophets, such as Jesus and Moses, was never fated to see the flock reach the promised land or achieve salvation.

This view of Woodsworth is fine as far as it goes. Perhaps it *does* give us some insight into the character of J.S. Woodsworth, but does it tell us anything concrete about the political struggles in which he was engaged? I think not. The class struggles of the first 40 years of this century are given a muddled treatment by Jeanine Locke. And the historical interpretation of just who and what Woodsworth represented is so confused as to be useless. J.S. Woodsworth a revolutionary? A subversive? A man who had caught the spirit of Ghandi or Lenin or Mao Tse-tung? Forget about Ghandi for now. However, I do suspect that if Lenin or Mao Tse-tung believed in the afterlife they would be raging about the heavens at such a presumptuous comparison. Woodsworth did believe in the afterlife — and he would be appalled. Let's get one thing straight. Woodsworth, like Tommy Douglas and Allan Blakeney, was a social democrat, a Fabian, that is, one who believes that the worst ills of the capitalist system can be cured through gradual amelioration brought about by parliamentary enactments; that, indeed, the basic features of the system can be maintained if only they are humanized. Does this mean that there is not a great difference between Woodsworth and MacKenzie King as Jeanine Locke implies? Not at all. MacKenzie King wanted to save capitalism. That is why he brought in old age pensions and the baby bonus. Woodsworth wanted to reform capitalism, and *that* is why he advocated these measures. Whatever the differing intentions of Woodsworth, King, Barrett and Trudeau we still have the same system. But I do recommend this film for both its entertainment and religious value, even while deploring its historical and political insights. History is not made by great men, no matter what social democrats may claim.

• • • •

May 3, 1977

HAVE I EVER LIED TO YOU BEFORE?

Before answering that question, may I open with a quote?

> . . . . The mass media increasingly reflect the attitudes and deal with the concerns of the affluent. We don't have mass media, we have class media — media for the middle and upper classes.

> The poor, the old, the young, the Indian, the Eskimo, the blacks are virtually ignored. It's as if they didn't exist. More importantly, these minority groups are denied expression in the mass media because they cannot command attention as the affluent can.

No, this citation is not that of a radical academic, nor is it the statement of the revolutionary elaborating on the insidious powers of bourgeois ideology, rather it is a quote from a presentation made by Jerry Goodis to the Senate Committee on the Mass Media. Yes, this is a quote from the man who brought us all those cute Hush Puppies ads, the man who humanized the London Life Insurance Company .. and who explained to Canadian women how life could be overflowing with the milk of happiness with wonderful, wonderful Wonderbra. In the National Film Board profile on Jerry Goodis entitled "Have I Ever Lied to You Before?", this contradiction between the man who understands full well the tricks, the gimmicks, and the chicanery involved in selling people products that they really do not want or need, and the man who is so successful at doing all of these things, is confronted . . . and what do we get? We get a cynical, not really convincing hour long commercial for Jerry Goodis.

We see that there is something inconsistent between Goodis' radical upbringing in the ghetto area of downtown Toronto and his present work as the advertiser for the federal Liberal Party, and yet throughout the whole hour not once is Goodis forced to explain this contradiction.

Maybe this is the best way to deal with the subject. The creative force of advertising is remarkable, but still it's clear that most national advertising is parasitic. It does not produce anything useful; it only sells products whose contribution to our well-being is dubious. And it certainly pushes a dream world life-style whose relationship with reality is tenuous. "Have I Ever Lied to You Before?" A zillion times.

•   •   •   •

July 25, 1977

CRTC INQUIRY

In ancient Rome, before Roman soldiers went out to battle the barbarians, the generals would call for the ritual killing of a sheep so as to determine from the entrails whether or not the time was ripe for a victorious battle. If the entrails suggested that the time was propitious, the Roman legions set off into the field. If the entrails indicated that the time was not ripe, another sheep was slaughtered and its entrails examined, and so on. From the reported responses of some cabinet ministers — the P.M., for one, and Jeanne Sauve, for another — to the CRTC's recently released report on broadcasting, it appears that the CBC will have to undergo yet another examination of its entrails in order to determine finally that there *are* separatists inside Radio Canada. This time, the CRTC, the hysterical outburst of some Liberal members of cabinet notwithstanding, found no specific separatist bias in Radio

Canada. For Madame Sauve, this was probably because the CRTC did not have the time for the kind of investigation that would root out such bias. The Prime Minister went further and stated that " . . . unless broadcasters are contributing to national unity, then they are aiding the separatist cause in this country".

To carry this extremely rigid formulation to its logical conclusion, "you must support national unity and if you don't explicitly and religiously, then you have no right to appear over the public airwaves". Frankly, I find this approach, apparently endorsed by some members of the cabinet, to be abhorent to the whole notion of freedom of the press. The CBC and all of the electronic media do not exist in order to crush the independence movement in Quebec; nor do they exist to promote this or that cabinet minister's understanding of national unity. Presumably, journalists in all of the media try, in as detached a manner as possible, to present the complex facts of the Canadian existence to all of this country's citizens. Because they are human beings with particular class and educational backgrounds, they may fail, on occasion, to be so detached; or perhaps they do not always have the time nor the inclination to properly research an item. Moreover, they do have employers who have class backgrounds.

But surely the answer to these human failings is *not* to impose upon these journalists, and thereby upon the nation, one man's or one party's particular view of what this country should look like? Unfortunately, the P.M.'s response to the CRTC report leads one to conclude that he does not share this view. I hope that 1984 is not going to be with us before 1984.

September 19, 1977

TAR SANDS

Last week, with little fanfare, the CBC quietly aired its exposé on the Canadian political process — "The Tar Sands". I must congratulate the CBC, the producer Ralph Thomas, and Larry Pratt, the author of the original book *The Tar Sands*. This documentary drama, which Barbara Frum begs us to believe is fiction, demonstrates for all those doubters just how relevant, how incisive, and indeed how entertaining a publicly owned network can be.

In brief, "The Tar Sands" tells the story of how a consortium of transnational oil companies brought the governments of Alberta and Ottawa to their knees and extracted a deal on Tar Sands oil development which will have economic and environmental consequences for Alberta and Canada for decades. The controversy surrounding this play will continue, ostensibly because some public figures known for their involvement in the Tar Sands project — Alberta Premier Lougheed, Syncrude head Spraggins, and the then Energy Minister Donald Macdonald — are depicted in the drama. The dialogue in the play is fictional, the events are not. In his book Pratt has masterfully documented how the oil companies cajoled, bullied, and threatened to get their way, which mainly involved the people of Canada taking all of the economic risks, weakening environmental standards, and emasculating trade union rights, while the gravy would eventually go to those same oil companies.

Bravo to the CBC for airing this drama! It should be rerun everytime the price of gas goes up at the pump. While I am in such a warm mood, let me also say a very few kind words about the "Bethune" production aired by CBC this past Sunday. This attempt to dramatize the life of Canada's greatest revolutionary hero is not a complete success — primarily because of the difficulty the writers appear to have had in resolving the contradictions between Dr. Bethune's early life as a maverick, individualist, and roué, and his later years of total dedication to the fight against fascism and to the cause of international revolution. However, this play takes a good shot at it and I suspect that the projected full length movie about Bethune will be better. By the way Donald Sutherland who played Bethune really has put his all into the role.

$$\bullet \quad \bullet \quad \bullet \quad \bullet$$

November 1, 1977

NEWSMAGAZINE ON THE RCMP

With the advent of television in the House of Commons, we are now in a position to see how our M.P.s actually deal with a crisis situation. Either the security service of the RCMP is totally out of the control of our elected officials or, and this is probably worse, the security service with the approval or under the direction of civilian authorities, has been systematically violating the law by committing arson, theft and burglary. "Mission Impossible" may be alive and well in Canada.

But back to the House of Commons for a moment. Last night's "Newsmagazine" had two obligations: (1) to make a rather frightening story coherent without sounding hysterical, and (2) to ensure that all four parties in the house were fairly represented. I think that "Newsmagazine" succeeded. The excerpts from the opposition's speeches made clear their concerns and we heard enough of the then solicitor-general Francis Fox's speech to be able to judge both his defense of the government and of the force. As to the latter's speech I was reminded of the old joke that emerged after World War II: "You can't condemn the whole SS because of a few bad apples". The CBC's choice of civil liberties general counsel Allan Borovoy as the background expert on this question was a good one. If this country was or is in a state of imminent sabotage and subversion, then let's hear about it. If not, then tell us what the police and their supposed bosses, the politicians are doing. This was Borovoy's message.

These are trying times for journalists. Our Watergate story is floating to the surface at a time when investigative journalism is no longer in such great favour, and when the beloved terms of some critics of the media are objectivity and lack of bias.

I hope that the journalists in television and in the other media who cover this RCMP story are committed, one might almost say biased, in favour of the preservation of those few rights we still have: the right to know, or at least to be reasonably certain, that police power is not running amuck. And I think that the CBC, both in last night's "Newsmagazine", and in the "National" that followed, proved that it is still capable of dealing with a very sensitive story in depth, with commitment, without prejudice, and, thank goodness, in a manner totally bereft of any phony objectivity.

* * * *

June 28, 1977

LAMARSH AND JOHNSON

It is no accident that both of these reports appeared almost simultaneously some two weeks ago. Indeed, unimpeachable sources in the broadcasting industry inform me that there was a great deal of jockeying between Al Johnson and Judy LaMarsh as to whose report was going to be released first. CBC, with the swiftness of a gazelle, won the race and came out with Al Johnson's *Touchstones for the CBC* at least 24 hours before Judy LaMarsh's misnamed *Royal Commission on Violence in the Media*.

Incidentally, these reports are by no means the last words on the subject. The CRTC's study of the CBC, which some have called soft core McCarthyism, is due to be submitted to the Government on Canada Day, July 1, 1977, while a royal commission on broadcasting in Canada is very definitely in the offing.

Let's be very clear about the Johnson report. There is very little in it with which I can disagree. Johnson has clearly given the matter serious thought and has come forward with an unimpeachable analysis of the situation complete with an action programme for its solution. The problem is that it has all been said many times before. For example, I certainly agree with Al Johnson when he advocates improvement of regional programming. My files and my head are stuffed full of fine sentiments by CBC executives regarding regional programming. What remains to be seen, of course, is whether anything concrete will ever transpire in this area.

The LaMarsh document is by far the more provocative of the two. While Johnson, the mild mannered social democratic bureaucrat, tries to move, step by step, into the future, LaMarsh wants to burn down existing structures and to create justice and right in the broadcasting media out of the ashes. Now, I do agree with those critics who point out that Ms. LaMarsh's conception of one centralized agency, Television Canada, which would effectively centralize all television programming in Canada, is reminiscent of George Orwell's 1984 (come to think of it, that's not too far off), but this proposition, while possibly eliminating violence from television programming, would in all likelihood further constrain the abilities of broadcasters to tackle subjects unacceptable to the mighty in our society. What is appealing about the LaMarsh report is its refreshingly frank analysis of why television is so rotten today. The LaMarsh report states that in broadcasting " . . . almost all major decisions are ultimately commercial ones with the public good appearing, if at all, well down the priority scale, certainly below the dollar signs". In other words, the spirit of private profit reigns supreme in the media, according to LaMarsh. Judy's solution, naturally, is not to confront that reality which prevails throughout Canadian society, but somehow through this proposed superagency we shall be able to transcend the values of capitalism. Of course, this is impossible. In conclusion, it appears that we shall have to live with the CBC's grey but sensible perennial promises for the future and reject the science fiction of Judy LaMarsh.

•   •   •   •

July 11, 1978

CBC-2

One year ago, CBC President Al Johnson came out with *Touchstone for the CBC,* his statement of what the corporation has been and what it should become in the future. Much of the document was well written, well thought out, and old hat. However, there was one idea that was novel and which certainly speaks to some of the criticisms I have been airing in this spot regarding the corporation's programming limitations.

Given that the CBC comes up for licence renewal before the CRTC this October, it is probably appropriate that we take a look at some of Johnson's more innovative proposals. One of my recurrent criticisms is the fact that the corporation persists in airing schlock American programmes such as "Bearcats". One of the reasons, I suspect, for such programmes being aired on CBC has to do with the relatively low purchase cost of such shows. A second reason, ironically is the advertising revenues that such programmes return to the corporation. Of course every time one of these programmes is run it takes up an hour which could be used to show quality Canadian productions, be they dramas, musicals, public affairs or news programmes. An excellent example was the series entitled "For the Record". Unfortunately, if you miss such programmes you usually have to wait for a year to see them again. Finally, there is a crying need for the lengthy in-depth interview-type programme, wherein, free from the constraints of time, politicians, writers, and other oddballs may be questioned. Commercial television just does not allow for these kinds of programmes and CBC, as it is now constituted, is commercial television. Johnson's answer is CBC-2, a second CBC channel initially intended for all those communities wired up for cable. There would be no commercials. Repeats of other CBC-1 programmes would dominate, allowing all Canadians the opportunity to view the best of the corporation's programs. At the same time the second channel would provide daily in-depth treatment of topical events and would allow for minority programming catering to the many specialized interests that make up this country. Why not a weekly programme that would discuss the arts in Canada, and another that would analyze developments in labour and in business? There are many other advantages that we could mention in connection with this TV-2 idea, not the least of which would be the opportunity to ensure that such programmes as the "Fifth Estate" are not pre-empted by the NHL playoffs. Millions could watch Les Canadiens, while thousands would still be able to get Adrienne Clarkson.

I believe that Johnson's point is well taken. Either the CBC gets a second non-commercial channel which will enable it to fulfill its cultural obligations to the nation, or the monetary constraints will force the single CBC channel we have now to continue to produce the hodgepodge of good and bad programming with which, apparently, nobody is happy.

* * * * *

January 23, 1979

THE ALBERTANS

Can Canadians produce television programmes on a sustained basis which can compete with slick American products? Can we produce "Kaz", "Vegas", "Dallas", and the rest? Unfortunately, yes. We can reproduce American schlock — just as slick and, basically, just as meaningless, and representing the same adman's view of the world. "The Albertans" proves it. Now before I really unload on this three part mini-series, let me say something positive about it. The series does deal with a current, pressing aspect of the Canadian reality, that is, the strivings of one section of the Western Canadian business class to conquer nature, to overcome the scepticism of our older Eastern ruling class, and to build petroleum-based heavy industry in Alberta. Furthermore, there is no doubt that alongside this tremendously vigorous development older economic formations — marginal farmers and ranchers — co-exist, and sometimes fail. And, of course, we cannot forget that the original Canadians, the native Indians, have been conned and cheated out of what has turned out to be very valuable land.

All of these forces, Alberta capitalists, struggling ranchers, and embittered Indians, are intricately involved in "The Albertans". Most of us are familiar enough with the news of the day to recognize that these are indeed genuine forces in the Alberta scene. For me, this closeness to reality is the most attractive aspect of the mini-series. "The Albertans" is a kind of one dimensional docu-drama without the documentation.

Because I identify some essence of reality in "The Albertans", I don't reject it totally as I do "Dallas", an American formula melodrama which could just as easily be taking place in an uptown New York apartment as in a Texas sky scraper.

However, "The Albertans" does have serious problems. Here we have a mini-series that it is trying to tell the whole history of Alberta. For this reason alone, as well, I suspect, because of the predelictions of the writer, Lyal Brown, the characters and the situations are painfully stereotyped. There are *good* open-minded Canadian capitalists and sleazy European wheeler dealers. There are crusty old ranchers and evil, racist, rural red necks. Finally there are bad revolutionary Indians and tame or confused good Indians.

Now don't get me wrong, I believe in good and evil. It's just that I am not completely convinced that the current Alberta model of development is the best available either for that province or, for that matter, for Canada, and one might have hoped that the writer of "The

Albertans" could have expressed at least some doubt about this model. But for all of that, I return to my first remark, this mini-series does prove that we can produce engaging drama, which, if not very deep, is at least visually pleasing and certainly capable of competing with the best or worst of its American counterparts. O.K., we've conquered the medium. Let's deal with the message.

NOTES

1. H. Ellison, *The Glass Teat*, p. 19.

2. In this article, primary attention will be paid to television. However, one can include radio, the daily press, religious institutions, the education establishment, fictional and non-fictional books, magazines, etc.

3. In the United States the ratings struggle amongst the three major networks is ferocious. However, it should not be forgotten that this competition to be Number 1 has to do with money. "Translated into dollars, a language T.V. folk feel . . . more comfortable speaking, each rating point in prime time is worth about $30 million in pretax profits over the course of the T.V. year. On the bottom line, it means, if the figures hold (for 1979) that ABC will ring up about $72 million more than CBS this year, and $102 million more than NBC". "CHAOS in Television", *Time*, March 12, 1979, p. 54. In 1978, ABC's profits were 185 million dollars; CBS's 135 million, and NBC's 65 million. *Time*, March 12, 1979, p. 57.

4. M. Landsberg, "The Tacky World of Kids' Saturday T.V.".

5. R. Milliband, *The State in Capitalist Society*, p. 238.

6. D. W. Smythe, "Communications: Blindspot of Western Marxism", pp. 1-28.

7. *Ibid.*, p. 3.

8. B. Livant, "The Audience Commodity: On the 'Blindspot' Debate", pp. 91-104.

9. "Networks Spending Spree Touches Off Worries Over Future Profits".

   However it is worth noting that some network executives do think about ideological messages. Witness the following remarks by Fred Pierce, President of ABC:
   > "Happy Days" and "Laverne and Shirley" really reinforce certain things within a family as they watch together. One of the most pleasing things is that not only is "Mork and Mindy" an enormous success, but that the social comment and moral point made at the end of the show *every week* are just overwhelming. It is a message about our society. The last time I happened to watch it, it was about Mork's own emotions coming out and how he felt freed. (My italics)

   "Talking Heads: A Triptych of Network Chiefs on Thrust, Appeal, Consensus, Risks, Holes, Fun Meaning, and . . ." *Time*, March 12, 1979, p. 58.

10. On the role of ideology see, for example, W. Clement, *The Canadian Corporate Elite*, pp. 270-286.

11. R. C. Cosbey, "Mass Media Stories — What are they Doing to our Heads?", pp. 12-15; see also his "Dreams and Other Stories", and "Myth and Literature".

12. *Ibid.*, p. 13.

I have observed Dr. Cosbey delivering his message to groups of rank and file trade unionists several times. What is encouraging and disturbing (depending on your point of view) is the positive response that Cosbey evokes from workers with his message of how they are being manipulated and yes, cheated by the mass media. People who read Harlequin romances and watch the "The Six Million Dollar Man" are shocked and then angered when they recognize the basic message being delivered through these seemingly 'innocent' stories. If a lifetime of a particular view of the world can be shaken by one (albeit) very good lecture by a quiet white bearded professor, what would happen if a pro-working class ideology was purveyed constantly over daily television, in the comics, etc.? This raises the question which cannot be discussed here, that perhaps the ruling class ideology is not as powerful as both its supporters and its critics claim.

13. A lot of water has flown under the bridge since this piece was written. From its inception as Canada's public network, the CBC has had a mandate from Parliament. To quote from the Broadcasting Act of 1968.

The Canadian broadcasting system must:

- safeguard, enrich and strengthen the cultural, political, social and economic fabric of Canada;
- provide reasonable, balanced opportunity for the expression of differing views on matters of public concern;
- use predominantly Canadian creative and other resources

There should be provided through a corporation established by Parliament for the purpose, a national broadcasting service that is predominantly Canadian in content and character.

The national broadcasting service must:

(i)   be a balanced service of information, enlightenment and entertainment for people of different ages, interests and tastes covering the whole range of programming in fair proportion,

(ii)   be extended to all parts of Canada, as public funds become available,

(iii)   be in English and French, serving the special needs of geographic regions, and actively contributing to the flow and exchange of cultural and regional information and entertainment, and

(iv)   contribute to the development of national unity and provide for a continuing expression of Canadian identity.

At the same time the Corporation does solicit advertising and in order to be successful in this endeavour it falls prey to the same ideological traps as do the private networks. For an overview of the CBC's accomplishments, problems, and promise see *Touchstone for the CBC* by A. W. Johnson, June 1977; *CBC — A Perspective.* Submission to the Canadian Radio-Television and Telecommunications Commission in Support of Applications for Renewal of Network Licences, CBC, May 1978. See also Maggie Siggins, "Does Sports Dominate the CBC?", *TV Guide,* August 18, 1978, pp. 2-4. For the longer historical view see F. Peers, *The Politics of Canadian Broadcasting 1920-1951,* and E. A. Weir, *The Struggle for National Broadcasting in Canada.*

There is some indication that the CRTC may be about to engage once again in some ritual muscle flexing. See R. Gwyn, "Programmes Must Improve — Board Tells CBC, CTV".

14. For a short, sharp critique of CBC's agricultural coverage see M. Siggins, "We Won't be Cowed!", pp. 2-4.

Readings

Boyle, Harris. J., "Other Countries Do It, So Why Don't We Do It?" *The Toronto Globe and Mail*, (September 9, 1978).

"Chaos in Television", *Time*, (March 12, 1979).

Clement, Wallace, *The Canadian Corporate Elite*, Toronto: McClelland & Stewart, 1975.

Cosbey, Robert C., "Dreams and Other Stories", *Sphinx*, No. 2, (1974).

Cosbey, Robert C., "Mass Media Stories — What Are They Doing To Our Heads?", *The Public Employee*, Vol. 1, no. 1, (Spring, 1978).

Cosbey, Robert C., "Myth and Literature", *Sphinx*, No. 1, (197[?]).

Ellison, Harlan, *The Glass Teat*, New York: Pyramid, 1975.

Ellison, Harlan, *The Other Glass Teat*, New York: Pyramid, 1975.

Landsberg, Michele, "The Tacky World of Kids' Saturday T.V.," *Toronto Star,* (September 22, 1978).

"Less Prime Time News", *Regina Leader Post*, (October 31, 1978).

Livant, Bill, "The Audience Commodity: On the 'Blindspot' Debate", *Canadian Journal of Political and Social Theory*, Vol. 3, No. 1, (Winter, 1979).

Metz, Robert, *CBC Reflections in a Bloodshot Eye*, Scarborough: Signet, 1976.

Milliband, Ralph, "The State in Capitalist Society, London: Weidenfeld & Nicolson, 1969.

Murdock, Graham, "Blindspots About Western Marxism: A Reply to Dallas Smythe", *Canadian Journal of Political and Social Theory*, Vol. 2, No. 2, (Spring, 1978).

"Networks Spending Spree Touches Off Worries Over Future Profits", *Wall Street Journal*, (Oct. 4, 1977).

Peers, Frank, *The Politics of Canadian Broadcasting 1920-1951*, Toronto: University of Toronto Press, 1969.

Porter, John, *The Vertical Mosaic*, Toronto: University of Toronto Press, 1965.

Reeves, Richard, "The Dangers of Television in the Silverman Era", *Esquire*, (April 25, 1978).

Sheppard, Robert, "New Committee Will Help Reform Communications", *Globe and Mail*, (Dec. 1, 1978).

Siggins, Maggie, "Does Sports Dominate the CBC?", *T.V. Guide*, (Aug. 18, 1978).

Siggins, Maggie, "We Won't be Cowed!", *T.V. Guide*, (Dec. 2-8, 1978).

Smythe, Dallas W., "Communications: Blindspot of Western Marxism", *Canadian Journal of Political and Social Theory*, Vol. 2., No. 2., (Spring, 1978).

Smythe, Dallas W., "Rejoinder to Graham Murdock", *Canadian Journal of Political and Social Theory*, Vol. 3., No. 1, (Winter 1979).

"Talking Heads: A Triptych of Network Chiefs on Thrust, Appeal, Consensus, Risks, Holes, Fun, Meaning and . . . .", *Time*, (March 12, 1979).

Weir, E. Austin, *The Struggle for National Broadcasting in Canada*, Toronto: McClelland & Stewart, 1965.

"Who Controls U.S. Television?", *Regina Leader Post*, (October 14, 1978).

Self-Care and Lifestyles: Ideological and Policy Implications

B. Singh Bolaria

B. SINGH BOLARIA is an Associate Professor and Head in the Department of Sociology at the University of Saskatchewan. His current research interests include Medical Sociology, Industrial Sociology, and Immigration of Ethnic Groups.

Introduction

Since the publication of the Lalonde Working Paper, *A New Perspective On the Health of Canadians*, there has been a renewed interest in individual lifestyles and self-imposed health risks.[1] Morbidity and mortality, for the most part, are attributed to individual life-styles and self-imposed risks, and consequently, the importance of the physical and social environment to an individual's health is downgraded.[2] The Working Paper contends that since the major risk factors causing mortality are under the personal discretion of the individuals, there would be a considerable decrease in mortality if individuals would focus their attention on changing those aspects of their lifestyles which are injurious to their health. As Lalonde argues,

> . . . individual blame must be accepted by many for the deleterious effect on health of their respective lifestyles. Sedentary living, smoking, over-eating, driving while impaired by alcohol, drug abuse and failure to wear seat-belts are among the many contributors to physical or mental illness for which the individual must accept some responsibility and for which he should seek correction.[3]

The underlying assumption is that the basic cause of much ill health is the individual. The solution to the problem, therefore, is to alter the individual's lifestyle and behaviour. As this explanation has received wide publicity through the mass media and has gained popular acceptance, it is bound to have far reaching consequences in policy decisions. As such it merits serious analysis and consideration. The promotion of this strategy — individual etiology and individual solutions — in the face of the national health-care "crisis" is more than merely coincidental. Suffice it to state here, that it obscures the extent to which health and illness depend upon socially determined ways of life, obfuscates the social causes of disease, shifts responsibility for health and illness back onto the individual, individualizes what is essentially a social problem, and promotes a course of action oriented toward changing individual behaviour and lifestyles rather than the existing social, economic, and political institutions and the health sector.

As the following discussion reveals, this is not a "new perspective," rather it is consistent with the basic tenets of "bourgeois individualism and freedom of choice". Our discussion further reveals that this ideology is pervasive in clinical medicine, and is coherent with prevailing ideologies in the social sciences and their applications to the analysis and explanation of various social issues and attendant policy formulations.

Individual Etiology in Medicine

This section evaluates the implications of the clinical paradigm, widely accepted in medical practice, that defines health and illness in individual terms. In this view illness is considered to be independent of the social context in which it occurs. As Turshen states: "This paradigm takes individual physiology as the norm for pathology (as contrasted with broader social conditions) and locates sickness in the individual's body".[4] Contemporary medicine operates on a mechanistic and individualistic model in which individuals are "atomized" and "decontextualized" for treatment. Under such a paradigm,

> . . . a living organism could be regarded as a machine which might be taken apart and reassembled if its structure and function were fully understood. In medicine, the same concept led further to the belief that an understanding of disease processes and of the body's response to them would make it possible to intervene therapeutically, mainly by physical (surgery), chemical, or electrical methods.[5]

This approach basically ignores social causes of much ill health, causes that are rooted in the structure of society itself. Many diseases are considered to have a "specific etiology", that is, the specific causes are sought in the body's cellular and biochemical systems. This "individual centered" concept of disease has led to an essentially "curative orientation", whereby people can be made healthy by means of "technological fixes".[6] Technical solutions are offered to many of the problems which stem from social conditions. As Fee states:

> ... complaints stemming from such environmental factors as poverty, sexism and racism, the nature of work inside and outside the home, crisis in housing and education, problems in personal relationships, and the like, can be 'treated' only by tranquilizers and placebos.[7]

Furthermore, the major response to many of these psychological disorders has been pharmacological — "antidepressants", "anti-anxiety agents", "stimulants", and "tranquilizers".[8-10] Women generally are prescribed and consume large quantities of these drugs.[11-12]

Many diseases are viewed as mere "technical defects in the body's machinery", and many treatments are oriented toward restoring the "normal" functioning of the human body. Rather than removing the external causes of illness, medical technology is used to destroy the capacity of the body organ to react to these causes.

> Ironically, many treatments for a variety of stress-related illnesses act not by removing the causes of illness but by destroying the capacity of the organ to respond to the cause, often by removing the organ or by severing its connection with the brain. Thus 'ultimate cures' for ulcer are vagotomy or removal of the duodenum; a response to hypertension may be blockage of the sympathetic nervous system; a response to severe mental disturbance may be psychosurgery.[13]

There has been increasing criticism of the clinical paradigm,[14-16] especially as it is applied to psychiatric treatment.[17-18] Despite much criticism, this orientation has pervasive influence in medical practice.[19]

Much research into non-psychological, or physical, illnesses reflects this orientation as well. There has been heavy emphasis on individual treatment and etiology of disease rather than on the causal nature of social and environmental factors, such as occupational and environmental exposure to pollutants, chemicals and other agents.[20] Similarly in the case of some cancer research, the major emphasis, both in research and educational campaigns, is placed on individual responsibility and behaviour, such as smoking and personal habits.[21]

It has been emphasized in the foregoing discussion that a mechanistic-individualistic conception of disease is pervasive in medical practice and research. This focus absolves the economic and political environment from the responsibility for disease. This disease-centered, high-technology, medical orientation undermines the social aspects of disease.

Individual Lifestyles Versus Environment

In the realm of medical practice, the clinical model discussed above attributes disease to "malfunctioning" of the human body, while in the social realm, disease is seen to lie in individual lifestyle and behaviours. In the former case the normal functioning of the body can be restored through "technological fixes"; while in the latter, the solution lies primarily in changing individuals' behaviors and lifestyles. Both approaches obscure the social nature of disease and undermine the importance of social and work environments to health and sickness.

With respect to deaths due to motor vehicle accidents, other accidents and suicides, the Working Paper states: "Since all these causes are mainly due to human factors, including carelessness, impaired driving, despair and self-imposed risks, it is evident that changes in these factors are needed if the rates of death are to be lowered".[22] Consider further the "self-imposed" risks regarding circulatory diseases discussed in this paper.

> While the causes of circulatory diseases are various, there is little doubt that obesity, smoking, stress, lack of exercise and high-fat diets, in combination, make a dominant contribution.[23]

Another exponent of individual epidemiology is a well-known health-economist, Fuchs, who states:

> It is becoming increasingly evident that many health problems are related to individual behavior. In the absence of dramatic break-throughs in medical science the greatest potential for improving health is through changes in what people do and do not do to and for themselves.[24]

Fuchs reiterated similar ideas elsewhere. ". . . the greatest potential for improving health lies in what we do and don't do for and to ourselves. The choice is ours."[25]

This emphasis on lifestyles and self-imposed risks masks the social aspects of disease and shifts the responsibility of maintaining health back onto the individual by denying that social factors have much to do with disease. This view is symptomatic of what William Ryan has called "blaming the victim" syndrome.[26] More importantly, Berliner states, "focussing on lifestyles serves only to reify the lifestyles as an entity apart from the social conditions from which it arises".[27] Berliner further states:

> Discussing changes in lifestyles without first discussing the changes in the social conditions which give rise to them, without recognizing that the lifestyle is derivative, is misleading and, in effect, victim blaming.[28]

This approach conceals the social context of disease. There is considerable evidence which suggests that many diseases are environmentally generated, in particular, by the work environment.

Workers constantly face hazardous working conditions, conditions which can hardly be attributed to their lifestyles. In 1973 workplace related illnesses and accidents accounted for 10.5 million man-days of lost-work in Canada as compared to 5.8 million days lost due to strikes and lockouts.[29] Thousands of workers work in unhealthy environments, where they are exposed to radioactive dusts, poor ventilation, inadequate safety, excessive dirt and other pollutants. Some of these pollutants are directly linked to various debilitating and fatal diseases, such as, asbestosis, silicosis, and black lung. In addition to these pulmonary diseases, many types of cancer are associated with environmental conditions.[30-32]

Occupational diseases are, for the most part, environmentally determined. The priority of profits over occupational safety and workers' satisfaction causes much of the disease.[33]

The nature and organization of work, job factors and job attitudes appear to have important relationships to general well-being.[34] Bosquet writes:

> So deep is the frustration engendered by work that the incidence of heart attacks among manual workers is higher than that in any other stratum of society. People 'die from work' not because it is noxious or dangerous . . . but because it is intrinsically 'killing'.[35]

Other investigators have shown a correlation between general economic conditions such as the unemployment rate, and cardiovascular and other mortality.[36-38]

Other conditions in the work environment serve to produce conditions which are widely known as "stress-related diseases". Many of these stress-related diseases such as heart disease, can be seen to be due to the needs of the capitalist system itself.

The competitive nature of production under capitalism, the continuous demand for increase in efficiency, the need for a "flexible" and "free" labour force, unemployment and job insecurity, all contribute to general stress in the population.

This is also evident in the social environment. Eyer and Sterling argue that economic and cultural forces in capitalist society create stress by disrupting communal ties and molding competitive, striving individuals.[39]

While competitiveness is associated with success in this system, at the same time much research has shown that it is a prime determinant of heart disease. Individual behavior patterns have been identified as one of the strongest risk factors in heart disease. In the literature, studies have shown that the chance of a person with "Type-A" behaviour (aggressive, competitive) having a heart attack is two to five times higher than that of a person with a "Type-B" behaviour (co-operative, easy going, relaxed, passive).[40] This indicates a contradiction between the needs of the economic system and what is healthy for the individual. It is in the interest of the individual, then, to take in Type-B behavior, but the interest of the system demands that individuals maintain Type-A behaviour. From this example, it is clear that the health effects of individual behaviour must be examined in the context of the social conditions from which this behavior arises.

Competitiveness and achievement orientation become an ideal and this is achieved through socialization in schools, religion, education and cultural values.[41–43] As noted earlier, social disruptions are produced by the process of maintaining a "free" and "flexible" labour force. To correct for such disruptions will hinder the capitalist pursuit of profits and productivity. "Similarly" as Eyer and Sterling state, "mass relaxation by the majority of men who share coronary prone behavior patterns would undermine productivity, the profits of capitalist firms, and thence the growth process itself".[44]

Those in this society who do not exhibit competitive achievement orientation may be considered as "maladjusted", and the individuals blame their failure on their own lack of initiative.[45] Therefore, the primary adaptation is competitive achievement orientation. There are those who cannot adapt or for whom the cost of adaptation is too high. The cost takes many forms other than coronary heart disease, such as, alcoholism, ulcer, mental illness and suicide.[46]

In addition to these factors, there is considerable evidence which shows the relationship of poverty to morbidity and mortality. As a representative of the Canadian Medical Association pointed out to the Special Senate Committee on Poverty:

> It so happens that even in the most affluent nations like Canada and the United States, 20 percent of the population are poor . . . and this 20 percent of the population suffers something like 75 to 80 percent of the major illnesses.[47]

Poverty, malnutrition and incidence of disease are all linked together.

> There is universal recognition that nutrition is a critical factor in poverty. Dietary inadequacies and undernutrition, combined with other deprivations attendant on poverty, cause health deterioration. This sets up the cycle of decreased performance of all activities, mental apathy, and incapacity for initiative or self-help. Medical research has linked malnutrition to anemia, low resistence to infectious diseases, mental retardation, and mental illness.[48]

Other evidence indicates that poverty is correlated with malnutrition, retarded growth, psycho-motor retardation, emotional problems and eyesight problems.[49] These problems are even more acute among the Native people, where poverty is combined with added exposure to environmental disruption. The Department of National Health and Welfare in their brief to the Special Senate Committee on poverty stated:

> The effects of a marginal existence, which is the common experience of most Indians and Eskimos, are apparent in related health statistics. The infant mortality in 1968 was 21 per 1,000 live births for all Canadians, 49 per 1,000 for Indians, and 89 per 1,000 for Eskimos. Among Indians as a whole, infant mortality has declined during the past decade from three times the national rate to just over twice the rate.[50]

The Native population, additionally, is subject to other pollutants. Mercury poisoning in White Dog and Grassy Narrows reserves in Ontario was given a great deal of publicity recently. The Native people in these two reserves were found to have 40 to 150 times more mercury in their blood than the average Canadian.[51-52] This problem is not confined to Northwestern Ontario. *The Medical Post* reports that there are 15 badly contaminated areas in Canada.[53]

Yet the reaction of the Ontario Minister of Health was to blame the people for their lack of concern for their own health. The Minister said he was "tired of people complaining about health hazards facing Indians in Northwestern Ontario while the complainers go on killing themselves with . . . diseases of choice by exercising too little and smoking too much."[54] According to him the "real" problem is the Native people.

> . . . One of the biggest frustrations the Government has faced in trying to cope with the problem is the attitudes of the Indians. 'We've just got to get through to them that they shouldn't eat certain fish,' he said.[55]

It may be noted here that most mercury pollution is caused by industrial enterprise. The Minister, however, is concerned about the Native attitudes and behaviour of the public rather than the attitude of the Reed Paper Company and that of his own Government. Again, it is the "blaming the victim" syndrome.

The differential use of medical services by the poor is often attributed to their lack of knowledge, lack of readiness to use services, lack of positive values toward health, cultural impediments and "fear" of immunization programs and dental clinics.[56] Though phrased somewhat differently, an attempt is made again to shift the responsibility for not using services back on to the poor people.

This approach to analyzing "social problems" is not confined to the health sector alone. It has been used in the sociological study of racism, education, inequality, welfare and poverty.[57] For instance, the sociologists, for the most part, focussed their analysis on the poor, their attributes and their way of life (culture) and lifestyles. Rather than looking into the socio-political and economic conditions which create inequality, poverty is explained in terms of personal attributes and deficiencies of the poor and their inappropriate ways of life. This view is best represented in Oscar Lewis' "culture of poverty" thesis.[58] Numerous variations of this perspective appear in other areas in the form of functionalist theory,[59] the I.Q. argument,[60] achievement syndrome[61] and personal pathologies,[62] just to mention a few.

Returning to the subject at hand, this singular emphasis in medicine on life-styles and self-imposed risks downgrades the importance of social and economic factors in disease. The review of selected studies presented above demonstrates this point. There is evidence which suggests that a change in lifestyles and elimination of so-called self-imposed risks might reduce only a small proportion of mortality rates. As a Task Force report indicates:

> In an impressive 15 year study of aging, the strongest predictor of longevity was work satisfaction. The second best predictor was overall 'happiness'. . . . Other factors are undoubtedly important — diet, exercise, medical care and genetic inheritance. But research findings suggest that these factors may account for only about 25% of the risk factors in heart disease the major cause of death. That is, if cholesterol, blood pressure, smoking, glucose level, serum uric acid, and so forth, were perfectly controlled, only about one-fourth of coronary heart disease could be controlled. Although research on the problem has not led to conclusive answers, it appears that work role, work conditions, and other social factors may contribute heavily to this 'unexplained' 75% of risk factors.[63]

Ideological and Policy Implications

The promotion of the causal role of lifestyles and self-imposed risks in relation to health and disease obscures the dependence of health and illness upon socially determined ways of life, and diverts attention from the social and economic structure. This approach shifts responsibility for health or lack of it back onto the individual, individualizes what is essentially a social problem, and promotes a course of action oriented toward changing individual behaviour and lifestyles rather than the existing social, economic and political institutions and the health sector.

During economic crises when the situation becomes even more critical and the health care crisis deepens, government programs designed to promote this type of individual emphasis gain dominance over others. An attempt is made "to shift the responsibility for disease back onto the worker, in this case through the victim blaming epidemiology and of individual solutions for the worker."[64] And as Ryan states: "It is a brilliant ideology for justifying a perverse form of social action designed to change, not society, as one might expect, but rather society's victim."[65]

This response to crises in health care is consistent with bourgeois individualism, and rather than weakening it, strengthens "the ideological construct of bourgeois individualism by which one is responsible for one's wealth or lack of it, for one's work or lack of it, and for one's health or lack of it."[66] Ideologically, it encourages the tendency to see problems and their solutions as individual and not social, thus it masks the social nature of disease. By focussing on workers' lifestyles and habits it diverts attention from unhealthy and unsafe work environments, by concentrating on safe driving and seat belts it ignores the automobile industry and unsafe cars, and by concentrating on individual diet it diverts attention from food monopolies and potentially harmful food additives.[67] As Navarro states:

> . . . [A]n ideology that saw the 'fault' of disease as lying with the individual and that emphasized the individual therapeutic response clearly absolved the economic and political environment from the responsibility for disease and channeled potential response and rebellion against that environment to an individual, and thus less threatening level. The ideology of medicine was the individualization of a collective causality that by its very nature would have required a collective answer.[68]

However, a focus on social, economic and political institutions will bring into question the legitimacy of the whole system and its health sector. By promoting individual responsibility, this strategy serves as a legitimizing function.

The policies are primarily geared toward changing lifestyles and this is achieved through educational campaigns. Popularization of this strategy, in the long run, would be instrumental in preparing the populace to accept further reductions in health services. Therefore, the burden of health crises may be borne by the individuals to the extent that they accept the proposition that what are actually to a great extent socially, economically and politically caused conditions can be solved individually either by medical intervention or by self-care and changes in lifestyles. This approach promotes a policy of "health education in prevention and clinical medicine in cure", rather than drawing attention to the organization of health care delivery systems, or the nature, function and composition of the health sector in this society and the overall economic and political forces which determine the state of healthiness.

Concluding Remarks

In this paper we have presented an analysis of one of the strategies — individual lifestyles and self-imposed risks — being largely popularized by the state and media at the present time in the area of medical care. The promotion of this strategy — individual etiology and individual solutions — in the face of the current health debate is more than coincidental. Our discussion indicates that this approach is consistent with the basic tenets of "bourgeois individualism and freedom of choice," and its singular emphasis on the individual obscures the extent to which health and illness depend upon socially determined ways of life. It diverts attention away from social causes of disease, and shifts responsibility for health and illness back onto the individual. In doing so it promotes a course of action oriented toward individual behavioural modification rather than changing the existing social, economic, and political institutions and the health sector.

At a broader political level, this strategy serves to legitimate existing class relations and the dominant political and economic structures. Ransacking existing social, economic and political institutions is likely to bring into question the legitimacy of the whole system and the health sector. The popularization of this ideology, in the long run, would be instrumental in preparing the population to alter their expectations regarding health care and, perhaps, accept reductions in health services. As Crawford states:

> These ideological initiatives, on the one hand, serve to reorder expectations and to justify the retrenchment from rights and entitlements for access to medical services, and, on the other, attempt to divert attention from the social causation of disease in the commercial and industrial sectors.[69]

The burden of health crisis may therefore be borne by individuals to the extent that they accept the proposition that illnesses that are actually the result of environmentally induced conditions can be solved individually by self-care or "wise living".

A final point must be made. In this paper we are not presenting a social deterministic behavior model. There are grounds to believe that changing "at-risk" behavior of certain individuals may improve their state of health. This, however, cannot be used as a substitute for improving the social and economic conditions that are responsible for so many health problems. Therefore we have criticized the political and ideological undercurrents inherent in the approach which continues to "atomize both causation and solution to illness" and the policy implications of changing individual behavior and not the social and economic environment.

NOTES

1. M. Lalonde, *A New Perspective on the Health of Canadians.*

2. *Ibid.*, pp. 14-17.

3. *Ibid.*, p. 26.

4. M. Turshen, "The Political Ecology of Disease", pp. 45-60.

5. T. McKeon, *Medicine in Modern Society*, p. 38.

6. M. Renaud, "On the Structural Constraints to State Intervention in Health", pp. 559-571.

7. E. Fee, "Women and Health Care . . .", pp. 115-132.

8. Waldron, "Increased Prescribing of Valium . . .", pp. 37-62.

9. R. L. Katz, "Drug Therapy . . .", p. 757.

10. L. A. Stroufe and M. A. Stewart, "Treating Children with Stimulant Drugs", p. 407.

11. Fee, "Women and Health Care . . .", pp. 115-132.

12. J. Handing, N. Wolf and G. Chan, "A Socio-Demographic Profile of People Being Prescribed Mood-Modifying Drugs . . .".

13. J. Eyer and P. Sterling, "Stress-Related Mortality . . .", p. 34.

14. I. Illich, *Medical Nemesis.*

15. R. Dubos, *Man, Medicine and Environment.*

16. J. Powles, "On the Limitations of Modern Medicine", pp. 1-30.

17. T. Szasz, *Myths of Mental Illness.*

18. R. D. Laing, *The Politics of Experience and the Bird of Paradise.*

19. Turshen, "The Political Ecology of Disease", pp. 45-60.

20. V. Navarro, "The Crisis of Western System of Medicine in Contemporary Capitalism", p. 205.

21. D. S. Greenberg and J. E. Randal, "Waging the Wrong War on Cancer".

22. Lalonde, *A New Perspective on the Health of Canadians*, p. 14.

23. *Ibid.*, p. 15.

24. V. Fuchs, "Health Care and the United States Economic System", p. 211-237.

25. V. Fuchs, *Who Shall Live?*

26. W. Ryan, *Blaming the Victim.*

27. H. S. Berliner, "Emerging Ideologies in Medicine", p. 119.

28. *Ibid.*, p. 119.

29. J. W. Rinehart, *The Tyranny of Work*, p. 60.

30. J. Cairns, "The Cancer Problem", pp. 64-72.

31. E. C. Hammond, "Epidemiologic Basis for Cancer Prevention".

32. G. Matanoski, "Lung Cancer by Census Tract. . . ."

33. A. Miller, "The Wages of Neglect . . .," pp. 1217-1220.

34. D. Coburn, "Work and General Psychological . . . Well-Being", pp. 198-212.

35. M. Bosquet, *Capitalism in Crisis and Everyday Life*, p. 102.

36. M. H. Brenner, "Economic Changes and Heart Disease Mortality", pp. 606-611.

37. J. Eyer, "Prosperity as a Cause of Death, pp. 125-150.

38. S. Deutscher, "Some Factors Influencing the Distribution of Premature Death . . .", pp. 150-157.

39. J. Eyer and P. Sterling, "Stress Related Mortality and Social Organization", pp. 1-44.

40. J. Eyer, "Hypertension as a Disease of Modern Society", pp. 539-558.

41. D. McClelland, *The Achieving Society*.

42. S. Bowles and H. Gintis, *Schooling in Capitalist America*.

43. R. W. Nelson and D. A. Nock, *Reading, Writing and Riches*.

44. Eyer and Sterling, "Stress Related Mortality . . .," p. 37.

45. E. Chinoy, *Automobile Workers and The American Dream*.

46. Eyer and Sterling, "Stress Related Mortality . . .", p. 37.

47. Canadian Medical Association . . ., *Poverty in Canada*, p. 124.

48. *Ibid.*, p. 124.

50. *Ibid.*, p. 124.

51. S. Moore, *Mercury Poisoning, Native People and Reed Paper Company*.

52. M. McDonald, "Massacre at Grassy Narrows", pp. 26-36.

53. D. Cassels, "Minamata", p. 25.

54. Moore, *Mercury Poisoning . . .*, p. 16.

55. *Ibid.*, p. 16.

56. Canadian Medical Association, *Poverty in Canada*, pp. 121-123.

57. Ryan, *Blaming the Victim*.

58. O. Lewis, *La Vida*.

59. K. Davis and W. E. Moore, "Some Principles of Stratification", pp. 242-249.

60. Bowles and Gintis, *Schooling in Capitalist America.*

61. B. C. Rosen, "The Achievement Syndrome . . .", pp. 203-211; and "Race, Ethnicity, and the Achievement Syndrome", pp. 47-60.

62. N. J. Davis, *Deviance.*

63. *Work in America*, pp. 77-79.

64. Berliner, "Emerging Ideologies in Medicine", p. 118.

65. Ryan, *Blaming the Victim*, p. 7.

66. Navarro, "The Crisis of the Western System of Medicine . . .", p. 206.

67. Berliner, "Emerging Ideologies in Medicine", p. 119.

68. Navarro, *Medicine Under Capitalism*, p. 207.

69. R. Crawford, "You Are Dangerous to Your Health . . .", pp. 663-680.

Readings

Berliner, Howard S., "Emerging Ideologies in Medicine," *The Review of Radical Political Economics*, Vol. 9, No. 1, (Spring 1977).

Berliner, Howard, "A Large Perspective on the Flexner Report," *International Journal of Health Services*, Vol. 5, (1975).

Blackburn, R. (ed.), *Ideology in Social Science*, New York: Random House, 1973.

Bosquet, M., *Capitalism in Crisis and Everyday Life*, Harvest Press, Sussex: 1977.

Bowles, Samuel and Herbert Gintis, *Schooling in Capitalist America*, Basic Books, 1977.

Brenner, M. Harvey, "Economic Changes and Heart Disease Mortality," *American Journal of Public Health*, Vol. 61, (1971).

Cairns, J., "The Cancer Problem," *Scientific American*, Vol. 233, No. 18, (1975).

Cassels, Derek, "Minamata", *The Medical Post*, (September 30, 1975).

Chinoy, E., *Automobile Workers and The American Dream*, New York: Doubleday and Company, 1955.

Coburn, David, "Job-Worker Incongruence: Consequences for Health", *Journal of Health and Social Behavior*, Vol. 16, (1975).

Coburn, David, "Work and General Psychological and Physical Well-Being," *International Journal of Health Services*, Vol. 8, No. 3, (1978).

Crawford, Robert, "You are Dangerous to Your Health: The Ideology and Politics of Victim Blaming," *International Journal of Health Services*, Vol. 7, No. 4, (1977).

Davis, Kingsley and Wilbert E. Moore, "Some Principles of Stratification," *American Sociological Review*, Vol. 10, (April, 1945).

Davis, Nanette J., *Deviance*, Dubuque, Iowa: Wm. C. Brown Company, 1975.

Drietzel, Hans Peter (ed.), *The Social Organizations of Health*, New York: MacMillan Company, 1971.

Dubos, R., *Man, Medicine and Environment*, Harmondsworth: Penguin Books, 1968.

Ehrenreich, Bauhava et. al., "Health Care and Social Control," *Social Policy*, (May-June, 1974).

Eyer, Joseph, "Hypertension as a Disease of Modern Society", *International Journal of Health Services*, Vol. 5, (1975).

Eyer, Joseph, "Prosperity As A Cause of Death," *International Journal of Health Services*, Vol. 7, No. 1, (1977).

Eyer, Joseph and Peter Sterling, "Stress-Related Mortality and Social Organization," *The Review of Radical Political Economics*, Vol. 9, No. 1, (Spring, 1977).

Fee, Elizabeth, "Women and Health Care: A Comparison of Theories", in Vincente

Navarro (ed.), *Health and Medical Care in the U.S.: A Critical Analysis*, New York: Baywood Pub. Co., Inc., 1977.

Fuchs, Victor, "Health Care and the United States Economic System", *Milbank Memorial Fund Quarterly*, Vol. 50 (2, Part 1), (1972).

Fuchs, Victor, *Who Shall Live?*, New York: Basic Books, 1974.

Greenberg, D. S., and J. E. Randal, "Waging the Wrong War on Cancer," *Washington Post*, (May 1, 1977).

Hammond, E. C., "Epidemiologic Basis For Cancer Prevention," *Cancer*, Vol. 33, No. 6, (1974).

Handing, J., N. Wolf and G. Chan, "A Socio-Demographic Profile of People Being Prescribed Mood-Modifying Drugs in Saskatchewan", Regina: Alcoholism Commission of Saskatchewan, November, 1977.

Illich, Ivan, *Medical Nemisis: The Expropriation of Health*, New York: Pantheon, 1976.

Katz, R. L., "Drug Therapy: Sedatives and Tranquilizers", *New England Journal of Medicine*, Vol. 286, (1972).

Kotelchuk, David (ed.), *Prognosis Negative: Crisis in the Health Care System*, New York: Vintage, 1976.

Laing, R. D., *The Politics of Experience and the Bird of Paradise*, Harmondsworth: Penguin Books, 1970.

Lalonde, Marc, *A New Perspective on the Health of Canadians*, Ottawa: Information Canada, 1974.

Lewis, Oscar, *La Vida*, New York: Random House, 1966.

McClelland, D., *The Achieving Society*, New York: Free Press, 1961.

McDonald, Marie, "Massacre at Grassy Narrows", *Maclean's*, (October 20, 1975).

McKeon, T., *Medicine in Modern Society*, London: Allen & Unwin, 1965.

Matanoski, G., "Lung Cancer by Census Tract in the City of Baltimore", *The Review of Radical Political Economics*, Vol. 9, No. 1, (Spring 1977).

Miller, A., "The Wages of Neglect: Death and Disease in the American Work Place", *American Journal of Public Health*, Vol.65, No. 11, (1975).

"Miller Fed Up", *Globe and Mail*, (October 16, 1975).

Miller, Lawrence G., "Negative Therapeutics", *Social Science and Medicine*, Vol. 5, (1975).

Moore, Steve, *Mercury Poisoning, Native People and Reed Paper Company*, Toronto Alliance Against Racism and Political Repression, Pamphlet No. 1.

Navarro, Vincente, "The Crises of the Western System of Medicine in Contemporary Capitalism", *International Journal of Health Services*, Vol. 8, No. 2, (1978).

Navarro, Vincente (ed), *Health and Medical Care in the U.S.: A Critical Analysis*, New York: Baywood Publishing Company, 1977.

Navarro, Vincente, *Medicine Under Capitalism*, New York: Prodist, 1976.

Nelson, Randle W. and David A. Nock, (eds.), *Reading, Writing and Riches*, [n.p.], Between the Lines, 1978.

O'Connor, James, *The Fiscal Crisis of the State*, New York: St. Martin's Press, 1973.

"Political Economy and Health", Special Issue, *The Review of Radical Political Economics*, Vol. 9, No. 1, (Spring 1977).

Powels, J., "On the Limitations of Modern Medicine," *Science, Medicine and Man*, 1973.

Renaud, Marc, "On the Structural Constraints to State Intervention in Health", *International Journal of Health Services*, Vol. 5, No. 4, (1975).

Rinehart, James W., *The Tyranny of Work*, Don Mills: Longman Canada, 1975.

Rosen, Bernard C., "The Achievement Syndrome: A Psychocultural Dimension of Social Stratification", *American Sociological Review* Vol. 21: (1956)

Rosen, Bernard C., "Race, Ethnicity, and the Achievement Syndrome," *American Sociological Review*, Vol. 24: (1959).

Ryan, William, *Blaming the Victim*, New York: Vintage Books, 1971.

Special Senate Committee on Poverty, *Poverty in Canada*, Ottawa: 1971.

Stroufe, L. A., M. A. Stewart, "Treating Children with Stimulant Drugs", *New England Journal of Medicine*, Vol. 289, (1973).

Szasz, T., *Myths of Mental Illness*, New York: Harper and Row, 1961.

Turshen, Meredith, "The Political Ecology of Disease", *The Review of Radical Political Economies*, Vol. 9, No. 1, (Spring, 1977).

Waldron, "Increased Prescribing of Valium, Librium, and other Drugs — An Example of the Influence of Economic and Social Factors on the Practice of Medicine", *International Journal of Health Services*, Vol. 7, No. 1, (1977).

Work in America, Cambridge, Mass.: M.I.T. Press, 1973.

Multinational Corporations and Canadian Food Policy

Harold E. Bronson

HAROLD E. BRONSON is an Assistant Professor
of Economics at the University of Saskatchewan.
His current research interests include Canadian
Agricultural Policy and Political Economy.

The rapid increase in Canadian retail food prices which began in
1972, and the subsequent intensification of the cost-price squeeze on
farmers, have led to renewed interest in the degree of responsibility
which should be attributed to farm suppliers, food processors and
food distributors. Since government policy, or lack of policy, is
involved in this question, the influence of these groups on governments is of particular concern.

Estimation of that influence requires identification of the most
powerful firms affecting the food system, followed by an examination
of the mechanisms which enable them to consolidate and strengthen
their control. Such a study requires inclusion of both corporate and
political interactions.

The Food Multinationals

Table 1 shows the 20 top multinational corporations (MNCs)[1]
involved in Canadian food and agriculture (ranked in order of sales
volume). Immediately it will be evident that their connections extend
beyond food and agriculture to the economy in general. In fact, the
first ten in this listing are among the top 20 of all non-Soviet industrial
and commercial enterprises in 1976.[2]

The prominence of oil and automotive companies in the list reflects
the importance of energy and machinery as components of food
production costs. Petroleum for fuel and lubricants accounted for 11.4
percent of all 1976 farm operating and depreciation costs in
Saskatchewan. All machinery costs, including operation, deprecia-

tion and repairs, added up to 33.4 percent of total costs (Statistics Canada, *Farm Net Income*). These facts are a reminder that in considering the role of the MNCs in the food industry, we are concerned with enterprises which are in a position to exert influence throughout the economy.

In addition to suppliers of energy and transportation, the selection of MNCs in Table 1 includes those providing most of the fertilizer, weedkillers and insecticides to Canadian farmers; together with those involved in processing and distributing the food products. Not listed are firms such as department stores, which include food and related items as a minor part of total sales. Also omitted are firms predominantly concerned with tobacco, beverages and pet foods.

TABLE 1
DOMINANT MULTINATIONAL CORPORATIONS INVOLVED IN
CANADIAN FOOD PRODUCTION AND DISTRIBUTION

	"Parent" Country	1976 Sales ($ millions)
1. Exxon (Imperial Oil)	U.S.	$48,631
2. General Motors	U.S.	47,181
3. Ford	U.S.	28,840
4. Texaco	U.S.	26,452
5. Mobil	U.S.	26,063
6. Gulf Oil	U.S.	16,451
7. Unilever	Britain	15,762
8. Chrysler	U.S.	15,538
9. International Tel. & Tel.	U.S.	11,764
10. Cargill[a]	U.S.	10,800
11. Safeway	U.S.	10,443
12. Shell Oil	U.S.	9,230
13. Du Pont	U.S.	8,361
14. Nestle	Switzerland	7,628
15. Imperial Chemical Ind.	Britain	7,465
16. Continental Grain[a]	U.S.	7,000
17. Procter & Gamble	U.S.	6,513
18. Tenneco	U.S.	6,389
19. International Harvester	U.S.	5,488
20. Essmark (Swift Canadian)	U.S.	5,301

Sources: *Fortune*, May, 1977; *Forbes*, May 15, 1977; Dun & Bradstreet, *Million Dollar Directory*, 1976.

[a]Cargill and Continental Grain are private companies and usually avoid public disclosure of their finances. Dun & Bradstreet show only their U.S. sales, but they both have large European and Latin American subsidiaries. Private information and legal investigations have enabled researchers at the North American Congress on Latin American (NACLA) to estimate their total sales as shown above. The Cargill figure is for the year ending May 31, 1976.

In a few cases, the connection between listed firms and the food and agriculture industries may not be clear. IT&T has extended its operations to include Wonderbread, Hostess Cakes[3] Continental Baking Co., and Morton frozen foods. Unilever has interests in tea and frozen foods. Tenneco has connections with the J.I. Case farm machinery enterprise and is also in fertilizers and packaging, as well as operating 86,000 acres of farmland. Du Pont produces weed killers, seed protectants and animal feed supplements. Procter and Gamble products include shortenings, oils, cake mixes, peanut butter, potato chips, coffee and animal feeds. ICI supplies fertilizers, insecticides and fungicides.[4]

Some firms which are clearly involved in one sector of food production, processing or distribution may also be integrating into other sectors. General Motors, the price leader in car and truck marketing[5] has become prominently connected with farm machinery through a subsidiary, White Motor Co., which controls the Oliver, Minneapolis-Moline and Cockshutt brands. Exxon (Imperial) not only leads the oil industry, but is also into fertilizers. And it has a wholly-owned "venture-capital" subsidiary which provides funds to approved enterprises, especially those which are developing new forms of energy (*Forbes,* Oct. 15/77).

In view of the widespread tendency to identify Canadian firms as the main culprits in the mistreatment of farmers and consumers, it is useful to compare the sales volumes of these firms with those of the leaders in Table 1. As well, the position of some smaller, but well known foreign firms may be of interest. Table 2 provides some examples, beginning with the largest Canadian MNC, George Weston Ltd., whose sales volume in 1976 was less than one-tenth of Exxon's.

TABLE 2
SOME LESSER BUT WELL-KNOWN FIRMS INVOLVED IN CANADIAN
FOOD PRODUCTION AND DISTRIBUTION

	"Parent" Country	1976 Sales ($ millions)
George Weston Ltd.	Canada	$4,345
Canadian Pacific	Canada	4,002
McDonald's	U.S.	3,063
Massey-Ferguson	Canada	2,695
Carnation	U.S.	2,167
Dominion Stores[a]	Canada	2,026
Campbell Soup	U.S.	1,636
Canada Packers	Canada	1,701
Del Monte	U.S.	1,430
Int. Multifoods (Robin Hood)	U.S.	847
Burns Foods	Canada	722

Sources: *Fortune,* May, 1977; *Financial Post 300,* Summer, 1977. For a more detailed discussion of foreign and Canadian MNCs in Canada's food industry, see John W. Warnock, *Profit Hungry,* Vancouver, New Star Books, 1978, especially Ch. 1.

[a] Wallace Clement has pointed out that by the 1930s, Dominion was one of the few important retailers in Canada that was not subsidiary to a foreign company. But nevertheless, it had 71 percent of its shares held in the U.S. (*Continental Corporate Power,* Toronto, McClelland & Stewart, 1977, p. 76.)

The vulnerability and weakness of the smaller "Canadian" MNCs is indicated by the experience of Weston in 1977. That firm was obliged to shut down 250 stores in the Chicago area after losing $28 million on them in that year. This "surgery" meant losing nearly 20 percent of the Weston wholesale and retail structure. Furthermore, Weston's subsidiary, Loblaw's, had to sell all of its common stock in Tamblyn Drugs as a result of losses in competition with U.S. drug chains. (*Financial Times*, May 2, 1977). The Loblaw supermarkets were also fighting a losing battle in Western Canada against the dominant Safeway chain.

Another "Canadian" MNC, Massey-Ferguson, has also shown vulnerability in a world dominated by the U.S. industrial-financial combinations. M-F entered 1978 showing losses and plummeting share values. During that year it continued to lose money at an average rate of a $½ million a day. (A high debt-equity ratio was identified as a major weakness. See *Financial Times*, September 18, 1978).

The Basis of Corporate Power

The above observations support a preliminary assumption that corporate economic and political power is directly related to size (which is most readily compared on the basis of sales volume). The decisive factor providing that influence seems to be an extension of what J. S. Bain has referred to as "pecuniary economies" of scale, which arise from the lower buying prices attainable by a multi-plant firm through its "bulk-buying power" (Bain, 1968: 170). The definition should be extended to include the coercive power which can be exerted by such a firm against its smaller rivals.

That development of pecuniary economies is facilitated by the extension of interlocking directorates, which often help to integrate some enterprises which seem to be Canadian-controlled with U.S. industrial-financial policy-making. Referring to the "U.S. stake in Canada's largest industrial companies", *Fortune* (August, 1976) concluded that Canadians "'control' even less of these companies than the numbers indicate". Some shares, it was noted, "are owned by investors who are neither Canadian or American". And the American ownership figures "represent shares owned by the U.S. parent, and do not include stock in the hands of other private investors".

In other words, a fragmented distribution of shares in Canada increases the ability of U.S. firms to exercise control with considerably less than 50 percent of the voting shares.[6] And extension of that control to entire industries is often possible.

That process is facilitated by the relatively high and increasing degree of industrial concentration in Canada. A 1977 report has shown that the largest four firms then controlled 77 percent of sales in supermarkets, 75.7 percent in convenience store outlets, 90 percent in breakfast cereals, and 77 percent in flour milling. Four of 170 fruit and vegetable companies accounted for 40 percent of sales, and four slaughtering and meat processors controlled 54 percent.[7] High concentration is also evident in farm machinery, fuel and fertilizers.

Aggregate concentration ratios were shown in a Statistics Canada study released early in 1978, which showed that out of 29,812 companies engaged in mining, manufacturing and forestry in 1972, 100 enterprises accounted for 46 percent of all the business activity. Of those 100, 66 were foreign-controlled. Among the next 100 companies, 74 percent were foreign controlled. The study also showed that on the average, foreign-controlled enterprises were much larger than Canadian-owned companies in the same industry, and that they were more diversified, and participated in more industries and multi-plant operations.

The supermarket structure in Western Canada provides an important example of the economic influence achievable in a highly concentrated industry by a dominant firm — in this case Safeway Stores of Oakland, California. Safeway's strength is derived from its international array (in 1974) of 2,838 stores in five countries (271 in Canada). It has recognized as dominant in the prairies and B.C. by both the Batten Report (1968)[8] and the Mallen Report (1976). Mallen showed Safeway with 248 of the 448 supermarkets in the prairies and B.C. in 1973.

Safeway is also an example of the extensive integration which the largest corporations have built up among suppliers, processors, distributors and financial institutions. It owns dairies, processing plants, bakeries and wholesale enterprises, including Lucerne Foods, Empress Foods, and Macdonald's Consolidated. It has directorship interlocks which include Del Monte, Caterpillar Tractor, Southern Pacific and J. G. Boswell Farms in California. Links have been identified between Safeway and three major U.S. banks, including Chase Manhattan.[9] With such backing, Safeway's dominance in Western Canada and its beginning penetration of the East is not surprising; nor is its success in driving its largest Canadian rival, Dominion Stores, out of Calgary and Edmonton.[10]

Similar control by dominant U.S. firms has been identified in the farm machinery industry. Before the sharp price increases of the 1970s, the Royal Commission on Farm Machinery had made the following assessment of that industry (where it found, in 1967, that the four largest firms, Deere, Ford, International Harvester and Massey-Ferguson supplied 68 percent of all the tractors sold, by value). "Tractor prices on the North American continent," it reported, "appear to be set by the two firms with the largest share of the market, International Harvester and Deere".[11]

Furthermore, the high price and profit levels maintained by these two firms enabled many smaller ones to stay in operation, with lower net returns. One result was highly inefficient output levels by most firms. The Commission's cost studies led to the conclusion that: "Between 5 and 10 firms of an efficient size could easily produce all the tractors currently sold in the non-Communist world. In fact, some 20 to 30 firms are now producing tractors in significant volume" (Report, 1969:96). Consequently, a cost saving of over 20 percent could have been achieved by firms advancing from 20,000 units to 90,000 (Report, 1969: 61.)

Yet some firms producing tractors were staying in business with annual outputs of 20,000 units. This meant that firms with larger outputs were making excess profits. For five tractor models in 1968, 67 percent of the extra price charged in North America, compared with Britain, reflected higher costs, and 33 percent represented higher profits. (Reports, 1969: 91.) And the Commission pointed out an additional adverse effect for Canada, namely, that all tractors sold here, except the large Versatiles, were manufactured in the U.S. (Report, 1969:14).

The Measurement of Corporate Power

The fact that conditions such as the above have been tolerated in Canada indicates the need to investigate the extent of MNC influence over government. To measure that influence with precision is a complex task, as shown in a study by Peter Mariolis entitled "Interlocking Directorates and Control of Corporations: the Theory of Bank Control" (*Social Science Quarterly*, December, 1975). In his paper, Mariolis compared several studies, paying special attention to the theory of bank control through stock ownership and corporate dependence on external financing. He also considered data concerning director interlocks among 797 financial and non-financial corporations.

The theory of bank control was neither disproved nor strongly supported in his study. It indicated the need for further examination of the role of insurance companies. But Mariolis concluded that the pervasiveness of interlocking directorates, and the resulting "high degree of cohesiveness" found among the larger corporations give continued support to a "minimum inference" made in 1965 by C. Wright Mills (*The Power Elite*, (1965:23.)

> 'Interlocking directorate' is no mere phrase: it points to a solid feature of the facts of business life, and to a sociological anchor of the community of interest, the unification of outlooks and policy, that prevails among the propertied class. . . . As a minimum inference, it must be said that such arrangements permit an interchange of views in

a convenient and more or less formal way among those who share the interests of the corporate rich.

In examining the extensive interlocking between Canadian and U.S. corporations, Wallace Clement emphasized that "the financial sector in Canada is the main source of origin for interlocks with U.S. dominants, accounting for almost half of all these interlocks". He indentified Calgary Power, MacMillan-Bloedel, Sun Life and Brascan as companies with three such interlocks; Toronto-Dominion Bank, Canada Life and Bell Canada with four; Canadian Pacific and Power Corporation with five. "Particularly active" were the Canadian Imperial Bank of Commerce and Trans-Canada Pipelines with seven each, and the Royal Bank with nine links to U.S. dominants (Clement, *Continental Corporate Power,* 1977:176).

It is usually contended that Canadian banks, with their legal requirements as to Canadian ownership, are thus one cornerstone of the country's independence. That assumption has little support in fact. The consistent endorsement of continentalism by these banks was typified in a statement by G. H. Eaton, president of the Canadian Commercial and Industrial Bank. He praised the anticipated Bank Act changes which would result in an estimated 45 to 65 foreign banks being established in Canada. "You cannot be a nationalist with respect to the affairs of money," Eaton said. (Saskatoon *Star-Phoenix,* October 8, 1977).

The Concentration of Corporate Power

Adding to the Mariolis study of corporate-financial interlocks was a 1973 U.S. Senate Study, "Disclosure of Corporate Ownership", which gave more prominence to the concept of bank domination. The study analyzed voting stockholders in 324 leading corporations and banks, and concluded that control was held primarily by eight institutions. These were: Morgan Guaranty Trust (New York); Bankers Trust Co. (New York); First National City Bank (New York); Chase Manhattan Bank (New York); Bank of New York; State Street Bank Trust Co. (Boston); Merrill Lynch, Pierce, Fenner & Smith; and Cede Company[12] (wholly owned by the New York Stock Exchange).

The 1973 Senate study concluded that the eight financial institutions listed had control not only of the 89 companies which reported fully, but also of the 177 corporations which replied only partially.[13] The corporations which made no reply included some of the biggest: Exxon, General Motors, Texaco, IBM, IT&T, General Foods, Aluminum Co. of America, and Morgan Guaranty Bank of New York.

Even if the eight financial institutions identified by the Senate study were not dominant, but merely supported and co-ordinated the 324 corporations under study,[14] they obviously constituted a focal point for a formidable concentration of economic and political power, with wide international connections. Referring to the 1,894 U.S. born and resident members of the economic elite with dominant director-ships in that country,[15] Clement found that 46 percent had multi-nationals as their main corporate affiliation, while only 24 percent had no connection with the MNCs (Clement, *Continental Corporate Power*:252). He also found that 7.3 percent of these directors held at least one Canadian post (Clement, *Continental Corporate Power*:253).

The main control mechanisms in the U.S. have been investigated by G. William Domhoff, who has concluded that "the owners and managers of large banks and corporations, with a little bit of help from their hired academics, lawyers and public relations people, dominate everything in this country that is worth dominating" (Domhoff, *Insurgent Sociologist*, No. 5, 1975.)

As to their international control, Domhoff observed that it was being co-ordinated by organizations such as the Council on Foreign Relations, the Council of the Americas and the Trilateral Commission. Economic directives were the function of the Conference Board, the Committee for Economic Development and the Brookings Institute. The Ford Foundation, three Carnegie Foundations and the Carnegie Council for Policy Studies in Higher Education were found dominant in that field. Domhoff concluded that: "Every one of these organiza-tions is financed and directed by the same few thousand men who run the major banks and corporations" (*Insurgent Sociologist*, No. 5, 1975).

The Trilateral Commission, described as "one of the most influen-tial organizations in the world" (*Maclean's*, October 17, 1977), has emerged as a key centre of international influence. It was set up in 1973 entirely at the initiative of David Rockefeller of the Chase Manhattan Bank. Its first objective was the improvement of relations between the U.S., Europe and Japan (hence the name "Trilateral"). Those relations had suffered as a result of Nixon's 1971 and 1973 devaluations of the dollar. But as *Monthly Review* has shown, the Trilateral's main task is to protect U.S. foreign investment.[16]

An obviously related example of that protection occurred in 1975 when a right-wing coup overthrew the radical Velasco government in Peru. Velasco had nationalized a Rockefeller oil subsidiary. After his overthrow, the new junta quickly reversed that legislation. Within one year, as reported by Shepherd Bliss, "the Peruvian economy was totally in the hands of a consortium of U.S. banks headed by Chase Manhattan" (*Guardian*, New York, November 17, 1976).

The Trilateral developed under 250 "Western" corporate and political leaders, including top officers of Fiat, Toyota, Caterpillar, the

Bank of America, Exxon, the Bank of Tokyo, Coca-Cola, Deere and Cargill. The Secretary-Treasurer of the AFL-CIO, and G.S. Franklin, an assistant to Nelson Rockefeller, were also members.

Initially, Canada had 12 members on the Trilateral, including R. W. Bonner, former chairman of MacMillan Bloedel; Jean-Luc Pepin; Doris Anderson, former editor of Chatelaine; and Alan Hockin, the executive vice-president of the Toronto-Dominion bank. When Pepin took on a position on the Anti-Inflation Board, he was replaced on the Trilateral by Mitchell Sharp, who became chairman of the commission's North American division. Early in 1978, the Canadian contingent was expanded to 15 with the addition of Donald Macdonald, just retired from the federal finance portfolio; John Fraser, the PC member for Vancouver South, and Donald Harvie, the deputy chairman of Petro-Canada (CP, Ottawa, March 13, 1978.)

The incorporation of Canadians into the Trilateral appears to have been a consolidation of Canada's "special status" in the U.S. "sphere of influence". As John Hutcheson has pointed out, that "status" began in 1940 with the Permanent Joint Board of Defence, and continued through NATO and NORAD. The U.S. demand for Canadian mobilization under these pacts during the Cuban missile crisis of 1962 was a major factor in the Conservative party split which defeated John Diefenbaker. It revealed that the Canadian government had "virtually lost ultimate authority over its own military forces". Diefenbaker's Secretary of State for External Affairs, H. C. Green, argued in vain that "if we go along with the Americans now we'll be their vassals forever".[17]

Alan Hockin, the Toronto-Dominion representative on the Trilateral, has been quoted as saying that Canadians see the organization as "an educating body", while "people like Rockefeller . . . see the commission having a direct influence on government decision-making" (Maclean's, October 17, 1977). Actually, in practice, both functions seemed to be accepted by the commission. Following the initiative of David Rockefeller, it recommended then Governor Jimmy Carter as "an ideal politician to build on". Zbigniew Brzezinski, a Trilateral director, originally described Carter as "educable". Brzezinski's appointment "was one of the first Carter made on coming to office" (Maclean's, October 17, 1977; April 17, 1978.)

With Carter established as president, more than normal interest was aroused by the array of Trilateralists in his cabinet, including Vice-President Walter Mondale, Secretary of State Cyrus Vance, Treasury Secretary W. M. Blumenthal, Defense Secretary Harold Brown, and U.N. representative Andrew Young. Brzezinski, not surprisingly, became National Security Adviser.[18]

The Application of Corporate Power

David Rockefeller subsequently indicated that he regarded the Canadian government as educable. Speaking to the Canadian Club early in 1978, he praised "a renewed vitality in Canadian-American relations" on many fronts, including trade, energy and public-private sector co-operation. He warned, however, that this could be undermined by Quebec seperatism. Uncertainty, he warned, could cause investors to react adversely.

But he praised the restraint policies of the Bank of Canada and federal restrictions on spending and on social programmes, all of which were raising Canadian unemployment while U.S. rates declined (CP, Toronto, February 4, 1978). At the same time, U.S. trade policies were resulting in a decline of the Canadian dollar relative to the American, thus causing sharp increases in the prices of Canadian imports, including fruit and vegetables.

Rockefeller also questioned the criticisms of MNCs "made in the name of the liberal tradition". The critics were showing "most illiberal ideas" by resisting "the growing internationalism and economic co-operation" promoted by the MNCs. Such "natural forces" should be freed of "crippling constraints" that will "diminish their influence and their capacity to lift the levels of world prosperity". All of this reflected "a distrust of free enterprise and the free market economy". He called for "a true world economy" and for policies which would let the MNCs "get on with this unfinished business".[19]

These circumstances indicate that influencing the political process, up to and including the selection of the U.S. president, is a matter of primary concern to the industrial-financial elite. Adept public relations, and awareness of the limits to public tolerance may induce manipulators like the Trilateralists to accept some token expressions of independence by political leaders.[20] Predictably, these turn out to be empty gestures. Witness, for example, the regular support for agricultural products marketing boards shown by Eugene Whelan, Canada's Agricultural Minister, in face of general opposition from the remainder of the cabinet and the Consumer's Association of Canada. But Whelan has also shown attitudes which are consistent with U.S. plans to control North American food exports as part of that nation's global power struggle.

Corporate-financial influence over political leaders has been further identified in the Canadian context by Eric Kierans, a former cabinet minister under Trudeau. In 1977 he asserted that the important economic decisions in Canada are being made by 311 corporations, 60 percent of which are foreign owned, and which earn almost half of the annual taxable income reported by all business. The government, he said, has put the country's destiny in the hands of multinational corporations.

He observed that the policy of switching cabinet ministers and deputy ministers every year or two was creating ideal conditions for the MNCs to get their way. "If you are the president of Imperial Oil," he explained, "nothing would be better than having a new energy minister every two or three years. You take the new minister to lunch and tell him what the score is" (*Daily Gleaner*, Fredericton, June 11, 1977). By thus focusing on the key Imperial Oil-Exxon-Rockefeller connection, Kierans seemed to indicate that even among the 311 dominant corporations, power was not distributed evenly.[21]

What Imperial Oil could do as an agent of Exxon-Rockefeller policy was indicated in the case of the Syncrude tar sands project. Taking advantage of a "crisis" caused by the withdrawal of one Syncrude partner, Atlantic Richfield, the Syncrude consortium, led by Imperial-Exxon, issued an ultimatum to the governments most directly concerned (Alberta, Ontario and Ottawa). In two weeks (by January 31, 1975) the project would be shut down unless these governments produced $1 billion in equity capital, together with exemptions from the new federal tax on formerly deductible provincial royalties. Furthermore, oil prices were to be allowed to rise until they reached world levels.

The three governments capitulated. They accepted a reorganization of Syncrude in which their combined shareholding would be 30 percent. They also put up commitments of equity, tax concessions and loans estimated to total $1,472 million, or 75 percent of the capital cost. Imperial received a share ownership increase from 30 to 31.25 percent, ensuring that company a margin of control over the three governments.[22]

The governments' commitments involved acceptance of company cost estimates for Syncrude, which had risen from $500 million late in 1972 to $2 billion by the end of 1974.[23] The then federal Minister of Energy, Mines and Resources, Donald Macdonald, admitted that he had "no real information to cross check" these cost increases. The government was "virtually dependent on the major international companies for its sources of information", he admitted.

There is every indication that even greater cost estimates will be made by the oil industry in the future. In completing the Alaska pipeline, the oil cartel's estimates increased from an original $1 billion in 1969 to $8 billion on completion in 1977. Combined with an added charge of $1.3 billion for interest during construction, this amounted to a 930 percent increase, which was described by the U.S. Bureau of Investigation and Enforcement as probably "the largest cost overrun in the history of a private business venture" (*Globe & Mail*, June 25, 1977).

That record may not last long, however. Preliminary demands on governments by Imperial-Exxon for another tar sands plant are already in the range of $4 billion, or double the amount set for Syncrude in 1975. In a report on the proposed project at Cold Lake, Alberta quoted Imperial as seeking an adaptation of Alberta's coal development fiscal formula, which involved special tax treatment. Imperial was also seeking exemption from prorationing, together with an Ottawa guarantee of access to world prices for the crude oil produced (*Globe & Mail*, December 6, 1977).

Do governments in Canada yield to MNC demands, as in the Syncrude case, because of economic or political threats, or because of inducements?[24] Do they submit as a result of coercion or through voluntary conformity to ideological guidelines? These questions cannot be answered indisputably. But in any event, the results support Clement's conclusion that for the dominant Canadian commercial and financial interests, "continued prosperity is now predicated on the ascendancy of the United States" (Clement, *Continental Corporate Power*: 291).

The Impact on Food Costs

The oil price increases allowed under the Syncrude formula have been of particular importance in the agricultral sector, where they add directly to the costs, not only of fuel, but also of petroleum-based fertilizers. To the extent that marketing boards enable such costs to be passed on, they add to the consumer's food bill, while compensating subsidies pass the burden on to the taxpayers.[25] The cost increases which remain to be borne by agriculture help to force financially insecure farmers off the land. (Rising fuel costs are also a major problem in that other major food producing area — the fishing industry).

The advance of the MNCs in the marketing sector also produces serious cost problems. Foremost in the marketing sector is the Cargill Grain Company of Minneapolis (see Table 1). Cargill, together with Continental Grain of New York, is in control of 50 percent of the world's international grain trade. Of particular interest to Western Canadians is the 1974 purchase by Cargill of 268 local elevators and a grain terminal from the National Grain Co. Further, Cargill has taken the lead in building "high throughput" elevators at Rosetown, Saskatchewan and Elm Creek, Manitoba, and has entered into a grain marketing contract with the farmer-owned Weyburn "inland terminal". In 1977 Cargill announced plans to build a network of high throughput elevators on the prairies in competition with the Wheat Pools.

Cargill, and other U.S. grain companies, expanded into a Canadian elevator system where excess capacity was already a problem. As expressed by Del Pound of the Canadian Grain Commission, the "chronic lack of profitability" in the system could only be resolved if the elevators could handle more bushels. Otherwise, handling charges would have to go up considerably. But since costs were rising rapidly, even increased volume would not be a final answer. As Pound concluded: ". . . Unless there is a total industry move to close down, say, half the elevators in Western Canada, there is little prospect of increasing efficiency significantly".[26]

Similarly, information supplied to the Saskatchewan Association of Rural Municipalities in Regina indicated that savings from a more centralized elevator system would be "minimized" if several companies set up at each delivery point. Instead, the most efficient system for the producer would be one elevator at each delivery point (CP, Regina, July 30, 1977).

In Saskatchewan, the Wheat Pool already had long range plans for a system of 500 high throughput elevators. Assuming conservatively that these would have an annual average throughput capacity of two million bushels, they could handle a total of one billion bushels. (Saskatchewan's production of all grains in 1976, an above average year, was 818 million bushels).

Evidently, a Cargill network in competition with the Pools at most delivery points would have created much excess capacity. Unless the higher unit costs were covered by greatly increased handling charges, there would be a struggle for survival in which Cargill would have the advantage. It is supported by 30 to 40 banks. including the First National Bank of Chicago and the First National Bank of Minneapolis. The "lead bank" for Cargill and for the whole U.S. grain industry is David Rockefeller's Chase Manhattan, which maintains close touch with Cargill in all its major financial moves.

Much of the company's grain inventory financing is done through these banks. For fixed assets such as elevators and terminals, it can rely on major insurance companies, as well as federal and state funds. Its international trade is strongly supported by subsidies from the U.S. Public Law 480 and by government lending programmes.[27]

Such are the financial and political resources which Cargill can mobilize in its economic "competition" with the Wheat Pools on the Canadian prairies. Most significant is its connection with the Trilateral Commission through its close contact with Vice-President Walter Mondale and the Chase Manhattan Bank. This indicates that like Imperial Oil (Exxon), Cargill can exert strong influence on Canadian politicians.

One of the Cargill objectives which is seen sympathetically by the Ottawa government is the advancement of the "user pays" principle to replace the Crow's Nest Pass freight rates on grain. In Vol. 2 of a federally commissioned report on transportation, Carl Snavely strongly advocated such a move, although Transport Minister Otto Lang, facing an election in 1978, admitted only that: "We commissioned it (the report) . . . and we put it out to get the reaction".

Following the release of Snavely's second volume, the senior vice-president of Cargill Grain (Canada) renewed the company's attack on the Crow Rates. He was reported to have told Alberta poultry producers that he had persuaded some senior government officials in Alberta and Manitoba that it would be worth considering the abandonment of the Crow Rates in those provinces (*Union Farmer*, March, 1978).

According to a Regina survey, abolition of the Crow Rates would cost prairie farmers an estimated $250 million a year. Also it would give railways the ability to charge relatively higher rates on less profitable lines, thus causing abandonment of some delivery points. "This tactic, coupled with the presence of large inland terminals, will force farmers to haul to the terminals . . .", while the resulting closure of local elevators "will have a serious negative impact on the nature and viability of rural life and small towns".[28]

Cargill must approve of this process because it is favourable to the company's present and planned high throughput system. Such developments could well lead to confirmation of the fears expressed by Saskatchewan Agriculture Minister Edgar Kaeding with reference to the fact that ten vertically integrated firms now control the entire North American poultry industry. These conglomerate operations, he said, ". . . are a warning that all other parts of farming may head on the same route" (*Free Press Report on Farming*, July 13, 1978). He subsequently warned at the University of Saskatchewan that: "In the U.S., 50 percent of agricultural production is grown on land which is owned by multinational agribusiness corporations" (*The Sheaf*, January 17, 1978).

Food as a Weapon

The route described by Kaeding is the one along which Canada is being taken by political leadership which accepts the guidance of manipulated "market" forces. That means dominance by those with the greatest financial resources. It also means that U.S.-based corporations will continue to grow at the expense of smaller, Canadian firms.

There is disagreement as to whether American MNCs dominate or serve that nation. But it is more important to determine the objectives pursued by that corporate-government combination. The U.S., in seeking to preserve and expand its neo-colonial empire, must depend on the multinationals to maintain economic control and to promote the political strategies necessary to protect its interests. Conversely, the MNCs must depend on their "home" nation for taxpayer support, for banking support, and in the final analysis for intelligence, "destabilization" and military support, if they are to remain secure in foreign ventures.

The U.S. national-corporate struggle to survive and expand takes place in confrontation with the Soviet Union, which advances against American interests in every continent. As these two superpowers compete in a world where most of the people are constantly close to hunger and starvation, each must recognize the potential power in concentrated control of exportable food. U.S. spokesmen have openly expressed determination to use that power.

At the 1974 World Food Conference in Rome, U.S. Secretary of Agriculture Earl Butz proclaimed that: "Food is a tool. It is a weapon in the U.S. negotiating kit". The Central Intelligence Agency has observed that the U.S. "near-monopoly" position as a food exporter "could give the U.S. a measure of power it never had before — possibly an economic and political dominance greater than that of the immediate post-World War II years. . . . Washington would acquire virtual life and death power over the fate of multitudes of the needy" (CIA Office of Policy Research, August, 1974).

Possibly the crudest actual use of the food weapon was in Chile before the coup which overthrew the regime of Salvador Allende in September, 1973. To weaken that regime, the U.S. cut off food credits to Chile, and just before the coup, as "a political decision of the White House", it refused cash sales of wheat to Chile. Those tactics were combined with sabotage of domestic food production by landowners opposing the government. Another major example occurred in Bangla Desh, where, in 1974, the U.S. refused loans for food unless that country stopped selling gunny sacks to Cuba.[29]

Seeking to strengthen the food weapon still further, the U.S. would obviously welcome developments which would bring its "near-monopoly" of exportable food even closer to full monopoly. Gaining control of Canada's exports would be a major step in that direction.[30] In that context, the advance of Cargill and other U.S. grain companies into Canada takes on even greater significance.

Food Policy Developments

Canadian government food policy has generally tended to develop in harmony with the U.S. policies outlined above. A major indication of that trend appeared with the Report of the Federal Task Force on Agriculture (1970).

The Report set out the "general objective" of an uninhibited continental market for grains, oilseeds, livestock and potatoes.[31] Free trade arrangements with the U.S. were also needed in "carrots, onions, turnips, cole crops and cranberries". (*Report*:441). While recognizing that apples were "virtually on a free trade basis", the Report neglected to discuss the problems thus created in Canada, where 12,000 apple growers were denouncing unfair foreign advantages, including the admitted fact that "over 70 percent of the pack of fruits and vegetables is processed in American-owned plants".[32]

The Report's only response was that the government "must be willing to subject other sectors of the Canadian economy to increased foreign competition" (*Report*:433). Rockefeller's Trilateralists could hardly have asked for more. Such advocacy of Canadian adjustment to the continental market meant, at that time, an adjustment to large U.S. grain export surpluses, coupled with the continuing capacity of the U.S. to absorb feeder cattle which could, in turn, consume some of that surplus.

With these factors in mind, it was recommended that "at least 10 million acres of prairie land . . . must be removed from wheat production". (This was indicated as a reduction from 30 million acres to 20 million by 1980). Some acreage would be diverted to hay and pasture for the production of up to 500,000 feeder cattle for export to the U.S. market, which would be "unlimited up to the capacity of Canadians to produce feeders", providing that prices fell by between $1.00 and $2.00 per hundred. Little hope was seen for major increases in the export of finished cattle which could have consumed some Canadian grain surpluses (*Report*: 163).

The continental market would also demand greater efficiency, including the ability to be competitive in exports. Thus the Report anticipated "the disappearance of approximately 40,000 small farm operators" in the 1966-71 period (*Report*:411). Actually, more than 64,000 disappeared during the five years in question. The study had seen only "a third or so" of the 430,000 farms that existed in 1966 as being large enough for "long run viability" (*Report*:409).

This search for more "efficient" management meant that a "high and rising proportion" of Canadian farmers would become "employees working for salaries and wages". They would be working in the "much larger units" which would result from "farm mergers and concolidation", and from "increasing formal and informal integration". Some family farms would survive, but all would be "rationally managed, profit oriented businesses" (*Report*:9).

Concerning those farmers who were to be forced off their farms, the Task Force modified its "market" orientation enough to recommend helping "at least some of them become capable of doing something else". This was presupposing "that jobs are available somewhere"

(Report:423-4). For the remainder, improved rural welfare services
were suggested, including the possibility of a guaranteed annual
income or negative income tax (Report: 424-5).

Thus the acceptance of a continental market was leading inevitably
toward acceptance of the U.S. type of corporate farming, and toward
the concept of providing food to those with money, while neglecting
the world's hungry millions who lack purchasing power. As observed
by the National Farmers' Union: "Canadian agriculture is to be
diverted from milk and grain for hungry people to meat products for
affluent Americans".[33] The Task Force plan was also moving Canada
toward the rural decay and unemployment which the MNCs had
already inflicted on most Third World countries. Subsequent policy
and recommendations have not varied in principle from these Task
Force guidelines.

In 1970, Operation LIFT (Lower Inventories for Tomorrow) was
introduced to deal with a world grain "surplus" which was made
worse by U.S. violation of International Grains Agreement pricing
in 1967-69. This left Canada with more than half of the wheat stocks
held by the four leading exporters (Bronson, 1972:127). LIFT reduced
Canadian wheat acreage from 24.4 million in 1969 to 12 million in
1970. At the same time the government promoted the Task Force
objective of expanded livestock production. However, even this subservience to "market" forces still failed to bring stability.

Pursuing the largest concentration of purchasing power, the
"market", led by Cargill and Continental, provided the Soviet Union
with 28 million tons of grain beginning in 1972. (That purchase can be
compared with total Canadian output of wheat and feed grains of 29.8
million tons in 1974-75). The Soviet sale created world "shortages"
and speculative price increases which reached a peak in the Chicago
market of $6.45 a bushel (for the March futures contract). Canadian
farmers went back to grain growing, with regrets for the production
lost during LIFT. By late 1976, wheat prices had dropped below $3.00,
well under the farmers' rising costs of production.

The Promotion of Free Trade

During these fluctuations, a renewed emphasis on the Task Force
"free trade" approach came from the Economic Council of Canada
(ECC). It was referring to conditions which "tended to increase the
interdependence of the Canadian and U.S. economies". These
conditions included the defence production sharing programme,
renewed in 1959, and the Canada-U.S. Automotive Agreement, signed
in 1965. The ECC noted, with apparent approval, the resulting "major
expansion of north-south trade".[34] It ignored the growing deficits

inflicted on Canada both in the Automotive Agreement[35] and in the purchase of U.S. military equipment.

The Council's only defense against more continental integration seemed to be an extension of multilateral free trade which "would provide the most remarkable improvement in the economic well-being of Canadians that could result from a single step by government today . . ." (Rea & McLeod, 1976:103). The Council's ultimate hope was "a totally free trade situation" in which Canada would become "truly competitive". This would mean the elimination of many non-competitive sectors of our industries and a shift to "increased specialization", *i.e.*, to virtually total integration with U.S. industry (Rea & McLeod, 1976:91, 104).

The dogmatic adherence to David Ricardo's theory of "comparative advantage"[36] completely ignored the imperialist-colonial relationship between the U.S. and Canada. It also neglected the fact that we could expect free trade, as in the case of the Auto Agreement, to be manipulated in favour of the dominant power. Increasingly, there is awareness of the need to substitute self-reliance for international specialization as long as there are great inequalities in the size and development of nations, and while the biggest and most advanced tend to use their power selfishly. As economic analyst Samir Amin has observed: ". . . Only when nations have reached the same level of development will it be possible for a new doctrine of specialization to be worked out".[37]

Referring to the Second and Fifth Annual Reviews of the ECC, Stephen Clarkson aptly noted that the Council's view was one of acceptance of a considerable lessening of Canada's independence through existing "advantageous interdependence in capital markets", combined with "extensive interconnections between business concerns across the border".[38]

Taking the same approach in 1977, a "confidential" report prepared by deputy ministers for government consideration (the "DM-10 Report") called for an end to long-term subsidies to agriculture, and the lifting of import quotas and tariffs. While the Task Force Report had accepted a cabinet-controlled marketing board system, the DM-10 was more critical, emphasizing the belief that these boards "are not synonymous with supply management and should not be used as instruments to stabilize or raise incomes directly" (The DM-10 Report).

To deal with farm input costs, the DM-10 called for a return to competitive marketing, with no indication of how this could be achieved except by applying the notoriously ineffective anti-combine laws. As it happened, that particular remedy was being further undermined by pressure from the big corporate lobbies. In 1977, after ten years of preparing amendments to the Combines Investigation

Act, and accepting changes proposed by the lobbies, the Ottawa government proposed to allow, for the first time, a merging and monopolization process if it could be shown to mean more efficient operation (CP, Ottawa, March 17, 1977).

Even this concession was not enough for Imperial Oil (Exxon). Its spokesmen subsequently told a Senate banking committee that the powers remaining to civil servants under the revised proposals were still "greater than necessary" (CP, Ottawa, June 16, 1977). Further delays in completing the legislation indicated that it would be weakened further.

The new tolerance for merging, monopolization and specialization, combined with a free trade approach, was also being accepted by the Progressive-Conservative opposition. That party's then economic adviser, James Gillies, was urging Canadians to be content to be "hewers of wood and drawers of water". In the past we had specialized in fish, fur, pulp and paper, minerals and oil. Such a policy was not disgraceful ". . . if that's where you have your comparative advantage," Gillies declared (CP, Ottawa, September 15, 1977).

It is thus evident that in the Canadian government and in the official opposition, the free trade-specialization doctrine prevails. In a world where nations vary greatly in economic and political power, that ideology serves imperialism and promotes the objectives of Rockefeller's Trilateral Commission.

To the extent that some degree of import restriction remains, the MNCs work persistently against it. One example was the purchasing strategy pursued in Alberta by Essmark (Swift Canadian) and Canada Packers. When they were paying more for imported U.S. hogs than for the domestic product, it was simply assumed that they were seeking to develop and extend their supply sources. Instead they were actually reducing Alberta farmers' bargaining power (*Union Farmer*, August-September, 1977).

Commenting on these tactics, the NFU observed that tariffs and quotas alone are not adequate, since processors and retailers are capable of charging consumers more, while paying less to producers. Ignoring price advantages, the MNCs were increasing their importation of hogs, cattle and meat products. Meanwhile, sharp reductions were occurring in Canadian production of these items, and in the number of participating farmers.

As in the Third World, MNC policy was creating idle lands and idle hands, thereby making Canadians increasingly dependent on corporate-controlled food imports. Such were the trends which led Professor Thomas Stout to declare, at the 1977 Canadian Meat-Grain Interface Project, that: ". . . If you really want free trade with the U.S. you almost have to say to hell with Canada". Less convincingly,

Stout concluded that political union with the U.S. would make ". . . good economic sense . . . and political sense too" (Saskatoon *Star Phoenix*, March 4, 1977).

Reviewing recent literature on the effects of tariff reduction, J. N. H. Britton has observed a general lack of concern with the possibility that foreign-owned subsidiaries might respond differently than domestic firms. "One gains the impression," he wrote, "that none of these trade monographs wishes to discuss the strength of the economic effects that derive from foreign ownership: rather, they treat this factor as a consequence of tariffs instead of treating it as an agent in its own right, reflecting different corporate goals and international strategies".[39]

Noting how attention has tended to focus on regional effects, Britton offered the view that ". . . it is not *regions* that would make the response to free trade but the *firms* contained within the various regions and for many of them it is their world corporate goals that will be emphasized . . ." (Britton, 1978:7 — Britton's emphasis).

Britton refused to accept the usual assumption of economic gains accruing to Canada under conditions of free trade with the U.S. He pointed to the economic decline which had occurred in the northeastern U.S., especially in New York, as manufacturing firms relocated in the south in response to that area's climatic advantages, combined with its lower wages and living costs, and declared that this experience should be contemplated by Canadians (Britton, 1978:11).

Britton also objected to comparison of a continental market in North America with the experience of the European Economic Community. The EEC ". . . embodies the union of more equally sized industrial economies, and/or ones whose industry is not dominated economically by the branches of one neighbour" (Britton, 1978:13).

Nevertheless, the perspectives criticized by Britton continue to prevail among those now developing, or likely to be developing, food policies and general economic strategies for Canada. A federal "Food Strategy for Canada" paper presented in parliament on June 10, 1977, rejected the principle of self-reliance and emphasized again the government's preference for free trade. This included an anticipated increase in grain exports and in the importation of other foods.

The paper noted without any sign of concern that only 38 percent of the food price paid at supermarkets reaches the farmer. It ignored farm complaints such as those registered by the Horticultural Council of Canada and the B.C. Coast Vegetable Marketing Board a few months earlier. Members of these groups had argued that Canada's fruit and potato producers are endangered because of the disadvantages they suffer as a result of the federal government's trade policies (*Free Press Report on Farming*, November 10, 1976).

New Policy Indications

Political resistance compels the legislators to proceed slowly toward their goal of a continental market. As one indication of this approach, the February, 1978 food strategy conference in Ottawa achieved consensus "only on vague, general 'motherhood' statements", according to one report (*Financial Post*, March 4, 1978). In the view of some critics, the 400 delegates representing 150 farm organizations were being subjected to "an attempt by the federal government to get an already decided upon federal food policy rubberstamped" (*Free Press Report on Farming*, March 1, 1978).

It is evident that the federal policy "already decided upon" is the continental market sought by the Trilateralists to improve the effectiveness of their food "weapon".[39] Wider awareness of that fact must be a first objective for those who reject the consequences of Canada becoming a neo-colonial appendage in a superpower struggle for world hegemony.

Such awareness would include recognition of the conclusion that most Canadians would benefit from the reduction and eventual elimination of the economic and political control over food and other products now exercised by MNCs in Canada. Otherwise, Canadian farmers will be forced off the land at an accelerating rate, while consumers are subjected increasingly to external price manipulation.

An obvious counterattack is the struggle for much greater self-reliance in Canada. As a prominent agricultural researcher has pointed out, two-thirds of Canada's food imports are made up of items which are grown commercially in Canada. Canadian food exports, on the other hand, are only 20 percent of total sales, so that the impact of retaliation by foreign buyers could be readily counteracted by adjusting production to replace imports.[40]

A self-reliance program would mean decisive action against the policies of the U.S.-based corporate-financial structures. Such action is not to be expected from parties committed to continentalism and the resulting dependency on foreign production. As in the Syncrude case, they are virtually forced to capitulate when faced with the threats and inducements which the MNCs can deploy.

To prevail against these forces, a political party would require strong popular backing for a self-reliance program. Economic pressures are creating the basis for that popular support, and it can be consolidated by political education. As part of that process, appropriate organizations are likely to develop boycotts of the MNCs. They will also seek to transform existing producer and consumer co-operatives into effective alternatives; or failing that, to create new types which will effectively challenge the MNCs. (Existing co-operatives in Canada often seem receptive to the continentalist approach. Referring to "co-operative" mergers in the U.S., Brian Clancey found a tendency among Canadian co-ops to develop "a vested interest in the well-being of their American counterparts"[41].

Some farm and labour unions, in their struggles against the MNCs, have begun to develop an essential organized base to support political action. Referring to MNC control of Canadian food production, National Farmers' Union President Roy Atkinson said in 1978 that it constitutes "a deliberate plan for underdevelopment in Canadian food production" which must result in "fewer full-time farmers, a greater dependence on foreign food supplies", and must contribute "to the total unemployment problem in the country" (*Union Farmer*, March, 1978).

Some Canadian Labour Congress (CLC) affiliates, notably those without AFL-CIO "parents", have actively supported public ownership of MNCs. But their efforts in this area have been hampered by the influence of AFL-CIO branches within the CLC. Some of these U.S. affiliates have a notorious record of collaboration with the MNCs and with the U.S. Central Intelligence Agency in the suppression of independence movements which have challenged the hegemony of the multinationals.[42]

On the other hand, a policy of support for public ownership has been unanimously endorsed by affiliates of the Confederation of Canadian Unions, an independent alternative to the CLC. A CCU brief to the federal cabinet (March 17, 1978) identified "public ownership of our economy, beginning with the oil and associated industries and marching through the basic segments of industry and commerce", as the only alternative to the present control over our economy by the United States.

Unity of pro-independence labour and farm organizations would be an essential first step in the development of a political base strong enough to resist the forces available to the MNCs. Another essential factor would be the establishment by these organizations of unified and effective communications media as an alternative to those now dominated by MNC advertising money. The new media could help to sustain nation-wide educational projects designed to counteract corporate-controlled propaganda.

A preliminary example of this educational process has appeared in the form of the People's Food Commission. Organized nationally in 1977 with support from farm, labour and church groups, the Commission was to conduct hearings and make recommendations regarding food policy. Among the suggestions on self-reliance submitted repeatedly to governments and also through the Food Commission were those put forward by the Saskatchewan Council for International Co-operation. It called for special attention by research organizations, community groups and governments to be directed to the promotion of domestic food production and distribution. Among the projects recommended for support were: waste-heat utilization for greenhouses, community gardens, family gardens, local food co-operatives and permanent farmers' markets (Brief to the Saskatchewan Government, March 15, 1978).

Financing of food self-reliance would mean that ties must be broken between the Canadian banking and financial system and the MNC power structure. That would seem to require a nationalized banking system dedicated to that policy and to mutually beneficial trade with the Third World. Underdeveloped countries, under similar but more extreme conditions, are being forced to nationalize their private banking systems.[43]

To deal with the all-important question of MNC-controlled farm input costs, no alternative seems practical except the nationalization of the industries involved, and their consolidation into fewer enterprises with larger, more efficient production runs. This would also permit standardization of machinery parts, and would thus make possible the development of more localized repair parts production and distribution. Government regulation of, or participation in, the present structures would seem to have no chance of breaking MNC control and influence, or of solving the problem of excessive costs arising from small scale production in fragmented branch plant industries.

A full discussion of the alternatives to the acceptance of increasing MNC influence over food policy must be premature until there has been more consideration and testing of the procedures involved. But we can start from the certainty that unless effective action is taken against MNC control in the food industries and in other vital sectors of the economy, Canada will continue to be steered toward Third World levels of poverty, unemployment, inflation and dependency.

NOTES

1. A "multinational corporation" (MNC) has been described as one with sales of at least $100 million annually, operating in six or more countries, with at least 20 percent of its assets in foreign branches. For a general discussion of their operations see Gurney Breckenfeld, "Multinationals at Bay", *Saturday Review*, January 24, 1976. A survey by the McGraw-Hill department of economics found that the 100 leading U.S.-based MNCs accounted for more than $50 billion of the $105 billion planned for investment by the 100 leading companies in each of 13 industrial countries (New York News Service, March 28, 1978.)

2. Ranked by 1976 sales ($ millions), the remaining ten are: Royal Dutch Shell (Netherlands-Britain), $36,087; American Telephone and Telegraph (U.S.), $32,816; National Iranian Oil (Iran), $19,761; Standard Oil of California (U.S.), $19,434; British Petroleum (Britain), $19,103; Sears, Roebuck (U.S.), $18,832; IBM (U.S.), $16,604; General Electric (U.S.), $15,697; Standard Oil of Indiana (U.S.), $11,532; Philips (Netherlands), $11,522.

3. This Hostess label should be distinguished from Hostess Food Products (Canada), a subsidiary of General Foods (New York).

4. Most of this corporate diversification is reported in Standard and Poor, *Corporate Records*; and Moody's *Industrial Manuals*.

5. As Douglas Mepham has reported (*Financial Post*, December 3, 1977), none of the "Big Three" auto makers will make a move to increase prices "until it sees what the industry leader, General Motors of Canada Ltd. plans".

6. Under U.S. law, the "general definition of control" is 25 percent of the foreign subsidiary's voting securities (see James Rusk, "Extraterritorial Aspect of U.S. Boycott Law is Affecting Canada", *Globe & Mail*, April 8, 1978).

7. *Free Press Report on Farming*, March 2, 1977. Using the categories developed by J. S. Bain, concentration would be "very high" where the first four firms account for 75 percent or more of an industry's sales. "High" concentration would include industries where the largest four firms have 65 to 74 percent (*Industrial Organization*, New York: John Wiley & Sons, 1968, pp. 138-39.) Other classifications of concentration do not differ greatly from Bain's. (See Bruce Mallen, "A Preliminary Paper on the Levels, Causes and Effects of Economic Concentration in the Canadian Retail Food Trade: a Study of Supermarket Market Power", Food Prices Review Board, Montreal: February, 1976, p. 21).

8. See *Report of the Royal Commission on Consumer Problems and Inflation*, Prairie Provinces Cost Study Commission, 1968.

9. See Margaret Lobenstein and John Schommer, *Food Price Blackmail*, San Francisco, United Front Press, 1973, p. 24. Wallace Clement has identified Safeway as one of 12 companies which, at the time of his survey, had nine interlocks with other dominant U.S. corporations (Clement, *Continental Corporate Power*, p. 31).

10. In that context, Walter Stewart has reported a description of industry gatherings which were "'wall to wall with Safeway guys and everybody kow-towing to them'" (Stewart, *Hard to Swallow*, Toronto: Macmillan, 1974, pp. 127-29).

11. Royal Commission on Farm Machinery, *Special Report on Prices*, Ottawa, Queen's Printer, 1969, p. 92. As an indication of price increases in the 1970s, farmers, comparing the same models and equipment, pointed out that in 1978 large combines had doubled in price during the preceding five years, while the price of smaller ones had doubled in three years (CTV, "Prime Time", March 12, 1978).

12. Cede Company, in 1972 was the largest stockholder in 32 corporations. Chase Manhattan was the largest in 20 (*Time*, January 30, 1978). A detailed example of the interlock system was provided in the consolidated statement of Morgan Guaranty Trust (December 31, 1977). Its list of directors included the chairmen of Coca-Cola, IBM, New York Life Insurance Co., Foreign Policy Association, Campbell Soup Co., Bethlehem Steel, and M.I.T., together with the former executive vice-president of Exxon, the president of Tenneco, and the chairman emeritus of Procter and Gamble.

13. The Senate letter of inquiry went to the 100 leading industrial corporations, and to the 50 top firms in each of four categories — transportation, public utilities, retailing and banking. It also went to the 24 major life insurance companies, excluding mutuals.

14. In *Continental Corporate Power*: pp. 315-32, Clement indentified 194 "dominant" U.S. corporations, including leaders in finance, transportation, natural resources and manufacturing.

15. Including other members of the U.S. economic elite who were not born or resident

there, Clement arrived at "2,450 persons who can be considered members" of that group. (*Ibid.*: p. 253.)

16. See Jeff Frieden, "The Trilateral Commission", and "Comment by the Editors", *Monthly Review*, December, 1977. Frieden reported the initiative by Rockefeller, and subsequent organization by Brzezinski. Both articles rejected a "conspiracy" interpretation of the Trilateral Commission. Conspiracy involves secrecy, and Trilateral objectives have been publicly proclaimed.

17. For more details see J. Hutcheson, "The Capitalist State in Canada", in R. Laxer, (ed.), *Canada Ltd.*, Toronto: McClelland & Stewart, 1973, pp. 153-77.

18. J. G. Endicott, the controversial Canadian missionary whose criticisms of the U.S. have been solidly supported by post-Viet Nam revelations, has identified Brzezinski as a former director of Columbia University's Research Institute on Communist Affairs, and an active counter-revolutionary. With such members, the Trilateral could well be "the 1978 equivalent, on a global scale, of the German monopoly industrialists like Thyssen, who financed the fascist movement of which Hitler was the head. Their stock-in-trade was anti-communism; so it is with Brzezinski" (*Canadian Far Eastern Newsletter*, February, 1978).

19. See "Multinationals Under Siege: A Threat to the World Economy", *Atlantic Community Quarterly*, Vol. 13, No. 3, (1975).

20. A major example, in 1977, was Carter's "denunciation" of the oil industry for aspiring to revenues of $150 billion a year by 1985. His own tentative and apparently ineffective proposals were based on assumed revenues of $100 billion, compared with $18 billion in 1973 (AP, New York: October 17, 1977).

21. Refuting assumptions of independence in a Canadian branch industry like Imperial Oil, Clement cited a case where Imperial's actions were being challenged in court by the Nova Scotia Power Corporation. The judge concluded that "Imperial does not have independence of action. . . . The ultimate decisions rested with Exxon Corporation" (Clement, *Continental Corporate Power*: p. 99).

22. For full discussion of this case, see Larry Pratt, *The Tar Sands*, Edmonton: Hurtig, 1976, pp. 164, 175-76, 192.

23. See G. R. Berry, "The Oil Lobby and the Energy Crisis", in K. J. Rea and J. T. McLeod, (eds.), *Business and Government in Canada*, Toronto: Methuen, 1976, p. 297.

24. On the question of bribery, the U.S. economic priorities board reported late in 1976 that during the 1970-76 period, 175 U.S. companies, including 117 from the top 500, made questionable payments abroad of $300 million.

25. Since subsidy money is largely diverted through farmers to the MNCs by way of debt repayments or purchase of new equipment and supplies, it can reasonably be argued that the government merely seeks to protect these corporations against excessive farm debt repudiation and bankruptcy; or against severe reduction in demand for their products and services.

26. Address to the Saskatchewan Association of Rural Municipalities, reported in Saskatoon *Star-Phoenix*, March 16, 1978.

27. See William Robbins, *The American Food Scandal*, New York: William Morrow, 1974, pp. 180-99; *Washington Post*, September 11, 17, 18, 1975; and NACLA, *U.S. Grain Arsenal*, New York: October, 1975.

28. See the Transportation Agency of Saskatchewan, *The Crow Rate and National Transportation Policy*, Regina: Queen's Printer, 1977.

29. See Francis M. Lappe and Joseph Collins. *Food First*, Boston: Houghton-Mifflin, 1977, p. 337.

30. Such a step seemed to be under serious consideration in the spring of 1978, when it was announced that the then Canadian Minister of Agriculture, Eugene Whelan, was supporting a proposed U.S.-Canadian cartel arrangement in the export of wheat (CP, Washington, March 15, 1978). The U.S. did not immediately agree, possibly because it has been able to maintain a considerable export advantage over Canada in wheat surplus periods. In 1967-68, for example, the U.S. increased its exports by two percent while total world exports declined by 15 percent. Canadian exports fell by 40 percent (see H. E. Bronson, "*Continentalism and Canadian Agriculture*", in G. Teeple, (ed.), *Capitalism and the National Question in Canada*, Toronto: University of Toronto Press, 1972, p. 127).

31. See *Canadian Agriculture in the Seventies*, Ottawa: 1970, p. 433.

32. *Canadian Agriculture in the Seventies*: p. 235.

33. See NFU brochure: "NFU Reveals Task Force Objectives", July, 1970.

34. Economic Council of Canada, "Looking Outward: a New Trade Strategy for Canada", Ottawa: Information Canada, 1975, in K. J. Rea and J. T. McLeod, *Business and Government in Canada*, 2nd. ed., Toronto: Methuen, 1976, p. 86.

35. Over 1965-75, the accumulated deficit amounted to $5 billion. Another $1 billion was added in 1976, and $1.1 billion in 1977 (*Financial Times*, April 17, 1978.)

36. A most thorough demolition of this theory of comparative advantage was done by Harry Magdoff (*Monthly Review*, December, 1971.) He emphasized how the imperialist-colonial relationships between England and Portugal must have distorted the cost relationships which Ricardo used to show the supposed benefits of English-imposed free trade.

37. Earlier application of that doctrine, Amin concluded, would amount to support of conditions similar to present central-periphery relationships (*Monthly Review*, February, 1978).

38. "The Two Solitudes: Foreign Investment through the Prism of Canadian Economists", a paper presented to the Learned Societies, Fredericton, New Brunswick, June 1977.

39. Of course, the continental market promoters consider not only food, but the whole range of products which made up $55 billion in trade between Canada and the U.S. in 1977. Thus James Flacke, the "counsellor for economic affairs" at the U.S. embassy in Ottawa, told the 1978 third annual Canadian-U.S. business conference in Minneapolis that the two countries might sign a separate pact "liberalizing" trade between the two countries (*Financial Times*, April 17, 1978).

40. Research data from Gordon MacEachern, president of the Agricultural Research Council of Canada (*Globe & Mail*, August 25, 1977). Wheat, as the major Canadian food export item is sold mainly to customers who would be unlikely to resent more self-reliance in Canada.

41. Clancey saw some Canadian co-operatives "taking on the hue of multinational corporations" through "a web of investments in U.S. co-ops and joint ventures" (see "The Co-op Connection", *Free Press Report on Farming*, April, 1978).

42. See Roger Howard and Jack Scott, "International Unions and the Ideology of Class Collaboration", *Capitalism and the National Question in Canada*; and George Morris, *CIA and American Labor*, New York, International, 1967.

43. In 1976, Guyana announced plans to nationalize foreign banks so that more money could be mobilized for development, including an advance toward self-sufficiency in food production. Jamaica began the same process by nationalizing Barclay's Bank in 1977 and the Bank of Montreal in 1978 (Jamaican *Weekly Gleaner*, November 30, 1976; January 30, February 20, 1978).

Readings

Clement, Wallace, *Continental Corporate Power*, Toronto: McClelland & Stewart, 1977.

Lappe, Francis M. and Collins, Joseph, *Food First*, Boston, Houghton-Mifflin, 1977.

Mills, C. Wright, *The Power Elite*, New York, Oxford University Press, 1965.

Rea, K. J. and McLeod, J. T. (eds.), *Business and Government in Canada*, Toronto, Methuen, 1976.

Robbins, William, *The American Food Scandal*, New York, Wm. Morrow, 1974.

Stewart, Walter, *Hard to Swallow*, Toronto, Macmillan, 1974.

Teeple, Gary (ed.), *Capitalism and the National Question in Canada*, Toronto, University of Toronto Press, 1972.

Warnock, John W., *Profit Hungry, The Food Industry in Canada*, Vancouver, New Star Books, 1978.

The Rural Depopulation of the Prairies

Gurcharn S. Basran

GURCHARN S. BASRAN is a Professor and former Head in the Department of Sociology at the University of Saskatchewan. His current research interests include Sociology of Development and Canadian Society.

A problem of increasing concern to social scientists, politicians and other students of rural areas is the continued depopulation of these rural areas and the accompanying decline of rural communities. Moreover migration of rural people is not only a problem for rural areas but it also creates problems in urban areas. We cannot stop the rural-urban migration but we at least can recognize some of the factors which are responsible for the depopulation of rural areas as well as look at some of the consequences of such migration. Ideas discussed in this essay may be of relevance to other provinces in Canada but they are developed in the context of the history, needs and problems of the Prairies in general and Saskatchewan in particular. It is particularly important to study rural depopulation in Saskatchewan from theoretical as well as from practical points of view as this province still depends heavily upon the agricultural industry as its main source of income.

The farm population in Canada is decreasing. By 1976 the number of farms in Canada had declined from the 1966 figure of 430,522 to 338,578, but the remaining farms were larger in average acreage than in 1966. According to the 1971 census, total farmland area for Canada as a whole declined to 169,086,823 acres in 1976 from 174,124,828 in 1966.

In 1971 the decline in farm numbers was common to all provinces and the territories. On the Prairies declines were 12.0 percent in Manitoba, 10.2 percent in Saskatchewan, and 9.7 percent in Alberta. The average acreage per farm in Saskatchewan increased to 938 acres in 1976 from 763 acres in 1966.

According to the 1976 census 4,416 farms in Saskatchewan (out of the total number of 76,970 farms) sold agricultural products valued at less than $2,500 a year. Although the total farm income has improved significantly since 1971, the prices of farm inputs have also gone up. Between 1962 and 1969 in the Prairies, cash receipts increased by 32 percent, while operating and depreciating costs went up 76 percent. The resultant cost-price squeeze has placed increasing economic burdens on smaller farm units in comparison with larger units which enjoy certain economies of scale. This has meant that many relatively young farm families who cannot realize satisfactory incomes from farming these smaller units have moved to other occupations, generally in the larger urban centers.

In addition, young people who may aspire to pursue farming as a career are unable to do so because of the high *initial investments* required: the average capital value of Saskatchewan farms in 1976 was $181,888. These young people, in search of available occupations and the educational requisites thereto, have in the past and continue to add to the rural-urban migration stream in increasing numbers. Between 1966 and 1971 in Saskatchewan the out-migration ratio of people between the ages of 20 and 34 was the highest in Canada.[1] Saskatchewan-born persons were the most likely to be found living in a province other than that of their birth (40 percent).[2]

Although rural-urban migration is by no means a phenomenon characteristic only of present-day rural areas it is of increasing importance when the characteristics of the migrants are taken into consideration. The migrants, as noted previously, are generally the younger individuals or family units who are also the better educated and/or skilled segments of their respective populations. This youthful migration has resulted in:

(1) An increasingly aged rural population (the average age of Saskatchewan farmers in 1971 was 50) with accompanying changes in the demands for various goods and services. This increasing age of farm operators is also of considerable concern within the agricultural community. The question now being asked is: Who will be the farmers of the future?

(2) A leadership vacuum in the rural areas whereby the available leadership positions go to the older, more conservative segments by "default" as the younger and more energetic segments, essential for the maintenance, growth or potential revitalization of rural communities, are removed.

(3) A general sense of alienation and powerlessness among the rural people as they do not have full control over forces which are related to depopulation of rural areas.

In addition to the apparent differential effects of migration on the rural communities, other variables which may be used to account for these differential growth patterns are transportation and distance to larger centers; and the increasing vertical integration and centralization of community centered organizations, institutions and services outwardly from the local area and the accompanying decline in the decision-making power of the individual and local community units.

People living in rural areas have a sense of powerlessness. They do not seem to have control over their socio-economic environment. This creates a sense of alienation, apathy and powerlessness on the part of individual farmers. They cannot relate to or control these giant bureaucracies and powerful organizations which control their destiny. Local organizations are not effective and relevant in bringing about important changes in rural communities. Another reason for the sense of apathy and powerlessness is the fact that some individuals, as noted previously, who have the ability to perform leadership roles in rural communities, leave for urban areas. This process leaves rural communities with traditional and sometimes out-dated leadership structures.

It is difficult to understand the depopulation of the Prairies without discussing the settlement of the west from an historical perspective. Problems which we face at this time are neither new nor unexpected. The Prairies were developed to play the role of hinterland to the central-eastern part of Canada and the U.S.A. It will be useful to look at some historical forces which were responsible for the settlement of the Prairies.

Around 1890 the Government of Canada decided to introduce tariff protection to aid industrialization. Tariff protection, looked on as an anti-Prairie measure, has been fought, albeit with limited success, by the Western Provinces. The Government of Canada also committed itself to the building of the Trans-Canada Railway and encouraged immigrants to settle these areas.

These three decisions — building of railways, introduction of tariffs and the encouragement of immigrant settlements — were partly taken as a result of changes which took place in the world economy. The strides in industrialization, which led to rises in the price of food stuffs and raw material after 1870, the decline in transportation costs, and the non-availability of land in the U.S. west — all these factors contributed to the development of the Canadian economic policy and the settlement of the west.

Long before Confederation the decision had been made to establish Canada's frontier region by the purchase of the British territory of Rupert's Land and Northwest Territory. The purchase which took place in 1870, marked a bold step in the settlement of the west, and subsequently led to the creation of Alberta and Saskatchewan as provinces.

Prairie economy was primarily agricultural in the early stage of its development. In the case of Saskatchewan, agriculture played an even more important role in the province's development. The agricultural sector did not enjoy the same federal governmental support and protection as did the industrial sector. This policy led to many problems such as a fluctuation in production and prices, cost-price squeezes and unstable and uncertain markets. The fluctuation in wheat output per acre ranged from 8.8 bushels in 1900 to a high of 25 bushels in 1925 down to the extreme low of 2.7 bushels per acre in 1937. The boom-bust cycle characterized the prairie economy in the early stages. The accelerated growth generated by World War I followed the boom that started in the opening years of the second decade of this century. The expansion of the twenties persisted till the depression of the thirties. Meanwhile, the U.S. tariff legislation of 1921 reduced the external markets for Canadian industrial, manufactured and primary products.

During the Depression the prairie provinces suffered greatly as they were primarily dependent upon agriculture. During these years the Prairie population declined by some 250,000 people. (The population of the Prairies in 1931 was 2.3 million). The province of Saskatchewan was hit by a combination of poor yield, the result of drought, and low prices which forced people to flee the province. Wheat earnings fell from the peak of $218 million in 1928 to a low of $17.8 million in 1937. As far as per capita earnings was concerned, Saskatchewan was the worst hit of all. While the national per capita average fell slightly below 50 percent between 1929 and 1933 and that of Alberta by about 60 percent, in Saskatchewan the decline was 72 percent.

The Second World War brought a repeat performance of the booms of the previous era. High prices and demand for wheat in foreign markets provided incentives for the expansion of wheat farms in the Prairies. However, partly because of the German blockade of British ports, a quota was introduced on wheat production, and compensation was paid for the reduction of wheat acreage. Subsidies were offered to stimulate increased dairy and livestock production. Even during this time of prosperity, and in face of population gains by all other provinces, Saskatchewan experienced a population decline of about 4 percent.

So the problems of depopulation of the Prairies are not new. They are part of our historical development and are the result of the functioning of our economic and political systems. Historically, the agricultural industry has been used to build the commercial and industrial systems in Canada. Fowke points out that "... what is clear from this analysis of the changing role of agriculture in Canadian society is that the agricultural industry has less power over other sectors of the Canadian economy as well as over its own destiny".[3]

Saskatchewan's economy is very sensitive to changes at the international level. It is dependent upon the export of grains to markets outside Canada. In 1976 export of agricultural grains to non-Canadian markets was worth $1,215 million compared to export of agricultural grains to local markets which was worth $250 million. This is also true with the livestock situation.[4]

In order to understand problems at the community or regional level, it is necessary to analyze macro-level variables. Such analysis is the main focus of this essay. People do not move from one place to another without experiencing pressures from outside. Many forces which operate at the local levels emerge from outside. Often local people do not have a great deal of control over these forces. As you will note in the section on theory in this essay, most of the studies in the area of internal and international migration concentrate on micro-level variables such as the age, education, intelligence, class, family type etc. of the migrants. The author's position is that such variables will not provide much explanation and insight into the problem of rural depopulation. One has to consider the following macro-level variables to be able to understand this problem:

(1) The historical development of the west
(2) The nature and function of the capitalist system
(3) The role of Canada (particularly the Prairies) as a hinterland to the U.S.A.
(4) Cost-price squeeze
(5) The role of multi-nationals in the system of production and distribution
(6) Policies of various governments.

The reader should refer to the articles by Fry (The Deterioration of Economic Stability in North America) and Bronson (Multinational Corporations and Canadian Food Policy) for a full discussion of some of these issues.

Theoretical Framework and Empirical Research in the Area of Migration

Social scientists have developed a number of theories of migration. Most of these theories deal with micro-level variables.[5] It will be difficult to review all these theories in detail but I will discuss some of them in this essay. The basic question which most of the theorists raise is: Why do people move from one place to another?[6] What motivates people to migrate? Economic, political, sociological, psychological, environmental and religious variables are all offered in the literature as an explanation of people's movement from one place to another. Most of the theories discussed in this section emphasize one or another discipline. One should note that the economic variables are given more importance in many theories of migration.

Samuel Stouffer[7] points out that the number of opportunities which a person perceives in a situation determine his plans to migrate. He proposes ". . . that the number of persons going a given distance is directly proportional to the number of opportunities at that distance and inversely proportional to the number of intervening opportunities". Stouffer's model is considered more useful than that of the distance model because of the reduction in the friction of space (better transportation). His theory has been validated by a number of sociologists.

David Sly[8] suggests that neither environmental nor technological factors affect migration directly. Rather, their effect on migration is produced through changes in organization which they generate. The research is done on southern black migration rates and the model is built on the ecological theory of Hawley (1950).

Wen Lang Li[9] supports E. G. Ravenstein's (1885) belief that each main migration stream has a counter stream — perhaps explainable by cultural contacts between the two points and the children of migrants moving back to point of origin. A Taiwan study established a high correlation between dominant and reverse streams. This correlation is greater for the old than the young and for women than for men.

Peter Uhlenberg[10] studied non-migration to understand migration. He takes the position that the push-pull theory is inadequate in cases where the reasons that caused migration at other times were present, but no migration took place. He hypothesizes that ". . . the stronger the person's ties with the community and the more involved one is in a network of family ties, the greater the constraints upon potential migration". He further hypothesizes that ". . . the less cosmopolitan and less able to adjust to new environments, the less likely that motivation for migration will reach migration". According to Uhlenberg those with (1) deep roots in the community; (2) strong kinship ties and ties with the local community; (3) large investment in the community; and (4) an inability to easily assimilate into a new social environment are likely to resist migration

Philip Martin[11] suggests that the best approach for understanding migration and non-migration may be through integration of economic and sociological views. For example the benefits of moving are greater for the young since they start at an earlier time in life. Generally, the costs of moving are less for the young. As people do not get complete information about the proposed place, and as uncertainty increases with distance, people generally do not move long distances. Worker migration often is determined by chains of friendship and relatives. The push-pull theory states that changes in wage differentials and/or employment opportunities induce interregional labour mobility toward areas yielding the highest net returns. But it is not enough that positive wage or employment differentials exist as these differentials can be offset by better working conditions, a favourable environment or lower living costs.

Schwarzweller and Brown[12] in their Kentucky study look at the relationship between social class origin and migration. According to them the social position of the family significantly influenced the pattern of out-migration and the economic life chances of individuals and families in the areas of destination. Upper class members of the community tended to move as family units whereas intermediate class members tended to move as individuals joining family members in other areas with some of the family remaining at the "homestead".

In his Pennsylvania study Sidney Goldstein[13] supports the assertion that out-migration from the community consisted largely of people who had been in-migrants in the previous decade. It means that high rates of in and out migration do not necessarily mean a high degree of population change or instability.

There are a number of studies which emphasize that centers which can provide services to the local people will survive. Gerald Hodge[14] takes the position that the center will survive on the basis of its ability to provide retail services. His ideas are derived from "Central Place Theory" which is based on the "range" of goods and the "demand threshold" concepts.

Charles Lemelin[15] uses P. A. Samuelson's interdependence model on migration from agriculture. According to him, in a situation where there is no injection of new capital into the economy, there will be migration from agriculture if there is transfer of capital from agriculture into industry.

Variables Related to Depopulation

In the previous section we have discussed some of the theories and research in the area of migration. We have noticed that most of these theories and empirical studies focus on micro-level variables. Some of them take the position that migration is the natural outcome of the working of our system as people move where the jobs are available and migrants make the best of their abilities and opportunities.

As discussed earlier, I take the position that migration is very much the function of macro-level variables which operate at the national as well as international levels. Ernest Mandel points out that our world economy is structured in an interdependent way and its different

TABLE 1
NET FARM INCOME, SASKATCHEWAN ($000,000's)

Year	Cash Income from Farm Products	Income in Kind	Value of Inventory Changes	Gross Income	Operating and Depreciation Expenses	Net Income Excluding Supplementary Payments	Supplementary Payments	Net Income Including Supplementary Payments
1935	111.0	24.2	5.3	140.5	116.2	24.3	-	24.3
1936	128.5	24.1	-25.9	126.7	115.4	11.3	-	11.3
1937	85.9	24.6	-41.3	69.2	104.2	-35.0	-	-35.0
1938	93.2	24.5	16.9	134.6	107.0	27.6	-	27.6
1939	157.9	24.5	35.6	218.1	115.8	102.3.	1.7	104.0
1940	149.7	26.5	29.4	205.6	117.5	88.1	7.1	95.2
1941	159.7	27.6	-20.1	167.1	115.5	51.6	18.4	70.1
1942	195.4	33.8	193.7	422.9	153.8	269.1	33.2	302.4
1943	327.4	39.3	-66.8	299.9	154.4	145.5	17.3	162.8
1944	543.2	43.9	-66.6	520.5	174.7	345.9	11.6	357.5
1945	409.6	45.3	-103.0	351.9	167.1	184.8	2.9	187.7
1946	387.6	49.0	-50.7	385.9	184.5	201.4	12.5	213.8
1947	428.5	53.7	-34.6	447.7	206.7	240.9	9.8	250.8
1948	534.0	61.4	-13.6	581.8	222.1	359.7	16.7	376.4
1949	566.1	56.5	-18.3	604.3	233.2	371.1	14.2	385.3
1950	412.5	55.6	51.8	519.8	258.4	261.3	8.2	269.6
1951	636.2	55.7	148.4	840.3	292.9	547.4	5.5	553.0

Source: *Saskatchewan Economic Review*, 1955, Table 26.

TABLE 2
CASH RECEIPTS AND NET INCOME OF SASKATCHEWAN FARM OPERATORS FROM FARMING OPERATIONS ($000,000's)

Year	Cash Receipts from Farm Products					Supplementary Payments	Total Cash Receipts	Income in Kind	Operating & Depreciation Charges	Realized Net Income	Value of Inventory Change	Total Gross Income	Total Net Income
	Wheat	Other Grains[a]	Livestock	Miscellaneous	Total								
	millions of dollars												
1952	461	119	77	45	702	2	704	51	317	438	170	925	608
1953	504	102	77	47	731	1	732	50	315	467	12	794	479
1954	264	74	80	45	463	1	464	47	291	220	-84	427	136
1955	216	74	80	46	416	22	438	48	311	175	152	638	327
1956	328	126	82	48	585	1	586	48	324	310	92	726	402
1957	283	94	102	47	526	1	527	49	320	255	-76	499	179
1958	313	67	134	52	566	32	598	51	331	318	-77	572	241
1959	307	72	126	51	555	13	568	50	344	274	-44	575	230
1960	312	80	103	48	543	42	585	52	371	265	68	704	333
1961	365	40	135	49	589	24	613	52	356	309	-209	456	99
1962	432	61	133	47	673	37	710	53	392	371	95	858	466
1963	465	66	112	50	692	6	698	56	434	321	231	986	552
1964	606	62	127	47	842	2	844	60	453	451	-109	795	342
1965	599	77	162	48	887	7	894	68	503	459	24	986	483
1966	629	87	183	50	949	1	950	73	558	465	118	1141	583
1967	642	87	198	49	976	2	978	77	576	480	-125	930	355
1968	553	88	196	57	893	5	899	78	611	365	97	1073	462
1969	317	171	172	52	712	6	718	73	623	169	240	1032	409
1970	353	88	190	55	686	37	723	91	591	222	14	827	236
1971	470	147	229	56	901	7	908	85	623	370	117	1111	488
1972	616	202	291	63	1172	31	1204	88	666	626	-220	1071	405
1973	824	162b	368	112	1466	2	1468	104	803	768	213	1784	982
1974	1340	228b	364	108	2039	2	2041	121	988	1174	-38	2125	1136
1975	1641	353b	378	96	2469	-	2469	137	1132	1475	44	2650	1519
1976	1302	512	455	15	2284	-	2284	159	1297	1148	275	2721	1424

aIncludes net cash advance payments on farm-stored grain.
bReduced by receipts from grain delivered during year deferred to following year.

Sources: *Saskatchewan Economic Review*, 1968, 1975 and 1976, Tables 34, 36 and 39. 1976 figures are preliminary

parts are sensitive to changes in the dominant systems. If someone sneezes on the New York Stock Exchange, 10,000 peasants are ruined in Malaya.[16] In Saskatchewan we will have to analyze the cost-price squeezes, boom and bust situation, the role of multi-national corporations, the role of Saskatchewan as hinterland, and the sense of alienation and powerlessness which local people develop as a result of centralization of power and decision making. People leave these small communities as they do not perceive any opportunity and future there. Edith Graber cites a 1972 gallop poll that indicated that 32 percent of Americans preferred to live in small towns if possible (this was more than any other category) whereas 23 percent preferred to live on farms. People who are forced to leave these communities experience a number of adaptive problems in the urban areas.[17]

The role of multinationals is discussed in Professor Bronson's article in reference to food policy. Their role in production and distribution is quite similar.

Boom and Bust in Saskatchewan Agriculture

As we have discussed in the introduction, Saskatchewan's agriculture and the province's economy have been subjected to a boom and bust situation.

There is no question that weather contributes to this situation in Saskatchewan, but the nature of our economic and political system is the main cause of these cycles. Any undiversified economy, such as Saskatchewan's, is subjected to the following problems:

(1) Fluctuation in production.
(2) Fluctuation in price (long range as well as short range).
(3) Inability to adapt to rapid changes in the economic structure at the national and international levels.

TABLE 3
INCOME OF FARM OPERATORS ($1000)

	1969-73	1974	1975	1976
1. Total cash receipts	1,004,517	2,040,975	2,468,996	2,223,042
2. Income in kind	92,489	121,356	137,431	153,604
3. Realized gross income (1+2)	1,097,006	2,162,331	2,606,427	2,376,646
4. Operating and depreciation charges	658,692	988,172	1,131,750	1,305,097
5. Realized net income (3-4)	438,314	1,174,159	1,474,677	1,071,549
6. Value of inventory changes	59,264	-37,717	44,056	367,549
7. Total gross income (3+6)	1,156,270	2,124,614	2,650,483	2,743,701
8. Total net income (7-4)	497,578	1,136,442	1,518,733	1,438,604

Prepared by author with information taken from the *Saskatchewan Economic Review*, 1976.

TABLE 4
INCOME OF FARM OPERATORS ($1000)

	1976	1977
1. Total cash receipts	2,223,042	1,900,000
2. Income in kind	153,604	160,000
3. Realized gross income (1+2)	2,376,646	2,100,000
4. Operating and depreciation charges	1,305,097	1,400,000
5. Realized net income (3-4)	1,071,549	700,000
6. Value of inventory changes	367,549	0
7. Total gross income (3+6)	2,743,701	2,100,000
8. Total net income (7-4)	1,438,604	700,000

Prepared by author with information taken from the *Saskatchewan Economic Review*, 1976.

(4) Such economies are more susceptible to national and international market instability and uncertainty.

Murray Bryck[8] points out that in 1942 net-farm income was almost twice that of 1943. This was followed by a doubling of net income for the year 1944. In 1945, net income was again halved to that of 1944. The 1952 net income of $608 million was not surpassed until 1973.

Transposing the new Western Grain stabilization plan as to the past 25 years, there would have been 11 or 12 bust years. Bust years in the case of the plan being defined as (those years when the net cash flow in total to the prairies from grain sales drops below the average level of 'net cash flow' for the immediately proceeding five year period. As Professor Thair[1] points out, we have not done much in Canada (in 1973-74) to mitigate the boom and bust situation. — the big problems are still with us. We still experience annual change (up or down) in realized net income (about 10 percent in the fifties and sixties and about 36 percent between 1971 and 1973). We have not done much to control cost-price squeeze, or to bridge the gap between the rich or poor farmers.

As the tables show, the boom years of 1974 and 1975 are now being followed by a downturn in the agricultural economy.

Cost-Price Squeeze

The cost-price squeeze is defined as the process wherein farm costs over the long run continually increase, while the prices of farm products remain relatively stable or at times decline or increase sporadically. It is a common experience to note that farm prices fluctuate because of internal and international pressures. We can see what happened to grain in 1976 and 1977 compared to 1973-75. But it is rare that farm costs will decrease or fluctuate very much. They

TABLE 5
FARM PRICES AND FARM COSTS (1961=100)

Year	Farm Prices of Agricultural Products Saskatchewan	Farm Costs, Western Canada				
		Total	Land and Farm Buildings	Farm Machinery and Motor Vehicles	Hired Farm Labour	Other Materials and Services
1965	101.6	114.1	136.7	107.7	117.0	106.8
1966	103.1	120.6	151.4	110.6	128.9	111.2
1967	106.9	121.6	137.9	114.1	140.2	116.0
1968	99.1	125.6	142.8	118.7	148.2	117.5
1969	96.3	130.2	153.0	121.2	155.7	120.6
1970	97.3	131.0	151.2	123.9	159.4	119.3
1971	96.4	135.9	159.7	127.4	167.9	122.2
1972	112.0	145.2	183.5	131.4	182.2	128.0
1973	189.5	162.9	199.9	136.1	208.3	165.1
1974	250.1	190.7	222.7	150.8	248.7	213.8
1975	230.0	210.7	230.5	175.8	295.3	227.2
1976	199.2	232.9	276.8	199.1	360.6	217.2

Source: *Saskatchewan Economic Review*, 1976, Table 19.

increase every year by 6 to 8 percent. Small farmers cannot survive under these conditions and are forced to move out of farming and sometimes from rural areas.

When you analyze this table carefully, it is not difficult to observe the squeeze farmers find themselves in. You will note that farmers experience fluctuation in farm prices of agricultural products from year to year whereas farm costs continue to increase. Hill points out that prices of inputs in farming went up faster than prices of farm products during the period 1946-65.[19]

So when we discuss rural depopulation it is imperative that we discuss these macro-level forces. The farmer has to expand to survive in the present situation. He has to use bigger machinery to economize an operational cost on a large farm.

Some important decisions are being made which will determine the future of farmers on the Prairies. But most of these decisions are made and will be made by federal or provincial governments along with some experts and specialists in agriculture. Farmers do not have much influence in the outcome of these decisions. Decisions such as railroad abandonment, Crows Nest Pass rates, status of grain elevators, centralization of various services[20] in rural areas, the role of inland terminals, the nature and cost of farm machinery, transport and communication systems, urbanization of rural values and the cost of owning and operating a farm are all very important decisions in reference to the future of prairie rural populations. But as most of these decisions are made outside rural communities, it is not surprising that rural people are apathetic and alienated. Let us look at some studies which have been conducted concerning the effects of railroad abandonment on the Prairies. Under the terms of the National Transportation Act of 1967 both railways (CP & CN) had applied to the Canadian Transport Commission for permission to abandon a number of branchlines. A federal government order in council issued in May, 1967 prohibited any such abandonment and froze 18,103 miles of rail lines in the three Prairie provinces for a seven year period.

The Commission on Grain Handling and Transportation was appointed in May, 1975 by the Canadian government under the chairmanship of E.M. Hall. The terms of reference of the commission were to study grain handling and transportation systems in the Prairies and make recommendations on branchline abandonment. A number of studies which have been conducted to determine the effect of branchline abandonment on rural communities all present conflicting conclusions. Stabler[21], in his study *Economic Effect of Rationalization of the Grain Handling and Transportation System on Prairie Communities*, concludes that the removal of rail and/ or elevator facilities will not alter the direction in which the communities are already moving.

Hodge's study of 1968 concludes that ". . . there is no definite indication (from this study) that a cessation of grain shipment functions would adversely affect community structure in Saskatchewan centres".[22] But Hodges in his earlier study[23] states "[t]he importance of the centre as a grain shipment point is also strongly related to its viability according to the scale". On the other hand, Pamela J. Smith's study indicates quite clearly that rail line abandonment will affect rural communities in a negative way. Smith concludes: ". . . the absolute annual loss of expenditures currently made by all sources in the 26 survey communities is $29,352,531 and that the absolute annual loss of expenditure in 124 communities is estimated to be $120,396,059. It must be remembered that these figures represent simply an annual loss and do not include any measurement of secondary and multiple effects"[24].

The Archer Report [25] (Report of the Rural Development Advisory Group, Sask. 1976) also supports Smith's position and points out ". . . the impact of railline and elevator abandonment would be felt differently by different communities but in general the smaller the centre, the greater the direct impact because of lost jobs and taxes".

There is another study[26] which the Hall Commission did not consider and which supports the position that railline abandonment will affect rural communities in a negative way, i.e., that it will cause loss of jobs, taxes, expenditures etc. These structural changes will affect rural communities in important ways. After reviewing some of these studies it is quite clear that the depopulation process will continue in the future. If the Snavely Report's recommendations are followed and the Crows Nest Pass Rates[27] are repealed and the railways are allowed to charge what the market can bear, the consequences for farmers on the Prairies can be quite serious. It will result in a decline of farm income by approximately 20 percent.

Conclusion

In conclusion I would suggest that the depopulation of the Prairies is the result of certain historical forces in Canada. It is the function of our economic and political system. To analyze the depopulation of the Prairies, we have to look primarily at macro-level structures which operate at the national and international levels rather than looking at the psychological, environmental and social characteristics of individuals who move from the Prairies. We have to analyze forces which compel these people to migrate. The important question is not whether people migrate or stay in rural communities, but why they move and what happens to them when they migrate from one area to another. When economic forces make these people migrate to other areas, how do they adapt to these areas? Depopulation of the Prairies will continue in the future. Forces which were responsible for the settlement of the West are still present with us. The Canadian government has not paid much attention to the problems of agriculture in Canada in general and the situation in Saskatchewan in particular. Under our present system of economic and political institutions, people will be forced to migrate from rural to urban areas and from one region to another. Such migration is in the best interest of people who control the system of production and distribution in Canada and who think in terms of profits and the material development of this country.

NOTES

1. Government of Canada 1971 Census, *Profile Studies Migration in Canada*, Cat. 99-705, Vol. 5, Pt. 1, Feb. 1977, p. 36.

2. *Canada Year Book, 1976-77* — 4.9.3., p. 182.

3. D.R. Whyte, "The Changing Role of Agriculture in the National Economy", p. 55.

4. Government of Saskatchewan, *Saskatchewan Economic Review 1977*, pp. 46-47.

5. R. Paul Shaw, *Migration, Theory and Fact: A Review and Bibliography of Current Literature.* See also Canada Department of Manpower and Immigration, *Internal Migration and Immigration Settlement.* For Saskatchewan study see R.G. Beck and J.C. Stabler, *Intraregional Migration Patterns in Saskatchewan,* Saskatoon: Extension Division, University of Saskatchewan, Publication No. 243, 1974; and a recent Canadian study by K. Grant and J. Vanderkamp, *The Economic Causes and Effects of Migration: Canada, 1965-71,* Ottawa: Economic Council of Canada, Copyright: Minister of Supply and Services, 1976.

6. R.Paul Shaw, "A Note on Cost-Return Calculations and Decisions to Migrate", pp. 167-169. On the basis of his study in Saskatchewan he concludes that there might be population sub-groups who either do not care to make cost return calculations to migration or who are unable to do so.

7. Samuel Stouffer, "Intervening Opportunities: A Theory Relating Mobility and Distance" pp. 845-867.

8. David Sly, "Migration and the Ecological Complex", pp. 615-628.

9. Weng Lang Li "A Differential Approach to the Study of Migration Streams", pp. 534-538.

10. Peter Uhlenberg "Noneconomic Determinants of Nonmigration: Sociological Considerations for Migration Theory", pp. 296-311.

11. Philip Martin, "Noneconomic Determinants of Nonmigration", pp. 353-359. Comments on Uhlengberg's article.

12. Harry Schwarzweller, James Brown "Social Class Origins, Rural-Urban Migration and Economic Life Chances: A Case Study", pp. 5-19.

13. Sidney Goldstein, "Repeated Migration as a Factor of High Mobility Rates", pp. 536-541.

14. Gerald Hodge "Do Villages Grow? Some Perspectives and Predictions", pp. 183-196.

15. Charles Lemelin, "Migration and Economic Development", pp. 36-54.

16. Ernest Mandel, *An Introduction to Marxist Theory,* p. 52.

17. J.A. Abramson, *Rural to Urban Adjustment,* p. 86.

18. Murray Bryck, Most of the information in a boom-bust and cost-price squeeze is taken from Bryck's unpublished M.A. Thesis, "A Conflict-Coercion Analysis of the Major Problems Affecting Agricultural Developments in Saskatchewan".

19. J.T. Hill "Trends in Prices Paid and Received by Farmers", p. 25.

20. M.P. Scharf, *A Report on the Declining Rural Population and the Implications for Rural Education.*

21. J.C. Stabler, *Economic Effect of Rationalization of the Grain Handling and Transportation System on Prairie Communities.*

22. Gerald Hodge, "Branch Line Abandonment: Death Knell for Prairie Towns?", pp. 54-70.

23. Gerald Hodge, "The Prediction of Trade Centre Viability in the Great Plains", pp. 87-115.

24. Pamela J. Smith, "The Socio-Economic Impact of Railline Abandonment Upon Saskatchewan Communities: Transportation and Community Viability", p. 22.

25. Government of Saskatchewan, *Report of the Rural Development Advisory Group,* (1976), p. 36.

26. Group Resources Consultant Service, "Pipestone Valley: a Pilot Study Concerning the Removal of Railroad Branchlines".

27. The Crows Nest Rates are approximately one half cent per ton mile. Hauling to Thunderbay this amounts to 12 cents and in the case of Vancouver it is 13½ cents per bushel. If these rates are repealed the cost to the farmers will go up from 14 cents to 40 cents per bushel.

Readings

Abramson, J.A., *Rural to Urban Adjustment,* ARDA Research Report No. RE-4 ARDA Project #37003, Ottawa: Department of Forestry and Rural Development, 1968.

Anderson, Theodore R., "Intermetropolitan Migration: a Comparison of the Hypotheses of Zipf and Stouffer", *American Sociological Review,* Vol. 20, No. (3), (June 1955).

Baker, Harold R. and June E. Bantjes, *Education for Rural Development: An Annotated Bibliography of Selected References,* Saskatoon: Rural Development Education Program, Extension Division, University of Saskatchewan, [197?].

Basran, G.S., "Adoption of New Farm Practices Among Farmers in Saskatchewan", Saskatoon: University of Saskatchewan, 1973. (Unpublished paper)

Berry, Brian J. L. and William L. Garrison, "A Note on Central Place Theory and the Range of a Good", *Economic Geography,* Vol. 34 (October 1958).

Berry, Brian J. L. and William L. Garrison, "Recent Developments of Central Place Theory", Papers and Proceedings of the Regional Science Association, Vol. 4, (1958).

Berry, Brian J. L., *Geography of Market Centers and Retail Distribution,* Englewood Cliffs, New Jersey: Prentice-Hall, 1967.

Bishop, C.E. (ed.), *Farm Labor in the United States,* New York: Columbia University Press, 1967.

Blevins, Audie L., "Socioeconomic Differences Between Migrants and Nonmigrants", *Rural Sociology* Vol. 36, No. 4 (December 1971).

Brewis, T.N., *Growth and the Canadian Economy,* Toronto: McClelland & Stewart, 1968.

Bronson, H.E., "Continentalism and Canadian Agriculture", in Gary Teeple (ed.), *Capitalism and the National Question in Canada,* Toronto: University of Toronto Press, 1972.

Brown, Alan A. and Egon Neuberger (eds.), *Internal Migration: A Comparative Perspective.* New York: Academic Press Inc, 1977.

Bryck, Murray Raymond, *A Conflict-Coercion Analysis of the Major Problems Affecting Agricultural Development in Saskatchewan,* M.A. Thesis. University of Saskatchewan, 1978.

Burley, Kevin H. (ed.), *The Development of Canada's Staples, 1867-1939,* Toronto: McClelland and Stewart, 1970.

Butler, James E. and Glenn V. Fuguitt, "Small-Town Population Change and Distance from Larger Towns: A Replication of Hassinger's Study", *Rural Sociology*, Vol. 35, No. 3 (September 1970).

Canada Department of Industry, Trade and Commerce, *Canada Year Book 1967-77, Special Edition*, Ottawa: Minister of Supply and Services, 1977.

Canada Department of Manpower and Immigration, *Internal Migration and Immigrant Settlement*, Canada Department of Manpower and Immigration in collaboration with the Ministry of State for Urban Affairs, Ottawa: Information Canada, 1975.

Canada. Economic Council of Canada, *The Economic Causes and Effects of Migration: Canada 1965-71*, by E. Kenneth Grant and John Vanderkamp, Economic Council of Canada, Ottawa: Minister of Supply and Services, 1976.

Canada. Statistics Canada, *1971 Census of Canada, Profile Studies, Migration in Canada*, Catalogue 99-705, Volume: V—Part: 1, (Bulletin 5. 1-5), Ottawa: Statistics Canada, 1977.

Chambers, Ernest John, *The Unexploited West*, Ottawa: Printed by J. de L. Tache, 1914.

Christian, William, Jr. and William Braden, "Rural Migration and the Gravity Model", *Rural Sociology* Vol. 31, No. 1, (March 1966).

Crawford, Charles O., "Family Attachment, Family Support for Migration and Migration Plans of Young People", *Rural Sociology*, Vol 31, No. 3, (September 1966).

Easterbrook, W.T. and Hugh G.J. Aitken, *Canadian Economic History*, Toronto: The Macmillan Company of Canada Limited, 1967.

Easterbrook, W.T. and M.H. Watkins (eds.), *Approaches to Canadian Economic History*, Toronto: McClelland & Stewart Limited, 1967.

Fowke, Vernon C., *The National Policy and the Wheat Economy*, Toronto: University of Toronto Press, 1957.

Furniss, I.F., "Trends in Farm Income", *Canadian Farm Economics*, Vol. 1, No. 5, (December 1966).

Galle, Omer R. and Karl E. Taeuber, "Metropolitan Migration and Intervening Opportunities", *American Sociological Review*, Vol. 31, No. 1, (February 1966).

Gibbs, Jack P., "A Note on Industry Changes and Migration", *American Sociological Review*, Vol. 29, No. 2, (April 1964).

Gibbs, Jack P., "Opinions of Community Leaders on the Causes of Migration", *Rural Sociology*, Vol. 29, No. 4, (1964).

Gilchrist, V., "A Pilot Study of Income Alternatives Affecting the Movement of Farm Operators Out of Agriculture", *Canadian Journal of Agricultural Economics*, Vol. 11, No. 1, (1963).

Gleave, David and Martyn Cordey-Hayes, "Migration Dynamics and Labour Market Turnover", *Progress in Planning*, Vol. 8, No. 1, (1977).

Goldstein, Sidney, "Repeated Migration as a Factor in High Mobility Rates", *American Sociological Review*, Vol. 19, No. 5, (October 1954).

Graber, Edith E., "Newcomers and Oldtimers: Growth and Change in a Mountain Town", *Rural Sociology*, Vol. 39, No. 4, (Winter 1974).

Grimshaw, Allen D., "Relationships Between Agricultural and Economic Indices and Rural Migration", *Rural Sociology*, Vol. 23, No. 4, (December 1958).

Group Resources Consultant Service, "Pipestone Valley: A Pilot Study Concerning The Removal of Railroad Branchlines", Prepared for the Deparment of Industry and Information, Province of Saskatchewan, 1964.

Hamilton, C. Horace, "County Net Migration Rates, Discussion", *Rural Sociology*, Vol. 30, No. 1, (1965).

Heady, Earl O. and Joseph Ackerman, "Farm Adjustment Problems and Their Importance to Sociologists", *Rural Sociology*, Vol. 24, No. 4, (December 1959). (See also "Discussion" by Charles P. Loomis, pp. 326-330).

Hill, J.T., "Trends in Prices Paid and Received by Farmers", *Canadian Farm Economics*, Vol. 1, No. 5, (December 1966).

Hillery, George A., Jr., James S. Brown, Gordon F. DeJong, "Migration Systems of the Southern Appalachians: Some Demographic Observations", *Rural Sociology*, Vol. 30, No. 1, (1965).

Hiscocks, G.A., "Supply Management — Definition, Techniques and Implications", *Canadian Farm Economics*, Vol. 5, No. 2, (June 1970).

Hodge, Gerald, "The Prediction of Trade Centre Viability in the the Great Plains", *The Regional Science Association*, Papers 15, 1965.

Hodge, Gerald, "Do Villages Grow? Some Perspectives and Predictions", *Rural Sociology*, Vol. 31, No. 2, (June 1966).

Hodge, Gerald, "Branchline Abandonment: Death Knell for Prairie Towns?", *Canadian Journal of Agricultural Economics*, Vol. 16, (1968).

Innis, Harold Adams, *Essays in Canadian Economic History*, Toronto: University of Toronto Press, 1956.

Innis, Hugh R. (ed.), *Regional Disparities*, (Consulting editor: Norman Sheffe), Toronto, McGraw-Hill Ryerson, 1972.

Iowa State University Center for Agricultural and Economic Adjustment, *Labour Mobility and Population in Agriculture*, Ames, Iowa: Iowa State University Press, 1961.

Jehlik, Paul J. "Patterns of Net Migration and Changes in Crude Birth Rates in the North Central States, 1940-1950, *Rural Sociology*, Vol. 20, (1955).

King, E.E.R., "Decreasing Farm Numbers and Incomes", *Canadian Farm Economics*, Vol. 1, No. 1, (April, 1966).

Lemelin, Charles, "Migration and Economic Development", *Canadian Journal of Agricultural Economics*, Vol. 13, No. 1 (1965).

Levitt, Kari, "Canada: Economic Dependence and Political Disintegration", *Canadian Dimension*.

Li, Wen Lang, "A Differential Approach to the Study of Migration Streams", *Rural Sociology*, Vol. 35, No. 4, (December 1970).

Lianos, Theodore P., "Stocks and Flows in Migration", *Canadian Journal of Agricultural Economics*, Vol. 16, No. 1, (February 1968).

Lianos, Theodore P., "Labor Mobility and Market Imperfections", *Canadian Journal of Agricultural Economics*, Vol. 18, No. 3 (November 1970).

Lipset, Seymour Martin, "Social Mobility and Urbanization", *Rural Sociology*, Vol. 20, (1955).

Lloyd, Peter E. and Peter Dicken, *Location in Space: A Theoretical Approach to Economic Geography*, New York: Harper and Row, 1972.

Mackintosh, William Archibald, *Prairie Settelement: The Geographical Setting*, Toronto: Macmillan Company of Canada, 1934.

Mackintosh, William Archibald, *The History of Prairie Settlement*, Toronto: Macmillan Company of Canada Limited, 1934-1940.

Mackintosh, William Archibald, *Economic Problems of the Prairie Provinces*, Toronto: Macmillan Company of Canada, 1935.

Mackintosh, William Archibald, *The Economic Background of Dominion-Provincial Relations*, Toronto: McClelland & Stewart, 1969.

Mandel, Ernest, *An Introduction to Marxist Economic Theory*, New York: Pathfinder Press, 1970.

Martin, Larry and Grant Devine, *Centralized Grain Collection Comes at a Cost*, Saskatoon: Extension Division, University of Saksatchewan, 1977.

Martin, Philip, "Noneconomic Determinants of Nonmigration: a Comment", *Rural Sociology*, Vol. 40, No. 3, (Fall 1975).

Martinson, Floyd M., "Personal Adjustment and Rural-Urban Migration", *Rural Sociology*, Vol. 20, (1955).

Metcalf, David, *The Economics of Agriculture*, Harmondsworth, Penguin Books, 1969.

Noble, Henry F., 1962 "Trends in Farm Abandonment", *Canadian Journal of Agricultural Economics*, Vol. 10 No. 1, (1962).

Olsen, H.D. and J.A. Brown, *A Study of the Growth of Selected Service Centers in Saskatchewan*, Saskatoon: Department of Agricultural Economics, University of Saskatchewan (Research Report RR: 75-03), 1975.

Petersen, William, "A General Typology of Migration", *American Sociological Review*, Vol. 23, No. 3, (1958).

Rose, Arnold M., "Distance of Migration and Socio-Economic Status of Migrants", *American Sociological Review*, Vol. 23 No. 4, (August 1958).

Rust, R.S., "A Review of Farm Credit and Income Relationships", *Canadian Farm Economics*, Vol. 5, No. 2, (June 1970).
Safarin, A.E., *The Canadian Economy in the Great Depression*, Toronto: McClelland & Stewart Limited, 1970.
Saskatchewan Agriculture, *Agricultural Statistics 1976*, Statistics Branch, Saskatchewan Department of Agriculture. Regina: Queen's Printer, 1976.
Saskatchewan Agriculture, *Farm Business Review for the Year 1976*, Regina: Statistics Branch, Saskatchewan Agriculture, 1976.
Saskatchewan Agriculture, *Services and Programs for Rural Saskatchewan 1978-79*, (Title page: Services and Programs for Rural Saskatchewan April 1, 1978. March 31, 1979), Regina: Saskatchewan Agriculture, 1978.
Saskatchewan Bureau of Statistics, *Saskatchewan Economic Review*, No. 31, Regina: Saskatchewan Bureau of Statistics, 1977.
Saskatchewan Economic Review, *Saskatchewan Economic Review*, No. 30, Regina: Saskatchewan Bureau of Statistics, 1976.
Saskatchewan Royal Commission on Agriculture and Rural Life, *Service Centers*, Report No. 12, Royal Commission on Agriculture and Rural Life, Regina: Queen's Printer, 1957.
Saskatchewan Rural Development Advisory Group. *Report of The Rural Development Advisory Group*, by J.H. Archer, V.W. Hay, R.F.E. Harvey and Roy Borrowman, 1976.
Scharf, M.P., *A Report on the Declining Rural Population and the Implications for Rural Education*, Regina: Saskatchewan School Trustees Association Research Center (Report No. 17-1974), 1974.
Schnore, Leo F. "Social Morphology and Human Ecology", *The American Journal of Sociology*, Vol. 63, No. 6, (May 1958).
Schulze, Rolf, Jay Artis, J. Allan Beegle, "The Measurement of Community Satisfaction and the Decision to Migrate", *Rural Sociology*, Vol. 28, No. 3, (September 1963).
Schwarzweller, Harry K. and James S. Brown, "Social Class Origins, Rural-Urban Migration and Economic Life chances: A Case Study", *Rural Sociology*, Vol. 32, No. 1, (1967).
Shaw, R. Paul, "A Note on Cost-Return Calculations and Decisions to Migrate", *Population Studies*, Vol. 28, No. 1, (March 1974).
Shaw, R. Paul, *Migration Theory and Fact: A Review and Bibliography of Current Literature*, Bibliography Series Number 5, Philadelphia: Regional Science Research Institute, 1975.
Shute, D.M., "Input Substitution and Productivity of Canadian Agriculture, 1961 to 1973", *Canadian Farm Economics*, Vol. 10, No. 1, (February 1975).
Sly, David F., 1972 "Migration and the Ecological Complex", *American Sociological Review*, Vol. 37, No. 5, (October 1972).
Sly, David F. and Jeff Tayman, "Ecological Approach to Migration Reexamined", *American Sociological Review*, Vol. 42, No. 5, (October 1977).
Smith, Mapheus, "Some Relationships Between Intelligence and Geographical Mobility", *American Sociological Review*, Vol. 8, No. 6, (December 1943).
Smith, Pamela J., "The Socio-Economic Impact of Railline Abandonment Upon Saskatchewan Communities: Transportation and Community Viability", presented at the 1977 Annual Meeting of the Canadian Sociology and Anthropology Association, June 10-14, 1977, Fredericton, New Brunswick, 1977.
Stabler, J.C., *Prairie Regional Development and Prospects*, prepared for the Royal Commission on Consumer Problems and Inflation, supporting study No. 1, 1968.
Stabler, J.C., *Economic Effect of Rationalization of the Grain Handling and Transportation System on Prairie Communities*, Saskatoon: Underwood McClelland Associates Limited, prepared for the Grains Group, Ottawa, 1972.
Stabler, J.C. and R.G. Beck, *Intraregional Migration Patterns in Saskatchewan*, Saskatoon: Extension Division, University of Saskatchewan, 1974.
Storey, Gary G., "Community Stability and Farm Size". (Unpublished paper)
Stouffer, Samuel A., "Intervening Opportunities: a Theory Relating Mobility and distance", *American Sociological Reivew*, Vol 5, (December 1940).

Stouffer, Samuel A., "Intervening Opportunities and Competing Migrants", *Journal of Regional Science*, Vol. 2, (Spring, 1960).

Stub, Holger R., "The Occupational Characteristics of Migrants to Duluth: A Retreat of Rose's Hypothesis", *American Sociological Review*, Vol. 27, No. 1, (February 1962).

Taeuber, Karl E., 1967 "The Residential Redistribution of Farm-Born Cohorts", *Rural Sociology*, Vol. 32, No. 1, (March 1967).

Tarver, James D., "Differentials and Trends in Actual and Expected Distance of Movement of Interstate Migrants", *Rural Sociology*, Vol. 36, No. 4, (December 1971).

Tarver, James D. and William R. Gurley, "The Relationship of Selected Variables with County Net Migration Rates in the United States, 1950 to 1960", *Rural Sociology*, Vol. 30, No. 1, (1965). "Rejoinder", pp. 17-22.

Tarver, James D. and Patrick M. Skees, 1967 "Vector Representation of Interstate Migration Streams", *Rural Sociology*, Vol. 32, No. 2, (June 1967).

The Telegram (Toronto) Canada 70 Team, *The Prairie Provinces: Alienation and Anger*, (Cover title: The Prairies: Alienation and Anger), Toronto: McClelland & Stewart Limited, 1969.

Thair, P.J., "Canadian Farm Income Levels — Implications", (paper delivered at the Canadian Agricultural Outlook Conference, Ottawa, January 28 and 29, 1974).

Uhlenberg, Peter, "Noneconomic Determinants of Nonmigration: Sociological Considerations for Migration Theory", *Rural Sociology*, Vol. 38, No. 3, (Fall 1973).

Whyte, D.R., "The Changing Role of Agriculture in the National Economy", in Rocco Louis Gentilcore (ed.), *Geographical Approaches to Canadian Problems*, Scarborough: Prentice-Hall of Canada, 1971.

Zimmerman, Carle C. and Garry W. Moneo, *The Prairie Community System*, Agricultural Economics Research Council of Canada, 1970.

Zipf, George Kingsley, The P_1P_2/D Hypothesis: On the Intercity Movement of Persons", *American Sociological Review*, Vol. 11, No. 6, (December 1946).

Canadian Immigration Policy and Assimilation Theories

Peter S. Li and B. Singh Bolaria

PETER S. LI is an Assistant Professor of Sociology at the University of Saskatchewan. His current research interests include Ethnic Inequality and the Chinese in Canada.

B. SINGH BOLARIA is an Associate Professor and Head in the Department of Sociology at the University of Saskatchewan. His current research interests include Medical Sociology, Industrial Sociology, and Immigration of Ethnic Groups.

The image of non-whites in Canada has been frequently distorted by both academics and policy makers. These distortions are based, in part, on assumptions of ethnic lives and cultures that are neither supported by empirical evidence nor theoretical arguments. Until the recent past, however, these assumptions have been unquestionably accepted by sociologists in their construction of assimilation models as basic tools to interpret the meanings of ethnicity.

Theoretical prejudices towards non-white ethnic groups are widely accepted not only by academics, but are also popular among many policy makers. Our examination of the Canadian immigration system suggests a striking similarity between the biases identified in the assimilation school, and those shared by immigration policy makers. Although such a 'coincidence' does not necessarily imply a causal relationship, it does point out a possible linkage between social science and social policy in that the former can provide ideological support to the latter by rationalizing social practice.

From a broader theoretical perspective, it can be seen that such racial biases, in academic theory and social practice, tend to facilitate exploitations of non-white labour in the capitalist market.

Fallacies of Assimilation Theories

It has been over half a century since Robert Park proposed his famous "race relations cycle", and more than a decade since Milton Gordon published *Assimilation in American Life*. Despite the radical changes in ethnic relations in North America, as exemplified by black militancy in the States during the sixties, and French separatism in Canada in the early seventies, sociologists have by and large adhered to the basic premises of the assimilation school in unravelling the meanings and implications of ethnicity.

The term "assimilation school" is probably a misnomer in that it encompasses a variety of conflicting theories which deal with the process of assimilation. These theories range from a popular concept such as "melting pot" to a formal theory such as Park's "race relations cycle" (1950). Between these polar extremes lies the treatise on assimilation by Gordon (1964) and the formulation of the triple melting pot by Kennedy (1944, 1952) and Glazier and Moynihan (1963). This rich and somewhat confusing theoretical tradition tends to camouflage the underlying assumptions of assimilation theories.

Rather than covering each theory (see, for example, Gorden, 1964 and Price, 1969), we shall identify the major camps within the assimilation school and examine their basic premise. The first camp includes those who argue the gradual dilution of cultural traits among ethnic immigrants. Anglo-conformists and melting-pot proponents, although differing on their emphasis on Anglo-Saxon culture versus an amalgamated product as the destination, have much in common in this respect — they both argue that immigrant groups are giving up their cultural traits in their assimilation into the new world. Among the second camp are the pluralists who stress the persistence of ethnic culture despite assimilation. Examples include, for instance, models of pluralism as formulated by Kuper and Smith, (1969), and the triple melting pot concept advanced by Kennedy, (1944, 1952), and Glazier and Moynihan, (1963). These authors argue that ethnic groups frequently maintain and develop ethnic institutions in their adaptation to the host society, and in doing so, produce a pluralistic structure characterized by various ethnic cleavages.

Despite the theoretical differences, these divergent views share one important aspect, that it is the *distinctiveness* of cultural origin which is being emphasized, that such distinctiveness, whether cultural or institutional, is an important determinant in explaining ethnic differences. In stressing the persistence or disappearance of cultural traits and institutions, proponents from both camps in fact recognize the importance of cultural origins in explaining subsequent behaviours of ethnic groups.

Discussions of ethnic inequality, as measured by economic and other differences, serve as a good example to illustrate the basic assumption in the assimilation school. The frequent explanation of ethnic inequality is to interpret it as differential degrees of assimilation or non-assimilation, depending on one's position within the assimilation school. In either case, it becomes important to identify those factors which are seemingly unique to a particular cultural origin as explanations of that group's economic success or failure. The classic example is the notion "culture of poverty", as developed by Oscar Lewis (1959, 1966), and used time and again as explanations of why groups like the Mexicans and Puerto Ricans are in an economically disadvantaged position. In the same vein, the apparent success of the Jews in North America is attributed to traditional Jewish scholarship (Herberg, 1960; Wagley and Harris, 1958), while the recent achievement of the Orientals in America is explained in terms of their cultural uniqueness (Hsu, 1972) and institutional heritage (Light, 1972). In the mobility literature, the assimilation perspective is expressed in various motivational hypotheses which stress value orientation differences among ethnic groups. One example of such hypotheses is the "achievement syndrome" argument as proposed by Rosen (1956, 1959), which suggests that variations among ethnic groups in achievement motivation, value orientation and educational-vocational aspiration account for the different rates of mobility.

The primary objection to the assimilation perspective is not so much whether assimilation as a process, however it is defined, takes place, or whether cultural origin as an attribute, exists or not. Rather, the challenge is based on the frequent allusion that the uniqueness in cultural origin is necessarily the cause of ethnic differences. There are mounting evidence and theoretical dispositions to suggest that the basic assimilationist position is false. For example, Yancey, Ericksen and Juliani (1976) show that among many groups the maintenance of ethnicity in America is attributed to the structural conditions of that society, particularly to the development of urbanization and modern transportation, rather than to some transplanted cultural heritage from the Old World. In the case of particular ethnic groups, Slater (1969) shows that traditional Jewish culture is antithetic to, and not complementary of, achievement ethics. Li (1976) argues that it is the historical exclusion of the Chinese in America, and not the sojourner orientation which channels them into ethnic businesses. Evidence pertaining to the Canadian situation reflects similar objections to the basic assimilationist position. Beattie's study of middle-level Anglophones and Francophones (1975) show that it is structural discriminations in the federal government bureaucracy, rather than value orientation differences which explain the income disparity between the two groups. Breton and Roseborough (1971) indicate that it is not cultural values which account for lower mobility among French-Canadians as compared to English-Canadians in a large corporation in Canada. The authors further conclude (Breton and Roseborough, 1971: 467) that ". . . there is sufficient evidence to suggest that Canadian ethnic groups . . . cannot automatically be assumed to hold different values, and that differences in values explain the differential assimilation in modern industrialized society".

The assimilationist position also suffers from a basic lack of clarity in the way the model is applied. The confusion arises from the causal application of the model as a description *and* explanation of the same ethnic phenomena. For example, the persistence of certain cultural traits (Fong, 1973) or cultural institutions (Breton, 1964) are sometimes used as indicators of the particular stage the ethnic group is in, along a continuum of integration or assimilation. Other times, cultural traits are interpreted as resultants of certain stages of assimilation in that certain groups maintain a certain cultural heritage because they are not as yet assimilated to the dominant culture. In this regard, the term "assimilation" has the same drawback as the term "culture". While the terms encompass multidimensions, it is a conceptual tautology to apply the terms as both causes and consequences. In speaking of this problem, Valentine (1968) lucidly argues that there is a distinct difference between those material conditions which exist prior to, and apart from culture, and culture itself. Similarly, one has to separate those conditions which are caused by specific ethnic culture, from others which are associated with, but not consequences of ethnic origin. While status differences are frequently *associated with* ethnic origins, such associations are not in themselves indications of causal relationships.

Ironically, assimilation theories frequently represent more idealistic projections of the future than objective realism of the present, or the past. To the extent that they are ethnocentric ideologies centred around the WASP culture, they are, as Lyman (1974:188) put it, ". . . mere projections of the dominant ethos of the larger society, an ethos which has too often been taken over uncritically by the sociologist".

The assimilation model has been criticized by others (for example Price, 1969) for its Social Darwinist overtone, its mechanical application to different ethnic lives as well as other theoretical confusions. Suffice to say that the basic model entails obvious theoretical flaws and ideological bias. The fact remains that for a long period of time the assimilation model has been the single most important framework in understanding ethnic lives in North America. The apparent inconsistency cannot be resolved on purely academic grounds. It is in examining a certain specific social policy that a fuller meaning and implication of assimilation theories begin to unfold.

Canadian Immigration Policy

The Canadian immigration policy, at least up to World War II, was aimed at excluding from entry into Canada those who did not come from Britain, the U.S. and Northern Europe. The line was clearly drawn between white and non-white immigrants, although among Caucasian immigrants, some (such as the British) were definitely more preferred than others (such as Jews and Italians).

The Canadian legislation pertaining to immigration prior to World War II clearly indicates a differential treatment of immigrants based on race. For example, by an order-in-council (P.C. 692) in 1931, the admissible classes were restricted to British, U.S. citizens, agriculturalists and certain immediate relatives such as wife and unmarried children under 18. Other groups, notably Asians, and in particular the Chinese, were subjected to severe legislative control. The Chinese Immigration Act of 1923 (S.C. 1923, c. 38), for example, prohibited the entry of practically all Chinese with the few exceptions of merchants, students, diplomats and children born in Canada of Chinese descent. Prior to 1923, the Chinese entering Canada were subjected to a head tax applied exclusively to them, and not to other groups. An order-in-council of 1907 required "Asiatic immigrants" to pay $200 landing money, with the amount being raised to $250 in 1919.

The exclusion and preference of immigrant groups, although generally affected by the labour market, does not necessarily correspond to the ebb and flow of the economy. It was during economic prosperity in 1923, for example, that the Chinese Exclusion Act was passed, and it was in the same year that the government of Canada actively recruited immigrants from Britain, the U.S. and Northern Europe. Various arrangements with the British government, transportation companies and land development companies were made to facilitate the immigration from these preferred countries (Manpower and Immigration, 1974a). The passage assistance available to British immigrants was a sharp contrast to the landing money required of Asiatic immigrants, and the head tax imposed upon the Chinese. Summarizing the period prior to World War II, a government report notes the following: "British and American immigrants were the most favoured. Northern Europeans were relatively well received. Other Europeans were accepted if no one else was available. Non-whites were not welcome" (Manpower and Immigration, 1974a).

The post-war immigration policy was summarized in the statement of Prime Minister MacKenzie King on May 1, 1947. After pointing out that future immigration should be related to the "absorptive capacity" of the country, King presented the government's position with respect to oriental immigration.

> There will, I am sure, be general agreement with the view that the people of Canada do not wish, as a result of mass immigration, to make a fundamental alteration in the character of our population. Large-scale immigration from the orient would change the fundamental composition of the Canadian population. Any considerable oriental immigration would, moreover, be certain to give rise to social and economic problems of a character that might lead to serious difficulties in the field of international relations. The government, therefore, has no thought of making any change in immigration regulations which would have consequences of the kind (Canada House of Commons Debates, 1947, p. 2646).

It is evident, from this statement, that a closed-door policy towards Asian immigration was to be maintained. Neither the 1952 Immigration Act, nor subsequent amendments in 1962, altered the basic preference of white to non-white immigrants. The 1962 bill, although removing some discriminatory clauses in the Canadian policy, still provided a wider range of sponsored relatives for European immigrants as compared to non-European immigrants (Hawkins, 1972). It was not until 1967 that an universal selection system was applied, theoretically at least, to immigrants of all ethnic origins.

The statistics on annual immigration to Canada indicate that preferential admissions are persistently given to immigrants from the United Kingdom and the United States, despite frequent claims, on the part of the Canadian government that the 1962 immigration act had laid down the basic selection criteria as educational and occupational qualifications, and the 1967 order-in-council had totally abolished differential selection based on national origins. Table 1 provides the figures of immigrants admitted annually to Canada since 1946, by country of last permanent residence. With the exception of a few years (1958 to 1961; 1971 to 1972), immigrants from the United Kingdom constituted the largest group admitted to Canada every year. It ranged from 65 percent of the total immigrants in 1946 to 19 percent in 1975. In contrast, Chinese immigrants, up to 1967, were no more than 3 percent of the total immigration figure. There was an increase in Asian immigrants as a consequence of the 1967 Act, resulting in 7 percent from China (largely from Hong Kong and Taiwan) and 6.6 percent from India and Pakistan in 1975. The immigration from Italy steadily increased after World War II, until it reached the peak in 1958 to 1961, surpassing the number of immigrants from the United Kingdom. But as Richmond (1967: 4) observes, "... whenever the proportion of British immigrants showed signs of falling, the Canadian government intensified its promotional

NUMBER OF IMMIGRANTS ADMITTED ANNUALLY TO CANADA BY SELECTED
COUNTRY OF LAST PERMANENT RESIDENCE[a], 1946-75[b]

Year	Total Immigrants	United Kingdom[d]	%	U.S.A.	%	Italy	%	China[c]	%	India Pakistan	%
1946	31081	20162	64.87	7454	23.98	58	.18	1	.00	1	.0032
1947	66990	47976	71.62	11410	17.03	142	.21	7	.01	7	.01
1948	79194	44788	56.55	9034	11.40	204	.25	24	.03	130	.16
1949	125603	40015	31.86	7305	5.82	5207	4.15	111	.09	63	.05
1950	73912	13427	18.17	7799	10.55	9059	12.26	1741	2.36	77	.1
1951	194391	31370	16.14	7732	3.98	24351	12.53	2697	1.39	97	.05
1952	164498	42675	25.94	9306	5.66	21383	13	2313	1.40	168	.10
1953	168868	47077	27.88	9379	5.56	24293	14.39	1929	1.14	139	.08
1954	154227	44593	28.91	10110	6.56	24595	15.95	1950	1.26	175	.11
1955	109946	30150	27.42	10392	9.45	20247	18.41	2575	2.34	245	.22
1956	164857	51319	31.12	9777	5.93	29806	18.07	2093	1.26	330	.20
1957	282164	72476	25.68	11008	3.90	29443	10.43	1662	.58	324	.11
1958	124851	26622	21.32	10846	8.68	28564	22.87	2615	2.09	451	.36
1959	106928	19361	18.10	11338	10.60	26822	25.08	2561	2.39	716	.66
1960	104111	20853	20.02	11247	10.80	21308	20.46	1370	1.31	673	.64
1961	71689	13295	18.54	11516	16.06	14630	20.40	861	1.20	744	1.03
1962	74586	15603	20.91	11643	15.61	13641	18.28	670	.89	584	.78
1963	93151	24603	26.41	11736	12.59	14426	15.48	1137	1.27	858	.92
1964	112606	29279	26.00	12565	11.15	19297	17.13	2674	2.37	962	.85
1965	146758	39857	27.15	15143	10.31	26398	17.98	4352	2.96	2664	1.81
1966	194743	63291	32.49	17514	8.99	31625	16.23	4094	2.10	2499	1.28
1967	222876	62420	28.00	19038	8.54	30055	13.48	6409	2.87	4614	2.07
1968	183974	37889	20.59	20422	11.10	19774	10.74	8382	4.55	3856	2.09
1969	161531	31977	19.79	22785	14.10	10383	6.42	8272	5.12	6400	3.96
1970	147713	26497	17.93	24424	16.53	8533	5.77	5377	3.64	6680	4.52
1971	121900	15451	12.68	24366	19.99	5790	4.75	5817	4.77	6281	5.15
1972	122006	18197	14.91	22618	18.54	4608	3.78	7181	5.89	6239	5.11
1973	184200	26973	14.64	25242	13.70	5468	2.97	16094	8.74	11488	6.23
1974	218465	38456	17.60	26541	12.15	5226	2.39	14465	6.62	15183	6.95
1975	187881	34978	18.62	20155	10.73	5078	2.70	13166	7.00	12309	6.55
TOTAL	4195700	1031630	24.59	429845	10.24	480414	11.45	122650	2.92	84957	2.02

a The figures from 1946-61 were based on ethnic origin, except for those from the U.S.A. The figures from 1962-75 were based on country of last permanent residence. For details, see annual reports of the Department of Mines and Resources (1946-49), Department of Citizenship and Immigration (1950-66), and Department of Manpower and Immigration (1967-75).

b The figures from 1946 to 1949 were compiled for the fiscal year ending March 31 of each year, from 1950-75 they were based on the calendar year ending December 31 of each year.

c Including those from Hong Kong and Taiwan.   d Percent based on total immigrants admitted each year.

campaign in the United Kingdom and re-established the primary position of the British immigrants."

That Canadian immigration policies have been patronizing certain immigrant groups is recognized by ministers in the administration. For example, Jean Marchand, the then Minister of Manpower and Immigration, said in 1966: "It is only fair to observe that the relatively favourable provisions for Europeans and residents of the United States, for instance, have developed over many years and have acquired the patina of tradition. Real non-discrimination in practice as well as on paper will not be effective overnight" (Canada, House of Commons, Minutes of Proceedings and Evidence, no. 1, 1966). It is interesting to note that the government developed over the years, not only a discriminatory policy of immigration, but also a theory to justify such a practice.

Such a justification springs from a basic dilemma. On the one hand, the government is dedicated to the democratic principles of equality and freedom, and on the other hand, it adopts an immigration policy which is discriminatory in nature. Putting it more bluntly, how could the government deny racial discrimination on the policy level, while at the same time keeping the Canadian door closed to some ethnic groups and opening it for others? The question is not so much to resolve this dilemma in practice, but rather, to rationalize it in theory. It is here that the assimilation arguments provide the necessary ammunition to defend the official position.

The official explanation for the Canadian immigration policy, both historically and contemporarily, may be summarized in the following premises. First, immigration to Canada is a privilege and not a right, and the government of Canada has the right to decide who to admit and exclude. Second, some groups, originating from areas which exhibit greater climatic and social differences, are less likely to be assimilated in the Canadian society. It follows, therefore, that immigrants from Europe and the United States are more welcome than other immigrants. This basic argument is used time and again by various ministers of immigration to justify the immigration policy. For example, as early as 1910, the Deputy Minister summarized the immigration policy in the following way:

> The policy of the Department at the present time is to encourage the immigration of farmers, farm labourers, and female domestic servants from the United States, the British Isles, and certain Northern European countries, namely, France, Belgium, Holland, Switzerland, Germany, Denmark, Norway, Sweden and Iceland.
>
> On the other hand, it is the policy of the Department to do all in its power to keep out of the country undesirables . . . those belonging to nationalities unlikely to assimilate and who consequently prevent the

building up of a united nation of people of similar customs and ideals (quoted in Manpower and Immigration, 1974a: 9-10).

Such a selective immigration policy based on the alleged "non-assimilability" of some groups is echoed in a 1923 statement by the then Minister:

> While there are some would-be immigrants into Canada who are not suited for the Dominion owing to physical, moral, or industrial unfitness or because they belong to races that cannot be assimilated without social or economic loss to Canada, there are at the same time in Great Britain and Continental Europe tens of thousands of skilled and unskilled workers (not agriculturalists) who would be an asset to Canada if steady employment could be found for them (quoted in Manpower and Immigration, 1974a: 14).

Despite the changes in immigration policy after World War II, the Minister of Immigration continued to reaffirm the traditional argument in favour of immigrants from Europe and the United States:

> We try to select as immigrants those who will have to change their ways least in order to adapt themselves to Canadian life and to contribute to the development of the Canadian nation. This is why entry into Canada is virtually free to citizens of the U.K., and the U.S., and France so long as they have good health and good characters. That is why deliberate preference is shown for immigrants from countries with political and social institutions similar to our own (Canada, House of Commons, 1955, quoted in Richmond, 1967: 3).

The striking similarity of these statements made at different years reflects more the same dilemma confronting the government than mere coincidence. It also shows that the government was forced to use the same assimilation argument to defend the official position. The argument is anchored upon the assumptions that (1) assimilation as a process is taking place in the Canadian society; and (2) the transplanted cultures of ethnic groups from outside Europe and the United States would impede the process of assimilation by creating adjustment problems. The argument shares with the academic position of the assimilation school in assuming that distinctiveness in cultural origins would necessarily make a difference in subsequent adjustments in the Canadian society.

Data on adjustments of immigrants in Canada indicate that there is little empirical support of the claim that non-white immigrants are necessarily less "assimilated". In a recent study of adjustments of immigrants after three years in Canada (Manpower and Immigration, 1974b), for example, it is reported that immigrants from Hong Kong, Taiwan, Yugoslavia and India are much more likely to feel that Canada is their home country than immigrants from France, Britain, Germany and the United States (see Table 2).

TABLE 2
SENSE OF BELONGING*, BY COUNTRY OF ORIGIN
(Percentage distribution)

	Sense of Belonging		
Country of Origin	At Home in Canada	Attached to Their Country of Origin	Undecided
Hong Kong & Taiwan	75	8	17
Yugoslavia	70	11	19
India	70	4	26
Portugal	64	10	26
France	58	16	26
Greece	53	10	37
Britain	50	16	34
Germany, Fed. Rep.	48	19	33
United States	48	24	28
Philippines	46	17	37
West Indies	43	11	46
Italy	39	19	42
Australia	25	39	36
Others	63	12	25
TOTAL	55	14	31

*Based on the following question:

Do you now feel that Canada is your "home" country, or do you feel as if you belong more to your former country?

—I now feel that Canada is my "home" country.
—I still feel that I belong to my former country.
—I am still undecided.

Source: Manpower and Immigration, Three Years in Canada, Ottawa: Information Canada, 1974, Table 11.11, pp. 107, 109.

Concluding Remarks

In summary, we are arguing that assimilation theories, in their monolithic emphasis on distinctiveness of cultural origin, are limited in explaining ethnic differences. There are both theoretical reasons and empirical evidence to suggest that the basic premise of the assimilation argument is false. One important implication of such theories has been to justify the Canadian immigration policy which was based upon differential selection on the basis of racial origins.

There is a tendency to dismiss racial biases, present in academic writings and social policy, as historical accidents or isolated thoughts, without considering the larger implications of racism on the capitalist labour market. One of the characteristics of such a market is to economize the cost of labour reserves for employers so that the overhead costs of labour can be passed from individual employers to the market (Pentland, 1959). This implies that a reserve labour force greatly benefits employers in that it supplies idle labour when labour demand increases, and it absorbs surplus labour when labour demand decreases. The maintenance of such a reserve pool of labour requires that sufficient workers are kept either from moving away from the pool, or are replenished in it when the size of the pool begins to shrink. One of the mechanisms of preserving the reserve labour force is to define a group of people as inferior or nonassimilable, thereby justifying various forms of institutional exclusion. Racism then, can be used effectively to recruit menial labour and to restrict immigrants to marginal participation in the labour market. It is in this larger context that racism has to be understood.

Although our analysis does not deal with the relationship between capitalism and racism directly, other studies have provided both theoretical explanation of and empirical support to our position. For example, Reich (1971) shows that one of the effects of racism in capitalist society is to divide the solidarity of the working class, and weaken union organization, thus strengthening the position of employers. Bonacich (1972, 1976) indicates that a split labour market operates in advanced capitalism, in which the price of labour for blacks is cheaper than that for whites. Symanski (1976) argues that capitalist society requires a group of oppressed workers to perform its menial tasks, and demonstrates that racism and sexism serve similar functions in producing such oppression. These studies clearly suggest the importance of understanding racism in the context of capitalism.

Readings

Beattie, Christopher, *Minority Men in a Majority Setting*, Toronto: McClelland & Stewart, 1975.

Blauner, Robert, *Racial Oppression in America*, New York: Harper & Row, 1972.

Bonacich, Edna, "A Theory of Ethnic Antagonism: The Split Labour Market", *American Sociological Review* Vol. 37, (1972).

Bonacich, Edna, "Advanced Capitalism and Black/White Race Relations in the United States: A Split Labour Market Interpretation", *American Sociological Review*, Vol. 41, (1976).

Breton, Raymond, "Institutional Completeness of Ethnic Communities and the Personal Relations of Immigrants", *American Journal of Sociology*, Vol. 70, (1964).

Breton, Raymond and Roseborough, Howard, "Ethnic Differences in Status", in B. Blishen, et al., (eds.), *Canadian Society, Sociological Perspectives*, Toronto: MacMillan of Canada, 1971.

Fong, Stanley L. M., "Assimilation and Changing Social Roles of Chinese Americans", *Journal of Social Issues*, Vol. 29, (1973).

Genovese, Eugene D., *The Political Economy of Slavery*, New York: Vintage Books, 1967.

Genovese, Eugene D., "Materialism and Idealism in the History of Negro Slavery in the Americas", *Journal of Social History*, Vol. 4, (1971).

Glaser, Nathan and Daniel P. Monihan, *Beyond the Melting Pot*, Cambridge, Mass: M.I.T. Press, 1970.

Gordon, Milton, *Assimilation in American Life*, New York: Oxford University Press, 1964.

Hawkins, Freda, *Canada and Immigration*, Montreal: Queen's University Press, 1972.

Herberg, Will, *Protestant, Catholic, Jew*, New York: Doubleday, 1960.

Hsu, Francis L. K., *Challenge of the American Dream: The Chinese in the United States*, San Francisco: Wadsworth, 1972.

Kennedy, Ruby J. R., "Single or Triple Melting Pot? Intermarriage Trends in New Haven 1870-1940", *American Journal of Sociology*, Vol. 49, (1944).

Kennedy, Ruby J. R., "Single or Triple Melting Pot? Intermarriage in New Haven, 1890-1950", *American Journal of Sociology*, Vol. 58, (1952).

Kuper, Leo and M. G. Smith (eds.), *Pluralism in Africa*. Oxford: Oxford University Press, 1969.

Lewis, Oscar, *Five Families: Mexican Case Studies in the Culture of Poverty*, New York: Basic Books, 1959.

Lewis, Oscar, *La Vida: A Peurto Rican Family in the Culture of Poverty*, San Juan and New York: Randon House, 1966.

Li, Peter S., "Ethnic Businesses Among Chinese in the U.S.", *Journal of Ethnic Studies*, Vol. 4, (1976).

Light, Ivan H., *Ethnic Enterprise in America: Business and Welfare Among Chinese, Japanese and Blacks*, Berkeley: University of California Press, 1972.

Lyman, Stanford, M., *Chinese Americans*, Toronto: Random House, 1974.

Manpower and Immigration, *The Immigration Program*, Ottawa: Information Canada, 1974[a].

Manpower and Immigration, *Three Years in Canada*, Ottawa: Information Canada, 1974[b].

Park, Robert E., *Race and Culture*, Glencoe, Illinois: Free Press, 1950.

Pentland, H. C., "The Development of a Capitalistic Labour Market in Canada", *Canadian Journal of Economics and Political Sciences*, Vol. 25, (1959).

Price, Charles, "The Study of Assimilation", in J. A. Jackson (ed.), *Migration*, Cambridge: Cambridge University Press, 1969.

Reich, Michael, "The Economics of Racism", in David Gordon (ed.), *Problems in Political Economy*, Lexington, Mass.: Heath, 1971.

Richmond, Anthony, *Post War Immigrants in Canada*, Toronto: University of Toronto Press, 1967.

Rosen, Bernard C., "The Achievement Syndrome: A Psychocultural Dimension of Social Stratification", *American Sociological Review*, Vol. 21, (1956).

Rosen, Bernard C., "Race, Ethnicity, and the Achievement Syndrome", *American Sociological Review*, Vol. 24, (1959).

Slater, Marian K., "My Son the Doctor: Aspects of Mobility Among American Jews", *American Sociological Review*, Vol. 34, (1969).

Szymanski, Albert, "Racism and Sexism as Functional Substitutes in the Labour Market", *Sociological Quarterly*, Vol. 17, (1976).

Valentine, Charles A., *Culture and Poverty*, Chicago: The University of Chicago Press, 1968.

Wagley, Charles and Marvin Harris, *Minorities in the New World*, New York: Columbia University Press, 1958.

Yancey, William L., E. P. Ericksen and R. N. Julian, "Emergent Ethnicity: A Review and Reformulation", *American Sociological Review*, Vol. 41, (1976).

The Crisis in Confederation*

Louis Feldhammer

LOUIS FELDHAMMER is an Assistant Professor of Sociology at Ryerson Polytechnical Institute. His current research interests include Canadian Political Economy and the State.

The victory of the Parti Québecois in the Québec provincial elections of November 15, 1976 brought to international attention a problem which has been developing in Canada for over 200 years — ever since the British conquest of New France in 1759. The P.Q. is totally and solely devoted to separating Québec from the rest of Canada and creating an independent Québec state. It has clearly indicated that all other considerations during its present tenure in office are to be subordinated to the achievement of Québec independence and of working to get a *yes* vote in a referendum to be held on this question sometime within the next four years. A crisis which threatens the continued existence of Canada is thus coming to a head. The repercussions of the outcome of this crisis, however, extend far beyond the borders of the Canadian state.

● ● ●

Accompanied by the genocidal crushing of the aboriginal tribes, Québec was slowly settled by emigrants from France — primarily Norman peasants. In 1663 there were only 2,500 settlers living in New France. By the time of the conquest the population had reached 63,000 and today the inhabitants of Québec number around 7 million, or almost one-third of the total population of Canada.

Under French rule New France experienced the development of a feudal system with seigneurial ownership of land. The Church was a major landowner. Taking the Marxist belief that material production is the basis of social life as a departure point, it can be seen that

---

*This paper was first presented at the annual meeting of the American Sociological Association held in Chicago in September, 1977.

the feudal conditions prevailing in New France during this period prevented the unity of economic life that is the essential condition for firm territorial unity and the stability of a cohesive national community. Feudal production relations, exemplified by seigneurial ownership of land, hindered the expansion of peasant tillage and peasant settlement of areas beyond the boundaries of the seigneurial lands. It was only with the emergence of capitalist relations, beginning in the second half of the seventeenth century, continuing with the conquest and the progressive institution of a national market, and, finally, capped by the enactment of the British North America Act in 1867 which established a single Canada-wide market, that the French-speaking population grew into full nationhood.

It is this existence of the reality of the French-Canadian *nation* which lies at the very heart of the Canadian crisis of confederation. Capitalists have long been aware of French-Canadians as members of a distinct nation. In the infamous Durham Report on responsible self-government in Canada, written in 1838, Lord Durham referred to ". . . two nations warring in the bosom of a single state". The reasons why Canadian monopoly capital is reluctant to publicly recognize French Canada as a nation will become clear in the course of this presentation.

But first it is absolutely crucial to establish what constitutes a nation. There has been, and continues to be, a tremendous amount of confusion on this question. Much of this confusion is deliberately fostered in order to maintain the *status quo* and avoid the implementation of a solution which would have a detrimental effect on the power and profits of the Canadian ruling class. Thus, Canadians are compelled to hear and read an abundance of ambiguous and unscientific information about "two founding 'races' ", or, as Trudeau recently stated, about how there are many nations in Canada, including the Indian and Innuit (let alone the Ukranian and Italian). Canada is also constantly referred to (with no regard for even minimal consistency) as a geographic entity, as a country, and as a single nation. All of this confusion inhibits the ability of Canadians to make a real analysis of the national question and, what is most significant, inhibits their ability to recognize *the bi-national character of the Canadian state.*

The concept of nation must be distinguished from the notion of "an independent sovereign state". The two are in no way synonymous and, as we know from numerous examples, more than one nation can inhabit a single state. The Soviet Union is, of course, the best and most successful example of this. Successful, because the ultimate resolution to the national problem is the attainment of that "consistent democracy" of which Lenin spoke and which only socialism can finally and completely guarantee. For as Lenin pointed out, communists must postulate the division of nations into oppressor and oppressed as basic, significant and inevitable under imperialism.[1]

The Marxist definition of a nation is precise and unambiguous: a nation is an historically constituted, stable community of people formed on the basis of a common language, territory, economic life, and world-view manifested in a common culture.

On this basis there can be no disagreement — the French-Canadian people are a nation.

The decisive significance of the existence of the French-Canadian nation — a fact recognized by Canadian communists for over 50 years — is now becoming more widely understood. For example, the General Estates of French Canada declared, in 1967, that: "(a) The French-Canadians constitute a nation; (b) Québec constitutes the national territory and the fundamental political environment of this nation."[2] What is still creating a tremendous problem in conceptual and, hence, ideological clarity is the already mentioned blurring of a "nation" with that of a "sovereign state".

That the French-Canadian nation is also an oppressed one in relation to the oppressor nation of English-speaking Canada is easily shown. Since most of the standard studies on French Canada include abundant data on this particular point only a brief selection of illustrative material will be referred to here.[3] This is in order not to divert excessive time away from more crucial propositions in our analysis. What these studies clearly demonstrate is that since the conquest there has persistently been a system of discriminatory structures and practices imposed against the French majority in Québec. The English language and the English minority have a privileged and profitable position while the francophone suffers from a cultural oppression and linguistic discrimination that goes far beyond strictly economic exploitation. For example, within Québec itself the privileged language of work has always been English and it has long been a generally understood rule that one has to speak English in order to get a decent job. Indeed, in 1969, the Report of the Royal Commission on Bilingualism and Biculturalism observed that a unilingual anglophone earns more than a bilingual francophone — or even a bilingual anglophone![4] Thus, French-Canadians in the main do not have the fundamental democratic right to work in their own language in their own nation.

The same government study also revealed that French-Canadians are at the bottom of the economic ladder: out of 14 ethnic groups in Québec they ranked twelfth in the scale of income earned.[5] Wage rates are consistently about 25 percent less for workers in Québec than for Canadian workers outside Québec. In addition the Report showed that in Montreal 17 percent of senior-level corporate management is francophone and 83 percent is anglophone — a "nice" statistic for a province where the population is 83 percent francophone and 17 percent anglophone!

In addition to the national oppression under which the people of

Québec suffer there is the important factor of the structural weaknesses of the Québec economy. The relative underdevelopment of French Canada vis-à-vis English Canada, especially Ontario, is a source of super-profits to capitalist monopolies, whether they be Canadian or multinationals. The maintenance of this low-wage area is more than sufficient reason for monopolies to resist acknowledging French-Canadian nationhood. Such acknowledgement would inevitably lead to the legitimation of demands for national rights and national equality. Further consequences would be the loss to the monopolies of a problem whose primary effect has been to divert working people away from class-based issues into those of bourgeois nationalism and, more importantly, to divide and, hence, weaken the working class movement across Canada.

Eighty-five percent of the industrial economy of Québec belongs to non-French speaking owners, be they anglophone Canadians, U.S. multi-nationals, or others.[6] The iron law of maximum profit reigns supreme. As a result the economic structure of Québec's material production is very unhealthy. In 1974, 63 percent of Québec working people were employed in the service sector, while 5 percent were employed in agriculture and mining, and a declining 31 percent in manufacturing and construction. Service sectors are extremely limited in their capacity to generate growth, and when they develop at a much higher pace than the industrial base, as in Québec, they generate accelerated inflation, deficits in the balance of payments, and increased unemployment.[7] Thus the Québec rate of unemployment is always one of the highest in Canada and poverty is widespread. For example, during the heyday of capitalism's period of affluence, the 1960s, the city of Montreal's population increased by 20 percent and its welfare recipients by 400 percent.[8]

The picture which our analysis thus far makes crystal clear is that ecomonic inequality and national inequality merge into a single whole. But it is absolutely imperative to avoid a vulgar "economism" by focussing on the economic factors alone. To speak only of economic inequality is to lose sight of the national element — the pressure that is bringing the crisis to a head. We will return to the nature of the relationship between the national and economic questions shortly.

In the face of the inevitable attempts by the French-Canadian people to change this rather grim *status quo* what have been the responses of the respresentatives of state-monopoly capitalism?

First and foremost has been a vague and ambiguous policy of "bilingualism". Officially, this is supposed to entail the active encouragement and support of the use of both languages amongst both nations of Canada. In reality, it has meant the continued imposition of English on the French majority in Québec. Furthermore, it has never been explained how the national aspirations or the economic exploitation of the Québec working class would in any way be affected by the opening of a French language class in Medicine Hat, Alberta. The policy of bilingualism is, in fact, designed to divert the attention of the Canadian people away from the fundamental reality of the bi-national character of Canada and focus it on superstructural epi-phenomena. Its major effect has been to intensify chauvinism and racism, already firmly implanted throughout much of English-Canada, by creating resentment and fears regarding the putative "forcing of French down our throats". Note that not only does the policy of bilingualism avoid the necessity of recognizing that French-Canada is a nation, but it also has the added quality of being a divide-and-rule tactic so beneficial to the bourgeoisie.

Indeed, every other bourgeois "solution" to the crisis facing Canada shares these two common characteristics: (1) they all equally deny or avoid recognizing the extant reality of the French-Canadian poeple as a nation, and (2) they all serve to enhance the traditional capitalist tactic of divide-and-rule. For example, as the policy of "bi-lingualism" appears more and more irrelevant, another option being pushed by the monopolies focusses on the slogan of "decentralization". This, again, by-passes the national question and turns the issue into one of greater provincial autonomy or more provincial rights. The more reactionary components of the Canadian ruling class, primarily resident in the Conservative (or Tory) Party, see the November 15 election results in Québec as an opening by which to tighten their control over the Canadian economy. Based on the viewpoints expressed by leading Tory spokesmen, their aim, apparently, is to shift the balance of power away from the federal government to the provinces. This line is advanced not only by an important part of the Canadian monopolies but also by the multi-nationals.[9] The effect of decentralization would be to create ten relatively autonomous provinces with a weak federal authority. Such an arrangement is ideal for strengthening the position of the multi-nationals and increasing their ability to control the Canadian economy, particularly in the fields of natural resources and energy.

A variant of the "decentralization" option is the proposal of "special status" under an amended BNA act. It is a solution offered by sectors of the French-Canadian bourgeoisie and, oddly enough, by the New Democratic Party — a social-democratic party. It, too, seeks to win more sovereignty for Québec by increasing the sovereignty of all ten provinces, in the expectation that only Québec would use its new power, thus achieving "special status". Like the other bourgeois solutions it provides neither national nor economic equality for French Canada and comes as too little, too late.

There is another option available to Canadian capitalists — an awesome and terrible one — which must be mentioned: the use of military power. Given the history of the relations between the two nations, during which the force of arms has been imposed on several occasions to thwart the aspirations of French Canada, from the rebellion of 1837-38, to the anti-conscription riots of World War I, to the FLQ crisis of 1970, such an alternative cannot be ignored. But more than history gives credibility to this potential eventuality. Ever since the P.Q. electoral victory, Pierre Trudeau has repeatedly, unbidden and with no one raising the question, stated his refusal to ever use force against Québec over the question of independence. Such well-exposed public denials to non-existent charges have caused many Canadians to feel it is becoming a case of "protesting too much". And while Mr. Trudeau makes his denials his government purchases 700 armoured cars whose only possible use could be for "crowd control" in urban warfare.[10] Furthermore, Mr. Joe Clark, leader of the Conservative Party, the other major political grouping representing monopolies in Canada, has stated he could not rule out the use of force "categorically and unequivocally".

Marx, writing on the Irish question, stated that a nation which oppresses another cannot itself be free. That fact is as true today as it was then. There can be no illusions on this score. Were the federal government to send troops into Québec it would mean civil war. The effects would be catastrophic. Minimally, it would accelerate the separation of Québec and the collapse of confederation. In spite of all this, and while it is not being suggested here that it is an immediate prospect, the use of force is an option that the most reactionary sectors of the Anglo-Canadian monopolies are clearly holding in reserve.

A real and lasting solution to the crisis of confederation in Canada can only be based on the recognition of two realities combined in a single dialectic: (1) French Canada is a nation, and (2) the class interests of the workers of both Canadian nations must be safeguarded and advanced.

With regard to the national component of the problem there can be little debate. For once the fact of French-Canadian nationhood is acknowledged then the basic principle of national rights flows directly out of it. And the most fundamental and universally-acknowledged right which must be accorded to all nations is, of course, *the right to self-determination.*

As Lenin said: "The class-conscious worker will answer the bourgeoisie — there is only one solution to the national problem (insofar as it can, in general, be solved in the capitalist world, the world of profit, squabbling and exploitation), and that solution is *consistent democracy*".[11] Clearly the rights of an individual in a nation can hardly be greater than the collective rights of the nation to which he belongs and there is no more fundamental principle of democracy than the principle of equality in rights, which implies the struggle against inequality, *i.e.*, the right to self-determination for a nation. Lenin was very specific about self-determination when he wrote "... it would be wrong to interpret the right to self-determination as meaning anything but the right to existence as a separate state."[12]

However, Lenin was also very careful to point out that the application in practice, of the national right to self-determination must be resolved concretely in each individual case, depending on the given historical conditions and on the working class struggle for socialism. And this is where the second component of our dialectic demands consideration. For separation is only one possible expression of genuine sovereignty, and it is far from always being the one that is in the best interests of the working people involved.

For while there can be no ambiguity that self-determination means, above all, recognition of the full equality of nations, regardless of size, *up to and including the right to secede*, Lenin went on to emphasize that, "... from the viewpoint of democracy in general ... recognition of the right to secession *reduces* the danger of the 'disintegration of the state' ".[13] He points out that, "... to accuse those who support freedom of self-determination, *i.e.*, freedom to secede, of encouraging separatism, is as foolish and hypocritical as accusing those who advocate freedom of divorce of encouraging the destruction of family ties".[14] In other words, recognition of the right to secession not only does not cause the "disintegration of the state", but, "on the contrary, strengthens it on a democratic basis, which is the only possible and durable basis in civilized society".[15] Finally, Lenin explicitly urged that the communists of a small nation must emphasize in their agitation that the "... voluntary union of nations ... must fight against small nation narrow mindedness, seclusion and isolation".[16]

The secession of Québec is not the answer to the inequality of the French-Canadian nation. On the contrary, it would intensify that inequality. To begin with, the separation of Québec would be economically disasterous for the province. Once removed from a Canada-wide internal market — albeit a market now weighted in favour of Ontario — Québec would have to fall back on an internal market limited only to the province. Tariff agreements, common market arrangements, and even monetary union would not prevent but actually increase the domination of any more powerful economic partner. (The European Common Market is an example of this.) A reduced internal market would either force Québec to produce everything for its own consumption, which is inconceivable, or make Québec more dependent on English-Canada and the U.S.. The living standards of the working people would fall.

Furthermore, separation would destroy the political unity of the working class of both nations against their common enemies —

Canadian monopoly capital and U.S. imperialism. This is particularly true in the case of the trade union movement, which by virtue of its position in both nations and its growing solidarity and unity in action — exemplified by the historically unprecedented massive political strike of over one million workers on October 14, 1976 — is able to play a decisive role in the solution of the crisis. And let there be no evasion of what this division and weakening of the working class across Canada signifies: it would mean delivering both peoples, English-speaking and French-speaking, into the total and suffocating embrace of U.S. imperialism.

Already there have been many disquietening signs of this develop-ment. The federal government has shifted considerably to the right since the P.Q. election victory. In its effort to gain U.S. monopoly support for the *satus quo* Canada has strained relations with Cuba, made a massive increase in its military contributions to *NATO* and *NORAD*, and, perhaps most significantly, has become much less resistant to U.S. pressures for a policy of "continentalism" in energy and natural resources. The Athabaska oil sands and Northern pipe line situations are examples of this.

Coupled with this right-wing shift is the attempt by the P.Q. to attain the same U.S. monopoly support, only in this case on behalf of separatism. Rarely has this hemisphere witnessed such a humiliating spectacle as the sight of René Lévesque, leader of the Québec govern-ment, scurrying down to the moneylenders at the New York Economic Club in order to reassure them that an independent Québec would be a good investment and safe for "free enterprise". He enthusiastically welcomed U.S. capital — one of the major causes of Québec's national oppression! — and even promised to guarantee the impossible, namely, "social peace" for U.S. investors. Bernard Landry, Minister of Economic Development in Québec, admitted that American capitalists saw the P.Q. as a means of breaking the kind of resistance they sometimes meet in their desire for northern expansion. He said it was an attitude of divide-and-conquer and saw nothing wrong with it.[17] No less a personage than David Rockefeller, the President of Chase Manhattan Bank, has stated: "Investors make little distinction between Québec and Canada and are more preoccupied with taxation on capital gains, and measures dealing with minerals and natural resources, than with separatism."[18]

It is essential to realize that if the right wing of the P.Q., which has always been in control of the party, succeeds in making an alliance with U.S. imperialism in order to achieve its aim of separation, it would transform Québec into an outpost of reaction. This would be a serious setback not only for the working class of Canada but for the forces of progress and socialism throughout the world. It might also be pointed out that the P.Q. campaign for separatism has the ancillary effect of diverting the working people away from a recognition of their class interests and the real source of their problems. While time does not allow for a detailed analysis of the somewhat diverse socio-economic composition of the P.Q., it is imperative to understand that the Parti Québécois is not a social-democratic party with a nationalist flavour based on the working class and the trade union movement. It is a party representing the interests of the petit-bourgeoisie and the professionals, particularly those in the state sector. Thus, the main leadership of the P.Q. rejects the class struggle and orients toward the multi-nationals and international financiers to provide a stable economic base for a French-Canadian monopoly capitalism which it hopes to manage and run. As Yvon Charbonneau, President of the powerful Centrale De L'Enseignement Du Québec (Quebec Teacher's Union), rightly asked: "Will independence be in the interests of the working people? Nothing in the P.Q. program indicates it".

A parenthetical comment, which is all that history ever gives them, should be made concerning the so-called "ultra-left". Their infantile "revolutionary" posturings and their eager willingness to sacrifice the interests of the working class on the altar of their own personal moral purity and self-esteem tends to reduce all social motion to one revolutionary and violent transfer of power from the bourgeoisie to the working class. (By working class, of course, they mean some kind of inchoate mass which ought to follow them if it would only stop watching hockey games on T.V.). For them there are no stages, no process, no history. A common position taken by many of these ultra-leftist sects is to portray Québec as an underdeveloped colony and to push for a revolution for independence. It should be sufficient to point out that this is advocating a national struggle bereft of class struggle. Since they see Québec, in defiance of both scientific taxonomy and plain common sense, as a colony, they consider the tasks of the Québec nation are those of a colonized people, regardless of class. But Québec is not a colony, and such a strategy effectively negates the position of the working class and prevents it from fulfilling its essential leadership role.

It is the ultra-left's ignorance of the crucial distinction (and, therefore, relationship) between the national and class struggles that propels it into the positions it holds. Thus, for the ultra-left grouplets there is either no national question and only the class struggle is considered, or the national struggle is perceived as being equivalent and synonomous with the class struggle. In either case, support for the immediate separation of Québec is the logical conclusion to this kind of pseudo-Marxism. (Equally absurd, of course, is the view held by some of them that all struggles for national rights and equality are, by definition, bourgeois and, therefore, reactionary).

The merging of the struggle for national equality and self-determination with the anti-monopoly and anti-imperialist struggle is the only winning strategy for the working class and its allies of both nations. This requires that the national aspirations of French Canada be recognized while at the same time the unity of the forces of labour and democracy in both nations is maintained. *In short, the democratic solution to the crisis of confederation in Canada is the scrapping of the present unrealistic provincial-federal system, formed under the hopelessly archaic BNA Act of 1867, and the creation of a bi-national state.* A new constitution, made in Canada, could easily do this.

The bi-national character of the country would be acknowledged, for example, under a confederal republic with a House of Commons based on representation by population and, to replace the present Senate, another chamber composed of an equal number of elected representatives from each of the two nations. Each chamber could initiate legislation, but both must adopt the legislation before it becomes law. Such a structure protects both democratic principles; equality of rights of nations regardless of their size, and majority rule.[19]

It is not without signficance that most workers in both English-speaking and French-speaking Canada, when they are allowed to be informed — and there is a real blackout by the mass media — as to what the Leninist position on the national question is — for that, fundamentally, is all that this presentation has been — immediately agree with it. For as Lenin realized: "From their daily experience, the masses know perfectly well the value of geographical and economic ties and the advantages of a big market and a big state. They will therefore resort to secession only when national oppression and national friction make joint life absolutely intolerable and hinder any and all economic intercourse. . . . The interests of the working class and of its struggle against capitalism demand complete solidarity and the closest unity of the workers of all nations".[20]

In conclusion, every alternative position advanced in Canada today ingores either the national specifics of the crisis, e.g., decentralization, or its class specifics, e.g., separatism, or both, e.g., bilingualism. *Only the bi-national solution deals with and satisfactorily resolves both elements of the question.*

Workers thus recognize that the analysis and solution given in this report, firstly, meet their national aspirations and, secondly, provide a highly practical and democratic way to achieve the basic goal of *a free union of two equal nations.*

NOTES

1. V.I. Lenin, "The Discussion of Self-Determination Summed Up", in *Critical Remarks. . .*, p. 203.

2. *Etats Generaux du Canada Francais*. Assisses Nationales (1967), Montreal, 1967.

3. Perhaps the most definitive, and certainly most widely used, source is the *Report of the Royal Commission on Bilingualism and Biculturalism*, Vol. III ("Work").

4. *Ibid.*, p. 22 (French edition)

5. *Ibid.* Despite the present campaign in the bourgeois press implying that the income gap is rapidly closing, the most recent data do not support their assertions. For example, the latest study, made available on April 30, 1977 (by Prof. Francois Vaillancourt of L'Université de Montréal), shows that French-Canadian males had actually dropped further behind other groups between 1961 and 1971. Prof. Vaillencourt's study gives the following figures:

National Origin and Languages Known	Total Mean Income	
	1960	1970
British, English only	6,049	9,088
British, Bilingual	5,929	8,506
French, French only	3,107	5,594
French, Bilingual	4,523	7,661

One can see from these results that the relative advantage of a unilingual Canadian of British origin increased in Québec from 1960 to 1970. (*Globe and Mail*, Toronto, July 25, 1977.)

6. W. Kashtan, "A Just and Lasting Solution of the National Question in Canada is Possible". p. 6.

7. Rodrigue Tremblay, L'Economie Québecoise, p. 8.

8. *Special Senate Committee Report on Poverty*, quoted in *Vancouver Sun*, Oct. 30, 1970.

9. For example, John P. Robarts, retired Conservative premier of Ontario and a member of the Board of Directors of several of the largest multi-nationals operating in Canada. Quoted in *Globe and Mail*, Jan. 15, 1977.

10. An editorial in the *Toronto Sun*, April 11, 1977 stated: "One of the most unexpected things the Trudeau government has done is make a deal to buy 700 armoured cars — the classy Piranha, the best in the business and used extensively by the British in Northern Ireland. . . . 700 armoured cars are a hell of a lot for Canada. Why this sudden interest in heretofore despised armour? Defense critic Mike Forrestall says they are intended for use in Québec in case of violence — or insurrection. . . the only realistic use for so many armoured vehicles is for possible domestic disorders. They are an urban weapon — for street fighting and against light weapons".

11. V.I. Lenin, *Critical Remarks on the National Question*, p. 12.

12. V.I. Lenin, "The Right of Nations to Self-Determination", in *Critical Remarks. . . .*, pp. 67-68.

13. *Ibid.*, p. 110.

14. *Ibid.*, p. 112.

15. *Ibid.*, p. 112.

16. V.I. Lenin, "The Discussion of Self-Determination Summed Up," in *Critical Remarks. . .*, pp. 241-242.

17. *La Presse*. Montreal, Jan. 25, 1977.

18. Centrale des Syndicats Nationaux, (Confederation of National Trade Unions), *Ne Comptons Que Sur Nos Propres Moyens*, p. 25.

19. This type of proposal is, of course, not original but is the long-standing position of the Communist Party of Canada. It is meeting with increasing support from key sectors of the trade union movement, particularly the U.A.W., U.S.W.A., and U.E., as well as from individual trade union leaders.

20. V.I. Lenin, "The Right of Nations to Self-Determination", p. 113-114.

Readings

Centrale des Syndicats Nationaux (Confederation of National Trade Unions), *Ne Comptons Que Sur Nos Propres Moyens*, Montreal, 1974.

Drache, Daniel (ed.), *Quebec — Only the Beginning: The Manifestos of the Common Front*, Toronto: New Press, 1972.

Etats Generaux de Canada Francais, Assisses Nationales, Montreal, 1967.

Gordon, Sheldon E., "Merger Before Referendum", in *The Financial Post*, 26 November, 1977.

Kashtan, W., "A Just and Lasting Solution of the National Question in Canada is Possible", in *Communist Viewpoint*, Vol. 9, No. 1, (January-February, 1977).

Lemoine, B. Roy, *The Growth of the State in Quebec*, Montreal: Black Rose Books, 1973.

Lenin, V.I., *Critical Remarks on the National Question — The Right of Nations to Self-Determination*, Moscow: Foreign Languages Publishing House, 1954. (There are many editions of Lenin's writings in print. All references and quotes from Lenin used in this paper are taken from the above work.)

Milner, Henry and Sheilagh Milner, *The Decolonization of Quebec: An Analysis of Left-Wing Nationalism*, Toronto: McClelland & Stewart, 1973.

Milner, Henry, *Politics in the New Quebec*, Toronto: McClelland & Stewart, 1978.

Royal Commission on Bilingualism and Biculturalism, *Report*, Vol. III, Ottawa: Queen's Printer, 1969.

Tremblay, Rodrique, *L'Economie Quebecoise*, Montreal: Editions du Jour, 1976.

Political Economy and Social Movements: Notes Towards Theory and Analysis

Gary B. Rush

GARY B. RUSH is an Associate Professor of Sociology at Simon Fraser University. His current research interests include Canadian Society, Political Economy and Social Movements.

In the literature of bourgeois sociology, it is virtually axiomatic that social movements are treated as aberrant phenomena; as irrational responses to strains in the social order. Invariably, as different forms of collective behaviour are arranged on the ubiquitous continua of normative regulation, social movements are relegated to the more deviant categories, exceeded only by riots and panic. Moreover, individual participation in movements becomes analyzed as deviant or, at best, misguided behaviour. In some fairness, perhaps, this approach might be justified by noting that social movements are not, in temperate North America at least, the most common of events. However, this may have as much to do with the pervasiveness of control mechanisms as it has to do with the imperial status of the region. Beyond this, it must be noted that American (and hence Canadian) sociology owes more of its tradition to the works of Durkheim, Weber and Spencer than it does to that of Marx. All were concerned with the dramatic — and frequently revolutionary — social, political and economic changes taking place in the eighteenth and nineteenth centuries, but not all from the same perspective. More recently, the twentieth century revival of interest in social movements dates to the emergence of European fascism, which was regarded with abhorrence by liberal social scientists, especially those who were refugees of the Nazi regime. Finally, it must be recognized that institutions such as academe exist at the sufferance of the ruling class and, as such, are subject to its ideology and control.

Irrespective of the ideological persuasion of social scientists, one fact they cannot dismiss is that change is a pervasive and immanent aspect of society. In fact, a great deal of the policy application of the social sciences is concerned with predicting and controlling processes of change. Moreover, few social scientists would deny that social movements are often dramatic and powerful vehicles of change, even though they are frequently aborted by the intervention of the state. Indeed, the vigilance maintained over incipient movements by various agents of the state would suggest that they are far from random and insignificant phenomena. In the final analysis, social movements are vital events in the process of historical change. For the functionalist, however, the bottom line is that they are aberrant responses to periodic strains in an essentially linear and progressive history. A more accurate reading, on the other hand, and one that is essential to undertaking any study of social movements from the perspective of political economy, is that history is a dialectical process, and that social movements are normal manifestations of the contradictions inherent in that process.

What follows shall be an attempt to develop some of the theoretical implications of this point of view, and to suggest certain lines of analysis that could apply to the study of social movements in Canada. This is in no way a final and comprehensive treatment, but represents more of a working paper for a larger project currently in progress.*

Definitions

One of the first Augean (and Procrustean) tasks that faces the student of social movements is the problem of definition. Perhaps the most universally acceptable feature of all movements is that they are collective attempts to bring about change in a society, or at least in some part of the social structure. However, not all collective attempts to promote change can be regarded as social movements. Essentially, there are two important elements that must be borne in mind when trying to sort this out: the arena of the dialectical process, and the fact that social movements themselves have a history.

Although all social relationships are dialectical, the field of social movements is limited to those collective actions which have a significant impact on the social order, or at least which evoke a significant response from those whose class interest (real or other-

---

*For some of the ideas contained herein, the author has drawn upon work originally undertaken in co-authoring, with R.S. Denisoff, *Social and Political Movements*, (Appleton-Century-Crofts, 1971, o.p.).

wise) lies in the maintenance of the social order. Basically, there are two levels where these kinds of collective struggles are played out — those of *class* and *nation*. Essentially, by *class* we refer to the unequal and exploitative divisions arising out of the social relations of production; by *nation* we refer to Ryerson's ". . . community of people, linked by a common cultural-linguistic historical experience of living and working together, whether or not in possession of their own state."[1] This distinction is not to deny that class and national movements can intersect and overlap, or that they can be either complementary or conflicting parts of the same process. Indeed, as we shall see, the impact of imperialism is particularly germane to class formation and social movements in Canada. However, setting aside for the moment the fact that imperial relations of domination condition the development of economic — hence class — relationships in subordinate states, the root nature of social movements is that they are manifestations of the class contradictions and antagonisms inherent in any society divided by class structures. Although any given movement may be typified by class coalitions and/or internal dissension, a common element of all movements is that action is directed upwards towards a superordinate class. Social movements are not generated from above, nor are they vehicles of expression for dominant class interests. This is not to say that dominant classes, by virtue of their monopoly of power, cannot transform, subvert, suppress, or otherwise deflect movement action directed towards them. From the outset, however, social movements are the actions of subordinate classes.

It goes without saying that these actions must be collective actions in order to constitute a social movement. If, we have argued, there is a class basis to such collective actions, we must then deal with the question of whether or not social movements embody class consciousness. Objectively, of course, class contradictions are inherent in and essential to the division between capital and labour in society. However, the mystification of class in capitalist society is pervasive, and does have an impact on the formation and history of social movements. Moreover, many class movements, and certainly all nationalist ones, involve class coalitions. Thus, although class interest is at the root of social movements, it cannot be said that this interest is always articulated as class consciousness. However, sooner or later, a movement must embody and communicate a class or national interest in order to be viable and enduring. This is, of course, an important reason why the state so jealously guards its implied mandate to articulate the national interest. In Canada, this point gains crucial importance when we consider the extent to which the federal prerogative in this area is becoming more and more challenged by regional and provincial interests.

Inherent in the discussion thus far has been the notion that social movements must involve action of some kind. Eventually, the dialectic must be engaged: collective, subordinate class action must be taken against a superordinate class, and a response evoked. It is at this point that collective action approaches a "crisis of legitimacy" — the *Catch 22* of social movements. In order to be viable, movements must attract adherents and, since class differences are manifest as power differences, must eventually confront the power structure of society. Internally, the crisis of legitimacy is bound up with attracting members to an organization whose ideology embraces the notion that existing power distributions are to some extent non-legitimate (or at least importunate). Externally, by corollary, the holders of power in society will perceive social movements as more or less non-legitimate — a perception which precipitates the exercise of that power. Thus, the crisis of legitimacy carries at least three implications: (1) social movements must operate outside of the legitimate channels of change in society, or at least attempt to use these channels in innovative ways; (2) the integral act of confronting the distribution of power in society invites retaliation; (3) in order to grow, a movement must attract followers from a general population who, by the very act of membership, become non-legitimate to the *status quo* of which they were so recently a part. This latter point is particularly relevant to the case of early farmer and labour movements in Canada, where the organizing vanguard frequently consisted of recent immigrants. Such persons not only brought an experience of militancy with them from Europe or the United States; they were also less integrated into the structure and ideology of power relationships in which non-immigrants had grown up.

Earlier, it was stated that social movements must eventually address these power relationships of society. To elaborate: class differences — the basis of social movements — stem from relationship to the means of production; power is the ability, arising out of ownership or control of these means of production, to control the flow of resources and material and social rewards available to a society at any given time. In class societies, the state is the primary instrument for facilitating and legitimating economic power, doing so through its political, administrative, judicial, coercive and ideological functions.* Thus, in attacking the class and power relationships of

---

*Of all social facts, power is perhaps the one that has been most mystified by bourgeois sociology. A detailed examination of the nature and exercise of power is beyond the scope of the present paper. However, for this, and particularly for the role of the state and its relationship to economic power, see Ralph Miliband, *The State in Capitalist Society*, (Quartet Books, 1973). Some exceptionally fine essays are also found in Leo Panitch (ed..), *The Canadian State: Political Economy and Political Power*, (University of Toronto Press, 1977). The author is also indebted to Erling Christensen, Ph.D. candidate in the Department of Sociology and Anthropology, Simon Fraser University, for discussions concerning class, power, and the state.

society, social movements are ultimately attacking the state; to this extent, all movements are political movements. This is an important point relative to the legitimacy of social movements. Any form of collective action which operates under the umbrella of legitimacy (such as pressure groups, political parties, trade unions, interest groups, etc.) cannot properly be considered social movements. This is not to say that such organizations cannot evolve into (or out of) movements — it is simply that nonlegitimacy, in the eyes of the economic and political *status quo*, is central to the dynamics of social movements.

Before attempting to gather these observations together for a tentative definition of social movements, one further point needs to be made regarding the nature of change sought through movement action. Since we have argued for the class basis of movements, and proposed that class differences are manifest as power differences, it seems reasonable to suggest that the changes sought by social movements will be, in the final analysis, changes in the distribution of power in society. This point will be taken up at greater length when we discuss types of social movements. For the moment, suffice it to say that such changes may vary from radical change of the economic and/or political base of social class and power, to attempts to ameliorate or modify existing or immanent class and power relationships, to denial and rejection of class and the economic, political and social structures which reflect and support class and power differences.

To summarize thus far, social movements are collective, political, subordinate class actions (reflecting class interest but not necessarily embodying class consciousness), mounted against superordinate classes in an attempt to change the distribution of power in society, which are consequently regarded and responded to as non-legitimate by the *status quo*, and relegated to operating outside of the accepted channels of political expression. Moreover, class movements are those in which a power confrontation between classes is carried out essentially within a state or culturally national territory; national movements are those in which the power confrontation is between a subordinate colony and a superordinate imperial metropole, in the course of which class coalitions are formed in the colonial hinterland.

Social Movements: Types, Relationships, Histories

Having defined the field, another consideration that the analyst must deal with is the fact that not all social movements are the same. Upon this realization, the first impulse is to construct a typology of social movements. Although it is probably impossible to deny this impulse, it should at least be resisted with bitter determination, and finally only yielded to with reluctance and qualification. Typologies — the legacy of Weberian methodology — have deficiencies in both time and space. In the first place, confining social phenomena to the cells of a row by column table — the "iron cross" of sociology — imparts a static quality to what is being studied, in spite of all protestations that typologies are only approximations of reality. This limitation may be excused when studying so-called routine, patterned and "normative" behaviour, but it can be a severe handicap when dealing with non-institutionalized and dynamic events such as social movements. In the second place, the construction of tabulations requires a certain stratification of variables. Minimally, the intersection of two dichotomized variables yields four "cells" into which observations or data may fall. However, while the stratification of variables increases arithmetically, the resulting production of cells increases geometrically. This kind of tinkertoy sociology can very quickly create some intriguing or amusing logical possibilities for which, however, no social reality would ever be found.

Bearing these limitations in mind, Figure 1 presents a tentative typology of social movements in an attempt to demonstrate not so much a classification of movements as a map of distinctions and relationships between them. From the previous definition of social movements, two variables seem essential: the type of change in power relationships sought by a movement, and the type of action taken against the superordinate *status quo* in order to bring about this change. Of the former, four types of change may be envisioned: institute new relationships, as in the establishment of a new social order; reinstate old relationships which existed, or are perceived to have existed, at some time in the past; modify existing relationships so as to make them operate more equitably; avoid existing relationships in favour of an alternate system. For the latter variable, three types of action are suggested: passive opposition, in which persuasion or reason are used to impress the need for change; active opposition, in which varying degrees of unilateral force may be used to seek redress; overthrow, in which force is used to attempt to remove and replace the existing superordinate power structure.

FIGURE 1.   A TYPOLOGY OF SOCIAL MOVEMENTS

Type of Change Sought in Power Relations	Type of Action Taken Against Status Quo		
	Passive Opposition	Active Opposition	Overthrow
Institute New	——	Rebellion	Revolution
Reinstate Old	——	Resistance	Reaction
Modify Existing	Reform	——	——
Avoid Existing	Expressive	——	——

Logically, the above permutation of variables should yield twelve types of social movements to be found in the real world. However, one would be hard-pressed to find instances of at least half of the possibilities. For example, passive opposition will not bring about a new social order or reinstate an old one, for, as we should be well aware, those who hold power in society are not about to give it up willingly. On the other hand, overthrow of the system is a somewhat extreme course of action if the goal is only to modify or avoid the present distribution of power. At best, the six types of movements distinguished in Figure 1 — rebellion, revolution, resistance, reaction, reform and expressive — do seem to exhaust the practical possibilities.

Some brief elaboration of these rather self-evident types of movements might be in order. In very general terms, rebellion and revolution can be considered movements of the "left", resistance and reaction movements of the "right", and reform and expressive movements of the "middle". Movements of the left are characterized by the goal of instituting new power relations for the purpose of achieving an idealized future society based on more or less total philosophical frameworks and conceptions of a logically developing universe. The problems of the existing society are seen as social and structural in origin (e.g., class differentiation), and capable of solution through collective action and structural change. On the other hand, movements of the right are characterized by the goal of reinstating old power relations for the purpose of counteracting existing trends in society and re-establishing a real or idealized past society which has been deviated from. Problems of the existing society are seen as moral and individual in origin (e.g., weak or sinister leaders), and capable of solution by force of individual determination. Within these distinctions, rebellion and resistance differ from revolution and reaction in terms of more limited goals, strategy, membership, class composition, ideological coherence, duration, and potential for success of the former compared to the latter. Characteristically, movements of the middle embody orientations of both left and right. The more liberally oriented reform movement seeks limited modifications in existing power relationships in order to make the system work more effectively or to extend certain rights and privileges to given groups. The ills of society are generally viewed as social in origin (e.g., poverty, lack of education), and capable of social solutions. The more conservative expressive movement may be seen as a symbolic statement of dissent which is not calculated to change a sick society, but rather to avoid it and its consequences for the individual. Although the origin of problems may be vaguely attributed to "society," the outcome is seen as manifest in the individual (e.g., powerlessness, alienation). Therefore, the solution is not to modify the society, but rather to modify one's relation to it, either subjectively (e.g., moral rearmament) and/or objectively (e.g., withdrawal).

One insight that emerges from the above discussion is that although all movements of a given historical period may be responses to the same objective "problem" situations, they differ in their analysis and ideology as to the sources and solutions of these problems. That is, reform, rebellion and revolution are linked by a common focus on social factors as the source of problems, and the need for a new, or at least modified, society as the solution. On the other hand, expressive, resistance and reactionary movements are linked to a certain extent by some common perception of the individual as, if not the source of problems, at least the vehicle of change. This suggests a potentially valuable line of analysis to pursue in considering the history of social movements, and particularly their relationship to the social order to which they are opposed.

Unquestionably, the central feature of all institutionalized society is conservatism, both ideological and structural. That is, the institutions of a society, and their supportive ideologies, are organized to conserve and perpetuate the interests of the dominant class of that society. In western societies, for example, the nineteenth century ascendancy of the industrial capitalist class has resulted in social relationships and ideologies which reinforce individualism and individual responsibility rather than collectivism and collective responsibility, hierarchy rather than equality, and progress rather than change.[2] Although all social movements oppose the dominant classes of society, and are therefore considered non-legitimate by them, movements in capitalist society which espouse the former of these orientations will fare somewhat better in their relationship to the status quo than those which espouse the latter. Of the movements we have identified, expressive (particularly religious) are the most consanguine with, and least threatening to, the interests of the capitalist class.* Of course, large-scale "opting out" can pose problems for the state and the economy, and the imposition of state power against an expressive movement can shift it from a position of passive opposition to one of active opposition, as, for example, the case of the Sons of Freedom sect of the Doukhobors illustrates. However, the limited membership and passive orientation of most expressive movements usually ensures state indifference, if not tacit approval, to this form of protest. Up to a point, reform movements

---

*The historical relationship between protestantism and capitalism has, of course, been well documented. Aside from Weber, *The Protestant Ethic and the Spirit of Capitalism*, note 2, and related literature, see also Liston Pope, *Millhands and Preachers*, (Yale University Press, 1958). To the student of Canadian political economy, the relationship of catholicism to capitalist development and social movements, especially in Quebec, should be of particular interest.

also enjoy a certain degree of freedom in capitalist society, inasmuch as they tend to express the liberal sentiments characteristic of the successful bourgeois revolution which gave industrial capitalism its structural and ideological foundations. However, the greater reception of the state to reform movements lies in the fact that, of all movements, they are the most amenable to co-optation. Paradoxically, of course, the liberalism of reform movements also makes them prone to co-optation by other, more activist, movements. Thus, until reform movements are safely "into the fold" of due legal and political process, they are met more with hostility than with blessings by the status quo. In this connection, it should be noted that the state will often attempt to co-opt the goals of an incipient movement as a means to guide it into a reform orientation, thus facilitating control over the specification of issues and the redress of grievances. In Canada, the histories of the women's suffrage and native rights movements provide ample evidence of this process.) Resistance movements, like their left-wing counterpart, rebellion, are usually too volatile to be met with any accommodation by the state. Reactionary movements, on the other hand, have enjoyed considerable liaison with the capitalist state. This may be attributed to a number of factors, not the least of which is the imperialist support, by capitalist metropoles, of reactionary movements and regimes in Third World hinterlands. Although a master of deceit, the state — especially in so-called "open" societies — cannot always maintain a mystical distinction between foreign and domestic policy, especially when domestic capitalists, both large and small, draw considerable profit from imperialism. Moreover, in spite of a professed condemnation of extremism by "democratic" governments, reactionary movements can be valuable instruments of domestic imperialism: they focus attention on scapegoats, and provide an alternative, both ideological and for potential membership, to the much more inimical possibility of revolution. Finally, reactionary movements in capitalist metropoles tend to extol the virtues of, and draw support from, the petit bourgeoisie. Although, under the incursion of corporate and state capitalism, this class is diminishing in size and declining in power, its memory is kept alive by a campaign of ideological bourgeoisification mounted by both the economy and the state. Thus, in a sense, the state in capitalist society encourages, in a variety of ways, the growth of reactionary movements.*

---

*The problem, of course, is to keep them under control. The history of fascist movements in Germany and Italy has provided eminent illustration of the failure to do so, but not as much attention has been given to successful manipulation and control, especially in Canada, where fascism enjoyed considerable vogue until the advent of war with Germany in 1939. One of the few works to address Canadian fascism of the 1930s in any detail is Lita-Rose Betcherman's *The Swastika and the Maple Leaf*, (Fitzhenry and Whiteside, 1975).

The relationship which a movement bears to the larger society of which it is a part has important consequences for the processes of movement development and demise. Figure 2 illustrates the possible lines of development between movements, in terms of both the relationships between movements previously discussed and state responses to different types of movements. In this figure, solid lines indicate the most likely paths of "natural" internal development between movements, broken lines indicate possible processes stemming from state intervention, and dotted lines indicate possible developments resulting from an interaction of internal and external factors.

FIGURE 2.   POTENTIAL MOVEMENT DEVELOPMENT

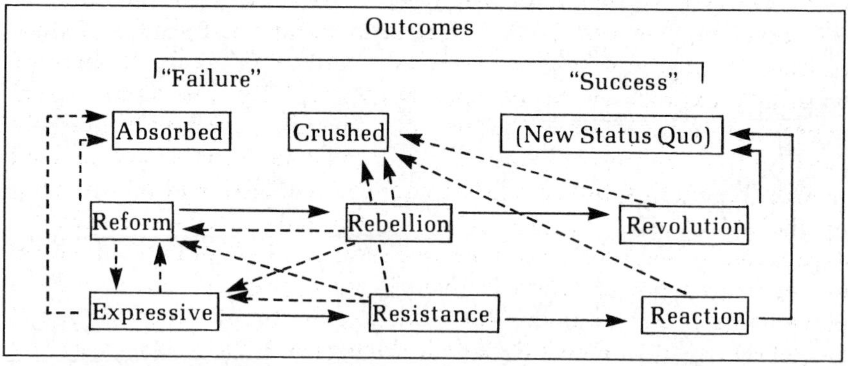

In brief, the potential outcomes for revolution and reaction — movements dedicated to the overthrow of the existing regime — are limited: they either succeed in their goal, and become the new regime, or are crushed by superior state force. Rebellion and resistance, on the other hand, are prone to several directions of development. Most frequently, they are quickly put down by the state. Alternatively, and usually in conjuction with repression of the leadership of such movements, the state strategy may be to attempt to subvert them by exerting pressures and incentives designed to transform them into more tractable and co-optable reform or expressive movements. Because of certain shared elements of ideology, the most usual course under these circumstances is for rebellion to become reform, and for resistance to become expressive. However, rebellion to expressive, or resistance to reform, are also possible, if infrequent, lines of development. The history of the agrarian protest movements on the Canadian Prairies during the early part of the twentieth century provides an illustration of the latter process. Initially organized around resistance to the National Policy — including specific issues such as land granting, taxation, railroad policy, tariffs, eastern financial and industrial hegemony, etc. — the farmers' movements eventually went political, in the course of which redress became sought less through attempting to change economic and political relationships and more through legislative and judicial channels.[3] If rebellion and resistance movements are not crushed or subverted, and gain momentum, their respective natural affinity with revolution and reaction will likely see them develop into these types of movements. The usual history of reform and expressive movements is co-optation and absorption into the *status quo*: the former via political parties, pressure groups, and/or legal process; the latter via the institutionalized church. Failing this, however, and if their goals cannot be met through passive opposition to the power structure, the adoption of more activist tactics may see them transform into rebellion or resistance movements. Under these circumstances, because of similarities in ideology and world view, reform is likely to become rebellion, expressive to become resistance. By the same token, expressive to rebellion, or reform to resistance, are highly unlikely possibilities. On the other hand, failure to achieve goals may not lead to a shift in tactics, but rather to a changed perception of relationship to the *status quo*. In this case, reform movements can become expressive, or expressive can become reform. The "spin off" of reform out of expressive or, more frequently, of expressive out of reform movements is not unusual. For example, the break-up of the social gospel reform movements in Canada during the 1920s was matched by a shift of many adherents into the more expressive pacifist and personal religion orientations which initially prompted the quest for reform.

Notwithstanding the potential for permanent revolution, the usual course of history of social movements is that they ultimately come to an end. This demise comes about either because the goals of the movement are not attained or, paradoxically, because they are. In the first instance, if the goals of a movement are so non-legitimate that they cannot be realized, the forces of social opposition will eventually bring about either its dissolution, or its transformation into a less societally threatening form. On the other hand — and this is perhaps the greatest irony of social movements — the success of a movement means that the new or modified structures and relationships which it institutes becomes the new *status quo*, and the viability of the movement as opposition comes to an end. The longevity of a movement, its potential for success, and the manner of its demise are dependent on a number of interacting factors, including the type of movement, its organizational and ideological structure, the nature of power distribution in or between the societies in which the movement emerges, and the manner in which this power is exercised.

A convenient dichotomy for considering the exercise of power lies in the apparent distinction between "absolutist" and "pluralist" systems. In the former, power is held by a relatively small and homogeneous elite, and is usually exercised in the form of superior force. This kind of power is exemplified in dictatorships, in the relationship between capital and labour in single industry towns, and in the imperial relationship between metropoles and dependent hinterlands. In pluralist societies, on the other hand, power is less centralized, being distributed among a multiplicity of interest groups, both economic and political, which formulate policies and manipulate decision-making to the extent of their differential power. Our reference to the *apparent* distinction between such systems is advisable: no matter how complex the machinery for exercising it, power basically adheres to ownership or control of the means of production in society. A more operative distinction between absolutist and pluralist states is that the latter tend to mystify control and the use of power by a sophisticated network of ideological and structural justifications, whereas the former do not. Nevertheless, the ideological and structural differences which do exist have a considerable impact on the type of movement likely to emerge in either society, the tactics employed by such movements, and state response to them. In absolutist societies, for example, the threat to state hegemony posed by *any* social movement will usually result in swift suppression. Under these circumstances, movements in such societies are advised to have considerable force or collective power behind them before they emerge. This is particularly true of revolutionary and reform movements. Revolutionary movements are also subject to state control in pluralist societies, sometimes through less direct means than immediate force. Reform movements in pluralist societies, as we have intimated, fare somewhat better, and may eventually become legitimated and included in the *status quo*. Given their opposition to ongoing social change, reactionary movements are customarily subject to state control in both absolutist and pluralist societies, except to the extent that they support the existing order against revolutionary or reform movements. This is more likely in long-established pluralist societies, where dominant groups who see their position under threat may tolerate or even openly support reactionary trends. Recently established revolutionary governments, on the other hand, will in most cases act to suppress any reactionary opposition to the programmes of change they are attempting to institute.

External pressures which can bring about the dissolution or transformation of a social movement may be conceptualized in terms of four processes: institutionalization, co-optation, discreditation, and repression. The demise of a social movement through institutionalization — the point of its succession to legitimacy — can come about in several ways. It may become part of the dominant power structure by developing into an interest group or political party. It may succeed in attaining its goals, and become the new *status quo* (as in the case of successful revolutionary or reactionary movements). Finally, the goals of the movement may become institutionalized into the policies of the existing *status quo*. This is frequently the history of reform movements in pluralist societies: since their goals usually have a certain legitimacy, they are commonly institutionalized by having these goals adopted either by the society as a whole, or by a legitimate political party. The course of the prohibition and women's suffrage movements in the early part of the twentieth century illustrate these processes. (In most cases, reform movements are rendered irrelevant by having their goals institutionalized, and decline into a phase of post-movement sectarianism. The Technocracy movement provides another notable example of this process.) Resistance movements also enjoy a certain degree of social legitimacy, particularly among formerly dominant classes, and they too are prone to institutionalization. Populist resistance movements on the Canadian Prairies, for example, finally emerged as the Social Credit and Co-operative Commonwealth Federation parties. From time to time, the goals of various Canadian-based annexationist movements — particularly that which followed the Rebellion Losses Act of 1849 and the subsequent burning of the parliament buildings by the disgruntled English-Canadian merchants of Montreal — have become institutionalized into the continentalist policies of the dominant American metropole.

Co-optation, the process of absorbing dissident elements into the *status quo*, is a common means of neutralizing social movements in pluralist societies, where a certain legitimacy is given to political competition. An inherent danger in competition, of course, is that it might be successful. Therefore, the dominant classes in pluralist societies have a considerable interest in establishing mechanisms to silence discontent and maintain stability. Co-optation may be applied not only to the leadership of a movement, but also to the issues it may address, and even to its ideology. An example of such multi-dimensional co-optation is provided by the response of the Canadian state to the so-called "youth movement" of the 1960s, wherein government jobs were found for leaders, funds were released for youth projects, and even a youthful image was created for key state leaders. Reform movements are the most amenable to co-optation, inasmuch as they have a specific, rather than a total, approach to change, and conform to at least a part of the ideology and structure of the *status quo*. On the other hand, rebellion and, particularly, revolutionary movements do not share a common interest with the dominant classes of society, and are not prone to co-optation. For this reason, a major strategy of the state for dealing with perceived revolutionary movements is a form of co-optation by infiltration, whereby *agents provocateurs* attempt to ferment dissent and incite tactically unwise acts.

The current McDonald Commission inquiry into the RCMP has, for example, revealed attempts at this in state dealings with the F.L.Q..

Discreditation as a means of suppressing social movements is most commonly applied in pluralist societies, where an extensive media network facilitates the dissemination and reinforcement of the dominant class point of view. The two most usual techniques are public denigration and ridicule of a movement or its leadership, and denigration or amelioration of the issue or issues which a movement addresses. The recent "National Unity" issue, manufactured to counter the apprehended threat of Quebec separatism, illustrates a blend of discreditation of the issues posed by the Parti Québécois (not to mention its leadership), and co-optation via the substitution of new issues.

Discreditation of labour has become commonplace in Canadian society, for example, where labour leaders invariably get bad press, and any threat of strike action is countered by appeals to the "public interest". The increasing role of the state as employer in Canada — whether it be at the federal, provincial or municipal level — enhances the discreditation of labour, inasmuch as it provides the illusion that it is no longer a sometimes suspect "business" against which labour is pitted, but rather the very citizenry which supposedly comprise the state. In the present state of economic crisis, labour — and other potentially dissident groups such as students, the unemployed and underemployed and minorities — also provides a convenient scapegoat for the ills of society. Denigration of these groups enables the state to co-opt the issues which they have publicized, to substitute new issues in their place, or to effect repressive legislation. Discreditation of movements may also stem from a decline in the social significance of the issues which gave rise to them. This is frequently the fate of post-movement "sects", which often continue to publicize issues long after they have declined in significance, and which are therefore objects of public ridicule, if they are indeed noticed at all. Because of their emphasis on "opting out" of society, expressive movements are particularly prone to discreditation. Reform movements have also been subject to discreditation, frequently through "innocent dupe" or "guilt by association" approaches. In either case, the leaders and/or issues addressed by reform movements have been portrayed to be in the grip of more sinister interests. The "Communist threat" approach, for example, has been used with considerable success in Western societies. In Canada, it was used effectively to purge the union movement after World War II, and to discredit the student movement of the late 1960s.

According to the temper of dominant class interests, resistance and reactionary movements are also subject to discreditation, usually by means of ridicule of their leadership. Since it relies on manipulating an essentially conservative "public" ideology, discreditation can be an effective technique for thwarting change. However, the attempt to arouse public antipathy is not without its hazards — the net effect may be that a hitherto unkown movement, or issue, can receive public attention and support. This problem is also inherent in the more overt repression of movements, particularly in pluralist societies.

Repression, as pointed out earlier, is most commonly used against social movements in absolutist societies, where the use of state force is less impeded by the necessity of justification. However, depending on the degree of threat which a social movement may pose to the dominant classes, repression is not unknown in pluralist societies. Among Western nations, Canada in particular has been marked by a singular use of force against social movements. Although we have not, as yet, experienced full-scale revolutionary struggle, force has been quickly applied to a number of rebellion movements, and particularly to labour. Since rebellion and revolution pose the greatest threat to the *status quo*, these are usually met with immediate and concerted force. Because of the immanence of state reprisal, these movements, when they emerge in absolutist societies, are frequently well organized and well armed. Thus, although leaders are the first targets for arrest and assassination, the dynamic of the movement can continue even though the original leadership is destroyed. For this reason, it is usually necessary for the state to crush or disperse as many members of a movement, including potential ones, as quickly as possible. In pluralist societies, on the other hand, repression of the leadership of an emergent movement is usually sufficient to bring about its demise. However, the use of direct force against domestic populations in pluralist societies poses certain problems in terms of the legitimation function of the state, inasmuch as it tends to undercut the mystique of democratic "freedom". For this reason, the pluralist state must mount an elaborate — and frequently hysterical — campaign to justify the use of force, usually citing the peril to democratic law and order supposedly presented by the group or groups against which it is applied. A case in point, if one considers Canada to be a pluralist society, is the "October Crisis" of 1970, where some 450 "terrorists" were rounded up by police arrest, resulting in about a dozen being charged. As pointed out earlier, another problem inherent in repression is that the use of state force may tend to legitimate a movement in the eyes of potential members. Moreover, opposition can have the effect of creating further cohesion in the ranks of those against whom it is applied. In the face of state force, a movement may "close ranks" and become even more effective as an instrument of change.

Canadian Political Economy and Social Movements

Before turning to a brief consideration of some of the significant elements in Canadian economic and political history, it may be helpful to recall our earlier reference to the role of class and nation in the formation of social movements. To elaborate at this point, it may be noted that class (and class interest) is an important determinant of the membership of a movement, whereas nation (and national interest) is more of a determinant of the type of movement to be expected in a region, and of superordinate (i.e., state) response to such movements. A significant aspect of both class and national relationships is the nature of exploitation inherent in them. To put it briefly, class manifests exploitation on a vertical, or hierarchical, plane, whereas nation manifests exploitation on a horizontal, or regional, plane. In recent years, the analysis of regional exploitation has been most successfully approached through the "dependency", or "metropolis/hinterland" model.[4] Essentially, this model assumes that hinterlands are dependent on the metropoles which dominate them, and that conditions in the metropoles determine economic, political, and other related developments in the hinterlands. In particular, the types of class relationships that develop in metropoles and hinterlands may be expected to be characteristically different. Inasmuch as metropoles are the more highly developed centres of the industry and trade, the class relationships which they manifest, while typifying the distinction between capital and labour, are more complex and stratified. For example, the accumulation and circulation of wealth characteristic of metropoles has led to the development of an increasingly large segment of the labour force engaged in service, as distinct from extractive and manufacturing, occupations. Concomitant with this has been the emergence of the state as employer — a development which complicates the distinctions and relationships between capital and labour. Moreover, metropoles have a significant petit bourgeois class — both merchant and technocratic — which tends to mediate the polarization between capital and labour.

Another mediating factor — of considerable importance to the study of social movements — is the greater wealth of metropoles, which facilitates not only the direct buying off of disaffected populations, but also an illusion of progressivism (not to mention the reality of employment) via the identification and treatment of "social problems". Finally, metropoles are characterized by a highly stratified division of labour, and a subsequent emphasis on individual mobility as a means of social betterment. For these reasons, as well as for the ideological factors discussed earlier, the class conflicts which underlie social movements are usually mitigated in metropoles. Moreover, the ascendancy or decline of social classes — which historically have been associated with, respectively, revolutionary and reactionary movements — tends to be moderated by the pervasive influence of the metropolitan state and economy. Consequently, the most common movements found in metropoles are of a reform or expressive nature. This is not to deny that these types of movements can also be found in hinterland regions. In particular, "cargo cults" are examples of expressive movements of hinterlands faced with the sudden incursion of metropole economic, political and cultural forces.

By comparison, class relationships and antagonisms in hinterland regions are frequently more stark and manifest. Rapid change, especially that associated with the imposition of metropolitan economic hegemony, is also characteristic of hinterland development. Frequently, under the impact of metropolitan demands for resources and markets, old aristocracies find themselves having to give way to an emerging comprador bourgeoisie, and former peasants are uprooted from the land to become extractive labourers or an urban lumpen proletariat. Alternatively, as has been the case with capitalist development in Canada, indigenous populations are decimated, and selective immigration is utilized to provide the necessary labour force. Under these conditions of exploitation and change, the potential for movements of a more radical nature — particularly rebellion and revolution — is intensified. Certainly, the increasing incidence of hinterland revolutionary and liberation movements during the twentieth century bears this out. However, any generalizations about social movements must be placed in historical context.

For example, the revolutionary and reform movements of England and Europe during the seventeenth to nineteenth centuries were carried out in the context of emerging industrial capitalist classes in metropole regions. The first American revolution (1776), on the other hand, was essentially one of a hinterland mercantile bourgeoisie, whereas the second American revolution (1860) consolidated the hegemony of the U.S. industrial bourgeoisie — and of the U.S. industrial heartland — in North America.

Hinterland development also predisposes resistance and reactionary movements, which are typical of erstwhile dominant, or at least secure, classes which have been "dispossessed" or disadvantaged by economic and class changes. However, these movements are also common to metropole regions, particularly during periods of economic crisis. Indeed, as we have pointed out earlier, imperialism encourages reactionary tendencies not only in the hinterlands which it dominates, but also, by extension, in the imperial metropole itself.

The history of Canada has been a history of a hinterland successively dominated by French, British and American empires. Moreover, the Canadian nation state itself is divided by an urban, industrial and financial metropole of central Canada dominating northern, western, and eastern hinterlands. Aside from this, Canadian metropole influence extends into other world hinterlands such as the Caribbean, Latin America and South Africa. However, Canadian overseas imperialism must be the subject of another investigation.

Undoubtedly, the salient feature of the Canadian economy has been its staple nature. In the trade relationships which developed between Canada and its successive metropoles, our major exports have always been staple goods, rather than manufactured goods. In return, we have imported the surplus industrial production, capital and, on occasion, population of the empires which colonized us. In short, the economic role of Canada has been to produce raw materials and to consume finished products. From the outset, this role has stimulated mercantile, rather than industrial, entrepreneurship in Canada. The merchant wars between Britain and France, which culminated in the British conquest of Canada, ensured the domination of the Canadian economy by British mercantile capital during the period of industrial expansion in the imperial metropole. Merchant class interests focus on the trade, financing and land speculation associated with industry, but not on creating industrial competition in the hinterlands. Mercantile capital is directed largely towards intermediary activities between producers and consumers. Moreover, it tends to seek short term, low risk investment, rather than the long term, high risk investment predicated by industrial development and competition. In simple terms, merchant capital will seek the safe bet of established industry, and is conservative and monopolistic rather than laissez-faire and competitive. Thus, during the formative years of the Canadian economy, financing was dominated by a conservative, monopolistic merchant class whose interest was in trade, and in the protection of this economic base.

This mercantile domination has had several important consequences for the growth of the Canadian economy. Among the first of these was the early centralization of typical merchant enterprises: banking, finance, transportation and utilities. To this day, these sectors remain heavily cartelized and monopolized with, at least in the case of the latter two, extensive public (i.e., state) ownership and control. Perhaps the most illustrative integration of the public sector with merchant capital was the building of the Canadian Pacific Railway. Railways, canals, and other components of a trade infrastructure provided some of the earliest employment in Canada. Resource extraction and transportation requirements were early determinants of immigration policies in Canada. Another consequence of the dominance of merchant capital in Canada has been the conservative political and economic policies which mercantile interests engender. As we have noted, the basis for accumulation of merchant capital is investment in short term, low risk enterprise. Moreover, the centralization of economic and political power in Canada served to minimize investment risk, particularly in the areas of government and financial institution securities. State protectionism encouraged extensive foreign portfolio investment (particularly British), but did not encourage the development of indigenous industry. Conservative protectionism also took the form of the tariff policy initiated by Macdonald's Tory government after 1878. Although its ostensible purpose was to protect infant Canadian industry, its more important role was to expand trade and capital accumulation by attracting foreign (primarily U.S.) capital. In the long run, the net effect of the tariff policy was to stimulate branch plant development in Canada. This process was abetted by American industry: by producing through Canadian subsidiaries, American manufacturers were able to break into the "most favoured" Commonwealth market. British portfolio capital continued to dominate foreign investment in Canada until World War I, after which it became increasingly replaced by U.S. portfolio capital. During World War II and the following rapid growth of U.S. monopoly corporations, American direct investment through the branch plant structure became the dominant form of foreign investment in Canada.

The interests of foreign metropoles, and the response to them by the Canadian state, has been perhaps the most significant element in the formation of class and national movements in

Canada. By way of conclusion, we shall look briefly at some of the implications of this for specific areas of movement activity.

(1) French Canada

The roots of the conflict between French and English Canada are not religious, linguistic or cultural, but economic. Language, religion and culture may intensify the perspective of French-Canadian nationalism, but they do not cause it. After the English conquest of New France in 1760, the French merchant bourgeoisie which deserted the colony were replaced by an English merchant ruling class, who merely continued the colonial policies of their pre-decessors — which was essentially to keep the colonists ascetic, disciplined, controlled and impoverished, and to extract the greatest profit of the colony out of staple resources. The English merchant presence in Canada was augmented by the influx of conservative United Empire Loyalists, who fled the rebellious English colonies at the time of the American Revolution. This revolution added a new dimension to the imperial concerns of Britain: the necessity to maintain a British presence in North America. In the ensuing conflict between Britain and America (e.g., the invasion of 1775, the War of 1812, the liberation effort of 1838, the Fenian raids of 1866), the French were less than eager to lend aid to the British cause. Successive imperial responses to the "French question" — including appeasement and bribery (Quebec Act of 1774), engulf-ment (Constitutional Act of 1791), and assimilation (Act of Union, 1840) — were framed by aristocrats and tended to strengthen colonial comprador aristocracies, such as the clergy and mercantile elite, and to subjugate the peasantry, labour and other underclasses. Under these circumstances, no indigenous francophone bourgeoisie of any numerical significance would emerge until the "Quiet Revolution" of the 1960s gave strength to a growing technocratic bourgeoisie. Although the roots of a potential nationalist revolution (presaged by the Rebellion of 1837) are to be found in the relatively class conscious national bourgeoisie of modern Quebec, the necessary support of other classes, particularly labour, is as yet questionable.

(2) Native Movements

As any student of Canadian history is aware, the earliest exploitation of native Indians in Canada was in the fur trade. This exploitation, reflected in the successive rivalries between French, British and American merchants, led to the Indian rebellions of 1747, 1763, 1791-94, and 1811, and to the successive abrogation of native territorial rights marked by diplomatic manoeuverings such as Jay's Treaty (1794) and the Treaty of Ghent (1814). As in the case of the French colonists, the fate of the native people in hinterland Canada became settled far away in an imperial metropole. Inter-imperial rivalry, and the resource and land settlement policies of the emerging Canadian state, were also prominent instigators of the Riel Rebellions. In order to secure a western trade route — trade with the Orient having been "opened up" for the British by the Opium War of 1839-42, and for the Americans by their trade treaty with China negotiated under threat in 1844, and the acquisition of the Oregon territory in 1846 — it became imperative for British and Canadian mercantile interests to press for the political and economic unification of Canada that eventuated in Confederation. Moreover, the threat of U.S. imperial "manifest destiny" was pressing in, not only from the south but also, with the acquisition of Alaska from Russia in 1867, from the north. Fearing the loss of territorial and political rights in the face of concerted western settlement, the Métis arose in 1870, and again in 1885 when it became apparent that their fears were justified. The swift suppression of the Métis — 1885 being the first military preparedness test of the nearly completed transcontinental railroad — reflects the considerable threat that any attempt at political sovereignty presented to the embryonic Canadian state. This threat was not only internal: the Fenian raids (1866) and American annexationist pressures augured that, once again, any internal disputation in Canada would be met with imperial incursion from some quarter or another.

Today, it is the Inuit and other peoples of northern Canada that are under threat from the resource and land demands of Canadian and American capital. State response to emerging Indian politicization ranges from repression to co-optation, and there are indications of potential for a simultaneous class and nationalist based movement of native people. In this respect, perhaps the major consideration must be whether or not there remains a sufficient population base to sustain such a movement.

(3) National Bourgeoisie

As pointed out earlier, the early foundations of the Canadian political economy were laid through an interaction of domestic merchant and financial classes and foreign merchant, financial, and, eventually, industrial classes. The overwhelming economic interest of these charter groups was, has been, and is now in resource extraction and the financial and commerical infrastructures associated with it, and not in the development of competitive industry. Thus, the development of any sizable industrial bourgeoisie in Canada has been forestalled. Moreover, although Canada is a significant world producer of agricultural products, control of this production has remained in the hands of, firstly, a commercial and financial elite and, latterly, monopoly corporations. The only significant nationalist bourgeois uprisings in Canadian history to date have been the abortive Rebellions of 1837, mounted by a reform coalition of industrial and agrarian entrepreneurs and labour against the Family Compact and the Château Clique. The swift suppression of these movements must again be seen in the light of annexationist pressures from the United States, this time in the form of the patriot movements, dedicated to the final liberation of that part of North America still remaining under British rule — a goal with which the rebellious Canadian bourgeoisie had considerable sympathy. With the exception of the French-Canadian case discussed earlier, there seems little likelihood of a bourgeois revolution taking place in Canada, for a number of reasons. In the first place, and especially with the increasing control of production in Canada falling under foreign ownership, there is little economic base for an indigenous industrial bourgeoisie. Even if this class were to emerge in strength, the state of Canadian industry is such that is it too non-competitive and dependent on foreign capital for its owners to turn against the hands that feed it. Moreover, in spite of tremors of anti-Americanism from some quarters, the class interest of the Canadian bourgeoisie seems to be fixated on regionalism — more often than not, their strategy is to threaten some form of secession in order to get a better deal out of the federal state.

(4) Agrarian Movements

The history of settlement of the Canadian west differs markedly from that of the American experience. Although, from time to time, the American state put constraints on western expansion, settlement usually followed a "frontier" pattern, with surplus populations pressing outward, and developing a certain degree of economic and political autonomy in the process. By contrast, settlement of the Canadian west was part of a concerted state plan — the National Policy — whereby political and economic unification of the country was to be accomplished by a number of deliberate strokes: Confederation, railroad building, tariff protection, selective immigration and settlement. All of these policies were to have a profound effect on the settlers lured to the prairie west by the promise of riches as independent commodity producers. As the history of agrarian resistance movements shows, they were systematically thwarted in their attempts for political autonomy by the constraints of Confederation, rendered into a condition bordering on indentured servitude by the land policies of the state and the C.P.R. (the "state on wheels"), and exploited by protected eastern industry, railroads, and financeers. Eventually, these circumstances — complicated by the end of the wheat boom, the onset of the great depression, and the adversity of nature — prompted a populist resistance movement that was to last for some fifteen years. However, the basically petit bourgeois class interest of agrarians predicated a movement amenable to eventual co-optation into the *status quo* of political parties. Today, the agrarian class in Canada has become so reduced in numbers that their significance as a force for change is in danger of becoming only a part of history. However, in spite of their inherent petit bourgeois inclinations, Canadian farmers do have a long history of organization, and still, from time to time, raise a loud voice of protest.

(5) Labour

The history of the labour movement in Canada is a rich and colourful one, but which has only recently received due attention. Perhaps one of the significant aspects of Canadian labour has been its militancy and long association with radical politics, in contrast to American labour which, by the turn of the century, had already begun to make its peace with capital in the form of Samuel Gomper's American Federation of Labour. This is not to deny the history of American labour radicalism, nor to say that Canadian labour has not accommodated to capital in some respects. Nevertheless, Canada still has one of the world's highest records of industrial conflict which, regardless of its source, reflects a continuing tension between capital and labour. The militancy of Canadian labour has been matched by a long and bloody history of labour repression by capital and its agent, the state. In a sense, the tenor of the ruling class approach to labour in Canada was set as early as the 1830s, when the implementation of the so-called "Wakefield policy" of labour and land settlement (which resulted in vast imperial land grants to settlement companies and other elites) ensured a landless and impoverished working class for the development of the resource-extractive infrastructure in

Canada.* Some of the earliest working class responses to this kind of exploitation — and resulting state repression of labour — occurred in Quebec (the Lachine and Beauharnois canal strikes of 1843) and British Columbia (sporadic outbreaks in the coal mines of Vancouver Island from the 1850s on). To this day, these two provinces remain centres of labour militancy, and some of the earliest union organizing dates to the metal mining industry of south-eastern British Columbia. The stark contrast between capital and labour, and the absence of mediating classes, the exploitative conditions of work, boom and bust economic cycles, and the importation of labour all contribute to the militancy of labour in resource extractive regions. In contrast, the Canadian manufacturing labour force, especially since the peak and subsequent decline of industry in the 1950s, has become more and more protectionist. This development is co-terminous with the increasing ownership or control of Canadian industry by American capital, and the con-comitantly increasing influence of American business unionism in Canadian labour relations. At the same time, however, one of the major struggles of the Canadian trade union movement has been to escape the domination of American international unions. Thus, the phenomena of breakaway unions and union raiding form a complex and often confusing pattern of intra-union relations in Canada. Finally, the increasing role of the state as employer — which has been discussed earlier — and the dramatic increase in the proportion of service workers in the labour force (Canada leads all other OECD countries in the shift into service employment) augurs a new arena of class conflict on the Canadian labour scene. Given the existing, and even increasing, class consciousness of a large part of the Canadian labour force, and the antagonism to American industrial unionism often displayed, there may be a considerable potential for class, and even nationalist, movements emerging from this sector of the population.

By means of conclusion, perhaps it can be said that if the foregoing observations are at all accurate, the field of Canadian social movements, especially when viewed in the light of political economy, promises to be a fruitful area of study and, for some, involvement.

---

*Essentially, Wakefield's theory was that labour would not remain wage dependent without restrictions on land settlement and ownership and that, if such restrictions were not imposed, a pool of workers for industrial development would not emerge in the colonies. One of Wakefield's contemporaries was, interestingly enough, Karl Marx.

NOTES

1. Stanley Ryerson, "Quebec: Concepts of Class and Nation", in Gary Teeple (ed.), *Capitalism and the National Question in Canada*, p. 212. See also Ryerson, *Unequal Union: Roots of the Crisis in the Canadas, 1815-1873*, (Progress Books, 1973), esp. "Postscript: Polemical", pp. 424-435. To some, the distinction between class and nation may beg the question of international class movements. Notwithstanding the possibility of such movements, they have been historically rare, and will not be taken up in this limited discussion.

2. This by no means exhausts the list of structures and ideologies pertinent to capitalism. One of the classics in the field, of course, is Max Weber, *The Protestant Ethic and the Spirit of Capitalism*, (Charles Scribner, 1958). See also Harry K. Girvetz, *The Evolution of Liberalism*, (Collier Books, 1963), and Georg G. Iggers, "The Idea of Progress: A Critical Reassessment", *American Historical Review*, Vol. 71, (October, 1965), pp. 1-17.

3. A very good recent work on this process is John F. Conway, *To Seek a Goodly Heritage: The Prairie Populist Resistance to the National Policy in Canada*, (Unpublished Ph.D. thesis, Simon Fraser University, 1978).

4. For an excellent review of the literature applying this model to Latin America, see Ronald H. Chilcote, "Dependency: A Critical Synthesis of the Literature", *Latin American Perspectives*, Vol. 1, No. 1, (Spring, 1974), pp. 4-29. Among the Canadian contributions, see Kari Levitt, *Silent Surrender: The Multinational Corporation in Canada*, (Macmillan, 1970), esp. pp. 92-115; R.T. Naylor, "The Rise and Fall of the Third Commercial Empire of the St. Lawrence", in Gary Teeple (ed.), *Capitalism and the National Question in Canada*, pp. 1-41; Robert M. Laxer (ed.), *(Canada) Ltd., The Political Economy of Dependency*, (McClelland and Stewart, 1973); Melville H. Watkins, *et al, Foreign Ownership and the Structure of Canadian Industry*, (Ottawa: The Queen's Printer, 1968).

Readings

Abella, Irving M., *Nationalism, Communism and Canadian Labour*, Toronto: University of Toronto Press, 1973.

Abella, Irving M., (ed.), *On Strike: Six Key Labour Struggles in Canada, 1919-1949*, Toronto: James Lorimer and Company, 1975.

Betcherman, Lita-Rose, *The Swastika and the Maple Leaf: Fascist Movements in Canada in the Thirties*, Toronto: Fitzhenry and Whiteside, 1975.

Clark, S.D., *Movements of Political Protest in Canada, 1640-1840*, Toronto: University of Toronto Press, 1959.

Clark, Grayson and Grayson, (eds.), *Prophecy and Protest: Social Movements in Twentieth-Century Canada*, Toronto: Gage Educational Publishing Ltd., 1975.

Garner, Roberta Ash, *Social Movements in America*, (second edition), Chicago: Rand McNally College Publishing Co., 1977.

Horowitz, Gad, *Canadian Labour in Politics*, Toronto: University of Toronto Press, 1968.

Innis, Harold A., (edited by Mary Q. Innis), *Essays in Canadian Economic History*, Toronto: University of Toronto Press, 1956.

Jamieson, Stuart, *Times of Trouble: Labour Unrest and Industrial Conflict in Canada, 1906-66*, Ottawa: The Queen's Printer, 1971.

McCormack, A. Ross, *Reformers, Rebels, and Revolutionaries: The Western Canadian Radical Movement, 1899-1919*, Toronto: University of Toronto Press, 1977.

Robin, Martin, *Radical Politics and Canadian Labour*, Queen's University at Kingston, Industrial Relations Centre, 1968.

Teeple, Gary (ed.), *Capitalism and the National Question in Canada*, Toronto: University of Toronto Press, 1972.